CONTENTS

PREFACE

Two methods were open to me for condensing the nine volumes of *The George Eliot Letters* (1954–78) into one. The easiest would have been simply to select some dozens from the thousands of letters and publish them complete without regard to their connection. The other method, which I have adopted, attempts to cover the principal epochs of George Eliot's life by giving the most interesting parts of hundreds of letters to provide a continuous narrative for the general reader as well as the essential details of the writing and publication of her works.

Everyone must be fascinated by the extraordinary love affairs of this far from beautiful woman and by the remarkable success story of the largely self-educated country girl who was acknowledged the greatest novelist of her time. Born 22 November 1819 in a farmhouse on the Warwickshire estate of the Newdegate family, for whom her father Robert Evans was agent, she was christened *Mary Ann* in the Chilvers Coton parish church. At various periods she also spelled her name *Mary Anne*, *Marianne*, and *Marian*, returning finally in 1880 to *Mary Ann*. Her close friends called her *Polly* or *Pollian*. For economy of space in the brief headnote to each letter I have used the acronym *GE*, and for George Henry Lewes, *GHL*.

To reproduce in type all the vagaries of manuscript is neither feasible nor desirable. Such contractions as *sh^d*, *w^d*, *y^r*, *vol.*, *&c.*, have been expanded. The names of months and days, *Xmas*, *Xt*, and *Xtian* have been spelled out, but other proper names (*Shakspeare*, *Esop*) have been left as she wrote them. All her life George Eliot used archaic forms like *dulness* or *burthen*. She wrote both *favor* and *favour*, *judgment* and *judgement*, *criticize*, *realize*, and *teaze*. Blackwood, the publisher of her novels, altered her spellings to conform to the new house style adopted in 1846. The *Oxford English Dictionary* sanctions *-ize* as the correct spelling, but its quotations from the books of George Eliot and many other Victorian authors represent them as spelling with the *-ise* form, which few of them ever used. The original readings given here offer material for an interesting study of the influence of printers' style upon English spelling of the nineteenth century.

Economy of space has also prompted some freedom in paragraphing the letters. All the closing forms but the one preceding the signature have been run into the final paragraph; the headings have been put in one line with vertical rules to indicate the original spacing; and engraved headings have been put in boldface type to distinguish them from manuscript. Quotations should be made from the complete edition, of which the volume and page numbers are given in the headnotes, except for eleven newly discovered letters that are here published for the first time.

CHRONOLOGY

1819 Nov 22	GE born at South Farm, Arbury, Warwickshire.
Nov 29	Baptized Mary Anne Evans at Chilvers Coton.
1820	Moves to Griff.
1828–32	At Mrs. Wallington's School, Nuneaton.
1832–35	At the Miss Franklins' School, Coventry.
1836 Feb 3	Her mother Mrs. Robert Evans dies.
1841 Mar 17	GE and her father move to Foleshill, Coventry.
Nov	GE meets the Charles Brays.
1842 Jan–May	Refuses to go to church with her father.
1843 Nov	Visits Dr. Brabant at Devizes.
1844 Jan	Begins translation of Strauss's *Das Leben Jesu.*
1845 March	A picture restorer proposes to GE.
1846 Jun 15	*The Life of Jesus* published.
1849 May 31	Robert Evans dies.
Jun 12	GE goes abroad with Brays; stays at Geneva.
1850 Mar 25	GE returns to Rosehill.
1851 Jan 8	Goes to John Chapman's at 142 Strand, London.
Mar 24	Driven away by his wife and mistress.
Sep 29	Returns to edit *Westminster Review* for him.
1852 Apr	Friendship with Herbert Spencer; rumored engaged.
Jul–Aug	At Broadstairs; Spencer visits GE.
Oct	Begins to see George Henry Lewes.
1853 Oct 17	Moves to 21 Cambridge St., Hyde Park.
	Intimacy with GHL begins.
1854 Jul	GE's translation of Feuerbach's *Essence of Christianity* published.
Jul 20	GE and GHL leave for Germany together.
Nov	At Berlin GE begins translation of Spinoza's *Ethics.*
1855 Mar 14	GE at Dover; GHL in London to sell his *Life of Goethe.*
Oct 3	GE and GHL take lodgings at 8 Park Shot, Richmond, their home till 5 Feb 1859.
1856 Sep 23	GE begins "Amos Barton," first of *Scenes of Clerical Life.*
1857 Jan 1	Part I published in *Blackwood's.*
1857 Feb 4	Pseudonym George Eliot assumed.
May 26	Writes Isaac Evans that she has a husband.
June 2	*Scenes* are ascribed to Liggins.
Oct 22	*Adam Bede* begun.
1858 Feb 28	GE reveals her identity to John Blackwood.
1859 Feb 1	*Adam Bede*, 3 vols., published.
Feb 11	Moves to South Fields, Wandsworth.
Sep 28	GE and GHL study rivers at Gainsborough.

1860	Mar 24	Leave for Italy.
	Apr 4	*The Mill on the Floss*, 3 vols., published.
	May 21	GHL suggests Savonarola as subject for a novel.
	Sep 30	GE begins *Silas Marner*.
1861	Apr 2	*Silas Marner* published.
	Apr 19	GE returns to Florence for notes on *Romola*.
	Jul	*Romola* begins in the *Cornhill*.
1863	Jul	*Romola*, 3 vols., published.
	Aug 21	GE and GHL buy the Priory, 21 North Bank.
	Oct 16	Thornton Lewes leaves for Natal.
1864	May 4	GE and GHL go to Italy with F. W. Burton.
	Jun	GE begins *Spanish Gypsy* as a play.
1865	Mar 29	GE begins *Felix Holt, the Radical*.
1866	Jun 15	*Felix Holt*, 3 vols., published.
	Dec 27	GE and GHL start for Spain.
1868	May 25	*The Spanish Gypsy* published.
1869	Mar–Apr	GE and GHL in Italy; meet John Cross.
	May 8	Thornton Lewes returns, ill. GE begins *Middlemarch* (Featherstone-Vincy part).
	Oct 19	Thornton Lewes dies.
1870	Dec 2	GE experimenting with "Miss Brooke."
1871	Dec 1	*Middlemarch*, Book I published.
1872	Dec 1	*Middlemarch*, concluded with Book VIII.
1873	May 12	Emanuel Deutsch dies.
	Aug	GE visits synagogues in Germany.
	Nov 11	GE "simmering towards another book."
1874	May	*The Legend of Jubal* published.
1876	Feb 1	*Daniel Deronda*, Book I published.
	Sep 1	Book VIII concludes *Daniel Deronda*.
	Dec 6	GE and GHL buy the Heights at Witley.
1877	May 15	Dine with the Princess Louise.
1878	May 31	Dine with the Crown Prince and Princess of Germany.
	Nov 30	GHL dies.
1879	Feb 23	GE sees Cross.
	Sep 2	Establishes Studentship at Cambridge.
1880	Apr 9	GE agrees to marry Cross.
	May 6	Married; start for Continent.
	Jun 16	In Venice Cross jumps into the Canal.
	Jul 26	Return to Witley.
	Dec 3	Move to 4 Cheyne Walk.
	Dec 22	GE dies.

SELECTIONS FROM
GEORGE ELIOT'S LETTERS

1

FROM FAITH TO DOUBT
Griff · Foleshill

Religion in the Evans family at Griff House was of the high-and-dry variety, suspicious of all extremes. But at the school in Nuneaton, only two miles away, where GE was sent at the age of nine, her teacher Maria Lewis was a fervid disciple of the new curate, whose evangelical enthusiasm was stirring lively controversy in the town. She inculcated in her young pupil an earnest piety that dominated GE's life till she was 22. Constant reading of the Bible in the King James Version formed the foundation of the future novelist's vigorous style. At 13 she went on to the school in Coventry conducted by Rebecca and Mary Franklin, daughters of the minister of the Baptist Chapel. There the religious tone was Calvinistic, dwelling much on conviction of sin and the atonement; the girls organized prayer meetings, at which GE's eloquence was conspicuous. But Miss Rebecca Franklin was surprisingly liberal in encouraging their reading, and GE acquired a thorough knowledge of English authors from Shakespeare and Milton to Scott and Byron. She won the first-year prize in French and became expert on the piano. Called home in her third year by the terminal illness of her mother, GE kept in touch with Miss Lewis and corresponded with several schoolmates, who in their letters set each other subjects for moralizing. At home she taught herself Latin and had weekly lessons in German and Italian. Proud of the achievements of his "little wench," her father let her buy whatever books she liked.

Her loss of faith, though sudden, was long in preparation. As a child she had wondered how heroic characters in stories could be noble without being Christians. Later she found that books which attempted to reconcile Genesis with geology and astronomy only encouraged speculation about the very doubts they meant to dispel. In 1841 her father turned his business over to his son Isaac and moved with GE to Foleshill, near Coventry. There she became acquainted with Charles Bray and his family, who were active in all good causes, and freethinkers. Before she met them GE had read *An Inquiry concerning the Origin of Christianity* by Mrs. Bray's brother Charles Hennell. This book precipitated her break with orthodoxy. On 2 January 1842 she refused to go to church with her father. For several months the "Holy War," as she later called it, raged before they reached a compromise which left her free to think what she pleased so long as she appeared respectably with him at church on Sunday. She felt "inexpressible relief" at being freed from the gloomy burden she had borne for so many years. Though return to the old faith was impossible, she came to regret the impetuosity of her collision with her father. She lived on at Foleshill, tenderly caring for him until his death eight years later. In 1843 Charles Hennell married Rufa Brabant, who had begun to translate *Das Leben Jesu* by David Friedrich Strauss, a friend of her father. Rufa was glad to turn the task over to GE. Published without her name in three volumes (1846), *The Life of Jesus* had a profound influence on religious thought in England.

TO MARIA LEWIS, 6 JANUARY 1836

This earliest-known letter of GE was written to her former teacher, who had left Nuneaton to be governess in the family of the Reverend Latimer Harper in Northamptonshire. Robert Evans's Journal describes his illness as "inflammation upon the kidneys." William Bucknill was the Nuneaton surgeon. [I, 3–4]

Griff Wednesday | January 6. / 36.

My dear Miss Lewis,

I am grieved and ashamed that we should have appeared so unmindful of your kindly expressed desire to hear from us respecting our dear Mother's health. I will not say that our silence was altogether unavoidable, for had we borne in mind our promise we had many opportunities of forwarding a note to you previous to your departure from Nuneaton; but I trust that the entire occupation of our minds on other and painful subjects will be a sufficient plea for our seeming neglect. Since we saw you at Griff, my dear Mother has suffered a great increase of pain, and though she has for the last few days been much relieved, we dare not hope that there will be a permanent improvement. Our anxieties on her account though so great have been since Thursday almost lost sight of in the more sudden and consequently more severe trial which we have been called to endure in the alarming illness of my dear Father. For four days we had no cessation of our anxiety, but I am thankful to say that he is now considered out of danger, though very much reduced by frequent bleeding and very powerful medicines.

My Mother and Sister unite with me in love to you, and my Brother begs me to present his kind regards. We all hope that your health is established by change of air and scene. I need scarcely apologize for the disgraceful untidiness of my note, as you may well imagine that neither my hand nor my head is in a very favourable state for writing; but I must tell you that I am compelled to send you this paper that looks so poverty-stricken in consequence of Mr. Bucknill's having drawn on my stock till it is quite exhausted.

Again begging you to accept my love and best wishes, I remain, my dear Miss Lewis

Yours very affectionately
Mary Anne Evans

We shall be glad to hear from you.

TO MARTHA JACKSON, 9 OCTOBER 1838

Though less homiletic than her letters to Miss Lewis, GE's correspondence with Martha Jackson, of Gobions, near Hertford, still reflects the religious tone of the Miss Franklins' School. [I, 8–10]

Griff, Tuesday evening, October 9th, 1838.

My dear Friend

I pursue the same plan with my letter as I used when a little child with my pudding, that of dispatching the part for which I had the least relish first, and therefore I will dispose of such dry crust-like subjects as my reasons for not responding sooner to your welcome and undeservedly kind proof of your remembrance of me, and of my inability now to do so in a way that would satisfy my gratitude, as speedily as possible, that we may discuss without interruption the little sweetmeat my ill-furnished store-room may afford. I am at all times, as you conjecture, an important personage at home, but especially now, from a cause you are probably not able to guess, as I fancy the custom of changing servants at Michaelmas is confined to Warwickshire. This one circumstance, added to your charity, which makes you look through green spectacles at the glaring defects of others, will serve to account for and excuse both my silence and my worthless mode of breaking it.

Many thanks for your warm and, I am certain, sincere invitations to Gobions. I hope it may not always be impossible to me to avail myself of them; at present my apparently harsh but doubtless well-meaning mistress Duty says, Stay at home. But you are under no such restriction, and therefore I may hope that you will have a little interval before spring summons you and the birds to migrate where you may have a permanent nest, in which you will be so denuded of allurements and obligations as to expend your ability of giving pleasure on me. I spent nearly three days with my Coventry friends last week, and I had the Miss Franklins successively at Griff to fill up a very short parenthesis in their half-year's engagements. . . .

On the last day I went with Miss Rebecca to an Oratorio at St. Michael's Church, where we heard Braham, Phillips, Mrs. Shaw and Mrs. Knyvett, and where, I think, I said farewell to all such expenditures of time and money. I think nothing can justify the using of an intensely interesting and solemn passage of Scripture, as a rope-dancer uses her rope, or as a sculptor the pedestal on which he places the statue, that is alone intended to elicit admiration. I think, too, that it is the duty of Christians individually to throw their weight, however dust-like, into that scale which as Christians they must profess to wish to preponderate; not to take the low ground of considering things merely with relation to existing circumstances, and graduating their scale of holiness to the temperature of the world; but to aim as perseveringly at perfection as if they believed it to be soon attainable. And if so, I ask myself can it be desirable, and would it be consistent with millenial holiness for a human being to devote the time and energies that are barely sufficient for real exigencies on acquiring expertness in trills, cadences, etc.? The only argument that seems to me to have any speciousness in favour of such exhibitions of skill is, that without them we should never have an opportunity of appreciating the beautiful powers of the human voice when carried to their highest point of improveability. But by once admitting such reasoning we disarm ourselves of every weapon against opera dancing, horse racing, nay, even against intemperance, which I have heard justified on the plea that since Providence has sent luxuries we are contemning them by abstinence.

But I am running on very selfishly with my own thoughts, without regarding the trouble I am giving you in expecting you to read what I dare say neither your theory nor your practice needs. I do know full well the variableness of mind and affection of which you speak; it is suited to humble and distress us, but may also quicken us to an increased ardour of exertion during our wakeful hours when eternity is realised by us in its awful nearness and importance; if such be the effect we shall have the joy of finding that as persons of riper years gradually lose that soundness and excess of sleep observable in growing children, so our intervals of spiritual drowsiness will decrease in duration and frequency. . . .

[Mary Ann]

TO MARIA LEWIS, 16 [MARCH 1839]

This pious homily on the evils of fiction, obviously suggested by her former teacher, exhibits GE's wide acquaintance with novels, beginning with *Waverley* in 1827. It should not be taken too seriously. [I, 21–24]

Griff February 16.

My dear Friend, . . .

In trying to guess as to the expedience of reading works of fiction I put out of the question all books of persons of perceptions so quick, memories so eclectic and retentive, and minds so comprehensive, that nothing less than omnivorous reading as Southey calls it can satisfy their intellectual maw, for (if I may parody the words of Scripture without profaneness), they will gather to themselves all facts and heap unto themselves all ideas. For such persons we cannot legislate. Again I would put out of the question standard works whose contents are matter of constant reference, and the names of whose heroes and heroines briefly and therefore conveniently describe characters and ideas. Such are Don Quixote, Butler's Hudibras, Robinson Crusoe, Gil Blas, Byron's Poetical romances, Southey's do. etc. Such too are Walter Scott's novels and poems. Shakespeare has a higher claim than this on our attention but we have need of as nice a power of distillation as the bee to suck nothing but honey from his pages. However as in life we must be exposed to malign influences from intercourse with others if we would reap the advantages designed for us by making us social beings, so in books. . . .

I am I confess not an impartial member of a jury in this case for I owe the culprits a grudge for injuries inflicted on myself. I shall carry to my grave the mental diseases with which they have contaminated me. When I was quite a little child I could not be satisfied with the things around me; I was constantly living in a world of my own creation, and was quite contented to have no companions that I might be left to my own musings and imagine scenes in which I was chief actress. Conceive what a character novels would give to these Utopias. I was early supplied with them by those who kindly sought to gratify my appetite for reading and of course I made use of the materials they supplied for building my castles in the air. . . .

As to the discipline our minds receive from the perusal of fictions I can conceive none that is beneficial but may be attained by that of history. It is the merit of fictions to come within the orbit of probability; if unnatural they would no longer please. If it be said that the mind must have relaxation, "Truth is strange—

stranger than fiction." When a person has exhausted the wonders of truth, there is no other resort than fiction; till then I cannot imagine how the adventures of some phantom conjured up by fancy can be more entertaining than the transactions of real specimens of human nature, from which we may safely draw inferences. I dare say Mr. James's Huguenot would be recommended as giving an idea of the times of which he writes, but as well may one be recommended to look at landscapes for an idea of English scenery. The real secret of the relaxation talked of is one that would not generally be avowed; but an appetite that wants seasoning of a certain kind cannot be indicative of health. Religious novels are more hateful to me than merely worldly ones. They are a sort of Centaur or Mermaid and like other monsters that we do not know how to class should be destroyed for the public good as soon as born. The weapons of the Christian warfare were never sharpened at the forge of romance. Domestic fictions as they come more within the range of imitation seem more dangerous. For my part I am ready to sit down and weep at the impossibility of my understanding or barely knowing even a fraction of the sum of objects that present themselves for our contemplation in books and in life. Have I then any time to spend on things that never existed?

I have written at random and have not said all I wanted to say. I hope the frequent use of the personal pronoun will not lead you to think that I suppose it to confer any weight on what I have said. I used it to prevent circumlocution and waste of time. I am ashamed to send a letter like this as if I thought more highly of myself than I ought to think, which is alas! too true. I long for Midsummer that I may see you. Do not talk of glimpses. I am grieved that your poor head is a frequent sufferer. Pardon all I ought not to have said and believe me

> Your very affectionate and sincere
> Mary Ann Evans.

In reading my letter I find difficulties in understanding my scribble that I fear are hopelessly insurmountable for another. Sir Walter Scott's life, of which I have read the 1st volume and here and there some pages of the succeeding ones, conveys some sad and useful lessons. The spiritual sleep of that man was awful; he does not at least betray if he felt any thing like a pang of conscience. All biography is interesting and instructive. Sir W. S. himself is the best commentary on the effect of romances and novels. He sacrificed almost his integrity for the sake of acting out the character of the Scotch Laird, which he had so often depicted. J'attends une réponse. Some persons are so provokingly phlegmatic that perhaps they should have stimulants.

TO MARTHA JACKSON, 27 FEBRUARY 1840

The complete text of this letter, recently discovered by Mr. John Dillon, of Trinity College, Dublin, is through his kindness here published for the first time. Joseph Brezzi came once a week from Leamington to give GE lessons in German and Italian. In Latin she was self-taught with the help of Locke's method and interlinear translations. Oneiza is a damsel in Southey's *Thalaba* (Book III, st. 20) who had woven Moath's tent. Jessie Barclay, another schoolmate at the Miss Franklins', was the daughter of a wholesale merchant of medicines in London.

Griff February 27th 1840

My dear Martha,

I think it will be politic for me, by way of exordium, to express my opinion that letters between friends should be as unpremeditated as their most familiar tête-à-tête, for then the haste and negligence which I foresee will characterize mine will borrow an air of sagesse as arising out of an abstract notion instead of a concrete sloth of mind and body. I must tell you too that I am going to send you another lucubration, that you may charitably excuse my dulness on the ground of my being destitute of Apollo's inspiring influence. I am not one of those birds of wisdom that can best exercise their faculties by night. I belong to the butterfly tribe and love to spread my "wings i' the eye of noon." I confess this is rather galling to me and I have had many a contest with "the dewy-feathered sleep," trying to prove Comus's assertion that he and Night have nothing to do with each other. Does my mental scent deceive me when it tells me that my merry little Martha's finely rounded compliment is strongly impregnated with the satire that she is continually, even though unconsciously, breathing out? Well, be it so, notwithstanding the paucity of my cerebrum in a certain part. I will not allow you tonight to disturb my self-complacency, but will answer your application with all gravity and importance. But why not ask Mr. Moginie's advice? The word classics has a very soaring air, but alas! we must crawl for some time up a rugged steep before we can catch a glimpse of the desired summit. We must get a Latin grammar and tax our memories with every word of it. This is all I have attempted at present with the exception of reading some of Esop with Taylor's literal translation. I have a series of elementary Latin books after Locke's method, published by Taylor and Walton; the set cost one guinea. As you are so spirited in determining to see every book that is mentioned to you, I will tell you the modern ones I have read since I last wrote. Three volumes of G. P. R. James's Life and Times of Louis Quatorze; there is a fourth and last which I shall I hope soon have. His reign you know was a focus on which were blended the brightest rays of France's military and literary glory. I devour it as a romance. I have now the life of Sir Richard Hill by the Revd Edwin Sidney and Scrope on Deer Stalking in the Highlands, which last you may fancy can be a book only for sportsmen and Amazons, but I rather think it is interesting.

I intend if spared to be busy with a Chart which I am anxious to complete and if I succeed to print it for a certain object. It gives a chronological view of Ecclesiastical History, and has not that I know of been forestalled. I have seen charts of profane History innumerable, or rather I should say secular History, but never one of Church History. Have you? I have a faint hope that Mr. Brezzi will be able to give me some time next month and if I am not disappointed I shall begin German with him and continue Italian. This I ardently long for. I know I shall have a reading companion in my dear Patty, and therefore we shall swim together admirably. I should like you to come when the flowery May is throwing from her green lap "the yellow cowslip and the pale primrose" and then we can pursue our occupation in my favorite drawingroom with the azure vaulted roof and the green carpet that not even the looms of Oneico [i.e., Oneiza] can equal.

Enough trifling—let me try to think of something good before I lie down. Sir R. Hill and his excellent sister are in their letters often exhorting their brother Rowland to diligence in his studies as calculated to increase his usefulness and recommend his piety. May we, my dear Martha, set before us the same worthy object in our little efforts, otherwise we shall be worse than triflers, we shall be criminally living to ourselves. Our dear Jessie's letters are always full of spiritual feeling and I rejoice that you share the same benefit as myself in being one of her correspondents. I am just now perturbed by circumstances that have called forth much emotion of a kind not favorable to the progress of the soul, either in earthly or heavenly acquirements. May I one day be a more useful friend! I beg you to credit me, dear Martha, when I tell you that my eyes have had a troublesome tendency to close all the time I have been writing and that I have felt the approach of sleep even to my digital extremities, so that you must really pardon me if I have sent you many illegible words. I rather chose to write under all these disadvantages than to defer answering your welcome letter. Good night, dear Patty.

Love your affectionate
Mary Ann.

TO MARIA LEWIS, 23 MARCH 1840

E. W. Short was the Nuneaton bookseller. GE's sister Chrissey Clarke had had a miscarriage. Elizabeth Tomlinson Evans, wife of GE's uncle Samuel Evans, was converted to Methodism in her youth and caused a stir by preaching in public. A story she told GE of visiting in prison a girl convicted of child murder became the germ of *Adam Bede*. Mrs. Evans, gravely ill, recovered and lived until 1849. [I, 42–43]

Griff March 23d 1840.

My very dear Friend,

Do you not know that fear is like some pseudo-prophecies, bringing to pass the very event it forbodes? I fear that I am going to send you another shabby selfish letter, and I dare to say my dread will deprive me of the little ability I might otherwise have to make the best of a bad season for writing. I really meant to give myself the treat of scribbling a long letter to you this week but I am obliged to send you one to-night that I may if possible obtain from you the full name, style and title of Dr. Pearson's Essay, with that of its publisher, for Mr. Short who seldom succeeds in getting me the right thing, having apparently a *pendant* to himself in London not at all inferior in stolidity, has sent me word that he cannot find out the birthplace of the work, and I am consequently losing a little time that might be more effectively employed, if I knew whether my ground had been preoccupied or not.

Many thanks for the rules, which I felt conscience-stricken to receive from you, knowing how precious is your modicum of leisure. I have just received my second lesson in German and while I think of it I will rectify a mistake that I remember imparting to you when we were together, respecting the *Sch.* In German these letters united are invariably pronounced as the sh in our *she*, so that Schiller is *Shiller*. Goethe, the German way of spelling which is Göthe, is pronounced as though the former vowel were the French eu in peu. The final e is not open, but like the common English pronunciation of er, when the r is not heard. Ch without the s varies according to its junction with certain vowels or consonants. Ei is pron[ounced] like i in *fine*, so that Freischutz is Frishutz. . . .

I am grieved to tell you that our dear Chrissey is in a very weak state from a kind of affliction second only to a confinement. I have not your letter at hand and am too hurried to fetch it, though I have an impression that it contains something I should like to notice, more than my memory furnishes to me. You remember hearing me speak of a dear Methodist Aunt in Derbyshire. She is now awaiting in peace and joy the summons that shall call her to be ever with the Lord. O to be followers of them who through faith and patience inherit the promises! And what promises! while we inflate ourselves with wind, and refuse the feast of fat things full of marrow, of wines on the lees well refined that the Saviour has placed within our reach.

Much love and promises of amendment from

Your own
Polly.

TO MARIA LEWIS, [30 MARCH 1840]

While work on the Chart continued, GE's reading of the Tractarians helped to undermine her evangelicalism. [I, 44–47]

Griff Monday Evening.

My very dear Friend, . . .

Your nice miniature chart which I shall carefully treasure up has quite satisfied me that Dr. Pearson at least has not realized my conceptions, though it has left me still dubious as to my own power of doing so. I will just (if you can bear to hear more of the matter) give you an idea of the plan, which may have partly faded from your memory. The series of perpendicular columns will successively contain, the Roman Emperors with their dates, the political and religious state of the Jews, the bishops, remarkable men and events in the several churches, a column being devoted to each of the chief ones, the aspect of heathenism and Judaism toward Christianity, the chronology of the Apos[tolical] and Patristical writings, schisms and heresies, General Councils, eras of corruption, under which head the remarks would be general, and I thought possibly an application of the Apocalyptic prophecies, which would merely require a few figures and not take up room. I think there must be a break in the chart after the establishment of Christianity as the religion of the Empire, and I have come to a determination not to carry it beyond the first acknowledgment of the supremacy of the Pope, by Phocas in 606 when Mahommedanism became a besom of destruction in the hand of the Lord, and completely altered the aspect of Ecclesiastical History. So much for this, at present, airy project, about which I hope never to teaze you more.

Mr. Harper lent me a little time ago a work by the Revd W. Gresley, begging me to read it, as he thought it was calculated to make me a proselyte to the opinions it advocates. I had skimmed the book before ("Portrait of An English Churchman") but I read it attentively a second time and was pleased with the spirit of piety that breathes throughout. His last work is one in a similar style, "The English Citizen," which I have cursorily read, and as they are both likely to be seen by you, I want to know your opinion of them. Mine is this: that they are sure to have a powerful influence on the minds of small readers and shallow thinkers, as, from the simplicity and clearness with which the author, by his beau idéal characters, enunciates his sentiments they furnish a magazine of easily wielded weapons for *morning calling* and *evening party* controversialists, as well as that really honest minds will be inclined to think they have found a resting-place amid the foot-balling of religious parties. But it appears to me that there is unfairness in arbitrarily selecting a train of circumstances, and a set of characters as a development of a class of opinions. In this way we might make atheism appear wonderfully calculated to promote social happiness. I remember, as I dare say you do, a very amiable atheist depicted by Bulwer in Devereux, and for some time after the perusal of that book, which I read 7 or 8 years ago, I was considerably shaken by the impression that religion was not a requisite to moral excellence. . . .

I am going to read a volume of the Oxford Tracts and the Lyra Apostolica; the former I almost shrink from the labour of conning, but the other I confess I am attracted towards by some highly poetical extracts that I have picked up in various quarters. I have just bought Mr. Keble's Christian Year, a volume of sweet poetry that perhaps you know; if not it is a dish both in ingredients and cooking that would suit you. Not more than 2/6 or 3s. The fields of poesy look more lovely than ever now I have hedged myself in the geometrical regions of fact, where I can do nothing but *draw* parallels and measure differences in a double sense. I shall soon hate heretics as vehemently as any papist can desire, for both their wide uniformity and their narrow differences are as Chrissey would say, *pestering*. Certain divines enjoin us to consult ecclesiastical records for the settling of our faith, a result the very opposite to what they appear likely to produce, in my humble and narrow apprehension. . . .

It is now twelve o'clock and the obtuseness of my faculties has reached its climax. I would ask you to forgive all the nonsense and bad English I have scribbled, but that you have interdicted all such appeals. The sooner I see your handwriting the better for

Your affectionate
Polly.

TO MARTHA JACKSON, 30 JULY 1840

In *The Language of Flowers* the name *Clematis*, which Martha bestowed on GE, signified mental beauty; *Ivy*, constancy. For a time GE called Maria Lewis *Veronica*, fidelity in friendship. [I, 60–61; IX, 332]

The Bower of Clematis, | July 30th, 1840.

My dear Ivy,

If you knew how the tendrils of your Clematis have been twisted out of their natural *inclination*, you would not wonder that she should concentrate all her sap for her own support under this racklike process, and thus become stunted instead of stretching out a branch to clasp even her Ivy. At length, however, she invites her fellow creeper (rather humbling by the bye that they must both be called *parasitic* plants) to try whether the same soil and air will suit the constitution of each. Without all travesty, dear Patty, if you can venture an experiment on Griff and its presiding nymph I shall be glad to welcome you hither on Wednesday week. . . .

There is an enchanting air of mystery about your note, my Ivy; you thought, I suppose, that you had shrouded your secret in the fashion of a Turkish lady, but I can tell you it wore only the thin gauze that tempts one to pry more closely. So some lord of the forest, some giant oak or elm, has discovered that *Ivy* has just the qualifications to make wedded bliss more than a dream! I perfectly agree with his oakship—for what should a wife be if not faithful, devoted, clinging to the last, even when the rich boughs that made the oak's beauty in the eyes of all beside, are leafless and withered? And what moreover if not of vigorous and fibrous mental contexture, conjoined with apparent fragility, lightness, and elegance? Shall I not do to write your epithalamium? Do secure me the office. Trèves de badinage! says my Patty, looking as sedate as becomes an "engaged young lady." Be it so. I confess I have need to remind you that I am your junior. However as Cowper wrote John Gilpin under a fit of mental depression, I may be believed when I say that malgré my attempt to sing to the tune of "Begone dull care" I am quite ready to slide into a minor key, and though I send you an awkward apology for a jet d'eau, my current really runs without one frisky ripple. Come and blow on me, and wrench the sorrowful weeds that nearly choke my stream. Send me that honeyed word yes, and you will gladden your drooping

Clematis.

TO SAMUEL EVANS, 10 AUGUST 1840

How thoroughly GE was steeped in the King James Version of the Bible is seen in the tissue of allusions in the letters to her Methodist uncle and aunt. [I, 61–62]

Griff August 10th 1840.

My dear Uncle,

Remembering the Apostle's declaration that "to be absent from the body is (for redeemed souls) to be present with the Lord," I cannot for her own sake regret that my dear Aunt is so near the very brink of Jordan; I would only pray that her Heavenly Father may, out of His tender consideration for His creatures, who "are but dust," lighten her weight of bodily suffering as far as may consist with His designs of mercy to her soul. Give to my dear Aunt if she should be able to receive it an assurance from me of my warm affection for her, and tell her I humbly resolve in the strength of the Lord to "seek his face evermore," that we may sing together a new song before His throne. For you, my dear Uncle, both my Father and myself truly feel, and I have endeavoured to pray that you may be powerfully sustained under a trial that will indeed bereave you of one who has been as the apple of your eye; but is it not to this end? "That God may be all in all" with you, and that having no earthly prop, you may walk entirely by faith? My Father bids me give his love to you, and tell you that you are passing through what he has already experienced. . . . I doubt not, my dear Uncle, that you will evidence the posses-sion of what belongs only to the Christian, "joy in tribulation," and that you will thus glorify the Lord God of Israel even in the fires. Truly the commandments of God are not grievous, for the Apostle sums them up by a "Rejoice in the Lord, and *again* I say rejoice," and though *this* may seem a great difficulty when the heart is bowed down and rent in twain by the loss of our earthly gourds, in *reality* that is the very time when we can best relish the waters that make glad the city of God. "Trials make the promise sweet," such promises as these, "To him that over-cometh will I grant to sit on my throne," and "the Lamb that is before the throne shall feed them, and God himself shall wipe away all tears from their eyes."

I am fearful of not being ready for the post so I must say good bye.

Your affectionate
Mary Ann.

TO MARTHA JACKSON, 20 OCTOBER 1840

Louis Aimé-Martin's book was *De l'Education des mères de famille, ou de la civilisation du genre humain par les femmes.* [I, 70; IX, 333]

Griff October 20th 1840

Have I really a friend Martha still, or is she become only a "bead of Memory's rosary"? I can ill spare her I confess for I am not rich in friends, and I am threatened with excision from Jessie's list for I have not heard from her since you dear Martha left me . . . and I cannot prevent a certain swelling of heart when the idea suggests itself that you have both determined to treat me after my deserts. . . . Every day's experience seems to deepen the voice of foreboding that has long been telling me "The bliss of reciprocated affection is not allotted to you under any form. Your heart must be widowed in this manner from the world or you will never seek a better portion; a consciousness of possessing the fervent love of any human being would soon become your heaven, therefore it would be your curse." Time only will prove the prophetic character of my presentiment. . . .

I was electrified a little while ago by an observation of Aimé Martin's: "I was resolved to be neither a Frenchman a Russian nor a Turk, but to be a Man!" May I

unceasingly aspire to unclothe all around me of its conventional human temporary dress, to look at it in its essence and in its relation to eternity, and thus in
perhaps rather a different sense from Wordsworth's "breathe the spirit of the
universe." By the bye Mr. Brezzi lent me Aimé Martin's work whence Woman's
Mission is drawn—I have been charmed by its stirring eloquence and its assertion
of neglected truths, *but* the author is not an orthodox Christian. I use this term to
imply that he saps the Gospel of all mystery, of all spirituality, if I rightly ap-
prehend him, and probably it is this that has given rise to the notion that
Woman's Mission is the work of a Socinian. Martin's opinions have been attributed to her. . . .

I am preparing an unwelcome task for you dear Martha in scribbling so much
that is scarcely legible—pardon it on the plea of real indisposition and believe me
even though discarded

> Your true and affectionate
> Clematis.

TO MARIA LEWIS, 27 OCTOBER 1840

Robert Evans retired in 1841, leaving his son Isaac as agent for the Newdegate family, while
he prepared to move to Coventry. These excerpts give a fair sample of GE's eclectic
reading. [I, 70–73]

> Griff | October 27th 1840.

My dear Veronica,

My only reason for writing on an evening that finds me with a mindful of the
accumulated scum of continued intercourse with the herd (I do not write superciliously) and with a head having a sore sensation as if from long pressure, is that I
may obtain from you a timely promise that you will spend your holidays chiefly
with me, that we may once more meet among scenes which now I am called on to
leave them, I find to have *grown in* to my affections. . . .

Carlyle says that to the artisans of Glasgow the world is not one of blue skies and
a green carpet, but a world of copperas-fumes, low cellars, hard wages, 'striking,'
and gin; and if the recollection of this picture did not remind me that gratitude
should be my reservoir of feeling, that into which all that comes from above or
around should be received as a source of fertilization for my soul, I should give a
lachrymose parody of the said description and tell you all seriously what I now tell
you playfully that mine is too often a world such as Wilkie can so well paint, a
walled-in world, . . . O how lusciously joyous to have the wind of heaven blow on
one after being *stived* in a human atmosphere, to feel one's 'heart leap up' after the
pressure that Shakespeare so admirably describes, "When a man's wit is not
seconded by the forward child understanding it strikes a man as dead as a large
reckoning in a small room." The poor Clown's distress that his Audrey was not
poetical is a type that is reacted daily under a thousand circumstances.

But it is time I checked this Byronic invective, and in doing so I am reminded of
Corinne's or rather Oswald's reproof, La vie est un *combat,* pas un *hymne.* We

should aim to be like plants in the chamber of sickness, dispensing purifying air even in a region that turns all pale its verdure and cramps its instinctive propensity to expand. . . .

I am reading Harris's Great Teacher, and am "innig bewegt" as a German would say by its stirring eloquence which leaves you no time or strength for a cold estimate of the writer's strict merits. I wish I could read some extracts to you. Isaac Taylor's work is not yet complete. When it is so, I hope to reperuse it and then will either write or *talk* to you of it. . . . I am reading *eclectically* Mrs. Hemans's poems, and venture to recommend to your perusal if unknown to you, one of her longest poems, "The Forest Sanctuary." I can give it my pet adjective, exquisite! I meant to write more; perhaps it is happy for you that I am constrained to close my extraordinarily illegible letter. I am going out early tomorrow morning. 'Tis now eight in the evening and my Daddy has laid by his papers.

Your true
Clematis.

TO MARTHA JACKSON, 4 MARCH 1841

The Reverend Walter Farquhar Hook, former Vicar of Holy Trinity, Coventry, left to become Vicar of Leeds in 1837. Abijah Hill Pears was Mayor of Coventry 1842–'43. GE's sister Chrissey, wife of Edward Clarke, a surgeon at Meriden, had her third child, Mary Louisa, 11 February. [VIII, 7–8]

Griff March 4th 1841.

My very dear Ivy

Imagination herself being only a combining faculty and entirely dependent on our much depreciated senses, I am hopeless that she could depict to you my condition and employ for the last three weeks, for right gladly do I believe that you have no materials in your memory wherewith she might construct a type of them. At length an islet of etherial blue seems to be emerging in the midst of my cloudy cope, and under its benign influence I have spirits to make an effort at writing a letter, not dreaming that I shall write one that would be worth the perusal except to a clinging friend, who can be satisfied with bare matter of fact concerning my whereabout, how, and whither. It has been determined for two months or more that our future residence shall be the house on the Foleshill Road formerly inhabited by Dr. Hook and next door to Mr. A. Pears. Thither we hope soon to remove, and thither some time I hope my Patty will come to regain her roses. . . .

Many thanks for your so kindly wishing to see me at Gobions—it would give me lively pleasure to visit you and see the rest of the Pleiades, one of which is so dear and interesting to me; but I dare not calculate on the indulgence at present. I cordially echo your feeling of comfort in knowing that our little concerns are in the hands of Him who doth all things well. To be so far a Quietist as to receive all with thankfulness is well, but we must stay then in the adoption of the system, and instead of sitting still actively go forward in whatever direction the finger of Providence points.

My dear Brother has mentioned you as one whom he admires, and my own dear

Father will I know be glad to welcome you again as my visitor, so do come amongst us. I shall have the cosiest hearth in Christendom, as quiet as a summer lake. My Sister wants to see you, and has recently presented us with a little girl, whom we shall be proud to display. . . . By the bye, I have read Buckland's Treatise on Geology with much pleasure, and I believe Lyell's is good though it differs in Theory, but alas the superficies of the earth are monopolizing my attention. I can neither delve nor soar.

Ever your true and affectionate
Clematis.

TO MARTHA JACKSON, 21 MAY 1841

Isaac Taylor's *Physical Theory of Another Life* anticipates in a future world a scheme adapted to the expanded powers of man after death. [I, 92–94]

Foleshill Road Coventry | May 21st 1841.

My very dear Martha

Being at length quite naturalized in this our adopted country, and at liberty to stretch the wings of thought and memory beyond my own nest and bush, I am determined to remind you of my existence and to enlighten you, as the metaphysicians say, concerning its modes. . . . Your undeserved affection will, I think, cause you to rejoice with me in the rich blessings that are continued and superadded to me in our new abode; you remember that I had forebodings as to the influence of a change on my dear Father. These are all dissipated, and I can decidedly say that I never before saw him so happy as he apparently is at present. Our next neighbours are Mr. and Mrs. Pears, gradually growing into friends, and I think valuable ones. If it were permissible to express a regret amid so many unmerited mercies, I should mention my lack of a free range for walking which I so enjoyed at Griff, with the deprivation of that 'prolixity of shade' of which I am a not less ardent lover than Cowper himself. I find too what I did not fully anticipate, a considerable disturbance of the usual flow of thought and feeling on being severed from the objects so long accustomed to call it forth. There is the same cope, imperial in its beauty, above me, the clouds are not less majestic or fleecy, the verdure of this month is even deeper and more luxuriant than any I have ever before seen, but I have never yet enjoyed that communion with them, viewed from my present position, that long familiarity rendered spontaneous in my early home.

Leaving this fruitless subject, I will not omit to tell you that you have instrumentally furnished me with the best soother under a rather severe attack of influenza in 'The physical theory of another life' which I had lent to a friend without reading it myself until about a month ago, when I nestled in my father's armchair and forgot headache cough and all their et ceteras in the rapture this precious book caused me, as intense as that of any school girl over her first novel. My chief trouble here ought to be my uselessness for I seem to have nothing to do but seek gratification, but to the willing spirit there is in every situation "room to deny ourselves, a road to bring us daily nearer God." . . .

It is the prerogative of friendship to dignify the gift even of a few hairs and I question whether, from a bald friend, we should not cherish the paring of a nail as a relic—hence I draw an inference favourable to the prospects of my worthless letter, which I venture to hope you will receive with pleasure as a proof of the remembrance and affection of your true

Clematis.

TO MARIA LEWIS, [13 NOVEMBER 1841]

Mrs. Pears introduced GE to her brother Charles Bray, a ribbon manufacturer and philanthropist, hoping that her evangelicalism might temper his heterodoxy. Mrs. Bray was a sister of Charles Hennell, whose *Inquiry concerning the Origin of Christianity* GE had already read. This was the engrossing inquiry that altered GE's belief and startled Miss Lewis. [I, 120–21]

Foleshill | Saturday.

My very dear Friend,

I fear you have thought me tardy in seeking further information about your prospects—at least if your goodness have not permitted this, my own wish to know them has made me fancy the eight or nine days that have elapsed since I had your letter unusually long. My whole soul has been engrossed in the most interesting of all enquiries for the last few days, and to what result my thoughts may lead I know not—possibly to one that will startle you, but my only desire is to know the truth, my only fear to cling to error. . . .

Think—is there any *conceivable* alteration in me that would prevent your coming to me at Christmas? I long to have a friend such as you are I think I may say alone to me, to unburthen every thought and difficulty—for I am still a solitary, though near a city. But we have the universe to talk with, infinity in which to stretch the gaze of hope, and an all-bountiful, all-wise Creator in whom to confide—He who has given us the untold delights of which our reason, our emotion, our sensations are the ever-springing sources. Hurry and darkness—so good-bye dear one. Why may we not talk without so much circumlocution, 'tis a very great compliment to the understanding of one's hearers to speak elliptically.

Ever yours
Mary Ann.

"An answer by return will oblige."

TO MARIA LEWIS, [18 DECEMBER 1841]

Miss Lewis was with the Evanses on Sunday 2 January, when Robert Evans wrote in his journal: "Went to Trinity Church in the forenoon. Miss Lewis went with me. Mary Ann did not go." [I, 123–24]

Foleshill Saturday Morning.

My dear Maria,

Come when it suits you best, and stay as long as your inclination and arrangements allow. I have no particular engagements in view but should any such occur I will apprize you. Please to send me word a day or so before you come that I may be at home to welcome you, as I shall do with great pleasure. Thank you very much for your kind enquiries about my health. I have been but poorly since I saw you, but I am decidedly better, and I am taking some medicine that seems beneficial.

My Father returned from his journey to Hallam last evening, and we have just breakfasted together for the first time since last Saturday, so that I have had a lonely week in which your company would have been very valuable, but it rather prevents one from being very urgent in giving invitations when one's own society is the only divertissement one has to offer. You however have kindly put up with me and my circumstances many times before this and will good naturedly do so again.

Goodbye and may Heaven bless you as it does by the sure laws of consequence bless every one who does his work faithfully and lives in loving activity.

Ever your affectionate
Mary Ann.

TO MRS. ABIJAH PEARS, [28 JANUARY 1842]

Mrs. Pears, away from Foleshill on a visit, wrote to GE about her altered religious view. [I, 124–26]

Foleshill | Friday Evening.

My very dear Friend,

Your kind note was put in my hand about an hour ago, and lest my reply should arrive to interrupt you on Sunday morning, I write very hastily that I may secure it a place in the letter-bag this evening. . . .

Never again imagine that you need ask forgiveness for speaking or writing to me on subjects to me more interesting than aught else—on the contrary believe that I really enjoy conversation of this nature; blank silence and cold reserve are the only bitters I care for in my intercourse with you. I can rejoice in all the joys of humanity; in all that serves to elevate and purify feeling and action; nor will I quarrel with the million who, I am persuaded, are with me in intention though our dialect differ. Of course I must desire the ultimate downfall of error: for no error is innocuous, but this assuredly will occur without my proselyting aid, and the best proof of a real love of the truth,—that freshest stamp of divinity,—is a calm confidence in its intrinsic power to secure its own high destiny,—that of universal empire. Do not fear that I will become a stagnant pool by a self-sufficient determination only to listen to my own echo; to read the yea, yea, on my own side, and be most comfortably deaf to the nay, nay. Would that all rejected *practically* this maxim! To *fear* the examination of any proposition appears to me an intellectual and a moral palsy that will ever hinder the firm grasping of any substance whatever. For my part, I wish to be among the ranks of that glorious crusade that is seeking to set Truth's Holy Sepulchre free from a usurped domination. We shall then see her resurrection! Meanwhile, although I cannot rank among my principles of action a fear of vengeance eternal, gratitude for predestined salvation, or a revelation of future glories as a reward, I fully participate in the belief that the only heaven here or hereafter is to be found in conformity with the will of the Supreme; a continual aiming at the attainment of that perfect ideal, the true Logos that dwells in the bosom of the One Father. I hardly know whether I am ranting after the fashion of one of the Primitive Methodist prophetesses, with a cart for her rostrum, I am writing so fast. Goodbye, and blessings on you, as they will infallibly be on the children of peace and virtue.

Ever, your affectionate
Mary Ann.

TO MARIA LEWIS, 18 FEBRUARY 1842

Charles Bray, an enthusiastic adherent of phrenology, had read GE's character from the bumps on her skull. Adhesiveness was the propensity to form attachments. Miss Lewis was now back at Nuneaton running a school. [I, 126–28]

Foleshill Road | February 18th 1842.

My dear Maria,

I dare say you have added subtracted and divided suppositions until you think you have a sure product—viz. a good quantum or rather a bad one of indifference and forgetfulness as the representation of my conduct towards you. If so, revise your arithmetic, for be it known to you that, having had my propensities sentiments and intellect gauged a second time, I am pronounced to possess a large organ of 'adhesiveness,' a still larger one of 'firmness,' and as large of conscientiousness—hence if I should turn out a very weather cock and a most pitiful truckler you will have data for the exercise of faith maugre common sense, common justice, and the testimony of your eyes and ears. I have not been in your neighbourhood since I wrote to you, though I imagine, from a message my sister Mrs. Isaac told me of, that you had the idea that I was at Griff when you received my parcel. . . .

My dear Sister is as you may imagine, but poorly. I shall have my children 2nd week in March. If you have any little ones with whom you commence teaching to read, use I earnestly recommend, Mrs. Williams's Syllabic Method. I have had a weary week and you have the fag end. At the beginning more than the usual amount of *cooled* glances, and exhortations to the suppression of self-conceit. The former are so many hailstones that make me wrap more closely around me the mantle of determinate purpose—the latter are needful and have a tendency to exercise forbearance that well repays the temporary smart. The heart knoweth its own whether bitterness or joy—let us, dearest beware how we *even with good intentions* press a finger's weight on the already bruised. The charity that thinketh no evil is loudly professed—but where is it in persons who to nurse their reliance on their own sentiments positively as I have heard a lady do today attribute perseverance in lovely conduct to a proud determination to disappoint the expectation of a fall? O this masquerade of a world! But I shall weary you. May you be happy and healthy and continue to love

Mary Ann.

TO ROBERT EVANS, [28 FEBRUARY 1842] ✓

After GE's refusal to go to Church family and friends argued against her changed opinion in vain. Ministers enlisted to reason with her found that she had already read the books they urged in support of their belief. Her brother Isaac called at Meriden, where GE was staying with her sister, and, as Robert Evans wrote in his Journal, "*schooled* Mary Ann." After an outburst of paternal authority her father lapsed into nine weeks of stony silence before GE wrote this letter, the only one to him that has survived. [I, 128–30]

Foleshill Monday Morning.

My dear Father,

As all my efforts in conversation have hitherto failed in making you aware of the real nature of my sentiments, I am induced to try if I can express myself more clearly on paper so that both I in writing and you in reading may have our judgements unobstructed by feeling, which they can hardly be when we are together. I wish entirely to remove from your mind the false notion that I am inclined visibly to unite myself with any Christian community, or that I have any affinity in opinion with Unitarians more than with other classes of believers in the Divine authority of the books comprising the Jewish and Christian Scriptures. I regard these writings as histories consisting of mingled truth and fiction, and while I admire and cherish much of what I believe to have been the moral teaching of Jesus himself, I consider the system of doctrines built upon the facts of his life and drawn as to its materials from Jewish notions to be most dishonourable to God and most pernicious in its influence on individual and social happiness. In thus viewing this important subject I am in unison with some of the finest minds in Christendom in past ages, and with the majority of such in the present (as an instance more familiar to you than any I could name I may mention Dr. Franklin). Such being my very strong convictions, it cannot be a question with any mind of strict integrity, whatever judgement may be passed on their truth, that I could not without vile hypocrisy and a miserable truckling to the smile of the world for the sake of my supposed interests, profess to join in worship which I wholly disapprove. This and *this alone* I will not do even for your sake—anything else however painful I would cheerfully brave to give you a moment's joy.

I do not hope to convince any other member of our family and probably not yourself that I am really sincere, that my only desire is to walk in that path of rectitude which however rugged is the only path to peace, but the prospect of contempt and rejection shall not make me swerve from my determination so much as a hair's breadth until I feel that I *ought* to do so. From what my Brother more than insinuated and from what you have yourself intimated I perceive that your establishment at Foleshill is regarded as an unnecessary expence having no other object than to give me a centre in society—that since you now consider me to have placed an insurmountable barrier to my prosperity in life this one object of an expenditure held by the rest of the family to be disadvantageous to them is frustrated—I am glad at any rate this is made clear to me, for I could not be happy to remain as an incubus or an unjust absorber of your hardly earned gains which might be better applied among my Brothers and Sisters with their children.

I should be just as happy living with you at your cottage at Packington or any where else if I can thereby minister in the least to your comfort—of course unless that were the case I must prefer to rely on my own energies and resources feeble as they are—I fear nothing but voluntarily leaving you. I can cheerfully do it if you desire it and shall go with deep gratitude for all the tenderness and rich kindness you have never been tired of shewing me. So far from complaining I shall joyfully submit if as a proper punishment for the pain I have most unintentionally given you, you determine to appropriate any provision you may have intended to make for my future support to your other children whom you may consider more deserving. As a last vindication of herself from one who has no one to speak for her I may be permitted to say that if ever I loved you I do so now, if ever I sought to obey the laws of my Creator and to follow duty wherever it may lead me I have that determination now and the consciousness of this will support me though every being on earth were to frown upon me.

Your affectionate Daughter
Mary Ann.

TO MRS. CHARLES BRAY, [12 MARCH 1842]

When her father put the lease of the Foleshill house up for sale and planned to move to a cottage at Packington, GE considered going into lodgings at Leamington and trying to support herself by teaching. [I, 131]

[Foleshill]
My dear Mrs. Bray,

My guardian angel Mrs. Pears has just sent for me to hear your kind note, which has done my aching limbs a little good. I shall be most thankful for the opportunity of going to Leamington, and Mrs. Pears is willing to go too. Since my morning's conversation with Mrs. P. I have been meditating on her kind plan of seeking an interview with my father, and owing to feelings and circumstances impossible for me to communicate fully, I am persuaded that the attempt to influence him would be unwise and could issue in no real good to any. I am unusually muddy to-night, and must wait for to-morrow to tell you more if even your benevolent ears are not weary of me and my woes—but woes I will not call them, there is but *one* woe, that of leaving my dear Father. All else, doleful lodgings, scanty meals, and *gazing-stockism* are quite indifferent to me. Therefore do not fear for me when I am once posited in my home, wherever it may be, and freed from wretched suspense.

Ever your grateful and affectionate
Mary Ann Evans.

We will be at your house by 10 o'clock.

TO MRS. CHARLES BRAY, [20 APRIL 1842]

Not wanting his sister to go into lodgings, Isaac invited her to return to Griff until her father sent for her. After some six weeks Mrs. Isaac Evans convinced him that to make her worldly interest dependent on changing her opinion was useless. A compromise was reached. GE agreed to accompany him to church as usual, and he tacitly conceded her right to think what she liked during the service. [I, 137–39]

[Griff]

My dear Mrs. Bray.

I wish I had you as a companion in a ramble through a precious little dingle that I have as a resort here, instead of doing what is only second best to talking with you. Before I had your kind letter, one of the ravens that hovered over me in my Saul-like visitation, was the idea that you did not love me well enough to bestow any time on me more than what I had already robbed you of, but that same letter was a David's harp that quite charmed away this naughty imagination. I know I am exposing myself very foolishly to contemptuous pity by telling such feelings, and the confessional too, according to the experience of all faithful Catholics is not the best check to frailty, but I am in earnest determining to o'er master this ugly habit of mind, that proceeds not from a want of self esteem, but a yearning for what is more than in sober reason and real humility I ought to desire.

You asked me in your first note to tell you about family matters—they are rather clearer to me than they were. My sister-in-law here, whose affection in spite of my excommunicated state I have been happy enough to win, having had some conversation with my Father wherein she represented to him what I have managed to make visible to herself—that if he be actuated by a love of truth, and desire that I should return to the profession of what he regards as truth, he could not place a more effective barrier to my 'conversion' than by making my apparent worldly interests in any way dependent on it. That the prospect of reinstalment in external comforts or in the good opinion of the world would be precisely the attendant on a change of opinion to create the most violent struggle in my mind ere I could confess such change, and that as regards society the attempt to interlace worldly interests with religious sentiment even more closely than in the present state of things is inevitable, would be an Ehud's homage to piety no other than a stab under the fifth rib. My Father consented and said that I had better return to him after a time, but he is bent, at present, more determinedly than is usual with him, on leaving Foleshill. A most lugubrious looking place at Fillongley (!) runs in his head as a desirable residence. Of course I shall not utter a word of discontent or claim a voice in the matter of a choice concerning his abode. I can quite appropriate Satan's sentiment, "What matter where if I be still the same." Or rather if I be attaining a better autocratship than that of the Emperor of all the Russias—the empire over self. But though disposed to be lamb-like in this matter, there is another on which I am warm and decided. When I came hither I did so in compliance with my Father's wish that I should retire for a time from a neighbourhood in which I had been placed on the very comfortable pedestal of the town gazing-stock and to be very plain but not less true, made a fool of by announcing my departure to everyone connected with me, but I never contemplated remaining here longer than a month, and I cannot be induced to prolong a *visit* farther than that. I must have a settled home if my mind is to become healthy and composed, and I shall therefore write to my Father in a week and request his decision. It is important, I know, for him as well as myself that I should return to him without delay, and unless I draw a circle round him and require an answer within it, he will go on hesitating and hoping for weeks and weeks. It was a sacrifice in the first instance to take up my abode with any of my family, and though I have every kindness here, there are feelings which are incommunicable that render it impossible for me to continue long an adjunct to a family instead of an integral part. . . .

Thank you for the note and *notes.* I shall think of Miss Brabant with grateful pleasure. Alas! I despair now of seeing your locks parted after my taste and like most other people (on other subjects) I am lost in astonishment that anyone can differ from me—that my ideas of the elegant and becoming are not shared by all the world. Nevertheless I can love you just as well, and I venture to say shall always love you however you might travesty the exterior of that something that utters, looks, smiles, and writes wisely and lovingly.

Do manage to cheer me with another little note.

Ever your affectionate,
Mary Ann Evans.

TO MRS. CHARLES BRAY, [SEPTEMBER 1842]

Mrs. Bray painted the first portrait of GE, now in the National Portrait Gallery, a water-color showing her blue eyes and light brown hair. [I, 145]

[Foleshill]

My own dear Heart's Ease,

I am too selfish to be sorry that you took the trouble to write to me, your looks and words of love are so precious to me. I am altogether ashamed of myself—do not tell any one that I am so silly as I appear to her whom I love best.

Dinner comes to take possession of the table and I cannot thank you half for your goodness but I will look my gratitude to-morrow afternoon, if you are inclined to finish the picture then.

Yours ever truly
Mary Ann.

TO SARA HENNELL, 3 NOVEMBER [1842]

Mrs. Bray's sister Sara Sophia Hennell, a handsome, intelligent woman, only seven years older than GE, had been governess in the Bonham Carter family, cousins of Florence Nightingale and Barbara Leigh Smith. She was a frequent visitor at Rosehill, the Bray's charming house overlooking Coventry, and soon replaced Maria Lewis as GE's chief correspondent. After Sara's brother Charles Hennell published the *Inquiry*, he met Rufa Brabant and proposed marriage to her. Her father Dr. R. H. Brabant opposed the match, finding Charles's lungs unsound. [I, 150–51]

Foleshill November 3.

My dear Sara,

I have been as slow to write as they tell me I am to speak, and that for two reasons—first, because bien-séance requires that we do not run up to kiss people who bow to us at the other side of the room, and next because I have been musing on many things and have been in high displeasure with myself, have thought my soul only fit for Limbo to keep company with other abortions, and my life the shallowest, muddiest, most unblessing stream. Having got my head above this slough of Despond, I feel quite inclined to tell you how much pleasure your letter gave me—it was so bright and good and loving, like yourself, you dear one. I think of you more and love you better than ever, and could almost turn Guebre and worship the sun for giving me a sight of my favourite glance.

I have had many pleasures since you wrote in the society of Mr. Hennell and Miss Brabant. You wish to know what conception or misconception I may happen to have about the character of the latter. The first empfindung was unfavourable and unjust, for in spite of what some caustic people may say, I fall not in love with every one, but I can now satisfy your affection by telling you that I admire your friend exceedingly; there is a tender seriousness about her that is very much to my taste, and thorough amiability and retiredness, all which qualities make her almost worthy of Mr. Hennell. . . .

You observe in your note that 'some persons say that the unsatisfied longing we feel in ourselves for something better than the greatest perfection to be found on earth is a proof that the true object of our desires lies beyond it.' Assuredly this earth is not the home of the spirit—it will rest only in the bosom of the Infinite. But the non-satisfaction of the affections and intellect being inseparable from the unspeakable advantage of such a mind as that of man in connection with his corporeal conditions and terrene destiny, forms not at present an argument with me for the realization of particular desires.

That huge Gryphon necessity that robs us of all the gold we dream of obliges me to stop short, for I only allow myself the time from tea to the departure of the letter bag to write. My love to all I know. I had a world more to say, but perhaps you are fortunate in being rescued from the trouble of reading another half sheet of scribble.

Ever your true and loving
Mary Ann.

TO MRS. CHARLES BRAY, [DECEMBER 1842]

Mrs. Bray shared GE's thirst for knowledge, read German and Italian with her, and played duets on the piano. At Rosehill GE was quickly drawn from provincial isolation into touch with the world of ideas. [I, 153–54]

[Foleshill]

As the apple tree among the trees of the wood so art thou my beloved, among the daughters, and I only wish you would change houses with the Mayor, that I might get to you when I would.

I send you the first part of Wallenstein with the proposition that we should study that in conjunction with the Thirty years' war, as I happen to have a loose copy. We had better omit the Lager and begin Die Piccolomini. The other part is Wallenstein's Tod. You shall have Joan of Arc, my grand favourite as a bonne bouche when you have got through Wallenstein, which will amply repay you for any trouble in translating it, and is not more difficult than your reading ought to be now. I have skimmed Manzoni, who has suffered sadly in being poured out of silver into pewter. The chapter on Philosophy and Theology is worth reading. Miss Brabant sent me my [Longfellow's] Hyperion with a note the other day. She had put no direction besides Coventry and the parcel had consequently been sent to some other Miss Evans and my choice little sentimental treasures alas! exposed to vulgar gaze. Miss B. begs me to tell her all I know of Rosehill and the inhabitants of "that Paradise." I shall hope to see its Eve to-morrow; in the meantime will you tell your Adam, who 'with front serene governs' in your Paradise, with my compliments or respects or love, whichever is proper and all three are true, that the trees are condemned to fall and be sold to Mr. Webb. Thank you for the Manual which I have had so long. I trust I did not bestow those scratches on the cover. I have been trying to find a French book that you were not likely to have read but I do not think I have one, unless it be Gil Blas which you are perhaps too virtuous to have read, though how any one can opine it to have a vicious tendency I am at a loss to conjecture. They might as well say that to condemn a person to eat a whole plum pudding would deprive him of all future relish for plain food.

Vale,
Mary Ann.

TO FRANCIS WATTS, [DECEMBER 1842]

The Reverend John Sibree, Independent minister of Coventry, appealed to Watts, a professor of theology at Birmingham, to persuade GE that her new belief was a mistake. After talking with her Watts confessed, "*She* has gone into the question." GE's offer to translate Vinet for him is the first of a series of similar offers made to others in later years, comprising writings of Strauss, Spinoza, Feuerbach, and Goethe. [I, 154–55]

Foleshill, Wednesday.

Revd and dear Sir,

I have received your valuable books quite safely and have already enjoyed some of their contents. I need not say how much I value such proofs of your kindness. I have copied Guizot's Address, but I return you the same rough papers that you had before because they may be bent and soiled at pleasure. I will not worry you with long letters, but I wish to express fully what I think I omitted to say in reply to a question of yours. If we should be so happy as to get one of Vinet's works published I beg you to understand that I consider myself *your* translator and the publication as yours, and that my compensation will be any good that may be effected by the work, and the pleasure of being linked to your remembrance.

I hope you will have a pleasant season of rest at Christmas and that I shall see you looking well before a very long interval has elapsed: some good deed to be done in this neighbourhood will draw you hither and remind you of me. Believe me, Revd and dear Sir,

Yours with respect and esteem
Mary Ann Evans.

The Revd F. Watts.

TO MRS. CHARLES BRAY, [8 NOVEMBER 1843]

Rufa Brabant went with GE, the Brays, and the Hennells on a tour of Wales in the summer of 1843, at the end of which her marriage to Charles Hennell was decided on. GE served as a bridesmaid at the wedding in London, after which she was invited to visit Dr. Brabant at Devizes "to take the place of his daughter." Mrs. Brabant, who was blind, did not attend the wedding. [I, 163–65]

Devizes Wednesday.

My dearest Friend,

Alas! I like not to tell you of my pleasant journey yesterday when I think that my parting from you was a beginning of sorrow to you. I hated myself for sitting so snugly in the coach and driving away from you like a very impersonation of selfishness, but I knew not what else to do. I will hope the best—that neither you nor Mr. Bray took cold from your wet walk and that as Mr. Hennell would say, "Forsan et haec olim meminisse juvabit." Perhaps as you are reading my note you will be seated so comfortably by your dining room fire that I should be discontented with my lot if I could have a picture of you. Should you like one of me? Well then, behold me at the table in Dr. Brabant's dining room with rather

aching limbs which is not wonderful, and in perfect good humour which *is*
wonderful. I should indeed have spleen enough to make me 'one of the most
remarkable women in this country' if I were not made happy by the warm welcome
and the delicate attentions I receive here. I have nothing to talk of yet but kind
words, kind looks, good fires and warm water, all which agrémens I have luxuri-
ated in since 7 o'clock last evening, for we did not reach Devizes until that
hour. . . .

I have been feasting my eyes on the Library this morning, and Dr. Brabant
insists that I shall consider that my room. What name do you think I have been
baptized withal? Rather a learned pun, Deutera, which *means* second and *sounds* a
little like daughter. Both my host and hostess seem pleased with me, or simulate it
so well, that their acting is as good as reality. I like Mrs. B. She talks so *neatly* and
is so perfectly polite. A dose of precision, *not* preciseness, will be the best thing in
the world for me. Dr. B's habits are of that regular and simple kind that always
indicate a healthy mind. He does not even sit in an easy chair; but here is
luncheon and I shall have to walk presently. I have written in a great hurry and
have not said one half of what I want to say, but I threaten you with a longer letter
in a few days, and to atone for its length it shall be more legibly written. I want
nothing but a letter from Father to make me happy—I have just been writing to
him to ask him the reason of his silence. Mrs. Brabant is talking, so I must leave off
scribbling.

> Love, love love from your
> Mary Ann

The people here are all so ugly! almost as ugly as I am.

TO MRS. CHARLES BRAY, 20 NOVEMBER [1843]

Brabant was regarded by Eliza Lynn, who had also visited him, as the original of Mr.
Casaubon in *Middlemarch*. He kept writing and rewriting a book intended to destroy all
superstition and dogma, which never got beyond the opening chapter. Mrs. Brabant's sister
Susan Hughes, alarmed at the intimacy between GE and Dr. Brabant, excited her jealousy.
Rufa ascribed it to GE's "simplicity of heart and ignorance of (or incapability of practising)
the required conventionalism," but blamed her father for acting as if the fault were GE's
alone. The visit ended two weeks earlier than she intended. [I, 165–66]

Devizes. Monday | November 20th.
Thank you, meine Liebe for your kind letter, so much longer and earlier than
you had allowed me to hope, but it was like you to be better than your promises. I
am in a little heaven here, Dr. Brabant being its archangel, but it would be a less
complete heaven if the recollection of you were not inwoven in the texture of my
happy thoughts. . . .

Mrs. Brabant is a most affectionate amiable being, too forgetful of herself to talk
of her loss, but really feeling it as much as any one. Of the Dr. what shall I say? for
the time would fail me to tell of all his charming qualities. We read, walk and talk

together, and I am never weary of his company. I have just written to Father to beg for a longer leave of absence than I had thought of when I came, but until I receive his answer I shall be uncertain about the time of my departure. If he should not wish for me sooner, I shall stay to the 13th of December. The journey will be rather formidable to a novice like me. Miss Hughes advises me to go by Cheltenham and Birmingham and I should like the novelty of that plan, but I hope I have yet three weeks to consider about the matter. . . .

The air of Devizes is very invigorating and I believe I am better than when I came, though I lost the first week in getting rid of my rakish languor. I am petted and fed with nice morsels and pretty speeches until I am in danger of becoming even more conceited than ever, and I shall want a month's mortification to make me endurable. Now then you know my whole status, and do you send me a letter just as full of Ichheit or I shall be wofully disappointed. I have written as fast as my pen [The rest of this letter is lacking.]

TO SARA HENNELL, [?9 APRIL 1844]

Rufa Brabant had begun to translate *Das Leben Jesu* by her father's friend David Friedrich Strauss. But after her marriage she was glad to hand it over to GE. Sara Hennell followed the book until its publication in 3 volumes, 15 June 1846, as *The Life of Jesus, Critically Examined.* [I, 174–75]

[Foleshill]

My dear Sara,

I have an impression that in tearing off that part of Strauss's first section which Mrs. Hennell wanted I was obliged to leave a page or so that was not translated. My first page is 257. Will you be so kind as to ascertain exactly how far Mrs. H's translation has proceeded, and send me the intermediate pages? Perhaps, however, I had better translate the whole §. It is the 34th about the magi—may they be anathema!

Thanks dear, for your pretty German note and for all other pretty and good things that you have done and said for me. I cannot stay to say more than that I am

Your affectionate
Mary Ann.

I meant to send this note by Mr. Bray, but he is gone without my knowledge.

TO CHARLES HENNELL, [APRIL 1844]

Joseph Parkes, M.P., contributed £150 towards the translation of *The Life of Jesus*, which John Chapman agreed to publish for "1/2 expense and 1/2 profit." [I, 175]

My dear Mr. Hennell,

Thank you for sending me the good news so soon and for sympathizing in my need of encouragement. I have all I want now and shall go forward on buoyant wing. I am glad for the work's sake, glad for your sake, and glad for 'the honourable gentleman's' sake, that matters have turned out so well. Pray think no more of my pens, ink and paper. I would gladly give much more towards the work than these and my English if I could do so consistently with duty.

Pray give my kindest remembrances to both the Mrs. Hennells and believe me

Yours very truly
Mary Ann Evans.

Foleshill | Friday Evening.

TO MRS. CHARLES BRAY, [18 JUNE 1844]

Mrs. Bray was visiting her mother in Hackney, where Charles Hennell and Edward Noel were also seen. Sara was preparing to go to Germany with Dr. Brabant and Susan Hughes. [I, 177–78]

[Foleshill]

My dear Friend,

It was very kind of you to think of me among so many pleasant people and pleasant sights. I am quite glad that you have Mr. Noel to double your enjoyment as well as have his own share. I went to your house as a marauder this morning, to carry off a book from the bookcase, and I found Hannah brimful of a theft that has been committed at your neighbour's Mr. Carter's. Some snapper up of unconsidered trifles from the fair I suppose, thought of running away with a silver fork and spoon but Jephcott has the glory of being the police officer in the case. Verily these are not days to hang up bracelets in the highways.

I do not think it was kind to Strauss (I knew he was handsome) to tell him that a *young lady* was translating his book. I am sure he must have some twinges of alarm to think he was dependent on that most contemptible specimen of the human being for his English reputation.

My love to Sara, and tell her I do not wish to distress her conscience with the purchase of an atheistic book, but I feel sure there is a '*Bauer's* Wesen des Christenthums' published at Berlin.

By the way, I never said that the canons of the Council of Nice, or the Confession of Augsburg, or even the 39 articles are suggestive of poetry. I imagine no *dogmas* can be. But surely Christianity with its Hebrew retrospect and millennial hopes, the heroism and Divine sorrow of its founder and all its glorious army of martyrs might supply and has supplied a strong impulse not only to poetry but to all the fine arts.

Mrs. Pears is coming home from Malvern to-night, and the children are coming to tea with me so that I have to make haste with my afternoon matters. Beautiful little Susan has been blowing bubbles and looking like an angel at sport. I am quite happy, only sometimes feeling "the weight of all this unintelligible world." That is Wordsworth's idea, and you must allow it to be vinous, not milk and watery as usual.

Love to Mr. Bray, although I am tremendously offended with his letter. Breakfast with you on Friday morning!

Mary Ann.

Tuesday afternoon.

TO SARA HENNELL, [SEPTEMBER 1844]

[I, 181]

Foleshill | Tuesday.

My dear Sara,
I think yours a very sensible proposition about the quotations from Josephus
etc. It has always seemed to me nonsensical to give so much Greek except on
debateable ground. You are an invaluable creature to me and save me a world of
anxiety. Do you mean that there are 26 quotations in the part already sent to you
or throughout the whole work? If Dr. Brabant would take the trouble to give an
English version of the notes, Strauss and I shall be much obliged to him, but do
not urge it if there be any symptoms of the *reputation ague*. I do not want the
'groups' and 'devils'—I sent for them merely that work might be dispatched. Are
not Mr. and Mrs. Hennell coming? If they are you shall have the rest of the
miracles and the Transfiguration by them.
I thought of you very much last night as I was driving home under the serene
light of the moon, Mars and Saturn. Do you not feel how hard it is not to give *full
faith* to every symbol?

Your
Mary Ann.

TO SARA HENNELL, [6 APRIL 1845]

The "affaire" GE mentions was with a young artist whom she met at the house of her half
sister Mrs. Houghton at Baginton. As Mrs. Bray described it to Sara, GE passed two days in
his company there, "and she thought him the most interesting young man she had seen and
superior to all the rest of mankind; the third morning he made proposals through her
brother in law Mr. Hooton—saying, 'she was the most fascinating creature he had ever
beheld, that if it were not too presumptuous to hope etc. etc., a person of such superior
excellence and powers of mind,' etc., in short, he seemed desperately smitten and begged
permission to write to her. She granted this, and came to us so brimful of happiness;—
though she said she had not fallen in love with him yet, but admired his character so much
that she was sure she should: the only objections seemed to be that his profession—a
picture-restorer—is not lucrative or over-honourable. We liked his letters to her very
much—simple, earnest, unstudied. She refused anything like an engagement on so short
an acquaintance, but would have much pleasure to see him as a friend etc.
"So he came to see her last Wednesday evening, and owing to his great agitation, from
youth—or something or other, did not seem to her half so interesting as before, and the

next day she made up her mind that she could never love or respect him enough to marry him and that it would involve too great a sacrifice of her mind and pursuits. So she wrote to him to break it off—and there it stands now. Poor girl, it has been a trying, exciting week to her and she seemed quite spiritless this morning: and we cannot help feeling that she has been over-hasty in giving it up. And yet—and yet—one does not know what to advise."
The name of GE's suitor is unknown. [I, 185–86; IX, 336–37]

Foleshill Sunday.

My dear Sara,

Glad am I that some one can enjoy Strauss! The million certainly will not, and I have ceased to sit down to him with any relish. I have been so idle from headache and other woes lately that I can possess my soul in patience about Mr. Parkes, though I should work much better if I had some proof sheets coming in to assure me that my soul-stupefying labour is not in vain.

I thought I had invariably put p. instead of s.—if not, s. would be better for all German works. I am very sorry my oversights or carelessness have given you so much tiresome labour. I think f. and ff. are not proper in an English translation. When I have supplied them at all I have put et seq. *Judaea and Peraea* not Judea and Perea. σ is correct for the middle of a word, ς for the end. They both represent sigma. I do not mind about any alterations that will satisfy your taste, though I am at a loss to know the rationale of some. According to dictionaries and grammars, '*as though*' is good gentlemanly English as well as '*as if*,' and if you heard more evangelical sermons, dear, you would find that it is invariably 1stly, 2dly, 3dly, 4thly, and *lastly*, not *finally*. It is St. Paul's Finally, my brethren, be strong in the Lord and in the power of his might, which has created your association. But about all these matters I am perfectly indifferent and quite glad to make your pencil marks ink. Only do not make Miss Rebecca Franklin's name into an opprobrious common noun, for I assure you she is not responsible for my faults.

I have never yet half thanked you for taking an interest in my little personal matters. My unfortunate 'affaire' did not become one 'du coeur,' but it has been anything but a comfortable one for my conscience. If the circumstances could be repeated with the added condition of my experience I should act very differently. As it is I have now dismissed it from my mind, and only keep it recorded in my book of reference, article '*Precipitancy, ill effects of.*' So now dear Sara, I am once more your true Gemahlinn, which being interpreted, means that I have no loves but those that you can share with me—intellectual and religious loves.

I want a walk before the next shower comes.

Goodbye
Mary Ann.

Is it worth while for me to see the translation again? You can judge whether I should like to do so. I have entire confidence in your judgment about the Greek and such things. I am more grateful to you than I can tell you for taking the trouble you do. If it had not been for your interest and encouragement, I should have been almost in despair by this time.

TO SARA HENNELL, 27 [MAY 1845]

The Brays had taken Sara to Hastings for a fortnight. "Baby," an illegitimate daughter of Bray, stayed at Rosehill with Mrs. Bray's acquiescence until 27 June, when she was taken back to her mother. Polly had long been a nickname for Mary; Sara transformed *Polly Ann* into *Pollian* in a pedantic pun on Apollyon, the Angel of Destruction, during the work on Strauss. [I, 194–95]

Foleshill | Tuesday | [May] 27th

My dear Sara

First let me deliver to you my budget of news from Rosehill. I had a most gracious reception this morning from Baby, and carried her to my great fatigue to pay our respects to the Cow. The Baby is quite well and not at all triste on account of the absence of Papa and Mamma, whom she invokes very lustily and shows no dismay that they do not come when she does call for them. Hannah desires me to send word that the Cow has not calved and that Mr. and Miss Bray spent Sunday at Rosehill, to Baby's great delight. The young lady's smiles were abundant this morning, interspersed however with frowns which I am afraid she is taught to think as amusing as the smiles. To me they are anything but interesting.

Thank you dear Sara for your last little note and the packet of papers. I think a great deal of Dr. B.'s translation is in the form of notes, but I have only read the first § and do not mean to read any more except in case of a difficulty. I find it teazes and disturbs me to read any other person's translation. It is like hearing another piano going just a note before you in the same tune you are playing. Nevertheless it is very advantageous to have references in a difficult passage, if such there be, and I am greatly obliged to Mrs. Hennell for letting me have the benefit of Dr. Brabant's loan. . . .

I am so very, very tired I can scarcely manage to write sense, for I have been making the most of a delightfully fair afternoon, and taking a long walk without my bonnet that the winds of heaven might visit my head. I hope it is as fair at Hastings. I guess you are all now seated round the tea-table, chatting very sociably, and poor I am going to my solitary one. Think of this and be grateful. I am fond of giving an exhortation now and then. Somebody write to me soon and tell me how you all are.

Your true
Pollian.

TO SARA HENNELL, [13 JUNE 1845]

Bray took GE to London 2–4 June to join Mrs. Bray and Sara. William Macready played Brutus at Birmingham 12 June. [I, 195–96]

[Foleshill]

My dear Sara,

I have just been looking over some of the *revise* and reading again your sweet letter to me from Hastings, and an impulse of gratitude and love will not let me rest without writing you a little note though my head has almost done its possible for the day under this intense heat. You do not guess how much pleasure it gives me to look over your pencillings—they prove so clearly that you have really entered into the meaning of every sentence, and it always gives one satisfaction to see the evidence of brain work. I am quite indebted to you for your care and I feel greatly the advantage of having a *friend* to undertake the office of critic. There is one word I must mention,—Azazel is the word put in the original of the O.T. for the scape-goat. Now I imagine there is some dubiousness about the meaning and that Strauss would not think it right to translate *scape-goat*, because from the tenor of his sentence he appears to include Azazel with the evil demons. I wonder if it be supposed by any one that Azazel is in any way a distinct being from the goat. I know no Hebrew Scholar, and have access to no Hebrew Lexicon. Have you asked Mr. Hennell about it?

It was sadly disappointing to me to have no more quiet intercourse with you in London—but we shall find time. . . . Where do you think we, i.e. Mr. and Mrs. Bray and I, went last night, wishing that you were with us? To Birmingham to see Macready act Brutus! I was not disappointed on the whole, and it was a real treat, notwithstanding a ranting Cassius and a fat, stumpy Caesar and a screeching Calpurnia. I am coughing myself into such heats that I cannot write any more. Ever, dear Sara,

Your affectionate
Pollian.

Friday.

TO SARA HENNELL, [25 SEPTEMBER 1845]

Proof began in September and was concluded in May 1846. *The Life of Jesus* (3 vols.) was published 15 June 1846. The trip to Scotland was delayed for GE by the bankruptcy of her brother-in-law Edward Clarke. [I, 199–200]

[Foleshill] Thursday.

My dear Sara,

I am delighted with the proof—the type and everything else are just what I wished. To see the first sheet is the next best thing to seeing the last which I hope we shall all have done this time next year. I have never yet been able to learn whether the volumes are to come out separately or all at once. Some time when you write to Rosehill or to me, do send me word. I see the Greek notes are given in the Introduction just as they are in the original. Will it not look rather queer to begin with giving Greek and then to alter the plan? I have been thinking over the matter of the notes and it seems to me that when, as is generally the case the substance or the leading idea contained in them is given in the text it would look very ungeschickt to translate *without at the same time giving the Greek*, since Strauss's object is to verify his assertions rather than to give information by the quotations at the foot. What thinkest thou?

There is a very misty vision of a trip to the Highlands haunting us in this quarter. The vision would be much pleasanter if Sara were one of the images in it. You would surely go if we went, and then the thing would be perfect. I long to see you. . . .

Ever dear Sara

Your true and affectionate
Mary Ann.

TO JOHN SIBREE, JR., [14 OCTOBER 1845]

John Sibree, Jr. (1824–95) was the son of the minister of the Independent Chapel in Coventry. GE had asked his help with some Greek notes in Strauss. She went with the Brays to Scotland 14 October, but their tour was cut short after ten days by news that her father had broken his leg the day she left. [I, 200]

Foleshill | Tuesday morning.
In the hurry of setting off suddenly for Scotland Miss Evans is anxious to express to Mr. J. Sibree her real gratitude for his prompt and efficient attention to her request. She is more obliged than her haste will allow her to tell. She has this moment received his second note for which she thanks him, and will give the notes a thorough examination on her return, so as to be able to avail herself of Mr. J. Sibree's kindness should any further question arise respecting them.

Miss E. is ashamed to send so hasty an acknowledgment of a great favour but she is *standing* for the two or three minutes which are left her for writing and is afraid of leaving twenty things undone.

TO SARA HENNELL, [31 DECEMBER 1845]

Sara and her mother had just moved from Hackney to Clapton. The Hebrew lexicon might have been borrowed from the Reverend William Drake, a master at the Free Grammar School in Coventry, who served as examiner in Hebrew at the University of London. [I, 203–04]

[Foleshill]

Dear Sara,
I do pity you with the drunken Christmas workmen, keeping you in this uncomfortable interregnum. But do not go distraught—the spring will really come and the birds—many having had to fly across the Atlantic which is farther than you have to go to establish yourself.

I could easily give the meaning of the Hebrew word in question, as I know where to borrow a lexicon, but observe, there are two Hebrew words untranslated in this proof. I do not think it well to give the English in one place and not in another where there is no reason for such distinction—and there is not here, for the note in this proof sounds just as fee-fo-fum-ish as the other, without any translation. I could not alter the troublesome, because it is the nearest usable adjective for schwierig, which stands in the German. I am tired of inevitable *importants* and cannot bear to put them when they do not represent the German. I have an invitation to refuse—just come.

Thine in haste
Mary Ann.

Wednesday.

TO SARA HENNELL, [APRIL 1846]

Sara claimed that in helping GE with the translation, she was her *fidus Achates*, amused that, while attacking orthodoxy, GE was *pius Aeneas*. As she neared the end, GE said that "she was Strauss-sick—it made her ill dissecting the beautiful story of the crucifixion." The translation is given correctly as "evening of the passover." [I, 213–14]

[Foleshill]
Dear Achates,

I have *no* doubt that Paschaabend must be translated the evening of the Passover, and I think if you look at the passage again you will see that it would make nonsense of it to translate *eve* of the passover. . . . Now the only question as to the time of the meal is whether it was eaten on the evening of the 14th Nisan i.e. *not* the *eve* of the passover, but the commencement of the Passover itself, or on the evening of the 13th Nisan, which would be what Strauss calls the *Vorabend* des Pascha.

The synoptists say that the last supper was taken at the proper time for eating the passover—John intimates throughout his story that it was taken on the evening before (Vorabend) that of eating the passover. "Paschaabend selbst" expresses the representation of the synoptists, and the *eve* of the passover was not the proper time for eating the Paschal meal. I am tired and hurried, but if I have not made the matter clear, your own logical faculty will do it. . . .

Do you think Mr. Chapman is advertising sufficiently: I hope he is not so penny wise as to economize in that particular.

Thine
Pollian.

Do not ask anybody about the meaning of Paschaabend because the nature of the subject is the only evidence.

TO CHARLES BRAY, [21 OCTOBER 1846]

The cheerful burlesque of this letter dispels any notion that GE lacked humor. The theme of the old pedant wooing a young lady was among her possible themes since she first thought of writing fiction; Professor Bücherwurm and Dr. Brabant foreshadow Mr. Casaubon in *Middlemarch*. [VIII, 12–15]

[Foleshill] Wednesday Evening.

My dear Friend

When I wrote to Cara I complained that I had no news to tell her—but oh the mutations of this giddy planet! little did I think that ere another week passed away I should be an actress in scenes so novel as those which it has now become a duty of friendship to relate to you. But a truce to prefaces and palpitations. I will plunge at once in medias res.

The other day as I was sitting in my study, Mary came with a rather risible cast of expression to deliver to me a card, saying that a gentleman was below requesting to see me. The name on the card ran thus—Professor Bücherwurm, Moderig University. Down I came, not a little elated at the idea that a live professor was in the house, and, as you know I have quite the average quantity of that valuable endowment which spiteful people call assurance, but which I dignify with the name of self possession, you will believe that I neither blushed nor made a nervous giggle in attempting to smile, as is the lot of some unfortunate young ladies who are immersed in youthful bashfulness.

And whom do you think I saw? A tall, gaunt personage with huge cheek bones, dull grey eyes, hair of a very light neutral tint, un grand nez retroussé, and very black teeth. As novel writers say, I give you at once what was the result of a survey carried on by degrees through a long interview. My professor's coat was threadbare enough for that of a first-rate genius, and his linen and skin dirty enough to have belonged to the Emperor Julian. A profound reverence. I begged him to be seated, and this very begrimed professor began in sufficiently good English, 'Madam, you can form no preconception of my design in waiting on you.' I bowed. 'About a fortnight ago I came to London to seek—singular as it may seem to you—a *wife*.' (Surely, thought I, this poor man has escaped from a lunatic asylum, and I looked alternately at the door and the poker, measuring my distance from the two.) 'But,' my professor continued, 'there were certain qualifications which were indispensable to me in the person whom I could receive into that relation. I am a voluminous author—indeed my works already amount to some 20 vols.—my last publication in 5 vols. was a commentary on the book of Tobit. I have also written a long dissertation on the Greek Digamma, a treatise on Buddhism shewing that Christianity is entirely derived from this monstrous oriental superstition, and a very minute inquiry into the date, life and character of Cheops. My chief work, however, and that by which I hope to confer a lasting benefit on mankind is yet on hand. It is a system of metaphysics which I doubt not will supersede the latest products of the German philosophic mind.

'But like most authors who, as our divine Schiller says, live citizens of the age to come, my books are not appreciated in my own country. Now I wish that England should at least have the opportunity of profiting by them, and as I can find no indifferent person who will undertake a translation I am determined if possible to secure a translator in the person of a wife. I have made the most anxious and extensive inquiries in London after all female translators of German. I find them very abundant, but I require, besides ability to translate, a very decided ugliness of person and a sufficient fortune to supply a poor professor with coffee and tobacco, and an occasional draft of schwarzbier, as well as to contribute to the expenses of publication. After the most toilsome inquiries I have been referred to you, Madam, as presenting the required combination of attributes, and though I am rather disappointed to see that you have no beard, an attribute which I have ever regarded as the most unfailing indication of a strong-minded woman, I confess that in other respects your person at least comes up to my ideal.'

At this the professor bowed and coughed as waiting for my reply. I said that certainly I was taken by surprise, having long given up all hope of such an application as the present, but that I was decidedly pleased with the business-like tone of my suitor, and I thought no woman had been wooed in a more dignified manner since the days of the amazons, who were won with the sword. I thought it possible we might come to terms, always providing that he acceded to my irre-vocable conditions. 'For you must know, learned Professor,' I said, 'that I require nothing more in a husband than to save me from the horrific disgrace of spinster-hood and to take me out of England. As negative conditions, my husband must neither expect me to love him nor to mend his clothes, and he must allow me about once in a quarter a sort of conjugal saturnalia in which I may turn the tables upon him, hector and scold and cuff him. At other times I will be a dutiful wife so far as the task of translation is concerned, and I promise to give to the English a lucid idea of your notions respecting Cheops and Tobit etc. As to my want of beard I trust that defect may be remedied, since I doubt not there must be creams and essences which gentlemen whose having in beard is but a younger brother's revenue employ to cherish the too reluctant down, and it is an interesting phys-iological experiment yet to be tried, whether the feminine lip and chin may not be rendered fertile by this top-dressing.'

So we agreed to refer the matter to my Father. He, considering that it would probably be my last chance, at length consented though the professor peremp-torily insisted on the wedding taking place next week, as he could not defer his literary projects for a longer period. My Father theorized a little on the undesir-ableness of long courtships, in order to reconcile his conscience, and accordingly the arrangements are made. On Wednesday next I become the Professorin and wend my way with my tocher and my husband to Germany—never more to appear in this damp atmosphere and dull horizon. So if you wish to utter a last farewell, you must come home before next Wednesday.

I have ordered a magnificent wedding dress just to throw dust into the eyes of the Coventry people, but I have gone to no further expense in the matter of trousseau, as the Professor prefers as a female garb a man's coat, thrown over what are justly called the petticoats, so that the dress of a woman of genius may present the same sort of symbolical compromise between the masculine and feminine attire of which we have an example in the breastplate and petticoat of the immortal Joan.

I have requested Sara to be my bridesmaid, but her notions are far too contracted for her to comprehend or sanction a scheme of matrimony so much beyond the views of the present age. But as I know that you, my dear Friend, hold the most enlightened and liberal views of these subjects, and regard all subjection to feeling in such affairs as a weakness, proper to small heads, under 20 inches in circumference, I doubt not you will honour my bridal with your presence.

TO SARA HENNELL, [5 NOVEMBER 1846]

John Chapman offered to supply GE with books. The L[iterary] L[ady] Eliza Lynn (later Mrs. Linton), who had just published her first novel, *Azeth the Egyptian*, boarded at Chapman's at 142 Strand. *The Fawn of Sertorious* was by Robert Eyres Landor. Sara sent GE a letter purportedly from Professor Bücherwurm "declining the engagement because she was not ugly enough after all." [I, 224–26]

[Foleshill]

Just been to Rosehill, dearest Sara, and read your letter of this morning. Thank Mr. Chapman for his kind offer and assure him that I shall have much pleasure in accepting it. Do you know if Mr. Chapman has any unusual facilities for obtaining cheap classics? Such things are to be got handsome and secondhand in London if one knew but the way. I want to complete Xenophon's works. I have the Anabasis—and I might perhaps get a nice edition of the Memorabilia and Cyropædia in a cheaper way than by ordering them directly from our own bookseller. But all this is very selfish and troublesome, and do not teaze yourself with it except when you want something to do or say.

I begin to be of your and Cara's opinion anent Dr. B[rabant]. You are my own best plainspoken friend and generally judge better for me than I can judge for myself. I hope Rufa knows the contents of my letter to you. Pray convince her and every one concerned in the matter that I am too inflatedly conceited to think it worth my while to run after Dr. Brabant or his correspondence. If I ever offered incense to him it was because there was no other deity at hand and because I wanted some kind of worship pour passer le temps. I always knew that I could belabour my fetisch if I chose, and laughed at him in my sleeve. Even that degree of inclination towards mock reverence has long since passed away and ridiculous as it may seem to every one else, I looked on my renewal of a correspondence with him as a favour *conferred* by me rather than *received*. I shall certainly take an opportunity of certifying him on which leg the boot was. You see I am getting horridly vulgar as well as proud.

Do not judge too harshly of the L. L. on a first interview. I am quite glad to hear of prettiness associated with learning and heresy. Is there genius too? If so, the gods are getting kinder to mortals.

I have been reading the 'Fawn of Sertorius.' I think you would like it, though the many would not. It is pure, chaste, and classic beyond any attempt at fiction I ever read. If it be Bulwer's he has been undergoing a gradual transfiguration, and is now ready to be exalted into the assembly of the saints.

You must write to me, *do*—there's a dear soul. Keep a bit of paper lying ready to scribble on for me. The Professor's letter transmitted through you, gave me infinite consolation—more especially the apt and pregnant quotation from Berosus. Precious those little hidden lakelets of knowledge in the high mountains, far removed from the vulgar eye, only visited by the soaring birds of love.

> Thine entirely
> Pollian.

Thursday.

TO SARA HENNELL, [15 NOVEMBER 1846]

GE wrote "the discourses of Jesus, *like fragments of granite,* could not be dissolved by the flood of oral tradition." Strauss has *"die körnigen Reden* (the gritty discourses)". [I, 227]

Dear Sara,

The review of Strauss contains some very just remarks, though, on the whole I think it shallow and in many cases unfair. The praise it gives to the translation is just what I should have wished—indeed I cannot imagine anything more gratifying in the way of laudation. Is it not droll that Wicksted should have chosen one of my interpolations or rather paraphrases to dilate on? The expression "granite," applied to the sayings of Jesus is nowhere used by Strauss, but is an impudent addition of mine to eke out his metaphor. . . .

You say in your note to Rosehill this morning that Mr. Chapman has sent me the books. I have not received them. There is some provoking fault somewhere, for I have not had a parcel which Dr. Brabant sent more than a week ago. Glad to hear that you are flourishing in body and mind. Love to Mrs. Hennell.

> Thine,
> Pollian.

Foleshill | Sunday.

TO SARA HENNELL, [28 FEBRUARY 1847]

Chapman's dealings as a publisher were always slippery. Using a copy of Spinoza's *Opera* borrowed from Brabant, GE began in 1843 to translate part of the *Tractatus Theologico-politicus* for Bray and resumed it in 1849 during her father's last illness. Brabant annoyed GE by the rude way he asked to have the book back. The phrenological Organs 6 and 7 were Combativeness and Destructiveness. [I, 231–32]

> Foleshill Sunday.

My dear Sara,

Mr. Hennell sent me a statement in black and white of the agreement between him and Mr. Chapman, but it was returned to him at his request. My strong impression was, that the first 250 copies were to be Mr. C's, the second 250, the subscribers'. We have a dispute here as to the number of copies printed. Was it 1000 or 2000? I hope Mr. Chapman will not misbehave, but he was always too much of the *interesting* gentleman to please me. Men must not attempt to be interesting on any lower terms than a fine poetical genius.

I certainly should have been delighted if the Spinoza parcel could have been sent at a high pitch of velocity to Devizes and found its mark somewhere above Dr. B's ear, so as to give a salutary bruise to his Nos. 6 and 7—but since cannon-ball speed is not attainable, I am not sorry that you should extract a little pleasure from his property before it reaches him. As you *have* detained it, will you take the trouble to ask Mr. Chapman to get me a copy of the same edition if possible— Mind, I really want this, and should have no end of difficulty in getting it in any other way. I never *meant* to write to Dr. B. on family matters—I merely said in my vicious, hyena fashion that I should like to send him an anathema maranatha. I am glad to hear you are better. Mr. Bray alarmed me about you. No more at present from thine

Pollian.

TO MARY SIBREE, 10 MAY [1847]

GE's caution about old people was provoked by Mary's quoting an opinion of the mother-in-law of Edward Delf, an Independent minister in Coventry. Exeter Hall was the scene of the annual May Meetings of the Church of England Missionary Society. GE found the word *guanoing* in Disraeli's *Tancred* (1847). [I, 233–35]

Foleshill May 10th.

My dear Mary

It is worth while to forget a friend for a week or ten days, just for the sake of the agreeable kind of startle it gives one to be reminded that one has such a treasure in reserve—the same sort of pleasure I suppose that a poor body feels who happens to lay his hand on an undreamt-of sixpence which had sunk to a corner of his pocket. When Mr. Sibree brought me your parcel, I had been to London for a week and having been full of Mendelssohn oratorios and Italian operas, I had just this kind of delightful surprize when I saw your note and the beautiful purse. Not that I mean to compare you to a sixpence—you are a bright golden sovereign to me, with edges all unrubbed, fit to remind a poor tarnished bruised piece like me that there are ever fresh and more perfect coinages of human nature forth-coming. . . .

I am glad to think of all your pleasure among friends new and old. Mrs. Delf's mother is I daresay a valuable person—but do not I beseech thee go to old people as oracles on matters which date any later than their 35th year—only trust them, if they are good, in those practical rules which are the common property of long experience. If they are governed by one special idea which circumstances or their own mental bias have caused them to grasp with peculiar firmness and to work up into original forms, make yourself master of their thoughts and convictions, the residuum of all that long travail which poor mortals have to encounter in their three score years and ten, but do not trust their application of their gathered wisdom, for however just old people may be in their *principles* of judgment, they are often wrong in their application of them, from an imperfect or unjust conception of the matter to be judged. Love and cherish and venerate the old, but never imagine that a worn-out, dried-up organization can be so rich in inspiration as one which is full fraught with life and energy. I am not talking like one who is superlatively jealous for the rights of the old, yet such I am I assure thee.

I heard Mendelssohn's new oratorio "Elijah," when I was in London. It has been performed four times in Exeter Hall to as large an audience as the building would hold—Mendelssohn himself the conductor. It is a glorious production and altogether I look upon it as a kind of sacramental purification of Exeter Hall, and a proclamation of indulgence for all that is to be perpetrated there during this month of May. This is a piece of impiety which you may expect from a lady who has been *guanoing* her mind with French novels. (This is the impertinent expression of d'Israeli, who writing himself much more detestable stuff than ever came from a French pen can do nothing better to bamboozle the unfortunates who are seduced into reading his Tancred than speak superciliously of all other men and things, an expedient much more successful in some quarters than one would expect.) But *au fond*, dear Mary, I have no impiety in my mind at this moment, and my soul heartily responds to your rejoicing that society is attaining a more perfect idea and exhibition of Paul's exhortation—Let the same mind be in you which was also in Christ Jesus. I believe the Amen to this will be uttered more and more fervently, "among all posterities for ever more." . . .

My pen tells me to leave off or be illegible, though perhaps this is not a mere possibility already. Goodbye, dear love,

Yours ever
Mary Ann Evans.

TO SARA HENNELL, 16 SEPTEMBER 1847

GE's scrupulous insistence on payment of even trifling debts was a lifelong characteristic. Robert Evans, now 74 and in failing health, demanded increasing attention. GE's signature *Husband*, like *Weib*, *Gemahlin*, *Sposa*, and other names, originated in the Bücherwurm correspondence. [I, 236–38]

Foleshill | September 16th 1847.
My dear Sara,

I cannot forgive you for not asking me for the two shillings which I owe you. You ought either to have felt sure that it was only an infirmity of memory which kept me in debt, or to have told me that I was too good-for-nothing to be your friend. I have given the two shillings to Mr. Bray and I beg that for my sake you will demand them from him when he goes to London. The fact was that I had asked him to pay you the carriage in the first instance when I sent Spinoza to you, and so I the more easily lost sight of the matter. But pray have the generosity another time to save me from the pain of finding that I have neglected to pay *even* my money debts, when there are so many others which I am unable to defray. Now I have scolded you I can talk of other things.

I have read the Inquiry again with more than interest—with delight and high admiration. My present impression from it far surpasses the one I had retained from my two readings about 5 years ago. . . . The book is full of *wit* to me, it gives me the exquisite kind of laughter which comes from the gratification of the reasoning faculties. . . . I think the Inquiry furnishes the utmost that can be done towards obtaining a *real* view of the life and character of Jesus by rejecting as little as possible from the Gospels. I confess that I should call many things "shining ether" to which Mr. Hennell allows "the solid angularity of facts," but I think he has thoroughly worked out the problem. Subtract from the New Testament the miraculous and highly improbable and what will be the remainder?

Father and I are going to the coast next week, but I do not yet know whether to Brighton or some where else. If you write to me, which you need only do if you feel that way inclined, send the note to Cara, and she will forward it to me.

> Thine ever affectionate
> Husband.

TO SARA HENNELL, 13 OCTOBER [1847]

GE took her father to the Isle of Wight for a fortnight, reading Scott's novels to him in the evenings. The work on philosophy she was thinking of was "The Idea of a Future Life," which she began in 1852 but never finished. The Swedish novels were translations of the works of Fredrika Bremer. [I, 239–40]

Foleshill | October 13.

Liebe Weib

Thy letter did not reach me by the 'breezy ocean' but it smiled on me, or rather, to be more literal, I smiled on it when I reached home on Saturday evening. I am reproaching myself for letting three days pass without thanking you for it, for I see it is now nearly a fortnight since you wrote it. I heartily wish you *had* been with me to see all the beauties which have gladdened my soul and made me feel that this earth is as good a heaven as I ought to dream of. I have a much greater respect for the Isle of Wight now I have seen it, than when I knew it only by report—a compliment which one can seldom very sincerely pay to things and people that one has heard puffed and bepraised. I do long for you to see Alum Bay. Though you have beheld many more beauties than I, I do believe that would be quite new to you. . . .

We staid at Brighton on our way home, and I very much enjoyed the sight of that splendid place, the only one of its kind, I suppose, in England. I find one very great spiritual good attendant on a quiet meditative journey among fresh scenes. I seem to have removed to a distance from myself when I am away from the petty circumstances that make up my ordinary environment. I can take myself up by the ears and inspect myself, like any other queer monster on a small scale. I have had many thoughts, especially on a subject that I should like to work out "The superiority of the consolations of philosophy to those of (so-called) religion." Do you stare? . . .

Thank you for putting me on reading Sir Charles Grandison. I have read five volumes and am only vexed that I have not the two last on my table at this moment that I might have them for my *convives*. I had no idea that Richardson was worth so much. I have had more pleasure from him than from all the Swedish novels together. The morality is perfect—there is nothing for the new lights to correct.

I seem to myself to have written very detestably, but you will rather have this disagreeable I-ish letter than think me ungrateful, which is *one* bad adjective that your Pollian does not deserve.

TO JOHN SIBREE, JR., [11 FEBRUARY 1848]

Sibree was a student at Spring Hill College, Birmingham, preparing to enter his father's profession as Independent minister. GE's letters to him at the period of revolutions on the Continent express her most radical political views. The Baroni are strolling acrobats adopted by Sidonia, the Jewish philanthropist in *Coningsby* and *Tancred*. Glums and Gawries are the males and females of the winged race inhabiting the Antarctic region in which the hero of *Peter Wilkins* is shipwrecked in the novel by Robert Paltock (1751). [I, 245–48]

Foleshill Friday.

Dear Mr. Sibree. . .

Begin your letters by abusing me, according to my example. There is nothing like a little gun-powder for a damp chimney and an explosion of that sort will set the fire of your ideas burning to admiration. I hate bashfulness and modesties as Sir Hugh Evans would say, and I warn you that I shall make no apologies, though from my habit of writing only to people who, rather than have nothing from me, will tolerate nothings, I shall be very apt to forget that you are not one of those amiably silly individuals. I must write to you *more meo*, without taking pains or laboring to be spirituelle when heaven never meant me to be so, and it is your own fault if you bear with my letters a moment after they become an infliction. I am glad you detest Mrs. Hannah More's letters. I like neither her letters, nor her books, nor her character. She was that most disagreeable of all monsters, a blue-stocking—a monster that can only exist in a miserably false state of society, in which a woman with but a smattering of learning or philosophy is classed along with singing mice and card playing pigs.

It is some time since I read Tancred, so that I have no very vivid recollection of its details, but I thought it very "thin" and inferior in the working up to Coningsby and Sybil. Young Englandism is almost as remote from my sympathies as Jacobitism as far as its form is concerned, though I love and respect it as an effort on behalf of the people. D'Israeli is unquestionably an able man, and I always enjoy his tirades against liberal principles as opposed to *popular* principles—the name by which he distinguishes his own. As to his theory of 'races' it has not a leg to stand on, and can only be buoyed up by such windy eloquence as 'You chitty-faced squabby-nosed Europeans owe your commerce, your arts, your religion to the Hebrews—nay the Hebrews lead your armies—' in proof of which he can tell us that Massena, a second-rate general of Napoleon's, was a Jew whose real name was Manasseh. Extermination up to a certain point seems to be the law for the inferior races—for the rest, fusion both for physical and moral ends. It appears to me that the law by which privileged classes degenerate from continual intermarriage must act on a larger scale in deteriorating whole races. The nations have been always kept apart until they have sufficiently developed their idiosyncrasies and then some great revolutionary force has been called into action by which the genius of a particular nation becomes a portion of the common mind of humanity. Looking at the matter aesthetically, our ideal of beauty is never formed on the characteristics of a single race. I confess the types of the 'pure races,' however handsome, always impress me disagreeably—there is an undefined feeling that I am looking not at *man* but at a specimen of an order under Cuvier's class, Bimana. The negroes certainly puzzle me—all the other races seem plainly destined to extermination or fusion not excepting even the "Hebrew-Caucasian." But the negroes are too important physiologically and geographically for one to think of their extermination, while the repulsion between them and the other races seems too strong for fusion to take place to any great extent.

On one point I heartily agree with D'Israeli as to the superiority of the Oriental races—their clothes are beautiful and ours are execrable. Did you not think the picture of the Baroni family interesting? I should like to know who are the originals. The fellowship of race, to which D'Israeli exultingly refers the munificence of Sidonia, is so evidently an inferior impulse which must ultimately be superseded that I wonder even he, Jew as he is, dares to boast of it. My Gentile nature kicks most resolutely against any assumption of superiority in the Jews, and is almost ready to echo Voltaire's vituperation. I bow to the supremacy of Hebrew poetry, but much of their early mythology and almost all their history is utterly revolting. Their stock has produced a Moses and a Jesus, but Moses was impregnated with Egyptian philosophy and Jesus is venerated and adored by us only for that wherein he transcended or resisted Judaism. The very exaltation of their idea of a national deity into a spiritual monotheism seems to have been borrowed from the other oriental tribes. Everything *specifically* Jewish is of a low grade.

And do you really think that sculpture and painting are to die out of the world? If that be sooth, let another deluge come as quickly as possible that a new race of Glums and Gawries may take possession of this melancholy earth. I agree with you as to the inherent superiority of music—as that questionable woman the Countess Hahn-Hahn says, painting and sculpture are but an idealizing of our actual existence. Music arches over this existence with another and a diviner. Amen too, to that ideen-voll observation of Hegel's. We hardly know what it is to feel for human misery until we have heard a shriek, and a more perfect hell might be made out of sounds than out of any preparation of fire and brimstone. When the tones of our voice have betrayed peevishness or harshness we seem to be doubly haunted by the ghost of our sins—we are doubly conscious that we have been untrue to our part in the great Handel chorus. But I cannot assent to the notion that music is to supersede the other arts, or that the highest minds must necessarily aspire to a sort of Milton blindness in which the "tiefste der Sinne" is to be a substitute for all the rest. I cannot recognize the truth of all that is said about the necessity of religious fervour to high art. I am sceptical as to the real existence of such fervour in any of the greatest artists. Artistic power seems to me to resemble dramatic power—to be an intuitive perception of the varied states of which the human mind is susceptible with ability to give them out anew in intensified expression. It is true that the older the world gets, originality becomes less possible. Great subjects are used up, and civilization tends evermore to repress individual predominance, highly-wrought agony or ecstatic joy. But all the gentler emotions will be ever new—ever wrought up into more and more lovely combinations, and genius will probably take their direction. Have you ever seen a head of Christ taken from a statue by Thorwaldsen of 'Christ scourged.' If not I think it would almost satisfy you. There is another work of his said to be very sublime of the archangel waiting for the command to sound the last trumpet. Yet Thorwaldsen came at the fag-end of time.

I am afraid you despise landscape painting—but to me even the works of our own Stanfield and Roberts and Creswick bring a whole world of thought and bliss—"a sense of something far more deeply interfused." The ocean and the sky and the everlasting hills are spirit to me, and they will never be robbed of their sublimity.

I am shocked to see how much paper I have covered with my sprawling "pattes de mouches." I shall really frighten you. I will be more forbearing another time. Have the students apartments at the college or have you lodgings elsewhere? I have no materials for imagining your whereabouts—a deficiency which always annoys me. Ah! I want doing good to in a thousand ways. Do not forsake the good work but write to me again as soon as you have any time to spare me.

> Always yours truly
> Mary Ann Evans

I am writing at midnight, so this cannot reach you till Sunday. Pardon its impertinence in presenting itself then and put it in your pocket till Monday.

TO JOHN SIBREE, JR., [8 MARCH 1848]

Carlyle's article was on Louis Philippe, who with his queen had been smuggled out of France and settled at Claremont, near Esher. "Albert, ouvrier" was the name signed on decrees of the revolutionists. In Glasgow unemployed workers rioted and broke into the gun shops; the cavalry was called to restore order. The Italians chased the Austrians out of Lombardy 17–22 March. [I, 252–56]

> [Foleshill] Wednesday.

Write and tell you that I join you in your happiness about the French Revolution? Very fine, my good friend. If I made you wait for a letter as long as you do me, our little échantillon of a Millennium would be over. Satan would be let loose again, and I should have to share your humiliation instead of your triumph. Natheless I absolve you, for the sole merit of thinking rightly (that is, of course, just as I do) about la grande nation and its doings. You and Carlyle (have you seen his article in last week's Examiner?) are the only two people who feel just as I would have them—who can glory in what is actually great and beautiful without putting forth any cold reservations and incredulities to save their credit for wisdom. I am all the more delighted with your enthusiasm because I didn't expect it. I feared that you lacked revolutionary ardour. But no—you are just as sansculottish and rash as I would have you. . . .

I thought we had fallen on such evil days that we were to see no really great movement—that ours was what St. Simon calls a purely *critical* epoch, not at all an organic one—but I begin to be glad of my date. I would consent, however, to have a year clipt off my life for the sake of witnessing such a scene as that of the men of the barricade bowing to the image of Christ "who first taught fraternity to men." One trembles to look into every fresh newspaper lest there should be something to mar the picture; but hitherto even the scoffing newspaper critics have been compelled into a tone of genuine respect for the French people and the Provisional Government. Lamartine can act a poem if he cannot write one of the very first order. I hope that beautiful face given to him in the pictoral newspaper is really his, it is worthy of an aureole. I am chiefly anxious about Albert, the operative, but his picture is not to be seen. I have little patience with people who can find time to pity Louis Philippe and his moustachioed sons. Certainly our decayed monarchs should be pensioned off: we should have a hospital for them, or a sort of Zoological Garden, where these wornout humbugs may be preserved. It is but justice that we should keep them, since we have spoiled them for any honest trade. Let them sit on soft cushions and have their dinner regularly, but for heaven's sake preserve me from sentimentalizing over a pampered old man when the earth has its millions of unfed souls and bodies. Surely he is not so Ahab-like as to wish that the revolution had been deferred till his son's days; and I think the shades of the Stuarts would have some reason to complain if the Bourbons who are so little better than they, had been allowed to reign much longer.

I should have no hope of good from any imitative movement at home. Our working classes are eminently inferior to the mass of the French people. In France, the *mind* of the people is highly electrified—they are full of ideas on social subjects—they really desire social *reform*—not merely an acting out of Sancho Panza's favourite proverb "Yesterday for you, to-day for me." The revolutionary animus extended over the whole nation, and embraced the rural population—not merely as with us, the artisans of the towns. Here there is so much larger a proportion of selfish radicalism and unsatisfied, brute sensuality (in the agricultural and mining districts especially) than of perception or desire of justice, that a revolutionary movement would be simply destructive—not constructive. Besides, it would be put down. Our military have no notion of "fraternizing." They have the same sort of inveteracy as dogs have for the ill-drest canaille. They are as mere a brute force as a battering ram and the aristocracy have got firm hold of them. Our little humbug of a queen is more endurable than the rest of her race because she calls forth a chivalrous feeling, and there is nothing in our constitution to obstruct the slow progress of *political* reform. This is all we are fit for at present. The social reform which may prepare us for great changes is more and more the object of effort both in Parliament and out of it. But we English are slow crawlers. The sympathy in Ireland seems at present only of the water toast kind. The Glasgow riots are more serious, but one cannot believe in a Scotch Reign of Terror in these days. I should not be sorry to hear that the Italians had risen en masse and chased the odious Austrians out of beautiful Lombardy. But this they could hardly do without help, and that involves another European war. But I am writing in utter misery with toothache and headache and the greasiest of pens— and all to give you the trouble of reading what is not worth that compliment.

Concerning the "tent-making," there is much more to be said; but am I to adopt your rule and never speak of what I suppose we agree about? . . . I want you to write me a Confession of Faith—not merely *what* you believe but why you believe it. I have no right in the world to make such a request, but your goodness will give me more than my mere right. Never mind what you write to me—your letters shall be quite sacred, and you see I write any nonsense that can come into a poor woman's brain to you.

I wish you would burn my letters when you have read them once through, and then you would not have time to find out how good for nothing they are, and there would be no risk of a critical third pair of eyes getting a sight of them, which would certainly be a death blow to my reputation for gravity and wisdom—not that I am very careful in this matter—for this bump of cautiousness with which nature has furnished me is of very little use to me. But I will be as careful for you as if I were ultra-cautious on my own behalf, so I say again utter, utter, utter, and it will be a deed of mercy twice blest, for I shall be a safety-valve for your communicativeness and prevent it from splitting honest peoples' brains who don't understand you and moreover it will be fraught with ghostly comfort to me. Forgive me for writing to you when I am hardly able to write rationally, and accept it as the more gracious alternative—rather than remaining silent another week.

Ever your sincere friend
Mary Ann Evans.

TO MRS. HENRY HOUGHTON, [17? APRIL? 1848]

John Bury was for many years a surgeon at Coventry. [I, 257]

[Foleshill] Monday.

My dear Fanny

Mr. Bury has put Father on a different system of diet—he takes no meat or wine and has had a Blister on the chest which I trust has already done a little good. I fear his illness is much more serious than I was led to believe and I am in very great anxiety, but Mr. Bury assures me there is no cause for immediate alarm. He says all is being done that can be and that the symptoms are a little subdued this morning. In his opinion it is the imperfect action of the *heart* that produces the difficult breathing. I am going to have a bed made up for him in the dining-room to prevent his having the exertion of going up stairs which Mr. Bury thinks injurious. He had a wretched night last night. I shall sleep on the sofa in his room until he is better. In a day or two when we can judge of his improvement I will write again. I need not say, Come to see him whenever you feel inclined—*that* you will of course do. Invitations in this case would be quite out of place. I have been in great agitation this morning, but Mr. Bury has comforted me, and therefore, you must take comfort on the same ground. Ever, dear Fanny

Your affectionate
Mary Ann

TO JOHN SIBREE, JR., [14? MAY 1848]

In attempting to formulate his reasons for believing Sibree found them inadequate, and after a time abandoned the ministry. His parents blamed GE for influencing John. He followed her advice, went to Halle, lived in a high attic, translated Hegel, took an M.A. at the University of London, married, and became a tutor at Stroud. [I, 260–61]

Foleshill, | Sunday Evening.

My dear Mr. Sibree,
   I might make a very plausible excuse for not acknowledging your kind note earlier by telling you that I have been both a nurse and invalid, but to be thoroughly ingenuous, I must confess that all this would not have been enough to prevent my writing, but for my chronic disease of utter idleness. I have heard and thought of you with great interest however, for Mary has not failed to make me a sharer in all her joys and anxieties on your account. You have my hearty and not inexperienced sympathy, for, to speak in the style of Jonathan Oldbuck, I am haud ignara mali. I have gone through a trial of the same genus as yours, though rather differing in species. I sincerely rejoice in the step you have taken—it is an absolutely necessary condition for any true development of your nature. It was impossible to think of your career with hope while you tacitly subscribed to the miserable etiquette (it deserves no better or more spiritual name) of sectarianism. Only persevere—be true, firm and loving—not too anxious about immediate usefulness to others—that can only be a result of justice to yourself. Study *mental hygiène*—take long doses of 'dolce far niente,' and be in no great hurry about anything in this 'varsal world! Do we not commit ourselves to sleep, and so resign all care for ourselves every night? lay ourselves gently on the bosom of nature or God? A beautiful reproach to the spirit of some religionists and ultra-good people.
   I like the notion of your going to Germany as good in every way, for yourself, body and mind, and for all others. O the bliss of having a very high attic in a romantic continental town, such as Geneva—far away from morning callers dinners and decencies; and then to pause for a year and think 'de omnibus rebus et

quibusdam aliis,' and then to return to life, and work for poor stricken humanity and never think of self again.

I am writing nearly in the dark, with the post-bag waiting. I fear I shall not be at home when you come home, but surely I shall see you before you leave England. However that may be I shall utter a genuine Lebewohl.

Yours truly

Mary Ann Evans.

TO THE BRAYS AND HENNELLS,' 8 JUNE [1848]

GE took her father to St. Leonard's for the sea air. The Brays were in London to hear Emerson's lectures, staying with Sara and her mother at Clapton. Charles Hennell was first bass, Bray, second. At 142 Strand, Bray met Emerson, who was boarding there with his publisher John Chapman, and invited him to stop at Coventry on his way to his ship at Liverpool. When GE was presented at breakfast 13 July, he fell into earnest conversation with her. Suddenly, something she said made him start: he had asked what book first awakened her to deep reflection, and when she answered "Rousseau's *Confessions*," he declared that Carlyle had told him that very book had had the same effect on his mind. GE went with them to Stratford "to see Shakespeare," and on his return Emerson expressed his admiration of her: "That young lady has a calm, serious soul." To Sara GE wrote the next day: "I have seen Emerson—the first *man* I have ever seen. [I, 266–67]

33 Marina | St. Leonard's | June 8th.

Dear Quartett of Friends—

I may still say so, though I fear your primo basso has departed, for I suppose your basso secondo will have arrived before my letter. It has been quite enough of joy to me to think of you receiving the pleasures of your fourth in that delightful way and of Mrs. Hennell looking on. . . .

Father is no better at all, indeed I think his cough is more troublesome than when we came. This is dispiriting for him and so he is doubly dragged backwards. The weather is so cruelly cold, that one can expect no good influence from the sea-breezes.

Dear Cara, your husband desired me to send you the newspaper paragraph about George Sand, and I obey—but if you disapprove, utter none of your blasphemies to me.

Poor Louis Blanc! The newspapers make me melancholy—but shame upon me that I say 'poor.' The day will come when there will be a temple of white marble where sweet incense and anthems shall rise to the memory of every man and woman who has had a deep '*ahnung*,' a presentiment, a yearning, or a clear vision of the time when this miserable reign of Mammon shall end. . . . I feel that society is training men and women for hell.

You are going to Teignmouth, I hope? do not give up that charming plan, I beg. The sun is beginning to shine and I go to my bath. Seen anything of Emerson? Love to all

Your

Mary Ann.

TO CHARLES BRAY, [11 JUNE 1848]

At the end of June the Brays spent ten days at Bishop's Teignton, Devon. GE's indignation over *Jane Eyre* was aroused by Rochester's inability to divorce his mad wife and Jane's refusal to live with him. The Duke of Wellington wrote to one lady that he could not read her letter and asked her to write in dark ink and few words. [I, 268–69]

33 Marina | St. Leonard's | Sunday.

Alas! mon ami, Father is not better as you imagine—on the contrary all his worst symptoms have returned—a bad cough, shortness of breath, languor and aching of the limbs. I fear I shall have to take him home as great an invalid as ever. I thought you went to London last Thursday, and wrote a letter for the community there, supposing you to be a part of it. It is very charming to hear of all Cara's pleasures past and to come, and it will be still better to think of them when you are sharing them. Her letter was as exhilarating to me as anything could be when Father's pale haggard looking face was opposite to me. . . . Persevere in the Devonshire plan pray. I think we shall surely have fine weather now. Today is crowned with the most beautiful of skies, light floating clouds setting off that perfect azure which must ever stand for hope in the language of colours.

I have read Jane Eyre, mon ami, and shall be glad to know what you admire in it. All self-sacrifice is good—but one would like it to be in a somewhat nobler cause than that of a diabolical law which chains a man soul and body to a putrefying carcase. However the book *is* interesting—only I wish the characters would talk a little less like the heroes and heroines of police reports.

Do not curse my pale ink and send me an answer in the style of the Duke of Wellington to Mrs. M.

Yours in secula seculorum
Mary Ann.

TO MRS. HENRY HOUGHTON, [?JULY 1848]

Mrs. Bray wrote to Sara that the doctors expected Robert Evans to die suddenly. GE "has the whole care and fatigue of nursing him night and day with this constant expectation." [I, 271–72]

[Foleshill]

My dear Fanny

Father has had another wretched night which has made him feel increasingly ill this morning. He generally gets easier in the afternoon. Mr. Bury and Mr. Clarke met here this morning. They agree in the opinion that Father's state is not referable to any one organ, but that the entire system is disordered. I have written to Robert to beg him to come, as I am sure he would wish to see Father if he knew how ill he is.

I trust dear Father will not have another night so trying as the last. I am to try a mustard plaister between the shoulders if he should not be able to sleep. You will come again soon—but it would be well to contrive so that there should not be too many together as Father is too weak to bear much hurry or excitement, and we have now only one downstairs sitting room. Could you come tomorrow dear?

Ever your affectionate
Mary Ann

Tuesday Morning.

✓ TO SARA HENNELL, [9 FEBRUARY 1849]

Sara did not share GE's enthusiasm for George Sand's *Jacques* and had criticized the hero's advocacy of free love. GE's copy of Thomas à Kempis with her inscription "February 1849" was given to Sara 20 June 1851 and is now in the Coventry Public Library. [I, 276–78]

[Foleshill]
Dear Sara

My life is a perpetual nightmare—always haunted by something to be done which I have never the time or rather the energy to do. Opportunity is kind, but only to the industrious and I alas! am not one of them. Else I might write to you oftener, if indeed you would thank me for doing so. I have sat down in desperation this evening though dear Father is very uneasy and his moans distract me, just to tell you that you have full absolution for your criticism which I do not reckon of the 'impertinent' order. I wish you thoroughly to understand that the writers who have most profoundly influenced me—who have rolled away the waters from their bed, raised new mountains and spread delicious valleys for me—are not in the least oracles to me. It is just possible that I may not embrace one of their opinions, that I may wish my life to be shaped quite differently from theirs. For instance it would signify nothing to me if a very wise person were to stun me with proofs that Rousseau's views of life, religion, and government are miserably erroneous—that he was guilty of some of the worst basses ses that have degraded civilized man. I might admit all this—and it would be not the less true that Rousseau's genius has sent that electric thrill through my intellectual and moral frame which has awakened me to new perceptions, which has made man and nature a fresh world of thought and feeling to me—and this not by teaching me any new belief. It is simply that the rushing mighty wind of his inspiration has so quickened my faculties that I have been able to shape more definitely for myself ideas which had previously dwelt as dim 'ahnungen' in my soul—the fire of his genius has so fused together old thoughts and prejudices that I have been ready to make new combinations.

It is thus with G. Sand. I should never dream of going to her writings as a moral code or text-book. I don't care whether I agree with her about marriage or not—whether I think the design of her plot correct or that she had no precise design at all but began to write as the spirit moved her and trusted to Providence for the catastrophe, which I think the more probable case—it is sufficient for me as a reason for bowing before her in eternal gratitude to that 'great power of God' manifested in her—that I cannot read six pages of hers without feeling that it is given to her to delineate human passion and its results—(and I must say in spite of your judgment) some of the moral instincts and their tendencies—with such truthfulness such nicety of discrimination such tragic power and withal such loving gentle humour that one might live a century with nothing but one's own dull faculties and not know so much as those six pages will suggest. The psychological anatomy of Jacques and Fernande in the early days of their marriage seems quite preternaturally true—I mean that her power of describing it is preternatural. Fernande and Jacques are merely the masculine and the feminine nature and their early married life an everyday tragedy—but I will not dilate on the book or on your criticism for I am so sleepy that I should write nothing but bêtises.

I have at last the most delightful "de imitatione Christi" with quaint woodcuts. One breathes a cool air as of cloisters in the book—it makes one long to be a saint for a few months. Verily its piety has its foundations in the depth of the divine-human soul.

Thine Ever
Pollian.

Do not suppose that I mean this as an answer to your criticism or that I do not understand it.

TO SARA HENNELL, [18 APRIL 1849]

GE wrote for the *Conventry Herald* a review of J. A. Froude's *Nemesis of Faith* (1849), a story of a young man at Oxford who loses his faith by contact with the Tractarians. The book was burned in the Hall of Exeter College, of which Froude was a Fellow. Through Chapman, his publisher, Froude sent a copy "To the Translator of Strauss," and in the ensuing correspondence begged GE to reveal her identity. His *Shadows of the Clouds* (1847) contains two unpleasant stories of life at Westminster School and Oxford. None of GE's translation of the *Tractatus* has been found. [I, 279–81]

Foleshill | Wednesday.

Dear love, . .

I have so liked the thought of your being with Mr. Hennell and yet more that of your enjoying the Nemesis of Faith. . . . You must read the 'Shadows of Clouds'—it produces a sort of palpitation that one hardly knows whether to call wretched or delightful. I cannot take up the book again though wanting very much to read it more closely. . . .

I am translating the Tractatus Theologico-politicus of Spinoza and seem to want the only friend that knows how to praise or blame. How exquisite is the satisfaction of feeling that another mind than your own sees precisely where and what is the difficulty—and can exactly appreciate the success with which it is overcome. One knows—sed longo intervallo—the full meaning of the "fit audience though few." How an artist must hate the noodles that stare at his picture with a vague notion that it *is* a clever thing to be able to paint.

The cold of this weather really enters into one's soul. Write to me—I feel as if writing would be very delightful now. I have a corresponding fit just come over me. Do you have a correspon*dent* fit?

> Yours in perennial silliness and love,
> Pollian.

TO THE BRAYS, [30 MAY 1849]

GE had written to her half brother Robert Evans asking him to come. The Brays were visiting the Hennells at Clapton. Lenette is the dull, unhappy woman in Richter's *Blumenfrucht und Dornenstüche,* incapable of understanding her noble-minded husband Siebenkäs, whose name is here applied to Sara. Mr. Evans died in the night. He was buried at Chilvers Coton 6 June. [I, 284–85]

[Foleshill] 1/2 past 9. | Wednesday Morning.

Dear Friends—

Mr. Bury told us last night that he thought Father would not last till morning. I sat by him with my hand in his till four o'clock, and he then became quieter and has had some comfortable sleep. He is obviously weaker this morning and has been for the last two or three days so painfully reduced that I dread to think what his dear frame may become before life gives way. My Brother slept here last night and will be here again tonight. What shall I be without my Father? It will seem as if a part of my moral nature were gone. I had a horrid vision of myself last night becoming earthly sensual and devilish for want of that purifying restraining influence. I write when I can but I do not know whether my letter will do to send this evening. Love to all—Mrs. Hennell, Mr. and Mrs. C. Hennell, and My Siebenkäs. By the bye, Siebenkäs, Cara is very *Lenettish* about sundry things. Season your conversation with a little salt for her advantage and tell her to let me strip myself of my pewter and table-napkins without so many scruples. Dear Cara, love to you and yours.

Father is very, very much weaker this evening.

2

HIGH ATTICS
Geneva · 142 Strand

Five days after Robert Evans's funeral the Brays took GE abroad. From Paris they went to Lyon, Avignon, Marseille, Nice, Genoa, Milan, over the Simplon Pass to Chamonix, and on to Geneva, where they left her to spend the winter. She lived for two months at Campagne Plongeon, a pension on the Lake. Her vivid letters describing the other guests foreshadow the novelist in their keen observations of character. In October she moved to the center of Geneva, boarding with the family of François D'Albert Durade, reading omnivorously, going to lectures, playing the piano, and widening her social experience in the intelligent circle of D'Albert's friends. In March 1850 he escorted her to England. After brief visits with Isaac, Chrissey, and Fanny, GE lived at Rosehill with the Brays for seven months.

John Chapman, having published a learned book by R. W. Mackay called *The Progress of the Intellect as Exemplified in the Religious Development of the Greeks and Hebrews*, came to Coventry in October to ask "the translator of Strauss" to review it. Her brilliant article in the *Westminster Review* shows the extraordinary range of her mind. She delivered the manuscript herself in London and spent two weeks with the Chapmans at 142 Strand. On the ground floor of this large house Chapman conducted his publishing and bookselling business. On the floors above Mrs. Chapman took in boarders. Emerson, Bryant, Horace Greeley, and Noah Porter are a few of the Americans who stayed there, and many English writers mingled with the guests at the evening parties. Here GE returned to board in January 1851, determined to earn her living by her pen.

Chapman was 29, handsome, tall, magnetic. His wife Susanna, whom he married in 1843, was fourteen years older. They had three children. The youngest, who was deaf and dumb, lived with an uncle. The elder two, aged six and five, were looked after by Elisabeth Tilley, a pretty woman of 30, who was also Chapman's mistress. Within a few days of GE's arrival Elisabeth showed signs of jealousy. In his Diary for 1851, almost the only source of information about GE at this time, Chapman wrote that Elisabeth had persuaded Susanna "that we are completely in love with each other, . . . which a little incident (her finding me with my hand in Marian's) had quite prepared her for." No one can say what happened, for several pages of the diary have been cut out. GE was probably guilty of some indiscretion more serious than holding hands. After ten weeks she was driven back to Coventry. Putting her on the train, Chapman told her "that I felt great affection for her, but that I loved E. and S. too, though each in a different way. At this avowal she burst into tears . . . but the train whirled her away very very sad."

TO CHARLES BRAY, 27 JULY [1849]

The long letters from Switzerland illustrate GE's faculty for eliciting confidence. Mrs. Nagle Lock, the elderly English lady; the Baronne de Ludwigsdorf; Cousin Rosa; and the Marquise de St. Germain appear in a list of possible subjects for a novel that GE drew up twenty-five years later. [I, 289–92]

Campagne Plongeon | July 27th.

Dear Friend

We forgot the passport after all—so I must give you the trouble of sending it by post as soon as you reach home. When shall I have done troubling you? One kind of trouble, however, I think I can put an end to—anxiety about my comfort here. I find no disagreeables, and I have every physical comfort that I care about. The family seems well-ordered and happy. Mde. de Vallière is really a lady in feeling and language, evidently accustomed to the society of superior people. She is of the Pays de Vaud, where her husband still lives for the sake of a government appointment. She had an establishment in her own country very superior to this, but the political troubles of the Canton deprived her of the class of guests she was in the habit of receiving and she was fain to leave her husband behind and come here with her eight children. All this I heard from a young lady half French, half English, the cousin of the Austrian Baronne. She has been staying here for some time and speaks very highly of Mde. de V.

I have made another friend, too—an elderly English lady [Mrs. Lock], who used to live at Ryde, and who has been staying here about a month—a pretty old lady with plenty of shrewdness and knowledge of the world. She began to say very kind things to me in rather a waspish tone yesterday morning at breakfast. I liked her better at dinner and tea, and today we are quite confidential. She has her little granddaughter with its nurse under her charge while the mamma is travelling. I only hope she will stay—she is just the sort of person I shall like to have to speak to—not at all "congenial" but with a character of her own. She has been quizzing the two American ladies who are here. One of them is the middle-aged lady whom you admired. She is kind, but silly—the daughter silly, but not kind, and they both of them chatter the most execrable French with amazing volubility and self-complacency. They are very rich, very smart, and very vulgar—just a specimen of Americanism according to the Tories. The daughter has been presented at Court and this was the way in which she contrived to convey the fact to Mrs. Lock (my nice elderly lady). Mrs. Lock observed that she thought the health of young ladies in England was deteriorated by their habits. Miss America replied, "I have been to court and the young ladies looked very healthy there!!" Oh, said Mrs. Lock, I belong to the gentry—I know nothing about the nobility.

Madame la Marquise is a very good-natured person evidently, but she has the voice almost of a market-woman. The tall, squinting man is the Marquis her husband. A grey-headed gentleman and a young lanky one are their friends, and are occupying my room that is to be. There are besides these, the old Swiss lady who has lived here several years—and a really interesting-looking young German, with a bright intelligent refined face and a huge benevolence. He is an ardent politician and so far as I can make out, a republican.

The going down to tea bores me, and I shall get out of it as soon as I can, unless I can manage to have the newspapers to read. The American lady embroiders slippers—the Mamma looks on and does nothing. The Marquis and his friends play at whist—the old ladies sew and Mde. Vallière says things so true that they are insufferable. She is obliged to talk to all and *cap* their niaiseries with some suitable observation. She has been very kind and motherly to me. I believe she has found out already that I do not know how to look after my own interests—but I am sure she is a straight forward person. I like her better every time I see her. I think this is a tolerable budget of good news considering that this is only the second day since I parted from you.

I have a charming tub of cold water to wash in, and the pretty rosy cheeked damsel smiles very kindly at me. I have quiet and comfort—what more can I want to make me a healthy reasonable being once more? I will never go near a friend again until I can bring joy and peace in my heart and in my face—but remember that friendship will be easy then. Dear Cara and dear Sara a thousand loves to you—that is to say as much love as a thousand people could give you if they were not separated from you. Let me hear of your safe arrival.

Your affectionate
Pollian.

I am obliged to write very hastily because I want my letter to go at 6 o'clock tomorrow morning, and I did not know till just now that my passport would be wanted. I am going down to tea and *stare.*

TO THE BRAYS, 5 AUGUST [1849]

[I, 292–95]

Plongeon Sunday August 5.

Dear Friends . . .

My life here would be delightful if we could always keep the same set of people, but alas, I fear one generation will go and another come so fast that I shall not care to become acquainted with any of them. My good Mrs. Lock is not going—that is one comfort. She is quite a mother to me—helps me to buy my candles and do all my shopping—takes care of me at dinner and quite rejoices when she sees me enjoy conversation or anything else. The St. Germains are delightful people— the Marquise really seems to me the most charming person I ever saw, with kindness enough to make the ultra-politeness of her manners quite genuine. She is very good to me and says of me, "Je m'interesse vivement à Mademoiselle." The squinting Marquis is the most well-bred, harmless of men. He talks very little— every sentence seems a terrible gestation, and comes forth fortissimo, but he generally bestows one on me, and seems especially to enjoy my poor tunes (mind you, all these trivialities are to satisfy your vanity—not mine, because you are beginning to be ashamed of having loved me). The grey-headed gentleman who was here when I came was the Chevalier de Berray, the uncle of Mde. la Marquise.

He got quite fond of talking philosophy with me before he went, but alas he and a very agreeable young man who was with him are gone to Aix-les-Bains.

The American ladies too are gone and in their place we have a lady from Frankfort with her daughter and governess. She arrived only yesterday so I have not yet said a word to her. The young German is the Baron de Herder—the veritable grandson of the great Herder. I should think he is not more than two or three and twenty—very good-natured, but a most determined enemy to all gallantry. I fancy he is a Communist, but he seems to have been joked about his opinions by Mde. de Vallière and the rest until he has determined to keep a proud silence on such matters. He has begun to talk to me and I think we should become good friends—but he too is gone on an expedition to Mont Rosa. He is expecting his brother to join him here on his return, but I fear they will not stay long. Mademoiselle Rosa is the only person who speaks English besides Mrs. Lock. She is about equally French and English—rather a nice creature, but with a mere woman's head and mind. Mlle. de Phaisan [Faizan] is a good old maid—a native of Geneva—she has spent three summers here—but she goes into the town for the winter. Mlle. Elise, the gouvernante, is a German with a moral region that would rejoice Mr. Bray's eyes. Poor soul! she is in a land of strangers and often seems to feel her loneliness. Her situation is a very difficult one, and 'die Angst' she says often brings on a pain at her heart.

Mde. de Vallière is a woman of some reading, and considerable talent—very fond of politics, a devourer of the journals—with an opinion ready for you on any subject whatever. The poor woman has her share of anxieties—her youngest child is not more than eighteen months old, her eldest son eighteen years—and between these there are six more one of whom is an epileptic patient. It will be a serious loss to her to part with the St. Germain family—there are three children and six servants, so that they occupy 6 or 7 rooms. I fear they will not stay longer than this month.

I should be quite indifferent to the world that comes or goes if once I had my boxes and all my books. A Mrs. Sydney, a Scotch lady who was here before I came, is gone to Bex, and has sent Mrs. Lock an account of the excellent living and accommodations to be had there for 3 francs a day. Mrs. Lock says she would go if there were an English clergyman there, but she does not feel good enough to do without a clergyman. So you see there is some use for these insipid sticks still. Last Sunday I went with Mde. de Vallière to a small church near Plongeon and I could easily have fancied myself in an independent chapel at home. . . .

I have told you almost everything, but whatever I have omitted may be summed up in the one assurance that I am perfectly comfortable, that every one is kind to me and seems to like me. Your kind hearts will rejoice at this I know. Only remember that I am just as much interested in all that happens to you at Rosehill, as you are in what happens to me at Plongeon. Dear Sara, write to me. I am tired to death and can hardly fashion a sentence, so good-night dear souls. Pray that the motto of Geneva may become mine—Post tenebras lux.

Your affectionate
Mary Ann.

TO THE BRAYS AND SARA HENNELL, 20 AUGUST [1849]

The "Cornelius" family was probably that of Peter Carl Grunelius, the banker at Frankfurt-am-Main. [I, 295–300]

Plongeon August 20th. Monday.

Dear Friends

I have no head for writing today for I have been keeping my bed for the last three days—but I must remember that writing to you is like ringing a bell hung in the planet Jupiter—it is so weary a while before one's letters reach. I have been positively sickening for want of my boxes and anxiety to hear of my relations. . . . There is a fresh German family from Frankfort here just now—Mde. Cornelius and her children. She is the daughter of the richest banker in Frankfort and, what is better, full of heart and mind with a face that tells you so before she opens her lips. She has more reading than the Marquise, being German and Protestant, and it is a real refreshment to talk to her for half an hour.

The dear Marquise is a truly devout Catholic—it is beautiful to hear her speak of the comfort she has in the confessional—for our têtes-à-tête have lately turned on religious matters. She says, I am in a "mauvaise voie sans le rapport de la religion. Peut-être vous vous marierez—et le mariage, chère amie, sans la foi religieuse—" She says I have isolated myself by my studies—that I am too cold and have too little confidence in the feelings of others towards me—that I do not believe how deep an interest she has conceived in my lot. She says Signor Goldrini (the young Italian who was here for a week) told her when he had been talking to me one evening—Vous aimerez cette demoiselle, j'en suis sûr—and she has found his prediction true. Their residence is a short distance from Turin. They were obliged to escape from Piedmont because her brother-in-law the Duke de Visconti was proscribed and the St. Germains were accused of harbouring him. An amnesty has been obtained and they are leaving for their own country on Wednesday. She hopes I shall go to Italy and see her, and when I tell her that I have no faith that she will remember me long enough for me to venture on paying her a visit if ever I should go to Italy again, she shakes her head at my incredulity. She was born at Genoa, where there are two palaces belonging to her family—one close to the cathedral of Sta. Maria del Carignano from which we had the view of the city. Her father was three years Sardinian Minister at Constantinople before she was married, and she speaks with enthusiasm of her life there—C'est là le pays de la vraie poésie—où l'on sent ce que c'est que de vivre par le cœur. The gouvernante of Mde. Cornelius's little girl is an excellent person, simple in her manners and very intelligent.

M. de Herder is returned from Mont Rosa, with a face and mouth such as we had at Chamouni. He would be a nice person if he had another soul added to the one he has by nature—the soul that comes by sorrow and love. I stole his book while he was gone—the 1 volume of Louis Blanc's History of Ten Years. It contains a very interesting account of the 3 days of July 1830. His brother is coming to join him, so I hope he will not go at present.

Two other young Germans—Prussians—are here—the eldest odious, with an eternal simper and a mouth of dubious cleanliness. He speaks French very little and has a miserable splutter between a grunt and a snuffle so that when he begins to speak to one one's brain begins to twist and one feels inclined to rush out of the room. His brother frowns instead of simpering and is therefore more endurable. I gave a description of them something like this to M. de Herder the first night he came back. I found to my dismay that he knew them—however he disclaimed any friendship for them. After all they are very harmless young men and I fancy very rich—'so the world will love its own.' Then we have a family from Holland, gone now on an excursion to Chamouni, but coming back. I hardly know yet whether I shall like this place well enough to stay here through the winter. I have been under the disadvantage of wanting all on which I chiefly depend—my books, etc. When I have been here another month I shall be better able to judge. When you write, have the goodness to send me the names of McCracken's agents, and also the number of Miss Massy's residence in the Rue St. Honoré. . . .

Poor Mrs. Lock, who is a thorough Englishwoman and can only speak French negro-fashion, begins to tire sadly of the bows and 'Bonjours' and 'Pardons.' Yet she has no intention of returning to England. She has had very bitter trials which seem to be driving her more and more aloof from society. She has not yet had courage to tell me herself what these trials are, but I have heard from Mlle. Rosa that her daughter married one of the French noblesse. The match was in every way highly advantageous—the husband excellent, fortune considerable. They lived happily for some time—she had two little girls—when an accursed cousin of the husband's came in the way and caused a separation within the last year. Mrs. Lock is one of the Heads—the same family as that of Sir Francis Head. Her brother Major Head wrote an "Overland Journey from India" which you may have seen. She has multitudes of relations in England, but I suppose shame at her daughter's disgrace makes all her old associations painful. No one likes her here— simply because her manners are brusque and her French incomprehensible. She means to go to Bex for economy. . . .

Poor dear Cara—to have had so much trouble about my muff and tippet—after all I remember that they are in a chest of drawers lined with cedar which I have lent to Chrissey. I hope you managed to get in the black velvet dress. The people dress and think about dressing here more even than in England. You would not know me if you saw me. The Marquise took on her the office of femme de chambre and drest my hair one day. She has abolished all my curls and made two things stick out on each side of my head, like those on the head of the Sphinx. All the world says I look infinitely better so I comply, though to myself I seem uglier than ever—if possible. Mr. Prévost has not been again—but I do not care much about it. I have enough of monde here. In fact that becomes one of the disagreeables. If people like one they buzz round one like flies round a sugar basin, and neither one's heart nor one's vanity inclines one to make oneself odious for the sake of being left in quiet. I am fidgeted to death about my boxes, and that tiresome man not to acknowledge the receipt of them. . . .

Your loving
Pollian.

TO THE BRAYS, 28 AUGUST [1849]

Mrs. Isaac Evans wrote to tell GE that Clara Christiana Clarke had died in her sixth year. [I, 300–03]

Plongeon Tuesday August 28th.

Dear Friends

It is so pleasant to write to you that I cannot resist the temptation to begin as soon as I have read your letter, though I have almost lost the use of my arms with rowing, and my pen straggles anywhere but in the right place. . . . Madame de Ludwigsdorf, the cousin of Mlle. Rosa and the wife of an Austrian Baron, has been here for two days, and is coming again. She is handsome, spirited and clever, pure English by birth, but quite foreign in manners and appearance. She and all the world besides are going to winter in Italy.

Nothing annoys me now—I feel perfectly at home and shall really be comfortable when I have all my little matters about me. There has been the sad grief of hearing that Chrissey has lost her sweetest little girl—a trouble which goes to my heart, both for my sister's sake and for the real loss to my own affections. She was an angelic little being. I learned this in a letter from my sister Sarah last week. All is well at Griff—but my heart aches to think of Chrissey with her children ill of scarlet fever—her husband almost frantic with grief and her own heart rent by the loss of this eldest little daughter. However I cannot regret that I am not there, for I am really good for nothing yet, and I feel that my future health and actions entirely depend on my recovering thoroughly my strength and spirit.

People alarm me by telling me of the terrible severity of the winters here—but there are three reasons that incline me to remain at Plongeon rather than move to Paris which would on many accounts be preferable. . . . Indeed there are so many advantages connected with being in Paris that if I thought my finances would hold out I should brave every thing else, though I confess I am more sensitive than I thought I should be to the idea that my being alone is odd. I thought my old appearance would have been a sufficient sanction and that the very idea of impropriety was ridiculous. Here however I am as sagely settled as possible, for Mde. de Vallière is quite a sufficient mother and the Swiss ideas of propriety are rigid to excess. Mde. de Vallière would not receive Mrs. Lock's daughter if she were to come, because she is separated from her husband. You may console the Mrs. T. Carters etc. therewith and assure them that I dare not look or say or do half what one does in England. As long as people carry a Mademoiselle before their name, there is far less liberty for them on the Continent than in England. . . .

The other day (Sunday) there was a Fête held on the lake—the Fête of Navigation. I went out with some other ladies in M. de Herder's boat at sunset and had the richest draught of beauty. All the boats of Geneva turned out in their best attire—two very large ones fitted up for the occasion—with a band and artillery. When the moon and stars came out there were beautiful fireworks sent up from the boats. The mingling of the silver with the golden rays on the rippled lake, the bright colors of the boats, the cannon, the music, the splendid fireworks, and the pale moon looking at it all with a sort of grave surprise, made up a scene of perfect enchantment—and our dear old Mont Blanc was there in his white ermine robe. I rowed all the time, and hence comes my palsy. . . .

I shall want very warm clothing if I stay here and I am concerned to think that I have made so little provision in that way. There were many things such as shawls which would have been very useful to me and they lie in my wardrobe—but I am of that happy race whom experience only can teach. . . . I suffer miserably from cold feet and am just this moment almost stupefied from want of circulation. This is not at all fair for I use cold water and walking enough. The middle of the day is frequently intensely hot here—the trees quite languishing for want of rain. Autumn has begun already.

Good-bye, dear creatures. Keep me for seven years longer and you will find out the use of me, like all other pieces of trumpery.

Your
Mary Ann.

TO THE BRAYS, 20 SEPTEMBER [1849]

Nelly, mentioned in the last paragrah of this letter, was Bray's second illegitimate child, born in Birmingham, brought to Rosehill with Mrs. Bray's consent 10 June 1846, and adopted. She lived with them until her death at the age of 19. [I, 307–11]

Plongeon Thursday September 20th.

Dear Friends . . .

Mde. de Ludwigsdorf is so good to me—a charming creature—so anxious to see me comfortably settled—petting me in all sorts of ways. She sends me tea when I wake in the morning, orangeflower water when I go to bed, grapes, and her maid to wait on me. She says if I like she will spend the winter after this at Paris with me and introduce me to her friends there—but she does not mean to attach herself to me, because I shall never like her long. I shall be tired of her when I have sifted her etc. She says I have more intellect than morale—and other things more true than agreeable—however she "is greatly interested in me"—has told me her troubles and her feelings, she says, in spite of herself—for she has never been able before in her life to say so much even to her old friends—it is a mystery she cannot unravel. She is a person of high culture according to the ordinary notions of what feminine culture should be. She speaks French and German perfectly, plays well, and has the most perfect polish of manner, the most thorough refinement both socially and morally. She reminds me of Cara in one thing, though not like her generally. Her character is really remarkably destitute of animalism and she has just that sort of antipathy towards people who offend her refined instincts which we know so well in another person. She is tall and handsome—a striking looking person but with a sweet feminine expression when she is with those she likes—dresses exquisitely—in fine is all that I am not. I shall tire you with all this, but I want you to know what good creatures there are here as elsewhere.

Then there are the Forbeses—Mr. Forbes with a fine moral and intellectual head but spoiled by immense pride and vanity, which betray themselves in his thin affected-looking lips at the first glance. Miss Forbes, for whose health they are travelling, is a good creature. They are very evangelical. Miss Forbes tells me that the first day she sat by my side at dinner she looked at me and thought to herself, "That is a grave lady. I do not think I shall like her much"—but as soon as I spoke to her and she looked into my eyes she felt she could love me. Then she lent me a book written by her cousin—a religious novel "Use and Abuse"—(by Miss Skene now living at Leamington)—in which there is a fearful infidel who will not believe and hates all who do etc. etc. Then she invited me to walk with her and came to talk in my room—then invited me to go to the Oratoire with them—till I began to be uncomfortable under the idea that they fancied I was evangelical and that I was gaining their affection under false pretenses—so I told Miss Forbes that I was going to sacrifice her good opinion and confess my heresies. I quite expected from their manner and character that they would forsake me in horror, but they are as kind as ever. They never go into the salon in the evening, and I have almost forsaken it, spending the evening frequently in Mde. de Ludwigsdorf's room, where we have some delightful tea. The tea of the house here is execrable—or rather as Mrs. Wood says, "How glad we should be it has no taste at all—it might have a very bad one." I like the Woods—they are very good-natured. Mrs. Wood a very ugly but ladylike little woman who is under an infatuation as it regards her caps, always wearing the brightest rose-colour or intensest blue, with a complexion not unlike a dirty primrose glove. . . .

I shall certainly stay at Geneva this winter, and shall return to England as early as the spring weather will permit always supposing that nothing occurs to alter my plan. I am still thin and my hair is falling off—so how much will be left of me by next April I am afraid to imagine. I shall be length without breadth—quite bald and without money to buy a wig—but Mr. Hennell will think that I am fancying myself unhappy. The cholera is not at Geneva—the medical men say it is cholera-proof. The place is crowded with foreigners, the Hotels quite full. . . .

I am glad to hear that Nelly is flourishing—give my love to her and tell her that I shall want her to tell me all the stories Mamma teaches her when I go back to England because I have no one to tell me stories here, so she must keep them all ready for me. . . . Write again soon I beseech you. Your letters are as welcome as Elijah's ravens—I thought of saying the dinner-bell, only that would be too gross. . . .

Goodbye, dear Souls. Dominus Vobiscum.

TO MRS. HENRY HOUGHTON, 4 OCTOBER [1849]

When the cooler weather began, GE moved to the center of Geneva, living with the family of François D'Albert Durade (1804–86), a portrait painter. [VIII, 18–20]

Plongeon | Thursday October 4th.

My dear Fanny

The blessed compensation there is in all things made your letter doubly precious for having been waited for, and it would have inspired me to write to you again much sooner, but that I have been in uncertainty about settling myself for

the winter and I wished to send you my future address. I have finally decided on
going to M. D'Albert's. He is a highly respectable artist, a man I am told of
beaucoup d'esprit, fond of music and possessing a circle of superior friends. His wife
is a very pleasing ladylike person with a most kind face. I shall be their only
pensionnaire and I am to have a nice apartment with an alcove, that continental
device for turning a bedroom into a sittingroom. Everything is to be provided for
me except firewood for 150f. i.e. £6 per month. One of the advantages of being in
Geneva alone is that people of a really high tone of manners and education
receive pensionnaires—the fruit of the revolution I believe, which has reduced
many fortunes. The D'Alberts are middle-aged, between 40 and 50, and have two
nice boys about 14 or 15. They seem pleased with the idea of having me and are
very anxious to accommodate me as far as possible. I am to move to my new home
on Tuesday the 9th and my address will then be M. D'Albert Durade, rue des
Chanoines, no. 107. I shall not at all regret leaving here, for my only favourite,
the Baronne de Ludwigsdorf will set off for Vienna on Saturday, for the season is
beginning to be rather sombre, though the glorious chestnuts here are still worth
looking at half the day.

You have heard of some of the people whom I have described in my letters to
Rosehill—but I do not think I have mentioned to you Mde. de Ludwigsdorf. She
is a very accomplished Englishwoman, who married about 10 years ago an Austrian Baron of large possessions. She has not at all the air of an English person—
dark as a Spaniard, with French manners and a perfect Parisian accent. She has
been quite a treasure to me for the last month, for something has drawn us
together in spite of all the disparities between us and I hardly think that I ever
became so quickly attached to anyone before. But alas, she seems to know so little
of her future that I am almost afraid our parting on Saturday will be a final one.
Her life has been a most interesting one, and I shall always yearn to know how the
woof is being spun out.

The society here is less distingué than usual just now. There are two French
families whom it is amusing enough to see now and then, but who excite no vivid
interest. The dear little old maid Mlle. de Faisan is quite a good friend to me—
extremely prosy and full of tiny details, but really people of that calibre are a
comfort to one occasionally, when one has not strength for more stimulating
things. She is a sample of those happy souls who ask for nothing but the work of
the hour however trivial—who are content to live without knowing whether they
effect anything, but who do really effect much good simply by their calm and even
maintien. I laugh to hear her say in a tone of remonstrance, "Mde de Ludwigsdorf
dit qu'elle s'ennuie quand les soirées sont longue—moi, je ne conçois pas comment on peut s'ennuyer quand on a de l'ouvrage ou des jeux ou de la
conversation." . . .

My health has been very wretched here, partly owing to the unseasonable
hours—10 o'clock for breakfast and 6 for dinner, but at present I am better, and I
have no doubt that I shall recover my strength when I have a few more bodily
comforts. I want to present a very robust appearance to you all in spring. And you
dear Fanny, I hope, are getting back again your moderate share of embonpoint.

When people who are dressing elegantly and riding about to make calls every day of their life, have been telling me of their troubles—their utter hopelessness of ever finding a vein worth working in their future life, my thoughts have turned towards many whose sufferings are of a more tangible character, and I have really felt all the old commonplaces about equality of human destinies—always excepting those spiritual differences which are apart not only from poverty and riches, but from individual affections.

I have had a second letter from Sara with one from Isaac. Dear Chrissey also has found time and strength to write to me—very precious her letter was, though I wept over it. "Deep abiding grief must be mine" she says and I know well it must be. The mystery of trial! It falls with such avalanche-weight on the head of the meek and patient. . . . I wish I could do something of more avail for my friends than love them and long for their happiness. You dearest Fanny have a very large share of that very unmarketable benefit. . . . Does not Willenhall look beautiful in the autumn? The trees on the knoll opposite your house must have fine effect now. I can hardly see the letters I am framing and am expecting the dinner bell so, dear Fanny, once more believe I love you, and tell Henry I love him for your sake when he is good to you.

Your
Mary Ann.

Love to Robert and Jane whenever you can give it for me.

TO THE BRAYS, [24 OCTOBER 1849]

This letter gives a fair picture of the D'Alberts and their evening parties. Charles Hennell was suffering from tuberculosis. James Anthony Froude married Charlotte Maria Grenfell, sister-in-law of Charles Kingsley and the original of Argemone in his *Yeast*. Bray had once thought him a possible match for GE. [I, 316–19]

Rue des Chanoines 107.

Dear Friends

I languished for your letter before it came and read it three times running—judge whether I care less for you than of old. It is the best of blessings to know that you are well and cheerful. . . . But to satisfy Cara I will give you some "vérités positives" in which alas! poor imagination has hitherto been able to do little for the world. I have every day an excellent breakfast—good coffee, delicious butter and confiture—a good luncheon—and a still better dinner—for example, always two kinds of meat thoroughly well cooked, nice vegetables and pudding. Everything is on a generous scale without extravagance. Mde. D'Albert anticipates all my wants and makes a spoiled child of me. I like these dear people better and better—everything is so in harmony with one's moral feeling that I really can almost say I never enjoyed a more complete bien-être in my life than during the last fortnight.

For M. D'Albert I love him already as if he were father and brother both. You must know he is not more than 4 feet high with a deformed spine—the result of an accident in his boyhood—but on this little body is placed a finely formed head, full in every direction. The face is plain with small features, and rather haggard looking, but all the lines and the wavy grey hair indicate the temperament of the artist. I have not heard a word or seen a gesture of his yet that was not perfectly in harmony with an exquisite moral refinement—indeed one feels a better person always when he is present. He was educated for theology and did not become an artist—did not even begin to draw till he was 21. He sings well and plays on the piano a little. It is delightful to hear him talk of his friends—he admires them so genuinely—one sees so clearly that there is no reflex egotism. His conversation is charming. I learn something every dinner-time.

Mde. D'Albert has less of genius and more of cleverness—a really lady-like person, who says everything well. She brings up her children admirably—two nice intelligent boys—the youngest particularly has a sort of Lamartine expression with a fine head. I have not said half I feel about these good creatures because I am afraid you will laugh at me. But it is so delightful to get among people who exhibit no meannesses—no worldlinesses that one may well be enthusiastic. For instance, I told you that Mde. D'Albert was to find me light for the 150 fr. She does this as if I were a visitor to whom she was anxious to be extremely polite. I have a large lamp and five bougies always in my room, 2 on the mantel-piece, two on my piano, and one on my dressing-table. She scolds me when she comes in and sees me reading by a single bougie. You will think me childish to talk of such things, but to me it is so blessed to find any departure from the rule of giving as little as possible for as much as possible. Their whole behaviour to me is the same spirit—as if I were a guest whom they delighted to honour.

Last night we had a little knot of their most intimate musical friends—a Mlle. Herpin who plays admirably, a gentleman who has a splendid bass voice, and two really remarkable men, a M. Chaponnière, a physician, and his Father, a fine old man, quite a subject for a sculptor, who has written an infinity of clever poetry in the style of Thomas Hood, some of which M. D'Albert has read to me. He has also been a composer of music. The son is an antiquarian, has written a history of Bonnivard, is scientific, is full of all sorts of knowledge, with a delightful bonhommie. He has a fine tenor voice and sings with facility very difficult operatic music. M. and Mde. D'Albert introduce me to their friends as if they wished me to know them, as if they wished me to like their friends and their friends to like me. Mde. Chaponnière, the younger one's wife, is an amiable looking little woman who brings her work and listens to the music. The people and the evening would have been just after your own hearts. In fact I have not the slightest pretence for being discontented, not the shadow of a discomfort. Even the little housemaid Jeanie is charming—says to me every morning, in the prettiest voice Madame a-t-elle bien dormi cette nuit? puts fire in my chauffe-pied without being told, cleans my rooms most conscientiously. There—I promise to weary you less for the future with my descriptions. I could not resist the temptation to speak gratefully of M. and Mde. D'Albert. . . .

It is a comfort to hear of Mr. Hennell's being at all better. Also it is good that

Froude should marry a respectability—only if he preach the new word at Manchester I hope he will preach it so as to do without an after-explanation and not bewilder his hearers in the manner of Mephistopheles when he dons the doctor's gown of Faust. . . .

Good-bye, dear loves—shan't I kiss you when I am in England again—in England! I already begin to think of the journey as an impossibility. Geneva is so beautiful now the trees have their richest colouring. Coventry is a fool to it—but then you are at Coventry and you are better than lake trees and mountains to your affectionate

Mary Ann.

TO CHARLES BRAY, [26 OCTOBER 1849]

[I, 319]

Rue des Chanoines 107 | Geneva.

Dear Friend . . .

We have had some delicious autumn days here. If the fine weather last I am going up the Salève on Sunday with M. D'Albert. You remember the Salève. On one side I shall have a magnificent view of the lake the town and the Jura—on the other the range of Mt. Blanc. The walks about Geneva are perfectly enchanting. Ah! says poor Mlle. de Faisan, nous avons un beau pays si nous n'avions pas ces Radicaux! The election of the Conseil d'Etat is to take place in November, and an émeute is expected. The actual Government is Radical, and thoroughly detested by all the "respectable" classes. Fazy, the vice president of the Conseil and the virtual head of the government, is an unprincipled clever fellow horribly in debt himself and on the way to reduce the government to the same position. Please to send the enclosed to Sara.

Adieu.

TO THE BRAYS, [4 DECEMBER 1849]

Ethan Allen Hitchcock had offered Chapman a translation of Spinoza's *Ethics* by his brother Samuel. [I, 321–22]

107 Rue des Chanoines.

Dear Mr. Bray

I write at once to answer your questions about business. Spinoza and I have been divorced for several months. My want of health has obliged me to renounce all application. I take walks, play on the piano, read Voltaire, talk to my friends, and just take a dose of mathematics every day to prevent my brain from becoming quite soft. Therefore I am by no means eager to supersede any other person's labours, and Mr. Chapman is absolved from observing any delicacy towards me about Spinoza or his translators. If you are anxious to publish the translation in question I could, after a few months, finish the Tractatus Theologico-Politicus to keep it company—but I confess to you, that I think you would do better to abstain from printing a translation. What is wanted in English is not a translation of Spinoza's works, but a true estimate of his life and system. After one has rendered his Latin faithfully into English, one feels that there is another yet more difficult process of translation for the reader to effect, and that the only mode of making Spinoza accessible to a larger number is to study his books, then shut them and give an analysis. For those who read the very words Spinoza wrote, there is the same sort of interest in his style as in the conversation of a person of great capacity who has led a solitary life, and who says from his own soul what all the world is saying by rote, but this interest hardly belongs to a translation. . . .

Dear Cara also. Your letter is very sweet to me, giving me a picture of your quiet life. How shall I enable you to imagine mine, since you know nothing of the localities? My good friends here only change for the better. Mde. D'Albert is all affection, M. D'Albert all delicacy and intelligence, the friends to whom they have introduced me very kind in their attentions. In fact I want nothing but a little more money to feel more at ease about my fires etc. etc. I am in an atmosphere of love and refinement—even the little servant Jeanie seems to love me and does me good every time she comes into the room. I can say anything to M. and Mde. D'Albert. M. D'A. understands everything and if Madame does not understand she *believes*—that is she seems always sure that I mean something edifying. She kisses me like a mother, and I am baby enough to find that a great addition to my happiness. Au reste, I am careful for nothing. I am a sort of supernumerary spoon, and there will be no damage to the set if I am lost. It is different with you, and I cannot help being saddened by the idea of losses and possible renunciations that may be required of you. My heart ties are not loosened by distance—it is not in the nature of ties to be so—and when I think of my loved ones as those to whom I can be a comfort or a help I long to be with them again. Otherwise I can only think with a shudder of returning to England. It looks to me like a land of gloom, of ennui, of platitude, but in the midst of all this it is the land of duty and affection, and the only ardent hope I have for my future life is to have given to me some woman's duty, some possibility of devoting myself where I may see a daily result of pure calm blessedness in the life of another. . . . All possible Christmas pleasures and comforts to you all.

Your affectionate
Mary Ann.

TO THE BRAYS AND SARA HENNELL, [22 DECEMBER 1849]

Arthur Auguste de la Rive resigned his professorship at the University of Geneva after the revolution. In 1849–50 he gave a course of 26 lectures intended particularly for ladies. The "Varieties" were notes in the *Coventry Herald,* which Bray owned. [I, 324–25]

Chez M. D'Albert Durade. | 107 Rue des Chanoines.

Dear Friends all

A thousand Christmas pleasures and blessings to you—good resolutions and bright hopes for the New Year! Amen. . . .

I am attending a course of lectures on Experimental Physics by M. le professeur de la Rive, the inventor amongst other things of the electro-plating. I do not tell you whether I enjoy them or not. The lectures occur every Wednesday and Saturday. It is time for me to go. I am distressed to send you this shabby last fragment of paper and to write in such a hurry, but the days are really only two hours long, and I have so many things to do that I go to bed every night miserable because I have left out something I meant to do. Good bye dear souls—Forget me, if you like, you cannot oblige me to forget you, and the active is worth twice of the passive all the world over.

Mary Ann.

The earth is covered with snow and the government is levelling the fortifications. This last fact will do to put among your "Varieties."

TO THE BRAYS, [15 FEBRUARY 1850]

The Times had reported houses swept away by avalanches and travellers devoured by wolves. Bray was born 31 January 1811. D'Albert's portrait of GE is in the National Portrait Gallery. [I, 329–31]

107 Rue des Chanoines | Geneva.

Dear Friends

If you saw the Jura today! The snow reveals its forest ravines and precipices, and it stands in relief against a pure blue sky. The snow is on the mountains only now, and one is tempted to walk all day, particularly when one lies in bed till 10, as your exemplary friend sometimes does. . . . Your stories about the wolves and the snow are apocryphal. The Radicals are the only wild beasts of whom the good citizens of Geneva are in fear, and the winter here, though severe, has been less so than at Trieste, for example, and other places farther south. . . .

You will be amused to hear that I am sitting for my portrait—at M. D'Albert's request—not mine. If it turns out well, I shall long to steal it to give to you—but M. D'Albert talks of painting a second and in that case I shall certainly beg one. The idea of making a study of my visage is droll enough.

I have the kindest possible letters from my brother and sisters promising me the warmest welcome. This helps to give me courage for the journey, but the strongest magnet of all is a certain little group of three persons whom I hope to find together at Rosehill. I shall be quite disappointed if Sara be not with you when I arrive. Something has been said of M. D'Albert's accompanying me to Paris, but I am afraid he cannot afford the journey—and alas! I cannot afford to pay for him.

I am saddened when I think of all the horrible anxieties of trade. M. D'A. tells me that a large proportion of the trade of St. Etienne has transported itself to Basle. If I had children I would make them carpenters and shoemakers—that is the way to make them Messiahs and Jacob Boehms. As for us who are dependent on carpets and easy chairs—we are reprobates, and shall never enter into the kingdom of heaven. I go to the Genevese churches every Sunday and nourish my heterodoxy with orthodox sermons. However there are some clever men here in the church, and I am fortunate in being here at a time when the very cleverest is giving a series of conferences.

I think I have never told you that we have a long German youth of seventeen in the house—he has been here ever since Christmas—the most taciturn and awkward of lads. He said very naïvely when I reproached him for not talking to a German young lady in a soirée, when he was seated next her at table, "Je ne savais que faire de mes jambes." They had placed the poor garçon against one of those card-tables—all legs, like himself. Write to me again soon a little scrap like mine. I enclose a little letter for Mr. Bray all to himself, to put him in a good humour. I shall annihilate little Cara with kisses, drown Sara with my eyes—and not quarrel with Mr. Bray all the first evening.

Your affectionate
Pollian.

TO CHARLES BRAY, 1 MARCH [1850]

Bray forwarded GE's quarterly income from her father's bequest of £2,000. [I, 331]

107 Rue des Chanoines | March 1st.
Dear Friend

The weather is so glorious that I think I may set out on my journey soon after the 15th. If you can get the money forwarded to me, will you do so as soon as possible, that I may be ready for departure. I am not quite certain yet that M. D'Albert will not be able to accompany me to Paris—in any case a package of so little value will get along safely enough. . . . I am so excited at the idea of the time being so near when I am to leave Geneva—a real grief—and see my friends in England—a perfectly overwhelming joy—that I can do nothing. I am frightened to think what an idle wretch I am becoming. And you all do not write me one word to tell me you long for me. Your hearts are perfect flint and you have no bowels. I have a great mind to elope to Constantinople and never see any one any more!

Your highly-deserving and very little-minded friend
Mary Ann Evans.

TO SARA HENNELL, [26 MARCH 1850]

D'Albert accompanied GE to England and spent two months there. Godfrey Windus, whom Ruskin called "the retired coachmaker of Tottenham," showed his collection of Turner drawings on Tuesdays. [I, 332]

[Coventry]
Dear Sara

No—I am not in England—I am only nearer to the beings I love best. I try to forget all geography and that I have placed myself irretrievably out of reach of nature's brightest glories and beauties to shiver in a wintry flat. I am unspeakably grateful to find these dear creatures looking well and happy in spite of worldly cares, but your dear face and voice are wanting to me. But I must wait with patience and perhaps by the time I have finished my visits to my relations, you will be ready to come to Rose Hill again. I want you, dear, to scold me and make me good. I am idle and naughty—on ne peut plus—sinking into heathenish ignorance and woman's frivolity—remember you are one of my guardian angels.

Will you send me word of the address of the gentleman who has a collection of Turner's pictures which he opens weekly to the public? I want M. D'Albert to see it. I mean the collection from which you stole my soap-bubbles. I was ill in London after our rough passage from Calais, and unable to move from the Hotel—I should have thought my sickness much harder to bear if I had known there was a possibility of seeing you and going to Mr. Chapman's. More next time

From your
Pollian.

TO SARA HENNELL, [11 APRIL 1850]

Chapman's price for board and room at 142 Strand was £2 10s per week with 3s. 6d. extra for fires in bedrooms. After her return GE visited Isaac Evans at Griff and Chrissey Clarke at Meriden before coming to Rosehill, where she stayed with the Brays until January 1851. [I, 334–35]

Griff | Thursday.

My dear Sara

Will you send the enclosed note to Mrs. C. Hennell? I am not quite sure about her direction, but I am anxious to thank her for her kindness in inviting me. Will you also send me an account of Mr. Chapman's prices for lodgers—and if you know anything of other boarding houses etc. in London will you tell me what you can? I am not asking you merely for the sake of giving you trouble. I am really anxious to know.

O the dismal weather and the dismal country and the dismal people. It was some envious demon that drove me across the Jura to come and see people who don't want me. However I am determined to sell everything I possess except a portmanteau and carpet-bag and the necessary contents and be a stranger and a foreigner on the earth for ever more. But I must see you first—that is a yearning I still have in spite of disappointments. My love to Mrs. Hennell.

Ever your faithful
Pollian.

TO THE BRAYS, [30 NOVEMBER 1850]

After the success of her brilliant review of R. W. Mackay's The Progress of the Intellect, a book Chapman published, GE resolved to go to London and earn her living as a free-lance writer. She made a two-weeks' trial visit at Chapman's house in the Strand. Eliza Lynn had written a third novel called *Realities,* which Chapman agreed to publish. "Literary Ladies" were caricatured by Dickens in such characters as Miss Codger in *Martin Chuzzlewit.* [I, 337]

142 Strand.

Dear Friends

I mean to set off by the train that starts from Euston Sq. at 40 minutes past 11 on Monday. I have bought the Lucifers and done my duty about the Lamp shade, but to get one it will be necessary to send the old one as a pattern. We had a large soirée last night, but I will not tell you anything till I am seated in the red arm chair with my feet on the fender. I only hope you are all well and jolly. I have enjoyed my visit very much and am to come again in January.

Miss Lynn was here last night. She says she was "never so attracted to a woman before as to me"—I am "such a loveable person." She is so different from all I had imagined her that I was quite startled. Spectacles! and altogether an L. L. looking person.

Ever your
Pollian.

TO MRS. CHARLES BRAY, [8 JANUARY 1851]

GE returned to the Chapmans', intending to stay for an indefinite period. William Ballantyne Hodgson, Principal of Chorlton High School, Manchester, met GE with the Brays in Liverpool in 1844 and hypnotized her. [I, 341]

142 Strand.

Dearest Cara

I send you Sara's letter at once though there is little in it besides her plans about our doings. Of course I came safely enough—explain it which way you will— 'Caesar and his fortunes,' or, Naught is never in danger. We have just dined and my weary body is capable barely of digestion.

My room looks charmingly comfortable—Dr. Hodgson is here, and a Mr. Jarvis, an American, evidently a noodle. There is besides a little old-young lady, a cousin of Mr. Chapman's. Mr. C. met me at the station and I had no trouble. Bless you, dear creatures. Do not forget your

Pollian.

TO THE BRAYS, [28 JANUARY 1851]

Francis William Newman, brother of John Henry Newman, was one of the founders of the Ladies' [now Bedford] College. Chapman published *Letters on the Laws of Man's Nature and Development,* by H. G. Atkinson and Harriet Martineau, which pretended to discover the phrenological centers by making hypnotized subjects describe their own brains. Eliza Lynn's *Realities* dealt so candidly with the sordid side of the London theater that Chapman refused to publish it. [I, 341–44]

142 Strand.

Dearest Friends

I take for granted that you will like to hear what I am doing. On Friday evening I got out of bed to go and hear Faraday lecture at the theatre of the Royal Society—Mr. Mackay having kindly given me a ticket. You must know Faraday's lectures are as fashionable an amusement as the Opera—so there was store of ladies, who according to Mr. Mackay rain quite an adverse influence and spoil the lectures. It always does one good to see a thoroughly enthusiastic man of science like Faraday. He told us we little knew how many hours he had spent in blowing minute soap bubbles—like a certain other philosopher of my acquaintance. When we got home we found Dr. [Henry] Travis and two or three other people. Dr. T. is a charming man—so spiritual and æsthetic looking that one is quite startled when he begins to retail dry Robert-Owenisms. . . .

I am attending Professor Newman's course of lectures on Geometry at the Ladies' College every Monday and Thursday. You will say that I can't afford this, which is 'dreadful true'—but the fact is that I happened to say I should like to do so and good-natured Mr. Chapman went straightway and bought me a ticket which he begged me to accept. I refused to accept it—and have paid for it—wherefore I must stint myself in some direction—clearly in white gloves and probably in clean collars. . . .

Miss Martineau's book is come out, but there was not so great a sale the first day as was anticipated. Mr. Chapman's feud with Miss Lynn about her novel is not yet terminated—I conclude Sara has told you something of the matter in her letter. Did she tell you that Shoberl the publisher said—"I assure you, Sir, I am most careful on the score of Politics, Religion, and indeed all the *proprieties.*"

When am I to have Mr. Bray's promised letter? or to see him in propria persona. I shall be so glad of either. There is really no time to do anything here I am a poor never-having-time-to-clean-myself potter's wessel.

Your
Pollian.

TO THE BRAYS, [15 FEBRUARY 1851]

Frederick J. Foxton was the author of *Popular Christianity*, published by Chapman. Thomas Wilson, a curate in Norwich, lost his faith and left the Church to teach English at Bedford College; he resigned 5 March 1851 when his orthodoxy was questioned. GE proposed to review W. R. Greg's *The Creed of Christendom*, one of Chapman's publications. William E. Hickson owned the *Westminster Review*; Henry J. Slack was its editor. Eliza Cabot Follen, abolitionist, travelled with Harriet Martineau during her visit to the United States, 1835–36. [I, 345–46]

142 Strand.

Dearest Friends . . .

Since Sara left on Monday, nothing very particular has happened—we have been rather duller than usual. Mrs. C. has had a bad cough, the drawing room has been turned topsy-turvy in the absence of visitors, and everything has been so-so, the weather included. Mr. Mackay has been very kind in coming and walking out with me and that is the only variety I have had. Last night, however, we had an agreeable enough gathering. Foxton came, smelling horribly of tobacco, and sat talking with me an hour and a half by the timepiece till I was half dead. I think him an ugly, médiocre man. He says George Dawson has invited Wilson (you know whom I mean?) to go down to Birmingham and preach for him. Foxton you know is trying with Carlyle and others to get a chapel for Wilson at the West End in which he is to figure as a seceding clergyman.

I enclose you two notes from Empson as a guarantee that I have been trying to work. Mr. Chapman wrote to him (he is the editor of the Edinburgh Review) sending him the article on Mackay, and proposing that I should write one for the Edinburgh either on Mackay again, on Miss Martineau's work or on another subject for which he had employed Mr. Chapman to get him an article. Again, I proposed to write a review of Greg for the Westminster not for money, but for love—of the subject as connected with the Inquiry. Mr. Hickson referred the matter to Slack again and he writes that he shall not have room for it and that the subject will not suit on this occasion, so you see I am obliged to be idle and I like it best. You will be pleased to see that Mr. C. spoke of me to Empson as a man. Miss Lynn's affair with Mr. C. is closed by her accepting £5 as compensation!

I hope Mr. Bray is coming soon to tell me everything about you. I think I shall cry for joy to see him. But do send me a little note on Monday morning. Does Betsy go on well? and do she and Jane agree? Mrs. Follen called the other day in extreme horror at Miss Martineau's book, quoting as very rich a motto for the title-page proposed by a gentleman of her acquaintance "There is no God, and Harriet Martineau is his prophet."

TO MRS. CHARLES BRAY, [12 MARCH 1851]

None of the half-dozen known letters written during GE's ten weeks in the Strand refers to the jealousies that drove her back to Rosehill 24 March. Alfred Hyman Louis, born in Birmingham, was converted by Charles Kingsley. In America in the 1870s he sometimes posed as G. H. Lewes and declared that he was GE's model for Daniel Deronda. [I, 346–47]

142 Strand.

Dearest Cara

Sundry matters have decided that I should stay here until Saturday week— resign yourself then to kissing and being kissed. You seem dearer to me every time I go back to you.

On Monday went to tea at Mr. Mackay's and called on Rufa by *her invitation* on our way home. Yesterday Mr. C. took me to Tottenham to see Mr. Windus's Turners. On Friday we had a new man—a Mr. Louis, born a Jew—believing in Christianity—that is to say as a set of symbols expressing his philosophic creed. Very accomplished, played on the piano to Mrs. Chapman's utter disgust—she hating Mendelssohnianism. Thornton Hunt came again and to my vexation went away without my being introduced to him—for which I reviled Mr. Chapman whereto he answers by revilings.

I hope you are all getting blooming again. I thought Rufa looking very pale— and invalidish. She told us Mr. Bray had pronounced Frank the most spoiled of all children he had seen.

Ever thy
Pollian.

There are no Visitors—i.e. who pay—yet.

TO ELINOR MARY BRAY, [12 MARCH 1851]

Bray's adopted daughter was five years old. Ernest and Beatrice were Chapman's children, seven and five. Rufa Hennell's son Frank was also five. [I, 347–48]

[142 Strand]

My Dear Nelly

You cannot think how pleased the old woman in the red cloak was with the nice little bag which you and Mamma sent her. She is glad too that you should have a tortoise if you like it, but for her part she thinks it rather an ugly pet. Ernest and Beatrice have a canary of which they are very fond. It is a pretty little thing, but I would rather see birds flying about free and happy in the trees than shut up in a cage. What do you think?

Frank told me he was very sorry to leave you when he came back to London, and I dare say you were not glad to part with him. He told me this one night when I went to see his Mamma. He was in bed and lifted his round rosy face from the pillow to watch us taking off our bonnets.

Good bye, dear Nelly. I often think of you because I very often think of Papa and Mamma and then little Nelly comes into my mind along with them like the little buds that *will* be gathered with the wide open carnations and roses in summer. You see I have no more room.

Your affectionate
Auntie Pollian.

3

THE WESTMINSTER REVIEW
John Chapman · Herbert Spencer

Soon after GE's forced departure from London, William Hickson, owner and editor of the *Westminster Review*, offered to sell it to Chapman for £300. Though he had long dreamed of promoting liberal reforms in writing for his own periodical, Chapman recognized that his meager education had not fitted him to continue an editorial tradition established by its founder John Stuart Mill. The person with the necessary knowledge and literary ability was the Translator of Strauss, now banished from the Strand by the jealousy of his wife and mistress. At Bray's invitation Chapman went to stay a fortnight at Rosehill to discuss his plans for the *Westminster* with GE. Eager to help, she consented to serve as an unnamed assistant, allowing Chapman to be the nominal editor. In August 1851, when she came with the Brays to see the Exhibition at the Crystal Palace, Chapman persuaded his wife and mistress to allow GE to return to the Strand. Understanding Elisabeth's relation now, GE treated her with a sympathy she never forgot. In October she was settled again in her old room and began assembling articles for her first number of the *Westminster*, January 1852. During the next two years, under her skilful guidance it regained the pre-eminence it had enjoyed under Mill's editorship.

At 142 Strand there was a constant stream of boarders, many of them from America, come to see the Great Exhibition. GE's letters to the Brays describe them amusingly as well as the guests at the Chapmans' evening parties.

The person she saw most of was Herbert Spencer, who lived just across the Strand over the office of the *Economist*, of which he was subeditor. Spencer's duties included reviewing the theatres and opera, to which he often invited GE to accompany him. They went on long walks, and were seen together so much that "all the world is setting us down as engaged." In July 1852, when GE took lodgings at Broadstairs for her holiday, Spencer came down twice to be with her. She was madly in love with him. Though he considered her "the most admirable woman, mentally, I ever met," Spencer, who died a bachelor in his 84th year, was unripe for matrimony. With her extraordinary power to forgive, GE accepted his rejection of her love, and they remained good friends, seeing each other as before. Once on his way to call on her, meeting George Henry Lewes, Spencer invited him to go along. This happened several times. On the third or fourth time, when Spencer rose to leave, Lewes said that he would stay. And so began the most important relation of her life.

TO JOHN CHAPMAN, 4 APRIL [1851]

GE wrote many of the summaries for *An Analytical Catalogue of Mr. Chapman's Publications*. He had sent GE Mrs. Chapman's letters berating him for his intimacy with GE. [I, 348]

Rosehill | April 4.

Dear Mr. Chapman

I send you in another envelope a note written under my first impression on reading your packet of letters. On further consideration I consent to continue the Catalogue, since I am ashamed of perpetual vacillations, on condition that you state or rather, I should hope, restate to Mrs. C. the fact that I am doing it, not because I 'like,' but in compliance with your request. You are aware that I never had the slightest wish to undertake the thing on my own account. If I continue it, it will be with the utmost repugnance, and only on the understanding that I shall accept no remuneration.

Yours etc.
Marian Evans.

TO JOHN CHAPMAN, 9 MAY [1851]

In April Edward Lombe, a rich eccentric, wrote to Chapman, offering to pay for a reprinting of Hennell's *Inquiry* and an abridgement of Strauss's *Life of Jesus*, and to help in supporting a quarterly review of liberal tone. When Hickson offered him the *Westminster Review*, Chapman acquired it for £300. The Great Exhibition in the Crystal Palace opened 1 May. [I, 349–50]

Rosehill | May 9.

Dear Mr. Chapman:

I often seem to write pettishly when I only mean to write emphatically, so your canons of interpretation must be liberal. I agree to write the article on Greg, etc., though I am rather indisposed to do anything in a hurry just now. I suppose it is highly desirable to have it ready for the next number, otherwise I should be glad to defer it until the next but one. Fine May days may come and tempt me to be idle.

I congratulate you on the acquisition of the Westminster. You do not tell me the terms on which you have obtained it—whether other parties besides yourself have been concerned in the matter.

There is some uncertainty about the arrangements for my seeing the exhibition. Of course, I wish to be in London at the same time with Mrs. Bray, but she and Mr. Bray are invited to stay with Miss Marshall, who has not accommodation for me—at least she has not asked me to accompany them. However, Mrs. Bray will manage for me somehow, and in the meantime I do not trouble myself.

I do not see that my letters bear so poor a proportion to yours. I generally answer you very promptly, and should do so if you wrote more frequently. Rosehill furnishes no chronicles worth sending to you—unless you care to know that a nightingale has fallen in love with our Paradise and sings to us night and day.

I make use of the stamp to send you my notice of the "Rationale" [by J. Martineau] which I hope you will approve. Pray be candid—that is the first, second and third thing I require, though I am a woman and seem pettish. You know you must allow me to criticize your criticism.

I am astonished that your house is not yet full, but it must surely soon be so. It will be vexatious if you have not some compensations for extra turmoil. I should think you are right glad to have Mrs. Chapman again to enliven you all. . . .

Yours truly
Marian Evans.

I am pretty well now.

TO JOHN CHAPMAN, 9 JUNE [1851]

Chapman sent copies of the prospectus for the *Westminster Review* to 11 likely supporters. James Martineau thought it "ill-written and poor in substance," and told Hickson that Chapman "does not know his limits, and is ambitious of a literary function for which he is not qualified." [VIII, 23]

Rosehill | June 9.

Dear Friend

The enclosed letter was all the Post brought this morning. I am sorry it did not come yesterday that we might have talked it over together. As you predicted, James Martineau's answer is the coldest of all—indeed he writes as if he felt some personal pique. His letter, however, reads less disagreeably the second time than the first. We all think that your writing from Rosehill and requesting him to send you an answer here has given him the idea that Mr. Bray has a special pecuniary interest in your project and is therefore likely to have some influence over the Review. But you will know better what he means when you have had an interview with him. Only tell him that contributors are to be well paid and I think he will not refuse to be one of them.

With regard to the secret of the Editorship, it will perhaps be the best plan for you to state, that for the present *you* are to be regarded as the responsible person, but that you employ an Editor in whose literary and general ability you confide. On these practical points, however, you are the best judge.

We seemed quite dull at dinner without you. I hope you found all well and prosperous at home. In haste.

Yours faithfully
Marian Evans.

TO JOHN CHAPMAN, 15 JUNE [1851]

This letter illustrates the guidance GE gave Chapman in editing the *Westminster Review*. [I, 351–53]

Rosehill | June 15.

My dear Friend:

If, as I suppose, you intend to rewrite the letter to Mill, would it not be better if the 1st Paragraph read thus—"joint aims, so as best to further the main purpose of the future proprietor, which is, to make the Review the organ of the ablest and most liberal thinkers of the time." For "organ" in the 2d paragraph read "medi-um." I wish, too, you would leave out the dashes, which weaken instead of strengthening the impression on the reader. In the 3rd Paragraph for "I am convinced *that*" read "that, I am convinced"; for "gratefully received," which sounds too much like a craving for alms, read "duly valued." "Securing air" is an absurd expression and is of course a slip of the pen. I should like the 4th Paragraph better if it began thus—"In the sketch submitted to you there is perhaps an unnecessary air of conservatism." I think Mr. Lombe is a capital man, who knows what he means and will not pay for what he does *not* mean. I do not see that he wants 'smoothing down,' or that he is a person on whom the process should be tried. Hickson's method with him seems not to have answered, since according to Mr. Lombe's account there had been letters of remonstrance from him, threaten-ing to remove his support unless his views were more fully represented. Why should you shirk the direct fulfilment of his proposition?—the obtaining as good articles as possible on his chosen subjects—since he seems to choose well. I thoroughly agree with him about the hereditary "legislators." I suppose when he wrote this letter he had not received your last.

I was disappointed not to have fuller details in your letter about your conver-sations with [Andrew] Johnson, Spencer, and the rest, but do not forget that you have told me nothing. [George] Combe's letter is pleasant and gentlemanly—Dr. Hodgson's friendly, but surprizingly uncritical for him. He is right about the clause on the suffrage—it is as vague as 'Render unto Caesar the things that are Caesar's'—*what* things are Caesar's being left undetermined.

Good Mrs. [Thornton] Hunt has left behind a very pleasant impression. I think she is the most thoroughly unaffected being I ever saw. I am afraid the Leader is not prospering. The names of Thornton Hunt, Lewes, Linton and several more were specified last week in the papers as withdrawing from partnership in the concern—which seems to imply a presentiment of failure. We are all amused at Thornton Hunt's illustration in yesterday's Leader of "boiled mutton chops"—that must be a peculiarly Hammersmith dish.

Mr. [Edward] Noel has written to say he is first coming to England. He is invited here with his three children and servant, so we shall probably soon have a house full again. He speaks of returning to Greece.

I shall be awfully poor this half year, more than £12 legacy duty being sub-tracted from my interest. Have you fixed on 'Independent Section' as a title? . . .

I want to get out into the air, so goodbye.

Yours faithfully,
Marian Evans.

TO JOHN CHAPMAN, 20 JUNE [1851]

Chapman offered GE £100 for an abridgement of her translation of Strauss's *Life of Jesus*. He had taken the room GE had occupied for his study. [I, 353–55]

Rosehill, June 20.

My dear Friend

Your last letter was just what I wanted—it paid up your arrears of news. . . .

Pray when are we to hear any more of the Strauss abridgment? I have been looking through the work in writing on it for the Catalogue and have been all the time thinking what a capital abridgment I could make.

I congratulate you on your migration, but I hope the room has been duly exorcised since I left it. I pity you, poor soul, with those dismal windows before you instead of chestnut trees and turf. This gold pen is a bad scribbling pen. You see it obstinately refuses to mark every now and then, but I like it exceedingly when I am writing rather slowly. I have delicious walks before breakfast these fine mornings and have said good bye to headache. Mr. Bray is out, Mr. Noel has not yet come, so we are having a charmingly quiet interval.

There would be the same objection to Miss Bronty as to Thackeray with regard to the article on Modern Novelists. She would have to leave out Currer Bell, who is perhaps the best of them all. It appears James Martineau was rather apologetic. I shall be glad to know the purport of your second interview with him.

I had left myself hardly time to write before tea, that is, before post time, but I reflected that it would be of no use to write tomorrow.

Yours in haste
Marian Evans.

TO JOHN CHAPMAN, 1 AUGUST [1851]

GE went to Bishop's Teignton with Mrs. Bray to visit Edward Noel. Ferdinand Freiligrath, German poet and revolutionist, expelled from Prussia, was staying with Andrew Johnson, a clerk in the bullion office of the Bank of England, who was a friend of Karl Marx and other emigrés; Johnson offered to put an article by Freiligrath into good English for the *Westminster Review*, but nothing came of it. The Summaries are reviews of recent books in England, America, Germany, and France. GE arrived in London 13 August to see the Exhibition; after a discussion, Mrs. Chapman and Elisabeth Tilley acquiesced in her return to the Strand for the winter to edit the *Review*. [I, 356–57]

Bishop Steignton | August 1.

My dear Friend

Our visit here has been most unfortunate. Mrs. Bray has been so ill that we have had to call in a medical man. She is better today, and I hope will go on well. I too have been a perfect wretch with a bad cold—a most unusual complaint for me—otherwise I should have answered your letter before.

My decision about Freiligrath would depend more on your wishes and motives in the matter than on anything else, since I know nothing of his general capabilities. If I did only one of the Summaries, I should certainly prefer that of the English literature. I agree with you that Lewes would be likely to do an article on Modern Novelists very well. I advise you to ask him, as I should not like to engage myself to write anything not *ex officio* for the first number.

We are to be in London on the 11th (Monday week). Mr. Noel tells me we shall be at the Paddington Station about 5 o'clock. Do not say anything about Mrs. Bray's illness to Mrs. C. Hennell—as that only causes a report to go from her to Rosehill and heighten alarms. I trust she will soon be well. We shall send Mr. Bray word today, but Mr. Noel advises me to make the very best of the matter as he is inclined to think it a very transient disorder. So do not mention it to any one.

This place is surrounded with trees and does not appear to suit us. But my ailments are of no consequence—they only make me inclined to drown myself. Still I have no doubt I shall survive the temptation and be pretty well to-morrow. I hope your eingeweide are restored to order, and that you are enjoying your brother's visit.

Yours faithfully,
Marian Evans.

TO JOHN CHAPMAN, 18 SEPTEMBER [1851]

Edward Lombe sent Chapman a check for £500 to be placed to the credit of Harriet Martineau in support of an abridgement of Comte's *Cours de philosophie positive*. Later Chapman learned that W. M. W. Call had already made such an abridged translation. George Combe, the phrenologist, and his wife Cecilia, a daughter of the actress Sarah Siddons, met GE at Rosehill 29 August. Describing her head in phrenological terms, he added that "altogether, with the exception perhaps of Lucretia Mott [the American abolitionist], she appears to me the ablest woman whom I have seen, and in many respects she excells Lucretia. She is extremely feminine and gentle, and the great strength of her intellect combined with this quality renders her very interesting." [I, 360–61]

Rosehill | September 18.

My dear Friend

The subject of the enclosed letters shall be sacred with me.

I think Call's plan—of a *condensed* translation—the best possible in the hands of a person having the requisite judgment and power of writing. It is true that Harriet Martineau's style is admirably adapted for the people, clear, spirited, idiomatic, but I should have less confidence in the equal fitness of her calibre of mind for rendering a trustworthy account of Comte's work. I should augur much greater depth in Call—knowing nothing of him, however, beyond his poetry and a letter or two. But, as Miss M. intimates, the question of what you are to do in the matter turns upon this other question—Does Call's version fulfil the conditions demanded by her and Mr. Lombe's views?—is it one fitted for circulation among the people? *That* you can only ascertain by stating the whole case to him—as I suppose you have done. If he had the prospect of seeing his work ushered into the world by Mr. Lombe's £500 he would perhaps not object to send a specimen to the parties interested. It would be a shame for his labour to be wasted if it be of the right kind. Miss Martineau disclaims any egotism in the affair, but she evidently thinks no one can be so fit for the work as herself. This I doubt—nor do I think her name in the title-page would be of much value now—at least not more than "a graduate of Oxford or Cambridge" as the case may be. Find out the quality of Call's translation if possible—and if it be satisfactory use your influence on his side—of course with all possible delicacy towards Harriet Martineau, who after all is an admirable woman worth twenty of the people who are sniffing at her.

The Combes are still here—Mrs. Bray in bed—and I rather bored.

Yours faithfully
M. E.

TO MRS. CHARLES BRAY, [3 OCTOBER 1851]

GE returned to the Strand 29 September. Mill reviewed Newman's *Lectures on Political Economy* in the October number. GE's article on Greg's *Creed of Christendom* in the *Leader* pointed out that he had used Hennell's *Inquiry*, though not mentioning it in the preface. [I, 363]

[142 Strand]

Dearest Cara

By an oversight I have left behind the two volumes of Flügel's German Dictionary, which you will find in my room. Will you have the goodness to send them to me by Railway, as they are too bulky for anyone to carry. Also my *scissors* for want of which I am tormented.

Robert Chambers called yesterday—a plain Scotchman with a strong Doric accent and small twinkling eyes. The Papers for the People are to be closed, not being so successful as some others of the Chambers publications—*only* 35,000 have been sold. Tell Mr. Noel that Mr. Chapman has been exerting himself about the work on mills—I hope, with some good result. Meanwhile the terrible 'Mill' hight John Stuart has ground F. Newman to powder in the Westminster!

When you send my Dictionary I wish you would ask Mr. Bray to let me have Mill's System of Logic which I don't suppose he wants at present. I shall be glad to have it by me for reference. I am training myself up to say adieu to all delights. I care for nothing but doing my work and doing it well.

Tell Sara especially that Greg wishes the writer of the notice in the Leader to know that he did not intend to omit Hennell for whose work he has a high esteem. I can't remember the exact words and have not his letter by me.

Frederika Bremer is not yet arrived. The house is only just exorcised of Dr. Brabant.

Ever thine
Marian.

I have no smaller envelope than this monster one.

TO CHARLES BRAY, [4 OCTOBER 1851]

GHL in the *Leader* devoted three articles to *Social Statics*. GE wrote a summary of it for the *Analytical Catalogue of Mr. Chapman's Publications*. [I, 364]

142 Strand.

Dear Friend . . .

Dr. Brabant returned to Bath yesterday. He very politely took me to the Crystal Palace, the theatre, and the 'Overland Route.' On Friday we had Foxton,

Wilson, and some other nice people, among others a Mr. Herbert Spencer, who has just brought out a large work on "Social Statics," which Lewes pronounces the best book he has seen on the subject. You must see the book if possible. Mr. Chapman is going to send you Miss Martineau's work, or rather Mr. Atkinson's, which you must review in the Herald. I have been reading the copy which was to be sent to you, but last night I managed very adroitly to inundate it with grease. Sic transitur—i.e. the money from my pocket. Whatever else one may think of the book it is certainly the boldest I have seen in the English language.

I get nothing done here, there are so many *distractions*—moreover I have hardly been well a day since I came. I wish I were rich enough to go to the coast and have some plunges in the sea to brace me. Nevertheless, do not suppose that I don't enjoy being here. I like seeing the new people etc. and I am afraid I shall think the country rather dull after it. . . .

Your affectionate
Pollian.

TO CHARLES BRAY, [8 OCTOBER 1851]

GE walked to Chelsea with Chapman and wandered up and down Cheyne Row while he tried to persuade Carlyle to do the article. Describing the visit, Carlyle wrote to Browning that Chapman has "an able Editor (name can't be given), and such an array of 'talent' as was seldom gathered before." Fredrika Bremer, the Swedish novelist, returning from America, stayed at 142 Strand. William Jeffs sold foreign books in the Burlington Arcade. [I, 366–67]

142 Strand | Wednesday.
Dear Friend . . .
I don't know how long Miss Bremer will stay, but you need not wish to see her. She is to me a repulsive person, equally unprepossessing to eye and ear. I never saw a person of her years who appealed less to my purely instinctive veneration. I have to reflect every time I look at her that she is really Fredrika Bremer.

Fox is to write the article on the Suffrage, and we are going to try Carlyle for the Peerage, [Frederick O.] Ward refusing, on the ground that he thinks the improvement of the physical condition of the people so all-important that he must give all his energies to that. Ward, you know, is the man of the Sewers. He says "Life is a bad business, but we must make the best of it"—to which philosophy I say Amen.

Dr. Hodgson is gone, and all the fun with him. He found in the Minutes of Council on Education the following rhymes, used as copies in one of the schools:

God made bees, | Bees make honey;
God made man, | Man makes money;

God made Satan, | Satan made sin;
God made a place | To put Satan in.

Kate Martineau has just been here. She inquires with great interest about Cara. Love to this last and to Sara. Kind thoughts and wishes to all.

I was introduced to Lewes the other day in Jeff's shop—a sort of miniature Mirabeau in appearance.

Your
Marian.

TO THE BRAYS AND SARA HENNELL, [22 OCTOBER 1851]

GE wrote the notice of Carlyle's *Life of Sterling*, which opens the Contemporary Literature of England article in the *Westminster Review* for January 1852. [I, 369–70]

142 Strand.

Dear Creatures all . . .

We have had three more £20 subscriptions since you left—Newman, Robert Cox, and a Mr. Birch, without sending circulars.

Professor [Edward] Forbes is to write us a capital scientific article whereat I rejoice greatly. The Peerage apparently will not 'get itself done' as Carlyle says. I begin to fear that the Lombe patronage will be rather a bondage. The peerage is not an urgent question, nor does one see that, if the undue influence of the Peers on the elections for the Commons were done away with, there would be much mischief from the House of Lords remaining for some time longer in statu quo.

I have been reading Carlyle's life of Sterling with great pleasure—not for its presentation of Sterling but of Carlyle. There are racy bits of description in his best manner and exquisite touches of feeling. Little rapid characterizations of living men too—of Francis Newman for example, "a man of fine university and other attainments, of the sharpest cutting and most restlessly advancing intellect, and of the mildest pious enthusiasm." There is an inimitable description of Coleridge and his eternal monologue, "To sit as a passive bucket and be pumped into, whether one like it or not, can in the end be exhilarating to no creature."

I can't write any more having to send an editorial missive to Greg. The business news is disquieting. Love to all from

Your
Pollian.

TO SARA HENNELL, [2 NOVEMBER 1851]

[I, 372–73]

142 Strand.

Dear Sara

I have been quite laid up for the last day or two or I should have written you a word or two yesterday.

I must tell you a good story Miss Bremer got from Emerson. Carlyle was very angry with him for not believing in a devil and to convert him took him amongst all the horrors of London—the gin-shops etc. and finally to the House of Commons plying him at every turn with the question "Do you believe in a devil noo?" Miss Bremer left this morning. She is to have £300 for the English edition of her book on America and Mary Howitt £150 for translating it!

There is a severe attack on Carlyle's Life of Sterling in yesterday's Times— unfair as an account of the book but with some truth in its general remarks about Carlyle. Perhaps Mrs. Hennell has her copy of the Life with her and so you may see it. . . .

I am reading with great amusement (!) J. H. Newman's Lectures on the Position of Catholics. They are full of clever satire and description. My table is groaning with books and I have done very little with them yet—but I trust in my star which has hitherto helped me to do all I have engaged to do. Pray remember to send by Mrs. C. Hennell (since she has been kind enough to say she will bring it) the M. S. translation of Schleiermacher's little book and also the book itself. . . .

Tell Mr. Bray this story. When Bentley gave a dinner to the writers in his Miscellany on its first being started, there was a discussion about the title. 'Let it be the Wits' Miscellany,' said one. 'But if it were not witty?' said another. 'Then,' said Bentley, 'suppose we call it Bentley's Miscellany.' 'No, d——— it,' said Douglas Jerrold. 'Don't go to the other extreme.'

TO SARA HENNELL, [24 NOVEMBER 1851]

GE's birthday was 22 November, Sara's, 23, and for many years they exchanged greetings at this time. Spencer was subeditor of the Economist, reviewing theater and music. The letters from Harriet Martineau and Carlyle have not been found. [I, 376]

[142 Strand] Monday.

Dear Sara

I did not forget and meant to have written, but on Saturday afternoon I was teazed, and then came Mr. Spencer to ask Mr. Chapman and me to go to the theatre—so I ended the day in a godless manner, seeing the Merry Wives of Windsor.

You must read Carlyle's denunciation of the opera published in—the Keepsake! The Examiner quotes it at length. I send you the enclosed from Harriet Martineau. Please to return it. The one from Carlyle you may keep till I come. He is a naughty fellow to write in the Keepsake and not for us—after I wrote him the most insinuating letter, offering him three glorious subjects.

Yesterday we went to Mr. Mackay's, Dr. Brabant being there. All blessings on thee, dear Sara.

Thy faithful
Pollian.

TO MRS. CHARLES BRAY, 27 NOVEMBER [1851]

GHL reviewed the theatre for the *Leader*, in which he reported this performance as "dreary" rather than "comic." [I, 376–77]

142 Strand | November 27.

Dear Cara . . .

Carlyle called the other day, strongly recommending Browning the poet as a writer for the Review, and saying "We shall see" about himself. In other respects we have been stagnating since Monday, and now I must work, work, work— which I have scarcely done two days consecutively since I have been here. Lewes says his article on Julia von Krüdener will be "glorious." He sat in the same box with us at the "Merry Wives of Windsor," and helped to carry off the dolorousness of the play by such remarks as "There's the swan preening," "The swan comes out now and then," and "The play is a farce in five acts. If it were in one act and one didn't see it, it would be very well" etc., etc.

You see I have nothing to tell you, so goodbye, dear deuter. Love—

Your affectionate
Marian.

TO SARA HENNELL, [21 JANUARY 1852]

After spending Christmas with the Brays, GE returned to the Strand 12 January. James Martineau's 65-page article was a third longer than Chapman wanted. Pierre Leroux fled from France after the coup d'état of 1851. [II, 4–7]

142 Strand | Wednesday.

Many thanks, dear Sara for the critique. It is amusing enough to compare the diverse and contradictory opinions given by people and journals on every single article in the Review. . . .

I have brought the James Martineau affair to a satisfactory termination. I convinced Mr. C. that he had expressed himself in a way calculated to mislead and that he owed an admission of this to J. M. He got up early one morning to write this with a renewed request that J. M. would accept the supplementary cheque which had been refused—was taken ill, unable to write, and finally asked me to write for him, he signing the letter. Yesterday came a very kind reply, accepting the cheque, which I had requested him to do in *justice* to Mr. C., and very graciously acknowledging Froude's compliment which I had sent him. Of course, there was the quotation "*Laudari a laudato viro.*" So ends the affair, Mr. C. having saved his colours. "C'était une grande affaire, ce crise drole."

Harriet Martineau called on Monday morning, with Mr. Atkinson—very kind and cordial, but unhappily not able to stay long enough to dispel the repulsion excited by the *vulgarity* (I use the word in a moral sense) of her looks and gestures. . . . I honour Harriet Martineau for her powers and industry and should be glad to think highly of her. I have no doubt that she is fascinating when there is time for talk.

We have had two agreeable soirées. Last Monday, I was talking and listening for two hours to Pierre Leroux—a dreamy genius. He was expounding to me his ideas. He belongs neither to the school of Proudhon which represents Liberty only, nor to that of Louis Blanc which represents Equality only, nor to that of Cabet which represents Fraternity. Pierre Leroux' système is the "synthèse" which combines all three. He has found the true 'pont' which is to unite the love of self with the love of one's neighbour. He is, you know, a very voluminous writer. George Sand has dedicated some of her books to him. He dilated on his views of the origin of Christianity—Strauss deficient because he has not shewn the *identity of the teaching of Jesus* with that of the *Essenes*. This is Leroux' favourite idea. I told him of your brother. He moreover traces Essenism back to Egypt and thence to India, the cradle of all religions, etc. etc. with much more which he uttered with an unction rather amusing in a soirée tête-à-tête. "Est-ce-que nous sommes faits pour chercher le bonheur? Est-ce là votre idée, dîtes moi." "Mais non—nous sommes faites, je pense, pour nous développer le plus que possible." "Ah! c'est ça." He is in utter poverty—going to lecture—autrement il faut mourir—has a wife and children with him. He came to London in his early days, when he was 25, to find work as a printer—all the world was in mourning for the Princess Charlotte, "et moi, je me trouvais avoir un *habit pomme-vert.*" So he got no work, went back to Paris, by hook or by crook founded the "Globe" journal, knew St. Simon, disagrees with him entirely as with all other theorists except Pierre Leroux.

We are trying Mazzini to write on Freedom v. Despotism. Don't tell, of course. Froude is too busy translating the "Wahlverwandschaften" for Bohn to do anything for us worth having. . . . I am afraid there is nothing to interest you much in this hasty scribble, but somehow the scum on the surface is all I can give anyone this morning. I have a sore finger which makes it a bore to write.

Thine
Pollian.

Love to Cara. I hope to hear from her on Monday morning.

TO GEORGE COMBE, 27 JANUARY 1852

Combe added two other titles to his "Secular Education," which was put at the head of the July number, but no mention of the Sandwich Islands. Though GE would gladly have abridged Strauss, Chapman's objections are explained here. [VIII, 33–35]

142 Strand | January 27. 1852.

My dear Sir

An important question connected with the bookselling business is so occupying Mr. Chapman, that he finds it impossible to secure an interval for writing to you to-day, and he has therefore requested me to answer for him your letter of Friday last. I cannot regret an opportunity of renewing by letter an intercourse which was so agreeable to me in person.

Mr. Chapman has instructed me to say, that he thinks it desirable to have other publications as well as Mr. Ellis's book at the head of your article, and he suggests to you, in addition to the pamphlet of which he has forwarded to you some proof sheets, the reprint of the Reports and Speeches of the National Public School Association and of their opponents, which, if you do not happen to have them by you, he will be happy to supply you with. He will also be glad if it should fall in with your plan to notice the Report of the State of Education in the Sandwich Islands. As to the matter of your article, he is quite sure that he shall best do justice to its subject, and to the interests of the Review, by giving you a *carte blanche*. The arrangements for the April number will render it convenient that your article should not exceed 20 pages in length, . . .

The last communication from Mr. Lombe to Mr. Chapman was a very peremptory demand that the abridgement of Strauss, for which he had advanced £100, should be forthwith completed and placed in his hands, or else that the £100 should be immediately paid in to his banker. I wrote a letter, declining to make the abridgment for immediate publication, on the ground both of Mr. Chapman's interests and my own—interests which I could not think outweighed by the probable advantage to the public—of superseding a complete translation by an abridgment of a work which at present is fitted for the few rather than for the many. I also explained, that I had never understood from Mr. Chapman that the abridgment was expected to be ready for publication before the translation should be sold out, and happily Mr. Chapman had a copy of his correspondence on the subject, which proved that he had been sufficiently explicit to Mr. Lombe in his statement, that until the remaining 350 copies of the translation were either disposed of or paid for by Mr. L., he could not consent to the publication of an abridgment. Mr. Chapman enclosed my letter with one from himself informing Mr. Lombe that the £100 had been paid to his banker. We have heard nothing of the irascible gentleman since. . . .

I hope Mrs. Combe's health, as well as yours, is better still than when I had the pleasure of seeing her. Pray tell her that it is a happiness to me to think of her and of her kind words to me. Believe me, my dear Sir,

Yours very truly,
Marian Evans.

TO BESSIE RAYNER PARKES, [29 JANUARY 1852]

Bessie Parkes was the daughter of Joseph Parkes, M. P., who had supported the translation of Strauss. His wife was a granddaughter of Joseph Priestley, the discoverer of oxygen. [II, 7]

[142 Strand] Thursday.

My dear Miss Parkes
    I too regretted that I happened to be out yesterday when you and Mrs. Parkes were kind enough to call on me. Another unfortunate coincidence is, that an evening party at Mr. Mackay's at which I have promised to be present, occurs on

Saturday evening. But for this I should have looked forward with pleasure to spending the evening with you.

Mr. Chapman's evening parties have commenced now, and we all wish very much that you could be amongst us now and then. Can you not manage this? Monday is the day fixed on, and if you would accept so informal an invitation as this and come any Monday evening that you had no pleasanter engagement, you would be doing a kindness to others if not to yourself. Dear Miss Parkes,

Yours very truly
Marian Evans.

TO GEORGE COMBE, [24 FEBRUARY 1852]

No room was found for either quotation. The article ran to 31 pages instead of the 20 asked for. Hunt, whose financial difficulties were increased by his liaison with Agnes Lewes, was paid £20 a month by the *Leader*. The Booksellers Association, which for years had fixed the discount rate at 10 percent, cancelled Chapman's membership because of his advertising books at cost plus a small commission. In the April *Westminster Review* he published his "The Commerce of Literature", exposing the shabby racket of the Association. [VIII, 35–36]

142 Strand.

My dear Sir

Your M.S. was sent to the printer on Saturday, but when we receive it 'in slip' I shall be able to insert the quotations from Montaigne—at least the first, which is remarkably piquant. I have read your article with great interest and admiration, as I have done everything else proceeding from your pen. I think it will serve at once the cause it advocates and the reputation of the Review. In consequence of your permission, I have rather regretfully suppressed one or two of the less telling quotations from Mr. Ellis's book. My reason for doing so was our great embarrassment from want of space for the unexpectedly large amount of matter which it is incumbent on us to insert in the April number. I feel sure that there is no omission which you will consider important, though your selections were all so good that one would have been glad to retain them under other circumstances.

Mr. Bray is with me just now and hearing that I am writing to you he begs me to say to you, that he does not think Mr. Thornton Hunt's difficulties are of his own creating but that they arise from his having worked gratuitously for the Leader for six months, from his having had several long illnesses, and from the living in common with persons over whose expenses he had not the same control as over his own. . . .

I am glad to tell you that Mr. Chapman's feud with the Booksellers is not on his part a mere struggle for self-interest. He is convinced that he is making a stand against a system of dealing ultimately injurious to the general Book Trade and to the Diffusion of Literature.

I am sorry to write in haste to you, but I am anxious not to lose the post. With kind regards to Mrs. Combe, I am, my dear Sir

Yours very sincerely
Marian Evans.

TO MRS. CHARLES BRAY, [28 FEBRUARY 1852]

Richard Cobden had been leader of the Anti-Corn Law League. George Dawson, a popular preacher and lecturer, had seen GE frequently at the Brays'. [II, 12–13]

[142 Strand] Saturday.

Dearest Cara

I long very much to see your hand-writing—to have a word from your own self. . . . We went to the meeting of the Association for the Abolition of the Taxes on Knowledge on Wednesday—I that I might hear Cobden in whom I was woefully disappointed. George Dawson's speech, which the Newspapers don't report, was admirable. Dobson Collett, too, was really clever.

I received a note from Miss Lynn last evening—owing, it appears, to Mr. Bray's having mentioned my intention to leave here. She wished to mention to me some friends of hers in Cavendish Sq. who have two rooms to let. I called on her this morning and had a long talk. But the lodgings are not at all what I want, and altogether I think it undesirable to fix on a London residence at present as I want to go to Brighton for a month or two next quarter. I am seriously concerned at my languid body and feel the necessity of taking some measures to get vigour. . . .

Lewes inquired for Sara last Monday in a tone of interest; he was charmed with her, as who would not be that has any taste. Do write to me, dear Cara—I want comforting—this world looks ugly just now, all people rather worse than I have been used to think them. Put me in love with my kind again, by giving me a glimpse at your own inward self since I cannot see the outer one. In haste.

Ever your
Marian.

TO MRS. PETER TAYLOR, 27 MARCH 1852

Peter Alfred Taylor, grandson of the founder of the Courtauld silk firm, was a radical in religion and politics. Margaret Fuller, who had been a friend of Mazzini in Rome, died in a shipwreck in 1850. At the *conversazione*, a meeting of the Friends of Italy, Mazzini, amidst loud cheers, declared the Papacy the curse of Italy. [II, 14–15]

[142 Strand]

I am grieved to find that you have to pay for that fine temperament of yours in attacks of neuralgia. Your silence did not surprise me, after the account you had given me of your domestic circumstances, but I have wished for you on Monday

evenings. Your cordial assurance that you shall be glad to see me sometimes is one
of those pleasant things—those life preservers—which relenting destiny sends
me now and then to buoy me up. For you must know that I am not a little
desponding now and then, and think that old friends will die off, while I shall be
left without the power to make new ones. You know how sad one feels when a
great procession has swept by one, and the last notes of its music have died away,
leaving one alone with the fields and sky. I feel so about life sometimes. It is a help
to read such a life as Margaret Fuller's. How inexpressibly touching that passage
from her journal—"I shall always reign through the intellect, but the life! the life!
O my God! shall that never be sweet?" I am thankful, as if for myself, that it was
sweet at last. But I am running on about feelings when I ought to tell you facts. I
am going on Wednesday to my friends in Warwickshire for about ten days or a
fortnight. When I come back I hope you will be quite strong and able to receive
visitors without effort—Mr. Taylor too.

I *did* go to the *conversazione;* but you have less to regret than you think.
Mazzini's speeches are better read than heard. Proofs are come demanding my
immediate attention, so I must end this hasty scribble.

TO MRS. CHARLES BRAY, [30 MARCH 1852]

Bessie Parkes wrote to Barbara Leigh Smith: "Miss Evans I see more of; and she becomes a
friend to me. . . . As I know her better, the harsh heavy look of her face softens into a very
beautiful tender expression". Of the £500 Lombe sent to Harriet Martineau for the translation of Comte Chapman persuaded her to keep only £150; the rest was invested in a trust to
be applied to the cost of publication. By a codicil to her will she appointed Atkinson and
GE trustees in case she died before the work was completed. GE stayed at Rosehill 3–14
April. [II, 16–17]

[142 Strand] Tuesday.
Dear Cara
I had two offers last night—not of marriage, but of music—which I find it
impossible to resist. Mr. Herbert Spencer proposed to take me on Thursday to
hear William Tell, and Miss Parkes asked me to go with her to hear the Creation
on Friday. I have had so little music this quarter and these two things are so
exactly what I should like that I have determined to put off, for the sake of them,
my other pleasure of seeing you. So pray keep your precious welcome warm for me
until Saturday, when I shall *positively* set off by the 2 o'clock train. Miss Martineau
(Harriet) has written me a most cordial invitation to go and see her before July,
but that is impossible. She has made me joint trustee with Mr. Atkinson of the
fund for the publication of Comte. I liked Atkinson very well the other day. You
see I am cautious. Of new acquaintances one can never be sure because one likes
them *one* day that it will be so the next. Of old friends one is sure that it will be the
same yesterday, today, and forever.

Love to Mr. Bray and Sara. I have not written to the latter this long time because I have been busy—but my heart has been inditing of many a good matter to her.

Thy affectionate
Marian

TO CHARLES BRAY, 17 APRIL [1852]

Combe wanted the *Westminster Review* to have an article on mesmerism. A panic in the ribbon trade and Bray's losses with the *Coventry Herald* forced him to give up his old office. *The Chain of Events* was a melodrama adapted from the French by GHL. [II, 17–18]

142 Strand | April 17.

Dear Friend

I send you your share of Geo. Combe's missive. Mine contains a sequel to the mesmeric case which is very interesting and which I will send you when I have done with it. A very kind letter is come from James Martineau this morning, shewing his thorough willingness to write for us, and his appreciation of the subject proposed to him, but one of his daughters is seriously ill and he cannot pledge himself to prepare anything by July.

There was an article on the Bookselling affair in the Times of yesterday which must be the knell of the Association. Dickens is to preside at a meeting in this house on the subject some day next week. Mr. Chapman called on him yesterday with Bentley, and found him very straight-forward and agreeable. Splendid library, of course, with soft carpet, couches etc. such as become a sympathizer with the suffering classes. How can we sufficiently pity the needy unless we know fully the blessings of plenty? . . .

The one source of my low spirits was the parting with you in the midst of such bad news about everything, and the thought I can do nothing but cry when sorrows come. However, I came home and went to sleep from sheer want of spirit to do anything else, and Providence in an hour or two took pity on me and sent Herbert Spencer to ask me to go to the Lyceum and see 'The Chain of Events.' It is a very long chain and drags rather heavily. No sparkle, but a sort of Dickens-like sentimentality all through—in short, I think it might please you. As a series of tableaux I never saw anything equal to it. But to my mind it is execrable moral taste to have a storm and shipwreck with all its horrors on the stage. I could only scream and cover my eyes. It was revolting to hear the cheers and clapping of the audience. But perhaps all that was pure philosophy, and they were so thoroughly imbued with your beloved optimism that they felt more than ever reconciled to the scheme of things. . . .

Of course this letter is for all. My blessings on you all.

Your affectionate
Marian. . . .

TO HERBERT SPENCER, [21 APRIL 1852]

After GE's death Spencer wrote to his friend Youmans that he frequently took her to the opera and theatres, "and we were also thrown together in matters concerning the *Westminster Review*. After a time I began to have qualms as to what might result from this constant companionship. Great as was my admiration for her, considered both morally and intellectually, and decided as was my feeling of friendship, I could not perceive in myself any indications of a warmer feeling, and it occurred to me that mischief would possibly follow if our relations continued. Those qualms led me to take a strange step—an absurd step in one sense. I wrote to her indicating, as delicately as I could, my fears. Then afterwards, perceiving how insulting to her was the suggestion that while I felt in no danger of falling in love with her, she was in danger of falling in love with me, I wrote a second letter, apologising for my unintended insult. She took it all smilingly, quite understanding my motive and forgiving my rudeness. The consequence was that our intimacy continued as before." [VIII, 42]

Dear Friend

Not for the "satisfaction of breaking a conventionalism," but for the sake of hearing Le Prophète and yet more of hearing it with you, I accept your kind proposal. I am not sure that I understand your note, or rather, I am sure that I do not. But prior to all further explanation, or, if you wish, to the exclusion of it, let me assure you that I never imputed to you an ungenerous thought. I felt disappointed rather than "hurt" that you should not have sufficiently divined my character to perceive how remote it is from my habitual state of mind to imagine that any one is falling in love with me. But perhaps I still misapprehend you, so I will run no risk of blundering further. I will only say, that I value your regard very highly, and that the more strictly truthful you are to me, both explicitly and implicitly, the better I like you.

Yours very sincerely
Marian Evans.

142 Strand | Wednesday

TO THE BRAYS, [27 APRIL 1852]

Bray's business had long been in Much Park Street, Coventry. Sarah Pugh, an abolitionist from Pennsylvania, was one of the female delegates whose credentials were refused at the World's Anti-Slavery Convention in 1840. At the last moment a dispute over Johanna Wagner's contract caused the substitution of *I Martiri* for *Le Prophète*. [II, 20–22]

142 Strand | Tuesday.

Dearest Friends

I find it very difficult to resign myself to the fact of your having parted with the old place in Much Park Street, and am still impatient and rebellious. Well, we will love each other the better, the more destiny chooses to flout us. . . .

Our fortunes here are as usual—chequered—"Twist ye, twine ye, even so | Mingle human weal and woe." In the first place, the Bookselling affair promises to be a complete triumph over the Association. . . . At the same time it must be confessed that our Review Treasury is almost exhausted and no new funds pour in. So it is really creditable to be jolly.

We had quite a brilliant soirée yesterday evening. W. R. Greg, Forster (of Rawdon), Francis Newman, the Ellises, and Louis Blanc were the stars of greatest magnitude. I had a pleasant talk with Greg and Forster. Greg was "much pleased to have made my acquaintance." Forster, on the whole, appeared to think that people should be glad to make *his* acquaintance. Greg is a short man, with a hooked nose and an imperfect enunciation from defective teeth, but his brain is large, the anterior lobe very fine and a moral region to correspond. Black, wiry, curly hair, and every indication of a first-rate temperament. But when you see him across the room, you are unpleasantly impressed, and can't believe that he wrote his own books. Mrs. Charles Hennell was here with her tall, honest-looking brother, Herbert. He strikes me more agreeably than any Brabant I have ever seen. We have some very nice Americans here—the Pughs, friends of the Parkes's—really refined, intellectual people. Miss Pugh, an elderly lady, is a great abolitionist, and was one of the Women's Convention that came to England in 1840 and was not allowed to join the *Men's* Convention. But I suppose we shall soon be able to say, '*Nous avons changé tout cela,*' in spite of Mr. Bray and all retrogradists.

I went to the opera on Saturday—I Martiri, at Covent Garden—with my "excellent friend Herbert Spencer," as Lewes calls him. We have agreed that we are not in love with each other, and that there is no reason why we should not have as much of each other's society as we like. He is a good, delightful creature and I always feel better for being with him. . . .

Bless you, dear ones.

`Ever your true
Marian.

Mrs. Chapman's thanks for the Fig-pudding.

TO THE BRAYS, 5 MAY [1852]

Reports of the meeting aroused public opinion against the Booksellers' Association. In Parliament Gladstone castigated their method. By the end of May they voted to dissolve. Chapman's statement was drawn up with the help of GE and Spencer, who were together constantly. Lord Campbell, Lord Chief Justice, helped get the Copyright Act passed in 1842. The Association was willing to submit the case to his decision. [II, 23–25]

Wednesday | May 5.

Dearest Friends,

The meeting last night went off triumphantly, and I saluted Mr. Chapman with "See the Conquering Hero Comes" on the piano at 12 o'clock, for not until then was the last magnate except Herbert Spencer out of the house. I sat *at* the door for a short time, but soon got a chair within it and heard and saw everything.

Dickens in the chair—a position he fills remarkably well, preserving a courteous neutrality of eyebrow, and speaking with clearness and decision. His appearance is certainly disappointing—no benevolence in the face and I think little in the head—the anterior lobe not by any means remarkable. In fact he is not distinguished looking in any way—neither handsome nor ugly, neither fat nor thin, neither tall nor short. Mr. Chapman read his statement very well and looked distinguished and refined even in that assemblage of intellectuals. Letters were read from R. Chambers, Geo. Combe, MacCulloch, Cobden, James Wilson, De Morgan etc. Babbage moved the first resolution—an ugly man and a bad speaker but a great authority. Charles Knight is a beautiful elderly man with a modest but firm enunciation, and he made a wise and telling speech which silenced one or two vulgar, ignorant booksellers who had got into the meeting by mistake. One of these—Willis—no—Southron—began by complimenting Dickens—"views held by such worthy and important gentlemen, *which is your worthy person in the chair.*" Dickens looked respectfully neutral. These four booksellers were a capital foil to all the other men in the room, and they happened to sit all in a row. Their faces contrasted with those of the authors were in every sense a primâ facie argument against them. The most telling speech of the evening was Prof. Tom Taylor's—as witty and brilliant as one of George Dawson's. Professor [Richard] Owen's too was remarkably good. He had a resolution to move as to the bad effect of the trade restrictions on scientific works, and gave his own experience in illustration. Speaking of the slow and small sale of scientific books of a high class, he said, in his silvery bland way, alluding to Willis's boast that the retail booksellers *recommended* the works of less known authors—"for which limited sale we are doubtless indebted to the kind recommendation of our friends, the retail booksellers"—whereupon these worthies, taking it for a bonâ fide compliment, cheered enthusiastically. Dr. Lankester, Prof. Newman, Robert Bell and others spoke well, and every resolution was carried. Owen has a tremendous head and looked, as he was, the greatest celebrity of the meeting. Geo. Cruikshank, too, made a capital speech, in an admirable moral spirit. He is the most homely, genuine looking man, not unlike the pictures of Captain Cuttle.

So now I hope poor Mr. Chap. will have a little time to attend to his business which is needing him awfully—in fact his private affairs are wearing a melancholy aspect. However he has worked well and in a good spirit at this great question and has shewn a degree of talent, and power of mastering a subject which have won him general admiration.

I forgot to say that the sense of the meeting was decidedly against a deputation to Lord Campbell—the absurdity of making an individual opinion of importance in the matter was very strongly expressed on all hands, so the resolutions are to be sent to him with the names of the authors giving their adhesion, and a short note from Charles Dickens. By the way, I shall be able to pick up some autographs for Sara.

I went to hear the Huguenots on Saturday evening. It was a rich treat. Mario and Grisi and Formes and that finest of orchestras under Costa. . . . I am going to a concert to-night—Jetty Trefts, Sivori, Formes etc. This is all very fine, but in the meantime I am getting as haggard as an old witch under London atmosphere and influences.

Write again very soon and tell me something about yourselves. I shall be glad to have sent me my Shakespeare, Goethe, Byron, and Wordsworth, if you will be so good as to take the trouble of packing them.

Ever your affectionate
Marian.

TO MRS. CHARLES BRAY, 27 MAY [1852]

As her intimacy with Spencer deepened, GE's consciousness of her want of beauty increased. Robert Mackay had married for the first time at the age of 50. Millais' painting at the Royal Academy shows the Huguenot Knight saying farwell to his lover on St. Bartholomew's day. [II, 29–30]

142 Strand | May 27.

Dearest Cara . . .

You talk of poor Mr. Chapman's laurels—alas, alas, he is suffering the most torturing anxiety, advertising for a partner in half-despair of getting another kind of aid from Mr. Gardner. (These are secrets of course). The immediate difficulty is how to pay the authorship of the next number of the W.R.—a sum of £250! He sits in the shop the greater part of the day now, and is about to part with Mr. Beveridge, as a step in retrenchment. I suppose I am telling you these things on the ordinary principle of consolation—"You see there are others as badly off as you"—but I am afraid this is no balm to you good creatures who have the weakness to care almost as much for other people's sorrows as for your own.

The weather is horrid and depresses me more than I have ever felt it before. I look like one of those old hags we used to see by the wayside in Italy—only a little worse, for want of the dark eyes and dark hair in contrast with the parchment. My brightest spot next to my love of *old* friends, is the deliciously calm *new* friendship that Herbert Spencer gives me. We see each other every day and have a delightful *camaraderie* in everything. But for him, my life would be desolate enough now, with poor Mr. C. so occupied and so sad—but he runs away with a great deal of my time.

Kate Martineau called the other day with a friend of hers. I have not been to see the Mackays yet. The Chapmans brought rather a melancholy account of him. They think him rather worse than otherwise for the marriage. I am so grieved to hear that Sara does not get better. What a wretched lot of old shrivelled creatures we shall be by-and-bye. Never mind, the uglier we get in the eyes of others the lovelier we shall be to each other—that has always been my firm faith about friendship, and now it is in a slight degree my experience.

Has Mr. Bray described to you Millais' picture of 'the Huguenot Knight'? The face of the woman is never to be forgotten—I wish you could see it. The Americans happily are pouring in now—hitherto there has been an alarming paucity of lodgers.

Miss Parkes had a grand ball last night. I was asked, but refused to go. I hug letters from you all with rapture—do let me hear as often as you can. Madame D'Albert has sent me the sweetest letter just like herself and I feel grateful to have such a heart remembering and loving me on the other side of the Jura. They are very well and flourishing.

A thousand loves to Sara and Mr. Bray.

Your
Marian.

TO THE BRAYS, [14 JUNE 1852]

[II, 34–35]

[142 Strand] Monday.

Dearest Friends

The opera, Chiswick Flower Show, the French play, and the Lyceum, all in one week, brought their natural consequences of headache and hysterics all yesterday. At 5 o'clock I felt quite sure that life was unendurable and that I must consider the most feasible method of suicide as soon as the revises are gone to press. This morning, however, the weather and I are both better, having cried ourselves out and used up all our clouds, and I can even contemplate living six months longer. Was there ever anything more dreary than this June? . . .

I am distressed to hear that you are all ailing with Influenza. I should like to see you very much—nay, it is fast becoming a necessity to me—so don't be surprised if I announce an intention of that sort by and bye. I told Herbert Spencer of your invitation, Mr. Bray, not mentioning that you asked him *with me.* He said he should like to accept it—but I think it would be better for him to go down when I am with you. We certainly could not go together, for all the world is setting us down as engaged—a most disagreeable thing if one chose to make oneself uncomfortable. 'Tell it not in Gath' however—that is to say, please to avoid mentioning our names together, and pray burn this note, that it may not lie on the chimney piece for general inspection.

Your faithful
Marian.

TO CHARLES BRAY, 23 JUNE [1852]

GE was looking forward to being with Spencer at Rosehill. Chapman had agreed to escort her to Broadstairs, where she was going to stay two months. [II, 37]

[142 Strand] June 23.

Dear Friend

I have assured Herbert Spencer that you will think it a sufficiently formal answer to the invitation you sent him through Mr. Lewes if I tell you that he will prefer waiting for the pleasure of a visit to you until I am with you—if you will have him then. *Entre nous,* if Mr. Lewes should not accept your invitation now, pray don't ask him when I am with you—not that I don't like him—*au contraire*—

but I want nothing so Londonish when I go to enjoy the fields and hedgerows and yet more, friends of ten years' growth.

Mr. Chapman says I can't leave before today week, as he will be unable to escort me—that is to say, he and Mrs. C.—before then. I wish you could all go with me instead.

I spent the evening at Mr. Parkes's on Monday. Yesterday Herbert Spencer brought his father to see me—a large-brained, highly informed man, with a certain quaintness and simplicity—altogether very pleasing.

Good Geo. Combe is making efforts for Mr. C. and I hope something will come of them. Love to Cara and Sara and a kiss for Nelly ☀

> Ever your affectionate
> Marian Evans.

I should be *so* grateful for a remnant of ribbon—white if possible.

TO SARA HENNELL, [29 JUNE 1852]

Mrs. Samuel Smith was an aunt of Florence Nightingale, who had returned from studying nursing in Germany and was attempting to formulate "a new religion for the Artizans of England." Sara Hennell had been governess to Florence's cousin, Hilary Bonham Carter. Another cousin, Barbara Leigh Smith, became one of GE's warmest friends. Lucy Field was the daughter of Mrs. William Field, at whose school in Leamington Bessie Parkes had been educated. [II, 39–40]

[142 Strand] Tuesday Morning.

My dear Sara

Mrs. S. Smith *had* called on me before she received your letter of introduction, and Miss Florence Nightingale with her. I like them both, especially Mrs. S. Smith, who has more freedom and simplicity than any *un*distinguished woman of her age I ever saw. By freedom and simplicity, I mean non-subjection to "formulas." They came again last night with Miss Carter, your Hilary—and Madame Mohl, whose *make-up* was certainly extraordinary, but I suppose she is a superior woman. We had quite a constellation, a beautiful American authoress, Miss Sara Clarke, alias Grace Greenwood, being the greatest star.

I went to Kew yesterday on a scientific expedition with Herbert Spencer, who has all sorts of theories about plants—I should have said a *proof-* hunting expedition. Of course, if the flowers didn't correspond to the theories, we said, '*tant pis pour les fleurs.*'

Mr. Chapman begged me to accept a dozen catalogues that I might present them to you and Mr. Bray, and I did not refuse, so you must do me the honour etc. Miss Parkes has introduced me to *Barbara* Smith, whose expression I like exceedingly. I hope to know more of her.

Can you send me Miss Field's address at Ramsgate? but don't say that I asked for it, as I should like to be free either to see her or not. I go to Broadstairs on

Saturday. I am sadly in want of the change, and would much rather present myself
to you all when I can do you more credit as a friend.

Ever your loving
Pollian.

TO MRS. CHARLES BRAY, [4 JULY 1852]

[II, 42]

Chandos Cottage | Broadstairs

Dear Cara

I warn you against Ramsgate which is a strip of London come out for an airing.
Broadstairs is perfect, and I have the snuggest little lodgings conceivable with a
motherly good woman and a nice little damsel of 14 to wait on me. There are only
my two rooms in this cottage, but lodgings are plentiful in the place. Miss Field
was once in these same lodgings and wanted to come here now, but that her
medical man prescribed Ramsgate. I have a sitting-room about 8 feet by 9 and a
bedroom a little larger, yet in that small space there is almost every comfort. Miss
Field called last night with her brother, but unfortunately I was out and so missed
her. I pay a guinea a week for my rooms, so I shall not ruin myself by staying a
month unless I commit excesses in coffee and sugar. I am thinking whether it
would not be wise to retire from the world and live here for the rest of my days.
With some fresh paper on the walls and an easy chair I think I could resign myself.
Come and tell me your opinion.

Your affectionate
Marian.

TO HERBERT SPENCER, [8 JULY 1852]

Since GE left 3 July the London temperature had been 78, 89, 85, 81 degrees. With the
careful vagueness which veils his *Autobiography* Spencer wrote: "Two of my weekly vaca-
tions were spent at the sea-side." GE's lighter reading included Harriet Martineau's *Deerbrook* and GHL's *Rose, Blanche, and Violet*, as well as Tennyson's poem. GE's serious reading
of William Warburton's *Divine Legation of Moses* was in preparation for her *The Idea of a
Future Life*, which Chapman had announced for publication. [VIII, 50–52]

Chandos Cottage | Thursday.

Dear Friend

No credit to me for my virtues as a refrigerant. I owe them all to a few lumps of
ice which I carried away with me from that tremendous glacier of yours. I am glad
that Nemesis, lame as she is, has already made you feel a little uneasy in my
absence, whether from the state of the thermometer or aught else. We will not
inquire too curiously whether you long most for my society or for the sea-breezes.
If you decided that I was not worth coming to see, it would only be of a piece with

that generally exasperating perspicacity of yours which will not allow one to humbug you. (An agreeable quality, let me tell you, that capacity of being humbugged. Don't pique yourself on not possessing it). But seriously and self-ishness apart, I should like you to have the enjoyment of this pleasant place. The heat, tempered as it is here by the sea-breezes, is not at all oppressive, and only serves to give one a delicious, voluptuous laziness. There are fresh wild flowers coming out every day—the dear little creeping convolvulus and mignonette and others known to me "by sight, but not by name." And then the sun-set over the plains of wheat and barley, and the sea studded with sails. Do come on Saturday, if you would like it. There is a nice hotel where you can have a bed, and shant I be proud to do hospitalities once more? I think the Boat is better than the Excursion train—in spite of the shorter time of the latter. The heat and dust stretch 3 hours into 6.

I am ashamed to give a report of myself, for I have done nothing but dream away my time since I came. I think of retiring from the world, like old Weller, if my good landlady will accept me as a tenant all the year round. I fancy I should soon be on an equality, in point of sensibility, with the star-fish and sea-egg—perhaps you will wickedly say, I certainly want little of being a *Medusa*. I have had a loathing for books—for all tagging together of sentences since I came, and have liked everything as indefinite as the sounds of an Aeolian harp. You see I am sinking fast towards "homogeneity," and my brain will soon be a mere pulp unless you come to arrest the downward process. I have read Deerbrook, and am sur-prized at the depths of feeling it reveals. Rose, Blanche and Violet, too—at least the two first volumes—the third I left behind and (damaging fact, either for me or the novel!) I don't care to have it. I have read a good deal of "In Memoriam"—which, believe it or not, has great beauties—though the artificiality of the form is unforgiveable. Froude's much talked of article on Spinoza too I have read at last, and find it a mere sketch of his life—picturesquely done but with the usual Froudian sentimentality and false veneration. This morning I determined to reform and plunged into Warburton. Henceforth I mean to live laborious days—that is to say until I have made up my mind to fraternize with the star-fish. In haste,

Ever yours truly
Marian Evans.

I am horrified to see how I have blotted my letter. Grâce—

TO HERBERT SPENCER, [?14 JULY 1852]

Spencer came to Broadstairs on Saturday 10 July. It is impossible to date this letter with certainty. As I reconstruct the episode, GE handed it to him after his rejection of her love. It has no address or salutation and ends without a period. In his letter to Youmans after GE's death Spencer wrote: "And then, by and by, just that which I had feared might take place, did take place. Her feelings became involved and mine did not. The lack of physical attraction was fatal. Strongly as my judgment prompted, my instincts would not respond." [VIII, 56–57]

[Broadstairs]

I know this letter will make you very angry with me, but wait a little, and don't say anything to me while you are angry. I promise not to sin any more in the same way.

My ill health is caused by the hopeless wretchedness which weighs upon me. I do not say this to pain you, but because it is the simple truth which you must know in order to understand why I am obliged to seek relief.

I want to know if you can assure me that you will not forsake me, that you will always be with me as much as you can and share your thoughts and feelings with me. If you become attached to some one else, then I must die, but until then I could gather courage to work and make life valuable, if only I had you near me. I do not ask you to sacrifice anything—I would be very good and cheerful and never annoy you. But I find it impossible to contemplate life under any other conditions. If I had your assurance, I could trust that and live upon it. I have struggled—indeed I have—to renounce everything and be entirely unselfish, but I find myself utterly unequal to it. Those who have known me best have always said, that if ever I loved any one thoroughly my whole life must turn upon that feeling, and I find they said truly. You curse the destiny which has made the feeling concentrate itself on you—but if you will only have patience with me you shall not curse it long. You will find that I can be satisfied with very little, if I am delivered from the dread of losing it.

I suppose no woman ever before wrote such a letter as this—but I am not ashamed of it, for I am conscious that in the light of reason and true refinement I am worthy of your respect and tenderness, whatever gross men or vulgar-minded women might think of me

TO SARA HENNELL, 16 JULY [1852]

The *tabooed* family was that of Benjamin Leigh Smith, a radical member of Parliament. In 1826, when a bachelor of 43, he saw Anne Longden, a beautiful milliner's apprentice of 17, "took her under his protection"; before she died in 1834, she bore him five children, of whom Barbara was the eldest. Though he never married, Smith was devoted to his family. When Barbara came of age in 1848, he gave her an independent allowance of £300 a year; after his death she inherited a large fortune. GE does not mention Spencer in this letter to her "Liebe Gemahl" of former years. [II, 45–46]

Broadstairs | July 16.

Dear Sara

I thought of you last night when I was in a state of mingled rapture and torture—rapture at the sight of a glorious evening sky, torture at the sight and hearing of the belabouring given to the poor donkey which was drawing me from Ramsgate home. You will hear from Miss Field that her sister Alice has joined her.

I had a note from Miss Florence Nightingale yesterday. I was much pleased with her. There is a loftiness of mind about her which is well expressed by her form and manners. My talk the evening Miss Carter was at Mr. Chapman's was chiefly with Miss Nightingale and Mrs. S. Smith. I have so profound a faith in your *likings*, if not in your *dis-likings*, that I am quite sure any unfavourable impression about your Hilary is the sign of a want in me rather than in her. Had she been a person whom you had not prepared me to respect, I should have thought her rather affected and the least bit snobbish—that is thinking of her conventional rank and afraid lest you should overlook it. I was the more surprized at this that her friends seemed so entirely the reverse. I am far more agreeably impressed with Barbara Smith—one of the *tabooed* family—who is Bessie Parkes's intimate friend.

Glad you are pleased with the Westminster. I do think it a rich number— matter for a fortnight's reading and thought. Lewes has not half done it justice in the Leader. To my mind the Niebuhr article is as good as any of them.

If you could see me in my quiet nook! I am half ashamed of being in such clover both spiritually and materially while some of my friends are on the dusty highways without a tuft of grass or a flower to cheer them. A letter from you will be delightful. We seem to have said very little to each other lately. But I always know—rejoice to know that there is the same Sara for me as there is the same green earth and arched sky when I am good and wise enough to like the best things.

Ever thine
Pollian.

TO JOHN CHAPMAN, [24–25 JULY 1852]

This long, calm letter planning the October number of the *Westminster* recalls GE's extraordinary ability to forgive, to separate her emotion from her intellect. Though, like Spencer, Chapman had rejected her love, she had vowed to serve as his "helpmate" in editing the *Review*. Her analysis of the mistake in its original outline proved true when James Martineau later started the rival *National Review*. Her efforts to enlist Charlotte Brontë as a writer and to get an article on Lamarck from GHL were unsuccessful. Fashion was eventually discussed in an article by Spencer. [II, 47–50]

Broadstairs | Saturday Evening.

Dear Friend

I laid Mr. Gilpin's note with the accompanying pamphlet on my desk the morning I left London, meaning to commend them to your care. I dare say you will find them in my room. If not, I believe the purport of Mr. Gilpin's note was that the writer of said pamphlet wished to know if an article on "Free Schools in Worcestershire" (the subject of the pamphlet) would be accepted for the Westminster. I am not sure whether it was requested that the pamphlet should be noticed by us.

I return Froude's letter and Martineau's. Of course you will let Froude have his 26 pages. As to Martineau, there is no doubt that he will write—"Self-interest well understood" will secure that. Pray, how came you to tell him that J. S. Mill was going to write? I have told you all along that he would flatly contradict Martineau and that there was nothing for it but to announce contradiction on our title-page. I think M. is right as to the 'idea' of a quarterly, but it is plain that the

Westminster can't realize that 'idea.' However, if I were its proprietor and could afford to make it what I liked, it should certainly not represent the Martineau "School of thought." Not that I mean to decry him, or to speak superciliously of one so immeasurably superior to myself—I simply mean that I can't see things through spectacles of his colour.

What do you think of sending the note which I enclose to Miss Bronty? The thrice-announced parcel has just arrived. As to my disgraceful mistake about the stamps, I can only say—peccavi, peccavi. The only excuse I have to make is that I just glanced at the envelope in which you forwarded the same M.S. to me, and saw only two stamps on it. I need not say that I did not pause to use my reasoning faculty in the matter. Don't suggest 'Fashion' as a subject to any one else—I should like to keep it.

Sunday—This morning came (with the Athenaeum and Leader, for which thanks) a letter from Geo. Combe announcing Dr. S. Brown's refusal to write said article for October. I enclose the letters of both. Please return Geo. Combe's with *the one of his which I sent you some time ago.* (See last page of my letter.) I am sorry for Dr. B's defection as I am very favourably impressed with the character of his mind. I wish Mr. Bastard would wait until January and still get Dr. B. to write. I shall say so to Geo. Combe. If yes, what do you say to Lewes on Lamarck?

I have noticed the advertisement of the British Quarterly this morning. Its list of subjects is excellent. I wish you could contrive to let me see the number when it comes out. They have one subject of which I am jealous—"Pre-Raphaelism in Painting and Literature." We have no good writer on such subjects on our staff. Ought we not, too, to try and enlist David Masson, who is one of the British Quarterly set? He wrote that article in the Leader on the Patagonian Missionaries, which I thought very beautiful. Seeing 'Margaret Fuller' among their subjects makes me rather regret having missed the first moment for writing an article on her life myself, but I think she still may come in as one of a triad or quaternion.

I feel that I am a wretched helpmate to you, almost out of the world and incog. so far as I am in it. When you can afford to pay an Editor, if that time will ever come, you must get one. If you believe in Free Will, in the Theism that looks on manhood as a type of the godhead and on Jesus as the Ideal Man, get one belonging to the Martineau 'School of thought,' and he will drill you a regiment of writers who will produce a Prospective on a larger scale, and so the Westminster may come to have 'dignity' in the eyes of Liverpool.

If not—if you believe, as I do, that the thought which is to mould the Future has for its root a belief in necessity, that a nobler presentation of humanity has yet to be given in resignation to individual nothingness, than could ever be shewn of a being who believes in the phantasmagoria of hope unsustained by reason—why then get a man of another calibre and let him write a fresh Prospectus, and if Liverpool theology and ethics are to be admitted, let them be put in the "dangerous ward," *alias,* the Independent Section.

The only third course is the present one, that of Editorial compromise. Martineau writes much that we can agree with and admire. Newman ditto, J. S. Mill still more, Froude a little less and so on. These men can write more openly in the Westminster than anywhere else. They are amongst the world's vanguard, though

not all in the foremost line; it is good for the
have every facility for speaking out. Ergo, sir
himself, it is good that there should be one whi
Westminster. The grand mistake with respect to this plan is the paragraph in the
Prospectus which announces the Independent Section and which thus makes the
Editors responsible for everything outside that railing—Ah me! how wise we all
are après coup.

If we don't have Lewes's article on Lamarck, I think you had better sound him
when he comes back and see what hope there is in him for October. Defective as
his articles are, they are the best we can get *of the kind.* . . .

I congratulate you on your ability to be cheerful *malgré tout.*

Yours etc.
Marian Evans.

TO HERBERT SPENCER, [?29 JULY 1852]

Note the sudden formality in "Mr. Spencer." He wrote to Youmans in 1881. "It was a most
painful affair, continuing through the summer of 52, on through the autumn, and, I think,
into the beginning of 53. She was very desponding and I passed the most miserable time
that has occurred in my experience; for, hopeless as the relation was, she would not agree
that we should cease to see one another. So much did I feel the evil that I had done
involuntarily, or rather, against my will, that I hinted at the possibility of marriage, even
without positive affection on my part; but this she at once saw would lead to unhappiness."
But he returned for another visit to Broadstairs. The *Canterbury Herald* reported 7 August
that reaping had become general in Kent with the most auspicious weather. [VIII, 61]

Broadstairs | Thursday Evening.

Dear Mr. Spencer

It would be ungenerous in me to allow you to suffer even a slight uneasiness on
my account which I am able to remove. I ought at once to tell you, since I can do
so with truth, that I am not unhappy. The fact is, all sorrows sink into insignifi-
cance before the one great sorrow—my own miserable imperfections, and any
outward hap is welcome if it will only serve to rouse my energies and make me less
unworthy of my better self. I have good hope that it will be so now, and I wish you
to share this hope if it will give you any satisfaction.

If, as you intimated in your last letter, you feel that my friendship is of value to
you for its own sake—mind on no other ground—it is yours. Let us, if you will,
forget the past, except in so far as it may have brought us to trust in and feel for
each other, and let us help to make life beautiful to each other as far as fate and the
world will permit us. Whenever you like to come to me again, to see the golden
corn before it is reaped, I can promise you such companionship as there is in me,
untroubled by painful emotions. I meant to write you a long letter and tell you a
great deal about my thoughts and feelings since we parted—but I have been ill for
the last three days and everything is an effort to me.

Ever yours faithfully
Marian Evans.

4

SOME ONE TO LEAN UPON
George Henry Lewes

After her turbulent summer at Broadstairs GE saw the October 1852 number of the *Westminster Review* through the press before going to visit the Combes at Edinburgh and Harriet Martineau at Ambleside. On her return to the Strand she began to see more and more of GHL, who had been a contributor since 1840 and supplied articles for every number under GE's editorship. He and his friend Thornton Leigh Hunt had founded the *Leader,* a radical weekly, for which GHL wrote the literary and theatrical pages. In 1841 he had married the beautiful Agnes Jervis, by whom he had a daughter, who lived only two days, and four sons, the youngest of whom died in infancy in 1850. A month later Agnes bore a fifth son, whose father was Thornton Hunt. Unwilling to stigmatize the child, GHL allowed him to be registered as Edmund Lewes. But the offence was repeated, and in 1852 after the birth of the second of her four or five children by Hunt, GHL ceased to regard her as his wife. But having condoned the adultery, GHL was precluded from asking a divorce. In this dreary, wasted period of his life he came to know GE.

At first she was repelled by his flippant cynicism, until she realized that it was merely a mask to cover the pain of his shattered marriage. In her lonely state— ignored by her family, her love rejected by Spencer—GE found in GHL the companionship she could not live without. The summer of 1853 she spent mostly at St. Leonard's, where GHL may have joined her occasionally and poured out the story of his wrecked life. In October she moved from the Strand to lodgings at 21 Cambridge Street, Hyde Park, where she could receive visitors without scrutiny of the Chapman household. Besides her editorial work she was translating Feuerbach's *Das Wesen des Christenthums* for Chapman's Quarterly Series, in which he had also announced *The Idea of a Future life,* an original book "by the Translator of Strauss." GHL was overworking to support Agnes and her mingled brood, to which a third child by Hunt had just been added. GE read proofs for him, and in the spring of 1854, when he fell ill and was sent to the country for two months, she wrote reviews for his columns in the *Leader.* He needed her as much as she needed him. After discussing the matter with Chapman and with Bray, she resolved to join her life with GHL's. They embarked together for Germany 20 July 1854 in a union unbroken until his death in 1878.

TO SARA HENNELL, 2 SEPTEMBER [1852]

In his letter to Youmans after GE's death Spencer wrote: "At length it happened that being with Lewes one afternoon when I was on my way to see her, I invited him to go with me (they were already slightly known). He did so. This happened two or three times; and then, on the third or fourth time, when I rose to leave, he said he should stay. From that time he commenced to go alone, and so the relation began—(his estrangement from his wife being then of long standing). When I saw the turn matters were taking it was, of course, an immense relief to me." [II, 53–55]

142 Strand | September 2

Dear Sara . . .

To tell you editorial secrets—the articles are raining in. Froude is good—writes very judiciously and pleasantly, except that at the end he brings on Bengal lights and goes off in a Carlylian flourish. Forbes too is come—but is poor—(on Botany). Herbert Spencer says *his* article will have a "light appearance" by reason of its quotations which break the page but I suspect it will be like those stone sweetmeats which cheat the children. Altogether this number is not likely to be anywhere near the last.

Mr. Chapman says he wrote to Mr. Bray last night, so you know the last of his affairs. It seems that he is to go on. He makes a great point of my remaining here till Christmas, at all events, and I cannot under present "cums" say no. But ever since I came back I have felt something like the madness which imagines that the four walls are contracting and going to crush one.

No sooner did I get in on Saturday than Mr. Atkinson called, and talked for 2 hours. He is very pleasant and intelligent and one can't help liking him. He shewed me a letter of Harriet Martineau's, in which she complains that she is overdone in her Irish peregrinations and in which she, with incomprehensible ignorance, jeers at Lewes for "introducing *Psychology* as a science in his Comte papers." Why Comte himself holds Psychology to be a necessary link in the chain of science—Lewes only suggests a change in its relations. *Entre nous* she writes very sillily on the subject. But I am frightened to have told you this, for everything I say to any one at Rosehill gets around by some incomprehensible means to Lewes—Lewes can tell you the whole state of your domestic affairs, if you like, of course with additions, if not emendations, by the editor or editors. I have heard nothing of the Combes yet. There is a great, dreary article on the Colonies by my side asking for reading and abridgement, so I can't go on scribbling—indeed my hands are so hot and tremulous this morning that it will be better for you if I leave off.

Dearest Sara, your little loving notes are very precious to me, but I say nothing about matters of feeling till my good genius has returned from his excursions—the evil one has possession just now. Love to all.

Your
Pollian.

TO THE BRAYS, 7 OCTOBER 1852

GE visited the Combes at 45 Melville Street, Edinburgh, for two weeks. Combe's nephew Robert Cox edited the *Phrenological Journal*. Icaria was a commune established in 1849 at Nauvoo, Illinois. [II, 59]

Edinburgh | October 7. 1852.

Dear Friends

Here I am in this beautiful Auld Reekie once more—hardly recognizing myself for the same person as the damozel who left it by the coach with a heavy heart some six years ago.

The Combes are all kindness and I am in clover—an elegant house, glorious fires, and a comfortable carriage—in short just in the circumstances to nourish sleek optimism, convince one that this is "le meilleur des mondes possibles" and make one shudder at the impiety of all who doubt it. Last evening Mr. Robert Cox came to tea, to be introduced to me as my *cicerone* through the lions of Edinburgh, and we are to set out on an expedition tomorrow morning. . . . The talk last night was pleasant enough, though of course all the interlocutors besides Mr. Combe have little to do but shape elegant modes of negation and affirmation like the people who are talked to by Socrates in Plato's dialogues—'Certainly, that I firmly believe' etc. I have a beautiful view from my room window—masses of wood, distant hills, the Firth, and four splendid buildings dotted far apart—not an ugly object to be seen. When I look out in the morning it is as if I had waked up in Utopia or Icaria or one of Owen's parallelograms. The weather is perfect—all the more delightful to me for its northern sharpness which is just what I wanted to brace me. I have been out walking and driving all day and have only time before dinner to send this "paar worte"—but I may have still less time to-morrow. Much love to you all.

Your ever affectionate
Marian.

TO BESSIE PARKES, 30 OCTOBER 1852

GE spent a week with Harriet Martineau at Ambleside before going to Rosehill. Lady Grandison is the sister of Sir Charles, the hero of Richardson's novel, and Harriet Byron the heroine. [II, 64–65]

Rosehill, Coventry | October 30, 1852.

Dear Bessie

I kept my resolution in spite of Edinburgh attractions and invitations, so the address on your letter was all right. . . . I have had a delightful month—nothing but petting and admiration, beautiful scenery and agreeable talks. See what it is to go among people who know little of one! The long drives I had in the neighbourhood of Edinburgh were just what I wanted for my health and spirits. The soft outline of the Pentland Hills, the rich hanging woods, the bracing air, and Mrs.

Combe's silvery voice and bright beautiful eyes were the best of medicines. They were the alternative—then came the tonic in the shape of Harriet Martineau with her simple, energetic life, her Building Society, her winter Lectures and her cordial interest in all human things.

Now I am here for a week among affectionate long-tried friends, and I feel brave for anything that is to come after. That is quite enough about myself. You perceive that I am thriving—that being extremely comfortable, I am resigned. I have noticed that my resignation always flourishes best in that kind of soil.

Like Sir Charles Grandison? I should be sorry to be the heathen that did not like that book. I don't like Harriet Byron much, she is too proper and insipid. Lady G. is the gem, with her marmoset.

Tell your noble-looking Barbara—I cannot call her Miss Smith, at least to you—that I only hope she will keep up her desire to make an "indelible impression" on me. It will be no hard task. The material she has to work upon is very impressible and I am sure the mould is first-rate. I don't love you while I am writing to you, but when I have finished my letter I shall be as ever,

Your affectionate Friend
Marian Evans.

Mrs. Bray sends kind remembrances to you.

TO THE BRAYS, [6 NOVEMBER 1852]

Charles Kingsley's Phaethon: Or, Loose Thoughts for Loose Thinkers. Thackeray's Henry Esmond. [II, 65–66]

[142 Strand] Saturday.
Dearest Friends

To get into a first class carriage, fall asleep, and awake to find oneself where one would be, is almost as good as having Prince Hussein's carpet. This was my easy way of getting to London on Thursday. Good Mr. C. at the station waiting for me and delighted to see me. By 5 o'clock I had unpacked all my boxes and made my room tidy, and then I began to feel some satisfaction in being settled down where I am of most use just now. After dinner came Herbert Spencer and spent the evening with me. Yesterday morning Mr. Greg called, on his way to Paris, to express his regret that he did not see me at Ambleside. He is very pleasing, but somehow or other he frightens me dreadfully.

Things seem to be going on tolerably well here. Mr. Chapman listens most amiably to my report of the fault people find with him. He is better than they think. I have read Kingsley's Phaethon this morning, and long to cut it up. Kingsley provokes me more and more. I am going to plunge into Thackeray's novel now, so good-bye.

God bless you all.

TO THE BRAYS, [13 NOVEMBER 1852]

[II, 67–68]

[142 Strand] Saturday.

Dear Friends

O this hideous fog! Let me grumble, for I have had headache the last three days and there seems little prospect of anything else in such an atmosphere. I am ready to vow that I will not live in the Strand again after Christmas. If I were not choked by the fog, the time would trot pleasantly withal, but what use are brains and friends when one lives in a light such as might be got in the chimney? . . .

'Esmond' is the most uncomfortable book you can imagine. You remember, Cara, how you disliked 'François le Champi' (George Sand's). Well, the story of Esmond is just the same. The hero is in love with the daughter all through the book, and marries the mother at the end.

Mr. Chapman's affairs are just like the fog. Instead of a *thousand,* he wants £1200 now! The Lord have mercy on him! . . .

Pollian.

TO THE BRAYS, [22 NOVEMBER 1852]

In his diary William Cullen Bryant mentions "a blue-stocking lady named Ellans and a Mr. Spencer, a bookseller." Joseph Neuberg, a wealthy retired business man from Hamburg, helped Carlyle with *Frederick the Great.* [II, 68–69]

142 Strand | Monday.

Dear Friends

I perceive your reading of the golden rule is "Do as you are done by," and I shall be wiser than to expect a letter from you another Monday morning when I have not earned it by my Saturday's billet. The fact is, both callers and work thicken— the former sadly interfering with the latter. I will just tell you how it was last Saturday and that will give you an idea of my days. My task was to read an article of Greg's in the North British on Taxation, a heap of newspaper articles and all that J. S. Mill says on the same subject. When I had got some way into this *magnum mare,* in comes Mr. Chapman with a thick German volume. "Will you read enough of this to give me your opinion of it?" Then of course I must have a walk after lunch, and when I had sat down again thinking that I had two clear hours before dinner—rap at the door—Mr. Lewes—who of course sits talking till the second bell rings. After dinner another visitor—and so behold me at 11 P.M. still very far at sea on the subject of taxation but too tired to keep my eyes open.

We had Bryant, the poet last evening—a pleasant, quiet, elderly man. To-day the supreme felicity of a call from Dr. Brabant. He is coming to stay next month, partly attracted by the fact that Mr. Neuberg is to spend the winter here. We shall be quite brilliant. . . .

In haste

Your faithful
Marian.

TO GEORGE COMBE, 21 DECEMBER 1852

GE sent Combe proofs of Greg's "Charity, Noxious and Beneficent." [VIII, 68]

142 Strand | December 21. 1852.

My dear Sir

I am glad to tell you that by some further efforts since I last wrote to you, we have succeeded in getting rid of the obnoxious paragraphs on capital punishments and prison discipline in Mr. Greg's article.

My mind is painfully preoccupied this morning by a family trouble. My sister's husband—a medical man, not more than forty years of age—died yesterday. My sister is left with six little children, and I am full of anxiety about a future provision for them. I shall be obliged to leave town on Thursday—an unfortunate moment for the Westminster affairs.

With kindest regards to Mrs. Combe, I am ever, my dear Sir,

Yours very truly
Marian Evans.

Geo. Combe Esq.

TO THE BRAYS, 25 DECEMBER [1852]

Edward Clarke had borrowed £800 from his father-in-law Robert Evans, who wrote in his Journal 5 November 1839: "he give me a Bond for it, and if he does not pay it to me in my Life time it must be stopd out of my Daughters fortune after my Death." GE spent the night at Rosehill and drove to Meriden December 24th. [II, 74–75]

Meriden | Christmas Day.

Dear Friends

Your love and goodness are a comforting presence to me everywhere—whether I am ninety or only nine miles away from you. Chrissey bears her trouble much better than I expected. Money matters are not in the *very* worst state. We hope that an advantageous arrangement may be made about the practice, and there is a considerable sum in debts to be collected. Scarcely anything, however, is to come from the father's property—almost all had been anticipated by loans.

I shall return to town on Wednesday by a train which leaves Hampton at 4.20. It would have been a comfort to see you again before going back, but there are many reasons for not doing so. I am satisfied now that my duties do not lie *here*— though the dear creatures here will be a constant motive for work and economy.

Ever your lovingest
Marian.

TO THE BRAYS, [31 DECEMBER 1852]

Isaac Evans inherited the house at Attleborough, left by her aunt Mrs. Evarard to Chrissey, who sold it to her father in 1842 for £250. [II, 75]

142 Strand | Friday Morning.

Dear Friends

I arrived here only yesterday. I had agreed with Chrissey that, all things considered, it was wiser for me to return to town—that I could do her no substantial good by staying another week, while I should be losing time as to other matters. Isaac, however, was very indignant to find that I had arranged to leave without consulting him and thereupon flew into a violent passion with me, winding up by saying that he desired I would never "apply to him for anything whatever"—which, seeing that I never have done so, was almost as superfluous as if I had said I would never receive a kindness from him. But he is better than he shewed himself to me and I have no doubt that he will be kind to Chrissey, though not in a very large way. The practice is sold for £1200, and we are hoping that with the interest of that and other money Chrissey will have about £100 a year independently of brothers and sisters. I trust I shall be able to add something to it. Chrissey is to live in a house of my brother's which was once her own—rent free, of course. That will be a great help, and the boys will go to a free grammar school. But I am crossing my note by mistake—so you will thank me to come to an end.

Your
Marian.

TO SARA HENNELL, [10 JANUARY 1853]

Sara's review of Thackeray's novel in the *Coventry Herald* praised his women characters. [II, 80–81]

[142 Strand] Monday morning.

My dear Sara

Pray do not lay the sins of the article on the Atomic Theory to poor Lewes's charge. How you could take it for his I cannot conceive. It is as remote from his style both of thinking and writing as anything can be. The real author is Dr. Samuel Brown. . . .

I have read your notice of Esmond—but, you know, I can't change my opinion without getting a fresh impression from the book itself. Pray thank Mr. Bray for the paper.

I am thinking of paying another visit to my sister by and bye, and then I hope I shall manage to see you all. In haste, dear Sara

Your affectionate
Marian.

TO CHARLES BRAY, [17 JANUARY 1853]

[II, 81–82]

[142 Strand] Monday Morning.
Dearest Friend

One word before the work or the pleasure of the day begins. I can't tell you how thankful I am that things are for once better than your fears. Now do be stingy and industrious this next year and throw as much energy into your silk-buying and ribbon-making as you do into your fight with the "parsons."

You are a fine fellow to talk of supporting the Westminster—*for my sake* too. Don't you know that the only thing you can do *for my sake* is to prosper and get comfortable the rest of your days? If you are to be grey and haggard and fretted "what good shall my life do me?" though I had the Westminster and the glory thereof all to myself. The reason I did not answer your last letter *specially* was, that having to write a 'general epistle,' I seemed to have no inspiration for a particular one. But now I am sorry, for I see you think it a neglect. And have you not "such a friend?"—(as I, I suppose you mean). I am sure nobody cares for nobody more than I care for you, and as for having one's dearest friends under the same meridian with one, that would be to have two *summa bona* at once, which is clearly contrary to the law or method of nature.

I shall write to you all in a day or two, so I tell you no news. This is only to assure you that your little notes are very precious to me, whether I answer them or not. I am sorely disappointed when I have none of your handwriting. In short you are the dearest, oldest, stupidest, tiresomest, delightfullest, and never-to-be-forgotten-est of friends to me—and I am ever

Your affectionate
Marian.

TO CHARLES BRAY, [24 JANUARY 1853]

[II, 83]

[142 Strand] Monday Morning.
Dear Friend

At last I have determined to leave this house and get another home for myself. Many reasons, besides my health, concur to make me desire this change. I suppose I must stay here, however, until the April number is out of our hands. You once said that you would help me in such a case, and if you do not repent of that word I shall be most grateful for the kindness. I hope you will arrange to spend a quiet hour with me when you come to town.

You ask why I think Miss Lynn in want of friends. I *know* that she has great difficulty in obtaining any literary employment, and one can easily see how this must seriously affect her comfort in many ways.

Ever yours affectionately
Marian.

TO MRS. PETER TAYLOR, 1 FEBRUARY 1853

Bray came and took GE to Rosehill 3 February. Forster's article in the January *Westminster* urged support for the Northern abolitionists and predicted that Southern defiance would bring on a war. The incisive criticism of Mrs. Gaskell's *Ruth* should be compared with GE's article on "Silly Novels by Lady Novelists" in 1856. Mrs. Taylor was an advocate of women's rights. [II, 85–86]

[142 Strand]

My complaint, of which I am now happily rid, was rheumatism in the right arm—a sufficient reason, you will see, for my employing a scribe to write that promise which I now fulfil. I am going into the country, perhaps for a fortnight, so that if you are kind enough to come here on Wednesday evening, I shall not have the pleasure of seeing you. All the more reason for writing to you, in spite of cold feet and the vilest pens in the world.

Francis Newman is likely to come once or twice in the season—not more. He has, of course, a multitude of engagements, and many more attractive ones than a *soirée* in the Strand. Never mention me to him in the character of Editress. I think—at least I am told—that he has no high esteem of woman's powers and functions. But let that pass. He is a very pure, noble being, and it is good only to look at such.

The article on Slavery, in the last number of the 'Westminster'—which I think the best article of them all—is by W. E. Forster, a Yorkshire manufacturer, who married Dr Arnold's daughter. He is a very earnest, independent thinker, and worth a gross of literary hacks who have the "trick" of writing. I hope you are interested in the Slavery question, and in America generally—that cradle of the future. I used resolutely to turn away from American politics, and declare that the United States was the last region of the world I should care to visit. Even now I almost loathe the *common* American type of character. But I am converted to a profound interest in the history, the laws, the social and religious phases of North America, and long for some knowledge of them. Is it not cheering to think of the youthfulness of this little planet, and the immensely greater youthfulness of our race upon it?—to think that the higher moral tendencies of human nature are yet only in their germ? I feel this more thoroughly when I think of that great Western Continent, with its infant cities, its huge uncleared forests, and its unamalgamated races. . . .

Of course you have read 'Ruth' by this time. Its style was a great refreshment to me, from its finish and fulness. How women have the courage to write and publishers the spirit to buy at a high price the false and feeble representations of life and character that most feminine novels give, is a constant marvel to me. 'Ruth,' with all its merits, will not be an enduring or classical fiction—will it? Mrs Gaskell seems to me to be constantly misled by a love of sharp contrasts—of "dramatic" effects. She is not contented with the subdued colouring—the half tints of real life. Hence she agitates one for the moment, but she does not secure one's lasting sympathy; her scenes and characters do not become typical. But how pretty and graphic are the touches of description! That little attic in the minister's house, for example, which, with its pure white dimity bed-curtains, its bright-green walls, and the rich brown of its stained floor, remind one of a snowdrop springing out of the soil. Then the rich humour of Sally, and the sly satire in the description of Mr Bradshaw. Mrs Gaskell has certainly a charming mind, and one cannot help loving her as one reads her books.

A notable book just come out is [J. J. S.] Wharton's 'Summary of the Laws relating to Women.' "Enfranchisement of women" only makes creeping progress; and that is best, for woman does not yet deserve a much better lot than man gives her. I am writing to you the last thing, and am so tired that I am not quite sure whether I finish my sentences. But your divining power will supply their deficiencies.

TO MRS. CHARLES BRAY, 15 FEBRUARY [1853]

Charlotte Brontë's *Villette* was published 1 February. [II, 87]

[142 Strand] February 15.

Dear Cara

I am glad to have the wool but still more glad to think of the kind heart that remembered my little want and took the trouble to supply it.

I am only just returned to a sense of the real world about me for I have been reading Villette, a still more wonderful book than Jane Eyre. There is something almost preternatural in its power.

I have never been out of doors since I entered them on Saturday—they say I must go, so I can only scribble these two or three words else I shall not get my walk before dusk.

Love to all.

TO GEORGE COMBE, 18 FEBRUARY 1853

August Theodor Stamm's *Die Religion der That* opens with the announcement: "People of the World, here is the book for which you have stretched out your arms with longing." William Hale White reported that at dinner Stamm defended his denial of immortality by saying: "I do tink it is a glorious ting to die and have a bad small." GE's copy of Combe's *An Inquiry into Natural Religion,* privately printed, has a number of marginal comments in her hand, questioning Combe's circular arguments. [VIII, 71–73]

142 Strand February 18. 1853.

My dear Sir

Your letter of the 27th came to me when I was confined to my bed by a rheumatic attack. Since then I have been into the country to see my sister, and have taken large doses of romping and doll dressing—the very best alteratives for me. I am come back quite well and hardy enough to enjoy the frost and snow. I fear, however, that they do not agree so well with your lungs and Mrs. Combe's as with mine.

Dr. Stamm has been domesticated at Mr. Chapman's for some time. He has the most amiable social qualities, beautiful simplicity and purity of character and considerable attainments; but he is not, I think, destined to have much influence over other men. He would by no means concur in this negative clause; on the contrary he thinks himself a prophet. I ventured to tell him that a translation of a work beginning *"Völker der Erde, hier ist das Buch, nach dem ihr mit Verlangen eure Arme ausstrecht,"* would be simply "nuts" to our reviewers, but he was evidently incredulous. You will perceive that he has no slight endowment of self-esteem, and this is unchecked by a fine sense of the ludicrous, without which even pure moral enthusiasm is apt to verge on the ridiculous in its manifestations. Still, Dr. Stamm is a charming being, and wins everyone's good will. Perhaps his droll English has something to do with this, and his handsome face still more. His resources are very narrow, and he is determined not to return to Germany until its political condition is more hopeful. Hence he is anxious to obtain some literary occupation in England or America and is working hard to get the mastery of our language. . . .

I am deeply interested in the prospect of seeing your work on Natural Religion. You promised that I should be one of the few who are to see it before its ultimate publication—a proof of regard which was very pleasant to me. . . . Yes, indeed— I *should* like to renew our conversations by the fire-side at Edinburgh, but I must not so indulge myself this spring. I shall see you and Mrs. Combe in London, though, shall I not? And that will be a compensatory pleasure. Pray tell Mrs. Combe that I hope she is reading "Villette," and will tell me what she thinks of it. I mean to be really industrious now—to write and get money—*not* for myself. Do encourage me if you can.

With kindest regards to Mrs. Combe, Ever, my dear Sir,

Yours truly
Marian Evans

TO THE BRAYS, [26 FEBRUARY 1853]

The report by GHL in the *Leader* of an American copyright law proved premature. This was GE's first meeting with Thomas Henry Huxley. Back from four years on H.M.S. *Rattlesnake,* he wrote an account of the voyage in "Science at Sea" for the *Westminster Review* (January 1854) and for some time reviewed the science books. [II, 89–90]

[142 Strand] Saturday.
Dear Friends

Do you observe that we are on the eve of having an American Copyright? In which case the fortune of the Westminster is made, always supposing that periodicals are not excepted—which would be a most unbecoming piece of envy in the Gods.

I suppose you got my last Saturday's note, which, it appears, was too late for the post. We had an agreeable evening on Wednesday—a Mr. Huxley being the centre of interest. Since then I have been headachy and in a perpetual rage over an article that gives me no end of trouble and will not be satisfactory after all. I should like to stick red hot skewers through the writer whose style is as sprawling as his handwriting. I send Sara another Mazzini autograph to replace the one I took from her.

Dear Chrissey writes me letters that agitate me. People have offered to send her little ones to the Infant Orphan Asylum—and the idea of the thing rends her heart. I think she ought to be provided for without any such measures. For the rest, I am in excellent spirits, though not in the best health or temper. Mrs. Chapman knows that I am going to leave, and I think I shall manage it in the beginning of April. I am in for loads of work next quarter, but I shall not tell you what I am going to do. Good-bye, dear souls. Write me some little scraps to-morrow.

Ever your
Pollian. . . .

TO THE BRAYS, 5 MARCH 1853

GHL wrote to Mrs. Gaskell about Charlotte Brontë; "I was invited to meet her at your house. You remember she asked you not to point me out to her, but allow her to discover me if she could. She *did* recognize me almost as soon as I came into the room. You tried me in the same way; I was less sagacious. However, I sat by her side a great part of the evening, and was greatly interested in her conversation." Charlotte Brontë told Ellen Nussey that GHL's face "is so wonderfully like Emily, her eyes, her features, the very nose, the somewhat prominent mouth, the forehead, even at moments, the expression." Col. Thomas Perronet Thompson, a former owner and editor of the *Westminster*, published over 100 articles in it. [II, 90–91]

[142 Strand] March 5. 1853.

Dear Friends . . .

I have been to Blandford Sq. (Leigh Smiths) to an evening party this week. These soirées are a terrible *corvée* even without gas-lights—especially when one gets introduced to a man who squints and one is haunted by the squint for an hour after getting home as one sometimes sees one's own eyes in the glass in an incipient bilious attack. Dined at Mr. Parkes's on Sunday, and am invited to go there again tonight to meet said Smiths, but I think I shall not go, the weather being wet and I ailing. . . .

I want to know what *you* think of Villette. Lewes was describing Currer Bell to me yesterday as a little, plain, provincial, sickly-looking old maid. Yet what passion, what fire in her! Quite as much as in George Sand, only the clothing is less voluptuous.

Pray what does Sara mean by saying that my having plenty to do must be a great treat to me? I will trouble her to be more respectful to my serene editorship. The Review is to be stunning this time—very superior to the last both in variety and general interest. I am going to write to Col. Thompson, who has asked leave to insert an article at the eleventh hour.

I am very jolly—and ever your affectionate

Marian.

TO THE BRAYS, [12 MARCH 1853]

GE had read *Uncle Tom's Cabin* in September 1852. The message in the riddle would go by whichever ran faster. [II, 92]

[142 Strand] Saturday.

Dear Creatures

It is nearly post time and I have only just remembered that it is my day for writing to you. I come from reading a letter of John Sibree's—to *me*, not to my editorship, a very pleasing letter, telling of his doings, his aspirations, and his little daughters.

Many things have happened this week but I can't think of them in a trice. Mr. Chapman went with Mr. Neuberg to Carlyle's the other night. Carlyle said he had had a letter from Dr. Stamm announcing an intended call—a letter which made him expect nothing less than *Elijah the Tishbite*. . . . Mrs. Follen shewed me a delightful letter which she has had from Mrs. Stowe telling all about herself. She begins by saying—"I am a little bit of a woman, rather more than forty, as withered and dry as a pinch of snuff—never very well worth looking at in my best days, and now a decidedly used up article." At 25 she married a man "rich in Hebrew, Greek and Latin, but alas! rich in nothing else." The proceeds of her first writings she devoted to buying her first feather bed! The whole letter is most fascinating and makes one love her.

Villette—Villette—have you read it?

Our next number is to be "grand, fundamental, and imposing." Mr. Bray deserves to be immortalized for inventing that phrase. . . . I must write three lines to Chrissey so there is no help for this stupid letter.

Ever your
Marian.

If you wanted to send a message would you send it by your eyes or by your nose? A dreadfully vulgar riddle.

TO CHARLES BRAY, [18 MARCH 1853]

Sophia Tilley was the sister of Chapman's mistress Elisabeth. GE was disappointed in GHL's badly constructed article on *Ruth* and *Villette*, in which the latter receives more cursory treatment. GHL, aware that his wife was pregnant with her third child by Thornton Hunt, quoted long passages from *Ruth* in which the heroine told her son that he was illegitimate. [II, 93]

[142 Strand] Friday.

Dear Friend

A younger sister of Miss Tilley's—a poor girl quite dependent on her own labour as a milliner—is going to Australia, where two of her brothers are already settled. She is recommended to take out a few goods, as of course any form of property is better than money at Sydney, and Mrs. Chapman has suggested that you would perhaps not object to sell her a few half pieces of ribbon. . . .

I have been ready to tear my hair with disappointment about the next number of the W. R. We are actually obliged to pay for one paper and put it in the fire. The English Contemporary Literature is worse than ever and the article on Ruth and Villette is unsatisfactory. Then one of the articles is half as long again as it ought to be. In short I am a miserable Editor.

Instead of changing my street, I have changed my room only, and am now installed in Mr. Chapman's. It is very light and pleasant, and I suppose I must be content for a few months longer. Indeed I think I shall never have the energy to move—it seems to be of so little consequence where I am or what I do. In a hurry

Ever your affectionate
Pollian.

TO SARA HENNELL, [28 MARCH 1853]

March 1853 was one of the coldest on record. It snowed every day from the 15th to the 27th. [II, 94]

[142 Strand] Monday Morning.

Dear Sara

On Saturday I was correcting proofs literally from morning till night—yesterday ditto—so I have been unable to earn my week's pennyworth. The Review will be better than I once feared, but not so good as I once hoped.

I send the enclosed autographs in the hope that one or two of them may be worth putting in your collection. I suppose the weather has chilled your charity as well as mine. I am very hard and Mephistophelian just now, but I lay it all to this second winter. We had a pleasant evening last Wednesday—Lewes, as always, genial and amusing. He has quite won my liking, in spite of myself. . . .

Love to the other dear creatures.

Ever your faithful and loving
Marian.

Of course Mr. Bray highly approves the recommendations of the Commissioners on *Divorce*.

TO MRS. CHARLES BRAY, [16 APRIL 1853]

Helen Faucit, the actress, married Theodore Martin in 1851. Charles Bray in his *Autobiography* describes "a fine old acacia, the sloping turf about whose roots made a delightful seat in summer time. We spread there a large bear-skin, and many friends have enjoyed a seat there . . . with the flow of talk unrestrained." [II, 97–98]

[142 Strand] Saturday Morning.

Dear Cara

My chief trouble is poor Chrissey. Think of her in that ugly small house with six children who are inevitably made naughty by being thrown close together from morning till night. To live with her in that hideous neighbourhood amongst ignorant bigots is impossible to me. It would be moral asphyxia and I had better take the other kind—charcoal myself and leave my money, perhaps more accept-able than my labour and affection. Then I dare not incur the *material* responsibil-ity of taking her away from Isaac's house and its attendant pecuniary advantages. My health might fail and other things might happen to make her, as well as me, regret the change. Yet how odious it seems that I, who preach self-devotion, should make myself comfortable here while there is a whole family to whom, by renunciation of my egotism I could give almost everything they want. And the work I can do in other directions is so trivial! . . .

We had an agreeable soirée last Wednesday. I fell in love with Helen Faucit. She is the most poetic woman I have seen for a long while. Her conversation is not remarkable in any way but there is the ineffable charm of a fine character which makes itself felt in her face, voice and manner.

I am taking doses of agreeable follies, as you recommend, dear Cara. Last night I went to the French Theatre and tonight I am going to the opera to hear William Tell. People are very good to me. Mr. Lewes especially is kind and attentive and has quite won my regard after having a good deal of my vituperation. Like a few other people in the world, he is much better than he seems—a man of heart and conscience wearing a mask of flippancy.

Herbert Spencer means to quit his position as sub-editor of the Economist and trust to writing. This is *entre nous*. I rather tremble for him—with his nature, article-writing for bread will be worse than he has just now persuaded himself to think. Still this editorship is a horrid *gêne* and tethers him to London all the year, with the exception of a few days' holiday now and then. . . .

I am going to write to George Combe to whom I am in debt two letters deep—so, dear Cara, good bye—and do not let my grumbling letters alarm you for me. Chrissey will never consent to go to Australia she says. When the warm days come and the bearskin is under the acacia you must have me again. Love to Sara. Her letter about Hippolytus was read to three gentlemen—so she must not think her writing thrown away.

Ever your faithful
Marian.

TO MRS. BRAY AND SARA HENNELL, [17 JUNE 1853]

Sir James Clark, physician in ordinary to Queen Victoria, was pleased with GE and frequently invited her to dinner. Neil Arnott, like Clark a Scot and physician in ordinary to the Queen, was an old friend of GHL, who named his second son Thornton Arnott Lewes. Oxford Terrace is now Sussex Gardens. GHL was a prolific playwright and knew all the theatres; he took GE behind the scenes in the intervals. In *Villette* the French actress Rachel is recalled in Vashti. Caroline Frances Cornwallis wrote several articles for the *Westminster*. [II, 103–04]

[142 Strand] Friday Morning.

Dear Cara and Sara

Mr. Barclay put an end to my pain in ten minutes by stopping my hollow tooth, and moreover consoled me by telling me that I need feel no anxiety about the state of my teeth in general. So I am radiant with benevolence, as it is so easy to be when one is perfectly comfortable. Not that I am quite *that,* for my cough has been worse again the last few days.

On Wednesday I dined at Sir James Clark's where the Combes are staying and had a very pleasant evening—nice Dr. Arnott and Mr. Barton being the other guests. At 10 o'clock the Clarks went to the Queen's ball and I had the amusement of seeing them in their court dresses. The Combes have taken lodgings in Oxford Terrace where I mean to go, and where I hope Sara will come to stay with me some time. It is better than the Strand—trees waving before the windows, and no noise of omnibuses.

Last Saturday evening I had quite a new pleasure. We went to see Rachel again, and sat on the stage between the scenes. When the drop-scene fell, we walked about and saw the green room and all the dingy, dusty paraphernalia that make up theatrical splendour. I have not yet seen the 'Vashti' of Currer Bell in Rachel, though there was some approach to it in Adrienne Lecouvreur.

We are going to have a party to-night to meet Mrs. Cornwallis—a lady who reads Egyptian hieroglyphs and for aught I know the arrow-headed and cuneiform characters to boot. I shall write again soon—these few lines to thank you both for writing to me.

Your faithful
Pollian.

TO SARA HENNELL, [25 JUNE 1853]

Robert Noel, a nephew of Lady Byron and a brother of Cara Bray's friend Edward Noel, was staying with the Leigh Smiths. Berlioz's *Benvenuto Cellini* was not a success. F. A. Pulsky, the Hungarian revolutionist, and his wife, fled to England with Kossuth in 1849. [II, 105–06]

[142 Strand] Saturday Morning.

Dear Sara . . .

When I was reading your congratulations that my teeth were "settled" I was racked with pain, and the next day I had the tooth which *Mr. Barclay had stopped* taken out by another dentist—a man with 'bowels' who will risk giving chloroform. I was quite unconscious during the extraction and only began to protest that I would not submit to the operation when the tooth was lying on the table before me.

This affair hindered me from dining at Sir J. Clark's again to meet the Combes and the Pulzskys—for which I was more sorry than for the loss of most diningsout. On Wednesday evening Mr. and Mrs. C. and I went to Blanford Sq. to meet Mr. R. Noel, who was more agreeable than I ever saw him before. Tell Mr. Bray that Mr. N. spoke very admiringly of him and inquired about him with much interest. He called on me the next day with Mrs. Jameson *twice* and I was unfortunately not in. Vexing that, for I wanted to see Mrs. J., and this is the third time I have missed doing so. I am going to hear Berlioz' new opera tonight—an 'experience' I have looked forward to with great expectation.

What do you mean by saying that you fear the Whitby trip will drop through? Surely not. Business is not disappointing? I take tea with the Combes tomorrow and am to see the Pulzskys at whom I am a little frightened—*she* being a genius and *he* an encyclopaedia.

Love to the good friends who think it worth having—and even if not—*love*.

Your faithful
Pollian.

TO SARA HENNELL, [18 AUGUST 1853]

GE spent six weeks of her holiday at St. Leonard's. Louisa Nesbitt, the actress, widow of Sir William Boothby, retired there in 1851; her friend was Sir Arthur Brooke, M.P. The *Mr. Goethe* may allude to his English exponent GHL, a possible visitor. [II, 114–15]

Spa Cottage | St. Leonard's

Dear Sara . . .

Yesterday it rained sans intermission, and of course I said *cui bono?* and found my troubles almost more than I could bear—but today the sun shines and there is blue above and blue below—consequently I find life very glorious and myself a particularly fortunate diabolessa.

Lady Boothby (Mrs. Nisbett) is here—is building a house on a hill and shews her fine form and very withered but still suggestive-of-prettiness face (highly rouged) on the parade every day. (There is a bit of news to interest Mr. Bray.) Mr. Brooke, a member of Parliament, is her friend and supplies her with £800 a year whereby she lives at ease. The landlord of my lodgings is a German—comes from Saxe-Weimar, knows well the Duchess of Orleans, and talked to me this morning of *Mr.* Schiller and *Mr.* Goethe. A propos of Goethe, there is a most true, discriminating passage about him in the said article on Shakespeare. *Mr.* Goethe is one of my companions here, and I had felt some days before reading the passage the truth which it expresses. Love to all.

Thy affectionate
Marian.

TO THE BRAYS, [19 SEPTEMBER 1853]

[II, 117–18]

[142 Strand] Monday.

Dear Friends . . .

I have not yet fixed on any lodgings, and I think of advertising, as a certain situation is a sine quâ non. I find it difficult to meet with anything at once tolerable and cheap. My theory is to *live* entirely—that is, pay rent and find food—out of my positive income, and then work for as large a surplus as I can get. Cheap and pleasant lodgings are obtainable enough if one doesn't mind going 4 miles away from the centre, but not so when one must be within a reasonable distance at the West End.

The next number of the Review will be better than usual. Froude writes on the Book of Job! He at first talked of an article on the three great *subjective* Poems— Job, Faust and Hamlet. An admirable subject—but it has shrunk to the Book of Job alone.

Herbert Spencer inquires after you. He made the pen with which I write. So you see he is a useful member of society. Mr. Bray says, with dreadful truth, that my letters are uninteresting. I'm very sorry, but it will be all the kinder of you if you will send me your interesting ones gratuitously. A visitor.

> Your faithful
> Marian.

TO SARA HENNELL, [1 OCTOBER 1853]

Spencer's "Universal Postulate" was the original sketch of his *First Principles*. According to Cross, who had GE's Journal, her work was reading *Leader* proofs for GHL. [II, 118–19]

> 142 Strand | Saturday Evening.

My dear Sara

I meant to write to you today in time for tonight's post, but I have been busied about my lodgings all afternoon. I am not going to Albion St., but to 21 Cambridge St., Hyde Park Square.

You will have seen by the papers that Savill and Edward's printing office was burnt down yesterday morning. The Westminster Review narrowly escaped the fate of the Leader, the Literary Gazette and poor Dr. Vaughan's elaborate article on the Religious Tendencies of the Age, intended for the next number of the British Quarterly.

I hope you will be pleased with our present number. If you don't think the Universal Postulate first-rate, I shall renounce you as a critic. Why don't you write grumbling letters to me when you are out of humour with life, instead of making me ashamed of myself for ever having grumbled to you? I have been a more good-for-nothing correspondent than usual lately—this affair of getting lodgings, added to my other matters, has taken up my time and thoughts. But I don't deserve to be punished for this by your not writing to me for the next six weeks.

I have promised to do some work tonight and tomorrow for a person who is rather more idle than myself, so I have not a moment to spare.

> Ever your loving
> Pollian.

TO CHARLES BRAY, 3 NOVEMBER [1853]

GHL won Harriet Martineau's dislike by two devastating reviews of her *Letters on the Laws of Man's Nature and Development* in the *Leader* and rivalry over translating Comte. GHL's *Comte's Philosophy of the Sciences* was published in September 1853; her abridged translation of *The Positive Philosophy* did not appear until 19 November. [II, 122–23]

21 Cambridge Street | November 3.

Dear Friend

Eh bien! I will welcome the Bookcase. Please to add to your other goodness that of letting me know when it will arrive, as the impenetrability of matter positively forbids my having two Bookcases in my room at once. Poor Mr. Chapman has just left me, looking fagged to death from having, as a bit of extra work yesterday, run along the Strand after a thief who had managed to get into the house and *out* of it with £8 worth of plate!

Hitherto I have been spending £9 per month—at least after that rate—but I have had frequent guests. I am exceedingly comfortable and feel quite at home now. Harriet Martineau has been very kind—called again on Tuesday, and yesterday sent to invite me to go to Lady Compton's, where she is staying, on Saturday evening. This, too, in spite of my having vexed her by introducing Mr. Lewes to her, which I did as a desirable bit of peacemaking.

Pray let me know of any opening in the clouds. Love to Cara and Sara.

Yours affectionately
Marian Evans

TO SARA HENNELL, [18 NOVEMBER 1853]

A second edition of GHL's A *Biographical History of Philosophy* (1845–46) appeared in 1852. [II, 125–26]

21 Cambridge St. | Friday.

Dear Sara . . .

Mr. Lewes was at Cambridge about a fortnight ago, and found that Herbert Spencer was a great deal talked of there, for the article on the Universal Postulate as well as other things. Mr. Lewes himself has a knot of devotees there who make his history of Philosophy a private text-book.

Miss Martineau's Comte is out now. Do you mean to do *it* or Mr. Lewes's? We can get no one to write an article on Comte for the next number of the Westminster—Bain, our last hope, refusing.

I dare say this gossip is not very interesting to you, but a headache this morning inclined me to fill up ten minutes by writing it.

Ever thy loving
Pollian.

TO SARA HENNELL, [25 NOVEMBER 1853]

Sara wrote to GE, who was 35 on November 22nd; GE had forgotten to write on Sara's birthday, 23 November. The Noels were staying with the Leigh Smiths in Blandford Square. The Hensleigh Wedgwoods were interested in the education of women and other liberal causes. It is not certain that Chapman had ever paid GE more than room and board for her editorial work. [II, 127–28]

21 Cambridge Street | Friday Morning.

Dear Sara

Sundry hindrances external and internal have prevented me from fulfilling my desire to write to you. Chiefly an uncomfortable state of body—indeed I am now writing on my knee because I don't feel able to sit up at the desk. But you know that my life is a perpetual *werden.* I have not the less felt all that your letter *said.* Thank you for it dear, and for all the helpful love you have given me for the last ten years. I begin this year more happily than I have done most years of my life. "Notre vraie destinée," says Comte, "se compose de *resignation* et *d'activité"*—and I seem more disposed to both than I have ever been before. Let us hope that we shall both get stronger by the year's activity—calmer by its resignation. I know it may be just the contrary—don't suspect me of being a canting optimist. We *may* both find ourselves at the end of the year going faster to the hell of conscious moral and intellectual weakness. Still there is a possibility—even a probability—the other way.

My ailments and the fog together have prevented me from going to Blandford Square to see Robert Noel and his wife and to Mrs. Wedgwood's where H. Martineau is staying. I have not seen H. M's Comte yet—she is going to give me a copy—but Mr. Lewes tells me it seems to him *admirably well* done. I don't know whether you noticed the article on Mahomedanism and the Greek Church extracted from the Daily News, in the Leader of last week. That was hers, and I think it excellent. James Martineau tells Mr. Chapman that he shall never write another book on theology! Don't you think that a good sign?

I told Mr. Chapman yesterday that I wished to give up any connection with the editorship of the Westminster. He wishes me to continue the present state of things until April, but admits that he is so straitened for money and for *assistance* in the mechanical part of his business that he feels unable to afford an expense on the less tangible services which I render. I shall be much more satisfied on many accounts to have done with that affair—but I shall find the question of supplies rather a difficult one this year, as I am not likely to get any money either for Feuerbach, which, after all, Mr. Chapman I think will be afraid of publishing in his Series, or for "The Idea of a Future Life," for which I am to have "half profits" = %!

Herbert Spencer writes me word that he has had an attack of palpitation of the heart—but is quite recovered. I am going to quote to him a passage I found in Sainte-Beuve which just fits him. "Quand j'ai dit qu'il n'avait jamais eu de passion et d'excès, je me suis trop avancé; il a eu un excès de *raison."*

Give my love to Cara and thank her for her kind letter. I shall write to her soon.

Love to Mr. Bray too. Tell him to send me word of any new phase in matters of business, and any leader as brilliant as the last I saw.

Ever your loving
Pollian.

I hope you will appreciate this *bon-mot* as thoroughly as I did—"C'est un homme admirable—il *se tait* en sept langues!"

TO JOHN CHAPMAN, [2 DECEMBER 1853]

[II, 130–31]

21 Cambridge Street | Friday Morning.

Dear Friend,

Have the goodness to confine the perusal of this letter to yourself, and not to leave it about for the amusement of your amateurs of *lettres inédites.* There is one subject which I omitted to mention to you yesterday, but which will perhaps be better committed to paper, as it will then be understood to be a matter of business. Friendship is not to be depended on, but business has rather more guarantees.

You seem to be oblivious just now of the fact that you have pledged yourself as well as me to the publication of another work besides Feuerbach in your Series. For the completion of the historical part of that work, *books* are indispensable to me. If I could do as I pleased I would much rather become myself a subscriber to the London Library and save both myself and you the trouble of speaking to you on the subject. But as this said work will occupy nearly the whole of next year and as I am to have no money for it—since the "half profits" are not likely to have any other than a conceptional existence, a "gedachtsein"—I don't see how I can possibly go to any expense in the matter.

I bitterly regret that I allowed myself to be associated with your Series, but since I have done so, I am very anxious to fulfil my engagements both to you and the public. It is in this sense that I wish you to publish Feuerbach, and I beg you to understand that I would much rather that you should publish the work and *not* pay me than pay me and not publish it. I don't think you are sufficiently alive to the ignominy of advertising things, especially as part of a subscription series, which never appear. The two requests then which I have to make are first, that you will let me know whether you can, *as a matter of business,* undertake to supply me with the necessary books, and secondly, that you will consider the question of Feuerbach as one which concerns our *honour* first and our pockets after.

I have been making a desk of my knee so I fear some of my words may be illegible, which will be a pity because of course you can't substitute any half as good.

Yours faithfully,
Marian Evans.

TO CHARLES BRAY, [9 DECEMBER 1853]

Slingsby Lawrence was a nom de plume GHL used for his plays. GE may have disliked this play by J. Stirling Coyne the more because it deals with a man who has a bastard palmed off on him as his son. Thornton Hunt's third child by Agnes Lewes was born in October and another child by his own wife in November 1853. [II, 131–32]

21 Cambridge Street | Friday Morning.

Dear Friend

If you went to the Haymarket on Wednesday I hope you didn't carry away the impression that that stupid play—the "Hope of the Family"—was by Slingsby Lawrence. I confess, the theatre is generally a very dreary amusement to me. The wit is generally threadbare as well as vulgar—the actors and actresses are neither men and women nor gentlemen and ladies. I mentally resolved last night that it should be a long while before I wasted another evening there. . . .

Ever yours affectionately,
Marian Evans.

TO JOHN CHAPMAN, [15 DECEMBER 1853]

In his Science section of the *Westminster Review* for January, Huxley, after a paragraph praising Harriet Martineau's *Comte*, devoted more than two pages to attacking the scientific errors of GHL's *Comte's Philosophy of the Sciences*, calling him "a mere book scientist." [II, 132]

PRIVATE   [21 Cambridge Street]
Dear Friend

May I beg that you will not send Mr. Huxley's M.S. to the printer until you have seen me again? I have found out that he is in the wrong in his remark on the embryological doctrine at p. 33 of Mr. Lewes's book, and also that the ridicule he throws on the remark about the gallionella ferruginea is not well founded. At all events I think you will wish for the sake of the Review as well as from your own sense of justice that such a *purely* contemptuous notice should not be admitted unless it be well warranted. The case is the more delicate as the criticism of Mr. Lewes comes after the unmitigated praise of Miss Martineau. I hope to see you tomorrow afternoon.

How came you to mention to Miss M. that you saw the proof of Mr. Lewes's book *"in Miss Evans's room"*? I think you must admit that your mention of my name was quite gratuitous.

So far you were naughty—but never mind.

Yours faithfully
Marian Evans.

TO JOHN CHAPMAN, [19 DECEMBER 1853]

The review was published unchanged. In a long letter in the *Leader* GHL replied that he had occupied himself with biology for eighteen years (he was a medical student briefly in 1835). Admitting that he had written sulphuric for sulphurous acid, he showed that the authorities Huxley relied on had been superseded within the last two years by French scientists unknown to him. [II, 133]

PRIVATE   21 Cambridge Street | Monday Morning.

Dear Friend

I am not well enough to go out, so that the deferring of our expedition suits me. I will take my chance of finding you disengaged if I am able to get to you tomorrow, which is very uncertain. I cannot write anything to be added to the present notice of Mr. Lewes's book, which (the notice) seems to me likely to be a regular "mess." The only wise thing to be done in the case, so far as I can see, would be to leave it out altogether. You are not bound by any obligation that I know of, to review the book, since you go on a principle of selection not of universal registry, and certainly Mr. Huxley's notice, mitigated or unmitigated, will be of no earthly advantage either to the Westminster Review or to its readers.

So far as your duty is concerned in the matter I think reasons of delicacy would at once present themselves to the reader for your merely mentioning Mr. Lewes's book as a manual containing a brief sketch of Comte's system interspersed with commentary and criticism. Do you really think that if you had been the publisher of Mr. Lewes's book and Bohn the publisher of Miss Martineau's, Mr. Huxley would have written just so? "Tell that to the Marines."

Yours faithfully
Marian Evans.

TO BESSIE PARKES, 25 DECEMBER [1853]

In her Journal GE wrote: "Spent Christmas Day alone at Cambridge Street." Cross prints the entry as part of a letter to Mrs. Bray. He destroyed all entries in the Journal between 1849 and July 1854. [II, 134]

21 Cambridge Street, Christmasday

Dear Friend

I dare say you will be surrounded with friends tomorrow, and it is hopeless that you will be able to come to me. But I shall be alone in the evening and should be delighted to see you if you are able and kindly willing to bestow an hour or two on me, at 6 or after. I am going to see my sister next week, and I fear to-morrow evening will be the only one I shall have at liberty before I go.

Ever your loving
Marian.

TO SARA HENNELL, [17 JANUARY 1854]

Edward FitzBall was a dramatist and miscellaneous writer. The story was probably told to GE by GHL. [II, 138–39]

[21 Cambridge Street]

My dear Sara

It has struck me while writing this morning that you may sometimes mistake Feuerbach's habitual amplification, *which I think it necessary to preserve,* for a "whichever-you-please-my-little dear" of my own, and so *play the devil* by crossing out what should be kept in. By the bye, let all your crossings be in *pencil* and then there will be no danger. This word to the wise will suffice. You will now be awake to the distinction. Pray get rid of as many dashes as possible. What I put in are always Feuerbach's.

Here is a story for you. Carlyle, meeting FitzBall said, "How is it I never see your name as a dramatic author now?" "Oh" (very much through the nose) "I'm comfortable now; *my mother's dead."* That musn't be put in the paper or told to any one. But it will make you all laugh for three minutes—not a trifling boon in this world.

Your faithful
Pollian.

TO SARA HENNELL, 18 JANUARY [1854]

Sara agreed to read GE's translation of Feuerbach as she had that of Strauss. [II, 137]

21 Cambridge Street | January 18.

Thank you, dear Sara, for your note. It made me sit down more cheerily to my work this morning. I felt some reluctance to ask [you] to read Feuerbach because I feared he might repel you, but *now,* I may tell you, that I shall feel it a real comfort to have your *prospective* sympathy while I am writing, so be assured you will have the whole cargo of MS. It will be a great one before you get to the end. There are 100 mortal pages of appendix, of closer print than the rest! Your impression of the book exactly corresponds to its effect in Germany. It is considered *the* book of the age there, but Germany and England are *two* countries. People here are as slow to be set on fire as a *stomach.* Then there are the reviewers, who set up a mound of stupidity and unconscientiousness between every really new book and the public. Still I think the really wise and only dignified course for Mr. Chapman would be to publish it in his *Series* as he has announced it.

Thine ever
Pollian.

TO BESSIE PARKES, [21 JANUARY 1854]
[II, 138]

21 Cambridge Street | Saturday Morning.

Dear Friend

I *meant* to call on you the first day I could manage it.

As I seldom do anything *en règle* perhaps it will seem only consistent in me if I ask permission to answer Mrs. Parkes's invitation through you. I want you to make her understand, as gracefully as you can, that I am really obliged and pleased by her kind attention in inviting me and that under other circumstances I should have liked immensely to be of the party on Tuesday. But the fact is, I have no ball-dress, nor anything that would pass muster as one, and I can't afford just now to buy one. It would be a crucifixion of my own taste as well as other people's to appear like a withered cabbage in a flower garden. At a dinner-party, when people think only of conversation, one doesn't mind being a dowdy, but it is the essence of a dance that every one should look fresh and elegant—at least as to their garments. I did not like to send a note to Mrs. Parkes simply declining, and I could only give my explanation to you. But if you think I had better write to Mrs. Parkes according to form, send me three words to say so.

Ever, dear Friend,

Yours faithfully
Marian Evans.

TO SARA HENNELL, 9 MARCH 1854

Spencer did not forget; in his *Principles of Psychology* he credited this version to "a distinguished lady—the translator of Strauss and Feuerbach." [II, 144–46]

21 Cambridge Street | March 9. 1854.

Dear Sara

Pray keep the M.S. another week. By the week after next I shall have a large parcel for you which I hope Mr. Bray will not object to carry. . . .

I am exceedingly well now and enjoying existence as an imperfectly developed stunted creature may. I like my independent life in lodgings better and better, and want nothing but a little more money. Miss Barbara Smith has lent me some of her pictures, of which I am very fond, to ornament my room with and suggest some prettier ideas than I can extract out of dingy walls and curtains. I am often longing for a little more of "le superflu, chose si necessaire"—much oftener than I remember that half the things I have are "le superflu" for the majority of mankind.

I must tell you a characteristic trait of Herbert Spencer. I happened to say in reference to a criticism I had given of a passage in his article on the Universal Postulate, which passage he expunged in consequence, that the better form for the axiom which is the basis of the syllogism as explained by Mill would be—"Things which have the same fixed relation to the same thing have the same fixed relation to each other." Mill gives "Things which *co-exist* with the same thing" etc. The next day he came to tell me in intense delight how important the suggestion was to him in his work on Psychology—how it had given him just the bridge he wanted etc.—and that he should put a *long note* in his book explaining how he came by the idea. Is he not a dear bit of conscientiousness and scrupulosity? . . .

I have no time to say any more. I fear you can't read even this.

Pollian.

TO MRS. CHARLES BRAY, [18 APRIL 1854]

GHL's symptoms of severe headaches and a "terrible singing in the ears," persisted for several years. Arthur Helps (Eton, Trinity College, Cambridge), of Vernon Hill, near Bishop's Waltham, was one of GHL's closest friends. [II, 150–51]

21 Cambridge St. | Saturday.

Dear Cara

I was delighted to have a letter from you, but I am not able to answer it as it deserves, for I am rather overdone with the week's work and the prospect of what is to come next. Poor Lewes is ill and is ordered not to put pen to paper for a month, so I have something to do for him in addition to my own work which is rather pressing. He is gone to Arthur Helps in Hampshire for ten days, and I really hope this total cessation from work in obedience to a peremptory order will end in making him better than he has been for the last year. . . . No opera and no fun for me for the next month! Happily I shall have no time to regret it. Plenty of bright sun on your anemone bed. How lovely your place must look with its fresh leaves!

Love to all from your ever affectionate

Pollian.

TO SARA HENNELL, [29 APRIL 1854]

Eleven lines equating Christ with modern man were omitted at the end of § 7 of the Appendix. [II, 153]

21 Cambridge St. | Saturday.

Dear Sara

I have yet another service to beg of you—a very great one. It is to read as quickly as you can the portion of the appendix which I send you by today's post, and to tell me how far it will be necessary to modify it for the English public. I have written it very rapidly and have translated it quite literally so you have the *raw* Feuerbach—not any of my cooking. I am so far removed from the popular feeling on the subject of which it treats that I cannot trust my own judgment. With the ideas of Feuerbach I everywhere agree, but of course I should, of myself, alter the phraseology considerably. Before I do this however, I want you to tell me what I *must* leave out. Mind, I want to keep in as much as possible. Send it me back as soon as possible, and don't think of the *style* but only of the matter and the crudity of expressions. In great haste,

Your ever grateful
Pollian.

TO MRS. CHARLES BRAY, [19 MAY 1854]

GE quotes Keble's *The Christian Year,* which reads *range* for *roam.* [II, 155–57]

21 Cambridge Street | Friday.

Dear Cara

My various aches determined themselves into an attack of rheumatism which sent me to bed yesterday; but I am better this morning and, as you see, able to sit up and write. My troubles are purely psychical—self-dissatisfaction and despair of achieving anything worth the doing. I can truly say, they vanish into nothing before any fear for the happiness of those I love. Thank you for letting me know how things are, for indeed I could not bear to be shut out from your anxieties. Mr. Bray is the best judge of what is right to be done and there is nothing for this as for all other difficulties but to be brave and patient. When I spoke of myself as an island, I did not mean that I was so exceptionally. We are all islands—
"Each in his hidden sphere of joy or woe,
    Our hermit spirits dwell and roam apart"—
and this seclusion is sometimes the most intensely felt at the very moment your friend is caressing you or consoling you. But this gradually becomes a source of satisfaction instead of repining. When we are young we think our troubles a mighty business—that the world is spread out expressly as a stage for the particular drama of our lives and that we have a right to rant and foam at the mouth if we are crossed. I have done enough of that in my time. But we begin at last to understand that these things are important only to one's own consciousness, which is but as a globule of dew on a rose-leaf that at mid-day there will be no trace of. This is no high-flown sentimentality, but a simple reflection which I find useful to me every day. . . .

Herbert Spencer is not quite recovered from his palpitations, but is better. He inquired after you all when he wrote. I expect to see Mr. Lewes back again today. His poor head—his only fortune—is not well yet, and he has had the misery of being ennuyé with idleness without perceiving the compensating improvement. Still I hope the good he has been getting has been greater than he has been conscious of.

Tell Sara I expect Feuerbach will be all in print by the end of next week and there are no skippings except such as have been made on very urgent grounds. . . .

I don't think you will have read to the end, for the scribble is unreadable. But read and believe that I am ever

Your affectionate
Marian.

TO SARA HENNELL, [3 JUNE 1854]

The Chapmans moved to 45 Blandford Square and the publishing business to 8 King William Street. John Balbirnie's most recent book was *The Water Cure in Consumption and Scrofula*. [II, 159–60]

21 Cambridge Street | Saturday Morning.
Dear Sara

Thanks in the first place for the better news about business. It is a ray of sunshine to me this morning which finds me on the whole in a cloudy state. The printers have been so dilatory with Feuerbach, that I am only just going to correct what I think will be the last sheet but one. . . .

How came you to imagine that I did the Belles Lettres in the Westminster? Mrs. Sinnett did them as usual—and she begs Mr. Chapman not to take this work from her at present, as the loss of it would make a serious deficit in her income. . . . I went to the Strand last night and found Mr. and Mrs. Chapman already in the bustle of their double removal. A well-to-do brother of Miss Tilley's is come from Australia and will do something for her, I hope.

Mr. Lewes is still suffering from his head and is ordered to go into the country again. He sets off on a visit to Oxford this morning and from there he will go to Malvern to see Mr. Bray's acquaintance, Dr. Balbirnie, of whom I have not a pleasant recollection.

Brain and legs and fingers all move heavily with me. I do nothing well but idling, and the consciousness of this is like a garment of lead about me. If I could only fancy myself clever, it would be better, but to be a failure of Nature and to know it is not a comfortable lot. It is the last lesson one learns, to be contented with one's inferiority—but it must be learned. In haste ever

Your
Pollian.

TO MRS. CHARLES BRAY, [28 JUNE 1854]

GE stayed at Rosehill 17–26 June. *Sunshine through the Clouds* was adapted by GHL from *La Joie fait peur*. Mme Vestris was manager of the Lyceum. [II, 162]

21 Cambridge St. | Wednesday.
Dear Cara

As long as you can't afford the express, always come to London by the 12.30 train. It eventuates a spanker. I reached the Euston Square Station as dusty as an old ledger but with no other "incommodity" and a civil porter attended to me without delay. Yesterday Mr. Combe called. He and Mrs. C. set out on their journey on Sunday. Mr. Chapman is looking brighter, having got another letter of the alphabet, as Mr. Combe says, a G. or H. to satisfy the claims of E. and F.

I went to the Lyceum last night to see "Sunshine through the Clouds"—a wonderfully original and beautiful piece by Madame de Girardin, which makes one cry rather too much for pleasure. Vestris acts finely the bereaved mother passing through all the gradations of doubt and hope to the actual recovery of her lost son.

My idea of you is rather bright just now and really helps to make me enjoy all that is enjoyable. That is part of the benefit I have had from my pleasant visit, which was made up of sunshine, green fields, pleasant looks and good eatables— an excellent compound. Best love to all from

Your ever affectionate
Marian.

Will you be so kind as to send my books by railway, *without* the Shelley?

TO SARA HENNELL, [10 JULY 1854]

The translation of Feuerbach's *The Essence of Christianity* is the only one of GE's books to bear her name "Marian Evans" on the title page. Sara's review in the *Coventry Herald* praised GE's unrivalled "power of dealing with the tough metaphysical German." Labassecour is Charlotte Brontë's name for Belgium in *Villette*. The Crystal Palace, moved to Sydenham, was opened by the Queen 10 June. "Vivian" was GHL's nom de plume in the *Leader*. [II, 164–65]

21 Cambridge St. | Monday.

Dear Sara

It seems very ungracious to say so, but it is the fact, that I am vexed Feuerbach has been noticed in the Herald, and especially that anything has been said about me. . . .

I am going to pack up the Hebrew Grammar, the Apocryphal Gospels, and your pretty Titian, to be sent to you. Shall I despatch them by Rail or deposit them with Mr. Chapman to be asked for by Mr. Bray when he comes to town? I shall soon send you a good bye, for I am preparing to go to "Labassecour."

This morning I feel very much as I (suppose) I should if I had been standing on my head for an hour, having paid for a visit to the Crystal Palace and the luxury of French Chocolate by a headache yesterday. What a creation it is! (The C.P. not the headache). Shakespeare, our Navy and the Crystal Palace are the three most *eigenthümliche* things we have produced.

Herbert Spencer's article on the Genesis of Science is a grand one. You must read it. He will stand in the Biographical Dictionaries of 1954 as "Spencer, Herbert, an original and profound philosophical writer, especially known by his great work x x x which gave a new impulse to psychology and has mainly contributed to the present advanced position of that science, compared with that which it had attained in the middle of the last century. The life of this philosopher, like that of the great Kant, offers little material for the narrator. Born in the year 1820 etc."

Vivian's head is not likely to be up to the pitch of Feuerbach, so it will fall to the lot of some other non-leading attaché of the Leader. I have not had a copy yet!

Ever your affectionate
Pollian.

TO THE BRAYS AND SARA HENNELL, [19 JULY 1854]

GE and GHL left London together on the *Ravensbourne* for Antwerp, 20 July. She had discussed her plan with Bray (but not Cara or Sara) and borrowed £100 from him in advance of her patrimony, paying him 5 percent interest. [II, 166]

21 Cambridge Street | Wednesday Evening.

Dear Friends—all three

I have only time to say good bye and God bless you. Poste Restante, Weimar for the next six weeks, and afterwards Berlin.

Ever your loving and grateful

Marian.

5

THE STRONG-MINDED WOMAN
Germany · Spinoza's *Ethics*

GE had told no one of her plan except Bray and Chapman, who forwarded her mail. GHL joined her at the ship. They went from Antwerp to Weimar, where for three months he worked on his life of Goethe. GE helped him by translating the passages of Goethe that he incorporated in the book. They lived very frugally. All GHL's earnings from articles sent to the *Leader* were paid to Agnes in London, so GE was grateful for an offer from Chapman to write for the *Westminster*. In Berlin, where they went in November, she began to translate Spinoza's *Ethics*, which GHL had agreed to do for Bohn's Library. Here he had many old friends from his student days, all of whom accepted his relation with GE without comment.

But in England the gossip mongers were buzzing furiously about the "strong-minded woman" who had lured GHL "to run away from his wife and children." Without inculpating Agnes there was no way to refute the malicious attacks openly. On their return GE stayed alone at Dover while GHL went up to London to sell his *Goethe* and borrow £300 to pay Agnes's bills, which Thornton Hunt blithely ignored. Until GE received definite word that Agnes would never again live with GHL, she would not go to London. When word came, she joined him there. For 24 years they lived happily together as man and wife. They had to remind the few friends who dared call on them not to ask for "Miss Evans." Chapman engaged her to do book reviews for the *Westminster*. For nearly four years they lived at 8 Park Shot, Richmond. The enforced isolation from society gave her time to read Sophocles and the other dramatists in Greek.

GHL's study of Goethe had turned his interest toward natural history. In May 1856, after GE had finished the Spinoza translation, they went to Ilfracombe on the Devonshire coast to zoologize. GHL's researches gave him material for a series of articles in *Blackwood's Magazine*, later reprinted as *Sea-side Studies*. At the end of June they went to Tenby for six weeks to continue the work. GHL had long urged GE to try to write a story. Lying in bed one morning, she imagined herself writing "The Sad Fortunes of the Reverend Amos Barton," and with GHL's encouragement she began her career as a novelist.

TO JOHN CHAPMAN, 6 AUGUST 1854

His letter was the first that GE received in Germany. Chapman was threatened with bankruptcy. Her article "Women in France: Madame de Sablé" in the *Westminster Review* for October 1854 discusses all three of the books mentioned. Kingsley's *Westward Ho!* formed part of the Belles Lettres section in July 1855, but the separate article on his works was never written. [VIII, 115–17]

62a Kaufgasse, Weimar | August 6. 1854.

Dear Friend

Your letter made me glad and sorry. It is the immemorial fashion of lady letter-writers to be glad and sorry in the same sentence, and after all, this feminine style is the truest representation of life. I was delighted to see your writing on the back of the letter which the Post-Beamter, like a conscientious man, refused to give me because I had not my passport in my pocket, and when at last I did get it, I opened it with all sorts of grateful, affectionate feelings toward you for having written to me so soon. But I was deeply saddened by what you tell me about yourself. I have always cherished the hope that you would work your way to independence by gradually paying all debts and anything short of that I can never regard as a relief for you. But I think I am able to enter sympathetically into your whole position, and to estimate both your inward and outward difficulties, so you may rely on always having a fair appreciation from one person in the world, as well as a sisterly interest, which is perhaps less worth having. I shall be very anxious to know how things turn out—but I know you will write to me when you can.

On reading your letter, we determined to get Cousin's book and to unite it with several others as a subject for an article *by me* on "French writers on women." Do you approve of this? If so, I will endeavour to send you the MSS. early in September. I happen to have the material at hand to make such an article piquant and fresh, which are perhaps the qualities likely to be most welcome to you. (Tell me what space you want filled). But you must know that this Weimar—this Athens of the North—is in fact a large village rather than a town, and we are laughing at ourselves for having said of this book and the other, "O we can get it at Weimar," the truth being that the Court-Bookseller (Hof-Buchhandler) has a shop with about as commanding a front as Mr. Tupling's in the Strand. However, . . . I have ordered Victor Cousin's book, Sainte Beuve's "Douze Portraits de Femmes" which I know to be charming, and Michelet's "Femmes de la Revolution." Besides these, we have several books with us which will give me valuable material and suggestions. When we are at Berlin I shall be able to get Kingsley's works, without which an article on them might be like themselves, more imaginative than solid. You know, I have not been an industrious writer, otherwise I might by this time have been adept enough to criticize a man's works not only without having them at hand, but without having seen them.

We have had enjoyment enough compressed into the last fortnight to make a year more than endurable, if it had been sprinkled over that space. Our route has been through Antwerp, Brussels, Namur, Liege, Cologne, up the Rhine to Coblentz and thence to Mainz, to Frankfort, and finally to Weimar, where we arrived on Thursday. We have a charming little lodging here and are enjoying the quiet, which is the more complete that all the *vornehme* people are away at the

Baths or elsewhere taking their summer pleasures. We think it likely that we shall stay here two or three months, but what is most likely is not always what comes to pass. . . .

Any London news will be welcome, but most of all what relates to yourself. Give my kind remembrances to Mrs. Chapman, if she will accept them, and believe me always

Your faithful and affectionate
Marian Evans.

JOURNAL, 10 AUGUST 1854

Franz Liszt, whom GHL knew in Vienna in 1839, had been followed to Weimar by the Princess Caroline Sayn-Wittgenstein, whose husband was about to divorce her. They lived openly together at the Altenburg. Liszt had been Director of the Court Theatre since 1848. GHL called on him 9 August; the next day Liszt returned the call and invited GHL and GE to breakfast. The Comtesse d'Agoult, one of his famous mistresses, by whom he had three children, describes the break of their liaison in her novel *Nélida*. [II, 169–70]

About 1/2 past 10 Liszt called, and after chatting pleasantly for some time invited us to go and breakfast at his house, the Altenburg. Talking of Mde. D'Agoût, he told us that when her novel Nélida appeared, in which Liszt himself is pilloried as a delinquent, he asked her "Mais pourquoi avez vous tellement maltraité ce pauvre *Lehmann?*"

On arriving at the Altenburg we were shewn into the garden, where in a saloon formed by overarching trees, the déjeûner was set out. We found Hoffmann von Fallersleben, the lyric poet, Dr. Schade, a Gelehrter who has distinguished himself by a critical work on the 11,000 virgins (!), and a Herr Cornelius, an agreeable looking artist. Presently came a Herr or Doctor Raff, a musician who has recently published a volume called Wagnerfrage. Soon after we were joined by Liszt and the Princess Marie, an elegant, gentle looking girl of 17, and last, by the Princess Wittgenstein with her nephew Prince Eugène and a young French (or Swiss?) artist, a pupil of Scheffer.

The appearance of the Princess rather startled me at first. I had expected to see a tall distinguished looking woman, if not a beautiful one. But she is short and unbecomingly endowed with embonpoint; at the first glance the face is not pleasing, and the profile especially is harsh and barbarian, but the dark, bright hair and eyes give the idea of vivacity and strength. Her teeth, unhappily, are blackish too. She was tastefully dressed in a morning robe of some semi-transparent white material lined with orange-colour, which formed the bordering, and ornamented the sleeves, a black lace jacket, and a piquant cap set on the summit of her comb, and trimmed with violet colour.

The breakfast was not sumptuous either as to the food or the apppointments. When the cigars came, Hoffmann was requested to read some of his poetry, and he gave us a bacchanalian poem with great spirit. I sat between Liszt and Miss Anderson, the Princess Marie's governess, an amiable but insignificant person. G. sat next the Princess and talked with her about Goethe, whom she pronounced to have been an egotist. My great delight was to watch Liszt and observe the sweetness of his expression. Genius, benevolence and tenderness beam from his whole countenance, and his manners are in perfect harmony with it. A little rain sent us into the house, and when we were seated in an elegant little drawing room, opening into a large music-salon, we had more reading from Hoffmann, and from the French artist who with a tremulous voice pitched in a minor key, read us some rather pretty sentimentalities of his own.

Then came the thing I had longed for—Liszt's playing. I sat near him so that I could see both his hands and face. For the first time in my life I beheld real inspiration—for the first time I heard the true tones of the piano. He played one of his own compositions—one of a series of religious *fantaisies*. There was nothing strange or excessive about his manner. His manipulation of the instrument was quiet and easy, and his face was simply grand—the lips compressed and the head thrown a little backward. When the music expressed quiet rapture or devotion a sweet smile flitted over his features; when it was triumphant the nostrils dilated. There was nothing petty or egoistic to mar the picture. Why did not Scheffer paint him thus instead of representing him as one of the three Magi?

TO JOHN CHAPMAN, [15 OCTOBER 1854]

The money was the £15 for her article on Mme de Sablé. The scandal about GE was spreading; both Combe and Robert Chambers had inquired of Chapman about it. Thomas Carlyle wrote to his brother John: "Lewes has certainly cast away his Wife here,—who indeed deserved it of him, having openly produced those dirty sooty-skinned children which have Th. Hunt for father, and being ready with a third [actually a fourth]; Lewes to pay the whole account, even the money part of it!" GHL's sons were all blond. Arthur Helps spent the day with GE and GHL 30 August. Thomas Wilson was teaching at a girl's school in Weimar. James Marshall, a Scot, was Secretary to the Grand Duchess Sophie. [VIII, 123–25]

62a Kaufgasse, Weimar.

Dear Friend

It was a comfort to have a letter from you. Pray do not be so long again without writing to me. There are two ways in which you may send me the money; either by Bank of England notes sent in halves by separate posts, or through Coutts's who would send it for me to their correspondents at Weimar. The advantage of the *former* plan is, that there would be no delay in it and consequently, no probability, as in the other case, of my being obliged to remain in Weimar longer than another week or ten days.

I am sorry that you are annoyed with questions about me. Do whatever seems likely to free you from such importunities. About my own justification I am entirely indifferent. But there is a report concerning Mr. Lewes which I must beg you to contradict whenever it is mentioned to you. It is, "that he has run away from his wife and family." This is so far from being true that he is in constant correspondence with his wife and is providing for her to the best of his power, while no man can be more nervously anxious than he about the future welfare of his children. The letters he has received from Mrs. Lewes since he has been away, as well as those which he has written to her, have confirmed everything he has told me about their past history and proved to me that his conduct as a husband has been in the highest degree noble and self-sacrificing. Since we have been here, circumstances (in which I am not concerned) have led to his determining on a separation, but he has never contemplated withdrawing the most watchful care over his wife and the utmost efforts for his children.

We have been told of a silly story about a "message" sent by me "in a letter to Miss Martineau" which letter has been shown at the Reform Club. It is hardly necessary to tell you that I have had no communication with Miss Martineau, and that if I had, she is one of the last persons to whom I should speak as to a confidante. The phrase "run away" as applied to me is simply amusing—I wonder what I had to run away from. But as applied to Mr. Lewes it is more serious, and I have thought it right to explain to you how utterly false it is. You are in possession of the broad facts of the case, but there are very many particulars which you do *not* know and which are perhaps necessary to set his character and conduct in their true light. Such particulars cannot be given in a letter. He has written to Carlyle and to Robert Chambers, stating as much of the truth as he can without too severely inculpating others. Helps already knew, and his sympathy was a great comfort when he passed through Weimar.

You ask me to tell you what reply you shall give to inquiries. I have nothing to deny or to conceal. I have done nothing with which any person has a right to interfere. I have surely full liberty to travel in Germany, and to travel with Mr. Lewes. No one here seems to find it at all scandalous that we should be together. Mr. Wilson and Mr. Marshall are as friendly and attentive as possible. But I do not wish to take the ground of ignoring what is unconventional in my position. I have counted the cost of the step that I have taken and am prepared to bear, without irritation or bitterness, renunciation by all my friends. I am not mistaken in the person to whom I have attached myself. He is worthy of the sacrifice I have incurred, and my only anxiety is that he should be rightly judged. . . .

Mr. Lewes was in doubt whether he should not return to London to refute the report of his having "run away," but his health is so far from being established and he is so unequal to spending a winter of worry and sadness there that he will not do so unless it should prove absolutely necessary. He has given up the Leader.

Do write to me when you can, and believe me always, sincerely

Your obliged friend
Marian Evans.

TO CHARLES BRAY, [16 OCTOBER 1854]

[II, 178–79]

62a Kaufgasse | Weimar.

Dear Friend

I yesterday wrote to my brother to request that he would pay my income to you on the 1st of December. I also requested that, in future, he would pay my half yearly income into the Coventry and Warwickshire Bank, that I might order it to be sent to me wherever I wanted it, as he has sometimes sent me a cheque which I could not get cashed in London. Is there anything to be done—any notice given to the Bank in order to make this plan feasible? . . .

Of course many silly myths are already afloat about me, in addition to the truth, which of itself would be thought matter for scandal. I am quite unconcerned about them except as they may cause pain to my real friends. If you hear of anything that I have said, done, or written in relation to Mr. Lewes beyond the simple fact that I am attached to him and that I am living with him, do me the justice to believe that it is false. You and Mr. Chapman are the only persons to whom I have ever spoken of his private position or of my relation to him, and the only influence I should ever dream of exerting over him as to his conduct towards his wife and children is that of stimulating his conscientious care for them, if it needed any stimulus.

Pray pardon this long letter on a painful subject. I felt it a duty to write it. I am ignorant how far Cara and Sara may be acquainted with the state of things, and how they may feel towards me. I am quite prepared to accept the consequences of a step which I have deliberately taken and to accept them without irritation or bitterness. The most painful consequence will, I know, be the loss of friends. If I do not write, therefore, understand that it is because I desire not to obtrude myself. Write to me soon and let me know how things are with you. I am full of affection towards you all, and whatever you may think of me, shall always be

Your true and grateful friend
Marian Evans.

TO SARA HENNELL, 31 OCTOBER [1854]

Sara, an ardent feminist, could not believe that anything that could be told to Bray and Chapman could not be entrusted to her. [II, 181–82]

62a Kaufgasse, Weimar | Tuesday October 31.
My dear Sara

The mode in which you and Cara have interpreted both my words and my silence makes me dread lest in writing more I should only give rise to fresh misconceptions. I am so deeply conscious of having had neither the feeling nor the want of feeling which you impute to me that I am quite unable to read into my words, quoted by you, the sense which you put upon them. When you say that I do not care about Cara's or your opinion and friendship it seems much the same to me as if you said that I didn't care to eat when I was hungry or to drink when I was thirsty. One of two things: either I am a creature without affection, on whom the memories of years have no hold, or, you, Cara and Mr. Bray are the most cherished friends I have in the world. It is simply self-contradictory to say that a person can be indifferent about her dearest friends; yet this is what you substantially say, when you accuse me of "boasting with what serenity I can give you up," of "speaking proudly" etc. The only reply I can give to such an accusation is an absolute denial that I have been actuated by such a spirit as you describe with regard to any one thing which I have written, done, or left undone.

You say: "You" shew that "you wish to have communication with Charles only." The reason why I wrote to Mr. Bray and not to you and Cara is simply this. Before I left England, I communicated, by Mr. Lewes's desire, certain facts in strict confidence to Mr. Bray and Mr. Chapman and I did so for special reasons which would not apply to any female friend. After your kind letters came to me, we heard much painful news from London as to reports which were partly a perversion of the truth, partly pure falsehood. I cannot, even now, see that I did anything deserving so severe a reproach as you send me, in writing to Mr. Bray who was already in possession of the main facts, and in intimating that my silence to you arose from no want of affection, but from what I, falsely perhaps, but still sincerely, regarded as the very reverse of *pride* and a spirit of *boasting*.

There is now no longer any secrecy to be preserved about Mr. Lewes's affairs or mine, and whatever I have written to Mr. Bray, I have written to you. I am under no foolish hallucinations about either the present or the future and am standing on no stilts of any kind. I wish to speak simply and to act simply but I think it can hardly be unintelligible to you that I shrink from writing elaborately about private feelings and circumstances. I have really felt it a privation that I have been unable to write to you about things not personal, in which I know you would feel a common interest, and it will brighten my thoughts very much to know that I may do so. Cara, you and my own sister are the three women who are tied to my heart by a cord which can never be broken and which really *pulls* me continually. My love for you rests on a past which no future can reverse, and offensive as the words seem to have been to you, I must repeat, that I can feel no bitterness towards you, however you may act towards me. If you remain to me what you have ever been, my life will be all the happier, and I will try not to be unworthy of your love so far as faithfulness to my own conscience can make me worthy of it.

I have written miserably ill, and I fear all the while I am writing that I may be giving rise to some mistake. But interpret my whole letter so as to make it accord with this plain statement—I love Cara and you with unchanged and unchangeable affection, and while I retain your friendship I retain the best that life has given me next to that which is the deepest and gravest joy in all human experience.

                                                                                Marian Evans.

TO CHARLES BRAY, 12 NOVEMBER 1854

Isaac Evans was less than obliging to GE. Chrissey Clarke's son Robert drowned at sea a few months later. Varnhagen, to whom GHL brought an introduction from Carlyle in 1839, welcomed them to Berlin and proved "a real treasure" to GHL, supplying him with books for his biography of Goethe. [II, 184–86]

                                        62 Dorotheen Gasse, Berlin | November 12. 1854.

Dear Friend

My brother in reply to my letter requesting him to pay you my income on the 1st of December when it is strictly due to me, sends word through my sister that "he will pay the money when he receives it." This makes me nervous lest you should not receive the payment in time to meet the bill, and should be inconvenienced on that account. I could send you the money to England and receive it again when my brother pays it, if that would save you any inconvenience. I really regret that I had the money in advance now that there is this anxiety about it. My brother has generally paid me a week or fortnight after the time; but whenever I asked him for it, he always sent me a cheque at once, which of course it is perfectly easy for him to do. But I will take care in future not to involve anyone else in the annoyance resulting from his disinclination to accommodate me.

He also sends me word through my sister that circumstances render it desirable for the trustees to call in £1500 of my money, which must consequently be placed in the funds until a new investment can be found for it. So next Midsummer my income will be less than usual. I only hope he will think it worth while to get another investment. For a considerable part of my sister's money he gets 5 per cent. Poor Chrissey has been in trouble about her boys. One of them has been ill and the other very naughty—so naughty that he has had to leave his situation and they have determined to send him to sea. I have felt this a greater trouble to me than all the denunciations of London gossips.

We reached Berlin last Saturday, or rather a week ago yesterday, and find much to enjoy here. Varnhagen von Ense and Fraulein v. Solmar, old friends of Mr. Lewes's, have received me very kindly, and as they are in the best society of Berlin, this is no slight advantage. Mr. Lewes has not yet had time to call on half his friends, but all whom he has seen appear delighted to meet him again. Fraulein v. Solmar has a *salon* which is open every evening but Thursday to persons who have been invited once for all. Varnhagen made a little party for us last Thursday, offers the use of his library, and is altogether cordial. He had corresponded with Carlyle for years before Carlyle came to Germany (in 1852) and was terribly disappointed when he came to know him in the flesh. Varnhagen is a courtier, wears an order round his neck and carries a gold headed cane, so you may imagine that Carlyle's roughness and petulance were rather shocking to him. Withal this Varnhagen is a theoretical democrat, and thinks "Past and Present" Carlyle's greatest work, while to his dismay he found that Carlyle talked the fiercest despotism etc. etc.

Last night we went to see "Nathan der Weise." You know, or perhaps you do not know that this play is a sort of dramatic apologue the moral of which is religious tolerance. It thrilled me to think that Lessing dared nearly a hundred years ago to write the grand sentiments and profound thoughts which this play contains for the people's theatre which he dreamed of, but which Germany has never had. In England the words which call down applause here would make the pit rise in horror.

It is amusing to see how very comfortable the Germans are without many of the things which England considers the safeguards of society. The Germans eat their Bratwurst and Küchen from house to house in gladness of heart though they have no episcopal establishment and though they *have* some other things which are thought very noxious with us. I think them immensely inferior to us in creative intellect and in the possession of the *means* of life, but they know better how to use the means they have for the end of enjoyment. One sees everywhere in Germany what is the rarest of all things in England—thorough *bien-être*, freedom from gnawing cares and ambitions, contentment in inexpensive pleasures with no suspicion that happiness is a vice which we must not only not indulge in ourselves but as far as possible restrain others from giving way to. There are disadvantages, of course. They don't improve their locks and carriages as we do, and they consider a room furnished when it has a looking glass and an escritoire in it. They put their knives in their mouths, write un-sit-out-able comedies and unreadable books; but they are decidedly happy animals and in spite of Pascal, that is perhaps better than being extremely clever ones—miserable and knowing their misery.

Berlin is a cold place, but the cold is dry and bracing. This morning the roofs are covered with snow, and soon I suppose we shall have a firm stratum of snow in the streets which will lie all winter. We work hard in the mornings till our heads are hot, then walk out, dine at three and, if we don't go out, read diligently aloud in the evening. I think it is impossible for two human beings to be more happy in each other. All I am anxious about is the certainty of work by which I may get money—and that just now does not present itself.

Best love to all. Forgive all my omissions and commissions and believe me ever

Your sincere and affectionate
Marian Evans.

TO JOHN CHAPMAN, 9 JANUARY [1855]

The date 1854 is an obvious error. The article on woman in Germany was never written, but Chapman paid her £20 for one on "Memoirs of the Court of Austria." [VIII, 133–35]

62 Dorotheen Strasse, Berlin | January 9. 1854.

Dear Friend

Glad to hear from you again, though I was casting no mental reproaches on you for your silence, as I was aware that you must be very busy at the high tide of your editorial affairs. I still think the "Ideals of Womanhood" a good subject and one I should like to treat, but I have been thinking lately of an article on another subject which I believe I could make interesting and which I could prepare for your next number if you agree with me that it is promising. Meanwhile, if you think well, I will *slowly* prepare the other article for some future number. The subject I now propose is "Woman in Germany"—not simply the modern German woman, who is not a very fertile subject (metaphorically speaking) but woman as she presents herself to us in all the phases of development through which the German race has run from the earliest historic twilight when it was still blended with the Scandinavian race—and its women were prophetesses, through the periods of the Volks wanderung and the romantic and *bürgerlich* life of the Middle Ages up to our own day. There is a great deal of picturesque material on this subject and I am just in the midst of it here, so that it would suit me perhaps better than any other just now. What say you?—No, of course, unless you heartily concur—and I shall equally remain etc. etc. as politeness says at the end of letters, meaning Go to the _____. The article would very likely not reach 32 pages, but I should be glad to be allowed that length of tether as it would be a disadvantage to the subject for me to feel cramped. . . .

Mr. Lewes's health has been variable, but I think he is on the whole better. He desires me to send his kind remembrances to you, as indeed he always does, and I always forget to give them. We like our Berlin life immensely—an ugly place it must be to any one who comes to it hipped or solitary or what is worse, with a disagreeable companion. But, to make a very novel quotation—"the mind is its own place" and can make a pretty town even of Berlin. The day seems too short for our happiness and we both of us feel that we have begun life afresh—with new ambition and new powers. I say so much to you, because I know you have a friendly interest in me, and to that extent I am not afraid of incurring the fatality which the Germans seem still to believe in. When any one is spoken of as being very happy, they say "Unberufen"—meaning "Don't talk of it, or their happiness will vanish."

It is distressing to see the multitude of soldiers here—to think of the nation's vitality going to feed 300,000 puppets in uniform. In the streets one's legs are in constant danger from officers' swords, and at tables d'hôte the most noise is always made by officers. Will you be kind enough to let me owe you a 1d stamp and send the enclosed letter to Miss Hennell?

We have just come from hearing "Fidelio," and I write tonight to save the working time in the morning. Pray let no one else see this hasty and unconsidered letter.

Ever yours sincerely
Marian Evans. . . .

TO SARA HENNELL, 9 JANUARY [1855]

Adolf Stahr, whom they met at Varnhagen's, had just published his *Torso*, on which GE wrote an article for the *Leader* called "The Art of the Ancients" and another, "The Art and Artists of Greece," for the *Saturday Review*. Stahr, having lived for some years with Fanny Lewald, married her in February 1855. Otto Gruppe was another acquaintance of GHL, to whom he gave his *Ariadne* in 1839. Christian Rauch, the sculptor, had done several statues of Goethe. [II, 191–93]

62 Dorotheen Strasse, Berlin | January 9. 1854.

Dear Sara . . .

We have been to hear Fidelio this evening—not well executed, except so far as the orchestra was concerned, but the divine music positively triumphs over the defects of execution. One is entirely wrapt in the *idea* of the composer. Last week we had Orpheus and Euridice and I heard for the first time at once an opera of Gluck's and Johanna Wagner. It is one of the glories of Berlin to give Gluck's operas, and it is also something of a glory to have "die Wagner." She is really a fine actress and a fine singer; her voice is not ravishing, but she is mistress of it. I thought of you that evening and wished you could hear and see what I know would interest you greatly—I refer rather to Gluck's opera than to Johanna Wagner.

The scene in which Orpheus (Johanna Wagner) enters Tartarus, is met by the awful shades, and charms them into ecstatic admiration till they make way for him to pass on, is very fine. The voices—except in the choruses—are all women's voices, and there are only three characters—Orpheus, Amor and Euridice. One wonders that Pluto does not come as a Basso, and one would prefer Mercury as a tenor to Amor in the shape of an ugly German soprano—but Gluck willed it otherwise and the music is delightful. The scene in Elysium is immensely absurd—Ballet girls dance in the foreground and in the background are Greek shades looking like butchers in *chemises*. But the worst of it is, that instead of letting it be a tragedy, Euridice is brought to life again and we end with another Ballet girl scene before Amor's temple.

I am reading a charming book by Professor Stahr—who is one of our acquaintances here—*Torso: Kunst, Künstler und Kuntstwerke der Alten*. It feeds the fresh interest I am now feeling in Art. Prof. Stahr is the *futur* of Fanny Lewald, the novelist. He is a very erudite man, and what is very much rarer amongst Germans, a good writer, who knows how to select his materials and has above all a charming talent for description. We saw at his house, the other night, the first portrait of Schiller which *convinces* me of a likeness to him. It is the copy of a miniature which has never been engraved. . . .

I am very much interested in Professor Gruppe as a type of the German *Gelehrter*. He has written books on everything—on the Greek drama—a great book on the Cosmic Systems of the Greeks—an epic, numberless lyric poems etc.—he has a philosophical work and a history of literature in the press—is professor of philosophy at the University—has invented a mode of staining paper beautifully for bookcovers—is enthusiastic about Boar-hunting, and has written a volume of hunting poems—and *ich weiss nicht was*. Withal he is as simple as a child. When we go to see them in an evening, we find him wrapt in a moth-eaten grey coat, once a great coat, now converted into a schlafrock, and a cap on his head. Then he reads us a translation of one of the Homeric hymns, and goes into the most naïve *impersonal* ecstacy at the beauty of his own poetry (which is really good). The other night he read us part of an epic which is still in MS. and is to be read before the King—such is the fashion here. And his little wife, who is about 20 years younger than himself, listens with loving admiration. Altogether, they and their two little children are a charming picture.

We have been to Rauch's atelier. He is now occupied on a group representing Moses with his arms held up by Aaron and Har. It is very interesting to see the original little clay model—the marvellous expression given in that rough way. My back aches and it is nearly 12 o'clock. Best love to Cara.

Ever your affectionate
Marian.

TO BESSIE PARKES, 16 MARCH 1855

Bessie had given Chapman her letter to forward to GE. [II, 195–96]

1 Sydney Place | Dover | March 16. 1855.

Dear Friend . . .

We reached Dover on Wednesday and I have taken lodgings here for a short time while Mr. Lewes makes some arrangements in town. Your letter came to me when we were in the hurry of paying farewell visits first to friends and then to galleries and museums, so that I was unable to write to you from Berlin. I am now rather enjoying the contrast of perfect quiet and of a bright sun shining on cliff and softly rounded hill and fringed sea after much paddling through the thawing snows of the Berlin streets. I dare say you know that rather tame and ugly place, for which, however, I have considerable affection on the score of many happy hours passed there and many kind people whose faces shone benevolently on me. . . .

I can dilate on nothing now. I will only say that if you knew everything, we should probably be much nearer agreement even as to the details of conduct than you suppose. In the mean time, believe no one's representations about me, for there is not a *single person* who is in a position to make a true representation. My mind is deliciously calm and untroubled so far as my own lot is concerned, my only anxieties are sympathetic ones.

I write tonight rather sleepily because I may have to send to Mr. Chapman tomorrow and in that case I will enclose this note to him, as I suppose you still wish me not to write to you directly. Ever, dear Friend,

Yours faithfully and affectionately
Marian Evans.

TO CHARLES BRAY, 4 APRIL 1855

GE refused to join GHL until she had definite assurance that Agnes would never live with him again. Agnes said "No, never, and she would be very glad if he could marry Miss Evans." The other "big book" was GE's translation of Spinoza's *Ethics*, which GHL had agreed to do for Bohn's Library. [II, 197]

1 Sydney Place, Dover | April 4, 1855.

Dear Friend . . .

Such a conjunction as the [Crimean] war and the extreme severity of the winter must have been terrible indeed for the Coventry trade. And the weather *will* not get warm, that the ladies might be obliged to throw off their rusty bonnets! I am very anxious to know that you have had no loss which will materially affect your comfort.

My half year's income is due at the beginning of June and the beginning of December. I shall be much obliged to you if you will say what is necessary to the Bank, before the first of those periods, and also if you will tell me how to frame my order for the payment of the money to me in London, when I am there. I suppose they will pay it into a London Bank, and I must call for it? I should not like to make a simpleton of myself to Messieurs les banquiers, and my ignorance particularly well qualifies me for doing so. I wrote to my brother to ask him always to pay my income into the Coventry and Warwickshire Bank, but as he is not precise in answering letters (mine at least) it is difficult to know what he will do.

Mr. Lewes is gone to Arthur Helps's at Vernon Hill for a week or ten days, and on his return I shall join him in London where—that is, in the environs—we shall establish ourselves till the big books are fairly through the press, when I hope our wings will be plumed for a new flight to the south of Germany and Italy, for which we both yearn. Poor Mr. Chapman's illness makes me fear that he really has the radical delicacy of constitution which we used to suspect in old days. And the burthen of business upon him! It is sad to think of.

Good night and love to you all from

Yours ever affectionately
Marian Evans. . . .

TO CHARLES BRAY, 1 MAY 1855

GE joined GHL for a fortnight at Victoria Grove Terrace, Bayswater, before going to East Sheen. She was anxious that Bray should not quote a disparaging remark she had made about GHL before she knew him. Rufa Hennell was the first lady to call on GE since their union. [II, 199–200]

8 V[ictoria] G[rove] Terrace | May 1. 55.

Dear Friend

We go tomorrow to our new home at East Sheen, a charming village close to Richmond Park. If you write to me, please to enclose the letter to G. H. Lewes Esq. | 7 Clarence Row | East Sheen | Richmond | Surrey. When you come to London again, I hope you will pay us a visit, for I think, apart from any regard for me it will be a pleasure to you to see that pretty place, and it is far less trouble to get there than to Bayswater. You have only to jump into the train at the Waterloo Bridge Station and in ten minutes you will be at Mortlake where you must get down. Mortlake, as I daresay you know, is a lovely village on the bank of the Thames, and East Sheen is its twin sister lying close to it. Ask the way to East Sheen and in three minutes you will be at our door. Then you shall have a nice dinner and a nice snooze after it, and then a stroll, along the river or in the Park, such as you can't get at Coventry even by the help of a carriage.

And pray, when I see you again, don't misquote something I said two or three years ago, which something you seem to have converted into a supercilious, impertinent expression of disapprobation on my part. If the discipline of years has taught me anything, it has taught me to be reverent to all good in others and perpetually mindful of my own need of tolerance, and surely few people can have had more opportunity than I have had for knowing the good in you, and still fewer can have put that goodness to an equally severe test.

We are panting to be in the country and resume our old habits of undisturbed companionship and work. Mr. Lewes has been much worse since he returned to town and the other evening he alarmed me terribly by fainting. Imagine that I had never seen any one faint before, and that I thought he was dead! You will be able then to understand my condition for three or four minutes until he returned to consciousness. However we hope that when we are far away from the roar of omni*bii* (as poor Joseph Hume is accused of calling them) we shall have no more of such attacks.

Mrs. Hennell called on me the other day, very kindly and nobly. I respect her for it. I was so stupefied and heated by having sat in-doors writing all day, that she must have carried away anything but a charming image of me, but that was of slight consequence—it was enough that she did a good action.

Best love to Cara and Sara for whom, of course, I write as well as for you.

> Ever your affectionate friend
> Marian.

Poor Mr. Chapman seems in an uncomfortable state both physically and mentally.

TO BESSIE PARKES, [1 MAY 1855]

Bessie, an enthusiastic feminist who insisted on calling GE by her maiden name, was her second caller. [II, 200]

> 8 V. G. Terrace | Tuesday Morning.

Dear Friend

I forgot to say yesterday that if you write to me at East Sheen, I must beg you to enclose the letter to G. H. Lewes Esq. I will tell you the reason of this when I see you. If you are ever able to come to me, let me know the day before, that I may be at home and meet you at the station.

I have not yet lost the glow of joy at the sight of you.

> Ever your affectionate
> Marian.

TO CHARLES BRAY, 17 JUNE 1855

David Nutt gave GHL £250 for the first thousand copies of his *Goethe*. Together with reprints, the book brought him £450 in two years. GE's Journal records on 13 June, "I began the second book of the Iliad in Greek this morning." GHL, stung by Huxley's sneer that he was only a "book-scientist," was beginning serious study of biology. Between them GE and GHL filled nearly half the Supplement to the *Leader*. [II, 202–03]

> 7 Clarence Row | East Sheen | June 17. 55.

Dear Friend

I want very much to know how business has been going on, and that it is not too late for you to benefit by the more cheerful state of things. Pray satisfy my curiosity, which springs, I assure you, from a most respectable region of the head.

To set you an example of communicativeness, I tell you that "Goethe's Life" is at length going to be published on thoroughly satisfactory terms, and that we shall soon "hail with delight," as sub-editors say, the appearance of the first proof sheet.

My brother has sent me an order on Jones, Lloyd and Co. for my half year's income, with a kind letter saying that he hopes to find a good investment for the money which has been called in.

I think we like East Sheen better and better, and are happier every day— writing hard, walking hard, reading Homer and science and rearing tadpoles. I read aloud for about three hours every evening, beginning with Boswell's Johnson, or some such enjoyable book, not unfriendly to digestion, then subsiding into the dreary dryness of Whewell's History of the Inductive Sciences and winding up with Heine's wit and imagination. We breakfast at 1/2 past 8, read to ourselves till 10, write till 1/2 past 1, walk till nearly 4, and dine at 5, regretting each day as it goes.

I hope you think the supplement of the Leader a respectable turnout. Mr. Lewes wrote the articles on Sydney Smith, Owen Meredith, Newton's Boyhood, and How to live a hundred years, and I wrote the one on Menander and Greek Comedy.

Are you not coming to London soon? You have often scolded me for not writing about my own affairs. See how I am improved! Best love to Cara and the enclosed letter to Sara.

> Ever yours affectionately
> Marian.

TO MRS. CHARLES BRAY, 4 SEPTEMBER [1855]

After one letter protesting GE's union, Cara Bray broke off correspondence with her for nearly a year. Under the pretext of asking what to do with some sheets GE had left at Rosehill Cara wrote again, evoking this eloquent defence of GE's position. George Combe was horrified that "the noblest woman that I have seen," whom he had introduced to his distinguished friends, was living in sin with the foremost opponent of phrenology, and asked Bray if there was insanity in GE's family, for he saw no other explanation for her conduct. [II, 213–15]

> 7 Clarence Row | September 4.

Dear Cara

No one has better reason than myself to know how difficult it is to produce a true impression by letters, and how likely they are to be misinterpreted even where years of friendship might seem to furnish a sufficient key. And it seems the more probable to me that I misinterpreted your letter to me at Berlin since I find that my answer to it produced totally false conclusions in your mind. Assuredly if there be any one subject on which I feel no levity it is that of marriage and the relation of the sexes—if there is any one action or relation of my life which is and always has been profoundly serious, it is my relation to Mr. Lewes. If any expression or parallel in my letter bore an opposite construction it must have been, because you interpreted as of general application what I intended simply in answer to what I considered Mr. Combe's petty and absurd views about the effect on his reputation of having introduced me to one or two of his friends. *Nothing* that I said in that letter was intended as a discussion of the principles of my conduct or as an answer to your opinions on the subject.

It is, however, natural enough that you should mistake me in many ways, for not only are you unacquainted with Mr. Lewes's real character and the course of his actions, but also, it is several years now since you and I were much together, and it is possible that the modifications my mind has undergone may be in quite the opposite direction to what you imagine. No one can be better aware than yourself that it is possible for two people to hold different opinions on momentous subjects with equal sincerity and an equally earnest conviction that their respective opinions are alone the truly moral ones. If we differ on the subject of the marriage laws, I at least can believe of you that you cleave to what you believe to be good, and I don't know of anything in the nature of your views that should prevent you from believing the same of me. *How far* we differ I think we neither of us know; for I am ignorant of your precise views and apparently you attribute to me both feelings and opinions which are not mine. We cannot set each other quite right on this matter in letters, but one thing I can tell you in few words. Light and easily broken ties are what I neither desire theoretically nor could live for practically. Women who are satisfied with such ties do *not* act as I have done—they obtain what they desire and are still invited to dinner.

That any unwordly, unsuperstitious person who is sufficiently acquainted with the realities of life can pronounce my relation to Mr. Lewes immoral I can only understand by remembering how subtle and complex are the influences that mould opinion. But I *do* remember this, and I indulge in no arrogant or uncharitable thoughts about those who condemn us, even though we might have expected a somewhat different verdict. From the majority of persons, of course, we never looked for anything but condemnation. We are leading no life of self-indulgence, except indeed, that being happy in each other, we find everything easy. We are working hard to provide for others better than we provide for ourselves, and to fulfil every responsibility that lies upon us. Levity and pride would not be a sufficient basis for that.

Pardon me, dear Cara, if in vindicating myself from some unjust conclusions, I seem too cold and self-asserting. I should not care to vindicate myself, if I did not love you and desire to relieve you of the pain which you say these conclusions have given you. Whatever I may have misinterpreted before, I do not misinterpret your letter this morning, but read in it nothing else than love and kindness towards me to which my heart fully answers yes. I should like never to write about myself again—it is not healthy to dwell on one's own feelings and conduct, but only to try and live more faithfully and lovingly every fresh day.

I think not one of the endless words and deeds of kindness and forbearance you have ever shewn me has vanished from my memory. I recall them often, and feel, as about everything else in the past, how deficient I have been in almost every relation of my life. But that deficiency is irrevocable and I can find no strength or comfort except in "pressing forward towards the things that are before," and trying to make the present better than the past. But if we should never be very near each other again, dear Cara, do bear this faith in your mind, that I was not insensible or ungrateful to all your goodness, and that I am one amongst the many for whom you have not lived in vain.

Those dreadful sheets and pillow cases! Pray give them away if you won't use them, for I don't want them, and can never set up housekeeping on that small stock. I am very busy just now, and have been obliged to write hastily. Bear this in mind, and believe that no meaning is mine which contradicts my assurance that I am your affectionate and earnest friend

Marian.

My love to Sara. I can't write more today but will write to her another day.

TO CHARLES BRAY, [15 OCTOBER 1855]

GE wrote "Evangelical Teaching: Dr. Cumming," the liveliest assault on the religion of her adolescence, and reviewed eighteen books for the Belles Lettres section of the *Westminster* before she went with GHL to Worthing for a fortnight. On their return, possibly because their landlady had objected to the irregularity of GE's position, they went into new lodgings at 8 Park Shot, Richmond, where they lived until February 1859. GE's second article was "German Wit: Heinrich Heine" for the January number. [II, 218]

Richmond | Monday.

Dear Friend

Since you have found out the "Cumming," I write by to-day's post just to say, that it *is* mine, but also to beg that you will not mention it as such to any one likely to transmit the information to London, as we are keeping the authorship a secret. The article appears to have produced a strong impression, and that impression would be a little counteracted if the author were known to be a *woman*. . . . I have had a letter addressed to "the author of article No. 4." begging me to print it separately for "the good of mankind in general." It is so kind of you to rejoice in anything I do at all well.

Tell Cara I am very pleased to have her nice long letter, which I shall answer another day, when I have more time. I am dreadfully busy again, for I am going to write an article for the Westminster Review again, besides my other work. We enjoy our new lodgings very much—everything is the pink of order and cleanliness. . . .

Ever yours affectionately
Marian.

TO CHARLES BRAY, 1 JANUARY 1856

GE went to Attleborough 24 December 1855 to spend Christmas with Chrissey Clarke and her children, returning to Richmond the 29th. Cara Bray was still cool towards GE, who never again visited her in Coventry. Besides her article on Heine for the January number of the *Westminster*, GE reviewed 27 books for the Belles Lettres section, including Browning's *Men and Women*, Longfellow's *Hiawatha*, and Thoreau's *Walden*, and wrote some shorter articles for the *Leader*. [II, 224]

8 Park Shot | Richmond | January 1. 56.

Dear Friend

A happy New Year to you and yours!

I have never answered your note in which you invited me to call at your house on my way to my sister's. I am sure that note was written with the kindest intentions, but if you had thought twice you would have seen that I was not likely to take a journey twice as long as necessary and walk all through Coventry in order to make a call where I had only the invitation of the master of the house. I went straight from London to Nuneaton by express in two hours and a half, and returned in the same way. In this season one likes to abridge railway journeying as much as possible.

You will be glad to hear that I found my sister and her children very well and comfortable. She mentioned your kindness in sending her a newspaper. I, as well as she, am obliged to you. While I have been away Mr. Lewes has I hope been getting a great deal of good from a visit to his friend Mr. Helps at his pleasant place in Hampshire. He returns to me on Friday or Saturday. Meanwhile I am trying to fill up the gap his absence makes by being as industrious as possible.

I hope you have enjoyed your Christmas and are beginning the year with pleasant prospects. With kind remembrances to all, visitors included, I am

Always yours affectionately
Marian E.

TO SARA HENNELL, [26 FEBRUARY 1856]

Edward Noel and his children spent the winter with the Brays. [II, 230–31]

Richmond | Tuesday.

Dear Sara

Mr. Lewes wishes me to write again—though I think it hardly necessary—to say that if Mr. Noel comes to see us—and we shall be very happy if he will do so— we hope you will impress on his memory that he must ask for *Mrs. Lewes* and not for Miss Evans, as a misunderstanding on this matter would be very painful. Excuse me for troubling you with this bit of personal anxiety.

Ever yours
Marian.

TO BESSIE PARKES, 22 MARCH 1856

Mrs. Croft, their landlady at 8 Park Shot, Richmond, was very friendly and tolerant of Lewes's biological studies. [II, 231–32]

Richmond | March 22. 56.

Dear Friend . . .

You will be surprized to hear that I have not been to town more than twice since last spring—once to call on Mr. Chapman, and once to call on the Molluscs in the Zoological Gardens. I have no other visits to pay and I shudder at shopping so there has been no motive for rushing into the smoke. Mr. Lewes goes to town once a week, and he does any errands for me. However, with the prospect of seeing you the streets would look brighter, and now the weather is getting pleasanter we may be able some day to arrange a meeting. I quite understand that you cannot come here. . . .

Your address to me as *Miss Evans* was unfortunate, as I am not known under that name here. We find it indispensable to our comfort that I should bear Mr. Lewes's name while we occupy lodgings, and we are now with so excellent a woman that any cause of removal would be a misfortune. If you have occasion to write to me again, please to bear this in mind. Letters are unsatisfactory modes of communication generally, but yours are always clear as daylight and just like yourself. If I had any cloudy feelings about you, a few words such as you have sent me would have dissipated them and made me what I have uninterruptedly been—

Your confiding and affectionate
Marian.

TO SARA HENNELL, [6 APRIL 1856]

Depression in the ribbon industry and other losses reduced Bray's income so much that he sold Rosehill and moved to Ivy Cottage, where Sara and her mother lived. GHL, looking for a school for his two elder boys, had written to GE's friend John Sibree, Jr., now a tutor at Stroud, who could not take them. Sara told them about the Hofwyl School, near Berne, where the Noels had been educated. [II, 236–37]

Richmond | Sunday.

Dear Sara

Thank you for taking the trouble to write me a full account of matters so interesting to me. . . . O dear dear—I hope you will be able thoroughly to enjoy this last precious summer on the pretty lawn where it is one of my pleasures on sunshiny days to think of you all strolling about or seated on the bearskin.

We are very thankful for the Hofwyl circular and have almost decided to send the two eldest boys there. But it is necessary to weigh all things carefully before coming to a determination, as, not being either swindlers or philanthropists, we don't like to incur obligations which there is not a reasonable certainty of our being able to meet. I am much obliged to Mr. Bray, too, for sending Mr. John

Sibree's letter. Mr. Lewes had already received an answer from him declining his proposition, but we were interested to read his very characteristic letter to his sister, which proved to Mr. Lewes that I had given him a correct description of the man.

We are headachy this morning and so are keeping Sabbath in Mr. Bray's fashion—enjoying the sunshine and reading the newspapers. I wish you saw the "Saturday." With best love to all,

Ever yours affectionately,
Marian.

TO CHARLES BRAY, 6 JUNE 1856

In May 1856 GE and Lewes set out for the North Devon coast to study marine biology for his articles in *Blackwood's Magazine*. The zoological curate was the Reverend George Tugwell, a young Oriel man. E. F. S. Pigott had taken over the financing and editing of the *Leader;* the yacht was his brother's. GE reviewed Hugo's *Contemplations* among the 19 books covered in her Belles Lettres article in July. [II, 252–53]

Runnymeade Villa | Ilfracombe | June 6. 56.
Dear Friend

I am very very sorry one of the consequences of our leaving Richmond so early was, that I missed the opportunity of seeing you, especially as such opportunities are rare. You will think I have been rather slow to tell you this but the statement is not the less true because it has been a long time coming. The fact is, when we arrived here I had not even read a great book on which I had engaged to write a long article by the beginning of this month, so that between work and zoology and bodily ailments, my time has been full to overflowing.

We are enchanted with Ilfracombe. I really think it is the loveliest sea place I ever saw, from the combination of fine rocky coast with exquisite inland scenery. But it would not do for any one who can't climb rocks and mount perpetual hills. For the peculiarity of this country is that it is all hill and no valley; you have no sooner got to the foot of one hill than you begin to mount another. But I suppose you know Ilfracombe. You would laugh to see our room decked with yellow pie-dishes, a *footpan,* glass jars and phials, all full of zoophytes or molluscs or annelids—and still more to see the eager interest with which we rush to our 'preserves' in the morning to see if there has been any mortality among them in the night. Mr. Lewes has been devoting a great deal of time to microscopic examination since we came, and in this way, as well as from our zoological expeditions on the rocks, we seem to have gained a large influx of new ideas. The partial rest from writing he has had, and the change of air, have already done him good, and I am hoping that with two more months of this life he may even get quite rid of that terrible singing in his ears which has never left him since the commencement of his illness two years ago.

We have made the acquaintance of a charming little zoological curate here, who is a delightful companion on expeditions and is most good-natured in lending and giving apparatus and "critturs" of all sorts. Mr. Pigott is coming here with his yacht at the end of June, and we hope then to go to Clovelly—Kingsley's Clovelly—and perhaps other places on the coast that we can't reach on foot. After this we mean to migrate to Tenby, for the sake of making acquaintance with its molluscs and medusæ, and at the beginning of August, we must return to town, as Mr. Lewes is to take the boys to Hofwyl towards the end of August.

Herbert Spencer is now gone on a yachting expedition with Mr. Pigott to Guernsey where I suppose they will make acquaintance with Victor Hugo and the rest of the French colony of emigrants—pleasanter, I fancy, than making acquaintance with Victor Hugo's two volumes of "Contemplations" which the Fates have unfortunately introduced *me* to. . . .

My best love to all. Tell Sara I will send her an autograph of Mr. Helps's when I can, but he keeps two secretaries and dictates everything, so that he seldom writes any but confidential letters. His writing is very fine—rather large—firm without stiffness and flowing without sprawlingness and a great many other things without a great many other things. Mr. Lewes sends you his kind regards.

Ever yours affectionately
Marian.

TO BARBARA LEIGH SMITH, 13 JUNE 1856

After two months at Ilfracombe GE and GHL went to Tenby, where Barbara spent a week with them. According to Mrs. Belloc Lowndes, Barbara wrote to Bessie Parkes: "I do wish, my dear, that you would revise your view of Lewes. I have quite revised mine. Like you, I thought him an extremely sensual man. Marian tells me that in their marital relationship he is unsensual, extremely considerate. His manner to her is delightful. It is plain to me that he makes her extremely happy." She added that they practise some sort of birth control and intend to have no children. Their satisfying sexual relation gave GE a sense of well-being she had never known before. If that house at 2 Bridge Street, Tenby, is still standing, it might well bear a plaque: "George Eliot was born here." Without GHL's encouragement she would never have written fiction. Barbara's sorrows and renunciations doubtless came from her love affair with John Chapman, which had ended in September 1855. [II, 254–55]

Runnymeade Villa | Ilfracombe | June 13th. 1856.

Dear Friend,

I was so glad to see your handwriting this morning and to hear how things have been going with you lately. Alas! I fear Ilfracombe is not a favourable place for delicate people. We find the air very harsh and trying et cetera. Mr. Lewes has felt so poorly for the last week that we think of going elsewhere—probably to Tenby—as soon as affairs will allow us to move. But it is a ravishingly beautiful place. I long to be a painter when I look at the exquisite colour and form of the rocks. The fascination of the scenery and zoology here have been terribly unpropitious to my work and I have been writing with only half of my brains. There is still work to be done for the next week, but after that I hope to have a thorough holiday from scribbling, and do nothing but drink in wonders and beauties on the rocky beach and along the lovely lanes.

I wish I could drink in the sight of you among other pleasant things; and perhaps if the weather will have the goodness to clear up, you can make a little expedition to Ilfracombe before we leave. I fear we shall not be able to get away until the end of June or nearly the end. I have seldom felt an air that seemed more unkind to me than this. On the most brilliant sunshiny days the wind has always been biting. I am heartily pleased to hear of the success your pictures have, and especially of Ruskin's encouragement. What books his two last are! I think he is the finest writer living.

I shall say nothing of sorrows and renunciations, but I understand and feel what you must have to do and bear. Yes—I hope we shall know each other better, and that you will know Mr. Lewes too, for he is far better worth knowing than I. . . .

Thank you dear friend for writing.

TO CHARLES BRAY, 1 SEPTEMBER [1856]

GHL left for Hofwyl with Charles and Thornton on 25 August. The article for the October *Westminster* was "Silly Novels by Lady Novelists," but GE also had 17 books to review for the Belles Lettres. She was eager to start writing "Amos Barton," her first fiction. [II, 261–62]

8 Park Shot | Richmond | September 1.

Dear Friend . . .

Last Monday Mr. Lewes started with the boys to Hofwyl, and I expect him home tomorrow or Wednesday. I had counted on this space of solitary time to get an article written which I had promised to let Mr. Chapman have for his next number. But lo! on Tuesday came seven large devils of toothache in place of one little devil that had been teazing me now and then, and from Tuesday till Saturday I was nothing but a frightful energumen. The doctor came and said it was neuralgia, and dosed me with quinine. That didn't do so we sent for the dentist, who decided that it was simply my good-for-nothing wisdom tooth. So I was chloroformed *twice*, and at last—on Saturday evening—the tooth was got out.

I had written to Mr. Chapman begging him to let me off and get a substitute, but he cruelly wrote back that he *must* have the article. So here am I on this blessed 1st of September, with this odious article to write in a hurry and with Mr. Lewes coming home to reduce my writing time to the minimum. *That* is why I am vexed you are coming on the 6th, for we MUST see you, if everything else goes wrong. Send me word exactly when you shall be here. Love and thanks to Sara. I will write to her another day. I am not yet well, and unable to begin my work. If it were not for the work I should be in excellent spirits at the idea of having got through this nasty business of chloroform and forceps while Mr. Lewes is away. Excuse incoherence.

Ever yours
Marian.

JOURNAL, 6 DECEMBER 1857

This first of a number of autobiographical accounts was written in December 1857 after the *Scenes of Clerical Life* were completed in *Blackwood's Magazine* and about to be reprinted in two volumes. [II, 406–10]

HOW I CAME TO WRITE FICTION

September 1856 made a new era in my life, for it was then I began to write Fiction. It had always been a vague dream of mine that some time or other I might write a novel, and my shadowy conception of what the novel was to be, varied, of course, from one epoch of my life to another. But I never went farther towards the actual writing of the novel than an introductory chapter describing a Staffordshire village and the life of the neighbouring farm houses, and as the years passed on I lost any hope that I should ever be able to write a novel, just as I desponded about everything else in my future life. I always thought I was deficient in dramatic power, both of construction and dialogue, but I felt I should be at my ease in the descriptive parts of a novel. My "introductory chapter" was pure description though there were good materials in it for dramatic presentation. It happened to be among the papers I had with me in Germany and one evening at Berlin, something led me to read it to George. He was struck with it as a bit of concrete description, and it suggested to him the possibility of my being able to write a novel, though he distrusted—indeed disbelieved in, my possession of any dramatic power. Still, he began to think that I might as well try, some time, what I could do in fiction, and by and bye when we came back to England and I had greater success than he had ever expected in other kinds of writing, his impression that it was worth while to see how far my mental power would go towards the production of a novel, was strengthened. He began to say very positively, "You must try and write a story," and when we were at Tenby he urged me to begin at once. I deferred it, however, after my usual fashion, with work that does not present itself as an absolute duty. But one morning I was lying in bed, thinking what should be the subject of my first story, my thoughts merged themselves into a dreamy doze, and I imagined myself writing a story of which the title was— "The Sad Fortunes of the Reverend Amos Barton." I was soon wide awake again, and told G. He said, "O what a capital title!" and from that time I had settled in my mind that this should be my first story. George used to say, "It may be a failure—it may be that you are unable to write fiction. Or perhaps, it may be just good enough to warrant your trying again." Again, "You may write a chef-d'œuvre at once—there's no telling." But his prevalent impression was that though I could hardly write a *poor* novel, my effort would want the highest quality of fiction—dramatic presentation. He used to say, "You have wit, description and philosophy—those go a good way towards the production of a novel. It is worth while for you to try the experiment." We determined that if my story turned out good enough, we would send it to Blackwood, but G. thought the more probable result was, that I should have to lay it aside and try again.

But when we returned to Richmond I had to write my article on Silly Novels and my review of Contemporary Literature for the Westminster; so that I did not begin my story till September 22. After I had begun it, as we were walking in the Park, I mentioned to G. that I had thought of the plan of writing a series of stories containing sketches drawn from my own observation of the Clergy, and calling them "Scenes from Clerical Life" opening with "Amos Barton." He at once accepted the notion as a good one—fresh and striking; and about a week afterwards when I read him the early part of 'Amos,' he had no longer any doubt about my ability to carry out the plan. The scene at Cross Farm, he said, satisfied him that I had the very element he had been doubtful about—it was clear I could write good dialogue. There still remained the question whether I could command any pathos, and that was to be decided by the mode in which I treated Milly's death. One night G. went to town on purpose to leave me a quiet evening for writing it. I wrote the chapter from the news brought by the shepherd to Mrs. Hackit, to the moment when Amos is dragged from the bedside and I read it to G. when he came home. We both cried over it, and then he came up to me and kissed me, saying "I think your pathos is better than your fun."

So when the story was finished G. sent it to Blackwood, who wrote in reply, that he thought the "Clerical reminiscences would do," congratulated the author on being "worthy the honours of print and pay," but would like to see more of the series before he undertook to print. However, when G. wrote that the author was discouraged by this editorial caution, Blackwood disclaimed any distrust and agreed to print the story at once. The first part appeared in the January number 1857. Before the appearance of the Magazine—on sending me the proof, Blackwood already expressed himself with much greater warmth of admiration, and when the first part had appeared, he sent me a charming letter with a cheque for fifty guineas, and a proposal about republication of the series. When the story was concluded he wrote me word how Albert Smith had sent him a letter saying he had never read anything that affected him more than Milly's death, and, added Blackwood, "the men at the [Garrick] club seem to have mingled their tears and their tumblers together. It will be curious if you should be a member and be hearing your own praises!" There was clearly no suspicion that I was a woman. It is interesting, as an indication of the value there is in such conjectural criticism generally, to remember that when G. read the first part of "Amos" to a party at Helps's, they were all sure I was a clergyman—a Cambridge man. Agnes thought I was the father of a family—was sure I was a man who had seen a great deal of society etc. etc. . . .

Blackwood was eager for the second story, and much delighted with the two first parts of "Mr. Gilfil's Love Story," which I sent him together. I wrote the fourth part at Scilly—the epilogue, sitting on the Fortification Hill, one sunshiny morning. Blackwood himself wrote in entire admiration of it, and in the same letter told us that Thackeray "thought highly of the series." When we were at Jersey, he was in London, and wrote from thence that he heard nothing but approval of "Mr. Gilfil's Love Story." Lord Stanley, among other people, had spoken to him about the "Clerical Scenes" at Bulwer's, and was astonished to find Blackwood in the dark as to the author.

I began "Janet's Repentance" at Scilly and sent off the first Part from Jersey, G. declaring it to be admirable, almost better than the other stories. But to my disappointment, Blackwood did not like it so well, seemed to misunderstand the characters, and be doubtful about the treatment of clerical matters. I wrote at once to beg him to give up printing the story if he felt uncomfortable about it, and he immediately sent a very anxious, cordial letter, saying the thought of putting a stop to the series "gave him quite a turn"—"he didn't meet with George Eliots every day"—and so on. . . . I had meant to carry on the series beyond "Janet's Repentance," and especially I longed to tell the story of the Clerical Tutor, but my annoyance at Blackwood's want of sympathy in the first two parts of "Janet," (although he came round to admiration at the third part) determined me to close the series and republish them in two volumes.

The first volume is printed, and the advertisements greet our eyes every week, but we are still wondering how the public will behave to my first book.

December 6. 57.

6

THE MAKING OF GEORGE ELIOT
Scenes of Clerical Life

The first part of "Amos Barton" was published in *Blackwood's Magazine* for January 1857, like all of its articles, anonymously. In thanking Blackwood for his report on its reception GE declared herself resolute in preserving her incognito and gave him in case of inquiries the name of *George Eliot*. She did not reveal her identity to him until a year later. In March, after "Mr. Gilfil's Love-story" began in *Blackwood's*, GE and GHL went for two months of zoologizing in the Scilly Isles, and then for two months more in Jersey. With the success of her stories evident, GE wrote to her brother Isaac Evans that she had changed her name and asked him to pay her income into GHL's bank account in London. Outraged that she had married without his knowledge, Isaac gave her letter to the family solicitor to answer, and for 23 years addressed not a single word to his sister.

Her chief correspondent was John Blackwood, who (cautioned by GHL about her diffidence) wisely fostered the talent of his new unknown author. In 1858, when the stories were reprinted as *Scenes of Clerical Life*, they were enthusiastically reviewed. Readers around Nuneaton soon recognized in them characters and events of an earlier generation. But the claim of an eccentric named Joseph Liggins that *he* had written the stories protected the pseudonym; not even the Brays suspected GE. She had already begun to write *Adam Bede* and gone with GHL to Germany to work on it while he continued his biological studies for articles in *Blackwood's*.

TO JOHN BLACKWOOD, [4 JANUARY 1857]

GHL had been dealing with John Blackwood over his *Sea-Side Studies* and had sent him "Amos Barton" on "behalf of a friend," whom Blackwood assumed to be a clergyman. [II, 288]

[8 Park Shot, Richmond]

My dear Sir

Your letter has proved to me that the generous editor and publisher—generous both in word and in deed—who makes the author's path smooth and easy, is something more than a pleasant tradition. I am very sensitive to the merits of cheques for fifty guineas, but I am still more sensitive to that cordial appreciation which is a guarantee to me that my work was worth doing for its own sake.

If the "Scenes of Clerical Life" should be republished, I have no doubt we shall find it easy to arrange the terms. In the meantime, the most pressing business is, to make them worth republishing. I think the particularization of the children in the deathbed scene has an important effect on the imagination. But I have removed all names from the 'Conclusion,' except those of Patty and Dickey, in whom, I hope, the reader has a personal interest.

I hope to send you the second story by the beginning of February. It will lie, for the most part, among quite different scenes and persons from the last—opening in Shepperton once more, but presently moving away to a distant spot and new people, whom, I hope, you will not like less than Amos and his friends. But if any one of the succeeding stories should seem to you unsuitable to the pages of Maga, it can be reserved for publication in the future volume, without creating any difficulty.

Thanking you very warmly for the hearty acceptance you have given to my first story, I remain, my dear Sir,

Yours very truly,
The Author of Amos Barton.

TO JOHN BLACKWOOD, 4 FEBRUARY 1857

Blackwood reported divided opinions of "Amos Barton" among his friends. GE again defended her simple realism by analogy with Dutch painting in *Adam Bede*, Chapter 17. This is the first appearance of the nom de plume *George Eliot*; she chose *George* because of GHL and *Eliot* because it was "a good mouth-filling, easily pronounced word." [II, 291–92]

[8 Park Shot, Richmond] February 4. 57.

My dear Sir

Thank you for your last kind letter, fulfilling your promise to let me know something of the criticisms passed on my story. I have a very moderate respect for "opinions of the press," but the private opinions of intelligent people may be valuable to me. In reference to artistic presentation, much adverse opinion will of course arise from a dislike to the *order* of art rather than from a critical estimate of the execution. Any one who detests the Dutch school in general will hardly appreciate fairly the merits of a particular Dutch painting. And against this sort of condemnation, one must steel oneself as one best can. But objections which point out to me any vice of manner or any failure in producing an intended effect will be really profitable. For example, I suppose my scientific illustrations must be a fault, since they seem to have obtruded themselves disagreeably on one of my readers. But if it be a sin to be at once a man of science and a writer of fiction, I can declare my perfect innocence on that head, my scientific knowledge being as superficial as that of the most "practised writers."

I hope to send you a second story in a few days, but I am rather behind-hand this time, having been prevented from setting to work for some weeks by other business; and having, since then, been retarded by a bilious attack—surely one of the worst among the 'calamities of authors.'

I shall be glad to know if people think the better of 'Amos' from reading it to the end—and even if they think the worse, it will be better for me to know it. Whatever may be the success of my stories, I shall be resolute in preserving my incognito, having observed that a *nom de plume* secures all the advantages without the disagreeables of reputation. Perhaps, therefore, it will be well to give you my prospective name, as a tub to throw to the whale in case of curious inquiries, and accordingly I subscribe myself, best and most sympathizing of editors,

Yours very truly,
George Eliot.

TO JOHN BLACKWOOD, 18 FEBRUARY 1857

In sending her the proof of "Mr. Gilfil's Love-story," Blackwood had suggested that she make the hero less "abjectly devoted" to a girl whose "heart is *openly* devoted to a Jack-anapes"; but he added that he must not speculate on her plot, having read only the first part of the story. GE removed the French phrases Blackwood had queried in proof, but refused to alter her conception of the characters. [II, 298–99]

[8 Park Shot, Richmond] February 18th 1857.
My dear Sir
First let me thank you very heartily for your letter of the 10th. Except your own cordial appreciation, which is so much beyond a mere official acceptance, that little fact about Albert Smith has gratified me more than anything else in connection with the effect of 'Amos.' If you should happen to hear an opinion from Thackeray, good or bad, I should like to know it. You will see that I have availed myself of your suggestions on points of language. I quite recognize the justice of your criticism on the French phrases. They are not in keeping with my story. But I am unable to alter anything in relation to the delineation or development of character, as my stories always grow out of my psychological conception of the dramatis personae. For example the behaviour of Caterina in the gallery is essential to my conception of her nature and to the development of that nature in the plot. My artistic bent is directed not at all to the presentation of eminently irreproachable characters, but to the presentation of mixed human beings in such

a way as to call forth tolerant judgment, pity, and sympathy. And I cannot stir a step aside from what I *feel* to be *true* in character. If anything strikes you as untrue to human nature in my delineations, I shall be very glad if you will point it out to me, that I may reconsider the matter. But alas! inconsistencies and weaknesses are not untrue.

I hope that your doubts about the plot will be removed by the further development of the story. Meanwhile, with the warmest thanks for your encouraging letters, I remain

Yours very sincerely
George Eliot.

I hope to send the 3d Part in a few days.

TO JOHN BLACKWOOD, 14 MARCH 1857

As editor of a family magazine, Blackwood was constantly on guard against anything that would offend sensibilities. With the proof of the final part of "Mr. Gilfil's Love-story" he expressed grave doubts about the dagger that Caterina took out, intending to kill the sleeping Wybrow, and suggested that she might merely *dream* of taking it. In sending a cheque for £45 for GHL to hand "to the mysterious George Eliot," he repeated his doubts about the "dadger." He added: "By all means let the incognito be kept. Shall I say to anxious inquirers that the *Scenes* are by one George Eliot of whom I know nothing?" [II, 309–10]

[8 Park Shot, Richmond] March 14. 1857.
My dear Sir

The cheque and the proof have reached me and I am much obliged by your ready attention in both matters. I am glad you retain a doubt in favour of the 'dadger,' and wish I could convert you to entire approval, for I am much more satisfied when your feeling is thoroughly with me. But it would be the death of my story to substitute a dream for the real scene. Dreams usually play an important part in fiction, but rarely, I think, in actual life. So many of us have reason to know that criminal impulses may be felt by a nature which is nevertheless guarded by its entire constitution from the commission of crime, that I can't help hoping my Caterina will not forfeit the sympathy of all my readers.

The answer you propose to give to curious inquirers is the best possible. For several reasons I am very anxious to retain my incognito for some time to come, and to an author not already famous, anonymity is the highest *prestige*. Besides, if George Eliot turns out a dull dog and an ineffective writer—a mere flash in the pan—I, for one, am determined to cut him on the first intimation of that disagreeable fact. The fates have willed that this shall be a very melancholy story, and I am longing to be a little merrier again. Ever, my dear Sir,

Yours very truly (incognito apart)
George Eliot.

TO MRS. CHARLES BRAY, 5 APRIL [1857]

Chrissey Clarke's eight-year-old Fanny died 28 March. [II, 313–14]

St. Mary's | Scilly Isles | April 5.

Dear Cara . . .

We are more and more in love with these little islands. There is not a tree to be seen, but there are grand granite piles on the coast such as I never saw before, and furze covered hills with larks soaring and singing above them, and zoological wonders on the shore to fill our bottles and our souls at once. Mr. Lewes seems already to have recovered the ground he had lost in health during our last few months at Richmond, and by and bye I hope I shall flourish too, but for some time I have been unusually weak and knock-up-able. Our landlady is an excellent woman, but, like almost all peculiarly domestic women, has not more than rudimentary ideas of cooking, and in an island where you can get nothing but beef, except by sending to Penzance, that supreme science has its maximum value. She seems to think eating a purely arbitrary procedure—an abnormal function of mad people who come to Scilly, and if we ask her what the people live on here is quite at a loss to tell us, apparently thinking the question relates to the abstruser portion of Natural History. But I insist, and give her a culinary lecture every morning, and we do in the end get fed. Altogether, our life here is so far better than the golden age that we work as well [as] play.

That is the happy side of things. But there is a very sad one to me, which I shall not dwell upon—only tell you of. More than a week ago, I received the news that poor Chrissey had lost one of her pretty little girls of fever, that the other little one—they were the only two she had at home with her—was also dangerously ill, and Chrissey herself and her servant apparently attacked by typhus too. The distressing part of it is our being here, away so far out of reach of post and out of possibility of my going to her! The thought of her in this state is a perpetual shadow to me in the sunshine. Best love to all. Ever, dear Cara,

Your affectionate
Marian.

TO ISAAC EVANS, 16 APRIL [1857]

Kate Clarke was not yet six years old. [II, 317–18]

St. Mary's | Scilly Isles | April 16.

My dear Brother

I have been looking anxiously for some further tidings of Chrissey since your last letter which told me that she and Kate were better, though not out of danger. I try to hope that no news is good news, but if you do not think it troublesome to write, I shall be thankful to have that hope changed into certainty.

Meanwhile to save multiplying letters, which I know you are not fond of, I mention now what will take no harm from being mentioned rather prematurely. I

should like Chrissey to have £15 of my next half-year's income due at the beginning of June, to spend in taking a change of air as soon as she is able to do so; and
perhaps if it were desirable for her to leave before the money has been paid in, you
would be so kind as to advance it for a few weeks. I am writing of course in
ignorance of her actual state, but I should think it must be good for her, as soon as
she is able to move, to leave that fever-infected place for a time with Katy, and I
know the money must have gone very fast in recent expenses. I only suggest the
change of air as the thing that I should think best for Chrissey, but in any case I
should like her to have the money to do what she pleases with it. If she is well
enough, please to give her the enclosed note, in which I have suggested to her
what I have just written to you.

I was much obliged to you for your last letter, and shall be still more so, if you
will write me word of Chrissey's present condition. Hoping you are all well at your
own home, I am ever

Your affectionate sister,
Marian Evans.

TO SARA HENNELL, 16 APRIL [1857]

GE was reading *Oedipus Rex* in Greek and was about to begin the *Coloneus*. In the evenings
she read aloud *Cranford, Northanger Abbey, Persuasion,* and some Shakespeare. In her
Charlotte Brontë Mrs. Gaskell published a lurid story of how the mother of Branwell's pupil
urged him to elope with her. Her husband the Reverend Edmund Robinson dismissed him
and in his will bequeathed his property to her on condition that she never again see
Branwell, who thereupon "began his career as an habitual drunkard and to drown his
remorse." Threatened with a libel suit, Mrs. Gaskell withdrew the passages. Sara's *Christianity and Infidelity* had been favourably reviewed. [II, 318–20]

St. Mary's, Scilly | April 16.
Dear Sara . . .

We are enjoying a retrogression to old-fashioned reading:—George buries
himself in big physiological books, German French and English, with broad pages
spreading like a prairie, unbroken by paragraph or quotation; I rush on the
slightest pretext to Sophocles and am as excited about blind old Oedipus as any
young lady can be about the latest hero with magnificent eyes.

But there is *one* new book we have been enjoying—and so, I hope, have you.
The "Life of Charlotte Bronte"! Deeply affecting throughout:—in the early part
romantic, poetic as one of her own novels; in the later years tragic, especially to
those who know what sickness is. Mrs. Gaskell has done her work admirably, both
in the industry and care with which she has gathered and selected her material,
and in the feeling with which she has presented it. There is one exception,
however, which I regret very much. She sets down Branwell's conduct entirely to
remorse, and the falseness of that position weakens the effect of her philippics
against the woman who hurried on his utter fall. Remorse may make sad work with
a man, but it would not make such a life as Branwell's was in the last three or four

years unless the the germs of vice had sprouted and shot up long before, as it seems clear they had in him. What a tragedy—that picture of the old father and the three sisters, trembling day and night in terror at the possible deeds of this drunken brutal son and brother! That is the part of the life which affects me most.

I have looked with anxiety for a letter from my brother, on each of the two post days since he wrote last, but nothing has come. I try to think that Chrissey must be going on well, but I am very uneasy. . . .

We have wonderful descriptions from Barbara Smith of the glorious scenery and strange picturesque life she finds in Algiers. It really seems an easy way of bringing the tropics near to one's imagination, to take that short journey. In less than a week's easy travelling you are among palms and Arabs and wild horses and lions and panthers, and I don't know what beside. She dashes down sketches with her pen and ink, making arrow-heads to indicate the bark of Jackals!

Tell me any news you hear about your book, and about other things too when you are inclined. You know you live in the thick of the world and 'Society' compared with us. Best love to Cara and to the gas-lighted-content-radiating-nap-after-dinner-taking-leg-rest-enjoying- and ever-by-Pollian-remembered-affectionately-presiding genius of Ivy Cottage. And love, also best, to you, dear successful author, from your old friend

Marian.

TO ISAAC EVANS, 26 MAY 1857

[II, 331–32]

Rosa Cottage | Gorey | Jersey | May 26th 1857.

My dear Brother

You will be surprized, I dare say, but I hope not sorry, to learn that I have changed my name, and have someone to take care of me in the world. The event is not at all a sudden one, though it may appear sudden in its announcement to you. My husband has been known to me for several years, and I am well acquainted with his mind and character. He is occupied entirely with scientific and learned pursuits, is several years older than myself, and has three boys, two of whom are at school in Switzerland, and one in England.

We shall remain at the coast here, or in Brittany for some months, on account of my health, which has for some time been very frail, and which is benefited by the sea air. The winter we shall probably spend in Germany. But any inconvenience about money payments to me may, I suppose, be avoided if you will be kind enough to pay my income to the account of Mr. G. H. Lewes, into the Union Bank of London, Charing Cross Branch, 4, Pall Mall East, Mr. Lewes having an account there.

I wrote to you many weeks ago from Scilly, enclosing a letter to Chrissey, which if you received it, you would of course put by for her, as it was written in ignorance of her extreme illness. But as I have not received any intimation that my letter reached you, I think it safest to repeat its chief purport, which was to request that you would pay £15 of my present half year's income to Chrissey. I shall also be much obliged if you will inform me how Chrissey is, and whether she is strong enough to make it desirable for me to write to her. . . .

We are not at all rich people, but we are both workers, and shall have enough for our wants.

I hope you are all well and that Sarah is recovered from her fatigues and anxieties. With love to her and all my tall nephews and nieces, I remain, dear Isaac,

Your affectionate Sister
Marian Lewes.

TO MRS. HENRY HOUGHTON, 2 JUNE 1857

This is the earliest reference to Joseph Liggins, who had been mentioned in the *Manx Sun* as the probable author of *Scenes of Clerical Life*. [II, 336–37]

Rosa Cottage | Gorey | Jersey | June 2. 57.

Dear Fanny . . .

Thanks—a thousand thanks, dear Fanny for your letter. I have just written to Chrissey, being unable to wait another post after hearing that I *might* write to her, and finding I have yet a few minutes I write to you also. I hope Chrissey *will* be able to have some change of air for I begged Isaac to pay her £15 from me for that purpose. I do trust the money will not be absolutely wanted for anything else. I wish I could do more, but my poverty, not my will restricts me. Pray do something, if you can to urge that the money should be so applied. I don't mean that you should do it *obviously* or directly, or that you should appear to know anything about that sum, but simply that you should insist on the importance of leaving that hotbed of fever for a time.

You are wrong about Mr. Liggins or rather your informants are wrong. We too have been struck with the "Clerical Sketches," and I have recognized some figures and traditions connected with our old neighbourhood. But Blackwood informs Mr. Lewes that the author is a Mr. Eliot, a clergyman, I presume. *Au reste,* he may be a relation of Mr. Liggins's or some other 'Mr.' who knows Coton stories.

Have you read Currer Bell's Life by Mrs. Gaskell? Do—it will deeply interest you.

With kindest regards and best wishes for Henry's recovery, I am ever, dear Fanny

Your affectionate Sister
Marian Lewes *alias* Polly.

TO MRS. CHARLES BRAY, 5 JUNE 1857

In March 1858 Eliza Lynn married William Linton, a widower with seven children. In 1866 he left her and went with his younger daughters to America. Like GE, Eliza had visited Dr. Brabant at Devizes. [II, 338–40]

Rosa Cottage | Gorey | Jersey | June 5. 57.

Dear Cara

I could have wished myself at Richmond even in this hot weather for the sake of seeing you, but no pleasure short of that could have made me wish to be in the hazy atmosphere of London environs. Richmond is *not* fascinating in "the season" or through the summer—it is hot, noisy and haunted with cockneys; but at other times we love the Park with an increasing love, and we have such a kind good landlady there that it always seems like going home when we return to Park Shot. She writes to us "I hope you will make your fortune—but you must always live with me," which, considering that she gets less out of us than other lodgers is a proof of affection in a landlady. We shall be obliged to return thither in the middle or at the end of July on business matters, but for a short time only; for at the end of August Mr. Lewes is going to take Bertie the youngest boy to join his elder brothers at Hofwyl, and we shall if possible remain in Germany till the end of October. Yes! we like our wandering life at present; it is fructifying and brings us material in many ways; but we keep in perspective the idea of a cottage among green fields and cows, where we mean to settle down (after we have once been to Italy) and buy pots and kettles and keep a dog. The boys are going on so well at Hofwyl, and write charming letters. They are sweet-natured clever lads; the third, Bertie, has been sickly and stupid at books hitherto, but there is no knowing what boys and girls will turn into. Wherever we are, we work hard—and at work which brings *present* money; for we have too many depending on us to be dilettanti or idlers. . . .

Your gossip was very interesting to us, for we hear scarcely anything but what gets into the weekly newspapers, and not much of that. We had only heard of Miss Lynn, that she was going to marry Linton, the engraver. Your description of her devotion to those seven children is very pretty. Her large-hearted energy is something to admire and love her for. I laughed heartily at the Brabantian recitation which "sounds very grand on the other side of the wall." . . .

You wonder how my face has changed in the last three years. Doubtless it is older and uglier, but it ought not to have a bad expression, for I never have anything to call out my ill-humour or discontent—which you know were always ready enough to come on slight call—and I have everything to call out love and gratitude. I seem to have said nothing, yet here I am at the end of my sheet. *My best love and Mr. Lewes's kind regards to Mr. Bray.* I must give the other sheet to Sara.

Ever your affectionate
Marian.

TO SARA HENNELL, [5 JUNE 1857]

Bessie Parkes's father "did not remain faithful" to her mother, who had no sympathy for Bessie's passionate altruism. [II, 341–42]

Dear Sara . . .

Barbara has written us such descriptions of the splendour and romance to be found in Algiers, that we can't help envying people who can 'do the Tropics' in miniature by going thither in 5 days for £12! Miss Parkes was there a little while, and is now I believe in Italy with Mrs. Jameson. I am so glad to think of her travelling with people who have hearts and souls, for the Savile Row establishment is not richly provided with those commodities. Alas! What skeletons there are in houses where things look so enviable! . . .

I have written to my brother and my two sisters, telling them that I have changed my name and have a husband. Fanny has already answered me in a very kind letter. I have not yet heard from my Brother. I feel satisfied to have done this, for they are now acquainted with what is *essential* in my position, and if any utterly false report reaches them in the first instance, their minds will be prepared not to accept it without reserve. I do not think Chrissey will give up correspondence with me in any case, and that is the point I most care about, as I shall still be able to help her as far as my means will allow.

The "rumours" you mention have I dare say come through the Smiths and Mrs. Pears—friendly head-shakings and regrets which are meant in the best spirit. I have kept the subject so long before my mind, and have learned to see how much of the pain I have felt concerning my own family is really love of approbation in disguise, that I look calmly on the most disagreeable issues. If I live five years longer, the positive result of my existence on the side of truth and goodness will outweigh the small negative good that would have consisted in my not doing anything to shock others, and I can conceive no consequences that will make me repent the past. Do not misunderstand me and suppose that I think myself heroic or great in any way. Far enough from that! Faulty, miserably faulty I am—but least of all faulty when others most blame.

Ever thine in headachiness
Pollian.

TO MRS. JOHN CASH, 6 JUNE 1857

Mary Sibree was married to John Cash, a ribbon manufacturer in Coventry, who had bought Rosehill from the Brays when they moved to Ivy Cottage close by. [II, 343–44]

Rosa Cottage | Gorey | Jersey | June 6. 57.

Dear Friend

Your letter was very sweet to me. The sense of my deficiencies in the past often presses on me with a discouraging weight, and to know that any one can remember me lovingly helps me to believe that there has been some good to balance the evil. I like to think of you as a happy wife and mother, and since Rosehill *must* have new tenants I like to think that you and yours are there rather than any one else, not only because of my own confidence in your nature, but because our dear friends love you so much as a neighbour. You know I can never feel otherwise than sorry that they should not have ended their days in that pretty home; but the inevitable regret is softened as much as possible by the fact that the home has become yours. . . .

I am very happy—happy in the highest blessing life can give us, the perfect love and sympathy of a nature that stimulates my own to healthful activity. I feel, too, that all the terrible pain I have gone through in past years partly from the defects of my own nature, partly from outward things, has probably been a preparation for some special work that I may do before I die. That is a blessed hope—to be rejoiced in with trembling. But even if that hope should be unfulfilled, I am contented to have lived and suffered for the sake of what has already been.

You see, your kind letter has made me inclined to talk about myself, but as we do not often have any communication with each other, I know it will be a gratification to your sympathetic nature to have a few direct words from me that will assure you of my moral well-being. I hope your little ones are just like you— just as fair and sweet-tempered. Goodbye, and believe me

> Always your affectionate friend
> Marian Lewes.

TO JOHN BLACKWOOD, 11 JUNE 1857

Blackwood confessed that he was "rather puzzled" by the first part of "Janet's Repentance" and urged GE to "*soften* your picture as much as you can. Your sketches this time are all written in the harsher Thackerayan view of human nature. . . . When are you going to give us a really good active working clergyman, neither absurdly evangelical nor absurdly High Church?" [II, 347–49]

> Rosa Cottage, Gorey | June 11. 57.

My dear Sir

I am not much surprised, and not at all hurt by your letter received today with the proof. It is a great satisfaction—in fact my only satisfaction, that you should give me your judgment with perfect frankness. I am able, I think, to enter into an editor's doubts and difficulties, and to see my stories in some degree from your point of view as well as my own. My answer is written after considering the question as far as possible on all sides, and as I feel that I shall not be able to make any other than *superficial* alterations in the proof, I will, first of all, say what I can in explanation of the spirit and future course of the present story.

The collision in the drama is not at all between "bigotted churchmanship" and evangelicalism, but between *ir*religion and religion. Religion in this case happens to be represented by evangelicalism, and the story so far as regards the *persecution*, is a real bit in the religious history of England that happened about eight-and-twenty years ago. I thought I had made it apparent in my sketch of Milby feelings on the advent of Mr. Tryan that the conflict lay between immorality and morality—irreligion and religion. Mr. Tryan will carry the reader's sympathy. It is through him that Janet is brought to repentance. Dempster's vices have their natural evolution in deeper and deeper moral deterioration (though not without softening touches) and death from intemperance. Everything is softened from the fact, so far as art is permitted to soften and yet to remain essentially true. The real town was more vicious than my Milby; the real Dempster was far more disgusting than mine; the real Janet alas! had a far sadder end than mine, who will melt away from the reader's sight in purity, happiness and beauty.

My sketches both of churchmen and dissenters, with whom I am almost equally acquainted, are drawn from close observation of them in real life, and not at all from hearsay or from the descriptions of novelists. . . . If I were to undertake to alter Dempster's language or character, I should be attempting to represent some vague conception of what may possibly exist in other people's minds, but has no existence in my own. Such of your marginal objections as relate to a mere detail I can meet without difficulty by alteration; but as an artist I should be utterly powerless if I departed from my own conceptions of life and character. There is nothing to be done with the story, but either to let Dempster and Janet and the rest be as I *see* them, or to renounce it as too painful. I am keenly alive, at once to the scruples and alarms an editor may feel, and to my own utter inability to write under any cramping influence, and on this double ground I should like you to consider whether it will not be better to close the series for the Magazine *now*. I daresay you will feel no difficulty about publishing a volume containing the story of Janet's Repentance, though you may not like to hazard its insertion in the Magazine, and I shall accept that plan with no other feeling than that you have been to me the most liberal and agreeable of editors and are the man of all others I would choose for a publisher. . . .

When I remember what have been the successes in fiction even as republications from Maga I can hardly believe that the public will regard my pictures as exceptionally coarse. But in any case there are too many prolific writers who devote themselves to the production of pleasing pictures, to the exclusion of all disagreeable truths for me to desire to add one to their number. In this respect, at least, I may have some resemblance to Thackeray, though I am not conscious of being in any way a disciple of his, unless it constitute discipleship to think him, as I suppose the majority of people with any intellect do, on the whole the most powerful of living novelists.

I will retain the proof until I receive an answer from you. In the meanwhile, I remain, my dear Sir,

Yours with sincere regard and obligation
George Eliot.

TO VINCENT HOLBECHE, 13 JUNE 1857

When drawing up her father's will, Holbeche had suggested that he leave GE £100 in cash instead of her share in household goods. [II, 349–50]

Rosa Cottage | Gorey | Jersey | June 13. 1857.

My dear Sir

I have just received your letter written to me by my brother's request, and I willingly reply to it at once by a statement of the facts concerning which you desire information; the more so, because I anticipated the probability of my having to correspond with you as joint Trustee under my Father's Will. My brother has judged wisely in begging you to communicate with me. If his feelings towards me are unfriendly, there is no necessity for his paining himself by any direct intercourse with me; indeed, if he had written to me in a tone which I could not recognize (since I am not conscious of having done him any injury) I must myself have employed a third person as a correspondent.

Mr. Lewes is a well-known writer, author among other things, of the 'Life of Goethe' and the 'Biographical History of Philosophy.' Our marriage is not a legal one, though it is regarded by us both as a sacred bond. He is unable at present to contract a legal marriage, because, though long deprived of his first wife by her misconduct, he is not legally divorced. I have been his wife and have borne his name for nearly three years; a fact which has been known to all my personal friends except the members of my own family, from whom I have withheld it because, knowing that their views of life differ in many respects from my own, I wished not to give them unnecessary pain. Other considerations, however, have at length determined me to inform them of my circumstances and of the responsibilities for life, which I have undertaken.

It may be desirable to mention to you that I am not dependent on any one, the larger part of my income for several years having been derived from my own constant labour as a writer. You will perceive, therefore, that in my conduct towards my own family I have not been guided by any motives of self-interest, since I have been neither in the reception nor the expectation of the slightest favour from them. Mr. Lewes, as I have already stated, has an account at the Union Bank of London, Charing Cross Branch, 4 Pall Mall East. I have requested that any money due to me may be paid to his account there, because, as we are frequently out of England and away from town, the transmission of cheques is attended with much inconvenience. I presume that I have a legal right to appoint the payment of interest due to me to any person I may choose to name. But if there is any point necessary to be taken into consideration, which I have overlooked or of which I am ignorant, you will be good enough to set me right.

I have satisfaction in communicating with you in this case, rather than with anyone else, not only because you kindly undertook, from friendship to my Father, to become my trustee, but because I learned from him that it was owing to your considerate suggestion that some provision was made for me during the first year after my Father's death. I daresay you have forgotten the circumstance, but I have always remembered gratefully that instance of thoughtfulness on my behalf, and am glad to have an opportunity of acknowledging it. I remain, my dear Sir,

Yours very faithfully
Marian Lewes.

Vincent Holbeche Esq.

TO JOHN BLACKWOOD, 16 JUNE 1857

To GE's suggestion that they close the *Scenes* Blackwood replied: "I do not fall in with George Eliots every day, and the idea of stopping the Series as suggested in your letter gave me 'quite a turn' to use one of Thackeray's favourite phrases. There is nothing in the part that can make me 'afraid' to publish it. . . . In continuing to write for the Magazine I beg of all things that you will not consider yourself hampered in any way." [II, 353]

Rosa Cottage | Gorey | June 16th/57.

My dear Sir
    Thanks for your kind letter. It shows that you have understood me, and will give me confidence for the future. I have attended, I think, to all your marginal observations except one, and have been able to make several omissions and introduce several touches which I hope you will find an agreeable modification of the second chapter, when you read it in revise. I wish I could send you more M.S., but unfortunately I have not enough in readiness for you, to make that worth while.
    The descriptions of character are not so alien to the drama as they possibly appear to you at present, and several other things that seem to have puzzled you will I dare say, become clear as the story proceeds. I will forward the next part as soon as I can possibly get it in a state of completeness and now I have your cordial words to give me confidence it will go on more swimmingly.
    I heartily respond to your wish that our literary intercourse may continue—for that wish includes many good things. It means that I shall go on writing what will stir men's hearts to sympathy as well as that I shall have all the pleasures and advantages involved in the possession of a generous editor. That that editor may one day become a personal friend is a prospect which I hope I may indulge without proving too sanguine. Ever, my dear Sir,

Yours very truly
George Eliot.

TO JOHN BLACKWOOD, 12 [JULY] 1857

When reprinted in *Scenes of Clerical Life* "the Misses Pittman" was restored to "the Miss Pittmans" etc. Blackwood had written that the lampoon of Mr. Tryan did not make him laugh, and that he wished the bishop "had been a better sample of the cloth." GHL added a postscript to a letter to Blackwood the same day: "Entre nous let me hint that unless you have any *serious* objection to make to Eliot's stories, *don't* make any. He is so easily discouraged, so diffident of himself, that not being prompted by necessity to write, he will close the series in the belief that his writing is not relished. I laugh at him for his diffidence and tell him it's a proof he is *not* an author. But he has passed the middle of life without writing at all, and will easily be made to give it up. *Don't allude to this hint of mine.* He wouldn't like my interfering." [II, 361–62]

Rosa Cottage | Gorey | Jersey | June 12. 57.

My dear Sir

By today's post I return the proof of Part 2. Part 1 was printed as I wished in every respect except one. The printer's reader made a correction after I saw the proof, and though he may sometimes do so with advantage, as I am very liable to overlook mistakes, I in this case particularly object to his alteration, and I mention it in order to request that it may not occur again. He has everywhere substituted the form— "the Misses So and So" for "the Miss So and Sos"—a form which in England is confined to public announcements, to the backs of letters, and to the conversation of schoolmistresses. It is not the conversational English of good society, and causes the most disagreeable jolt in an easy style of narrative or description.

I think you have rather mistaken the intention of the jokes in the play-bill. They are not meant by any means as Attic wit, but as *Milby* wit, and any really fine sarcasm would be out of place. I have altered the conclusion a little to prevent that mistake in the reader. It would not do, I think, to substitute vagueness for particularity in this instance, and omit the play-bill. In the real persecution, a play-bill of an equally insulting kind was printed and circulated and thought the finest joke imaginable. My own impression on rereading very carefully the account of the confirmation is, that readers will perceive, what is the fact—that I am not in the least occupying myself with confirmation in general, or with Bishops in general, but with a particular confirmation, and a particular Bishop.

Art must be either real and concrete, or ideal and eclectic. Both are good and true in their way, but my stories are of the former kind. I undertake to exhibit nothing as it should be; I only try to exhibit some things as they have been or are, seen through such a medium as my own nature gives me. The moral effect of the stories of course depends on my power of seeing truly and feeling justly; and as I am not conscious of looking at things through the medium of cynicism or irreverence, I can't help hoping that there is no tendency in what I write to produce those miserable mental states. The interest of the next part will turn entirely on Janet and Mr. Tryan. . . .

Ever, my dear Sir,

Yours very truly
George Eliot.

TO JOHN BLACKWOOD, [5 SEPTEMBER 1857]

This is the earliest reference to *Adam Bede*. For the three stories in *Maga* Blackwood had paid GE a total of £263. [II, 381]

[Richmond]

My dear Sir

I am much obliged to you for your letter of the 31st enclosing a cheque for £20. Part IV will have reached you, I hope, by the time you receive this letter. With Part V the story will end. Unless there be any strong reason to the contrary, I should like to close the series with this story. According to my calculation, which however may be an erroneous one, the three stories will make two good volumes, i.e. good as to bulk.

I have a subject in my mind which will not come under the limitations of the title "Clerical Life," and I am inclined to take a large canvas for it, and write a novel. In case of my writing fiction for Maga again, I should like to be considerably beforehand with my work, so that you can read a thoroughly decisive portion before beginning to print.

According to my calculation, a page of Maga makes three good pages of a novel, and in that case the three stories would make 2 volumes of 300 pages each. But if I am wrong, you will be good enough to set me right. Ever, my dear Sir,

Yours very truly
George Eliot.

TO BESSIE PARKES, [24 SEPTEMBER 1857]

Bessie had joined Emily Faithfull in editing the *Waverley Journal*, "Conducted by Women," in which she tried to enlist GE's interest. Accompanied by GHL, she called at the office and was introduced by Bessie to her partner as "Miss Evans." [II, 384–85]

8 Park Shot | Richmond | Thursday.

Dear Bessie

This letter comes by way of postscript to our interview yesterday. First, it did me good to see you—the warm unmistakeable affection in your face was a sweet cordial to me.

Secondly, you must please not call me *Miss Evans* again. I have renounced that name, and do not mean to be known by it in any way. It is Mr. Lewes's wish that the few friends who care about me should recognize me as Mrs. Lewes, and my Father's Trustee sends me receipts to sign as Marian Lewes, so that my adoption of the name has been made a matter of business. There is not much probability of such a chance as that of your having to introduce me should occur again. But I think it better to write on the subject to you while it is in my memory, to prevent the possibility of a future mistake.

There is another thing I want to say, though perhaps it is superfluous. Mr. Lewes was afraid you would misunderstand my words about "Providence bringing you to Richmond" as an invitation, which it would be quite indelicate in me to give in the present state of our relative circumstances—i.e. of *your* circumstances and *mine*. I don't think you would misunderstand me so far—you know that I would not for the world have you do anything that should cause "your good to be evil spoken of." I meant that some unforeseen good luck might bring you to Richmond and that I might see you without causing offence to any one.

Ever your loving
Marian E. Lewes.

TO JOHN BLACKWOOD, 17 OCTOBER 1857

GHL's hint to Blackwood about GE's diffidence was heeded. On reading the concluding chapters of "Janet's Repentance" he wrote: "I was a little puzzled when I came to the climax about the bottle of brandy but you have rearranged it beautifully and it contributes to the air of truth. Should there be so much of Dempster's delirium? I daresay the effect would be lessened if it was shortened. Tryan's death is finely painted and I think few can fail to be affected by the closing scenes of the good man's life." He was eager to hear about the new novel. Through GHL's shrewd advice GE secured £180 for a first edition of 1,000 copies of *Scenes of Clerical Life* and retained the copyright. [II, 387–88]

[Richmond] Saturday | October 17. 57.

My dear Sir

I am very much gratified that my Janet has won your heart and kept up your interest in her to the end. I return the proof by today's post.

My new story haunts me a good deal, and I shall set about it without delay. It will be a country story—full of the breath of cows and the scent of hay. But I shall not ask you to look at it till I have written a volume or more, and then you will be able to judge whether you will prefer printing it in the Magazine, or publishing it as a separate novel when it is completed.

By the way, the sheets of the "Clerical Scenes" are not come, but I shall not want to make any other than verbal and literal corrections, so that it will hardly be necessary for me to go through the sheets *and* the proofs, which I must of course see. I enclose a title page with a motto. But if you don't like the motto, I give it up. I've not set my heart on it.

I leave the number of copies to be published, and the style of getting up, entirely to your discretion. As to the terms, I wish to retain the copyright, according to the stipulation made for me by Lewes when he sent "Amos Barton," and whatever you can afford to give me for the first edition, I shall prefer having as a definite payment rather than as half profits. You stated, in a letter about "Amos Barton," your willingness to accede to either plan, so I have no hesitation in expressing my wishes. I remain, my dear Sir,

Always yours truly
George Eliot.

TO CHARLES BRAY, 30 OCTOBER 1857

Bray's pamphlet on *The Industrial Employment of Women* contrasted conditions in the watch trade, in which they were not employed, and the ribbon trade, in which they were. Barbara Bodichon's *Women and Work* referred to ill-done work as the plague of human society. "People are grasping after some grandiose task, something 'worthy' of their powers, when the only proof of capacity they give is to do small things badly." [II, 396]

Richmond | October 30. 57.

Dear Friend

Thank you for sending me your pamphlet, which I have read with much interest. It brings forward some important points for the consideration of our reformers. The picture you give of the results of female labour in factories is sad enough. How is it that the results have been so different at Lowell?

That passage you quote from Mrs. Bodichon's book about "doing small things badly" is mine. She did me the honor to copy it from a letter I wrote to her, and that word—"Conscience goes to the hammering in of nails" is my Gospel. There can be no harm in preaching *that* to women, at any rate. But I should be sorry to undertake any more specific enunciation of doctrine on a question so entangled as the "Woman Question." The part of the Epicurean gods is always an easy one; but because I prefer it so strongly myself, I the more highly venerate those who are struggling in the thick of the contest.

"La carrière ouverte aux talents," whether the talents be feminine or masculine, I am quite confident is a right maxim. Whether "La carrière ouvert à la sottise," be equally just, when made equally universal, it would be too much like 'taking sides' for me to say.

Ever your affectionate Friend
Marian Lewes.

Charles Bray Esq.

TO JOHN BLACKWOOD, 7 NOVEMBER 1857

[II, 399–400]

[Richmond] November 7. 1857.

My dear Sir

It is pleasant to have the first sheet of one's proof—to see one's paragraphs released from the tight lacing of double columns, and expanding themselves at their ease. I perceive clearly the desirableness of the short number—for my observation of literary affairs has gone far enough to convince me that neither critical judgment nor practical experience can guarantee any opinion as to rapidity of sale, in the case of an unknown author; and I shudder at the prospect of encumbering my publishers' bookshelves.

My new story is in progress—slow progress at present. A little sunshine of success would stimulate its growth, I daresay. Unhappily, I am as impressionable as I am obstinate, and as much in need of sympathy from my readers as I am incapable of bending myself to their tastes. But if I can only find a public as cordial and agreeable in its treatment of me as my editor, I shall have nothing to wish. Even *my* thin skin will be comfortable then.

The page is not a shabby one, after all, but I fear the fact of two volumes instead of three is a fatal feature in my style in the eyes of librarians. Ever, my dear Sir,

Yours truly
George Eliot.

TO SARA HENNELL, [23 NOVEMBER 1857]

Sara's birthday was 23 November, GE's, 22; they had long exchanged greetings on the occasion. Chapman thought that she was a year younger than she was. Cross had 1820 engraved on her coffin instead of 1819, the date of her birth. [II, 404–05]

Richmond | Monday.

Dear Sara

The chinks of my time yesterday were so filled up with things I was obliged to attend to—proof-readings, etc. that I couldn't write to you. But I didn't forget to think of you gratefully, as we walked in the mild sunshine and looked at the purple and gold along the river.

Sometime, I *do* mean, if I can, to send you an ugly photograph, since you desire it, having perhaps a savage pleasure in perceiving how "the individual withers." I didn't give your letter to Mr. Lewes or tell him it was my birthday, for except you, I don't like anybody to say anything about it or make a fuss and congratulate me. Anniversaries are sad things—to one who has lived long and done little. . . .

Ever thine
Marian.

TO JOHN BLACKWOOD, 9 JANUARY 1858

At the prepublication subscription 580 copies were taken, 350 of them by Mudie's Library. In addition to Helps, copies were sent to Froude, Dickens, Thackeray, Tennyson, Ruskin, Faraday, Albert Smith, and Mrs. Thomas Carlyle. [II, 418–19]

Richmond | January 9. 1858.

My dear Sir

Thanks for your letter, and not less for the satisfaction I feel in the handsome getting up of the 'Scenes.' The two volumes are entirely agreeable to my eyes. The subscription far exceeds my highest hopes, and certainly hitherto everything has been auspicious. But we have of course still to wait for the proof of a real success.

As a matter of business I think it will be wise to send a copy to M. Emile Forgues, Bureau de la Revue des deux Mondes. I should also like a copy addressed to "The Author of Companions of my Solitude" (NOT *to Arthur Helps Esq.*), to be sent to Messrs. J. W. Parker and Son, and one to Professor Faraday. Besides these, I do not at present think of any one to whom I desire a copy to be sent on *literary* grounds, and I send none on private grounds. When I wish to drop my incognito, I will take a few intimate friends into my confidence, but not till then; and I shall not feel that wish for a long time to come. . . .

My new story goes on with a pleasant andante movement. I have read the early chapters to Lewes, who is a safer test than Molière could find in his housekeeper, I imagine, and he pronounces them to be better than anything I had done before. That is the best thing I have to tell you about it, and the next best is, that my heart is in the story. But I fear this last has been the case with very poor writers and very poor stories.

Always yours truly
George Eliot.

TO SARA HENNELL, 17 JANUARY 1858

The article in the January *Westminster* on "The Religious Weakness of Protestantism" was by F. W. Newman; that on Shelley by J. R. Wise. Charles Reade's novel *White Lies*, later made into a play, *The Double Marriage*, owed much to French playwrights. The strong laissez faire opinions in Spencer's article "State Tamperings with Money and Banks" stands in strong contrast to Ruskin's socialism. [II, 421–23]

Richmond | January 17. 58.

Dear Sara

Your letters are always seasonable whether it is the new year or the old or the middle-aged. "A pretty letter," Mr. Lewes said, when I read it to him. . . .

I fear many people will share your opinion about the article on the Religious Weakness of Protestantism; I don't know *who* wrote it. I confess it is very repugnant to me, though I abstained from saying so to Mr. Chapman, because I pity the sorrows of an editor. I have long ceased to feel any sympathy with mere antagonism and destruction, and all crudity of expression marks, I think, a deficiency in subtlety of thought as well as in breadth of moral and poetic feeling. The article on Shelley is a perfect puddle for an unfortunate editor to have fallen into. Can anything be more feebly foolish or foolishly feeble than that stuff about the 'blood-red hand of the baronet *covering up* atheism' and that false sarcasm on the same page about a mésalliance? I have not, of course read the article—I have only dipped in here and there, but a mere taste of an undone cake made with rancid butter is enough. . . . How could you waste your pretty eyes in reading 'White Lies'? Surely they are too precious to be spent on the inflated plagiarisms of a man gone mad with restless vanity and unveracity.

Herbert Spencer dined with us last week, and I had a talk with him about his monetary article, which interests me strongly. It is better written than his things have been of late, probably because it was written more rapidly. He cleared up several questions for me, and inclined me to think that he must be in the right. But I have not time at present to think of the subject except in a scrambling way. Apropos, I don't know whether you look out for Ruskin's books whenever they

appear. His little book on the Political Economy of Art contains some magnificent passages, mixed up with stupendous specimens of arrogant absurdity on some
economical points. But I venerate him as one of the great Teachers of the day—
his absurdities on practical points do no harm, but the grand doctrines of truth
and sincerity in art, and the nobleness and solemnity of our human life, which he
teaches with the inspiration of a Hebrew prophet, must be stirring up young minds
in a promising way. Mr. Lewes has been enjoying a week's holiday at Vernon Hill,
and was very pleased to find Alice Helps the eldest daughter there, a girl of
seventeen, become an enthusiastic student of painting under Ruskin, and stoutly
battling against the falsity that paints what the painter does not see. The two last
volumes of Modern Painters contain, I think, some of the finest writing of this
age. He is strongly akin to the sublimest part of Wordsworth, whom, by the bye,
we are reading now with fresh admiration for his beauties and tolerance for his
faults. . . .

Our present plans are:—to remain here till about the end of March, then to go
to Munich, which I long to see. We shall live there several months, seeing the
wonderful galleries in leisure moments. Our living here is so much more expensive
than living abroad that we save more than the expenses of our journeying, and as
our work can be as well done there as here for some months, we lay in much more
capital in the shape of knowledge and experience by going abroad. . . .

Ever your loving
Marian.

TO JOHN BLACKWOOD, 21 JANUARY 1858

In thanking the author for the Scenes, Dickens expressed his admiration of their extraordinary merit. "The exquisite truth and delicacy, both of the humour and the pathos of those
stories, I have never seen the like of. . . . I should have been strongly disposed, if I had
been left to my own devices, to address the said writer as a woman. I have observed what
seem to me to be such womanly touches, in those moving fictions, that the assurance on
the title-page is insufficient to satisfy me, even now. If they originated with no woman, I
believe that no man ever before had the art of making himself, mentally, so like a woman,
since the world began." Dickens was alone in this suspicion. [II, 424–25]

Richmond | January 21. 58.

My dear Sir
I'm sure you will be interested in Dickens's letter which I enclose, begging you
to return it as soon as you can, and not to allow any one besides yourself and Major
Blackwood to share in the knowledge of its contents. There can be no harm, of
course, in every one's knowing that Dickens admires the "Scenes," but I should
not like any more specific allusion made to the words of a private letter.

There can hardly be any climax of approbation for me after this, and I am so
deeply moved by the finely-felt and finely expressed sympathy of the letter, that
the iron mask of my incognito seems quite painful in forbidding me to tell Dickens

how thoroughly his generous impulse has been appreciated. If you should have an opportunity of conveying this feeling of mine to him in any way, you would oblige me by doing so. . . .

I remain, my dear Sir,

Yours very truly
George Eliot.

JOURNAL, 1 MARCH 1858

To his wife John Blackwood wrote: "I drove to Richmond to see Lewes, and was introduced to George Eliot—a woman (the Mrs. Lewes whom we suspected). This is to be kept a profound secret, and on all accounts it is desirable, as you will readily imagine. She is a most intelligent pleasant woman, with a face like a man, but a good expression. I am not to tell Langford the secret even. . . ." [II, 435–36]

On Sunday the 28th Mr. John Blackwood called on us, having come to London for a few days only. He talked a good deal about the "Clerical Scenes" and George Eliot, and at last asked, "Well, am I to see George Eliot this time?" G. said, "Do you wish to see him?" "As he likes—I wish it to be quite spontaneous." I left the room, and G. following me a moment, I told him he might reveal me. Blackwood was kind, came back when he found he was too late for the train, and said he would come to Richmond again. He came on the following Friday, and chatted very pleasantly—told us that Thackeray spoke highly of the "Scenes" and said *they were not written by a woman.* Mrs. Blackwood is *sure* they are not written by a woman. Mrs. Oliphant, the novelist, too is confident on the same side. I gave Blackwood the M.S. of my new novel to the end of the second scene in the wood. He opened it, read the first page, and smiling said, "This will do." We walked with him to Kew, and had a good deal of talk. Found, among other things, that he had lived two years in Italy when he was a youth, and that he admires Miss Austen.

TO MRS. CHARLES BRAY, 27 MARCH [1858]

The "lady of my acquaintance" was a photograph of GE taken 26 February 1858, which she inscribed: "To my sisters Cara and Sara." [VIII, 199–200]

[Richmond] March 27.

Dear Cara,

Your letter was very sweet to me, coming spontaneously, not a propos of a parcel. The feeling that you and Sara have been and always will be the women I have loved best in the world—the women I have had most reason to love and admire—strengthens instead of fading with time and absence. It is impossible ever to revive the past, and if we could recover the friend from whom we have parted we should perhaps find that we could not recover precisely the old relation. But that doesn't hinder the past from being sacred and belonging to our religion. I have some faith, too, that we should never lose our old fitness for each other, and that our talks together, and looks at each other must always be fuller of mutual understanding than we could find elsewhere.

In this faith I shall venture to recommend to you and Sara, a lady of my acquaintance in whom I have a peculiar interest. She will present herself to you shortly, with a note from my hand, and I believe that for my sake you will receive her with indulgence. I can't say much that is good of her, but I am confident that she will not misconduct herself in your society. She will sit in modest silence, looking ready to enjoy any joke that is passing.

Marian.

TO CHARLES BRAY, [29 MARCH 1858]

Though knowing that GE was writing busily, her friends were unable to identify any of her work in the *Westminster Review* and suspected that she might be writing a novel. The exposure of her psuedonym would have been disastrous. [II, 442–43]

[Richmond]

My dear Friend. . . .

Apropos, when do you bring out your new poem? I presume you are already in the Sixth Canto. It is true, you have never told me you intended to write a poem, nor have I heard any one say so who was likely to know. Nevertheless, I have quite as active an imagination as you, and I don't see why I shouldn't suppose you are writing a poem, as well as you suppose that I am writing a novel, and when the second edition of your Philosophy of Necessity comes out, I shall consider that a surreptitious affair, got up by a pseudo-Charles Bray, the real one being deeply engaged on his epic.

Seriously, I wish you would not set false rumours, or any other rumours afloat about me. They are injurious. Several people, who seem to derive their notions from Ivy Cottage, have spoken to me of a supposed novel I was going to bring out. Such things are damaging to me. It is true we *are* happy, but I don't know how you found it out from the book.

Ever yours
Marian.

TO MRS. CHARLES BRAY, [29 MARCH 1858]

Mrs. Bray had invited GE to Coventry before they went abroad. [II, 443]

[Richmond] Monday.

Impossible, my dear Cara, though I give you twenty spiritual kisses for wishing it. We set out next Monday, and there are all sorts of insuperable reasons why I couldn't leave home in the interim. But the aforesaid lady will not fail to make her appearance at Ivy Cottage and *she* will not turn Nelly out of her bed. . . .

In haste, ever your loving

Marian.

TO CHARLES BRAY, 31 MARCH [1858]

[II, 443–44]

Richmond | March 31.

Dear Friend

Thanks for your disclaimer. It shows me that you take a right view of the subject, and I feel sure that Sara too will on reflection see it in the same light. There is no undertaking more fruitful of absurd mistakes than that of "guessing" at authorship, and as I have never communicated to any one so much as an *intention* of a literary kind, there can be none but imaginary data for such guesses.

If I withhold anything from my friends which it would gratify them to know you will believe, I hope, that I have good reasons for doing so, and I am sure those friends will understand me when I ask them to further my object—which is not a whim but a question of solid interest—by complete silence. I can't afford to indulge either in vanity or sentimentality about my work. I have only a trembling anxiety to do what is in itself worth doing and by that honest means, to win very necessary profit of a temporal kind. "There is nothing hidden that shall not be revealed"—in due time. But till that time comes—till I tell you myself "This is the work of my hand and brain"—don't believe anything on the subject. There is no one who is in the least likely to know what I can, could, should or would write.

It would have been a great pleasure to me to see you all, but you perceive it was impossible. Goodbye, and love to all from

Yours ever affectionately
Marian Lewes.

I should have thought it might have been seen that Mr. Lewes is hardly in a vein for novel-writing. He is now engaged on a series of physiological papers for Blackwood, which are to be published separately as the "Physiology of Common Life."

TO JOHN BLACKWOOD, 1 APRIL 1858

As editor of a family magazine Blackwood had to be cautious about its moral tone. He wrote to GE: "The Captain's unfortunate attachment to Hetty will I suppose form a main element in the tragic part of the story. I am not quite sure how far I like the scenes in the wood, and I hope things will not come to the usual sad catastrophe." He urged GE to give him a sketch of the plot, but half expected this reply. GHL wrote: "I will give G.E. your message. You are the right sort of person to deal with him, for you perceive his Pegasus is tender in the mouth, and is apt to lay back his ears in a restive ominous style if even the reins be shaken when he is at work. Some people's Pegasus seems to have the mouth (as well as the *pace*,) of a cart horse; but your thoroughbred—all bone and nerve—requires other treatment." [VIII, 201–02]

Richmond | April 1. 58.

My dear Sir

I am obliged to you for the cheque for £60—the final payment for the first edition of Clerical Scenes.

Your appreciatory criticism of "Adam Bede" is highly gratifying to me. I am especially pleased that you appear to feel with me about my pet characters—Adam and Dinah. But I entertain what I think is well-founded objection against telling you in a bare brief manner the course of my story. The soul of art lies in its treatment and not in its subject. If a dramatist were to tell a manager that he had a fine tragedy in preparation, the subject of which was a man with a sore foot on a desert island, it is probable the manager would not feel any very brilliant hopes. Yet the Philoctetes is one of the finest dramas in the world. It is true my theme is not so meagre as a sore foot, nor am I Sophocles; but the mere skeleton of my story would probably give rise in your mind to objections which would be suggested by the treatment *other* writers have given to the same tragic incidents in the human lot—objections which would lie far away from my treatment. The Heart of Midlothian would probably have been thought highly objectionable if a skeleton of the story had been given by a writer whose reputation did not place him above question. And the same story told by a Balzacian French writer would probably have made a book that no young person could read without injury. Yet what girl of twelve was ever injured by the Heart of Midlothian? Of artistic writing it may be said pre-eminently—"to the pure writer all things are pure."

I am not arguing against your hesitation to publish "Adam Bede" in Maga, but simply stating my reasons for objecting to tell more of the story than I have already told you—namely, that it is partly tragic. It is natural that you should not have sufficient confidence in me to enter on the publication without more precise foreknowledge though you can certainly not be more solicitous about the moral spirit of what you publish in the Magazine, than I am about the moral spirit of what I write. Under the circumstances, it will perhaps be better definitively to give up the idea of monthly publication, and await the printing of the book in three volumes. Do not for a moment suppose that I look exclusively from my own point of view and fail to appreciate yours. But the nature of the writer is stronger than all circumstances. I could not write at all under a sense of doubt and distrust.

I shall forward you the amount of another part to-morrow. It is possible the perusal of that may in some degree modify your views. In any case I am always very heartily

Yours, with obligation
George Eliot.

TO SARA HENNELL, 17 APRIL 1858

GHL came to Munich armed with a number of letters of introduction. *The Life of Goethe* was so well known that the best intellectual society of the city showed him attention. [II, 449–52]

15, Luitpold Strasse | Munich | April 17. 1858.

Dear Sara . . .

We arrived here on Sunday night from Nürnberg—that town of towns—and of course the first thing to be done on Monday morning was to look out for lodgings. We walked ourselves weary all round by the Englischer Garten and the streets leading from the Ludwig Strasse, till we began to think it a hopeless business. . . . At last we found "zwei elegant möblirte Zimmer," where there has been an immense expenditure on wax and china ornaments and the least possible outlay in basins. We have two time-pieces under glass shades, several crucifixes also under glass shades, several bouquets of artificial flowers under glass shades, a Schranke with glass doors crammed full of the most brittle and tiny articles to be found in the German shops, selected apparently for their brittle-minuteness, and seventeen bad pictures. These are the chief advantages of our lodgings. As secondary ones, we have a very clean old maid as our landlady, and a goodnatured ruddy *dummes mädchen* for servant; we have a clean Abtritt(!) and two very large gilt framed mirrors hung in dark corners.

Our only discomfort of a serious kind, is that our box of books dispatched a fortnight ago has not yet arrived. We only want that to make us feel quite settled. Mr. Lewes has introductions to some of the best people here—von Siebold, and Bodenstedt and eminences of that sort—and Oldenburg is going to introduce him to Liebig, who is now one of the University professors here. So I dare say we shall have quite as much society as we shall care for.

We have been just to take a sip at the two Pinacotheks (the new one devoted to modern art is just finished) and at the Glyptothek, have bought our catalogues, and glanced here and there at the chief attractions. At present the Rubens-Saal is what I most long to return to. Rubens gives me more pleasure than any other painter, whether that is right or wrong. To be sure, I have not seen so many pictures and pictures of so high a rank, by any other great master. I feel sure that when I have seen as much of Raffaelle, I shall like him better, but at present Rubens more than any one else makes me feel that painting is a great art and that he was a great artist. His are such real, breathing men and women—men and women moved by passions, not mincing and grimacing and posing in mere apery of passion! What a grand, glowing, forceful thing life looks in his pictures—the men such grand bearded grappling beings fit to do the work of the world, the women such real mothers. . . .

The general aspect of Munich is distasteful to me. The buildings are generally huge, expensive and ugly, and one feels everywhere that the art is something superinduced by royal patronage. Such a contrast to Nürnberg! . . . We staid there only twenty-four hours, and I felt sad to leave it so soon. *There* one sees a real mediæval town, which has grown up with the life of a community as much as the shell of a nautilus has grown with the life of the animal; and the result is just as beautiful. No uniform barrack-like lines of houses there. Every house has a physiognomy—there is no end to the varieties which the vista of every street presents—but it is a variety like Nature's, showing general unity presiding over an endless play of individual variety. A pity the place became protestant, so that there is only one Catholic church where one can go in and out as one would. We turned into the famous St. Sebald's for a minute, where a Protestant clergyman was reading in a cold formal way under the grand gothic arches. Then we went to the Catholic church, the Frauenkirche, where the organ and voices were giving forth a glorious mass, and we stood with a feeling of brotherhood among the standing congregation, till the last note of the organ had died out. . . .

Mr. Lewes sends his kind regards. By the bye, did the "lady" present herself duly at Ivy Cottage? Love to all from

Your affectionate
Marian.

TO SARA HENNELL, 10–13 MAY 1858

King Maximilian II of Bavaria gathered many distinguished German scholars as honorary professors at the University of Munich. Among them were Justus von Liebig, chemist, whom the Leweses met at the house of Oldenburg, the publisher; Emanuel von Geibel, philosopher; Paul Heyse, novelist; F. M. von Bodenstedt, poet and journalist; Franz von Löher, lawyer; Karl von Siebold, biologist; Wilhelm von Kaulbach, painter; and Karl von Martius, botanist. [II, 452–56]

Luitpold Strasse, 15 | Munich | May 10th 1858.
Dear Sara . . .

Our life here is very agreeable—full of pleasant novelty, although we take things quietly, and observe our working hours just as if we were at Richmond. People are so kind to us that we feel already quite at home, sip Baierisch Bier with great tolerance, and talk bad German with more and more aplomb. The place, you know, swarms with professors of all sorts—all gründlich, of course, and one or two of them great. There is no one we are more charmed with than Liebig. Mr. Lewes had no letter to him—we merely met him at an evening party—yet he has been particularly kind to us, and seems to have taken a benevolent liking to me. We dined with him and his family yesterday, and saw how men of European celebrity may put up with greasy cooking in private life. He lives in very good German style, however, has a handsome suite of apartments, and makes a greater figure than most of the professors. His manners are charming—easy, graceful, benignant, and all the more conspicuous because he is so quiet and low-spoken among the loud talkers here. It is touching to look at his hands, the skin begrimed and the nails black to the roots. He looks best in his laboratory with his velvet cap on, holding little phials in his hand and talking of Kreatine and Kreatinine in the same easy way that well bred ladies talk scandal. He is one of the professors who have been called here by the present king, Max, who seems to be a really sensible man among kings—gets up at five o'clock in the morning to study, and every Saturday evening has a gathering of the first men in science and literature, that he may benefit by their opinions on important subjects. At this "Tafel-rund," every man is 'required' to say honestly what he thinks—every one may contradict every one else—and if the King suspects any one of a polite insincerity, the too polished man is invited no more. Liebig, the three poets—Geibel, Heyse, and Bodenstedt, and a Professor Löher, a writer of considerable mark, are always at the Tafel-rund, as an understood part of their functions; the rest are invited according to the King's direction. Bodenstedt is one of our best friends here—enormously instructed after the fashion of Germans, but not at all stupid with it. Like all the best men here, he is a North German, and has not acquired the Bavarian habit of spending his evenings at the Kneipe, drinking beer, smoking tobacco, and trying to talk down his companions. That is the understood mode of life for all genuine Bavarians, however cultivated, and you may imagine what is the character of the women *dabei*. It is quite an exception to meet with a woman who seems to expect any sort of companionship from the men, and I shudder at the sight of a woman in society, for I know I shall have to sit on the sofa with her all the evening listening to her stupidities, while the men on the other side of the table are discussing all the subjects I care to hear about. And the stupidity of a Bavarian woman——

13th. I think I was going to say that the stupidity of a Bavarian woman has not the virtue even of German cabbage—it is not copious, liberal, abundant—it is stingy, feeble, barren of propositions. But there are exceptions to this dreadful description. And happily there is such a colony of North Germans among the educated people that one hopes there may be a gradual modification through their influence.

Mr. Lewes is in a state of perfect bliss this morning. He is gone to the Akademie to see wonders through von Siebold's microscope and watch him dissecting. We were at his house last night to meet a party of celebrities, and, what was better, to see the prettiest little picture of married life—the great comparative anatomist (von Siebold) seated at the piano in his spectacles, playing the difficult accompaniments to Schubert's songs, while his little round-faced wife sang them with much taste and feeling. They are not young—von Siebold is grey, and probably more than fifty, his wife perhaps nearly forty, and it is all the prettier to see their admiration of each other. She said to Mr. Lewes, when he was speaking of her husband, "Ja, er ist ein netter Mann, nicht wahr?"

We take the Art in very small draughts at present, the German hours being difficult to adjust to our occupations. We are obliged to dine at *one!* and, of course, when we are well enough, must work till then. There is no moving for two hours afterwards, and then all the great public exhibitions are closed—except the churches. . . . But alas! I *cannot* admire much of the modern German art. It is for the most part elaborate lifelessness. Kaulbach's great compositions are huge charades, and I have seen nothing of his equal to his own Reineke Fuchs. It is an unspeakable relief, after staring at one of his huge pictures, the Destruction of Jerusalem, for example, which is a regular child's puzzle of symbolism, to sweep it all out of one's mind—which is very easily done, for nothing grasps you in it—and call up in your imagination a little Gerard Dow that you have seen hanging in a corner of one of the cabinets. Kaulbach himself is not much liked here: some are jealous, of course, for he has made a very large fortune, while others who think themselves equal to him are in poverty, getting no royal orders to execute; others have been offended by his whims etc. etc.—At Munich, as well as in London, one must listen with a grain of scepticism. We have been to his atelier, and he has given us a proof of his *Irrenhaus*, a strange sketch which he made years ago, very terrible and powerful. He is certainly a man of great faculty, but is, I imagine carried out of his true path by the ambition to produce "Weltgeschichtliche Bilder," which the critics (German) may go into raptures about. . . .

I must tell you something else which interested me greatly as the first example of the kind that has come under my observation. Among the awful mysterious names hitherto known only as marginal references, whom we have learned to clothe with ordinary flesh and blood is Prof. Martius ("Spix and Martius"), now an old man, and rich, after the manner of being rich in Germany. He has a very sweet wife—one of those women who remain pretty and graceful in old age—and a family of three daughters and one son—all more than grown up. I had suspected that Frau Martius was a Catholic, yet it seemed to me, from the Professor's *Wesen*, impossible that he could be a Catholic too. So the other night, I asked the charming Frau, and learned that she *is* Catholic, that her daughters are Catholic, and her husband and son Protestant, the children having been so brought up according to the German law in cases of mixed marriage. I can't tell you how interesting it was to me to hear her tell of her experience in bringing up her son conscientiously as a Protestant, she herself being Catholic all the while, and then to hear her and her daughters speak of the exemplary priests who had shown them such tender fatherly care when they were in trouble. They are the most harmonious affectionate family we have seen, and one delights in such a triumph of human goodness over the formal logic of theorists.

But I go on scribbling in a meagre way what is present in my own imagination, forgetting that this bit of paper will carry no picture to you. Goodbye, and God bless you—Love to all.

Your affectionate
Marian. . . .

TO JOHN BLACKWOOD, 28 MAY 1858

In a letter to GHL Blackwood wrote: "The following will perhaps interest and amuse G.E. I was smoking my cigar and watching the betters in the enclosure in front of the Stand on the Derby day when I was accosted by Newdigate, the member for Warwickshire, who after some talk on politics etc. said, "Do you know that you have been publishing a capital series of stories in the Mag., the Clerical Scenes, all about my place and County." My disbelief availed nothing. He knew the author, a Mr. Liggers. This is I think the same unfortunate patronymic that the *Manx Cat* selected as the author's. . . . The perfect conviction of Newdigate in the truth of his surmises was very curious, and G.E. must write me a line with a message to him." Blackwood had sent GHL an article from the *Manx Sun*, 4 July 1857, declaring that Joseph Liggins (there misspelled *Liggers*) was the author of *Scenes of Clerical Life*. [II, 459–60]

[Munich] May 28th/58.

My dear Sir

You were right in believing that I should like to hear Mr. Newdegate's opinion of the Stories. His testimony to the spirit in which they are written is really valuable, for I know he deserves the character you give him.

As to details, he seems, from what you say, as likely to be mistaken about them as he is about the authorship; but it is invariably the case that when people discover certain points of coincidence in a fiction with facts that happen to have come to their knowledge, they believe themselves able to furnish a key to the whole. That is amusing enough to the author, who knows from what widely sundered portions of experience—from what a combination of subtle shadowy suggestions with certain actual objects and events, his story has been formed. Certain vague traditions about Sir Roger Newdegate (him of "Newdegate-Prize" celebrity) which I heard when I was a child are woven into the character of Sir Christopher Cheverel, and the house he improved into a charming Gothic place with beautiful ceilings, I know from actual vision—but the rest of "Mr. Gilfil's Love Story" is spun out of the subtlest web of minute observation and inward experience, from my first childish recollections up to recent years. So it is with all the other stories. It would be a very difficult thing for me to furnish a key to them myself. But where there is no exact memory of the past any story with a few remembered points of character or of incident may pass for a history.

Surely there has been a sale of the Clerical Scenes in Scotland so as to make up the 800, of which I had received a confident impression that they had been sold, some time before I left England? If not, I shall be really uncomfortable on the subject since I had written to you under that confident impression.

We pay for our sight of the snowy mountains here by the most capricious of climates. English weather is steadfast compared with Munich weather. You go to dinner here in summer and come away from it in winter. You are languid among trees and feathery grass at one end of the town, and are shivering in a hurricane of dust at the other. This inconvenience of climate, with the impossibility of dining (well) at any other hour than one o'clock, is not friendly to the stomach—that great seat of the imagination, and I shall never advise an author to come to Munich except *ad interim*—when he is writing nothing, and only gathering materials for a picture of society where it is held a recreation to drink tea without flavour and tell jokes without point. There is something else worth studying—the great Saal full of Rubens's Pictures, and two or three precious bits of sculpture; and the sky on a fine day always puts one in a good temper—it is so deliciously clear and blue, making even the ugliest buildings look beautiful by the light it casts on them.

Ever yours truly
George Eliot.

TO SARA HENNELL, 14 JUNE 1858

Sara had written announcing the death of her mother Mrs. James Hennell. GE's reference to the death of her own mother is interesting. [II, 464–65]

15 Luitpold Strasse | Munich | June 14. 58.

Dear Sara

My thoughts were very often with you in conjectures not far from the truth, before your letter came. It is a long while since it came—for I have been very poorly and have not had energy to put a letter on paper, though I have been sometimes writing one in my mind. Words are very clumsy things—I like less and less to handle my friends' sacred feelings with them. For even those who call themselves 'intimate' know very little about each other—hardly ever know just *how* a sorrow is felt, and hurt each other by their very attempts at sympathy or consolation. We can bear no hand on our bruises. And so I feel I have no right to say that I know *how* the loss of your mother—'the only person who ever leaned on you'—affects you. I only know that it must make a deeply felt crisis in your life, and I know that the better, from having felt a great deal about my own mother and father and from having the keenest remembrance of all that experience. But for this very reason, I know that I can't measure what the event is to you, and if I were near you I should only kiss you and say nothing. I cried over your letter and felt myself with you in all you were telling me about. People talk of the feelings dying out as one gets older—but at present my experience is just the contrary. All the serious relations of life become so much more real to me—pleasure seems so slight a thing, and sorrow and duty and endurance so great. I find the least bit of real human life touch me in a way it never did when I was younger. . . . Cara I dare say, is like you, worn and in need of rest and change. I hope she means to allow herself some by and bye. Give my best love to her and divide between you twenty kisses. . . .

Whenever you can spare me half an hour to tell me something about yourself, you will be doing a good deed.

Ever your affectionate
Marian.

TO SARA HENNELL, 28 JULY 1858

Of the *Sistine Madonna* GE wrote in her Journal: "I sat down on the sofa opposite the picture for an instant, but a sort of awe, as if I were suddenly in the presence of some glorious being, made my heart swell too much for me to remain comfortably, and we hurried out of the room." Theodor Bischoff, the anatomist and physiologist, and Emil Harless, whose major study was nerve and muscle physiology, guided GHL's researches. GE's German was now fluent; in her conversation with Strauss when Dr. Brabant introduced them in Cologne in 1854 she had hardly been able to speak. [II, 471–73]

5B Waisenhaus Gasse | Dresden! | July 28th 1858.

Dear Sara

Just received your letter, which by a quite miraculous inspiration of practicality in Bavarian officials, has been sent on to me here, though we omitted to leave any directions at the P.O. Since I wrote to you last I have lived through a great deal of exquisite pleasure. First, an attack of Cholerine during our last week at Munich— which I reckon among my pleasures because I was nursed so tenderly. Then a fortnight's unspeakable journey to Salzburg, Ischl, Linz, Vienna, Prague, and finally Dresden, which is our last resting place before returning to Richmond, where we hope to be at the beginning of September. Dresden is a proper climax, for all other art seems only a preparation for feeling the superiority of the Madonna di San Sisto the more. We go three days a week to the gallery, and every day after looking at other pictures, we go to take a parting draught of delight at Titian's Zinngroschen and the *Einzige* Madonna. In other respects I am particularly enjoying our residence here—we are so quiet, having determined to know no one, and give ourselves up to work. We both feel a happy change in our health from leaving Munich, though I am reconciled to our long stay there by the fact that Mr. Lewes gained so much by his intercourse with the men of science there— especially Bischoff, v. Siebold, and Harless. I remembered your passion for autographs, and asked Liebig for his on your account. I shall send it you from Richmond. I was not sure that you would care enough about the handwriting of other luminaries, for there is such a thing as being European and yet obscure—a fixed star visible only from observatories.

You will be interested to hear that I saw Strauss at Munich. He came for a week's visit before we left. I had a quarter of an hour's chat with him alone, and was very agreeably impressed by him. He looked much more serene, and his face had a far sweeter expression than when I saw him in that dumb way at Cologne. He speaks with very choice words, like a man strictly truthful in the use of language. Will you undertake to tell Mrs. Call from me that he begged me to give his kindest remembrances to her and to her father, of whom he spoke with much interest and regard as his earliest English friend. Or perhaps, I had better reserve the message until I write to her myself on my return to Richmond. . . .

We shall probably leave here on the 30th or 31st of August. So don't write after then. Anything before that time will be gratefully received.

Your loving friend
Pollian.

TO JOHN BLACKWOOD, 8 SEPTEMBER 1858

George Simpson, Blackwood's confidential clerk and manager in Edinburgh, was in London, where GHL delivered to him the manuscript of Vol. II of *Adam Bede*. [II, 480]

Richmond | September 8th. 58.
My dear Sir
I hope you will soon receive, through Mr. Simpson, the M.S. of 'Adam Bede,' up to what must be the end of the second volume. I wish it reached to the end of the third instead of the second, for the story is so closely knit together that it must lose by being read in fragments. But since I am behindhand, it is important to use

every means of saving time, and it will be some saving if you will be so good as to read this portion at your earliest convenience.

Mr. Lewes tells me I shall lose a considerable advantage if the book does not appear in the Christmas season, and I shall work with the hope of being ready in time for that. I suppose the three volumes could be printed in six weeks, when the preliminaries were once arranged? If you had not assured me that you retain a vivid recollection of the first part, I should have entreated you to re-read it, hard as that entreaty would be on you, for the early part of this new portion would suffer especially from a dim notion of what precedes.

I am always, my dear Sir

Yours very truly
George Eliot.

TO JOHN BLACKWOOD, 5 NOVEMBER 1858

On October 29th GHL took Volume III of *Adam Bede* (through page 216) to London to send to Edinburgh. There were still 45 pages to finish the story. Blackwood was delighted with it and wrote an enthusiastic letter offering £800 for the copyright for four years. The specimen page was identical with those of the *Scenes*. [II, 493]

Richmond | November 5th 1858.

My dear Sir

Thank you for your letter. I care for the fact that my story has touched you, not merely as a guarantee of success, but as a matter of personal sympathy.

The specimen page you have sent me distresses me, I confess. It looks shabby by the side of the pages of Clerical Scenes. I suppose the calculations have been based on a fair *average* of my MS. pages which are very unequal, the size of my writing varying with my moods. If so, there is no help for it, but to make the volumes rather thinner for the sake of getting a handsome page. On looking at the novels we have by us, I find them usually of not more than 300 pages to the volume—a very respectable size. But your experience and judgment are a better guide than my own notions on these subjects: and on the time of publication also, though I was rather disappointed to find that a delay was desirable. Still, I have no motive for haste that would outweigh your opinion as to what is best for the book.

I enclose an acceptance of your proposition, with a slight modification of the terms, which I hope will not be otherwise than agreeable to you. Thank you once more for writing me such cordial words of admiration. I *was* rather desponding, now I am singing 'Viva la joia, fidon la tristessa.' Ever, my dear Sir,

Yours very truly
George Eliot.

TO JOHN CHAPMAN, 5 NOVEMBER 1858

GE had confided to Spencer that she was the author of the *Scenes*. When he came to dine with them, he brought the unpleasant news that Chapman had asked him point blank if she wrote the book. GE sent this note the same day. [II, 494]

[Richmond]

Dear Friend

I have just learned that you have allowed yourself to speak carelessly of rumours concerning a supposed authorship of mine. A little reflection in my behalf would have suggested to you that were any such rumours true, my own abstinence from any communication concerning my own writing, except to my most intimate friends, was evidence that I regarded secrecy on such subjects as a matter of importance. Instead of exercising this friendly consideration, you carelessly, certainly, for no one's pleasure or interest, and to my serious injury, contribute to the circulation of idle rumours and gossip, entirely unwarranted by any evidence. . . . Should you like to have unfounded reports of that kind circulated concerning yourself, still more should you like an old friend to speak idly of the merest hearsay on matters which you yourself had exhibited extreme aversion to disclose?

Marian Lewes.

TO JOHN BLACKWOOD, 25 NOVEMBER 1858

Blackwood forwarded the offer of Tauchnitz's agent of £30 for the Continental edition of *Scenes of Clerical Life*. The final pages of *Adam Bede* were finished November 16th and sent to Edinburgh. Proof of the first 32 pages of Volume I arrived on the 23rd. In softening the dialect as Blackwood suggested, GE changed such words as *goo* to *go*, *al'ys* to *allays*, and *belave* to *believe*. In subsequent editions it was softened further. [II, 499–500]

Richmond | November 25. 58.

My dear Sir

I shall be much obliged if you will accept for me Tauchnitz's offer of £30 for the English reprint of C.S. And will you also be so good as to desire that Tauchnitz may register the book in Germany, as I understand that is the only security against its being translated without our knowledge, and I shudder at the idea of my books being turned into hideous German by an incompetent translator.

I return the proofs by today's post. The dialect must be toned down all through in correcting the proofs, for I found it impossible to keep it subdued enough in writing. I am aware that the spelling which represents a dialect perfectly well to those who know it by the ear, is likely to be unintelligible to others. Mr. Lewes is a good test, being innocent of dialects, and he is good enough to run over the proofs for the sake of checking unintelligibility. I hope the sheets will come rapidly and regularly now, for I dislike lingering, hesitating processes.

Your praise of my ending was very warming and cheering to me in the foggy weather. I'm sure if I have written well, your pleasant letters have had something to do with it.

Ever yours truly
George Eliot.

Can anything be done in America for Adam Bede? I suppose not—as my name is not known there.

JOURNAL, 30 NOVEMBER 1858

[II, 502–05]

HISTORY OF "ADAM BEDE."

The germ of "Adam Bede" was an anecdote told me by my Methodist Aunt Samuel (the wife of my Father's younger brother): an anecdote from her own experience. We were sitting together one afternoon during her visit to me at Griff, probably in 1839 or 40, when it occurred to her to tell me how she had visited a condemned criminal, a very ignorant girl who had murdered her child and refused to confess—how she had stayed with her praying, through the night and how the poor creature at last broke out into tears, and confessed her crime. My Aunt afterwards went with her in the cart to the place of execution, and she described to me the great respect with which this ministry of hers was regarded by the official people about the gaol. The story, told by my aunt with great feeling, affected me deeply, and I never lost the impression of that afternoon and our talk together; but I believe I never mentioned it, through all the intervening years, till something prompted me to tell it to George in December 1856, when I had begun to write the "Scenes of Clerical Life." He remarked that the scene in the prison would make a fine element in a story, and I afterwards began to think of blending this and some other recollections of my aunt in one story with some points in my father's early life and character. The problem of construction that remained was to make the unhappy girl one of the chief *dramatis personæ* and connect her with the hero. At first I thought of making the story one of the series of "Scenes," but afterwards, when several motives had induced me to close these with "Janet's Repentance," I determined on making what we always called in our conversations "My Aunt's Story," the subject of a long novel: which I accordingly began to write on the 22d October 1857.

The character of Dinah grew out of my recollections of my aunt, but Dinah is not at all like my aunt, who was a very small, black-eyed woman, and (as I was told, for I never heard her preach) very vehement in her style of preaching. She had left off preaching when I knew her, being, probably, sixty years old, and in delicate health; and she had become, as my father told me, much more gentle and subdued than she had been in the days of her active ministry and bodily strength, when she could not rest without exhorting and remonstrating in season and out of season. I was very fond of her, and enjoyed the few weeks of her stay with me greatly. She was loving and kind to me, and I could talk to her about my inward life, which was closely shut up from those usually round me. I saw her only twice again, for much shorter periods: once at her own home at Wirksworth in Derbyshire, and once at my Father's last residence, Foleshill.

The character of Adam, and one or two incidents connected with him were suggested by my Father's early life; but Adam is not my father any more than Dinah is my aunt. Indeed, there is not a single *portrait* in "Adam Bede"; only the suggestions of experience wrought up into new combinations. When I began to write it, the only elements I had determined on besides the character of Dinah were the character of Adam, his relation to Arthur Donnithorne and their mutual relation to Hetty, i.e. to the girl who commits child-murder: the scene in the prison being of course the climax towards which I worked. Everything else grew out of the characters and their mutual relations. Dinah's ultimate relation to Adam was suggested by George, when I had read to him the first part of the first volume: he was so delighted with the presentation of Dinah and so convinced that the readers' interest would centre in her, that he wanted her to be the principal figure at the last. I accepted the idea at once, and from the end of the third chapter worked with it constantly in view.

The first volume was written at Richmond and given to Blackwood in March. He expressed great admiration of its freshness and vividness, but seemed to hesitate about putting it in the Magazine, which was the form of publication he, as well as myself, had previously contemplated. He still *wished* to have it for the Mag., but desired to know the course of the story; at *present*, he saw nothing to prevent its reception in Maga, but he would like to see more. I am uncertain whether his doubts rested solely on Hetty's relation to Arthur, or whether they were also directed towards the treatment of Methodism by the Church. I refused to tell my story beforehand, on the ground that I would not have it judged apart from my *treatment*, which alone determines the moral quality of art; and ultimately I proposed that the notion of publication in Maga should be given up, and that the novel should be published in three volumes, at Christmas, if possible. He assented.

I began the second volume in the second week of my stay at Munich, about the middle of April. While we were at Munich, George expressed his fear that Adam's part was too passive throughout the drama, and that it was important for him to be brought into more direct collision with Arthur. This doubt haunted me, and out of it grew the scene in the Wood between Arthur and Adam: the fight came to me as a *necessity* one night at the Munich opera when I was listening to *William Tell*. Work was slow and interrupted at Munich, and when we left I had only written to the beginning of the dance on the Birthday Feast: but at Dresden, I wrote uninterruptedly and with great enjoyment in the long, quiet mornings, and there I nearly finished the second volume—all, I think, but the last chapter, which I wrote here in the old room at Richmond in the first week of September, and then sent the M.S. off to Blackwood. The opening of the third volume—Hetty's journeys—was, I think written more rapidly than the rest of the book, and was left without the slightest alteration of the first draught. Throughout the book, I have altered little, and the only cases, I think, in which George suggested more than a verbal alteration, when I read the M.S. aloud to him, were the first scene at the Farm and the scene in the Wood between Arthur and Adam, both of which he recommended me to "space out" a little, which I did.

When, on October 29, I had written to the end of the love scene at the Farm, between Adam and Dinah, I sent the M.S. to Blackwood, since the remainder of the third volume could not affect the judgment passed on what had gone before. He wrote back in warm admiration, and offered me, on the part of the firm, £800 for four years' copyright. I accepted the offer. The last words of the third volume were written and dispatched on their way to Edinburgh November the 16th, and now on this last day of the same month I have written this slight history of my book. I love it very much and am deeply thankful to have written it, whatever the public may say to it—a result which is still in darkness, for I have at present had only four sheets of the proof. The book would have been published at Christmas, or rather, early in December, but that Bulwer's "What will he do with it?" was to be published by Blackwoods at that time, and it was thought that this novel might interfere with mine.

8 Park Shot, Richmond. | November 30. 1858.

TO JOHN BLACKWOOD, 1 DECEMBER 1858

The contract with Tauchnitz required the author's signature. As GHL wisely refrained from connecting his name with George Eliot, the agent was persuaded to accept Blackwood's signature. The rumor of her authorship was spreading in London, too. Having wormed the secret out of Spencer, Chapman was gossiping about it. Sir Walter Scott to protect his secret denied flatly that he was the author of the Waverley novels. [II, 505]

Richmond | December 1. 1858.

My dear Sir

Mr. Lewes thinks it better that he should not put his name as a witness to my signature. If a name be necessary, will you be kind enough to insert yours?

I am very nervous about the preservation of the incognito, for I have reason to believe that some rumour of the authorship of C.S. has escaped from a member of my own family, who, however, could only speak on *suspicion*.

This makes me anxious that the publication of 'Adam' should not be delayed longer than is necessary after the Christmas Holidays, for I wish the book to be judged quite apart from its authorship.

Ever yours truly
George Eliot.

John Blackwood Esq.

P.S. The rumour to which I refer is slight and, I believe, confined to an unimportant quarter. If it reach us in the way of question, it will be met with direct contradiction, for I am of Scott's opinion on that point. An incognito can be maintained on no other condition, and in such a case one ought to say 'No' to an impertinent querist as one would decline to open one's iron chest to a burglar.

7

"GENIUS OF THE HIGHEST ORDER"
Adam Bede · *The Mill on,the Floss*

Scenes of Clerical Life had drawn the warm interest of many discriminating readers, and the continued discussion of who the unknown author might be, carried along by the champions of Liggins with letters to *The Times*, kept curiosity alive. When *Adam Bede* appeared in February 1859, it quickly became the best-seller in a year that included Dickens's *A Tale of Two Cities* and Meredith's *The Ordeal of Richard Feverel*. *The Times* declared in a review filling three of its huge columns: "It is a first-rate novel, and its author takes rank at once among the masters of the art." Blackwood had offered GE £800 for four years' copyright, but the success of the book was so extraordinary that he doubled the amount and returned the copyright to his unknown author. The haunting fear that the circulating libraries and the critics would boycott her books because of the irregularity of her life with Lewes was dispelled by tbe enthusiastic reception of *The Mill on the Floss* in April 1860, which earned her £4,000 within the year. *The Times* review began: "George Eliot is as great as ever." After years of stringent economy the Leweses celebrated with a two-months' holiday in Italy. They stopped in Switzerland and brought home with them GHL's eldest son Charles, who with the help of Anthony Trollope soon found a good place in the Secretary's department of the Post Office.

TO JOHN CHAPMAN, 1 JANUARY 1859

After Chapman left unanswered her protest of his gossip about her authorship, GE wrote in her Journal: "I shall not correspond with him or willingly see him again." But his tardy excuses brought this reply. He had secured an M.D. degree at St. Andrews in May 1857 and specialized in the disorders of women. [III, 3]

Richmond | January 1. 1859.

Dear Friend

I have received your letter of the 30th, in which you state the reasons that, in your opinion, justified you in leaving unanswered my letter written two months ago. If that letter of mine implied any misconception or contained any word not strictly just, I beg so far, to apologize for it.

Several of your observations and statements I have read with much surprise, but I forbear commenting on them, since it does not seem likely that further letter-writing would advance our mutual understanding. I remain

Yours very sincerely
Marian Lewes.

John Chapman Esq. M.D.

TO JOHN BLACKWOOD, 31 JANUARY 1859

Blackwood sent £400, the first half of the payment for *Adam Bede*, which was published 1 February. Her acknowledgment is signed "George Eliot." She asked to have presentation copies inscribed "From the Author" sent to Dr. John Brown, Mrs. Carlyle, Dickens, Froude, Charles Kingsley, Richard Owen, and Thackeray. Forgues was dropped from the list because he had reviewed the *Scenes* as an example of the evils of a married clergy! [III, 6–7]

Richmond | January 31. 1859.

My dear Sir

Enclosed is the formal acknowledgment, bearing my signature, and with it let me beg you to accept my thanks—*not* formal but heartfelt—for the generous way in which you have all along helped me with words and with deeds. The impression 'Adam Bede' has made on you and Major Blackwood—of whom I have always been pleased to think as concurring with your views—is my best encouragement, and counterbalances, in some degree, the depressing influences to which I am peculiarly sensitive. I perceive that I have not the characteristics of the "popular author," and yet I am much in need of the warmly expressed sympathy which only popularity can win.

I have sent to Mr. Langford a list of seven persons whom I wish to receive presentation copies. I have substituted Emile Montégut, of the *Revue des Deux Mondes* for Emile Forgues. Montégut is the better writer of the two, but 'Adam' is not very likely to suit any Frenchman's palate.

Can you imagine why Mudie has almost always left the Clerical Scenes out of his advertised list, although he puts in very trashy and obscure books? I hope it is nothing more than chance. A good subscription would be cheering, but I can understand that it is not decisive of success or non-success. Thank you for promising to let me know about it as soon as possible.

With my best regards to Major Blackwood, I am

Yours very truly
George Eliot.

John Blackwood Esq.

TO MRS. CHARLES BRAY, 24 FEBRUARY [1859]

This is one of several letters about GE's difficulty in finding a servant for Holly Lodge, into which they had moved 5 February. [III, 22–23]

Holly Lodge [Wandsworth] | February 24.

Dear Cara

One word of gratitude to *you* first, before I write any other letters. Heaven and earth bless you for trying to help me. I have been blasphemous enough sometimes to think that I had never been good and attractive enough to win any little share of the honest disinterested friendship there is in the world: one or two examples of late had given that impression, and I am prone to rest in the least agreeable conviction the premisses will allow. The advertisement in the Herald is a business-like way of proceeding. Perhaps it would be worth while to mention that the servant is wanted for a *lady and gentleman only.* I need hardly tell you what I want—you know it so well: a servant who will cause me the least possible expenditure of time on household matters. *Cooking* is a material thing, not because Mr. Lewes is epicurean (for he is stupid of palate) but because he is, amongst his other eminences, eminently dyspeptic. I am anxious therefore to have a cook who is not only honest but soup-making and full of devices—as good a cook as your Hannah of old time. Honesty and cleanliness are the two other emphatic requirements and a not unimportant one is a power of keeping simple accounts—the spelling *ad libitum.*

I wish I were not an anxious fidgetty wretch, and could sit down content with dirt and disorder. But anything in the shape of an *anxiety* soon grows into a monstrous vulture with me, and makes itself more present to me than my rich sources of happiness, such as too few mortals are blessed with. You know me.

Ever your grateful
Marian. . . .

Since I wrote this I have just had a letter from my Sister Chrissey—ill in bed—consumptive—regretting that she ever ceased to write to me. It has ploughed up my heart.

TO JOHN BLACKWOOD, 24 FEBRUARY 1859

Mrs. Carlyle's response to *Adam Bede* [III, 17–19] was even more enthusiastic than that to *Scenes of Clerical Life*. Blackwood sent her passages copied from GE's letter. Her sister Chrissey Clarke, who was dying of consumption, broke the silence since 1857 and wrote to her. [III, 23–24]

[Wandsworth] February 24. 59.

My dear Sir

Mrs. Carlyle's ardent letter will interest and amuse you. I reckon it among my best triumphs that she found herself "in charity with the whole human race" when she laid the book down. I want the philosopher himself to read it because the *pre*-philosophic period—the childhood and poetry of his life—lay among the furrowed fields and pious peasantry. If he *could* be urged to read a novel! I should like, if possible, to give him the same sort of pleasure he has given me in the early chapters of *Sartor*, where he describes little Diogenes eating his porridge on the wall in sight of the sunset, and gaining deep wisdom from the contemplation of the pigs and other "higher animals" of Entepfuhl. . . .

I needed your letter very much, for when one lives apart from the world, with no opportunity of observing the effect of books except through the newspapers, one is in danger of sinking into the foolish belief that the day is past for the recognition of genuine truthful writing, in spite of recent experience that the newspapers are no criterion at all. . . .

It is a wretched weakness of my nature to be so strongly affected by these things—and yet, how it is possible to put one's best heart and soul into a book and be hardened to the result—be indifferent to the proof whether or not one has really a vocation to speak to one's fellow-men in that way? Of course one's vanity is at work; but the main anxiety is something entirely distinct from vanity. You see, I mean you to understand that my feelings are very respectable, and such as it will be virtuous in you to gratify with the same zeal as you have always shown. . . .

I wonder if all your other authors are as greedy and exacting as I am. If so, I hope they appreciate your attention as much as

Yours ever truly
George Eliot.
P.T.O.

I have reopened my letter to ask you if you will oblige me by writing a line to Mrs. Carlyle for me. I don't like to leave her second letter (she wrote a very kind one about the C.S.) without any sort of notice. Will you tell her that the sort of effect she declares herself to have felt from "Adam Bede" is just what I desire to produce—gentle thoughts and happy remembrances; and I thank her heartily for telling me so warmly and generously what she has felt. That is not a pretty message—revise it for me, pray, for I am weary and ailing and thinking of a sister who is slowly dying.

TO JOHN BLACKWOOD, 25 FEBRUARY 1859

GHL shielded GE from reviews that he knew would discourage her. [III, 25–26]

[Wandsworth] February 25. 59.

My dear Sir

The folio of notices duly came and are returned by today's post. The friend at my elbow ran through them for me, and read aloud some specimens to me, some of them ludicrous enough. The Edinburgh Courant has the ring of sincere enjoyment in its tone, and the writer there makes himself so amiable to me that I am sorry he has fallen into the mistake of supposing that Mrs. Poyser's original sayings are remembered proverbs! I have no stock of proverbs in my memory, and there is not one thing put into Mrs. Poyser's mouth that is not fresh from my own mint. Please to correct that mistake if any one makes it in your hearing.

I have not ventured to look into the folio myself, but I learn that there are certain threatening marks in ink by the side of such stock sentences as "best novel of the season" or "best novel we have read for a long while," from such authorities as the Sun or Morning Star or other orb of the newspaper firmament—as if these sentences were to be selected for reprint in the form of advertisement. I shudder at the suggestion. Am I taking a liberty in intreating you to keep a sharp watch over the advertisements that no hackneyed puffing phrase of this kind may be tacked to my book? . . . I shall be grateful to you if you will save me from the results of any agency but your own—or at least of any agency that is not under your rigid criticism in this matter.

Pardon me if I am overstepping the author's limits in this expression of my feelings. I confide in your ready comprehension of the irritable class you have to deal with.

Ever yours truly
G. E.

TO SARA HENNELL, 26 FEBRUARY [1859]

The "external influence" was their brother Isaac Evans. [III, 26]

Holly Lodge | February 26.

I think not, dear Sara, thank you. I have written to Chrissey and shall hear from her again. She has the materials for knowing and inferring all that is necessary.

I think her writing was the result of long quiet thought—the slow return of a naturally just and affectionate mind to the position from which it had been thrust by external influence. She says, "My object in writing to you . . . was to tell you how very sorry I have been that I ceased to write and neglected one who under all circumstances was kind to me and mine. *Pray believe* me when I say it will be the greatest comfort I can possibly receive to know you are *well* and *happy*. Will you write once more etc. etc." I wrote immediately, and I desire to avoid any word of reference to anything with which she associates the idea of alienation. The past is abolished from my mind—I only want her to feel that I love her and care for her. . . .

Mr. and Mrs. Richard Congreve have called on us. We shall return the call as soon as we can.

Ever your loving
Pollian.

TO CHARLES BRAY, [28] FEBRUARY [1859]

Monday was February 28th, when GHL's Journal records their calling on the Congreves—"found them both charming and likely to be agreeable neighbours." His wife Maria was the daughter of John Bury, the Coventry physician who had attended Robert Evans in his last illness. Richard Congreve, a contemporary of Clough and Arnold at Oxford, resigned his fellowship at Wadham College to marry, earning his living by taking private pupils. [III, 27]

[Wandsworth] Monday | February 27.
Dear Friend

I have written to Chrissey and await another letter from her. If she expresses a wish to see me, I shall go—as soon, that is, as I can leave Mr. Lewes for two days, of which he stoutly resists the mere notion so long as the present servant is in the house. It is a terrible sacrifice to me to leave home at all—quite like the prospect of a tooth-drawing; and much as I should like to sit with you all by your own fire, I am afraid the necessity of hurrying back and making two unbroken railway journeys of it, will forbid me that pleasant renewal of the past. People who have been inseparable and found all their happiness in each other for five years are in a sort of Siamese-twin condition that other people are not likely to regard with tolerance or even with belief. . . .

I have not seen the Congreves, for we were out when they called and have not yet been able to return their visit. We shall go this morning.

Ever yours affectionately
Marian Lewes.

Charles Bray Esq.

TO SARA HENNELL, [21 MARCH 1859]

Chrissey Clarke died 15 March. Her daughters Emily and Kate were sent to school by GE in Lichfield. Edward, the eldest son, went to Australia in 1861. The second, Christopher Charles, followed him in 1864. [III, 38]

[Wandsworth]
Dear Sara

It was worth your while to write me those feeling words—for they are the sort of things that I keep in my memory and feel the influence of a long long while.

Chrissey's death has taken from the possibility of many things towards which I looked with some hope and yearning in the future. I had a very special feeling towards her, stronger than any third person would think likely. The eldest girl writes me very nice, simple letters—grave and womanly, but in her own words, and not in borrowed sentences. The eldest boy is almost of age—finishes his apprenticeship this April. The second is being well educated at Ewell College. The eldest girl is between 14 and fifteen—old enough to take care of her one little sister.

No more now—dear Sara. I will write when my thoughts are happier.

Ever your affectionate
Pollian.

TO JOHN BLACKWOOD, 31 MARCH [1859]

William Lucas Collins reviewed *Adam Bede* in *Blackwood's Magazine*, April 1859. The "new novel" was *The Mill on the Floss*, which GE had begun in January before the last proofs of *Adam Bede* came. The *jeu de mélancolie* was *The Lifted Veil*. [III, 40–41]

[Wandsworth] Thursday Night | March 31.

My dear Sir

I should like you to convey my gratitude to your reviewer. I see well he is a man whose experience and study enable him to relish parts of my book which I should despair of seeing recognized by critics in London back drawing rooms. He has gratified me keenly by laying his finger on passages which I wrote either with strong feeling or from intimate knowledge, but which I had prepared myself to find entirely passed over by reviewers. Surely I am not wrong in supposing him to be a clergyman? The review in the "Universal" is better written than usual, and contains some good critical remarks. It will help the sale of the second edition, if the magazines and quarterlies will take up the book, and I shall be anxious to know that the new five hundred move off the shelves. . . .

About my new story, which will be a novel as long as Adam Bede, and a sort of companion picture of provincial life, we must talk when I have the pleasure of seeing you—a pleasure which Major Blackwood has promised on your behalf at the end of April. It will be a work which will require time and labour.

But I have a slight story of an outré kind—not a *jeu d'esprit*, but a *jeu de mélancolie*, which I could send you in a few days for your acceptance or rejection as a brief magazine story—of one number only. I think nothing of it, but my private critic says it is very striking and original, and on the strength of that opinion, I mention it.

Do write me good news as often as you can.

Ever yours hungrily
George Eliot.

I owe thanks to Major Blackwood for a very cheering letter.

TO SARA HENNELL, [9 APRIL 1859]

Liggins matriculated at St. Catharine's College, Cambridge in 1824, but never took a degree. His father was a miller or baker at Attleborough, where Chrissey Clarke lived. [III, 45–46]

Holly Lodge | Saturday Evening.

Dear Sara

We are just come home from the Isle of Wight! Whither we rushed in desperation after Mr. Lewes had suffered days and days from a burning head and burning mouth—the symptoms, as the doctors tell him, of debility and indigestion. He hoped that a sniff of the sea breezes, idleness and change of scene might serve as a better tonic than doctors' stuff, and they really seem to have done him good, though we have been absent only four days. . . .

Mr. Lewes has read Adam Bede, and is as dithyrambic about it as others appear to be so I must refresh my soul with it now, as well as with the Spring tide. Mr. Liggins I remember as a vision of my childhood—a tall black coated genteel young clergyman-in-embryo.

Ever thine
Pollian.

TO JOHN BLACKWOOD, 10 APRIL 1859

Sara Hennell had written about Joseph Liggins, who was claiming to be the author of both *Scenes of Clerical Life* and *Adam Bede*. At first the Leweses were amused by the claim because it diverted attention from the true GE. Joseph Langford was Blackwood's London agent. [III, 43–44]

[Wandsworth] April 10th 59.

My dear Sir . . .

The other day I received a letter from an old friend in Warwickshire containing some striking information about the author of "Adam Bede." I extract the passage for your amusement.

"I want to ask you if you have read 'Adam Bede' or the 'Scenes of Clerical Life,' and whether you know that the author is Mr. Liggins. . . . A deputation of dissenting parsons went over *to ask him to write for the Eclectic*, and they found him washing his slop-basin at a pump. He has no servant and does everything for himself, but Mr. Rosevear" (one of said parsons) "said that he inspired them with a reverence that would have made any impertinent question impossible. The son of a baker, of no mark at all in his town, so that it is possible you may not have heard of him. You know he calls himself 'George Eliot.' It sounds strange to hear the Westminster doubting whether he is a woman, *when here he is so well known.* But I am glad it has mentioned him. *They say he gets no profit out of 'Adam Bede,' and gives it freely to Blackwood, which is a shame.* We have not read him yet, but the extracts are irresistible."

Conceive the real George Eliot's feelings, conscious of being a base worldling—

not washing his own slop-basin, and *not* giving away his M.S.! Nor even intending to do so, in spite of the reverence such a course might inspire. I hope you and
Major Blackwood will enjoy the myth.

The story will be ready in a few days—would have been ready now, but for
illness of my own and of others, sadly interrupting all work.

Mr. Langford sent me a letter the other day from Miss Winkworth, a grave lady
who says she never reads novels—except a few of the most famous—but that she
has read 'Adam' three times running. One likes to know such things—they show
that the book tells on peoples' hearts and may be a real instrument of culture. I
sing my 'Magnificat' in a quiet way, and have a great deal of deep, silent joy, but
few authors, I suppose, who have had a real success, have known less of the flush
and the sensations of triumph that are talked of as the accompaniments of success.
I think I should soon begin to believe that "Liggins" wrote my books—it is so
difficult to believe what the world does *not* believe, so easy to believe what the
world keeps repeating.

Ever yours truly
George Eliot.

TO JOHN BLACKWOOD, 20 APRIL 1859

After the 3-column review in *The Times* the Reverend Henry Anders wrote a letter
declaring that its author was Liggins; he and the characters he paints "are as familiar there
as the twin spires of Coventry." This brought a reply (written by GHL but signed "George
Eliot") denying that Liggins had ever seen a line of the books until they were printed. Then
Charles Bracebridge, the squire of Atherstone, wrote to Blackwood assuring him that
Liggins was the author. Blackwood replied, "You and your neighbours are mistaken." But
he was reluctant to publish a point-blank denial because if any one should stumble upon the
real name, a less decided denial would be an admission. [III, 53–54]

[Wandsworth] April 20. 59.

My dear Sir

I know good Mr. Bracebridge, and dined at his house in my sallet days, though
I'm sure he has no recollection of me. He is a kindhearted, patronizing man—of
wealth and old family—who once tried to make a figure politically (as a liberal) in
his county and succeeded—only the figure was a very poor one.

But this myth about Liggins is getting serious and must be put a stop to. I think
an explicit denial should be given to Mr. Bracebridge. We are bound not to allow
sums of money to be raised (or perhaps a place given) on a false supposition of this
kind. Don't you think it would be well for *you* to write a letter to the "Times" to
the effect that, as you find in some stupid quarters my letter has not been received
as a bonâ fide denial, you declare Mr. Liggins not to be the author of Clerical
Scenes and Adam Bede; further, that any future applications to you concerning
George Eliot will not be answered, since that writer is not in need of public
benevolence. Such a letter might save us some future annoyance and trouble; for I
am rather doubtful about Mr. Liggins's character. The last report I heard of him

was that he spent his time in smoking and drinking. I don't know whether that is one of the data for the Warwickshire logicians who have decided him to be the author of my books.

The last letter you enclosed to me was from the "Constitutional Press," asking me for a story on my "own terms"! Only think what I lose by my anonymity.

Ever yours truly
George Eliot.

TO JOHN BLACKWOOD, 29 APRIL 1859

"The Lifted Veil" was published in *Blackwood's* in July. *The Leader* declared concealments of authorship "a species of literary fraud. . . . Let him tell the truth as to his name, and shame Mr. Anders." The sentence about Adam's belief in the willow wand was added in Chapter 4. [III, 60–61]

[Wandsworth] April 29. 59.

My dear Sir

Herewith the dismal story, which I did not send before because I thought you were already choked with the proofs for Maga, just issued.

Thank you for sending me Sir Edward Lytton's letter, which has given me real pleasure. The praise is doubly valuable to me for the sake of the generous feeling that prompted it.

I think you judged rightly about writing to the "Times." I would abstain from the remotest appearance of a "dodge." But you alarm me about the "Critic" and "Leader." What have they been saying? I am anxious to know of any *positive* rumour that may get abroad, for while I would willingly, if it were possible—which it clearly is not—retain my incognito as long as I live, I can suffer no one to bear my arms on his shield.

There is *one* alteration or rather one addition—merely of a sentence—that I wish to make in the 12s/. edition of "Adam Bede." It is a sentence in the chapter where Adam is making the coffin at night, and hears the willow wand. Some readers seem not to have understood what I meant, namely—that it was in Adam's peasant blood and nurture to believe in this, and that he narrated it with awed belief to his dying day. That is not a fancy of my own brain, but a matter of observation, and is in my mind an important feature in Adam's character. There is nothing else I wish to touch. I will send you the sentence some day soon, with the page where it is to be inserted. . . .

Ever yours truly
George Eliot.

John Blackwood Esq.

TO MME EUGÈNE BODICHON, 5 MAY 1859

In 1857 Barbara Leigh Smith had married Eugène Bodichon, a French physician, and gone to live in Algiers. There she read a review of *Adam Bede* in an obscure newspaper in which the quoted passages made her exclaim "That is written by Marian Evans, there is her great big head and heart and her wise views." Weeks later after reading the reviews in *The Times* and the *Westminster* (where Chapman, who had wormed the secret out of Spencer, hinted that GE was a woman), Barbara wrote to her, triumphing in her triumph. GHL added a postscript to this letter, reminding her that "you must not call her Marian Evans again: that individual is extinct, rolled up, mashed, absorbed in the Lewesian magnificence!" [III, 63–65]

Holly Lodge, May 5. 59.

God bless you, dearest Barbara, for your love and sympathy. You are the first friend who has given any symptom of knowing me—the first heart that has recognized me in a book which has come from my heart of hearts. But keep the secret solemnly till I give you leave to tell it, and give way to no impulses of triumphant affection. You have sense enough to know how important the *incognito* has been, and we are anxious to keep it up a few months longer.

Curiously enough, my old Coventry friends who have certainly read the 'Westminster' and the 'Times' and have probably by this time read the book itself, have given no sign of recognition. But a certain Mr. Liggins whom rumour has fixed on as the author of my books and whom they have believed in, has probably screened me from their vision—I am a very blessed woman, am I not? to have all this reason for being glad that I have lived, in spite of my sins and sorrows—or rather, by reason of my sins and sorrows. I have had no time of exultation; on the contrary these last months have been sadder than usual to me, and I have thought more of the future and the much work that remains to be done in life than of anything that has been achieved. But I think your letter today gave me more joy—more heart-glow, than all the letters or reviews or the other testimonies of success that have come to me since the evenings when I read aloud my manuscripts—to my dear dear husband, and he laughed and cried alternately and then rushed to kiss me. He is the prime blessing that has made all the rest possible to me—giving me a response to everything I have written, a response that I could confide in as a proof that I had not mistaken my work. . . .

But we will talk of everything when you come. Remember, you can have a bed. And do make the dear Doctor come with you to England. It is so sad to think of his staying behind, and we want to see him again. These are cogent reasons, in *our* opinion, for his coming, and like the rest of the world, we expect men to be guided by *our* reasons rather than their own. Ever dear Barbara

Your loving and grateful
Marian.

TO JOHN BLACKWOOD, 21 MAY 1859

As *Adam Bede* became the best-seller of the year, the Blackwoods wrote that they meant to add £400 to the £800 paid for the copyright for four years, "although we do leave Mr. Liggins in penury." [III, 69–70]

[Wandsworth, 21 May 1859]
My dear Sir
   Thank you: first, for acting with that fine integrity which makes part of my faith in you; secondly, for the material sign of that integrity. I don't know which of those two things I care for most—that people should act nobly towards me, or that I should get honest money. I certainly care a great deal for the money, as I suppose all anxious minds do that love independence and have been brought up to think debt and begging the two deepest dishonours short of crime.
   I look forward with quite eager expectation to seeing you—we have so much to say. Pray give us the first day at your command. The excursion, as you may imagine, is not ardently longed for in this weather, but when "merry May" is quite gone, we may surely hope for some sunshine; and then I have a pet project of rambling along by the banks of a river, not without artistic as well as hygienic purposes.
   Pray bring me all the Liggins Correspondence. I have an amusing letter or two to show you,—one from a gentleman who has sent me his works; happily the only instance of the kind. For as Charles Lamb complains, it is always the people whose books *don't* sell who are anxious to send them to one, with "foolish autographs" inside.

Ever yours truly
George Eliot

TO JOHN BLACKWOOD, [5 JUNE 1859]

Letters to *The Times* continued. When Blackwood called on the Leweses at Wandsworth 5 June, he drew up a reply which was sent with this letter of GE's, denying Liggins's claim. They were published together 6 June. [III, 75]

[Wandsworth]
My dear Mr. Blackwood,
   As it seems my statement that Mr. Liggins is not the author of "Scenes of Clerical Life" and "Adam Bede" is by certain persons flatly contradicted, I wish you would add the weight of your testimony to the truth of what I have stated.
   It is the more painful to me that Mr. Liggins, or any one else, should be receiving charitable donations on the ground that your treatment of me has not been sufficiently liberal, because I, for my part, can only wish that every author had equal reason to be satisfied with his publisher. If those benevolent persons who persist in attributing the authorship of the works in question to Mr. Liggins,

will induce Mr. Liggins to write one chapter of a story, that chapter may possibly do what my denial has failed to do.

Yours most sincerely
George Eliot.

TO WILLIAM BLACKWOOD, 6 JUNE 1859

Tauchnitz, who had paid £30 for the reprint of the *Scenes* in Germany, gave £50 for *Adam Bede*. Mrs. Gaskell's letter was signed "Gilbert Elliot." [III, 76]

[Wandsworth] June 6. 59.

My dear Major Blackwood

I shall be much obliged to you if you will accept for me this amended offer on Tauchnitz' part.

The "Liggins business" *does* annoy me, because it subjects you and Mr. John Blackwood to the reception of insulting letters and the trouble of writing contradictions. Otherwise, the whole affair is really a subject for a Molière-comedy— "The wise men of Warwickshire," who might supersede the "Wise men of Gotham."

The letter you sent me was a very pleasant one from Mrs. Gaskell, saying that since she came up to town she has had the compliment paid her of being suspected to have written "Adam Bede." "I have hitherto denied it: but really I think, that as you want to keep your real name a secret, it would be very pleasant for me to blush acquiescence. Will you give me leave?" I hope the inaccuracy with which she writes my name is not characteristic of a genius for fiction, though I once heard a German account for the bad spelling in Goethe's early letters by saying that it was "genial"—their word for whatsoever is characteristic of genius.

Yours very sincerely
George Eliot.

TO JOHN GWYTHER, [15 JUNE 1859]

The Curate of Chilvers Coton, John Gwyther, who officiated at Mrs. Evans's funeral and Chrissey's wedding, had recognized himself as "Amos Barton" when the story appeared in *Maga*. He suspected that W. H. King, Curate of Nuneaton at the time, had written it, and when Liggins's claim was being discussed, wrote to ask Blackwood if King was the author. The letter was sent to GE for acknowledgement, and a copy of hers was sent to Gwyther. [III, 85–86]

[Wandsworth]

The author of the "Scenes of Clerical Life" and "Adam Bede" begs me to inform you that he is not the Rev. W. H. King, but a much younger person, who wrote "Amos Barton" under the impression that the clergyman whose long past trial suggested the groundwork of the story was no longer living, and that the incidents, not only through the license and necessities of artistic writing, but in consequence of the writer's imperfect knowledge, must have been so varied from the actual facts, that any one who discerned the core of truth must also recognize the large amount of arbitrary, imaginative addition.

But for any annoyance, even though it may have been brief and not well-founded, which the appearance of the story may have caused Mr. Gwyther, the writer is sincerely sorry.

TO SARA HENNELL, [24 JUNE 1859]

The Brays and Sara Hennell came to Sydenham for the Handel Festival 20 June and invited the Leweses to dine at their lodgings after the concert. GE wrote in her Journal, "I told them I was the author of *Adam Bede* and *Clerical Scenes*, and they seemed overwhelmed with surprize. This experience has enlightened me a good deal as to the ignorance in which we all live of each other." Sara had looked forward to this first meeting in five years to discuss the manuscript of her *Thoughts in Aid of Faith;* GHL had the disagreeable task of telling her of their decided disapprobation. [III, 90]

[Wandsworth]

Dear Sara

There is always an after-sadness belonging to brief and interrupted intercourse between friends—the sadness of feeling that the blundering efforts we have made towards mutual understanding have only made a new veil between us—still more the sadness of feeling that some pain may have been given which separation makes a permanent memory. We are quite unable to represent ourselves truly— why should we complain that our friends see a false image?

I say this, because I am feeling painfully this morning that instead of helping you when you brought before me a matter so deeply interesting to you, I have only blundered, and that I have blundered, as most of us do, from too much egoism and too little sympathy. If my mind had been more open to receive impressions instead of being in overhaste to give them, I should more readily have seen what your object was in giving me that portion of your M.S., and we might have gone through the necessary part of it together on Tuesday. It seems of no use to write this now—and yet, I can't help wanting to assure you that, if I am too imperfect to do and feel the right thing at the right moment, I am not without the slower sympathy that becomes all the stronger from a sense of previous mistake.

Dear Sara, believe that I shall think of you and your work much, and that my ear and heart are more open for the future because I feel I have not done what a better spirit would have made me do in the past.

Yours,
Marian.

TO CHARLES BRAY, [24 JUNE 1859]

The Brays had long known Thornton Hunt and his wife and had discussed his liaison with Agnes Lewes. [III, 91]

[Wandsworth]

Dear Friend

Pardon me for troubling you with a few words just to say that I am uneasy at having listened with apparent acquiescence to statements about poor Agnes which a little quiet reflection has convinced me are mingled with falsehood—I fear of a base sort. And I am also angry with myself for having spoken of her faults—quite uselessly—to you and Cara. All such talk is futile. And I always hate myself after such attempts to vindicate one person at the expense of another. Justice is never secured in that way—perhaps not in any other. So much, not to remove any impression from your two minds—but to satisfy myself by protesting against a momentary acceptance of gratuitous evil speaking either by myself or others.

Yours—

M. L.

TO THE BRAYS AND SARA HENNELL, [27 JUNE 1859]

On the train back to Coventry, the Brays reported, one lady told them that Isaac Evans had been heard to say after reading *Adam Bede*, "No one but his Sister could write the book." The two portraits in the *Scenes* are those of John Gwyther (Amos Barton) and James Buchanan (Robert Dempster). [III, 99]

Holly Lodge | Monday Evening.

Dear Friends—all three of you—

Thanks for your packet of heart-felt kindness. That is the best of your kindness—there is no sham in it. It was inevitable to me to have that outburst when I saw you for a little while after the long silence, and felt that I must tell you then or be forestalled, and leave you to gather the truth amidst an inextricable mixture of falsehood. But I feel that the influence of talking about my books even to you and Mrs. Bodichon has been so bad to me that I should like to be able to keep silence concerning them for evermore. If people were to buzz round me with their remarks, or compliments, I should lose the repose of mind and truthfulness of production without which no good healthy books can be written. Talking about my books, I find, has much the same malign effect on me as talking of my feelings or my religion.

I should think Sara's version of my brother's words concerning Adam Bede is the correct one—"that there are *things in it about my father*" i.e. being interpreted, things my father told us about his early life, not a "portrait" of my father. There is not a single portrait in the book, nor will there be in any future book of mine. There are *two* portraits in the Clerical Scenes; but that was my first bit of art, and my hand was not well in—I did not know so well how to manipulate my materials.

As for the incognito—things must take their course. We can't help people saying *now* that the books are mine, but the one point to secure is that we and our friends make no categorical statement, which can be taken as absolute authority. As soon as the Liggins falsehood is annihilated of course there will be twenty new ones in its place; and one of the first will be that I was not the sole author. The only safe thing for my mind's health is to shut my ears and go on with my work.

So much, and no more. Think of me always as a sharer in your evil and your good.

Marian.

TO CHARLES BRAY, 5 JULY 1859

Bray sent GE a letter from Charles Bracebridge with comments on *Adam Bede* by Florence Nightingale, whom he and Mrs. Bracebridge had accompanied to the Crimea in 1854. A coolness had arisen between the Leweses and Spencer because of his jealousy of their success and his betrayal of the pseudonym to Chapman. GHL went to Hofwyl to see his sons, leaving GE at Lucerne with their neighbours the Congreves. [III, 110–11]

H. L. | July 5. 59

Dear Friend

Thanks for the letters. They have given me one pleasure—that of knowing that Mr. Liggins has not been *greatly* culpable—though Mr. B's statement that only "some small sums" have been collected, does not accord with what has been written to Blackwood from other counties. But "O I am sick!" Take no more trouble about me—and let every one believe—as they will in spite of all your kind efforts—*what they like to believe.*

It is amazing, after the experience we have all had when we have lived a good number of years in the world, that our minds still rush to accept statements and repeat them. I feel so deeply the duty of doubting everything to the disadvantage of another until demonstration comes, that I beg you not to regard the last thing Mr. Lewes told you about Herbert Spencer, as a thing incapable of being so explained as to make it more consistent with our previous conviction concerning his character. Mr. Lewes and I both hope in the possibility of such an explanation. And I need hardly say that anything we have told you about him, has been told in full confidence that you would allow no symptom of such knowledge to escape you either to him or others. *We* shall be doubly careful to speak only of what we admire in him to the world generally. The rest we have told to no one but Mrs. Bodichon, you, and Blackwood. Blackwood we were obliged to tell in order to account for the betrayal of the anonymity. . . . We intend to start for Switzerland on Saturday—nothing hindering—to remain away not more than ten days, I imagine.

I can't tell you how much melancholy it causes me that people are, for the most part, so incapable of comprehending the state of mind which cares for that which is essentially human in all forms of belief, and desires to exhibit it under all forms with loving truthfulness. Free-thinkers are scarcely wider than the orthodox in this matter—they all want to see themselves and their own opinions held up as the true and the lovely. On the same ground that an idle woman with flirtations and flounces likes to read a French novel because she can imagine herself the heroine, grave people, with opinions, like the most admirable character in a novel to be their mouth-piece. If Art does not enlarge men's sympathies, it does nothing morally.

I have had heart-cutting experience that opinions are a poor cement between human souls; and the only effect I ardently long to produce by my writings, is that those who read them should be better able to *imagine* and to *feel* the pains and the joys of those who differ from themselves in everything but the broad fact of being struggling erring human creatures.

Yours ever
G. E.

My *name* is Marian Evans *Lewes*.

TO JOHN BLACKWOOD, 23 JULY 1859

Blackwood's check combined £50 from Tauchnitz with £37 10s. for "The Lifted Veil." In his letter John Blackwood offered to advance the payments for *Adam Bede* if GE needed money. The success of the book consoled her for the vulgar personal attack by William Hepworth Dixon in the *Athenaeum* Gossip Column declaring that it was a tale "such as a clever woman with an observant eye and unschooled moral nature might have written . . . a rather strong-minded lady, blessed with abundance of showy sentiment and a profusion of pious words, but kept for sale rather than use . . . , Miss Biggins." From Lucerne GHL went to Hofwyl to see his sons "and unburthened myself about Agnes to them. They were less distressed than I had anticipated and were delighted to hear about Marian." GE once said to Blackwood that she wished some nobleman would admire *Adam Bede* enough to send her a pug, and he declared that she should have one. [III, 118–19]

[Wandsworth] July 23. 59.

My dear Sir

I thank you for the cheque for £87..10, which awaited me here. You would conclude that nothing but absence could be the cause of my slowness in acknowledgement. I thank you also for your offer about the money for Adam, but I have intentions of stern thrift, and mean to want as little as possible. When "Maggie" is done, and I have a month or two of leisure, I should like to transfer our present house into which we were driven by haste and economy, to some one who likes houses full of eyes all round him. I long for a house with some shade and grass close round it—I don't care how rough—and the sight of Swiss houses has heightened my longing. But at present I say, avaunt, to all desires.

I carried away with me the comfort of knowing that 5000 of Adam had gone in a fortnight, and *that* was enough to console me for all the inflictions of Dixonian or other enmity—even for the inflictions of friendship, which are certainly the hardest of all. While I think of it, let me beg of you to mention to the superintendent of your printing office, that in case of another reprint of "Adam," I beg the word "sperrit" (for "spirit") may be particularly attended to. Adam never said "speerit," as he is made to do in the cheaper edition, at least in one place—his speech at the birthday dinner. This is a small matter, but it is a point I care about.

Words fail me about the not impossible pug, for some compunction at having mentioned my unreasonable wish will mingle itself paradoxically with the hope that it may be fulfilled.

I hope we shall have other interviews to remember this time next year, and that you will find me without aggravated symptoms of the "author's malady"—a determination of talk to my own books, which I was alarmingly conscious of when you and the Major were here. After all, I fear authors must submit to be something of monsters not quite simple, healthy human beings; but I will keep my monstrosity within bounds if possible. With kindest remembrances to Major Blackwood, I am ever, my dear Sir,

Yours very truly
George Eliot.

TO MME EUGÈNE BODICHON, 23 JULY 1859

On her honeymoon in the United States Barbara wrote frequent letters describing conditions there in 1857. She asked the Leweses to help get them published. [III, 119]

Holly Lodge | July 23. 59.

Dear Barbara

We reached home last night, and one of my first thoughts is naturally about you. Did you get your three volumes of American Letters? Mr. Lewes thought we had better send them even without your commands, and we sent them by the carrier accordingly.

I am wonderfully inspirited and strengthened by our rapid run—Mr. Lewes less so, but still conscious of benefit. Some quiet days of talk with the Congreves, in sight of the Lucerne lake and mountains, was a soothing change to me, and I sit down to my desk with fresh courage and fresh enjoyment. You are getting the same sort of repose in the green country, I hope. Let me hear of it, and enrich my life with your pleasures.

The 4th edition of 'Adam Bede' (5000) sold in a fortnight! These are the results that give one fortitude to endure one's enemies—even to endure one's friends. I will not call you a friend—I will rather call you by some name that I am not obliged to associate with evaporated professions and petty egoism. I will call you only Barbara, the name I must always associate with a true, large heart. Some mean, treacherous Barbara may come across me, but she will only be like a shadow of a vulgar woman flitting across my fresco of St. Barbara.

Ever yours,
Marian.

TO JOHN BLACKWOOD, 30 JULY 1859

Blackwood enlisted the services of his cousin Colonel Steuart to find Pug, which cost him 30 g. "But *Adam Bede* flourishes, so I grins and bears it," he wrote to Langford, who brought the dog to the Leweses' and stayed for lunch, 29 July. [III, 124–25]

[Wandsworth]

My dear Sir

Pug is come!—come to fill up the void left by false and narrow-hearted friends. I see already that he is without envy, hatred, or malice—that he will betray no secrets, and feel neither pain at my success nor pleasure in my chagrin. I hope the photograph does justice to his physiognomy. It is expressive, full of gentleness and affection, and radiant with intelligence when there is a savoury morsel in question—a hopeful indication of his mental capacity. I distrust all intellectual pretension that announces itself by obtuseness of palate!

I wish you could see him in his best *pose*,—when I have arrested him in a violent career of carpet-scratching, and he looks at me with fore-legs very wide apart, trying to penetrate the deep mystery of this arbitrary, not to say capricious, prohibition. He is snoring by my side at this moment, with a serene promise of remaining quiet for any length of time: he couldn't behave better if he had been expressly educated for me. I am too lazy a lover of dogs and all earthly things to like them when they give me much trouble, preferring to describe the pleasure other people have in taking trouble.

Alas! the shadow that tracks all earthly good—the possibility of loss. One may lose one's faculties, which will not always fetch a high price; how much more a *Pug* worth unmentionable sums—a PUG which some generous-hearted personage in some other corner of Great Britain than Edinburgh may even now be sending emissaries after, being bent on paying the kindest, most delicate attention to a sensitive mortal not sufficiently reticent of wishes.

All I can say of that generous-hearted personage No. 2 is, that I wish he may get—somebody else's Pug, not mine. And all I will say of the sensitive, insufficiently-reticent mortal No. 2 is, that I hope he may be as pleased and as grateful as

George Eliot.

TO CHARLES LEWES, 30 JULY 1859

GE's first letter to GHL's eldest son is in reply to one from him beginning "Dear Mother" and saying that he is learning Mozart's Sonata in D for piano and violin. The journey was the School's annual outing in the Alps. [III, 125–27]

Holly Lodge, | Wandsworth, | July 30, 1859.

Dear Charlie,

I look forward to playing duets with you as one of my future pleasures, and if I am able to go on working, I hope we shall afford to have a fine grand piano. I have none of Mozart's Symphonies, so that you can be guided in your choice of them entirely by your own tastes. I know Beethoven's Sonata in E flat well. It is a very charming one, and I shall like to hear you play it. That is one of my luxuries—to sit still and hear some one playing my favourite music; so that you may be sure you will find willing ears to listen to the fruits of your industrious practising. There are ladies in the world, not a few, who play the violin, and I wish I were one of them, for then we could play together sonatas for the piano and violin which make a charming combination. The violin gives that *keen edge* of tone which the piano wants.

I like to know that you were gratified by getting a watch so much sooner than you expected. It was the greater satisfaction to me to send it you because you had earned it by making good use of these precious years at Hofwyl. It is a great comfort to your father and me to think of that, for we, with our grave old heads, cannot help talking very often of the need our boys will have for all sorts of good qualities and habits in making their way through this difficult life. It is a world, you perceive, in which crossbows *will* be *launisch* sometimes and frustrate the skill of excellent marksmen—how much more of lazy bunglers?

The first volume of the "Physiology of Common Life" is just published and it is a great pleasure to see so much of your father's hard work successfully finished. He has been giving a great deal of labour to the numbers on the Physiology of the Nervous System, which are to appear in the course of two or three months, and he has enjoyed the labour in spite of the drawback of imperfect health which obliges him very often to leave the desk with a hot and aching head. It is quite my worst trouble that he has so much of this discomfort to bear; and we must all try and make everything else as pleasant to him as we can, to make up for it. Tell Thornton he shall have the book he asks for—if possible—I mean the book of moths and butterflies; and tell Bertie I expect to hear about the wonderful things he has done with his pocket-knife. Tell him he is equipped well enough to become king of a desert island with that pocket-knife of his; and if, as I think I remember, it has a corkscrew attached, he would certainly have more instruments than he would need in that romantic condition.

We shall hope to hear a great deal of your journey with all its haps and mishaps. The mishaps are just as pleasant as the haps when they are past; that is one comfort for tormented travellers. You are an excellent correspondent, so I do not fear you will flag in writing to me; and remember you are always giving a pleasure when you write to your loving mother

Marian Lewes.

TO JOHN BLACKWOOD, 16 AUGUST 1859

GE began *The Mill on the Floss* in January 1859, when she went to the British Museum to study accounts of floods. In June she gave Blackwood the first 110 pages, which delighted him. He wrote to his brother: "She honestly confesses to a most deep seated anxiety to get a large price for the new Tale, and I think we will be well able to afford to give it. It should be a little fortune to her." In the ensuing weeks he asked eagerly about its progress. Caspar Hauser, a German foundling who said that he had been shut up in a dark room for 16 years, claimed to be the hereditary Prince of Baden. [III, 132–33]

[Wandsworth] August 16.59

My dear Sir . . .

I'm glad my story cleaves to you. At present, I have no hope that it will affect people as strongly as Adam has done. The characters are on a lower level generally, and the environment less romantic. But my stories grow in me like plants, and this is only in the leaf-bud. I have faith that the flower will come. Not enough faith, though, to make me like the idea of beginning to print till the flower is fairly out—till I know the end as well as the beginning.

Pug developes new charms every day. I think, in the pre-historic period of his existence, before he came to me, he had led a sort of Caspar Hauser life, shut up in a kennel in Bethnal Green, and he has had to get over much astonishment at the sight of cows and other rural objects on a large scale, which he marches up to and surveys with the gravity of an "own correspondent" whose business it is to observe. He has absolutely no bark—but *en revanche*, he sneezes powerfully and has speaking eyes, so the media of communication are abundant. He sneezes at the world in general, and he looks affectionately at *me*. . . .

Ever yours truly
George Eliot. . . .

TO MRS. CHARLES BRAY, 23 AUGUST [1859]

Leaving his children's old nurse Baker in the house to look after Pug, the Leweses went 26 August to Wales for a holiday. Cara had accepted the liaison and invited the Leweses to visit at Coventry. [III, 137]

Wandsworth | August 23.

Dear Cara

Our great difficulty is *Time*. I am little better than a sick nigger with the lash behind him, at present. If we go to Penmaenmawr, we shall travel all through by night, in order not to lose more than one day, and we shall pause at Lichfield on our way back. If we decide against Pen etc. (which I don't think probable) Lichfield will be a separate journey some time in October.

To pause at Coventry would be a real pleasure to me, but I think even if we could do it on our way home, it would be better economy to wait until the sense of hurry is past, and make it a little reward for work done. The going to the coast seems to be a wise measure, quite apart from indulgence—we are both so feeble—but otherwise, I should have kept my resolution, and remained quiet here for the next six months. Ever, dear Cara

Your affectionate
Marian.

They have sold 3000 more of Adam and are printing a 6th Edition!

TO JOHN BLACKWOOD, 13 SEPTEMBER 1859

The Leweses stayed only a week in Wales; to find lodgings was difficult and the weather cold. They stopped in Lichfield to see GE's nieces Emily and Kathy Clarke at Miss Eborall's School, and went on to Weymouth for a fortnight. There GE worked at her novel, looked over several mills, and discussed with GHL plans for publication. Since the loss of her anonymity the Blackwoods were less eager to have *The Mill on the Floss* in *Maga* and had made no definite offer for it. [III, 151–52]

39, East Street | Weymouth | September 13. 59.
My dear Sir

The very large sale of "Adam Bede" has necessarily modified my prospects as to the publication of my next book, and before troubling you with further manuscript, I want to tell you my thoughts on the subject. I have now so large and eager a public, that if we were to publish the work without a preliminary appearance in the Magazine, the first sale would infallibly be large, and a considerable profit would be gained even though the work might not ultimately impress the public so strongly as "Adam" has done.

Now surely publication in Maga, in the case of a new writer concerning whose works there is some expectation and curiosity, would inevitably reduce what would otherwise be the certain demand for three-volumed copies. The Magazine edition would be devoured, and would sweep away perhaps 20,000—nay, 40,000—readers who would otherwise demand copies of the complete work from the libraries. To say the least, there is enormous risk that the sale of the completed novel would be diminished. Again, the book might be in some respects superior to Adam, and yet not continue in the course of periodical reading to excite the same interest in the mass of readers, and an impression of its inferiority might be spread before republication:—another source of risk. The large circulation of "Adam" renders the continual advertisement afforded by publication in a first-rate periodical—an advertisement otherwise so valuable—comparatively unimportant.

I don't at all know what are your views as to the amount you could afford to pay me for publishing in the Magazine—I have no doubt you would do the utmost for me consistently with publishing rules—but in my ignorance I am unable to believe that you would find it worth while to compensate to me for the inevitable subtraction from subsequent proceeds. I shall be much obliged to you if you will let me know precisely what arrangement you contemplate.

You see, I speak to you without circumlocution, and I am sure you will like that best. You know how important this money question is to me. I don't want the world to give me anything for my books except money enough to save me from the temptation to write *only* for money. Ever, my dear Sir,

Yours very truly
George Eliot.

John Blackwood Esq.
We return to Wandsworth on Friday.

TO JOHN BLACKWOOD, 22 SEPTEMBER 1859

Though Blackwood wrote to his brother that he would rather give £4,000 than lose *The Mill on the Floss* for the Magazine, he offered GE £3,000 for its publication there and the copyright for four years. With a singular lapse of tact, he added, "In the Magazine we would not put any author's name, and it would be great fun to watch the speculations as to the author's life." [III, 161–62]

Holly Lodge | Wandsworth | September 22. 59.

My dear Sir
When I wrote to you I felt no disposition to publish in the Magazine beyond the inclination to meet your wishes—if they still pointed in that direction, and if I could do so without sacrifice. Your letter confirms my presupposition that you would not find it worth your while to compensate me for the renunciation of the unquestionable advantages my book would derive from being presented to the public in three volumes with all its freshness upon it. It was an oversight of mine not to inform you that I do not intend to part with the copyright, but only with an edition. As, from the nature of your offer, I infer that you think my next book will be a speculation attended with risk, I prefer incurring that risk myself.

I don't know whether you have had any glimpse of the annoyances I am still suffering from Mr. Bracebridge and the other friends of Liggins. Mr. Bracebridge still maintains that Liggins gave me my materials! But, worse than this, he has taken a journey into Staffordshire, and has busied himself among people named Poyser in order to identify my supposed portraits! He has discovered that I had an aunt and uncle who were Wesleyans, and is informing his acquaintances that Dinah and Seth are portraits of my aunt and uncle—two aged people, dead these twelve years, with no other resemblance to my characters than that they were pious Wesleyans. Mr. Irwine, it appears, is a "Rev. George Hole," of whom I never heard in my life—etc.—etc. I hope the world is getting a great deal of good out of Adam Bede—it will signify less, then, that the author gets so much pain out of it. Mr. Bracebridge has had a severe letter written to him, calling on him to apologize for the implication he casts on me, of using other people's materials and disavowing them. Whether it will be effective passes the bounds of sane conjecture. He appears to be so nearly an idiot, that it would not be safe to predict his mental processes.

Ever yours truly
George Eliot.

John Blackwood Esq.

TO CHARLES BRAY, [30 SEPTEMBER 1859]

In a letter to Bray Bracebridge spoke of GE as "a living phenomenon, a self-educated farmer's daughter." Combe noted Bray's description of her in his Journal, 29 August 1851. [III, 168–69]

[Wandsworth] Friday.

Dear Friend

Amidst the prevaricating and low-minded imbecility of Mr. Bracebridge's letters, concerning which I do not intend to write another word, there is one phrase which I am prompted to notice by my feeling towards my Father's memory. He speaks of my Father as a "farmer." Now my Father did not raise himself from being an artizan to be a farmer: he raised himself from being an artizan to be a man whose extensive knowledge in very varied practical departments made his services valued through several counties. He had large knowledge of building, of mines, of plantation, of various branches of valuation and measurement—of all that is essential to the management of large estates. He was held by those competent to judge as *unique* amongst land-agents for his manifold knowledge and experience, which enabled him to save the special fees usually paid by landowners for special opinions on the different questions incident to the proprietorship of land. I mention this subject to you, because I have some reason to believe that in using the phrase "self-educated farmer's daughter" Mr. Bracebridge was borrowing from you. My reason is, that long ago George Combe told me you had spoken of my father to him as a "mere farmer," and I had to explain to George Combe what my father really was. So far as I am personally concerned, I should not write a stroke to prevent any one, in the zeal of antithetic eloquence, from calling me a tinker's daughter; but if my Father is to be mentioned at all—if he is to be identified with an imaginary character, my piety towards his memory calls on me to point out to those who are supposed to speak with information, what he really achieved in life.

Yours affectionately
Marian Evans Lewes.

Charles Bray Esq.

TO HERBERT SPENCER, 2 OCTOBER 1859

Almost eight months after its publication Spencer finally read *Adam Bede*. In a long letter to GE 30 September he wrote: "At length I have read Adam Bede—finished it last night in considerable alarm at the probable consequences of having read a volume and a half in the day: consequences however which were not so bad as I expected. . . . And now that I have read it what am I to say. That I have read it with laughter and tears and without criticism. Knowing as you do how constitutionally I am given to fault finding, you will understand what this means. That I who am so little given to enthusiastic admiration, should not know how adequately to say how much I admire, will give you some idea of my feeling respecting it. It comes up to my ideal of a work of art—possesses *all* the requisite qualities in due balance; which is more than I can say of any fiction I ever read. . . . And then let me not forget the moral effect. I feel greatly the better for having read it; and can scarcely imagine any one reading it without having their sympathies widened and their better resolves strengthened. Not only in the interests of literature but in the interests of progress I hope that we shall have many more such books from you." Spencer protested that he was unaware of any change in his attitude towards the Leweses, accounting for it by his long absences from town. "I should feel it a serious misfortune if anything were to dissolve our friendship." [VIII, 247]

Holly Lodge, South Fields | Wandsworth | October 2. 59.

Dear Friend

    Your words about 'Adam Bede' are very precious, and they came opportunely, for I have been much worried of late. To have written a book that can move people as they say they are moved by 'Adam Bede' ought to be happiness enough for me—ought to make me strong against minor personal griefs. But I have a new proof of the predominance of an egoistic sensitiveness in me, in the power these minor griefs retain over me. Yet I did feel very happy this morning, in spite of previous depression, when I came to that part of your letter where you say you felt the better for reading my book. It will always be one of the things I shall think of when I want to gather courage.

    I have often accounted to myself for the change I imagined in your manner towards me by the supposition that I had made myself disagreeable in some way. I should not have trusted my own inferences, because I know I am rather morbid in such matters; but George, who is not apt to err in the same way, had a similar impression, and long ago, at Richmond, we used to try and recal some possible offence on my part.

    Never mind: it is enough that you are not conscious of any change in feeling.

Ever yours sincerely
Marian Evans Lewes.

Herbert Spencer Esq

TO MRS. CHARLES BRAY, [?3 OCTOBER 1859]

The photograph that Marian gave the Brays had hung in the dining room. On 1 October Sara wrote that, though she grieved to change its place, "we have agreed that it should come to my bedroom for the present." [III, 170–71]

[Wandsworth]

Thank you, dear, dear Cara, for your words of sympathy. And the things you tell me at the end of your note are just such as I need to know—I mean, about the help my book is to the people who read it.

    The weight of my future life—the self-questioning whether my nature will be able to meet the heavy demands upon it, both of personal duty and intellectual production, presses upon me almost continually in a way that prevents me even from tasting the quiet joy I might have in the work done. Buoyancy and exultation, I fancy, are out of the question, when one has lived so long as I have. But I am the better for every word of encouragement, and am helped over many days by such a note as yours. I often think of my dreams when I was four or five and twenty. I thought then, how happy fame would make me! I feel no regret that the fame, as such, brings no pleasure, but it is a grief to me that I do not constantly feel strong in thankfulness that my past life has vindicated its uses, and given me reason for gladness that such an unpromising woman-child was born into the world. I ought not to care about small annoyances, and it is chiefly egoism that makes them annoyances.

Tell Sara, I won't write to her today, but I know she will like to hear that I had quite an *enthusiastic* letter from Herbert Spencer the other day about "Adam Bede." He says he feels the better for reading it—really words to be treasured up. . . .

Tell Sara, I leave the decision about the portrait to her—but I *do not* like it to be in a public place.

Ever thine
Marian.

I must tell you, *in confidence,* that Dickens has written to me the noblest, most touching words about 'Adam'—not hyperbolical compliments, but expressions of deep feeling. He says the reading made an epoch in his life. Mind, I tell you *in confidence.*

TO SARA HENNELL, 7 OCTOBER 1859

After GE's death, when the obituary accounts revived the charge that she had copied Dinah's sermon from her aunt's notes, Sara Hennell published this letter in the *Pall Mall Budget*. [III, 174–77]

Holly Lodge, | October 7, 1859.
Dear Sara,—

I should like, while the subject is vividly present with me, to tell you more exactly than I have ever yet done, *what* I knew of my aunt, Elizabeth Evans. My father, you know, lived in Warwickshire all my life with him, having finally left Staffordshire first, and then Derbyshire, six or seven years before he married my mother. There was hardly any intercourse between my father's family, resident in Derbyshire and Staffordshire, and our family—few and far-between visits of (to my childish feelings) strange uncles and aunts and cousins from my father's far-off native country, and once a journey of my own, as a little child, with my father and mother, to see my uncle William (a rich builder) in Staffordshire—but *not* my uncle and aunt Samuel, so far as I can recall the dim outline of things—are what I remember of northerly relatives in my childhood.

But when I was seventeen or more—after my sister was married and I was mistress of the house—my father took a journey into Derbyshire in which, visiting my uncle and aunt Samuel, who were very poor, and lived in a humble cottage at Wirksworth, he found my aunt in a very delicate state of health after a serious illness, and, to do her bodily good, he persuaded her to return with him, telling her that *I* should be very, very happy to have her with me for a few weeks. I was then strongly under the influence of Evangelical belief, and earnestly endeavouring to shape this anomalous English-Christian life of ours into some consistency with the spirit and simple verbal tenor of the New Testament.

I *was* delighted to see my aunt. Although I had only heard her spoken of as a strange person, given to a fanatical vehemence of exhortation in private as well as public, I believed that we should find sympathy between us. She was then an old woman—above sixty—and, I believe, had for a good many years given up preaching. A tiny little woman, with bright, small dark eyes, and hair that had been black, I imagine, but was now grey—a pretty women in her youth, but of a totally different physical type from Dinah. The difference—as you will believe—was not *simply* physical: no difference is. She was a woman of strong natural excitability, which I know, from the description I have heard my father and half-sister give, prevented her from the exercise of discretion under the promptings of her zeal. But this vehemence was now subdued by age and sickness; she was very gentle and quiet in her manners—very loving—and (what she must have been from the very first) a truly religious soul, in whom the love of God and love of man were fused together.

There was nothing highly distinctive in her religious conversation: I had had much intercourse with pious Dissenters before: The only freshness I found, in our talk, came from the fact that she had been the greater part of her life a Wesleyan, and though *she left the society when women were no longer allowed to preach,* and joined the New Wesleyans, she retained the character of thought that belongs to the genuine old Wesleyan. I had never talked with a Wesleyan before, and we used to have little debates about predestination, for I was then a strong Calvinist. Here her superiority came out, and I remember now, with loving admiration, one thing which at the time I disapproved: it was not strictly a consequence of her Arminian belief, and at first sight might seem opposed to it, yet it came from the spirit of love which clings to the bad logic of Arminianism. When my uncle came to fetch her, after she had been with us a fortnight or three weeks, he was speaking of a deceased minister, once greatly respected, who from the action of trouble upon him had taken to small tippling, though otherwise not culpable. 'But I hope the good man's in heaven for all that,' said my uncle. 'Oh yes,' said my aunt, with a deep inward groan of joyful conviction. 'Mr. A's in heaven—that's sure.' This was at the time an offence to my stern, ascetic hard views—how beautiful it is to me now!

As to my aunt's conversation, it is a fact, that the only two things of any interest I remember in our lonely sittings and walks, are her telling me one sunny afternoon how she had, with another pious woman, visited an unhappy girl in prison, stayed with her all night, and gone with her to execution, and one or two accounts of supposed miracles in which she believed—among the rest, *the face with the crown of thorns seen in the glass.* In her account of the prison scenes, I remember no word she uttered—I only remember her tone and manner, and the deep feeling I had under the recital. Of the girl she knew nothing, I believe—or told me nothing—but that she was a common coarse girl, convicted of child-murder. The incident lay in my mind for years on years, as a dead germ, apparently—till time had made my mind a nidus in which it could fructify; it then turned out to be the germ of 'Adam Bede.'

I saw my aunt twice after this. Once I spent a day and night with my father in the Wirksworth cottage, sleeping with my aunt, I remember. Our interview was less interesting than in the former time: I think I was less simply devoted to religious ideas. And once again she came with my uncle to see me—when Father and I were living at Foleshill: *then* there was some pain, for I had given up the form of Christian belief, and was in a crude state of free-thinking. She stayed about three or four days, I think. This is all I remember distinctly, as matter I could write down, of my dear aunt, whom I really loved. You see how she suggested Dinah; but it is not possible you should see as I do how entirely her individuality differed from Dinah's. How curious it seems to me that people should think Dinah's sermon, prayers, and speeches were *copied*—when they were written with hot tears, as they surged up in my own mind!

As to my indebtedness to facts of locale, and personal history of a small kind, connected with Staffordshire and Derbyshire—you may imagine of what kind that is, when I tell you that I never remained in either of those counties more than a few days together, and of only two such visits have I more than a shadowy, interrupted recollection. The details which I knew as facts and have made use of for my picture were gathered from such imperfect allusion and narrative as I heard from my father, in his occasional talk about old times.

As to my aunt's children or grandchildren saying, if they *did* say, that Dinah is a good portrait of my aunt—that is simply the vague easily satisfied notion imperfectly instructed people always have of portraits. It is not surprising that simple men and women without pretension to enlightened discrimination should think a generic resemblance constitutes a portrait, when we see the great public so accustomed to be delighted with *mis*-representation of life and character, which they accept as representations, that they are scandalized when art makes a nearer approach to truth.

Perhaps I am doing a superfluous thing in writing all this to you—but I am prompted to do it by the feeling that in future years 'Adam Bede' and all that concerns it, may have become a dim portion of the past, and I may not be able to recall so much of the truth as I have now told you. Once more, thanks, dear Sara.

Ever your loving
Marian.

TO JOHN BLACKWOOD, 16 OCTOBER 1859

GE was always concerned about the text of her novels, though willing to soften the dialect to make easier reading. *The Mill on the Floss* was still without a title. All her previous letters to the Blackwoods had been signed "George Eliot," and the new signature indicated that she intended to make no secret of her authorship. Dr. J. J. Guggenbühl founded an establishment for cretins near Interlaken. [III, 184–85]

Holly Lodge | October 16. 59.

My dear Sir

The other day, happening to take up the 2 volume edition of "Adam," I read on a good way, and shuddered not a little, every now and then, to find how many misprints had crept even into this first of the 2 volume editions. Unless something can be done to refresh the official Reader's care, the text will become corrupt to an extent that will really mar many passages of the book. Conceive an author's feelings at findings such changes as "vale" for "veil," making him guilty of bad metaphors! Will you "sharpen it into" the right persons, that in correcting the press a copy of the *first* 3 volume edition must be used, and that great care must be taken of the dialect, though this is less vital than nouns and verbs. Still it is a blemish, to see such things as "theed'st" constantly printed for "thee'dst."

I wish you had read the letter you enclosed to me—it is really curious. The writer, an educated person, asks me to "perfect and extend" the benefit Adam Bede has "conferred on society," by writing a *sequel* to it, in which I am to tell all about Hetty after her reprieve—"Arthur's efforts to obtain the reprieve and his desperate ride after obtaining it—Dinah on board the convict ship—Dinah's letters to Hetty—and whatever the author might choose to reveal concerning Hetty's years of banishment." "Minor instances of the incompleteness which induces an unsatisfactory feeling may be alleged in the disposal of the *locket and ear-rings*—which everybody expects to re-appear—and in the incident of the *pink silk neckerchief*, of which all would like to hear a little more"!! . . .

If you were living in London instead of at Edinburgh, I should ask you to read the first volume of "Sister Maggie" at once, for the sake of having your impressions; but it is inconvenient to me to part with the M.S. The great success of "Adam" makes my writing a matter of more anxiety than ever: I suppose there is a little sense of responsibility mixed up with a great deal of pride. And I think I should worry myself still more if I began to print before the thing is essentially complete. So on all grounds it is better to wait. . . .

You must no longer believe in Pug's portrait—he is so much handsomer, to say nothing of the new "mind, the music breathing from his face." Considering that when he came, he was a sort of crétin, fit for Dr. Guggenbühl's establishment, I am proud of the advance he has made in three months of our intellectual soceity. Ever, my dear Sir,

Yours very truly
Marian Evans Lewes.

John Blackwood Esq.

TO FRANÇOIS D'ALBERT DURADE, 18 OCTOBER 1859
[III, 186–88]

Holly Lodge, South Fields | Wandsworth, Surrey
October 18, 1859.

My dear Friend

Does it ever happen to you now to think of a certain Englishwoman, née Marian Evans? She seems perhaps to deserve that you should forget her, seeing that she has let years pass without making any sign of her existence. . . . But in these last three years a great change has come over my life—a change in which I cannot help believing that both you and Madame d'Albert will rejoice. Under the influence of the intense happiness I have enjoyed in my married life from thorough moral and intellectual sympathy, I have at last found out my true vocation, after which my nature had always been feeling and striving uneasily without finding it. What do you think that vocation is? I pause for you to guess.

I have turned out to be an artist—not, as you are, with the pencil and the pallet, but with words. I have written a novel which people say has stirred them very deeply—and *not a few* people, but almost all reading England. It was published in February last, and already 14,000 copies have been sold. The title is "Adam Bede"; and "George Eliot," the name on the title page, is my *nom de plume.* I had previously written another work of fiction called, "Scenes of Clerical Life," which had a great *literary* success, but not a great *popular* success, such as "Adam Bede" has had. Both are now published by Tauchnitz in his series of English novels.

I think you will believe that I do not write you word of this out of any small vanity:—my books are deeply serious things to me, and come out of all the painful discipline, all the most hardly-learnt lessons of my past life. I write you word of it, because I believe that both your kind heart and Madame d'Albert's too, will be touched with real joy, that one whom you knew when she was not very happy and when her life seemed to serve no purpose of much worth, has been at last blessed with the sense that she has done something worth living and suffering for. And I write also because I want to give both you and her a proof that I still think of you with grateful affectionate recollection. . . .

Farewell, dear friend. Ask Madame d'Albert to accept my affectionate regards, and believe me faithfully yours

Marian E. Lewes.

TO JOHN BLACKWOOD, 28 OCTOBER 1859

John Blackwood wrote that instead of £400 additional payment for *Adam Bede* they intended to give GE £800. The printers had been reprimanded for the mistakes in the 2-volume edition of the book. A publisher named Newby had just announced *Adam Bede, Junior. A Sequel.* GHL thought that Blackwood should seek an injunction, but his legal friends agreed with him that it was better to let the rubbish die. Dickens wrote a letter with warm praise of *Adam Bede,* which he told GE had made an epoch in his life. He was eager to get her next novel for his magazine, *All the Year Round.* [III, 191–92]

Holly Lodge, South Fields | Wandsworth | October 28. 59.

My dear Sir

I beg that you and Major Blackwood will accept my thanks for your proposal to give me a further share in the success of "Adam Bede," beyond the terms of our agreement, which are fulfilled by the second cheque for £400, received this morning. Neither you nor I ever calculated on half such a success, thinking that the book was too quiet and too unflattering to dominant fashions ever to be very popular. I hope that opinion of ours is a guarantee that there is nothing hollow or transient in the reception "Adam" has met with. Sometimes when I read a book which has had a great success and am unable to see any valid merits of an artistic kind to account for it, I am visited with a horrible alarm lest "Adam" too should ultimately sink into the same class of outworn admirations. But I always fall back on the fact that no shibboleth and no vanity is flattered by it, and that there is no novelty of mere form in it, which can have delighted simply by startling.

Mr. Lewes *had* written to you (to St. Andrews') about Newby's advertisement. I wish it *could* be put a stop to without much trouble. People in the provinces, I fear, know no difference between "Newby" and "Blackwoods" and can't see the moral impossibility of the sequel being mine. . . . I should have thought the advertisement might be stopped by a mere letter to Newby threatening him with an injunction. That would be a private affair, not liable to Dixonian comments. *More* trouble than that, perhaps, the injury is hardly worth. One wouldn't mind if the author of said sequel could be forced to put his name to it, as Reynolds did to "Pickwick Abroad."

Apropos of Pickwick, and quite *entre nous,* think a little kindly of Dickens on this ground: he has both written and spoken with the warmest, most generous admiration of "Adam." As a bit of justice too, I must tell you that the friend who caused me to make so much *mauvais sang* by his want of sympathy has come round to strong expression of even *benefit* from the reading of the book, which he has at last accomplished. I don't think he was conscious of the negations which wounded me; so we must forgive him his trespasses. But I am really too lengthy in my talk.

Ever yours truly
Marian Evans Lewes.

John Blackwood Esq.

TO MRS. ELIZABETH GASKELL, 11 NOVEMBER 1859

When Mrs. Gaskell, long a dupe of the Liggins myth, learned that Marian Evans was the author of *Adam Bede,* she wrote a generous letter telling how "earnestly, fully, and humbly" she admired her books. "I never read anything so complete and beautiful in fiction in my whole life before." But she could not resist adding, "I should not be quite true to my ending, if I did not say before I concluded that I wish you *were* Mrs. Lewes. However that can't be helped, as far as I can see, and one must not judge others." [III, 198–99]

Holly Lodge, South Fields | Wandsworth. | November 11. 59.

My dear Madam

Only yesterday I was wondering that artists, knowing each other's pains so well, did not help each other more, and, as usual, when I have been talking complainingly or suspiciously, something has come which serves me as a reproof. That "something" is your letter, which has brought me the only sort of help I care to have—an assurance of fellow-feeling, of thorough truthful recognition from one of the minds which are capable of judging as well as of being moved. You know, without my telling you, how much the help is heightened by its coming to me afresh, now that I have ceased to be a mystery and am known as a mere daylight fact. I shall always love to think that one woman wrote to another such sweet encouraging words—still more to think that you were the writer and I the receiver.

I had indulged the idea that if my books turned out to be worth much, you would be among my willing readers; for I was conscious, while the question of my power was still undecided for me, that my feeling towards Life and Art had some affinity with the feeling which had inspired "Cranford" and the earlier chapters of "Mary Barton." That idea was brought the nearer to me, because I had the pleasure of reading Cranford for the first time in 1857, when I was writing the "Scenes of Clerical Life," and going up the Rhine one dim wet day in the spring of the next year, when I was writing "Adam Bede," I satisfied myself for the lack of a prospect by reading over again those earlier chapters of "Mary Barton." I like to tell you these slight details because they will prove to you that your letter must have a peculiar value for me, and that I am not expressing vague gratitude towards a writer whom I only remember vaguely as one who charmed me in the past. And I cannot believe such details are indifferent to you, even after we have been so long used to hear them: I fancy, as long as we live, we all need to know as much as we can of the good our life has been to others. Ever, my dear Madam,

Yours with high regard
Marian Evans Lewes.

Mrs. Gaskell.

TO JOHN BLACKWOOD, 26 NOVEMBER 1859

Nearly half of The Mill on the Floss was written when, unable to bear the uncertainty, GE wrote this letter. [III, 215]

Holly Lodge | November 26. 59.

My dear Sir

As the time for publication of my next work is not very far removed, and as thorough frankness is the condition of satisfactoriness in all relations, I am induced to ask you whether you still wish to remain my publishers, or whether the removal of my incognito has caused a change in your views on that point.

I have never myself thought of putting an end to a connection which has hitherto not appeared inauspicious to either of us, and I have looked forward to your being my publishers as long as I produced books to be published; but various indications, which I may possibly have misinterpreted, have made me desire a clear understanding in the matter. I remain, my dear Sir,

Always yours truly
Marian Evans Lewes.

John Blackwood Esq.

TO JOHN BLACKWOOD, 30 NOVEMBER 1859

Blackwood protested that he had been hurt at the tone in which his offer of £3,000 has been received, "and also at the very dry way in which our conduct in doubling the purchase money of Adam Bede was acknowledged." He added: "As to the withdrawal of the incognito, you know how much I have been opposed to it all along. It may prove a disadvantage and in the eyes of many it will, but my opinion of your genius and confidence in the truly good, honest, religious, and moral tone of all you have written or will write is such that I think you will overcome any possible detriment from the withdrawal of the mystery which has so far taken place." Instead of sending The Times a letter denying that GE wrote Adam Bede, Jr., Blackwood merely had the Athenaeum and the Daily News publish a paragraph saying, "We are requested to state that a book advertised as Adam Bede, Jun.: a Sequel, is not by the author of Adam Bede." [III, 217–19]

Holly Lodge | November 30. 59.

My dear Sir

It is clear that there has been a misunderstanding between us, and I will try to explain my part of it. The first thing that hurt me was this. When you were in town and we were discussing the publication of my next book, you declared yourself strongly desirous to have it for the Magazine, and in answering Mr. Lewes's arguments for serial publication, you observed that you thought you could make the appearance of my story in Maga answer quite as well for me in a monetary point of view. Some months afterwards, when the success of "Adam Bede," having been in a perpetual crescendo, had heightened the prospects of my next book, I began to have increased doubt as to the prudence of publishing in Maga, thinking that, with my assured public, you would hardly be able to compensate me for certain disadvantages, some of which I had already mentioned to you as connected with the periodical publication of my story. Still, as you had seemed to wish it strongly, I desired to lay before you all my thoughts on the matter, that you might reconsider it. It was possible that you had contemplated an arrangement which would supersede my objections. I therefore wrote to you from Weymouth, putting before you as clearly and frankly as I knew how, all the reasons which disinclined me to publish in Maga, and expressing my doubt whether you would find it worth your while to give me such extra remuneration on the ground of that publication as would neutralize these reasons. In your reply, you took no notice whatever of the specific contents of my letter, but stated that you would give me "at least as much" for publication in Maga as in any other way. I think you will perceive, on reconsideration, that this reply was a stultification of my letter. Your proposition at the same time to publish the story without the name of George Eliot seemed to me (rendered doubly sensitive by the recent withdrawal of my incognito) part of a depreciatory view that ran through your whole letter, in contrast with the usual delicacy and generosity of your tone.

Still, I am aware that letters are peculiarly liable to misinterpretation, and in writing to decline your proposition, I had no thought of any breach, or of any inference on your part that I did not look forward to your publishing "Maggie" in three volumes. At that time I had received no offer from publishers but such as you were aware of, hence, you will perceive that the words in your letter of yester-day—"I would be the very last man who would wish for a moment to stand in the way of your doing what you thought best for yourself, but I think I should have been told so frankly, instead of having my offer treated as if it were worth no consideration at all"—are words which have no proper application to any con-duct of mine. I have never written to you with any double or suppressed intention. In fact, I had not dreamed that there was any doubt in your mind as to my expectation that you would publish "Maggie" until Mr. Langford, a short time ago, in conversation with Mr. Lewes, appeared to presuppose that you would *not* publish it.

After this, came what appeared to us, a manifestation of indifference to my wishes, if not to my interests, in the matter of Newby, which was hardly what was due from publisher to author or from friend to friend. On all hands we have heard surprize expressed at your silence. And, in declining to write to the Times, to write to the Athenæum, a paper which has grossly insulted me, to ask them to insert a paragraph without the mention of your name, indicated, I thought, a forgetfulness which implied a very considerable alteration of feeling toward me.

This is the chapter of my unpleasant impressions, which at length became so strong, that I determined to write and ask you a simple question, that our mutual feeling might be ascertained. But up to this moment, I have said to every one that the Messrs. Blackwood are my publishers, and that I see no reason to leave them; but the contrary. It was important to me on every ground to know that I was not speaking on a false basis; for if you did *not* wish to publish for me, I should necessarily be in a different attitude towards proposals which I have hitherto waived.

I prefer, in every sense, permanent relations to shifting ones, and have the strongest distaste for the odour of mere money speculation about my writing. Moreover, I should be sorry to entertain any exorbitant notions, inconsistent with a rational, just regard to other people's motives and interests. But I may say without cant—since I am in a position of anxiety for others as well as myself—that it is my duty to seek not less than the highest reasonable advantage from my work. It did appear to Mr. Lewes and myself that, for the sum you mentioned, it would be unwise to give up my book for *five* years, losing time also by a slow form of publication.

I must express my sincere regret that my mode of acknowledging to yourself and Major Blackwood your honourable intention to give me a further sum of £400, doubling the sum you were under agreement to give me, should have appeared to you curt and unresponsive. I had expressed myself, I thought, so strongly on previous occasions, that I had no apprehension of your suspecting me of insusceptibility on such points, and the simple "thank you" seems the most natural thing between people who understand each other.

I hope, at all events, that we have cleared the air, and that whatever may seem dubious in future may not be left without an immediate request for explanation. There is no reason, that I can see, for anything but the utmost frankness and explicitness on both sides.

Always yours truly
Marian Evans Lewes.

John Blackwood Esq.

TO JOHN BLACKWOOD, [5 DECEMBER 1859]

Her long letter arrived just as Blackwood was setting out for a weekend with Charles Newdegate at Arbury Hall. In his answer he treated each point made in her letter with care, explaining why he thought it wisest to have the new novel anonymous in *Maga*, though he now saw how it might have fallen disagreeably upon her. "I regretted the partial removal of the incognito, but I never thought of ceasing to be your publisher on that account nor did I dream that such an idea would ever occur to you." GE had sent her own letter to *The Times* about the Newby *Sequel*; Blackwood still thought that it would have been best to "let the rubbish die a natural death." If they could not agree on a fair sum for the novel, "possibly we may arrange some plan for a certain payment in the first instance and further instalments according to the sale of the book." [III, 224]

Holly Lodge | Monday.

My dear Sir

I hope you will be able to be with us at luncheon on Wednesday. Our time, you know, is half past one. It will be a great comfort to see you, and exchange our "winged words" in a less blind and ambiguous fashion than by letter.

I congratulate [you] on having seen that fine old place, Arbury. You must have passed by my brother's house, too—my old, old home.

Ever yours truly
George Eliot.

John Blackwood Esq.

TO FRANÇOIS D'ALBERT DURADE, 6 DECEMBER 1859

D'Albert wrote that in some pages of *Adam Bede* he could not recognize her. When she lived with them in Geneva, her ideas about the state of the soul during and after this life had verged on pantheism. [III, 230–32]

Holly Lodge, South Fields | Wandsworth | December 6. 59.

Dear Friend . . .

I can understand that there are many pages in "Adam Bede" in which you do not recognize the "Marian" or "Minie" of old Geneva days. We knew each other too short a time, and I was under too partial and transient a phase of my mental history, for me to pour out to you much of my earlier experience. I think I hardly ever spoke to you of the strong hold Evangelical Christianity had on me from the age of fifteen to two and twenty and of the abundant intercourse I had had with earnest people of various religious sects. When I was at Geneva, I had not yet lost the attitude of antagonism which belongs to the renunciation of *any* belief—also, I was very unhappy, and in a state of discord and rebellion towards my own lot. Ten years of experience have wrought great changes in that inward self: I have no longer any antagonism towards any faith in which human sorrow and human longing for purity have expressed themselves; on the contrary, I have a sympathy with it that predominates over all argumentative tendencies. I have not returned to dogmatic Christianity—to the acceptance of any set of doctrines as a creed, and a superhuman revelation of the Unseen—but I see in it the highest expression of the religious sentiment that has yet found its place in the history of mankind, and I have the profoundest interest in the inward life of sincere Christians in all ages. Many things that I should have argued against ten years ago, I now feel myself too ignorant and too limited in moral sensibility to speak of with confident disapprobation: on many points where I used to delight in expressing intellectual difference, I now delight in feeling an emotional agreement. On that question of our future existence, to which you allude, I have undergone the sort of change I have just indicated, although my most rooted conviction is, that the immediate object and the proper sphere of all our highest emotions are our struggling fellowmen and this earthly existence. So much in reply to your questions on those matters. I hope I shall not have made myself more obscure by my explanation.

We are very anxious to get an accomplished translator for "Adam Bede," and a little while ago Mr. Lewes wrote to Emile Montégut whose answer we are expecting on the subject. Hitherto I have rejected propositions of translation, from the dread of having one's sentences metamorphosed into an expression of somebody else's meaning instead of one's own. I particularly wish my books to be well translated into French, because the French read so little English, and if there is any healthy truth in my art, surely they need it to purify their literary air! . . .

I am writing a new work, which will not be published till next Easter, so that just now my hands and brain are full. At Easter our eldest boy will come home from school, and that will make a new epoch in our domestic life, for hitherto we have lived alone. I hope my heart will be large enough for all the love that is required of me.

Ever, dear Friend,

Yours with lasting regard
Marian Evans Lewes.

TO JOHN BLACKWOOD, 20 DECEMBER 1859

After a long interview with the Leweses at Holly Lodge 7 December, Blackwood carried away a volume and a half of MS. "She said her wish was to make some arrangement always to publish with us," he wrote to William Blackwood, and "she was determined that no publisher should ever lose by her." Bradbury & Evans had offered her £4,500 for publication in *Once a Week*, but she had rejected the offer. GHL had a notion of publication in monthly shilling numbers, but she felt that her story would tell better in a mass. After reading the MS, John sent her an offer of £2,000 for an edition of 4,000 copies and the same rate for every copy above that number in the 3-volume edition at 31/6. For the 2-volume edition at 12/, £150 a thousand, and for the 1-volume at 6/, £60 a thousand. When he called the next day, they accepted the terms—if they decided not to try the 1/ numbers plan. "She is a fine character—all my former good opinion of her is restored," John wrote to William. "I am sure I cannot be mistaken both in her language and the expression of her face." The next day GE sent this letter. [III, 236]

Holly Lodge, South Fields Dec. 20.59

My dear Sir

I think we have fairly dissipated the Nightmare of the Serial by dint of much talking. So we may consider the publication of Maggie settled according to the terms of your letter of the 14th December, understanding (I presume?) that the sums specified are to be paid at the date of publication.

I hope you have enjoyed your wintry visit more than you expected.

Ever yours truly
Marian Evans Lewes.

TO JOHN BLACKWOOD, 3 JANUARY 1860

With his check doubling the agreed payment for *Adam Bede*, Blackwood announced that they would return the copyright to GE for the remainder of the four years. The £2,000 for *The Mill on the Floss* they agreed to pay, not on date of publication, but in two installments, rather than the three the Blackwoods had proposed. The title was still undecided. [III, 240–41]

Holly Lodge | January 3. 1860.

My dear Sir

I never before had so pleasant a New Year's greeting as your letter containing a cheque for £800, for which I have to thank you today. On every ground—including considerations that are not at all of a monetary kind—I am deeply obliged to you and to Major Blackwood for your liberal conduct in relation to "Adam Bede."

With regard to the payments for the new book, it is of importance to me that they should rather be made in two sums of £1000, at six and nine months after the date of publication; and I hope this arrangement will not be inconvenient to you.

As, owing to your generous concession of the copyright of "Adam Bede," the three books will be henceforth on the same footing, we shall be delivered from further discussion as to terms.

I suppose it will be well to announce the new book in February (in Maga), will it not? We are demurring about the title. Mr. Lewes is beginning to prefer *"The House of Tulliver, or, Life on the Floss,"* to our old notion of "Sister Maggie." *"The Tullivers, or, Life on the Floss,"* has the advantage of slipping easily off the lazy English tongue, but it is after too common a fashion (The Newcomes, the Bertrams, etc. etc. etc.). Then, there is *"The Tulliver Family, or Life on the Floss."* Pray meditate and give us your opinion. . . .

Hoping that this 1860 may be a white year to you and Major Blackwood, and that my new novel may help to make it so, I am ever

Yours truly
Marian Evans Lewes.

John Blackwood Esq.

TO JOHN BLACKWOOD, 6 JANUARY 1860

Blackwood wrote: "It suddenly came across me that *The Mill on the Floss* would be an appropriate Title and in some respects more appropriate and curiously exciting than any of those suggested. It has too a sort of poetical sound." GE consulted an attorney about the legal details of Mr. Tulliver's bankruptcy. Blackwood proposed reprinting 1,000 copies of *Scenes of Clerical Life* in the 12/-edition. Sir Edward Bulwer Lytton told Blackwood that he would like to call on GE. [III, 245–46]

Holly Lodge | January 6. 60.
My dear Sir

"The Mill on the Floss" be it then! The only objections are, that the Mill is not *strictly* on the Floss, being on its small tributary, and that the title is of rather laborious utterance. But I think these objections do not deprive it of its advantage over "The Tullivers, or Life on the Floss,"—the only alternative, so far as we can see. Pray give the casting vote.

Easter Sunday, I see, is on the 8th April, and I wish to be out by the middle or end of March. Illness apart, I intend to have finished volume 3 by the beginning of that month, and I hope no obstacle will impede the rapidity of the printing. Perhaps, as I wish the attorney to see the earlier sheets of volume 2, it will be well to begin the printing before the writing is done.

Your plan about the Clerical Scenes is thoroughly satisfactory to me. Nothing else occurs to me to say on business this morning. The prospect of seeing Sir Edward is very agreeable to us both.

Ever yours truly
Marian Evans Lewes.

J. Blackwood Esq.

TO JOHN BLACKWOOD, 12 JANUARY 1860

To help GE decide between *The Mill on the Floss* and *The Tullivers, or Life on the Floss* Blackwood had the two titles set up as specimens for the advertisement. [III, 248–49]

Holly Lodge | January 12.60.

My dear Sir

Thank you for letting me see the specimen advertisements; they have helped us to come to a decision, namely, for "The Mill on the Floss." The disadvantage of titles with several words in them is, that in small advertisements they are apt to be divided—running on to the second line. But this is not so very long after all, and I suppose that mischance can be avoided by sufficient care. I agree with you that it will be well not to promise the book in March—not because I do not desire and hope to be ready, but because I set my face against all pledges that I am not *sure* of being able to fulfil. The 3d volume is, I fancy, always more rapidly written than the rest. The 3d volume of "Adam Bede" was written in six weeks, even with headachy interruptions, because it was written under a stress of emotion—which first volumes cannot be. I will send you the first volume of "The Mill" at once. The second is ready, but I would rather keep it as long as I can.

I suppose, rejecting "March," you will simply put "In the press"? Besides the advantage to the book of being out by Easter, I have another reason for wishing to have done in time for that. We want to get away for two months to Italy, if possible, to feed my mind with fresh thoughts, and to assure ourselves of that fructifying holiday before the boys are about us, making it difficult for us to leave home. But you may rely on it that no amount of horse-power would make me *hurry* over my book, so as not to do my best. If it is written fast, it will be because I can't *help* writing it fast.

Always yours truly
Marian Evans Lewes.

John Blackwood Esq.

TO JOHN BLACKWOOD, 23 FEBRUARY 1860

GE foresaw Blackwood's preference for a happy ending to *The Mill on the Floss*, which from the first conception she intended to end with the flood. [III, 264–65]

[Wandsworth] February 23. 60.

My dear Sir

I hope it will not be forgotten in the printing office that Mr. Sheard, the attorney is to have a copy of the next batch—*only* the next batch—of proofs, as I shall keep mine, waiting for his hints or corrections.

Sir Edward Lytton called on us yesterday. The conversation lapsed chiefly into monologue, from the difficulty I found in making him hear, but under all disadvantages I had an agreeable impression of his kindness and sincerity. He thinks the two defects of "Adam Bede" are the dialect and Adam's marriage with Dinah; but of course I would have my teeth drawn rather than give up either.

Jacobi told Jean Paul that unless he altered the dénouement of his "Titan," he would withdraw his friendship from him, and I am preparing myself for your last enmity on the ground of the tragedy in my third volume. But an unfortunate duck can only lay blue eggs, however much white ones may be in demand.

Ever yours truly
Marian Evans Lewes.

John Blackwood Esq.

TO JOHN BLACKWOOD, 22 MARCH 1860

The final chapter was sent to Edinburgh Wednesday, 21 March, without GE's having reread it. The changes she requested were made, and by the marvellous speed of printer and post, the proof was in her hands Friday evening, 23 March. Early the next morning they set off for Paris on their way to Italy. [III, 278–79]

Holly Lodge | March 22. 60.

My dear Sir

Your letter yesterday morning helped to inspire me for the last 11 pages—if they have any inspiration in them. They were written in a furor, but I dare say there is not a word different from what it would have been if I had written them at the slowest pace. It makes me rather miserable that I can't see the proofs, for though Mr. Lewes read the last 11 pages after I had written them, I did not. Lying awake in the night and living through the scene again, three corrections occurred to me, and I hope there will be time for you to make them.

1st. In Maggie's speech—mental speech—*before* she falls on her knees, strike out the "O God" before the words "How shall I have patience and strength?" It spoils the climax in the next paragraph.

2d. Please to insert "wooden" before "machinery," if I have not put it. I mean the machinery that upsets the boat.

3d. In the "Conclusion," it occurs to me that I have written, "bear the *stamp* of the past rending." For "stamp" please put "marks."

We expect to start on Saturday morning, and to be in Rome by Palm Sunday—or else by the following Tuesday. Of course we shall write to you when we know what will be our address in Rome. In the meantime news will gather. I don't mean to send the "Mill on the Floss" to any one, except to Dickens, who has behaved with a delicate kindness in a recent matter, which I wish to acknowledge. Mr. Langford has had word of that, but I just mention that I don't mean to send any copies about, because, if *you* present any, I should be glad if you would particularly enjoin "From the Publisher" to be written in them, that they may not be imagined to come from me.

I am grateful and yet rather sad to have finished—sad that I shall live with my people on the banks of the Floss no longer. But it is time that I should go and absorb some new life and gather fresh ideas.

Pray give my kind remembrances to Major Blackwood and believe me

Always yours truly
Marian Evans Lewes.

J. Blackwood Esq.

8

ITALY
Silas Marner · Romola

Before *The Mill on the Floss* was published, the Leweses were in Italy again, reaching Rome for Holy Week. After a chilly month they went to Naples in search of warmer weather and then to Florence. GHL, reading about Savonarola, suggested to GE that he and his times afforded fine material for a historical romance. She caught at the idea with enthusiasm. They collected books and pictures and visited the scenes of his life, making careful notes. At home again GE studied the period deeply and began planning *Romola.* But the story would not get started. She was greatly depressed. In September 1860 her childhood recollection of a linen weaver with a bag on his back and an expression that had made her think him an alien from his fellows thrust itself across her notes on the 15th century. Within four months *Silar Marner* was written and published. It brought critical acclaim and larger sales than any of her earlier books. In April the Leweses were again in Florence to make further research for *Romola.* Back in London GE went to the British Museum to study costumes; GHL described her as "buried in the Middle Ages." Despite his best efforts she was "utterly desponding" and almost resolved to give the book up. In January 1862 George Smith called and offered her £10,000 for publishing it in the *Cornhill Magazine* in 16 installments, "the most magnificent offer ever yet made for a novel." She refused on the ground that it would not be worth that sum, but finally accepted £7,000 for dividing it into 12 parts. In the event 14 were required, from July 1862 to August 1863. Blackwood's courteous reply to the announcement of her defection shows his sterling character at its best.

TO JOHN BLACKWOOD, 3 APRIL 1860

The Leweses left London 24 March, went from Paris to Culoz by train, over the Mont Cenis Pass by diligence and sledge to Susa, and by rail to Turin and Genoa. After two days' rest they went by packet boat to Leghorn, made a brief excursion to Pisa by rail, and reached Civita Vecchia on 1 April. They were in Rome at noon. [III, 284–86]

117, San Carlo al Corso | Rome | April 3. 60.

My dear Sir

I can now give you our address for the next month or more, for I foresee that it will not be easy to forsake Rome. . . . Our journey was entirely prosperous: we saw the summit of Mount Cenis in due time under the morning starlight, and rested two days at Genoa, under unbroken sunshine, hearing from fellow-travellers sad stories of what their friends had suffered who made the same journey a few weeks earlier. One party was nearly 24 hours passing Mount Cenis, with no food except a small loaf which one of them shared with the rest. I had seen Genoa the superb before; but it was new to Mr. Lewes, and his rapturous delight in those streets of palaces and the amphitheatre of softly shadowed hills gave it the best sort of novelty to me.

I think Rome will at last chase away Maggie and the Mill from my thoughts: I hope it will, for she and her sorrows have clung to me painfully. As for the book, I can see nothing in it just now but the absence of things that might have been there. In fact, the third volume has the material of a novel compressed into it. I tremble rather, to hear of its reception, lest high hopes should be speedily checked. But then, I am always in a state of fear, more or less rational; and if any good news comes, it will be the more welcome. You will hardly have anything to tell by the time you receive this letter, and perhaps it will be worth while for you to wait till something more than the fact of the subscription has turned up. But I know you will write just as soon as the kindest consideration can prompt. . . .

We both hope to hear that you as well as the book are entirely prosperous, and begging you and the Major to accept our kind regards, I am ever, my dear Sir,

Yours truly
Marian Evans Lewes.

John Blackwood Esq.

TO MRS. RICHARD CONGREVE, 4–6 APRIL 1860

After resigning the premiership of Sardinia in 1859 in dissatisfaction over the peace terms imposed by Napoleon III, Cavour had just resumed the office. Prince Carignan had been a representative at the Great Exhibition in London in 1851. Mrs. Browning's enthusiasm for Napoleon III had aroused comment in the English and American press. [III, 286–89]

[Rome]

I shall tell you nothing of what we have seen. Have you not a husband who has seen it all, and can tell you much better? Except, perhaps, one sight which might have had some interest for him, namely, Count Cavour, who was waiting with other eminences at the Turin station to receive the Prince de Carignan, the new Viceroy of Tuscany. A really pleasant sight—not the Prince, who is a large stout "moustache," squeezed in at the waist with a gold belt, looking like one of those dressed-up personages who are among the chessmen that the Cavours of the world play their game with. The pleasant sight was Count Cavour, in plainest dress, with a head full of power, mingled with bonhomie. We had several fellow-travellers who belonged to Savoy, and were full of chagrin at the prospect of the French annexation. Our most agreeable companion was a Baron de Magliano, a Neapolitan who has married a French wife with a large fortune, and has been living in France for years, but has now left his wife and children behind for the sake of entering the Sardinian army, and, if possible, helping to turn out the Neapolitan Bourbons. I feel some stirrings of the insurrectionary spirit myself when I see the red pantaloons at every turn in the streets of Rome. I suppose Mrs Browning could explain to me that this is part of the great idea nourished in the soul of the modern saviour Louis Napoleon, and that for the French to impose a hateful government on the Romans is the only proper sequence to the story of the French Revolution.

Oh, the beautiful men and women and children here! Such wonderful babies with wise eyes!—such grand-featured mothers nursing them! As one drives along the streets sometimes, one sees a madonna and child at every third or fourth upper window; and on Monday a little crippled girl seated at the door of a church looked up at us with a face full of such pathetic sweetness and beauty, that I think it can hardly leave me again. Yesterday we went to see dear Shelley's tomb, and it was like a personal consolation to me to see that simple outward sign that he is at rest, where no hatred can ever reach him again. Poor Keats's tombstone, with that despairing bitter inscription, is almost as painful to think of as Swift's. . . .

Friday. Since I wrote my letter we have not been able to get near the post-office. Yesterday was taken up with seeing ceremonies, or rather with waiting for them. I knelt down to receive the Pope's blessing, remembering what Pius VII. said to the soldier—that he would never be the worse for the blessing of an old man. But altogether, these ceremonies are a melancholy, hollow business, and we regret bitterly that the Holy Week has taken up our time from better things. I have a cold and headache this morning, and in other ways am not conscious of improvement from the Pope's blessing. I may comfort myself with thinking that the king of Sardinia is none the worse for the Pope's curse. It is farcical enough that the excommunication is posted up at the Church of St John Lateran, out of everybody's way, and yet there are police to guard it.

TO FRANÇOIS D'ALBERT DURADE, [17 APRIL 1860]

Receiving a request from Mme. Adèle Roch of Geneva for permission to translate *Adam Bede*, GE consulted D'Albert, who described her as the daughter of a lady's maid and a coachman, quite unsuited to the task, which he himself volunteered to undertake. On 7

February GE sent him formal authorization for the exclusive French translation. There
were three editions of it in Russian in 1859. [VIII, 263–64]

[Rome]
[My dear Friend]
I think you have made rapid progress with the translation, seeing that you can
only use fringes of time for it. It is a very sweet thought to me that the work may be
a source of some pleasure to you and Maman (I am very glad to be assured that I
may still say "Maman," for that is the name by which she has always gone in my
silent memory). It will interest you, perhaps, to know that it is translated into
Hungarian, and the first volume is fairly rendered into German—possibly the
second also by this time. You see I am counting on your and Maman's interest in
everything that belongs to me. I do not write about Rome: you have read much
better things on that subject than I can tell you. But no one can tell you about
myself, unless *I* take upon me that agreeable labour.
What a delight it would be to take the old walks in Geneva once more! But I
fear there are many changes that would check the current of my memory. And the
change from the old to the new is always painful to us who are getting old and
living more and more in the past. Tell Maman I enter now into her conservative
feelings, which I used inwardly to disapprove in my revolutionary mood—the
mood I was in when you knew me.
You will forgive me for writing hastily and briefly, and will understand that
temporary preoccupation with the wonderful place I am in is not *indifference* to
other things. With affectionate regards to Maman, I am always yours, with sincere
and faithful friendship,

[Marian Evans Lewes]

TO WILLIAM BLACKWOOD, 27 MAY 1860

The review of *The Mill on the Floss* in *The Times*, like that of *Adam Bede*, was by E. S. Dallas.
In his Journal 21 May GHL wrote: "This morning while reading about Savonarola it
occurred to me that his life and times afford fine material for an historical romance. Polly at
once caught at the idea with enthusiasm. It is a subject which will fall in with much of her
studies and sympathies; and it will give fresh interest to our stay at Florence." The next day
they studied a portrait of Savonarola at the Accademia, and at San Marco she remained in a
room where the Fra Angelico *Crucifixion* may be seen by ladies "while I went over the
monastery and took notes for her." They then spent some time buying books on Savonarola. [III, 299–300]

Florence | May 27. 60.
My dear Major Blackwood
I am much obliged to you for writing at once, and so scattering some clouds
which had gathered over my mind in consequence of an indication or two in Mr.
John Blackwood's previous letter. The "Times" article arrived on Sunday. It is
written in a generous spirit, and with so high a degree of intelligence, that I am
rather alarmed lest the misapprehensions it exhibits should be due to my defective

presentation, rather than to any failure on the part of the critic. I have certainly fulfilled my intention very badly if I have made the Dodson honesty appear "mean and uninteresting," or made the payment of one's debts appear a contemptible virtue in comparison with any sort of "Bohemian" qualities. So far as my own feeling and intention are concerned, no one class of persons or form of character is held up to reprobation or to exclusive admiration. Tom is painted with as much love and pity as Maggie, and I am so far from hating the Dodsons myself, that I am rather aghast to find them ticketed with such very ugly adjectives.

We intend to leave this place on Friday (3d) and in four days after that we shall be at Venice—in a few days from that time, at Milan—and then, by a route at present uncertain, at Berne, where we take up Mr. Lewes's eldest boy, to bring him home with us. . . .

There has been a crescendo of enjoyment in our travels, for Florence, from its relation to the history of modern art, has roused a keener interest in us even than Rome, and has stimulated me to entertain rather an ambitious project, which I mean to be a secret from every one but you and Mr. John Blackwood. . . . Mr. Lewes unites with me in kind regards, and I am always

Yours very truly
Marian Evans Lewes.

TO JOHN BLACKWOOD, 23 JUNE 1860

On their second day in Berne, the Leweses returned with the boys to the School and spent the evening there. Blackwood had reported that there was much balancing of opinion about the relative merits of *The Mill* and *Adam Bede*. Samuel Laurence lunched with the Leweses 5 March, 1860, meeting GE for the first time. She gave him nine sittings in August. [III, 306–07]

Berne, June 23. 60.

My dear Sir

We arrived here only a few hours ago, so that your letter has probably been awaiting me several days. It has just come to fill up my time agreeably while Mr. Lewes is gone to Hofwyl to fetch the boys. . . .

I am really vexed to think that you will have left London before our return, which can hardly be managed before the 29th or 30th—the more vexed because it is likely to be so long before we have an opportunity of chatting together again. We had hoped to be at home by the 25th, but we were so enchanted with Venice, that we were seduced into staying there a whole week instead of three or four days, and now we must not rob the boys of their two days' holiday with us. . . .

I don't think I can venture to tell you what my great project is by letter, for I am anxious to keep it a secret. It will require a great deal of study and labour, and I am athirst to begin.

As for "The Mill" I am in repose about it now I know it has found its way to the great public. Its comparative rank can only be decided after some years have passed, when the judgment upon it is no longer influenced by the recent enthusiasm about "Adam," and by the fact that it has the misfortune to be written by me instead of by Mr. Liggins. I shall like to see Bulwer's criticism, if you will be kind enough to send it me, but I particularly wish *not* to see any of the newspaper articles.

I will consult Mr. Lewes about the photograph. It would be a pleasure to me to meet a slight wish of yours; but I have rather a horror of photography. Mayall took one a couple of years ago, and we have several copies of it on paper, but it is not thoroughly satisfactory. Lawrence, the portrait painter, wished very much to take my portrait before we left England, but I had no time to give him the six (!) sittings he required. However, Mr. Lewes promised him that I should sit to him on our return. It is to be a chalk drawing, like his portrait of Thackeray, which you know well. . . .

Ever yours truly
Marian Evans Lewes.

John Blackwood Esq.

TO JOHN BLACKWOOD, 9 JULY 1860

In his letter to Blackwood, 14 March 1860 [VIII, 261–63], Bulwer Lytton praises the earlier account of Maggie and Tom, but finds that they later fail in the principle that characters should never violate "the Becoming," the conception readers have already formed of them. "But this is unimportant compared to the error, as I think, of her whole position towards Stephen. It may be quite natural that she should take that liking to him, but it is a position at variance with all that had before been heroic about her. The *indulgence* of such a sentiment for the affianced of a friend under whose roof she was, was a treachery and a meanness according to the Ethics of Art, and nothing can afterwards lift the character into the same hold on us. The refusal to marry Stephen fails to do so." [III, 317–18]

Holly Lodge | July 9. 60.
My dear Sir
I return Sir Edward's critical letter, which I have read with much interest. On two points I recognize the justice of his criticism. First, that Maggie is made to appear too passive in the scene of quarrel in the Red Deeps. If my book were still in MS., I should—now that the defect is suggested to me—alter, or rather expand that scene. Secondly, that the tragedy is not adequately prepared. This is a defect which I felt even while writing the third volume, and have felt ever since the MS. left me. The "*epische Breite*" into which I was beguiled by love of my subject in the two first volumes, caused a want of proportionate fullness in the treatment of the third, which I shall always regret.

The other chief point of criticism—Maggie's position towards Stephen—is too vital a part of my whole conception and purpose for me to be converted to the condemnation of it. If I am wrong there—if I did not really know what my heroine would feel and do under the circumstances in which I deliberately placed her, I ought not to have written this book at all, but quite a different book, if any. If the ethics of art do not admit the truthful presentation of a character essentially noble but liable to great error—error that is anguish to its own nobleness—*then*, it seems to me, the ethics of art are too narrow, and must be widened to correspond with a widening psychology.

But it is good for me to know how my tendencies as a writer clash with the conclusions of a highly accomplished mind, that I may be warned into examining well whether my discordancy with those conclusions may not arise rather from an idiosyncrasy of mine, than from a convicition which is argumentatively justifi-able. I hope you will thank Sir Edward on my behalf for the trouble he has taken to put his criticism into a form specific enough to be useful. I feel his taking such trouble to be at once a tribute and a kindness. If printed criticisms were usually written with only half the same warrant of knowledge, and with an equal sincerity of intention, I should read them without fear of fruitless annoyance. I remain, my dear Sir,

Always yours truly
Marian Evans Lewes.

John Blackwood Esq.

TO CHARLES BRAY, 18 JULY 1860

In addition to losses in the ribbon business Bray had lost a libel suit against him for an article in the *Coventry Herald*, with damages set at £150. Thornton Lewes was to be placed in the High School at Edinburgh to prepare for a post in the Civil Service. [III, 325]

Holly Lodge | July 18. 60.

Dear Friend

Your letter of this morning has interested me painfully, making more distinct to me the causes of anxiety which have been pressing on you during these last months. But I don't write now for the sake of saying sentimental phrases. In practical matters, the only thing for friends to do is, either to help, or else clearly to define the impossibility of help.

First, about the investment. I know no capitalist to whom I could mention it, so that the question confines itself to my personal circumstances. At present I have no money that I could invest, the sums which I am to receive for my last work not being yet due. But I have a small sum in the Bank of Deposit, which we keep there to supply extra calls, and from this I could manage, on due notice, to lend you £100, if that would fill up any temporary deficit caused by this payment for libel. I am sure you will not think me too plain and blunt in mentioning this possibility of small help, just by way of saving time or doubt, in case circumstances should happen to make it useful.

We are quite uncertain about our plans at present. Our second boy, Thornie, is going to leave Hofwyl and to be placed in some more expensive position in order to the carrying on of his education in a more complete way, so that we are thinking of avoiding for the present any final establishment of ourselves, which would necessarily be attended with additional outlay. Besides, these material cares draw rather too severely on my strength and spirits. But until Charley's career has taken shape, we frame no definite projects.

> Ever your affectionate Friend,
> Marian.

TO MME EUGÈNE BODICHON, [17 AUGUST 1860]

Asked by GHL about the possibility of a place for Charles in the Post Office, Anthony Trollope wrote to the Duke of Argyll, the Postmaster General, and secured a nomination for a supplementary clerkship in the Secretary's Office. The competitive examination included spelling, arithmetic, and composition, for which GHL and GE trained Charles. She began sitting for her portrait early in August. [III, 332]

> Holly Lodge | Friday.

Dear Barbara

I know you will rejoice with us that Charley has won his place at the Post Office, having been at the head of the list in the examination. Magnificat anima mea! The dear lad is fairly launched in life now.

I trusted to your being frightened at the rain on Wednesday, as I was. I am going to Lawrence's tomorrow at 1/2 past 2, and can't help wishing you would meet me, for I long to see or hear something of you.

We go to Miss Bayley's to lunch today. In haste

> Ever yours
> M. E. L.

TO JOHN BLACKWOOD, 28 AUGUST 1860

The English story was not *Silas Marner*, which came to GE later. She gave Laurence the eighth sitting, but he demanded still another. Replying to this letter Blackwood wrote: "I had an idea that the secret was an Italian story and I hoped that you might intend it for the Magazine, but I was entirely out as to the date of the story." He and his brother William rejoiced in the idea of such a series and in the prospect of another story of English life. [III, 339–40]

> Holly Lodge | August 28. 60.

Private
My dear Sir

I am grieved to hear of Major Blackwood's illness, for more important reasons than our own disappointment of the pleasure we had looked forward to in seeing him. Mr. Langford had sent us word of the illness, but had not given us the idea that it was so serious as it has been. I hope when you write again you will be quite freed from anxiety.

I think I must tell you the secret, though I am distrusting my power to make it grow into a published fact. When we were in Florence I was rather fired with the idea of writing a historical romance—scene, Florence—period, the close of the fifteenth century, which was marked by Savonarola's career and martyrdom. Mr. Lewes has encouraged me to persevere in the project, saying that I should probably do something in historical romance rather different in character from what has been done before. But I want first to write another English story, and the plan I should like to carry out is this: to publish my next English novel when my Italian one is advanced enough for us to begin its publication a few months afterwards in Maga. It would appear without a name in the Magazine, and be subsequently reprinted with the name of George Eliot. I need not tell you the wherefore of this plan—you know well enough the received phrases with which a writer is greeted when he does something else than what was expected of him. But just now I am quite without confidence in my future doings, and almost repent of having formed conceptions which will go on lashing me now until I have at least tried to fulfil them.

I am going to-day to give my last sitting to Lawrence, and we were counting on the Major's coming to look at the portrait, and judge of it. I hope it will be satisfactory, for I am quite set against going through the same process a second time.

We are a little distracted just now with the prospect of removal from our present house, which some obliging people have at last come to take off our hands.

Always yours truly
M. E. Lewes.

TO FRANÇOIS D'ALBERT DURADE, 18 SEPTEMBER 1860

The translation of *Adam Bede* was published in Paris by Dentu and in Geneva by Georg. On 26 September the Leweses moved to 10 Harewood Square, now covered by Marylebone Station. D'Albert had asked 3,000 francs per year for Thornie, which GHL could not afford. [III, 346–48]

Holly Lodge | Wandsworth | September 18. 60.

Dear Friend

I was really relieved to see your handwriting, for, remembering the wish you had expressed to send me a copy of your translation, I feared that either a parcel from you might have miscarried, or that you might have supposed me neglectful because I had not yet written you word of our new address. . . .

I could not write earlier, because we have always been thinking ourselves on the eve of a decision as to our future residence, and yet have never decided until today. At last I can tell you that our next address, probably for six months, will be 10 Harewood Square, London. We have taken a furnished house there, in order to try the experience of how far a town life will be endurable to us, since that seems on the whole the most desirable thing for Charles, who has a good place in the Post Office, after passing a government examination with high credit. His working hours are from 10 till 4, and of course we are anxious to provide a home for him that shall be the best moral education in the critical years between seventeen and twenty one. Thornton, the second boy, is coming from Hofwyl in a fortnight, to be immediately placed at Edinburgh. I quite understood the difficulty you were under, in your expensive house, with the inability to receive many boarders at once. At first it was a great regret to me that Thornton should not be placed with you; but our observation of Charles, since he came home, has convinced us that, as we hope Thornton will be able to pass an examination for the Indian service, it will be best for him to be prepared in the routine of *English* teaching. The English methods, especially in mathematics, are not the best; but a boy whose intelligence is really more cultivated than that of the average, is still under a disadvantage in his native country, if native words and practices are not the readiest to him. . . .

Alas! for the harvest, and for the poor people whose lot is so deeply affected by its failure. . . . Assure Maman of my deep and constant gratitude and affection, and believe me, dear friend, yours ever with cherished memories,

M. E. Lewes.

TO JOHN BLACKWOOD, 27 SEPTEMBER 1860

With his check for £1,000, the first installment for *The Mill on the Floss,* Blackwood wrote that it left £2,250 still to be paid, and that they would be happy to make the other payments earlier to suit her convenience. On 30 September GHL took Thornie to Edinburgh to board in the house of George Robinson. The writer in the *North British Review* ranked GE with Cervantes, Shakespeare, and Goethe among the more powerful intellects, placing Hawthorne in the second order of imagination. The children in *The Mill* are praised in contrast with those in *Dombey and Son.* [III, 351]

10 Harewood Square | September 27. 60.

My dear Sir

The precious cheque arrived safely today. I am much obliged to you for it, and also for the offer to hasten further payments. I have no present need of that accommodation, as we have given up the idea of buying the house which attracted us, dreading a step that might fetter us to town, or to a more expensive mode of living than might ultimately be desirable.

I think I have never had a clear understanding as to the period of payment to me for the 12s/. and 6s/. editions of my books. Perhaps some time when you are writing to me, you will be good enough to state what is the arrangement on that head. I wish to know it, because I like to be able to calculate with precision about my incomings.

I hope Mr. Lewes will bring me back a good report of Major Blackwood's progress towards re-established health. In default of a visit from him, it was very agreeable to have him represented by his son, who has the happy talent of making a morning call one of the easiest pleasantest things in the world.

I wonder if you know who is the writer of the article in the N. British, in which I am reviewed along with Hawthorne. Mr. Lewes brought it for me to read this morning, and it is so unmixed in its praise that if I had any friends, I should be uneasy lest a friend should have written it. Ever, my dear Sir

Yours truly
M. E. Lewes.

J. Blackwood Esq.

JOURNAL, 28 NOVEMBER 1860

The Mill on the Floss alone had brought GE £3,685 in 1860 and *Adam Bede*, £1,705. Anthony Trollope soon became a warm friend of the Leweses. Arthur Helps was appointed Secretary of the Privy Council in June 1860, a post which threw him into close touch with the Queen. [III, 360]

November 28. Since I last wrote in this journal I have suffered much from physical weakness accompanied with mental depression. The loss of the country has seemed very bitter to me, and my want of health and strength has prevented me from working much—still worse, has made me despair of ever working well again. I am getting better now by the help of tonics, and I should be better still if I could gather more bravery, resignation and simplicity of striving. In the meantime my cup is full of blessings: my home is bright and warm with love and tenderness, and in more material vulgar matters we are very fortunate. I have invested £2000 in East Indies Stock, and expect shortly to invest another £2000, so that with my other money, we have enough in any case to keep us from beggary.

Last Tuesday, the 20th, we had a pleasant evening. Anthony Trollope dined with us, and made us like him very much by his straightforward, wholesome *Wesen*. Afterwards Mr. Helps came in, and the talk was extremely agreeable. He told me the Queen had been speaking to him in great admiration of my books, especially the Mill on the Floss. It is interesting to know that Royalty can be touched by that sort of writing—and I was grateful to Mr. Helps for his wish to tell me of the sympathy given to me in that quarter.

Today I have had a letter from M. d'Albert, saying that at last the French edition of Adam Bede is published. He pleases me very much by saying that he finds not a sentence that he can retrench in the first volume of "The Mill."

I am engaged now in writing a story, the idea of which came to me after our arrival in this house, and which has thrust itself between me and the other book I was meditating. It is "Silas Marner, the Weaver of Raveloe." I am still only at about the 62d page, for I have written slowly and interruptedly of late.

TO MME EUGÈNE BODICHON, 26 DECEMBER 1860

Barbara wrote from Algiers. The Leweses moved 17 December to 16 Blandford Square, near the Leigh Smith house at number 5. Barbara's sister Nannie and her friend Bessie Parkes were much drawn to the Catholic Church. "Bessie has not entered the CC,"

Barbara wrote, "but really she is more Catholic than 900 out of every 1,000 of the Pope's children." Mrs. Benjamin Brodie, daughter of a serjeant-at-law, had discussed the possibility of GHL's getting a divorce abroad. [III, 365–67]

16 Blandford Square | December 26. 60.

My dear Barbara

Your letter came this evening and if I were a journalist, I should say that I "hailed it with delight." . . . The bright point in your letter is, that you are in a happy state of mind yourself. For the rest, we must wait, and not be impatient with those who have their inward trials though everything outward seems to smile on them. It seems to those who are differently placed that the time of freedom from strong ties and urgent claims must be very precious for the ends of self-culture, and good, helpful work towards the world at large. But it hardly ever is so. —As for the "forms and ceremonies," I feel no regret that any should turn to them for comfort, if they can find comfort in them: sympathetically, I enjoy them myself. But I have faith in the working-out of higher possibilities than the Catholic or any other church has presented, and those who have strength to wait and endure, are bound to accept no formula which their whole souls—their intellect as well as their emotions—do not embrace with entire reverence. The highest "calling and election" is to *do without opium* and live through all our pain with conscious, clear-eyed endurance.

You say nothing about the Doctor, so I hope he is flourishing and free from neuralgic pains. We are all right—comfortable enough in our new house with the prospect of two old-maidish servants, who will want no looking after. And our dear boys are a joy to us—Charley more good and loving every day—Thornie prospering at Edinburgh, etc. etc. etc.—In fact we have no sorrows just now, except my constant inward worret of unbelief in any future of good work on my part. Everything I do seems poor and trivial in the doing, and when it is quite gone from me and seems no longer my own—then I rejoice in it and think it fine. That is the history of my life.

By the way, we have consulted a barrister, very accomplished in foreign and English law, about that matter broached by your friend Mrs. Brodie. He pronounces it *impossible*. I am not sorry. I think the boys will not suffer, and for myself I prefer excommunication. I have no earthly thing that I care for, to gain by being brought within the pale of people's personal attention, and I have many things to care for that I should lose—my freedom from petty worldly torments, commonly called pleasures, and that isolation which really keeps my charity warm instead of chilling it, as much contact with frivolous women would do. . . .

God bless you, Think often of your affectionate Friend.

M. E. Lewes. . . .

TO JOHN BLACKWOOD, 12 JANUARY 1861

The new story was *Silas Marner*. [III, 371–72]

16, Blandford Square, | N.W.
January 12. 1861.

My dear Sir . . .
I am writing a story which came *across* my other plans by a sudden inspiration. I don't know at present whether it will resolve itself into a book short enough for me to complete before Easter, or whether it will expand beyond that possibility. It seems to me that nobody will take any interest in it but myself, for it is extremely unlike the popular stories going; but Mr. Lewes declares that I am wrong, and says it is as good as anything I have done. It is a story of old-fashioned village life, which has unfolded itself from the merest millet-seed of thought. I think I get slower and more timid in my writing, but perhaps worry about houses and servants and boys, with want of bodily strength, may have had something to do with that. I hope to be quiet now.

Mr. Lewes is busy with his microscope again and very happy in his work; but everybody we meet tells him how old and thin he looks—which is not encouraging.

Always yours truly
Marian Evans Lewes.

J. Blackwood Esq.

TO RICHARD OWEN, 22 JANUARY 1861

Owen inscribed this copy of his book on the giant ground-sloth "To the Author of Adam Bede, from an obliged friend." To GHL, who brought her the book, Owen spoke of his pleasure in *The Mill on the Floss*. He had sent her a number of his earlier writings. [III, 373]

16, Blandford Square, | N.W.
January 22. 1861.

My dear Sir
I have seldom in my life had a kind attention that has caused me keener pleasure than your gift of the "Memoir on the Megatherium," sent through Mr. Lewes the other day, as a sign of the pleasure you had had in "The Mill on the Floss." One likes to be read by the many, for strong reasons, impersonal as well as personal, but there is another sort of encouragement in the sympathy of the few, which is very much needed as an assurance that one has not been writing *down* to the many. And if I had been allowed to choose my "few," since I should have chosen them among the most accomplished minds I know of, I should certainly have chosen the giver of the Memoir—which, besides, though my scientific ignorance is by no means insignificant, I am not quite too ignorant to value for its own sake.

It is a very good and graceful thing for the greater worker to help the less in this
way, and you will not be surprized that I wanted to tell you, I am grateful.

Yours faithfully
George Eliot.
(Marian Evans Lewes)

Professor Owen.

TO SARA HENNELL, 8 FEBRUARY 1861

Mary Marshall, Sara's cousin, called for the letters written to Sara during the 1840s, which
had been returned to GE. After her death Sara gave them to John Cross for the biography.
The collapse of the ribbon trade brought serious unemployment to Coventry. [III, 376–77]

16, Blandford Square, | N.W.
February 8. 61.

My dear Sara

Miss Marshall called yesterday and I delivered over to her the "Strauss letters."
I have not read them since you gave them to me, years ago, and I would rather not
know what is in them since I have not the right to destroy them. The knowledge
would only give a more definite repugnance to the idea of their falling into other
hands after your death. I have destroyed almost all my friends' letters to me,
simply on that ground—because they were only intended for my eyes, and could
only fall into the hands of persons who knew little of the writers, if I allowed them
to remain till after my death. In proportion as I love every form of piety—which is
venerating love—I hate hard curiosity; and unhappily my experience has impressed me with the sense that hard curiosity is the more common temper of mind.
But enough of that.

The reminders I am getting from time to time of Coventry distress have made
me think very often, yearningly and painfully, of the friends who are more
immediately affected by it, and I often wonder if more definite information would
increase or lessen my anxiety for them. Send me what word you can from time to
time, that there may be some reality in my image of things round your hearth.
Give my best love to Cara and Mr. Bray, and tell Cara I often have a longing to
write, and yet feel a letter hardly justifiable with so little to say as I have. . . .

Ever yours
Pollian.

TO JOHN BLACKWOOD, 15 FEBRUARY 1861

Silas Marner was published in 364 pages on 2 April, two days after Easter. Though the subject of GHL's lecture is not known, his use of diagrams on a blackboard suggests natural history or physiology. [III, 377–78]

16, Blandford Square, | N.W.
February 15. 1861.

My dear Sir

I send you by Post today about 230 pages of M.S. The entire story will make 100 pages more—equal to one volume of the Mill. I send the M.S. because in my experience printing and its preliminaries have always been rather a slow business, and as the story, if published at Easter at all, should be ready by Easter Week, there is no time to lose. I shall be glad to hear that the packet has arrived, and also to know how the story impresses you. . . .

Send us better news of Major Blackwood, if you can. We feel so old and rickety ourselves that we have a peculiar interest in invalids. Mr. Lewes is going to lecture for the Post Office this evening, by Mr. Trollope's request. I am rather uneasy about it, and wish he were well through the unusual excitement.

Ever yours truly
M. E. Lewes.

TO SARA HENNELL, [20 FEBRUARY 1861]

Emily Clarke was at Miss Eborall's School in Lichfield. Frederick Denison Maurice preached at St. Peter's Chapel in Vere Street. [III, 381–82]

16, Blandford Square, | N.W.
Wednesday.

Dear Sara

I am grateful to you for your letters. They are just what I want, and prevent me from feeling so far away from you, and so shut out from your lives, as I have sometimes felt. Mr. Lewes got through his Lecture with perfect ease, and I have been all the happier since the task has been done.

My niece Emily did not come at Christmas—the weather was too discouraging for a long journey. But if we are at home at Easter, I think she will come for a week then. Her father's brother is very kind to her, and I think he and his wife contemplate taking her into their family; for her aunt told Emily that she need not think of being a governess, as there were plenty of friends to take care of her. I should have been inclined to have her with me a good deal, but our boy puts that out of the question. At present she is still at school, at Lichfield.

I am glad to hear that Mr. Maurice impressed you agreeably. If I had strength to be adventurous on Sundays, I should go to hear him preach, as well as others. But I am unequal to the least exertion or irregularity. My only pleasure away from our own hearth is going to the Zoological Gardens. Mr. Lewes is a fellow, so we turn in there several times a week, and I find the birds and beasts there most congenial to my spirit. There is a shoe-bill, a great bird of grotesque ugliness, whose top-knot looks brushed up to a point with an exemplary deference to the demands of society, but who I am sure has no idea that he looks the handsomer for it. I cherish an unrequited attachment to him. Best love to Cara and Mr. Bray. One touch of biliousness makes the whole world kin—I dare say there was a close resemblance in our experience.

Ever thine
Pollian.

TO JOHN BLACKWOOD, 24 FEBRUARY 1861

Blackwood offered £800 for an edition of 4,000 copies of *Silas Marner* to sell at 12/6—a royalty of 33 percent. From the beginning he had "felt the want of brighter lights and some characters of whom one can think with pleasure as fellow creatures." The only Nemesis is Eppie's refusal to accept Godfrey Cass as her father. Major William Blackwood, no longer able to read, died in April. [III, 382–83]

16, Blandford Square, | N.W.
February 24. 61.

My dear Sir

It is not possible, I think, that Silas will make more than one volume; and I hope you will have the entire M.S. in your hands in ten days. Is it wise (you, of course, are the best judge) to charge more than 10/6? Though, certainly, the volume is likely to be rather larger than one volume of a three-volumed novel.

I don't wonder at your finding my story, as far as you have read it, rather sombre: indeed, I should not have believed that any one would have been interested in it but myself (since William Wordsworth is dead) if Mr. Lewes had not been strongly arrested by it. But I hope you will not find it at all a sad story, as a whole, since it sets—or is intended to set—in a strong light the remedial influences of pure, natural human relations. The Nemesis is a very mild one. I have felt all through as if the story would have lent itself best to metrical rather than prose fiction, especially in all that relates to the psychology of Silas; except that, under that treatment, there could not be an equal play of humour. It came to me first of all, quite suddenly, as a sort of legendary tale, suggested by my recollection of having once, in early childhood, seen a linen-weaver with a bag on his back; but, as my mind dwelt on the subject, I became inclined to a more realistic treatment.

My chief reason for wishing to publish the story now, is, that I like my writings to appear in the order in which they are written, because they belong to successive mental phases, and when they are a year behind me, I can no longer feel that thorough identification with them which gives zest to the sense of authorship. I generally like them better at that distance, but then, I feel as if they might just as well have been written by somebody else.

It would have been a great pleasure to me if Major Blackwood could have read my story. Have you advertised it in the next Maga?

Ever yours truly
M. E. Lewes.

J. Blackwood Esq.

TO JOSEPH LANGFORD, 27 MARCH 1861

Langford, Blackwoods' London manager, forwarded the final pages of *Silas Marner* to Edinburgh on 10 March. On the 18th all the proof had been read by GE, and she went off with GHL to Hastings. On the 25th she received her first copy of the book. GE's fears about the price were groundless; it sold more than 8,000 copies at 12/-. The books on costume were for *Romola*. [III, 393–94]

16, Blandford Square, | N.W.
March 27. 61.

Dear Mr. Langford
Thank you for the cheering words you sent me with the copy of Silas. I am rather uncomfortably constituted; for while I am unable to write a sentence for the sake of pleasing other people, I should be unable to write at all without strong proofs that I had touched them. I confess I shudder a little at the high price of the book, but it is a comely volume, with a delightful type.

I don't wish for any presentation copies, except one for Mr. Lewes's mother. Her address is: Mrs. Willim, | 51 Clifton Road East | St. John's Wood. We should also, by and by, like a couple of copies to be sent here. But there is no hurry about them.

I have not yet had an opportunity of thanking you for those nice old-fashioned costumes you were so good as to look up for me. You would oblige and help me very much if you would keep your eyes open for all books or fragments that will serve as memoranda of costume either mediaeval or modern. In the London Library they have nothing better than Fairholt's scanty book, and unhappily, with my temperament, I fear it would be next to impossible for me to go to the British Museum. I would go to some expense for a good book on mediaeval costumes.

Yours very sincerely
Marian Evans Lewes.

TO MRS. PETER ALFRED TAYLOR, 1 APRIL 1861

Clementia Doughty, wife of the wealthy radical politician Peter Taylor, knew GE in her *Westminster Review* days and in 1856 wrote her a sympathetic letter. On 4 April 1861 she called at Blandford Square. [III, 395–96]

[16 Blandford Square]

It gave me pleasure to have your letter, not only because of the kind expressions of sympathy it contains, but also because it gives me an opportunity of telling you, after the lapse of years, that I remember gratefully how you wrote to me with generous consideration and belief at a time when most persons who knew anything of me were disposed (naturally enough) to judge me rather severely. Only a woman of rare qualities would have written to me as you did on the strength of the brief intercourse that had passed between us. It was never a trial to me to have been cut off from what is called the world, and I think I love none of my fellow-creatures the less for it: still I must always retain a peculiar regard for those who showed me any kindness in word or deed at that time, when there was the least evidence in my favour. The list of those who did so is a short one, so that I can often and easily recall it.

For the last six years I have ceased to be "Miss Evans" for any one who has personal relations with me—having held myself under all the responsibilities of a married woman. I wish this to be distinctly understood; and when I tell you that we have a great boy of eighteen at home who calls me "mother," as well as two other boys, almost as tall, who write to me under the same name, you will understand that the point is not one of mere egoism or personal dignity, when I request that any one who has a regard for me will cease to speak of me by my maiden name.

TO JOHN BLACKWOOD, 4 APRIL 1861

The check was for £1,350 for *The Mill on the Floss*. With the news of the sale of *Silas Marner* Langford, who came to lunch 2 April, also brought them a box for the opera—opening night, *Le Prophète*—to which the Leweses went with Charles. [III, 396–97]

16, Blandford Square, | N.W.
April 4. 61.

My dear Sir

I am much obliged to you for your punctuality in sending me my precious cheque. I prize the money fruit of my labour very highly as the means of saving us dependence or the degradation of writing when we are no longer able to write well or to write what we have not written before.

Mr. Langford brought us word on Tuesday that he thought the total subscription (including Scotland and Ireland) would mount to 5500. That is really very great. And letters drop in from time to time giving me words of strong encouragement—especially about the Mill; so that I have reason to be cheerful, and to believe that where one has a large public, one's words must hit their mark. If it were not for that, special cases of misinterpretation might paralyze me. For example, when you read McMillan, pray notice how my critic attributes to me a disdain for Tom: as if it were not *my* respect for Tom which infused itself into my reader—as if he could have respected Tom, if I had not painted him with respect; the exhibition of the *right* on both sides being the very soul of my intention in the story. However, I ought to be satisfied if I have roused the feeling that does justice to both sides. . . .

Mr. Lewes begs me to ask you to let him see the Times if there should be a review of "Silas" in it; as otherwise the review may pass by and he may not know of it.

Ever yours truly
M. E. Lewes.

John Blackwood Esq.

TO MRS. PETER ALFRED TAYLOR, 6 APRIL 1861

Mrs. Taylor become a regular visitor. GHL sometimes went to the Taylors' evening parties, and Charles Lewes's London social experience began at their house. [III, 397–98]

[16 Blandford Square]

I feel more at ease in omitting formalities with you than I should with most persons, because I know you are yourself accustomed to have other reasons for your conduct than mere fashion, and I believe you will understand me without many words when I tell you what Mr Lewes felt unable to explain on the instant when you kindly expressed the wish to see us at your house—namely, that I have found it a necessity of my London life to make the rule of *never* paying visits. Without a carriage, and with my easily perturbed health, London distances would make any other rule quite irreconcilable for me with any efficient use of my days; and I am obliged to give up the *few* visits which would be really attractive and fruitful in order to avoid the *many* visits which would be the reverse. It is only by saying, "I never pay visits," that I can escape being ungracious or unkind—only by renouncing all social intercourse but such as comes to our own fireside, that I can escape sacrificing the chief objects of life.

I think it very good of those with whom I have much fellow-feeling, if they will let me have the pleasure of seeing them without their expecting the usual reciprocity of visits; and I hope I need hardly say that you are among the visitors who would be giving me pleasure in this way. I think your imagination will supply all I have left unsaid—all the details that run away with our hours when our life extends at all beyond our own homes, and I am not afraid of your misinterpreting my stay-at-home rule into churlishness.

TO SAMUEL LAURENCE, 8 APRIL 1861

GHL, like the Blackwoods, was opposed to any publication of a portrait of GE. When permission was asked by Laurence to exhibit his at the Royal Academy, she wrote this letter. Blackwood wanted a portrait for the collection of his authors at 45 George Street, Edinburgh. His nephew Willy Blackwood and Langford reported favourably on it. When GHL declined to purchase it, Laurence sold it to John Blackwood. It appears as the frontispiece in Haight's *George Eliot. A Biography*, 1968. Another sketch, signed by Laurence and dated 1857 (4 years before he met GE), is at Girton College, Cambridge. [III, 401]

16, Blandford Square, | N.W.
April 8. 61.

My dear Sir

I have mentioned to Mr. Lewes your wish to exhibit my portrait at the Royal Academy, and he has stated to me—what he had not stated before—namely, his reasons for originally stipulating with you that the portrait should not be exhibited, or exposed to the risk of being copied. These reasons are entirely unconnected with you, or with the character of the likeness: they would apply to any portrait of me, by any artist whatever, and they are reasons which, now that he has fully stated them to me, I feel to be as strong as they appear to him.

I must therefore decline to give my consent that my portrait should be exhibited anywhere beyond the doors of your own atelier. I remain, my dear Sir

Yours sincerely
M. E. Lewes.

Samuel Lawrence Esq.

TO JOHN BLACKWOOD, 19 MAY 1861

The Leweses set out again for Florence 19 April 1861 to make further studies for *Romola*, returning 14 June. Mrs. Anna Blackwell had inquired about translating GE's novels into French. [III, 416–18]

Florence | May 19. 61.

My dear Sir

"Adam" and "The Mill" *are* translated into French. The former was published some time ago, the latter will be published soon. The translator is an old friend of mine in whose family I lived for some months at Geneva after my father's death, and since he is an accomplished man and the work of translating my books brings some extra happiness to himself and his wife, I don't mean to take it away from him, though I give up any share in payment. By this time I have no doubt he has begun to translate "Silas." But if Mrs. Blackwell, who, I imagine, is a competent person, would like to translate the "Scenes of Clerical Life," I am under no obligation to reserve them for M. d'Albert, and, if I live, I dare say there will be something else for him to do. . . .

I was ill for a week with a sort of influenza which was prevalent in Florence when we arrived, but since I have been well, we have been industriously foraging—in old streets and old books. I feel very brave just now and enjoy the thought of work—but don't set your mind on my doing just what I have dreamed. It may turn out that I can't work freely and fully enough in the medium I have chosen, and in that case, I must give it up; for I will never write anything to which my whole heart, mind, and conscience don't consent, so that I may feel that it was something—however small—which wanted to be done in this world, and that I am just the organ for that small bit of work. . . . Mr. Lewes is kept in continual distraction by having to attend to my wants—going with me to the Magliabec-chian library, and poking about everywhere on my behalf—I having very little self-help about me of the pushing and inquiring kind. . . .

We are grieved to read of the bad weather in England, and the destruction of the fruit blossoms. Here we have had bright mild days for more than a week, but no great heat such as we found here this time last year. I look forward with keen anxiety to the next outbreak of war—longing for some turn of affairs that will save poor Venice from being bombarded by those terrible Austrian forts. Thanks for your letters; we both say, "More, give us more."

Ever yours truly
M. E. Lewes.

TO CHARLES LEWES, 27 MAY 1861

[III, 418–19]

Florence, May 27. 61.

Dearest Boy

Jubilate! we shall soon be at home again—if indeed you are not learning to do without us so well that our presence will hardly be matter of jubilation. . . . This evening we have been mounting to the top of Giotto's tower—a very sublime getting-upstairs indeed, and our muscles are much astonished at the unusual exercise; so you must not be shocked if my letter seems to be written with dim faculties, as well as with a dim light.

It made me feel hot and tired to read of your being out late three nights running! Nevertheless we have rejoiced at your having pleasant musical evenings—especially at your hearing Formes and your prospect of hearing Fidelio. You perceive, you need be in no anxiety about the payment for your lessons as we shall be home before they are at an end.—Tell Grace and Amelia to get everything in order at once—curtains up etc. by the 10th so that if we should write to say we are coming before the 15th, they may be in no hurry or confusion. Ask Amelia to send my muslin dress to the wash, as I shall want thin clothes in the London heat—more difficult to bear, I imagine, than the Florentine.

Our life has varied little since Pater wrote you his last description. We have seen no one but Mrs. [Thomas] Trollope and her pretty little girl Beatrice, who is a musical genius. She is a delicate fairy about ten years old, but sings with a grace and expression that make it a thrilling delight to hear her. . . . We have had glorious sunsets shedding crimson and golden lights under the dark bridges across the Arno. All Florence turns out at eventide, but we avoid the slow crowds on the Lung' Arno and take our way "up all manner of streets"—to please a certain wilful pig, of course. You must write to us again, but Pater is going to add his say, and he will give you directions about the address. I have said nothing, after all—but here is the pith of all possible letters from me—that I am

Your loving
Mutter.

JOURNAL, 19 JUNE 1861

Blackwood called the day after the Leweses returned to London and had a fascinating conversation with GE about the way in which she realized her characters. The invitation to dinner at Greenwich on the 17th was his effort to entertain the firm's most valuable author and introduce her to John Delane, editor of *The Times*. [III, 427–28]

June 14th, we reached home, and found all well there. Blackwood, having waited in town to see us, came to lunch with us, and asked me if I would go to dine at Greenwich on the following Monday, to which I said "Yes" by way of exception to my resolve that I will go nowhere for the rest of the year. He drove us there with Colonel Stewart, and we had a pleasant evening—the sight of a game at Golf in the Park, and a hazy view of the distant shipping with the Hospital finely broken

by trees in the foreground. At dinner Colonel [Edward Bruce] Hamley and Mr.
[Moncrieff] Skene joined us: Delane who had been invited, was unable to come.
The chat was agreeable enough, but the sight of the gliding ships darkening
against the dying sunlight made me feel chat rather importunate. I think, when I
give a white bait dinner I will invite no one but my second self, and we will agree
not to talk audibly.

This morning for the first time I feel myself quietly settled at home. I am in
excellent health, and long to work steadily and effectively. If it were possible that
I should produce *better* work than I have yet done! At least there is a possibility
that I may make greater efforts against indolence and the despondency that comes
from too egoistic a dread of failure.

This is the last entry I mean to make in my old book in which I wrote for the first
time at Geneva, in 1849. What moments of despair that life would ever be made
precious to me by the consciousness that I lived to some good purpose! It was that
sort of despair that sucked away the sap of half the hours which might have been
filled by energetic youthful activity: and the same demon tries to get hold of me
again whenever an old work is dismissed and a new one is being meditated.

June 19th 1861.

TO SARA HENNELL, 2 JULY 1861

James Martineau moved from Manchester to London in 1853 and became pastor of the
Little Portland Street Chapel in 1860. [III, 432–33]

16, Blandford Square, | N.W.
July 2. 61.

Dear Sara

That was a pretty bit of human fellowship—to send us word about the comet.
But alas, our London sky was murky last night, and though we sat up till near
midnight and looked out the last thing, there were no lamps in heaven—only
terrestrial lamps, particularly a red one at a distant gin-shop. However, we will
hope for better luck this evening, and I am grateful to you for giving us notice. . . .

You will be amused with what befel me and Charley last Sunday morning.
Intending to go to James Martineau's chapel, we turned by mistake into an
Episcopalian Proprietary chapel, where there was a broad-chested young Irish
preacher fresh from lessons in elocution, who gave us a polite sermon on "ini-
quity" and prayer in the approved stage tones with an occasional climax after
Macready's manner! Fancy me shut up in a very narrow pew under these circumstances with the sense of a healthy youth beside me who had no room to stretch his
limbs, and is "quite sure" that "nobody" was ever moved by the Church Service! I
can endure any amount of sitting in churches and chapels when I am not fidgetty
about my companions, for I can dream and think without risk of interruption, and
I should go to all sorts of places of worship if I could go alone.

Give my best love to Cara and Mr. Bray, and let me know whenever anything pleasant happens to any one of you. I won't expect anything that is not pleasant.

Ever yours
Pollian.

TO SARA HENNELL, 30 JULY 1861

Thornie came home from Edinburgh 26 July and stayed until 20 August, when he went to Hofwyl for a holiday. At the Princess's Theatre GE found herself sitting next to Mrs. Thomas Carlyle when Charles Fechter played *Hamlet*. GHL regarded it as one of the finest performances he had ever seen. [III, 441–42]

16, Blandford Square, | N.W.
July 30. 61.

Dear Sara . . .

Thornie, our second boy is at home from Edinburgh, for his holidays, and I am apt to give more thought than is necessary to any little change in our routine. We had a treat the other night which I wish you could have shared with us: we saw Fechter in Hamlet. His conception of the part is very nearly that indicated by the critical observations in Wilhelm Meister, and the result is deeply interesting— the naturalness and sensibility of the *Wesen* overcoming in most cases the defective intonation. And even the intonation is occasionally admirable; for example, "and for my soul, what can he do to that etc." is given by Fechter with perfect simplicity, whereas the herd of English actors imagine themselves in a pulpit when they are saying it.

Apropos of the pulpit, I had another failure in my search for edification last Sunday. Mrs. Bodichon and I went to Little Portland St. Chapel, and lo, instead of James Martineau there was a respectable old Unitarian gentleman preaching about the dangers of ignorance and the satisfaction of a good conscience in a tone of amiable propriety which seemed to belong to a period when brains were untroubled by difficulties and the lacteals of all good Christians were in perfect order. I enjoyed the fine selection of Collects he read from the Liturgy. What an age of earnest faith, grasping a noble conception of life and determined to bring all things into harmony with it, has recorded itself in the simple pregnant, rhythmical English of those Collects and of the Bible! The contrast when the good man got into the pulpit and began to pray in a borrowed washy lingo—ex tempore in more senses than one!

Ever yours
Pollian.

TO JOHN BLACKWOOD, 12 SEPTEMBER 1861

As the question of republication of GE's first four books was being considered, she inquired whether the Blackwoods would like to acquire the copyrights. The writing of *Romola* was still uncertain. The Leweses were at Malvern trying the hydropathic cure for GHL's ailments. [VIII, 289–90]

Malvern | September 12. 1861.

My dear Sir

Your letter enclosing the cheque for £600 reached me here this morning. You will have heard from Mr. William Blackwood that there were reasons for not sending me the order for £1000, as you proposed. Many thanks for your promptness, and a sincere Amen to your wishes for our mutual future. I can desire nothing more satisfactory to myself than that our relations should continue as long as my writing life.

And now, for the new edition of my books. Mr. Lewes's suggestion is, that a 6/. edition might be published in moderate numbers, which, if stereotyped, might be reproduced on thinner paper as the 2/6 edition—one set of types thus serving for two editions. You, of course, will weigh the merits of this suggestion against those of any other plan you may have in your mind.

Meanwhile, reconsideration has changed my views as to the retention of copyrights, and made me wish to consult you on a question which has arisen. As we have no young children and as our responsibilities for others lie in the present rather than in the distant future, I feel that the profits henceforth to be gained on my four published books will be less valuable to me spread over the long term of copyright, than in the form of an immediate sum calculated in due proportion to the probable amount of those profits. And I should like to know from you whether you consider that it would be for the advantage of your firm to give me such a sum for my copyrights as it would be for my advantage to receive at this early stage of their existence. . . .

You can't possibly think more of the "great work" than I do, or than Mr. Lewes does. He thinks hopefully; I think doubtfully. On the whole I should recommend to your attention the supplementary beatitude "Blessed is he that expecteth nothing" etc.—if it were not that I *never* expect anything, but don't find myself beatified in consequence. All work will go on better when I can once be easier about Mr. Lewes's health. I congratulate you on being obliged to stay in the country.

I may venture to send through you, or through this letter, my kind regards to Mr. William Blackwood and thanks for his explanation about the order. Mr. Lewes unites with me in all kind remembrances.

Ever yours truly
Marian Evans Lewes

TO JOHN BLACKWOOD, 25 SEPTEMBER 1861

The check was for £1,000, making up to £1,760 for 8,000 copies of *Silas Marner*. Thornie, back from his holiday at Hofwyl, stayed a week in Blandford Square before returning to Edinburgh. The evidence that GE read carefully all four of her books before they were printed in the so-called Cheap edition establishes its textual importance. [VIII, 290–91]

16, Blandford Square, | N.W.
September 25. 61.

My dear Sir

Thanks for the precious cheque, which has just been safely deposited in Mr. Lewes's pocket on its way to the bank. . . .

We have our noisy hopeful, Thornie— "Sturm und Drang" as one of our friends has christened him—just come home from Switzerland, which will cause the parental meditations a few days of distraction—happily not of an unhealthy kind.

I have read carefully all through "Adam Bede" and "The Mill" and have marked all the *errata* I have discovered. I hope the new editions will be carefully printed after these corrected copies, which I shall presently send. I have also marked in the Clerical Scenes some corrections which Mr. Lewes noted when he last read them. But I cannot read these and Silas Marner through, as I have done the other two books—I find this reading excite me too much and carry me away from the present. I am very glad, however, that I have given the needful time to "Adam" and "The Mill," for there were several mistakes which affected the sense in an important manner. It has moved me a good deal—reading the books again after a long interval, but it has done me good, for I can say a full Amen to everything I have written. I shall await your letter about the new editions and then send the corrected copies. . . .

We are having frequent rain here. I hope you are more fortunate, and have moisture in no other form than that of white morning mists, soon dispersed by sunshine.

Ever yours truly
Marian E. Lewes.

John Blackwood Esq.

TO JOHN BLACKWOOD, 17 OCTOBER 1861

GE was greatly agitated about the sale of her copyrights. Blackwood offered £3,000 to be paid over two years, beginning with the new editions. But in consequence of GHL's consultation with Bradbury & Evans, she wrote to refuse. GHL was planning to write a history of science, of which his *Aristotle* (1864) was the first part. Though GE read little fiction by her contemporaries, this letter indicates that she had read some of Mrs. Oliphant's novels in *Blackwood's*. [VIII, 292]

16, Blandford Square, | N.W.
October 17. 61.

My dear Sir

I have been considering the offer contained in your last letter, and the result is, that I do not think it advisable for me to part with my copyrights. I can quite understand that it would not answer, as a business speculation, to advance on a prospective benefit, a sum which it would be wise in me to accept. The inducement on my part to entertain the idea was not any immediate want of money, but the possibility that my copyrights might be worth a sum which, in addition to what I already possess, would have given us a secure income, that might have enabled Mr. Lewes to give the larger proportion of his time to an important work which he has long been meditating. But now, dismissing this episodic idea, we had better lose no time in arranging about the terms for the cheaper editions.

I have not read the last number of the Chronicles of Carlingford, not having much time for extra reading, but I read the previous number, and thought the scene between the Rector and his deaf mother delightful.

I hope you in Scotland are sharing our pleasant weather.

Ever yours truly
M. E. Lewes.

TO JOHN BLACKWOOD, 18 NOVEMBER 1861

Dumas had attached himself to Garibaldi, who appointed him Director of the Museum at Naples, where Carlo Arrivabene, the Italian patriot, was serving as correspondent for the *Daily News*. GHL thought Fechter's Hamlet "one of the very best, and his Othello one of the very worst I have ever seen." With his French accent and slight physique Fechter lacked the personality for Othello, playing him as young, not black, and "bearing himself like the hero of French *drame.*" [VIII, 292–93]

16, Blandford Square, | N.W.
November 18. 61.

My dear Sir

Your explanatory letter to Mr. Lewes leaves, I think, nothing more to be discussed about this long-agitated business of the new editions. I agree with you that the £4. saved on the paper will be best applied in improving the binding. We can hardly expect a very large sale of the 6s/. editions, so it will be wisest to proceed on the basis of modest hopes in the printing. Let us understand, then, that I accept the proposition of £60 per thousand for all the four books in their 6s/. edition i.e. if you at length decide on fixing "Silas" at that price.

You will perhaps be interested and amused, as I was, to hear that one of the most ardent among the admirers of "Adam Bede" is—Alexandre Dumas, the elder. Count Arrivabene brought us that information from Naples yesterday. Dumas declaimed about it, after his peculiar fashion, with the book in his hand, translating here and there, especially from Hetty's journey—and pronouncing the book to be the greatest novel of the age. After this I will never venture to predict who will like or dislike my books. But imagine what I escaped: by some means or other it was reported by telegraph that we were coming to Naples, and Dumas was preparing to announce my arrival in an article. I shudder at the thought. Pray appreciate the picture of my frightened self accosted by that journalistic whirlwind. It was too piquant a bit of gossip for me to resist telling it you, though I am plunged in the glooms of sick headache.

Mr. Lewes has finished his article on Hamlet and Othello, and will despatch it tomorrow. It is really important that there should be some truthful writing about Fechter's Othello. I think the performance positively injurious to the half-cultivated people who make up the mass of his audiences. That a tragedy like that, should produce a series of small titters in its moments of highest pathos, is an outrage on Shakespeare and is demoralizing to the titterers. I could perceive that most of the elegantly dressed people around me were totally unacquainted with the play and were being introduced to Shakespeare by Fechter. They were in a state of utter obfuscation.

Ever yours truly
M. E. Lewes.

TO SARA HENNELL, 22 NOVEMBER 1861

According to their custom, Sara had remembered GE's birthday—her 42nd, the day before her own. Arthur Hugh Clough, the poet, and his wife met Spencer in 1860 when he was visiting Barbara's uncle Octavius Smith in Scotland. [III, 466–67]

16, Blandford Square, | N.W.
November 22. 61.

My dear Sara
Your loving words of remembrance find a very full answer in my heart—fuller than I can write. The years seem to *rush* by now, and I think of death as a fast-approaching end of a journey: double and treble reason for loving, as well as working, while it is day. . . .

You have heard, probably, of Mr. Clough's death at Florence whither his poor wife had gone to join him after her confinement. Mr. Herbert Spencer dwells on the death as one brought on by excessive work, but he is perhaps over-apt to assign this as a cause for illness. He himself has just returned from a visit to Paris, where he had intended to stay until after Christmas; but he seems to have found that brilliant place as dull as brilliant places usually are to lonely strangers. We went to see Fechter's Othello the other night. It is lamentably bad. He has not weight and passion enough for deep tragedy, and to my feeling, the play is so degraded by his representation that it is positively demoralizing—as indeed all tragedy must be when it fails to move pity and terror. In this case, it seems to move only titters among the smart and vulgar people who always make the bulk of a theatre audience. Of course the newspapers don't tell the truth about the matter. Please give my thanks to Mr. Bray for his pamphlet. The letter on spirit-rapping I had read before. . . .

Love to all: special thoughts to you, dear Sara, on this morning when memories and prospects come crowding more thickly than usual

Pollian.

TO SARA HENNELL, 6 DECEMBER 1861

Bulwer Lytton's A *Strange Story* was appearing serially in Dickens's *All the Year Round*. Wilkie Collins came frequently with Pigott and Redford to the Leweses' Saturday evenings. [III, 467–70]

Blandford Sq. | December 6. 61.

Dear Sara . . .

I must tell you a story which Mr. Wilkie Collins told us about Bulwer the other night. I don't know whether you are reading "The Strange Story," which from its air of lofty science along with representations of preternatural power, is, in our opinion of rather unwholesome tendency for popular reading—and indeed would be wicked it if were not done by Bulwer in perfectly good faith, as it is. He is quite caught by the spirit of the marvellous, and a little while ago, at Dickens's house, was telling of a French woman who could raise the dead, but only at *great expense.* "What," said Dickens, "is the cause of this expense in raising the dead?" "The Perfumes!" said Bulwer, with deep seriousness, stretching out his hand with his usual air of lofty emphasis.—I feel as if I ought not to tell you this, for if you repeat it to anybody else, I don't know what sort of monstrosity it may be turned into by the time it gets to the fifth narrator. I ought also to tell you, by way of balance to this absurdity, that Bulwer has behaved very nicely to me, and that—quite apart from that personal question—I have a great respect for the energetic industry with which he has made the most of his powers. He has been writing diligently in very various departments for more than thirty years, constantly improving his position, and profiting by the lessons of public opinion and of other writers.

Mr. Spencer is coming to lodge in Harewood Square close by us, but as we exclude visitors except on a Saturday we shall not, I dare say, see the more of him. He is very delightful when we don't get on art and classical literature—subjects on which there is a great gulf fixed between us. I don't mind it when we are alone, but I am always uneasy for *him* when I see he is boring other people. For, to my thinking, it is more pitiable to bore than to *be* bored.

I am writing on my knees with my feet on the fender and in that attitude I always write very small—but I hope your sight is not teazed by small writing. Give my best love to Cara

Ever your loving
Pollian.

TO JOHN BLACKWOOD, 1 JANUARY 1862

In her Journal GE wrote: "Mr. Blackwood sent me a note enclosing a letter from Montalembert [author of *Les Moines d'occident*] about Silas Marner, and a few hours after a china pug as a memorial of my flesh and blood Pug, lost about a year ago. *I began my Novel of Romola.*" Nothing is known of Pug's fate. [IV, 3]

16, Blandford Square, | N.W.
January 1. 62.

My dear Sir

The year opens with good auguries. I have begun my novel this morning, and now a second Pug is come to be a faithful companion through my life—reminding me always of two things that I care for a good deal—the memory of my poor black-nosed pet, and the kindness of the Friend who gratified my too extravagant desires.

Montalembert's words are very precious to me coming after I have learned to admire his book as I do.

All happiness to you and Mrs. Blackwood in this coming year. I wish I could believe that I shall contribute to it by writing a book you will like to read.

Ever yours truly
M. E. Lewes.

TO SARA HENNELL, 14 JANUARY 1862

The first volume of F. Max Müller's *Lectures on the Science of Language* appeared in 1861. Trollope draws Mr. Moulder, the fat commercial traveller from Houndsditch, and his wife in a broad Dickensian vein. Spencer's *First Principles* was published in parts. He brought his father to the Leweses' Saturday evening party 11 January. Spencer, who lived to be 83, would stop in the midst of company to feel his pulse, or if he thought the conversation too exciting, close his ears with stoppers. [IV, 8–9]

16 Blandford Sq. | January 14. 62.

Dear Sara

I am grieved to think of the sprain. Pray let me know, when you can, that it is better, for I have a dread of the possible persistence attributed to sprains. I hope you are able to enjoy Max Müller's great and delightful book during your imprisonment. It tempts me away from other things. I have read most of the numbers of Orley Farm, and admire it very much, with the exception of such parts as I have read about Moulder and Co., which by the way, I saw in glancing at a late

Spectator, the sapient critic there selects for peculiar commendation. There is no mistake an author can make but there will be some newspaper critic to pronounce it his finest effort. Anthony Trollope is admirable in the presentation of even, average life and character, and he is so thoroughly wholesome-minded that one delights in seeing his books lie about to be read. . . .

You have never told me what impression Mr. Spencer's book makes on you as it proceeds. I am anxious to know whether the elaborate proof of generalities which are accepted as soon as stated will not cause some of the later numbers to be wearisome for the majority of readers. I hope not, for it is touching to see how his whole life and soul are being poured into this book and into keeping himself well that he may write it. The very watching against disease is becoming a disease in itself. He has had his father in London lately, and the old gentleman, seated upright on a small chair, looks almost the younger of the two.

I am going to be taken to a pantomime in the day-time, like a good child, for a Christmas treat, not having had my fair share of pantomime in the world. Farewell—let me know about the sprain, and think of me always as

Your loving
Pollian.

JOURNAL, 17–26 FEBRUARY 1862

At this time the guests at the Saturday evenings included few ladies. GE's dejection was not dispelled even by George Smith's offer to purchase *Romola* for £10,000 for the *Cornhill Magazine*. [IV, 15, 17]

February 17. Monday. I have written only the two first chapters of my novel besides the Proem, and I have an oppressive sense of the far-stretching task before me, health being feeble just now. On Saturday, Dr. Wyatt, Mr. F. Chapman, and Mr. Boner from Munich were our visitors. I was much fatigued and consequently not well on Sunday. We walked to Hampstead in a very cold wind. Today there has been constant rain and fog, and I have not been out of doors.

19. This evening I read aloud to G. again, at his request the first 45 pages of my romance, Charlie also being present. The rain has been constant all day. Nevertheless we have been to the B. Museum, and I have picked some details from Manni's life of Bartolommeo Scala—also from Borghini's Discorsi, about the simplicity of the Florentine table equipage.

I have lately read again with great delight Mrs. Browning's Casa Guidi Windows. It contains amongst other admirable things a very noble expression of what I believe to be the true relation of the religious mind to the Past.

26. I have been very ailing all this last week and have worked under impeding discouragement. I have a distrust in myself, in my work, in others' loving acceptance of it which robs my otherwise happy life of all joy. I ask myself, without being able to answer, whether I have ever before felt so chilled and oppressed. . . . I have written now about 60 pages of my romance. Will it ever be finished?—ever be worth anything?

TO JOHN BLACKWOOD, 19 MAY 1862

GE's initial refusal was based on fear that the story would not tell in the 16 installments of 24 pages which Smith wanted, and accepted £3,000 less to have it in 12; finally it ran to 14 installments. Blackwood's reply the next day shows his sterling character at its best:

My Dear Madam

I am of course sorry that your new Novel is not to come out under the old colours but I am glad to hear that you have made so satisfactory an arrangement.

Hearing of the wild sums that were being offered to writers of much inferior mark to you, I thought it highly probable that offers would be made to you, and I can readily imagine that you are to receive such a price as I could not make remunerative by any machinery that I could resort to.

Rest assured that I feel fully satisfied of the extreme reluctance with which you would decide upon leaving your old friend for any other publisher, however great the pecuniary consideration might be, and it would destroy my pleasure in business if I knew any friend was publishing with me when he thought he could do better for himself by going elsewhere. We have had several most successful enterprises together and much pleasant correspondence and I hope we shall have much more.

In a few days we go to Derbyshire where we leave the children with their aunts and intend to move on London about the end of next week. I hope therefore to see you soon and trust I shall find you in good health and spirits with your work progressing.

always yours truly
John Blackwood.

Mrs. Lewes.

[IV, 34–36]

16 Blandford Square | May 19. 1862

My dear Sir

I fear this letter will seem rather abrupt to you, but the abruptness is unavoidable. Some time ago I received an offer for my next novel which I suppose was handsomer than almost any terms ever offered to a writer of Fiction. As long as I hesitated on the subject I contemplated writing to you to ascertain your views as to the arrangement you would be inclined to make for the publication of the same work; since I was not willing to exchange my relations with you for any new ones without overpowering reasons. Ultimately I declined the offer (on various grounds) and there was therefore no need to write.

But another offer, removing former objections, has been made, and after further reflection, I felt that, as I was not at liberty to mention the terms to you, and as they were hopelessly beyond your usual estimate of the value of my books to you, there would be an indelicacy in my making an appeal to you before decision. I have consequently accepted the offer, retaining however a power over my copyright at the end of six years so that my new work may then be included in any general edition.

I know quite well from the feeling you have invariably shewn, that if the matter were of more importance to you than it is likely to be, you would enter fully into the views of the case as it concerned my interests as well as your own.

I remain, my dear Sir

Always yours very truly
M. E. Lewes.

TO SMITH ELDER & CO., 21 MAY 1862

Uncertain about how to name GE, the publisher included GHL's name in the agreement and left a blank for hers, which she filled in with "Marian Evans" before they both signed. [VIII, 301]

It is agreed between Mrs. Marian Evans Lewes and George Henry Lewes Esq. and Messrs. Smith Elder & Co.

That Mrs. Lewes shall write a novel of sufficient length to fill 384 pages of "the Cornhill Magazine" and deliver the Manuscript to Smith Elder & Co. in twelve monthly portions.

That Smith Elder & Co. are to have the copyright of the Novel (for Great Britain and the Continent) both for publication in "the Cornhill Magazine" and for publication in separate form for a period of six years after the appearance of the last part in the Magazine, and the right of disposing of early sheets for America.

After the expiration of the six years the copyright is to revert to Mrs. Lewes, but Smith Elder & Co. are to continue to sell the copies they may then have, and may reprint and sell the Book during the whole term of copyright in any one form they may determine on.

Smith Elder & Co. are to pay Mrs. Lewes for such copyright as is secured to them by this agreement £583.6.8 (five hundred and eighty three pounds six shillings and eight pence) on delivery of each portion of the Manuscript, and such copyright is to be formally transferred to Smith Elder & Co. should they at any time require it.

London | May 21st 1862

Marian Evans Lewes.
G. H. Lewes.

TO FREDERIC LEIGHTON, [?5 JUNE 1862]

At first GE tried to guide Leighton's conception of the illustrations for *Romola*, but soon realized the wisdom of letting him choose the subjects and follow his own conception of the text. Leighton, who had studied in Florence from the age of 14 and knew it better than she, was paid £40 for each number. [IV, 41]

16 Blandford Square, N.W.
Thursday.

Dear Mr. Leighton,

Unmitigated delight! Nello is better than my Nello. I see the love and care with which the drawings are done. After I had sent away my yesterday's note, written in such haste that I was afterwards uncomfortable lest I had misrepresented my feelings, the very considerations you suggest had occurred to me and I had talked them over with Mr. Lewes—namely, that the exigencies of your art must forbid perfect correspondence between the text and the illustration; and I came to the conclusion that it was these exigencies which had determined you as to the position of Bardo's head and the fall of Romola's hair. You have given her attitude transcendently well, and the attitude is more important than the mere head-dress.

I am glad you chose Nello's shop; it makes so good a variety with Bardo and Romola. In a day or two you will have the second part, and I think you will find there a scene for Tessa "under the Plane Tree." But perhaps we shall see each other before you begin the next drawings.

Ever yours truly,
M. E. Lewes.

TO GEORGE SMITH, 10 JULY 1862

Smith had Leighton's drawings on the woodblocks photographed before they were engraved and sent a set of them mounted to GE. Rossetti's book was *The Early Italian Poets*, which Smith published in 1861. [IV, 48]

16, Blandford Square, | N.W.
July 10. 1862.

My dear Sir
I cannot rest without thanking you for the Photographs, which I had been pleased to think of possessing even as simple pieces of paper to be inserted in a book. But your kind and pretty device has quite outstripped my imagination. I am really obliged to you. The revival of the first impression from the drawings makes one sympathize with poor Mr. Leighton's chagrin at the engraver's rendering of Nello—and Bardo, too, is far less feeble in the original than in the translation.

I am also in arrear of acknowledgment for your gift of Mr. Rossetti's book, which I am very glad to possess. I remain, My dear Sir,

Yours very sincerely
M. E. Lewes.

TO GEORGE SMITH, [25 JULY 1862]

On his doctor's advice GHL stayed at Spa, Belgium, 17 July–4 August. [IV, 51]

16, Blandford Square, | N.W.
Friday Evening.

My dear Sir
Having gathered from a note of Mr. Leighton's accompanying one of his drawings, that the last proofs sent to me have not yet been forwarded to him, I have given him my copy. Will you be kind enough to order that another copy may be sent to me?

I have the best news from Mr. Lewes every day. He accuses you of being a "gourmet" because I told him you had pronounced the Spa commons to be miserable. He is getting quite strong—walks like a postman and eats like a German.

Yours very truly
M. E. Lewes.

TO FREDERIC LEIGHTON, 10 SEPTEMBER 1862

The Leweses had gone to Littlehampton on the Sussex coast to work in quiet. At the end of Chapter 15 Savonarola takes the crucifix from the hand of Romola's dying brother and gives it to her. [IV, 55–56]

Park Hotel, Little Hampton, | Sussex,
September 10, '62.

Dear Mr. Leighton,

Thanks for your letter, which I have received this morning. My copy of Vasari has a profile of Piero di Cosimo, but it is of no value, a man with a short beard and eyes nearly closed. The old felt hat on his head has more character in it than the features, but the hat you can't use.

Of Niccolo Caparra it is not likely that any portrait exists, so that you may feel easy in letting your imagination interpret my suggestions in the First and the Fifth Parts of Romola. There is probably a portrait of Piero di Cosimo in the portrait room of Uffizi, but in the absence of any decent catalogue of that collection it was a bewildering and headachy business to assure oneself of the presence or absence of any particular personage.

If you feel any doubt about the *new* Romola, I think it will be better for you to keep to the original representation, the type given in the first illustration, which some accomplished people told me they thought very charming. It will be much better to continue what is intrinsically pretty than to fail in an effort after something indistinctly seen. If you prefer the action of *taking out* the crucifix, instead of the merely contemplative attitude, you can choose that with safety. In the scene with Piero di Cosimo, I thought you might make the figures subordinate to those other details which you render so charmingly, and I chose it for that reason.

But I am quite convinced that illustrations can only form a sort of overture to the text. The artist who uses the pencil must otherwise be tormented to misery by the deficiencies or requirements of the one who uses the pen, and the writer, on the other hand, must die of impossible expectations. *Apropos* of all that, I want to assure you again of what I had said in that letter, which your naughty servant sent down the wind, that I appreciate very highly the advantage of having your hand and mind to work with me rather than those of any other artist of whom I know. Please do not take that as an impertinent expression of opinion, but rather as an honest expression of feeling by which you must interpret any apparent criticism.

The initial letter of the December part will be W. I forgot to tell you how pleased I was with the initial letter of Part V. . . . I am really comforted by the thought that you will mention doubts to me when they occur to you. My misery is the certainty that I must be often in error. Mr. Lewes shares my admiration of the two last illustrations.

Ever yours truly,
Marian E. Lewes.

TO BESSIE PARKES, 24 NOVEMBER 1862

Bessie's interest in the Roman Catholic Church, stirred by her friendship with Adelaide Procter, led to her conversion in 1864. The Parkes family were all Unitarians and like many of Bessie's freethinking friends disapproved of her Catholic leaning. Joseph Dunn was a bookseller in Islington. Bessie was planning to visit Barbara Bodichon in Algiers, but her family were afraid to let her go alone. [VIII, 307]

16, Blandford Square, | N.W.
November 24. 62.

Dear Friend

Thanks for the precious books. They are just what I wanted—showing me the practical aspect of the Catholic Church in England in these times, and telling me many details that I care to know. I keep the Dunn's Catalogue, because I have marked some books in it that I want to have. I hope you are keeping well so that you may brave the January voyage without fear of being too much shaken.

God bless you. Ever yours with affectionate remembrance

M. E. Lewes.

TO MME EUGÈNE BODICHON, 26 NOVEMBER 1862

William Allingham lived at this time in Ireland, but made almost annual visits to London. After 1868 he called frequently on the Leweses. The Peter Taylors gave fortnightly parties at Aubrey House, Notting Hill. Charles Lewes, now well established in the Post Office, was interested in the social and educational causes the Taylors supported. [IV, 64–65]

16 Blandford Sq. | November 26. 62.

Dear Barbara . . .

I don't see what we can do towards making ourselves agreeable or useful to Mr. Allingham just yet, but when we begin to receive visitors again, we will try and ask him to come on an evening when he will meet somebody worth talking to. Mr. Lewes has taken down his address and will write to him on the strength of *your* letter. . . .

Pray don't ever ask me again not to rob a man of his religious belief, as if you thought my mind tended towards such robbery. I have too profound a conviction of the efficacy that lies in all sincere faith, and the spiritual blight that comes with No-faith, to have any negative propagandism in me. In fact, I have very little sympathy with Free-thinkers as a class, and have lost all interest in mere antagonism to religious doctrines. I care only to know, if possible, the lasting meaning that lies in all religious doctrine from the beginning till now. . . .

Our big boy is gone to Mrs. P. Taylor's gathering to-night. He has been telling us a story of an old supplementary clerk at the P.O. who is called "maid of all work" in the Correspondence Branch. The waiter at the dining room offered him the newspaper; whereupon he replied, "I didn't come 'ere to 'ear the news. I came to *heat!*"—It was the boy's twentieth birthday on Monday—a very happy date to us, for we think he gets better with the years. He was rather discontented that he did not say goodby to you.

You left a handkerchief at our house. I will take care of it till next summer. I look forward with some longing to that time when I shall have lightened my soul of one chief thing I wanted to do, and be freer to think and feel about other people's work. We shall see you oftener, I hope, and have a great deal more talk than ever we have had before to make amends for our stinted enjoyment of you this summer.

We are very well and unspeakably happy. I know you care to think of other people's happiness—therefore I tell you such private news. George is plunged in dingy books of science—sends his loving remembrances to you both, nevertheless. God bless you, dear Barbara. You are very precious to us.

Ever yours
M. E. Lewes.

TO SARA HENNELL, 26 NOVEMBER 1862

The club GE describes soon collapsed. Richard Congreve had become a leader of the English Positivists. The Leweses were regularly in the audience of the Saturday concerts at St. James's Hall. [IV, 65–67]

16 Blandford Sq. | November 26. 62.

Dear Sara . . .

You will be interested to know that there is a new muster of scientific and philosophic men lately established, for the sake of bringing people who care to know and speak the truth as well as they can, into regular communication. Mr. Lewes was at the first meeting at Clunn's Hotel on Friday last. The plan is to meet, and dine moderately and cheaply; and no one is to be admitted who is not "Thorough" in the sense of being free from the suspicion of temporizing and professing opinions on official grounds. The plan was started at Cambridge: Mr. Huxley is president, and Charles Kingsley is vice. If they are sufficiently rigid about admissions the club may come to good—bringing together men who think variously, but have more hearty feelings in common than they give each other credit for. Mr. Robert Chambers (who lives in London now) is very warm about the matter. Mr. Spencer too is a member. . . .

Mr. Congreve came to have a long chat the other day, and I was pleased to find that he had been for a week to Oxford, where he was very cordially received by the men of the liberal party, in spite of his heresy. Few people outside the University can imagine how much an Oxford man gives up when he leaves an Oxford clique for conscience' sake.

Mr. Lewes sent your "Buddhism" today by post. Thanks for it. If I had not been dull of sense, I might have found it on the table, when you wanted it. We have been to a "Monday Pop" this week, to hear Beethoven's Septett, and an amazing thing of Bach's played by the amazing Joachim. But there is too much "Pop" for the thorough enjoyment of the chamber music they give. With love generally,

Yours ever
Pollian.

TO SARA HENNELL, 26 DECEMBER 1862

William Howard Russell, whose letters to *The Times* from the Crimea inspired Florence Nightingale's work, had just published *My Diary North and South*. His frank account of the battle of Bull Run had made him unpopular in the Northern states, but, though *The Times* supported the Southern cause, Russell did not soften his detestation of slavery. [IV, 70–72]

16 Blandford Sq. | December 26. 62.

Dear Sara

It is very sweet to me to have any proof of loving remembrance. That would have made the Book-marker precious even if it had been ugly. But it is perfectly beautiful—in colour, words and symbols. Hitherto I have been discontented with the Coventry Book-marks, for at the shop where we habitually see them they have all got "Let the people praise Thee, O God" on them and nothing else. But I can think of no motto better than those three words. I suppose no wisdom the world will ever find out will make Paul's words obsolete "Now abide" etc. "but the greatest of these is Charity." . . .

If my book marker were just a little longer I should keep it in my beautiful Bible in large print, which Mr. Lewes bought for me in provision for my old age. He is not fond of reading the Bible himself but "sees no harm" in my reading it.

He has just finished reading Russell's American Diary which is intensely interesting—full of strange pictures. Some one told me on oracular authority that if I had to be born again, I ought to pray to God to be born an American. I should sooner pray to be born a Turk or an Arab.

Farewell, dear Sara. Give my love and best wishes for the coming year to Cara and Mr. Bray. I am always yours affectionately

Pollian.

TO CHARLES BRAY, 29 DECEMBER 1862

The textile workers, especially in Lancashire, were suffering from the cotton famine caused by the American Civil War. [IV, 72–73]

16 Blandford Sq. | December 29. 62.

Dear Friend

I obey your instructions literally, and send a pound, but another is ready whenever you will tell me to send it. I have been fearing that Coventry would be minus of help, from the concentration of effort in Lancashire. Poor "Lizzie"! I am disappointed with that clause "no wittles"—I had hoped she was well off.

I am not quite sure what you mean by "charity" when you call it humbug. If you mean that attitude of mind which says "I forgive my fellow-men for not being so good as I am," I agree with you in hoping that it will vanish, as also the circumstantial form of almsgiving. But if you are alluding to anything in my letter to Sara, I meant there what charity meant in the elder English and what the translators of the Bible meant in their rendering of the XIII [th] chapter of I Corinthians—*Caritas,* the highest love or fellowship, which I am happy to believe that no philosophy will expel from the world. . . .

Ever yours sincerely
M. E. Lewes.

C. Bray Esq.

TO JOHN BLACKWOOD, 6 FEBRUARY 1863

Though *Romola* had still six months to run in the *Cornhill,* the Blackwoods kept in touch with GE despite her desertion. The volume with *Scenes of Clerical Life* was issued as she requested in April. Montalembert's *Le Père Lacordaire* was reviewed in *Maga* in February. [IV, 76]

16, Blandford Square, | N.W.
February 6. 1863.

My dear Sir

I missed the pleasure of seeing Mr. William Blackwood yesterday, being gone out for a walk when he called, but he left two questions with Mr. Lewes, which I suppose it is best for me to answer by writing to head quarters.

We think it may be well to place the "Scenes" first in the forthcoming volume, as they are perhaps more novel to the public than "Silas." I corrected Silas carefully for the last edition, so that the reprint may be made from that without any need for my revision.

I was pleased to see the article on Lacordaire in the last Maga; it has made me desire to see Montalembert's book, for the sake of its personal touches, which must be profoundly interesting, presented as he knows how to present things. Always my dear Sir,

Yours very truly
M. E. Lewes.

John Blackwood Esq.

TO SARA HENNELL, 9 MARCH 1863

Charles Lewes had been on holiday in Switzerland. The Prince of Wales met the Princess Alexandra at Gravesend 7 March, and they made a progress through London from Southwark to Paddington. Their wedding took place at Windsor 10 March. John William Colenso, Bishop of Natal, was publishing his criticism of the pentateuch in parts, stirring up a great controversy in the press. Harriet Beecher Stowe's protest against English sympathy for the South was answered by Frances Power Cobbe's assurance that English women still sympathized with the North's struggle against slavery. [IV, 77–78]

16 Blandford Sq. | March 9. 63.

Dear Sara . . .

We have had a week at Dorking, returning a few days ago to welcome Charlie home after his holiday—*not* to see the procession, which I should have liked well enough to see if I had had more strength of mind and body to endure being driven through crowded streets and sitting at a window with people who would have a long while to stare at one before the procession came. . . .

That scheme of a sort of Philosophic Club that I told you of went to pieces before it was finished, like a house of cards. So it will be to the end I fancy, with all attempts at combinations that are not based either on material interests, or on opinions that are not merely opinions but *religion*. —I think I have no news to tell but such as is in the newspapers. Doubtless you have been interested in the Colenso correspondence and perhaps in good Miss Cobbe's Rejoinder to Mrs. Stowe's Remonstrating Answer to the Women of England. I was glad to see how free the answer was from all tartness or conceit. . . . With best love to all,

Ever yours
Pollian.

JOURNAL, 6–18 MAY 1863

Much of *Romola* was written at Littlehampton and Dorking, where GE could be free of housekeeping and callers. [IV, 83–84]

[16 Blandford Square]

May 6. We have just returned from Dorking whither I went a fortnight ago, to have solitude while George took his journey to Hofwyl to see Bertie. The weather was severely cold for several days of my stay, and I was often ailing. That has been the way with me for a month and more and in consequence I am backward with my July number of Romola—the last part but one.

7. At the 37th page, having made a large excision of matter for the sake of rapidity.

10. Sunday. Wrote this morning the beginning of the Trial by Fire. I am very feeble, finding the latter half of the day all weariness.

14. Read Part XIII to G. up to the moment when Spini gives the order about Tito.

16. Finished Part XIII. Killed Tito in great excitement!—Went to see the Priory, North Bank, a house we think of buying.

18. Began Part XIV—the last! Yesterday George saw Count Arrivabene, who wishes to translate Romola, and says the Italians are indebted to me.

TO MME EUGÈNE BODICHON, 12 MAY 1863

Barbara had met a Mr. and Mrs. Webster in Algiers and given them a letter to GE. In Rabelais's *Pantagruel*, when Panurge throws overboard the sheep he has bought, all the others follow and are drowned. The reaction reflects GE's growing conservatism. [IV, 84–85]

16 Blandford Sq. | May 12. 63.

My dear Barbara

I was very much in want of that proof in black and white that you were not only "all right" but that part of the rightness consisted in sometimes thinking of me. Yes! we shall be in town in June. Your coming would be reason good enough, but we have others—chiefly, that we are up to the ears in Boydom and imperious parental duties. All is as happy and prosperous with us as heart can lawfully desire, except my health. I have been a mere wretch for several months past. You will come to me like the morning sunlight and make me a little less of a flaccid cabbage plant. . . .

I am terribly frightened about Mrs. W.[ebster]. She wrote to me telling me that we were sure to suit each other, neither of us holding the opinions of the "moutons de Panurge." Nothing could have been more decisive of the opposite prospect to me. If there is one attitude more odious than any other of the many attitudes of "Knowingness" it is that air of lofty superiority to the vulgar. However, she will soon find out that I am a very commonplace woman.

I have been fasting so long from all news about you, that I shall have a voracious appetite for all you can tell of these six months.

Our boy, who brightens up at your name, is as good or better than ever, only his beard grows with a vicious rapidity—the downy time forever gone! George shares all my loves and cares, you know—and not least those which concern you and the dear Doctor—our image of human uprightness, bodily and spiritual.

Ever yours
Marian.

JOURNAL, 20 MAY–9 JUNE 1863

Wiseman was Cardinal-Archbishop of Westminster. [IV, 86–87]

[16 Blandford Square]

20. Mr. and Mrs. Bray lunched with us.

24. Sunday. We went to St. Mary's Moorfields in the morning, and heard Beethoven's Mass in C and Cardinal Wiseman's wretched Sermon on the Day of Pentecost. Coming home, we found Mrs. Bray waiting for us. Drove her to Hampstead.

25. Heavy and good for nothing. Only at p. 18.

June 1. I have not yet finished Romola, and am made stupid and depressed by a slight cough. I have written up to the moment when Tessa and the children are taken home by Romola.

June 6. We had a little evening party, with music, intended to celebrate the completion of Romola, which however is not absolutely completed, for I have still to alter the Epilogue.

7. Sunday. Ill with hemicrania, unable to do anything all day.

8. Still suffering from my cough and headache.

9. Tuesday. Put the last stroke to Romola. *Ebenezer!* Went in the evening to hear La Gazza Ladra.

TO CHARLES LEWES, 21 JUNE 1863

Thackeray's *Henry Esmond* was published in 1852, *The English Humourists* in 1853. [IV, 90–91]

Niton, | Isle of Wight. | June 21, 1863.

Dearest Boy,

I am very happy in my holiday finding quite a fresh charm in the hedgerow grasses and flowers after my long banishment from them. We have a flower garden just round us and then a sheltered grassy walk, on which the sun shines through the best part of the day; and then a wide meadow, and beyond that trees and the sea. Moreover, our landlady has cows and we get the quintessence of cream— excellent bread and butter also, and a young lady with a large crinoline to wait upon us. All for twenty-five shillings per week; or rather, we get the apartment in which we enjoy those primitive and modern blessings for that moderate sum.

I am glad you enjoyed "Esmond." It is a fine book. Since you have been interested in the historical suggestions, I recommend you to read Thackeray's "Lectures on the English Humorists," which are all about men of the same period. There is a more exaggerated estimate of Swift and Addison than is implied in "Esmond"; and the excessive laudation of men who are considerably below the tip-top of human nature both in their lives and genius, rather vitiates the Lectures, which are otherwise admirable and are delightful reading.

Thy
Mutter.

9

SOCIETY YIELDS
Felix Holt, the Radical

Since she began to write fiction, GE had earned more than £16,000, and GHL about £4,000. Most of his earnings had gone to Agnes and her illegitimate brood and to his own sons' schooling in Switzerland. In 1863 when *Romola* ended, they bought the Priory, a pleasant house and garden at 21 North Bank, Regent's Park, where they soon began to receive friends on Sunday afternoons. At first there were few ladies among the guests, for Victorian propriety could not overlook GE's honest and open defiance of the marriage convention. Much of the ostracism she suffered could have been avoided had she been willing to live the clandestine life adopted by other famous and more discreet contemporaries. Never unmindful of the legal obstacle to their marriage, she considered her union with GHL a permanent and sacred bond. As her fame increased she welcomed the increasing number of visitors, but paid no calls and accepted no invitations. Regard for her achievement gradually wore down the unjust disapproval. In the 1870s her drawing room was crowded with what Lord Acton called the most remarkable society in London. "Poets and philosophers united to honour her," he wrote; "the aristocracy of letters gathered round the gentle lady, who was justly esteemed the most illustrious figure that has arisen in literature since Goethe died." Two of Queen Victoria's daughters, eager to meet her, contrived to have the Leweses invited to dinner parties with them.

In 1865 at GHL's prompting GE set to work on a tragic drama for Helen Faucit, but after six discouraging months abandoned it for another English novel, *Felix Holt, the Radical*, laid in Warwickshire during the Reform Bill agitation of the 1830s. When the first two volumes were written, she sent them to Blackwood, who was happy to have his old author back, and offered her £5,000 for five years' copyright.

TO SARA HENNELL, [11 JULY 1863]

Ellen Allen, the heroine of this little romance, married Herman Bicknell, a sperm oil merchant, of Clyde House, Upper Norwood, 6 August 1863. The French actress who played Juliet was Stella Colas. The Italian tragedienne Adelaide Ristori played Adrienne Lecouvreur. Gounod's *Faust* was being given by rival companies with Gassier as Mephistopheles at Her Majesty's Theatre and Faure at Covent Garden. [IV, 91–93]

16 Blandford Sq. | Saturday.

Dear Sara . . .

A pretty thing has happened to an acquaintance of mine, which is quite a tonic to one's hope. She has all her life been working hard in various ways as housekeeper, governess, and several et ceteras that I can't think of at this moment: a dear little dot about 4 ft. 11. in height, pleasant to look at and clever; a working woman, without any of those epicene queernesses that belong to the class. Her life has been a history of family troubles, and she has that susceptible nature which makes such troubles hard to bear. More than once she has told me that courage quite forsook her—she felt as if there were no good in living and striving; it was difficult to discern, or believe in, any results for others, and there seemed none worth having for herself. Well! a man of fortune and accomplishments has just fallen in love with her, now she is 33—it is the prettiest story of a swift, decided passion, and made me cry for joy. She is so much above vulgar feeling about such things, that she was not at all sure at first that she would have him, "splendid match" as he is; but now she has accepted and yesterday Mrs. Bodichon and I went with her to buy her wedding-clothes. Barbara has for years been her best friend, and it is *her* school that this clever little curly-haired woman has been managing. The future husband is also 33—old enough to make his selection an honour, fond of travelling and science and other good things such as a man deserves to be fond of who chooses a poor woman in the teeth of grand relatives: brought up a Unitarian, just turned Catholic! Last, not quite least, he settles £150 a year on his future mother-in-law. If you will only imagine everything I have not said, you will think this a very charming fairy tale.

We are going this evening to see the French actress in Juliet, who is astonishing the town. Last week we saw Ristori, the other night heard the Faust, and next week we are going to hear the Elisir d'Amore and Faust again! So you see we are trying to get some compensation for the necessity of living among bricks in this sweet summer-time. I can bear the opera better than any other evening entertainment, because the house is airy and the stalls are comfortable: we both feel now that we are too old to find pleasure in bad air and with cramped limbs. The opera is a great, great product—pity we can't always have fine *Weltgeschichtliche* dramatic motives wedded with fine music, instead of trivialities or hideousnesses. Perhaps this last is too strong a word for anything except the Traviata. Rigoletto is unpleasant, but it is a superlatively fine tragedy in the Nemesis—I think I don't know a finer.

Best love to Cara, and tell her I rejoice to think of her being so far on in her work. We are really going to buy the Priory after all:—she would think it very pretty if she saw it now with the roses blooming about it.

Ever yours lovingly
Marian.

You know, of course, that there is to be another number of Romola?

TO MRS. PETER ALFRED TAYLOR, 30 JULY 1863

GE had read aloud to GHL Renan's *Essais de morale et de critique* in 1859 and *Etudes d'histoire religieuse* in 1861. [IV, 94–95]

[16 Blandford Square]
I have wanted for several days to make some feeble sign in writing that I think of your trouble. But one claim after another has arisen as a hindrance. Conceive us, please, with three boys at home, all bigger than their father! It is a congestion of youthfulness on our mature brains that disturbs the course of our lives a little, and makes us think of most things as good to be deferred till the boys are settled again. I tell you so much to make you understand that "omission" is not with me equivalent to "neglect," and that I *do* care for what happens to you.

Renan is a favourite with me. I feel more kinship with his mind than with that of any other living French author. But I think I shall not do more than look through the Introduction to his 'Vie de Jésus'—unless I happen to be more fascinated by the constructive part than I expect to be from the specimens I have seen. For minds acquainted with the European culture of this last half-century, Renan's book can furnish no new result; and they are likely to set little store by the too facile construction of a life from materials of which the biographical significance becomes more dubious as they are more closely examined. It seems to me the soul of Christianity lies not at all in the facts of an individual life, but in the ideas of which that life was the meeting-point and the new starting-point. We can never have a satisfactory basis for the history of the man Jesus, but that negation does not affect the Idea of the Christ either in its historical influence or its great symbolic meanings. Still such books as Renan's have their value in helping the popular imagination to feel that the sacred past is of one woof with that human present, which ought to be sacred too. . . .

TO RICHARD HOLT HUTTON, 8 AUGUST 1863

Hutton's article on *Romola* appeared in the *Spectator*, 18 July 1863. [IV, 96–97]

[16 Blandford Square]
After reading your article on 'Romola,' with careful reference to the questions you put to me in your letter, I can answer sincerely that I find nothing fanciful in

your interpretation. . . . It is the habit of my imagination to strive after as full a vision of the medium in which a character moves as of the character itself. The psychological causes which prompted me to give such details of Florentine life and history as I have given, are precisely the same as those which determined me in giving the details of English village life in 'Silas Marner,' or the "Dodson" life, out of which were developed the destinies of poor Tom and Maggie. But you have correctly pointed out the reason why my tendency to excess in this effort after artistic vision makes the impression of a fault in 'Romola' much more perceptibly than in my previous books. And I am not surprised at your dissatisfaction with Romola herself. I can well believe that the many difficulties belonging to the treatment of such a character have not been overcome, and that I have failed to bring out my conception with adequate fulness. I am sorry she has attracted you so little; for the great problem of her life, which essentially coincides with a chief problem in Savonarola's, is one that readers need helping to understand. But with regard to that and to my whole book, my predominant feeling is,—not that I have achieved anything, but—that great, great facts have struggled to find a voice through me, and have only been able to speak brokenly. That consciousness makes me cherish the more any proof that my work has been seen to have some true significance by minds prepared not simply by instruction, but by that religious and moral sympathy with the historical life of man which is the larger half of culture.

TO SARA HENNELL, [23 AUGUST 1863]

Sara wrote that in *Romola* GE had painted a goddess, and not a woman. Her admiration of the book was in contrast to that of the general public, by whom, GHL noted in his Journal, it "has been flatly received." Frederick Denison Maurice, the founder of Christian Socialism and one of the greatest spiritual influences of the Victorian era, wrote her two letters, which GHL said "are among the most exquisite things I ever read. His sister, Archdeacon Hare's widow, has also written with great fervor, and asked Polly to go and see her." None of these letters has been found. [IV, 103–05]

16 Blandford Sq. | Sunday.
Dear Sara . . .

You are right in saying that Romola is ideal—I feel it acutely in the reproof my own soul is constantly getting from the image it has made. My own books scourge me.

I value very much your assurance that you are "satisfied." The various *strands* of thought I had to work out forced me into a more ideal treatment of Romola than I had foreseen at the outset—though the "Drifting away" and the Village with the Plague belonged to my earliest vision of the story and were by deliberate forecast adopted as romantic and symbolical elements.

A very deep delight, which I think you will share with me, has come to me in the (to me) unexampled beauty of Frederick Maurice's conduct towards me. I should think there are very few men living who would do just as fine a thing as he

did in writing a certain letter which you shall see some time. I don't like the thing
talked about, because it seems as if I cared to tell it for my own glorification, and I
can say quite genuinely that I rejoice more in the deed itself than in the fact that
my personality is concerned in it. I think everything we admire profoundly has
that sort of effect. The contemplation of whatever is great is itself religion and lifts
us out of our egoism. The pity of it is that one perpetually sinks back behind the
dust-heaps, seeing nothing great.—Mr. Maurice's sister, the widow of Julius
Hare, long imprisoned in her room by terrible chest ailments and loss of voice has
also written to me with womanly tenderness.

These things *entre nous.* I tell them you because I know you feel an interest in
certain relations between conduct and religious belief which have been much
urged on my notice by the experience of the last eight years. . . .

Your affectionate
Pollian. . . .

TO SARA HENNELL, 16 OCTOBER 1863

GE tutored Thornie for his examinations for the India Service, but having set his heart on
going to Poland to fight the Russians, he failed miserably. Mme Bodichon persuaded him
that he would enjoy life in Natal, where farming could be combined with shooting big
game, and he went off in high spirits. GHL's third son Herbert was taken out of Hofwyl and
sent to learn farming in Scotland before going to join Thornie in Natal. Owen Jones, who won fame for the decoration of the Crystal Palace in 1851, took over
that of the Leweses' new house, the Priory, designing the wallpaper, choosing elegant
draperies, and even prescribing a splendid "grey moiré antique" gown for GE. [IV, 108–10]

16 Blandford Sq. | October 16. 63.

Dear Sara . . .

Well, our poor boy Thornie parted from us today and set out on his voyage to
Natal. I say "poor" as one does about all beings that are gone away from us for a
long while. But he went in excellent spirits with a large packet of recommendato-
ry letters to all sorts of people, and with what he cares much more for—a first-rate
rifle and revolver—and already with a smattering of Dutch and Zulu picked up
from his grammars and dictionaries. . . .

I am taking a deep bath of other peoples' thoughts, and all doings of my own
seem a long way off me. But my bath will be sorely interrupted soon by the
miserable details of removal from one house to another. Happily Mr. Owen Jones
has undertaken the ornamentation of our drawing room and will prescribe all
about chairs, etc. I think, after all, I like a clean kitchen better than any other
room.

We are far on in correcting the proofs of the new edition of the "Goethe" and
are about to begin the printing of the Aristotle which is to appear at Christmas or
Easter. But Mr. Lewes is even now retouching it—always finding something to

add or to modify. I hope he will have some thorough peace now, for he has been a good deal harassed. Best love to all, and many thanks to Cara for her last letter. Ever, dear Sara

Yours
Pollian.

TO ANTHONY TROLLOPE, 23 OCTOBER 1863

Rachel Ray had just been published in two volumes by Chapman & Hall. *The Small House at Allington* was still appearing serially in the *Cornhill*. [IV, 110–11]

16 Blandford Sq. | October 23. 63.

Dear Mr. Trollope

I received your kind letter some days before I received "Rachel Ray." But now I have read the book and can thank you both for your remembrance of me and for the gift. I value both.

Rachel has a formidable rival in "The Small House," which seems to me peculiarly felicitous in its conception, and good for all souls to read. But I am much struck in "Rachel" with the skill with which you have organized thoroughly natural everyday incidents into a strictly related, well-proportioned whole, natty and complete as a nut on its stem. Such construction is among those subtleties of art which can hardly be appreciated except by those who have striven after the same result with conscious failure. Rachel herself is a sweet maidenly figure, and her poor mother's spiritual confusions are excellently observed.

But there is something else I care yet more about, which has impressed me very happily in all those writings of yours that I know—it is that people are breathing good bracing air in reading them—it is that they (the books) are filled with belief in goodness without the slightest tinge of maudlin. They are like pleasant public gardens, where people go for amusement and, whether they think of it or not, get health as well. It seems rather preachy and assuming in me to say that, out of all the other things I might say. But it is what I feel strongly, and I can't help thinking that it is what you care about also, though such things are rather a result of what an author *is* than of what he intends.

We shall soon be in the agonies of moving, and after that I hope we shall contrive to see you, by planning.

Always yours very truly
M. E. Lewes.

TO BESSIE PARKES, 15 NOVEMBER 1863

Bessie's name does not appear among the 17 guests at Charles Lewes's birthday party, though there were five other ladies. The violinist Jansa played. The house was greatly admired. "Besides the trouble and vexation incident to moving," GHL wrote in his Journal

13 November, "we have had extra annoyances. The tuner was sick over our elegant drawing room paper, which Owen Jones had decorated, and over the carpet! This obliges us to have fresh paper made, as there are no remnants of the old, and it was originally made for us." [IV, 114]

The Priory, | North Bank, | Regents Park.
November 15. 1863.

Dear Bessie

You would like to meet Mr. Anthony Trollope, I think, should you not? We expect him to be one of a small gathering we shall have on the evening of the 24th, to make some brightness on the day Charlie comes of age. If you would like to come, and have no reason to the contrary, do. If not, there has been no harm done by an invitation *entre nous*.

Ever yours
M. E. Lewes.

TO MME EUGÈNE BODICHON, 4 DECEMBER 1863

When Leopold Jansa played at the Priory, he agreed to give George Eliot lessons in accompanying the violin. William George Clark, a Fellow of Trinity College, Cambridge, and Public Orator of the University, had been a friend of the Leweses since 1861. [IV, 118–20]

The Priory, 21 North Bank | December 4. 1863.

Dearest Barbara . . .

I am rather ashamed to hear of anyone trying to be useful just now, for I am doing nothing but indulge myself—enjoying being petted very much, enjoying great books, enjoying our new pretty quiet home and the study of Beethoven's Sonatas for piano and violin with the mild-faced old Jansa—and not being at all unhappy, as you imagined me.

We had a house-warming celebration of Charlie's birthday on the 24th: it was a birthday extraordinary introducing a new era for him, for he became twenty-one! Our youngest lad Bertie seems to have had his wits a little sharpened by change of circumstances and writes as if he liked his Scotch farming and Scotch domesticity. Of Thornie we cannot well hear until the end of January or beginning of February, so that our parental minds are for the moment at ease.

The "Life of Goethe" is about to appear in one handsome volume, and George is correcting the proofs of the "Aristotle." The correction is a slow business, because the proofs are read by several people: our friend Mr. Clark of Cambridge reads them to make us easy about the Greek accents, and Huxley and Tyndal read some of them for the sake of scientific criticism. Meanwhile George sits in a comfortable room delightfully free from irritation of organs and street cries, making further studies for his History of Science, and I sit in another room taking deep draughts of reading—Politique positive, Euripides, Latin Christianity and so forth, and remaining in glorious ignorance of "the current literature." Such is our life: and you perceive that instead of being miserable, I am rather following a wicked example and saying to my soul, "Soul, take thine ease." . . .

I am sorry to think of you without any artistic society to help you and feed your faith. It is hard to believe long together that anything is "worth while" unless there is some eye to kindle in common with our own, some brief word uttered now and then to imply that what is infinitely precious to us is precious alike to another mind. I fancy that, to do without that guarantee, one must be rather insane—one must be a bad poet, or a spinner of impossible theories or an inventor of impossible machinery. However it is but a brief space either of time or distance that divides you from those who thoroughly share your cares and joys—always excepting that portion which is the hidden private lot of every human being. In the most entire confidence even of husband and wife there is always the unspoken residue—the *undivined* residue, perhaps of what is most sinful, perhaps of what is most exalted and unselfish.

All blessings on you and yours, dear Barbara. George is gone into town, or he would send his message.

Ever your loving
Marian.

TO SARA HENNELL, 22 JANUARY 1864

Robert Buchanan, born in Staffordshire in 1841, lived ten years in Glasgow before coming to London. GHL met him through the articles he submitted to the *Cornhill*, of which the account of *David Gray* in February 1864 was one. [IV, 128–29]

The Priory, | North Bank, | Regents Park.
January 22. 64.

Dear Sara . . .

We have been interested lately in a young poet, Robert Buchanan, a Scotchman who came up to London 4 years ago in the faith that he should find the greatest and most generous minds there, and who has gone through the usual trials of disappointment in that faith. He seems to have kept a beautiful seriousness and simplicity of nature, and to add to one's grounds of sympathy for him, he has just married as a refuge from the loneliness of London life. He is a delicate looking creature, not more than four and twenty. I was especially pleased with the venerating affection he expressed for Miss Mulock—for her earnest religious feeling, and her strength of character. "She has taught me," he said, "to see good in other women—good that I never saw before." Wasn't that pretty?—I mention him to you that, if you happen to see in the Cornhill an account of a young Scotch poet who died of consumption, you may know that it was written by Mr. Buchanan, and that *he* is the Robert Blank who figures (very modestly) as the friend of the dead. Tell me any news of yourself or others, when the spirit moves you, and believe me

Always yours lovingly
Pollian. . . .

TO MRS. ROBERT EVANS II, 12 FEBRUARY 1864

GE's half brother Robert Evans, born 1802, died 29 January 1864. His son Robert III wrote to tell GE of his father's death and gave his mother's address. Mrs. Evans replied 15 March with gratitude for GE's letter [VIII, 316–17]: "I must tell you that the last Book he looked at was 'Adam Bede.' He had expressed a wish that I should fetch it and read 'Dinah's Prayer and Sermon' and when I had done so I was called from the room—and he said 'Give me the Book, I shall like to read it again.' When I returned he had gone to sleep with the Book in his hand, he was never able to hold another." [IV, 133–34]

The Priory | North Bank | Regents Park. | February 12. 1864.
My dear Mrs. Evans

I have deferred writing to you, fearing to be obtrusive after I had already sent a message to you through your son. But I cannot be quite easy without expressing to yourself directly—so far as a few written words can express it—my sincere sympathy with you in the greatest of all partings that has just befallen you.

You have many dear ties and abundant friends around you, but I think there can hardly be one whose memory of the husband you have lost stretches so far back as mine. For in all the years I have lived I remember nothing that is much earlier than the knowledge that I had a brother Robert, and I have always thought of him, throughout the years we have been separated, as one whose heart had on every opportunity shown its ready kindness towards me, and besides that, I have cherished the memory that we had one dear Father whom we both venerated.

I will not believe that you will think there is no good in my saying these things to you, for good is always felt from the simple utterance of feelings that bind us poor struggling men and women to one another—And you must be very changed from what I remember you if you do not give a very gentle and loving welcome to any word or look of affection. But I cannot imagine you much changed—even your face I fancy would look familiar to me and bear few traces of the years that have passed since we last saw each other. To see you again or to hear from you, if ever you had the prompting or opportunity, would be a very sweet renewal of the past. May you be blest in all that remains to you after this supreme loss! I am comforted to think that very much must still remain in the love and prosperity of your children. Ever dear Mrs. Evans

Sincerely yours
M. E. Lewes.

TO MRS. PETER ALFRED TAYLOR, 25 MARCH 1864

GE had read the Greek dramatists carefully in the 1850s. After *Romola* was finished, she resumed daily reading of Greek and kept up the practice throughout the rest of her life. Mrs. Taylor was a strong upholder of the Union side in the Civil War, and her husband was the first M.P. to associate himself with the Federalists. [IV, 139]

[The Priory]
Fog, east wind, and headache: there is my week's history. But this morning, when your letter came to me, I had got up well, and was reading the sorrows of the aged Hecuba with great enjoyment. I wish an immortal drama could be got out of my sorrows, that people might be the better for them two thousand years hence. But fog, east wind, and headache are not great dramatic motives.

Your letter was a reinforcement of the delicious sense of *bien être* that comes with the departure of bodily pain; and I am glad, retrospectively, that beyond our fog lay your moonlight and your view of the glorious sea. It is not difficult to me to believe that you look a new creature already. Mr Lewes tells me the country air has always a magical effect on me, even in the first hour; but it is not the air alone, is it? It is the wide sky and the hills and the wild flowers which are linked with all calming thoughts, just as every object in town has its perturbing associations.

I share your joy in the Federal successes—with that check that attends all joy in a war not absolutely ended. But you have worked and earned more joy than those who have been merely passives.

TO SARA HENNELL, 30 APRIL 1864

Frederic William Burton met the Leweses while he was living in Munich in 1858. They became warm friends, and he was a constant caller at the Priory. The reviewers were less enthusiastic than GE about his watercolour *Hellelil and Hildebrand*. Burton had never before been to Italy. Their two weeks together in Venice taught GE a good deal about how to look at pictures. He was Director of the National Gallery 1874–94. [IV, 147]

The Priory, | 21. North Bank, | Regents Park.
April 30. 64.

Dear Sara

Only think! next Wednesday morning we start for Italy. The move is quite a sudden one. We need a good shake for our bodies and minds and must take the Spring-time before the weather becomes too hot. We shall not be away more than a month, or six weeks at the utmost. Our friend Mr. Burton, the artist, will be our companion for at least part of the time. He has just painted a divine picture— better than Millais' Huguenots—which is now to be seen at the Old Water- Colour Exhibition. The subject is from a Norse Legend, but that is no matter— the picture tells its story. A knight in mailed armour and surcoat has met the fair tall woman he secretly loves on a turret stair. By an uncontrollable movement he has seized her arm and is kissing it. She, amazed, has dropped the flowers she held in her other hand. The subject might have been made the most vulgar thing in the world—the artist has raised it to the highest pitch of refined emotion. The kiss is on the fur-lined *sleeve* that covers the arm, and the face of the knight is the face of a man to whom the kiss is a sacrament. . . .

Your ever affectionate
Pollian.

TO FRANÇOIS D'ALBERT DURADE, 24 JUNE 1864

Burton rejoined the Leweses in Milan and accompanied them home. GHL's stepfather Captain John Willim, after serving in Bengal for eight years, was retired in 1811; he died 9 February 1864, aged 86. Charles Lewes was engaged to Gertrude Hill, a sister of Octavia Hill and granddaughter of Dr. Southwood Smith. D'Albert Durade wanted permission from Smith & Elder to publish his French translation of *Romola*. [IV, 153–55]

21. North Bank | Regent's Park | June 24. 1864.

Dear Friend

Yes! We have been absent, and if this, your second letter had come a day earlier, it would not have found us at home. We have been away seven weeks and have been like you, in Italy; moreover, twice—on our way to and from Venice—we spent some days in Milan. If either of those stays had happened to coincide with your visit and we had met at a turning of the street! But on Corpus Christi Day we were in Venice, nearly at the end of our fortnight's sojourn there, which we enjoyed not at all the less because we had been there four years ago. In spite of the years that have made us older, Venice and her art seemed more beautiful to us than the images our memory had retained. We entered the more thoroughly into the art from having a friend with us who is like yourself, a brother of the brush, and having never been in Italy before felt an ardour of curiosity and enjoyment that was an added stimulus to his companions. Our route was from Paris to Turin, Milan, and Venice without pause at the intermediate Lombard towns, which we reserved to vary our return homewards. I had half set my heart on seeing Ravenna, but Mr. Lewes's health was too delicate for us to venture on the inconvenient journeying necessary to get to that out of the world place. So we returned from Venice in the easiest and most luxurious manner, pausing at Padova, Verona, and Brescia, and going from Milan by Lakes Como and Lugano over the St. Gothard to Lucerne, where we rested well, and so on to Paris again. You can imagine that London does not look pretty after such a journey, and the gratification we get in returning home must be such as comes from the sense of duties to be fulfilled there.

We have many such duties. Mr. Lewes has an aged mother who has lately become a widow and makes large demands on his time, both for personal attentions and for the management of her monetary affairs. And our family prospects have complicated themselves even during our short absence in a way that will not, I think, be entirely without interest to Maman and you. Our "boy" Charles in this his twenty-second year has become engaged to a young lady, for whom we had observed that he had a growing penchant, but who we suspected would hardly fall in love with our amiable bit of crudity. That was a mistake, a parental notion, however. She *has* fallen in love with him, and it is very pretty to see their fresh young happiness. She is in my opinion remarkably handsome and has the rare gift of a splendid contralto voice. She is 4 years older than Charles, which under all the circumstances is an advantage, for she seems to have been brought up in such a way as to have preserved all that is best in youthfulness while she has had much domestic experience. One never knows what to wish about marriage—the evils of an early choice may be easily counterbalanced by the vitiation that often comes from long bachelorhood. So Mr. Lewes and I fix our minds chiefly on the good we see instead of the possible ills which we may never see. . . .

Yours with affectionate memory
M. E. Lewes.

I have little doubt that MMrs. Smith and Elder will answer your letters favourably.

TO SARA HENNELL, 13 JULY [1864]

Nelly was Charles Bray's illegitimate daughter, whom with Cara's consent they adopted in 1846. In 1863 she contracted pulmonary tuberculosis. John Henry Newman was gratuitously assailed in a review by Charles Kingsley, who attributed to him the statement that "Truth, for its own sake, has never been a virtue of the Roman Catholic clergy." After an exchange of letters and pamphlets, Newman published his *Apologia pro Vita Sua*, which effectively demolished Kingsley's arguments. William Ullathorne was assigned in 1841 to set up a Roman Catholic mission in Coventry, where he soon became acquainted with the Brays. He was consecrated bishop in 1846, and on the restoration of the hierarchy was translated to the newly created see of Birmingham. [IV, 158–59]

The Priory, | North Bank, | Regents Park.
July 13

Dear Sara

Your letter interested me deeply. I can't help thinking very often of the time when Nelly was a bright little child, playing with Fly on the lawn. That part of her life, I think, was really joyous—and how much you did for her then! I used to feel your elevation above me continually in the attitude of mind you showed about Nelly's education and your sense of your relation towards childhood generally. These are the lasting things—the true thoughts, the true feelings, the good deeds, which live in others even when they have gone quite away from the mind in which they were born, so that sometimes the man or woman who is sitting in desolation is doing the office of a glorified Saint for those who *remember*. . . .

I have been reading Newman's Apologia pro Vita Suâ, with such absorbing interest that I found it impossible to forsake the book until I had finished it. I don't know whether the affair between him and Kingsley has interested you, or whether you have shared at all my view of it. I have been made so indignant by Kingsley's mixture of arrogance, coarse impertinence and unscrupulousness with real intellectual incompetence, that my first interest in Newman's answer arose from a wish to see what I consider thoroughly vicious writing thoroughly castigated. But the Apology now mainly affects me as the revelation of a life—how different in form from one's own, yet with how close a fellowship in its needs and burthens—I mean spiritual needs and burthens. At the end there is a beautiful letter written by our old acquaintance Dr. Ullathorne, Bishop of Birmingham, intended as a public testimony to Newman's active life since he entered the Catholic Church.

Yesterday we went to see Holman Hunt's picture which he has been labouring at intermittently of course for five or six years. He calls it the Afterglow in Egypt, but the chief thing is what the afterglow shines upon—a Nubian girl carrying a bundle of gleaned wheat which has attracted a flight of pigeons towards her. . . . It is a bit of existence, not of action, and is painted with immense elaboration, yet with shortcomings in the midst of elaboration that prevent it from being a triumph. That is always rather a sad thing to say when there has been so much study, so much hard work, so much heroism as must always go to the doing of anything difficult. But Inspiration is a rare incalculable thing—it will flash out sometimes in a mere bit of sky and water and weed, and leave you only to wonder at its absence in a picture where all sorts of rare and beautiful things have been brought together and studied with immeasurable pains. . . .

My best love and deep sympathy to Cara and Mr. Bray. Write again on the first movement of your will that way.

Ever thine
Pollian.

TO SARA HENNELL, [2 OCTOBER 1864]

In Venice while looking at an *Annunciation* by Titian, the idea of *The Spanish Gypsy* occurred to GE. She worked at it all summer, with more than the usual pangs that afflicted her when writing. On Sara's recommendation they went to try the water cure at Harrogate and later went to Scarborough. [IV, 164–65]

The Priory, | 21. North Bank, | Regents Park.
Sunday Morning.

Dear Sara

If I had not written too hastily and carelessly to you from Scarbro' I should have told you that I received your nice letter addressed to Benwell House, giving me hints about the things to be seen in the neighbourhood of Harrogate. . . . It makes me very, very happy to see George so much better, and to return with that chief satisfaction to the quiet comforts of home.

I have had a fit of Spanish history lately and have been learning Spanish grammar—the easiest of all the Romance grammars—since we have been away. Mr. Lewes has been rubbing up his Spanish by reading Don Quixote in these weeks of idlesse, and I have read aloud and translated to him, like a good child. I find it so much easier to learn anything than to feel that I have anything worth teaching.

I hear and read with deep interest any details about Nelly, and am always grateful to you for taking the trouble to write me any. All is perfectly well with us, now the "little Pater" is stronger, and we are especially thankful for Charlie's prospect of marriage. We could not have desired anything more suited to his character, and more likely to make his life a good. But this blessing which has befallen us only makes me feel the more acutely the cutting off of a like satisfaction from the friends I chiefly love.

Ever, dear Sara your
Pollian.

TO FRANÇOIS D'ALBERT DURADE, 12 JANUARY 1865

GHL gave up his work as consulting editor of the *Cornhill* in October 1864. But Smith was already projecting an evening paper, the *Pall Mall Gazette*, on which he offered him a post as consultant at £300 a year. The trip to Paris was to persuade the editor of the *Revue des deux mondes* to contribute articles. The new periodical GE mentions was the *Fortnightly Review*, which Anthony Trollope and other friends were planning. [IV, 175–76]

The Priory | North Bank N.W. | January 12. 1865.
Dear Friend . . .
We are exceedingly well prepared to sympathize both in joy about sons and in sickness, for we have had much of both those different experiences. Charles is to be married in April, and his engagement is an increasing source of satisfaction to us. We have good news from Thornie, who is happy and active at Natal; and our third son Bertie has just been with us for his Christmas visit, gratifying us highly by his improvement in health and morale. As for sickness, that has been an almost incessant companion with us since I last wrote to you. . . .
I never write in periodicals. That is to say, I have not done it for many years, and of late Mr. Lewes has not contributed to the Cornhill until this month, the number for which contains an article by him on "Shakspeare in France." I am now occupied with writing, but rather to please myself than the public, and I am not certain whether what I am doing will be published.
Mr. Lewes has been earnestly requested to take the editorship of a new periodical which is in some respects to form a sort of English "Revue des deux Mondes," and after decidedly refusing from fear of an undertaking which would make too great demand on his time, he is now inclined to consent under certain arrangements which will save him from excessive work.
Tomorrow we shall start for Paris for a stay of about ten days, so I have written in haste this morning lest you should wonder at my silence if I deferred writing till my return. You see, we are happy and prosperous and I shall feel all the happier now that I have had good news of you. Pray give my best love to Madame D'Albert, and beg her to accept with you my husband's very high and kind regards. Believe me, dear Friend,

Ever yours gratefully and affectionately
Marian E. Lewes.

TO SARA HENNELL, 6 FEBRUARY [1865]

Cara's patient was Nelly Bray. The gaieties of Paris in addition to the galleries included six evenings out of ten at the theatres. [IV, 177–78]

The Priory, | 21. North Bank, | Regents Park.
February 6.

Dear Sara

I suspect you have come to dislike letters, but until you say so, I must write now and then to gratify myself. I want to send my love, lest all the old messages should have lost their scent, like old lavender bags. I wonder how poor Cara's patient bears the winter with its rapid alternations from severity to mildness, and how Cara herself is under all vicissitudes.

Since I wrote to you last we have actually been to Paris! A little business was an excuse for getting a great deal of pleasure, and I, for whom change of air and scene is always the best tonic, am much brightened by our wintry expedition, which ended just in time for us to escape the heavy fall of snow. We are very happy, having almost recovered our old tête-à-tête, of which I am so selfishly fond, that I am beginning to feel it an heroic effort when I make up my mind to invite half a dozen visitors. But it is necessary to strive against this unsocial disposition, so we are going to have some open evenings.

There is great talk of a new periodical—a fortnightly apparition, partly on the plan of the Revue des deux Mondes. Mr. Lewes has consented to become its editor if the preliminaries are settled so as to satisfy him. . . .

Ever yours affectionately
Pollian.

TO SARA HENNELL, 2 MARCH 1865

Nelly Bray died 1 March 1865. [IV, 180]

The Priory, | 21. North Bank, | Regents Park.
March 2. 1865.

Dear Sara

I feel too acutely what death is to write vain words to Cara. This sorrow seems to have happened to me too—it calls up such long memories of the time when we were very near each other. I shall be anxious to know how both Cara and Mr. Bray are after another week—when you can spare me a few minutes.

Surely, dear Sara, both to you and Cara there must be the sense of having tried to the utmost to give value to that young life which was brought so close to you. But we make sad mistakes in attempting to judge of each other's consolations. Ever, in my deepest heart

Your sister
Pollian.

TO MRS. CHARLES BRAY, 18 MARCH 1865

[IV, 182–84]

The Priory, | 21. North Bank, | Regents Park
March 18. 65.

My dear Cara

You see I have let the weeks go by—thinking of you, but not writing to you. I believe you are one of the few who can understand that in certain crises, direct expression of sympathy is the least possible to those who most feel sympathy. If I could have been with you in bodily presence, I should have sat silent, thinking silence a sign of feeling that speech, trying to be wise, must always spoil. The truest things one can say about great death are the oldest simplest things that everybody knows by rote, but that no one knows really till death has come very close. And when that inward teaching is going on, it seems pitiful presumption for those who are outside to be saying anything. There is no such thing as consolation, when we have made the lot of another our own as you did Nelly's. The anguish must be borne—it will only get more and more bearable as other thoughts and feelings recover some power.

I don't know whether you strongly share, as I do, the old belief that made men say the gods loved those who died young. It seems to me truer than ever, now life has become more complex and more and more difficult problems have to be worked out. Life, though a good to men on the whole, is a doubtful good to many, and to some not a good at all. To my thought, it is a source of constant mental distortion to make the denial of this a part of religion, to go on pretending things are better than they are—like talking of "your Majesty's happy reign" to a successful monarch whose reign has been one of blood and fire to half a population, who happen to be at a distance and out of sight. So to me, early death takes the aspect of salvation—though I feel too that those who live and suffer may sometimes have the greater blessedness of *being* a salvation. But I will not write of judgments and opinions. What I want my letter to tell you is that I love you truly, gratefully, unchangeably. And to show me you believe it, you must not write till you feel inclined—not think I shall mind if you don't answer this at all, for indeed there is nothing to answer.

Sara spent an hour or two with us. She struck me as looking remarkably well in health, but with less ability than usual to receive impressions. I mean, that she seemed nervously absorbed, and dim of apprehension for everything outside her. I hope this stay at the coast will be a renovation for her.

It has been a grief to me to read in the parliamentary debates, the statement of Coventry distress, and the absence of any strong hope as to the revival of trade there. I wish I had had some clothes to send, as Mr. Bray desired; but I really get rapidly fleeced of spare wool. The few things I could have parted with were rather for those who required to look "respectable."

With love to him, always, dear Cara, your old

Marian.

JOURNAL, 25, 29 MARCH 1865

GE's Journal does not mention Charles's marriage in the Rosslyn Hill Unitarian Chapel to Gertrude Hill, 20 March, but GHL's does: "The day was remarkably brilliant, but piercingly cold from a bitter and fierce east wind. No one was invited to the wedding except Polly and I, the Aunts, Gertrude's mother and sisters; yet there were many people in the Church. We went back to Church Row and had a quiet and pleasant talk with them all. The young couple started at 1/2 past 1 for Folkestone on their way to Italy. Happier prospects never smiled upon a marriage. Polly and I then called on Mother. Drove home and were quiet and cozy together all day." The Aunts were Mary and Margaret Gillies, with whom Gertrude had lived since childhood at 25 Church Row, Hampstead. As editor of the *Fortnightly* GHL had a salary of £600 a year with a subeditor and clerk. GE contributed a few light fillers to help start the *Pall Mall Gazette*. The novel she had begun was *Felix Holt, the Radical*. [IV, 184]

[The Priory]

25 March. During this week the commencement of the Fortnightly Review, of which George has been prevailed on to be the editor, has been finally decided on. I am full of vain regrets that we did not persist in original refusal, for I dread the worry and anxiety G. may have. About myself I am in deep depression, feeling powerless. I have written nothing but beginnings since I finished a little article for the Pall Mall on the Logic of Servants. Dear George is all activity, yet is in very frail health. How I worship his good humour, his good sense, his affectionate care for every one who has claims on him! That worship is my best life.

29. Sent a letter on Futile Lying from Saccharissa to the Pall Mall. *I have begun a Novel.*

TO MRS. PETER ALFRED TAYLOR, 10 JULY 1865

In the general election Peter Taylor was returned as M.P. for Leicester, a seat he held 1862–84. John Stuart Mill was M.P. for Westminster 1865–68. GE had been rereading his *Political Economy*. GHL's articles in the *Fortnightly* were "The Principles of Success in Literature." [IV, 196–97]

[The Priory]

Success to the canvassing! It is "very meet and right and your bounden duty" to be with Mr Taylor in this time of hard work, and I am glad that your health has made no impediment. I should have liked to be present when you were cheered. The expression of a common feeling by a large mass of men, when the feeling is one of good-will, moves me like music. A public tribute to any man who has done the world a service with brain or hand, has on me the effect of a great religious rite, with pealing organ and full-voiced choir.

I agree with you in your feeling about Mill. Some of his works have been frequently my companions of late, and I have been going through many *actions de grâce* towards him. I am not anxious that he should be in Parliament: thinkers can do more outside than inside the House. But it would have been a fine precedent, and would have made an epoch, for such a man to have been asked for and elected solely on the ground of his mental eminence. As it is, I suppose it is pretty certain that he will *not* be elected.

I am glad you have been interested in Mr Lewes's articles. His great anxiety about the "Fortnightly' is to make it the vehicle for sincere writing—real contributions of opinion on important topics. But it is more difficult than the inexperienced could imagine to get the sort of writing which will correspond to that desire of his.

TO MRS. PETER ALFRED TAYLOR, 1 AUGUST 1865

Guiseppe Mazzini, the Italian patriot, had been a friend of Peter Taylor since 1845. The caution this letter shows may have been induced by GHL's position on the *Fortnightly* and GE's growing circle of more conventional friends. [IV, 199–200]

[The Priory]

I received yesterday the circular about the Mazzini Fund. Mr. Lewes and I would have liked to subscribe to a tribute to Mazzini, or to a fund for his use, of which the application was defined and guaranteed by his own word. As it is, the application of the desired fund is only intimated in the vaguest manner by the Florentine committee. The reflection is inevitable, that the application may ultimately be the promotion of conspiracy, the precise character of which is necessarily unknown to subscribers.

Now, though I believe there are cases in which conspiracy may be a sacred, necessary struggle against organized wrong, there are also cases in which it is hopeless, and can produce nothing but misery; or needless, because it is not the best means attainable of reaching the desired end; or unjustifiable, because it resorts to acts which are more unsocial in their character than the very wrong they are directed to extinguish: and in these three supposable cases it seems to me that it would be a social crime to further conspiracy even by the impulse of a little finger, to which one may well compare a small money subscription.

I think many persons to whom the circular might be sent would take something like this view, and would grieve, as we do, that a proposition intended to honour Mazzini should come in a form to which they cannot conscientiously subscribe. I trouble you and Mr Taylor with this explanation, because both Mr Lewes and I have a real reverence for Mazzini, and could not therefore be content to give a silent negative.

TO MME EUGÈNE BODICHON, [3 AUGUST 1865]

Mme Bodichon painted a watercolor landscape for the Priory. Théodore de la Villemarqué had written the *Contes populaires des anciens Bretons* (1842) and *La Légende celtique en Irlande, en Cambrie, et en Bretagne* (1864). This was the first time they had seen Tom Trollope since his wife's death in April. [VIII, 349–50]

The Priory, | 21, North Bank, | Regents Park.
Thursday.

Dear Barbara

You did not come again, but the picture came. We are both very much pleased with it and grateful to the soul and the hand that produced it for us. It is deliciously fresh and airy and happy. It is settled now that we go for a month's holiday in Normandy and Brittany starting next Thursday. So I am reading Villemarqué and setting my mind towards Celtic legends, that I may people the land with great shadows when there are no solid Bretons in sight.

Yesterday the two Trollopes dined with us and we had a good deal of pleasant talk, or rather shouting. Also I sat for the last time for my portrait, and Mr. Burton was disappointed to find that you had left town before he had been able to call on you and see certain oil sketches. I gave him your address that he might write to you. Let me know how you get on.

Ever yours
M. E. Lewes.

JOURNAL, 14–15 OCTOBER 1865

GE had been reading widely for *Felix Holt* but had written little. Browning first called on the Leweses in Blandford Square in December 1862 and came to dinner with them a few weeks later. [IV, 205]

[The Priory]

October 14. At p. 74 of my novel. The last fortnight has been almost unproductive from bad health.

15. Sunday. In the evening walked home with Browning, went into his house, and saw the objects Mrs. Browning used to have about her, her chair, tables, books etc. An epoch to be remembered. Browning showed us her Hebrew Bible with notes in her handwriting, and several of her copies of the Greek dramatists with her annotations.

TO MRS. CHARLES BRAY, 10 NOVEMBER [1865]

Mrs. Congreve's sister Emily Bury had been severely ill with a fever. Mr. Congreve passed his examination and was admitted to the Royal College of Physicians in 1866. Sara Hennell's friends had concluded that her religious monomania made rational discussion hopeless. The tenant had taken the Bray's house at Sydenham, which was often unlet. [IV, 207–08]

The Priory, | 21. North Bank, | Regents Park.
November 10.

My dear Cara

When your kind letter came into my hands I had just returned from my first visit to Mrs. Congreve and Miss Bury. The poor patient is recovering, but still needs great care. Both Mr. and Mrs. Congreve have suffered less physically than I feared they would. You may imagine what the strain on Mr. Congreve is when I tell you that he expects in a month to undergo the Examination of his Medical Studies.

I wrote a long letter to you nearly a fortnight ago, and burnt it, because I hesitated whether I ought to say what I had said in it. Yet I think I will tell you that the gist of it—of course confided to you with perfect trust in your loving discretion—was to beg of you not to accept our dear Sara's statements about her friends' words or their condition, because I felt convinced that her mental habits were of a kind that absolutely forbid her getting any accurate impressions about things outside her own theoretic world. That word will suffice—is perhaps more than enough—by way of additional caution to your own indisposition towards hasty judgments. I had also told you in that burnt letter, that the best compensation for not seeing you was to hear that the reason was a Tenant. Gaudeamus! . . .

Unfailing memory, dear Cara, from

Your affectionate
Marian.

JOURNAL, 15–24 NOVEMBER 1865

D. F. Strauss's *Leben Jesu für das deutsche Volk*, 1864, was a popular rather than scholarly book. Rufus Lyon's story is Chapter 6 of *Felix Holt*. [IV, 208–09]

[The Priory]

15. During the last three weeks George has been very poorly, but now he is better. I have been reading Fawcett's Economic Condition of the Working Classes, Mill's Liberty, looking into Strauss's Second Life of Jesus, and reading Neale's History of the Puritans of which I have reached the fourth volume. Yesterday the news came of Mrs. Gaskell's death. She died suddenly while reading aloud to her daughters.

* 16. Writing Mr. Lyon's story, which I have determined to insert as a narrative. *Reading the Bible.*

22. Sara Hennell lunched and dined with us. At the end of Chapter VII.

24. Finished Neale's History of the Puritans: began Hallam's Middle Ages.

TO FRANÇOIS D'ALBERT DURADE, 17 DECEMBER 1865

Translations of *Romola* into German and Dutch had been published, but D'Albert's French translation remained unpublished until 1878. The *Fortnightly* was the first English periodical to insist on signed articles. Edmond Schérer had been literary critic of *Le Temps* since 1860. Mlle Bohn's enthusiastic opinion of *Romola* was given during her call at the Priory in July 1865. Thornton Lewes had joined a commando group in Natal to fight the Basutos, on being promised a right to land for his service. While they were in Italy, Frederic Burton had asked GE if he might take her portrait. The first sitting was 19 June 1864; a year later she was still sitting, clearly for a fresh study in chalks, which shows GE's fair complexion, light brown hair, and blue-gray eyes. The reproduction in color proved impractical. The portrait was given to the National Portrait Gallery in 1883. [IV, 210–12]

The Priory, North Bank | St. John's Wood. | December 17. 1865.
My dear Friend
  Your kind letter came to me yesterday. I wish there had been no family trouble to disturb the happiness of which your previous letter had given me an idea. . . .
"The Fortnightly" is a great *succès d'estime;* the principle of signature, never before thoroughly carried out in England, has given it an exceptional dignity, and drawn valuable writers. It is a thoroughly serious periodical, intended for the few who will pay a high price, and is supported by proprietors unconnected with the publishing trade. It is still a question whether it will succeed commercially. I think I told you that Mr. Lewes accepted the editorship on urgent request, after having previously refused it, and has nothing to do with it as a speculation. He likes the work very well, now he has entered into it, finding that superior contributors present themselves and brave the supposed perils of signature. I am occupied, in a leisurely way, with my own writing, and, as you know, am not in the habit of contributing to periodicals.
  It grieves me that you have had your trouble in vain in translating Romola. I have had at least four applications from France for permission to translate it. But in fact the permission has always belonged to Smith and Elder; and now, no permission is needed. A short time ago we had a visit from Mlle. Bohn, the niece of Professor Schérer, residing with him at Versailles. She says that, by herself and in her circle, Romola is valued more than any of my previous books. It is rather a cruel thing that she, like so many others, inquired whether my books had been translated into French—I mean, it is cruel for you, that after your conscientious labour your publishers have not been able to make better arrangements for you with Parisian houses. I have received numerous letters asking me to give my authority to translations of the Clerical Scenes, or Silas Marner, or the Mill. I only tell you this as so much information that you might perhaps use, in your relations with your publishers.
  Our eldest son Charles is extremely happy in his marriage, and we see more and more reason to rejoice in his early establishment. Thornton has had some calamities to encounter in Natal, owing to a monetary crisis in the colony and a war with the natives. But he is well in health and shows much spirit. These conditions in Natal cause us to waver in our intention of sending out the youngest who is now old enough to go, and is better fitted for colonial than for English life, at least as far

as the means of pushing his fortune are concerned. He is a fine fellow physically, and has pleasant social qualities, but he is not suited to any other life than that of a farmer, and in England farming has become a business that requires not only great capital but great skill to render it otherwise than hazardous.

These are the chief points in our present circumstances. Besides these, perhaps it will interest you to know that what my friends consider a remarkably fine portrait of me (in crayons) has been executed by an artist named Frederick Burton, a friend of ours, and that the portrait is to be published by a process which professes to produce facsimiles of such drawings. See how I chat about myself! But you wish me to do so.

Mr. Lewes unites with me in kindest feelings and wishes. Send my best love to Madame d'Albert when you write, and believe me dear friend—with a thorough response to your wish that we may meet again—

> Your true and affectionate friend
> Marian E. Lewes.

TO MRS. CHARLES LEWES, 21 DECEMBER [1865]

Gertrude's sister Octavia Hill, later co-founder of the National Trust, had just interested Ruskin in the problem of improving housing for the London poor. Octavia was strongly influenced by F. D. Maurice and the Christian Socialists. [IV, 213–14]

The Priory, | 21. North Bank, | Regents Park.
December 21.

Dearest Gertrude . . .

It has occurred to me since you were with us the other day, that something I said about "Church people" at Canterbury N. Z. was open to misapprehension. Your sister Octavia once said to me "Have you never known any earnest church people?"—and lest you should be unable to correct the sort of misconception implied in her question, I want to tell you that I was brought up in the Church of England, and never belonged to any other religious body. I care that this should be known, not at all on personal grounds, but because, as I have been, and perhaps shall be, depicting dissenters with much sympathy I would not have it supposed that the sympathy springs from any partiality of association.

As to its origin historically, and *as a system of thought,* it is my conviction that the Church of England is the least morally dignified of all forms of Christianity i.e. all considerable forms dating from the Reformation; but as a portion of my earliest associations and most poetic memories, it would be more likely to tempt me into partiality than any form of dissent. What I referred to as dreading in a New Zealand settlement was the peculiar aspect which any religious body assumes when it is quite dominant in a new country, and is not under the stringent criticism of dissidents.

Perhaps all this explanation was needless, but lest it should not have been, I prefer to give it. Best love to all.

Always, dearest Chick,
Your loving
Mutter.

TO MME EUGÈNE BODICHON, 15 JANUARY 1866

For nearly two years Bessie Parkes had been undecided about accepting an offer of marriage. Lord Edward Seymour died in India after being bitten by a bear he was shooting. Philip Hamerton had met GE (though she did not recall it) a dozen years before at 142 Strand. He was one of the writers brought to the Priory by GHL's editorship of the *Fortnightly.* [VIII, 358–60]

21 North Bank | January 15. 1866.

My dear Barbara . . .

I have been delighted to know of Bessie's final decision against the marriage. She seems bright and happy, and courageous in the hope of working with her pen so as to eke out her income.

You remembered the beautiful-eyed, clever, amiable Lord Edward Seymour? Did you see the account of his death—after amputation of a leg, made necessary by a gunshot? I was grieved by his death. He was not one of the ordinary young Liberals, who echo the catchwords of a party. He had genuine opinions, and strove after their precise expression. . . .

Yesterday, Mr. Hamerton, whose books and (bad) pictures you are acquainted with, came to be introduced to me. He is a very unaffected man, but not of transparent porcelain, rather of good honest earthenware. He really writes well, but I have been told by others as well as you that his pictures are a painful *non sequitur* to all his able theorizing. "So vast is art, so narrow human wit." We were much interested by your account of all you gathered about Courbet, and after reading your letter I was less sceptical as to Proudhon's conception of his genius. Apropos of Proudhon, in the Revue Contemporaine, there are four interesting papers by Sainte Beuve, giving a sketch of Proudhon from his correspondence which was unusually copious and representative of the man. If the last 4 Numbers of the Revue Contemporaine come in your way, read them.

Always, dear Barbara

Your faithfully affectionate
Marian.

TO FREDERIC HARRISON, 22 JANUARY 1866

Harrison, a young barrister, was a friend and disciple of Richard Congreve in the Positivist movement. He had lately been writing an article on trade unions for the *Fortnightly.* When he called at the Priory early in January, he offered to advise GE on the legal aspects of the plot of *Felix Holt.* This led to a long correspondence. He came by invitation 18 January and spent two hours reading the earlier chapters of *Felix Holt.* The next day he wrote: "I feel even at this moment as if I had been present and seen some great tragedy . . . the highest art for the first time consciously devoted to the deepest moral problems." Bertie Lewes was going to study with a farmer at Snitterfield. [IV, 221–22]

The Priory, | 21. North Bank, | Regents Park.

January 22. 66.

My dear Mr. Harrison

I had not any opportunity, or not enough presence of mind, to tell you yesterday how much I felt your kindness in writing me that last little note of sympathy. In proportion as compliments (always beside the mark) are discouraging and nauseating, at least to a writer who has any serious aims, genuine words from one capable of understanding one's conceptions are precious and strengthening. Yet I have no confidence that the book will ever be worthily written. And now I have something else to ask. It is, that if anything strikes you as untrue in cases where my drama has a bearing on momentous questions, especially of a public nature, you will do me the great kindness to tell me of your doubts.

On a few moral points, which have been made clear to me by my experience, I feel sufficiently confident—without such confidence I could not write at all. But in every other direction, I am so much in need of fuller instruction as to be constantly under the sense that I am more likely to be wrong than right.

Hitherto I have read my M.S. (I mean of my previous books) to Mr. Lewes, by 40 or 50 pages at a time, and he has told me if he felt an objection to anything. No one else has had any knowledge of my writing before their publication (I except, of course, the publishers). But now that you are good enough to incur the trouble of reading my M.S. I am anxious to get the full benefit of your participation.

Our boy goes into Warwickshire to-morrow morning, and we shall start for Tunbridge Wells at half past eleven.

Always sincerely yours

M. E. Lewes.

TO MRS. CHARLES LEWES, [? MARCH 1866]

Gertrude's first pregnancy was the secret. [IV, 234]

The Priory, | 21. North Bank, | Regents Park.

Monday.

Dearest Gertrude

When Pater was with Grandma the other day she was full of a great, great secret. I hope you have no objection to Mutter's knowing that secret and telling you of her deep desire that it may be the fulfilled beginning of new and very high joys to you and Charlie.

I am a good-for-nothing friend, too weary to be of use to any one else than Pater, and my sympathy is all fruitless. But I cherish for myself the happiness of being

Always your loving

Mutter.

TO MME EUGÈNE BODICHON, 10 APRIL 1866

Felix Holt was about two-thirds finished. [IV, 236–37]

21 North Bank | April 10. 66.

My dear Barbara . . .

We have been going on as usual—both of us better and worse by turns. Yet happier and happier. As soon as we can leave, we shall go away, probably to Germany, for six weeks or so. But that will not be till June. I am finishing a book, which has been growing slowly like a sickly child, because of my own ailments; but now I am in the later acts of it. I can't move till it is done. . . .

Our children at Hampstead are gone for their month's holiday to the Isle of Wight. Dear Gertrude, who shows herself more and more of a treasure, has the joy now of expecting a little one—but not till the autumn. We are getting patriarchal, and think of old age and death as journeys not far off—all knowledge, all thought, all achievement seems more precious and enjoyable to me than it ever was before in life. But as soon as one has found the key of life "it opes the gates of death." Youth has not learned the *art* of living, and we go on bungling till our experience can only serve us for a very brief space. That is the "external order" we must submit to.

I am too busy to write except when I am tired, and don't know very well what I say. So you must not be surprized if I write in a dreamy way. Kind remembrances to all whom you know me to remember, especially to your sister. George sends his love with mine.

Always your affectionate
Marian.

TO FREDERICK LEHMANN, 19 APRIL [1866]

Frederick Lehmann was the husband of Nina Chambers, eldest daughter of Robert Chambers, the Edinburgh publisher and author of *Vestiges of the Natural History of Creation*. Nina remembered GHL, and when she found herself sitting next to him at Covent Garden in 1864, invited the Leweses to dinner the following Sunday. In 1866, when Nina was forced to spend the winter in southern France, Lehmann used to come to the Priory and play duets with GE with only GHL for audience. This letter, now in the British Library, is here published complete for the first time.

The Priory, | 21. North Bank, | Regents Park.
April 19

My dear Mr. Lehmann

Please understand me to be waiting in the hope that you may possibly foresee an evening when nothing more agreeable solicits you than the bringing your violin to us, and that you will let me know of it. But I am reasonable enough to imagine that just now your engagements are too numerous for you to afford us that pleasure.

Visitors and various time-taking nothings have kept me away from the piano, but I shall try to make the keys less strange to my fingers in the faint hope that I may have the indulgence of accompanying you.

I know you write to your dear wife daily. Will you give my love to her and tell her that her letter is much valued, and everything about the 'Tottemses' as well as herself has been read more than once. I should write again but that I am a feeble creature, and can never get into the day half the things I want to do.

Always yours sincerely
M. E. Lewes

F. Lehmann Esq.

TO JOHN BLACKWOOD, 25 APRIL 1866

With the two first volumes completed, GHL wrote to Blackwood, who after sending GE an appreciative letter, offered £5,000 for the five-years' copyright. [IV, 243–44]

The Priory, | 21. North Bank, | Regents Park.
April 25. 66.

My dear Sir

It is a great pleasure to me to be writing to you again, as in the old days. After your kind letters, I am chiefly anxious that the publication of "Felix Holt" may be a satisfaction to you from beginning to end. Mr. Lewes writes about other business matters, so I will only say that I am desirous to have the proofs as soon and as rapidly as will be practicable. They will require correcting with great care, and there are large spaces in the day, when I am unable to write, in which I could be attending to my proofs.

I think I ought to tell you that I have consulted a legal friend about my law, to guard against errors. The friend is a Chancery barrister, who "ought to know." After I had written the first volume, I applied to him, and he has since read through my M.SS.

I remain, my dear Sir,

Yours very truly
M. E. Lewes.

John Blackwood Esq.

TO JOHN BLACKWOOD, 27 APRIL 1866

The slip inserted in *Blackwood's Magazine* and sent to other journals announced *Felix Holt, the Radical* by GE to be published early in June. To his London manager Langford Blackwood wrote: "The book is a perfect marvel. . . . Her politics are excellent and will attract all parties. Her sayings would be invaluable in the present debate." [IV, 247–48]

The Priory, | 21. North Bank, | Regents Park.
April 27. 66.

My dear Sir

The slip, I think, is perfect, and pray tell the provident Mr. Simpson that I admire his choice of colour.

How very good it was of you to write me a letter which is a guarantee to me of the pleasantest kind that I have made myself understood. The tone of the prevalent literature just now is not encouraging to a writer who at least wishes to be serious and sincere, and, owing to my want of health, a great deal of this book has been written under so much depression as to its practical effectiveness, that I have sometimes been ready to give it up.

Your letter has made me feel, more strongly than any other testimony, that it would have been a pity if I had listened to the tempter Despondency.—I took a great deal of pains to get a true idea of the period. My own recollections of it are childish, and of course disjointed, but they help to illuminate my reading. I went through the Times of 1832–33 at the British Museum, to be sure of as many details as I could. It is amazing what strong language was used in those days, especially about the Church. The Times is full of turgid denunciation: "bloated pluralists," "stall-fed dignitaries" etc. are the sort of phrases conspicuous in the leaders. There is one passage of prophecy which I longed to quote, but I thought it wiser to abstain. "Now the beauty of the Reform Bill is, that under its mature operation the people must and will become free agents"—a prophecy which I hope is true, only the maturity of the operation has not arrived yet.

Mr. Lewes is well satisfied with the portion of the 3d volume already written, and as I am better in health just now I hope to go on with spirit, especially with the help of your cordial sympathy. I trust you will see, when it comes, that the 3d volume is the natural issue prepared for by the 1st and 2d.

Mr. Lewes is in a sadly delicate state. There is nothing organically wrong, but he has been continually suffering, as I have, from the malaise of indigestion, and has gone on getting thin. I rely on a holiday for him in June—a holiday of cheerful idleness and chalybeate waters.

Always yours truly
M. E. Lewes.

J. Blackwood Esq.

TO JOHN BLACKWOOD, 30 APRIL 1866

Blackwood consulted not only the aged Sir Archibald Alison, but John Hill Burton, both of whom wrote to GE in Dorking. Harrison too gave his opinion about prisoners of war under Napoleon, as well as transportation. [IV, 251–52]

The Priory, | 21. North Bank, | Regents Park.
April 30. 66.

My dear Sir

Tomorrow we go—Mr. Lewes's bad health driving us—to the Rookery Farm, Westcott, Dorking, Surrey where everything will reach me as quickly as in London.

I am in a horrible fidget about certain points which I want to be sure of in correcting my proofs. They are chiefly two questions which a lawyer and historian like Sir A. Alison would be able to answer at once. There are two reasons why clever people in London can't always answer one's questions: first, they are too busy, and secondly, they don't know. Could you make an appeal to Sir A. Alison, not of course mentioning me? I wish to know

1. Whether in Napoleon's war with England, after the breaking up of the treaty of Amiens, the seizure and imprisonment of civilians was exceptional or whether it was continued throughout the war?

2. Whether in 1833, in the case of transportation to one of the colonies, when the sentence did not involve hard labour, the sentenced person might be at large on his arrival in the colony?

It is possible you may have some one near at hand who will answer these questions without your taking the trouble of writing to Sir A. Alison. I am sure you will help me if you can, and will sympathize in my anxiety not to have even an allusion that involves practical impossibilities. One can never be perfectly accurate, even with one's best effort, but the effort must be made. Always, my dear Sir

> Yours very truly
> M. E. Lewes.

TO FREDERIC HARRISON, [?23 MAY 1866]

In his *Memories and Thoughts* (1906) Harrison says that he wrote the "opinion" of the Attorney-General in Chapter 35 as a guide to the language used in Lincoln's Inn, and GE inserted it bodily in the book. [IV, 259–60]

> **The Priory, | 21. North Bank, | Regents Park**
> [?23 May 1866]

My dear Mr. Harrison

This trial scene has been written under horrible pressure owing to ill health with its hindrances. Will you cast your eyes over it and see if there is anything wrong or absurd? I found, in time to correct some allusions in the previous dialogue, that felons were not allowed to have counsel till 1836.

Will you let me have the M.S. again today? I have not read it all over myself.

> Yours sincerely,
> M. E. Lewes.

10

INCREASING CONSERVATISM
The Spanish Gypsy

After seeing GHL's youngest son Bertie dispatched to join Thornie in Natal, GE again took up *The Spanish Gypsy*, a tragic play in blank verse, laid in 1487. Though she insisted that the plot was entirely her own, it smacks a little of the melodramas that GHL used to write. Fedalma, the heroine, betrothed to Duke Silva, learns that she is really the daughter of Zarca, a captive chief of the Gypsies. Forced to choose between love and duty, she abandons all to escape with her father and work for the Gypsy cause. Published in April 1868, the poem was received with surprising favor.

The stigma of her open breach of the marriage convention gradually yielded to recognition of GE's great genius. With the natural conservatism of her country background she welcomed the talented and famous visitors who crowded her drawing room. Some of her friends, deluded by her union with GHL, sought her support in the campaign for women's rights. But GE made plain her belief that there must always be a difference between the function of male and female in society. At Blackwood's request, after the passage of the Reform Bill of 1867, she wrote "Address to Working Men. By Felix Holt," appealing to them through the mouth of her most conservative "radical" to use their new political power with restraint.

She had long since abandoned the hostility to religion of the translator of Strauss and Feuerbach. Though return to the old faith was impossible, she could look with reverence upon any sincere effort towards a religion combining feeling with intellect, and sympathized even with those seeking comfort in the older forms. The Positivists strove vainly to enlist her in their movement. Her friendship with the wife of Richard Congreve drew her interest in, but not her adhesion to his Religion of Humanity. Frederic Harrison tried repeatedly to persuade her to write prayers or ceremonial liturgy for his branch of Positivism. Though it was not written for him, "O May I Join the Choir Invisible" came as close as she ever got to the idea. She was more receptive to efforts to secure the higher education of women, working actively with Barbara Bodichon and Emily Davies to establish what became Girton College, Cambridge.

TO MRS. CHARLES BRAY, 5 JUNE 1866

Leaving 7 June, the Leweses travelled leisurely through Belgium and Holland, and divided a month between Schwalbach and Schlangenbad. Rufa Hennell Call wrote about the death of her father Dr. Robert Brabant at Bath 13 May. [IV, 267–68]

The Priory, | 21. North Bank, | Regents Park.
June 5. 66.

My dear Cara

We start on Thursday! I finished writing on the last day of May, after days and nights of throbbing and palpitation—chiefly I suppose from a nervous excitement which I was not strong enough to support well. As soon as I had done and read the last page to George, I felt better, and have been a new creature ever since, though a little overdone with visits from friends and attention (miserabile dictu!) to petticoats etc.

Along with your letter the post brought me a very kind one from Rufa, written under the supposition that I must already know of her father's death. It is not wonderful that I was in ignorance, for I have no acquaintances who know anything of our Bath friends.

I can't help being a little vexed that the course of things hinders my having the great delight of seeing you again—during this visit to town. Now that my mind is quite free, I don't know anything I should have chosen sooner than to have a long, long quiet day with you.

Bless you, dear Cara. Believe me always,

Your affectionate
Marian.

TO JOHN BLACKWOOD, 25 JULY 1866

Blackwood wrote that "The chorus of applause upon *Felix* waxes loud and strong. The 'Great British Public' is not yet sufficiently aware of the existence of the book to affect the sale, but the expressions of public and private opinions which are pouring forth will I think get at the monster speedily." On 21 July he reported that about 4,400 had been sold. "Doubtless the War has affected us." The Leweses' holiday practically coincided with the Austro-Prussian War, by which Bismarck excluded Austria from the North German Confederation. Blackwood felt desperately sorry for the Austrians, who had lost 40,000 men in the battle of Königgrätz alone. [IV, 290–92]

Chaudfontaine, near Liège | July 25. 1866.

My dear Sir. . .

We are staying at this pretty quiet place for a couple of days to avoid the King of the Belgians, who is winning the hearts of his subjects by making a "progress" through the chief towns in his busy flourishing little dominions. On Friday we intend to resume *our* progress through Louvain, Ghent, Bruges and Ostend, hoping to be at home again by the 1st of August. If I were wishing entirely for my own sake, and not at all for yours, I should wish that you were still in London, that we might have a long talk about "Felix" and the amusing variety I dare say you have found in the interpretations and preferences of reviewers and drawing-room critics. But I am too magnanimous not to be glad for your sake that you have been enjoying the quiet and freshness of Strathtyrum, which, I imagine, is as delightful as many of the places we have come far to see.

We stayed our fortnight at Schwalbach, going thence to Schlangenbad, and although we had no special alarm about ourselves, it so happened that our departure from both places was so timed as to save us from personal inconvenience. We left Schlangenbad just early enough to be able to go down the Rhine to Bonn by the Dutch Steamer, and soon after we were on board we saw the Prussian troops marching to take Eltville, which we had quitted ten minutes before. One is conscious of making rather an ignoble figure as a pleasure-seeking foreigner in the midst of such events, and nothing but the excuse of having come for the sake of health could make one friendly with oneself under these circumstances.

I share your feeling of pity for the Austrians. My heart goes to the losing side, even when it feels bound to fight with the winners. Amid national calamities, it is the helpless and not the guilty who are the chief sufferers. The care the Prussians are said to have for the wounded Austrians is one of the proofs one likes to register, that we are slowly, slowly, growing out of barbarism. I have been reading Motley's "Rise of the Dutch Republic" since I have been away, and one of the best compensations for dwelling on the barbarities of Spanish and Flemings in the glorious 16th century, is the sense that such horrors are no longer possible in any European nation. . . .

Mr. Lewes, coming to tell me that dinner awaits us, begs me to thank you for your letter and to send his best remembrances.

Always yours truly
M. E. Lewes.

John Blackwood Esq.

TO ANTHONY TROLLOPE, 5 AUGUST 1866

In a highly laudatory letter 3 August Trollope wrote that "the unrivalled success of *Felix Holt* must have touched you. For, as far as I can make an estimate of such things, I think its success is unrivalled." He comments on most of the principal characters, doubting only Esther's delay after she knows that she loves Felix. Trollope adds that he has just got 8,000 cigars from Cuba, which he will share with GHL. [IV, 296]

The Priory, | 21. North Bank, | Regents Park.
August 5. 66.

My dear Mr. Trollope

All goodness in the world bless you! First, for being what you are. Next for the regard I think you bear towards that (to me) best of men, my dear husband. And after those two chief things, for the goodness and sympathy you have long shown both in word and act towards me in particular. That is the answer I at once made inwardly on reading your letter so I write it down without addition.

The Little Man hopes to speak to you on that tender subject, the cigars, on Wednesday, perhaps, at one?

Always yours in affectionate friendship
M. E. Lewes.

TO SARA HENNELL, 10 AUGUST 1866

In his *On Actors and the Art of Acting* (1875, pp. 207–12) GHL describes the performance of the Oberammergau company, consisting of 18 tableau vivants without dialogue. [IV, 296–99]

The Priory, | 21. North Bank, | Regents Park.
August 10. 66.

My dear Sara . . .

Mr. Bray will wonder less that Mr. Lewes could be so long away when he knows that he had arranged the programmes of all the numbers beforehand, save for such circumstantial demands as Mr. Anthony Trollope undertook to meet; and that there is always on the spot a subeditor (Mr. Dennis) who has the unfailing interest of a shareholder in the proprietorship of the Review. Mr. Lewes is much better, and I am quite well—"looking." Grace says, "just like my portrait," from which I conclude that my face has some of that "fleshiness" which Cara found objectionable. . . .

I thought of you—to mention one occasion amongst many—when we had the good fortune at Antwerp to see a placard announcing that the company from the Oberammergau, Bavaria, would represent that Sunday evening the *Lebensgeschichte* of our Saviour Christ at the Théâtre des Variétés. I remembered that you had seen the representation with deep interest, and these actors are doubtless the successors of those you saw. Of course we went to the theatre. And the Christ was, without exaggeration, beautiful. All the rest was inferior and might even have had a painful approach to the ludicrous, but both the person and action of the Jesus were fine enough to overpower all meaner impressions. Mr. Lewes, who, you know, is keenly alive to everything "stagey" in physiognomy and gesture, felt what I am saying quite as much as I did, and was much moved.

I forgot what was your exact route to Cologne, and how far you saw the Belgian towns, besides Antwerp. To me, these towns remain superior in interest to anything in Holland. Rotterdam with the grand approach to it by the broad river, the rich brick of the houses, the canals uniformly planted with trees and crowded with the bright brown masts of the Dutch boats, is far finer than Amsterdam. The colour of Amsterdam is ugly: the houses are of a chocolate colour, almost black (an artificial tinge given to the bricks) and the woodwork on them screams out in ugly patches of cream-colour; the canals have no trees along their sides, and the boats are infrequent. We looked about for the very Portuguese Synagogue where Spinoza was nearly assassinated as he came from worship. But it no longer exists. There are no less than three Portuguese Synagogues now—very large and handsome. And in the evening we went to see the worship there. Not a woman was present, but of devout *men* not a few, curious reversal of what one sees in other temples. The chanting and the swaying about of the bodies—almost a wriggling—are not beautiful to the sense; but I fairly cried at witnessing this faint symbolism of a religion of sublime far-off memories. The skulls of St. Ursula's eleven thousand virgins seem a modern suggestion compared with the Jewish Synagogue. . . .

Our Gertrude expects to have her baby at the end of September and is remarkably well. And we have found no greater domestic calamity on our return, than the distortion of our white blinds and curtains by cleaning, and the extortions of a wicked gardener's bill. I wish Mr. Bray did not hint at vexations of this latter sort for him too. We enter thoroughly into his need for quiet above all things. I fear age is making us too impatient of our fellow-men's society. . . .

Best love to all.

Always your
Pollian.

TO ROBERT EVANS III, 14 AUGUST 1866

The younger generation of the Evans family did not share the animosity towards GE felt by her brother Isaac and her half sister Fanny Houghton. [IV, 299]

The Priory, | 21. North Bank, | Regents Park.
August 14. 66.

My dear Nephew

I was much pleased to receive your kind letter and invitation. It would gratify me to shake your hand and to make the acquaintance of your wife. But we have just returned from a two months' journey on the Continent, and are about to be immediately occupied with the preparation of our youngest son for his departure to Natal, so that we must deny ourselves any further absence from our home at present.

If you have a few minutes to spare, I should be very much obliged to you if you would write me a few lines to tell me where your Mother and your Aunt Houghton are now residing, and whether they are both well. I have mislaid the address your Mother sent me, when she last wrote, and am moreover uncertain whether she may not have changed her residence since then.

I beg you to present my kindest acknowledgments to your wife for her share in your willingness to receive Mr. Lewes and myself. I assure you that we both feel your attention.

Always yours sincerely
M. E. Lewes.

TO FREDERIC HARRISON, 15 AUGUST [1866]

After the warmest praise of *Felix Holt*, Harrison in an earnest ten-page letter urged GE to write a poetic drama in which he believed she should embody the fundamental principles of Positivism. GHL had been an early English disciple of Comte, and GE too agreed with the ethical elements of the cult; but neither of them was willing to accept the religious extension Congreve imposed. In resuming work on *The Spanish Gypsy* GE tried to prevent it from lapsing "anywhere from the picture to the diagram." In her adherence to Positivism, as Congreve admitted after her death, GE "never accepted the details of the system, never went beyond the central idea." [IV, 300–02]

21 North Bank | August 15.

My dear Mr. Harrison

I have read several times your letter of the 19th which I found awaiting me on my return, and I shall read it many times again. Pray do not ever say, or inwardly suspect, that anything you take the trouble to write to me will not be valued. On the contrary, please to imagine as well as you can the experience of a mind morbidly desponding, of a consciousness tending more and more to consist in memories of error and imperfection rather than in a strengthening sense of achievement—and then consider how such a mind must need the support of sympathy and approval from those who are capable of understanding its aims. I assure you your letter is an evidence of a fuller understanding than I have ever had expressed to me before. And if I needed to give emphasis to this simple statement, I should suggest to you all the miseries one's obstinate egoism endures from the fact of being a writer of novels—books which the dullest and silliest reader thinks himself competent to deliver an opinion on. But I despise myself for feeling any annoyance at these trivial things.

That is a tremendously difficult problem which you have laid before me, and I think you see its difficulties, though they can hardly press upon you as they do on me, who have gone through again and again the severe effort of trying to make certain ideas thoroughly incarnate, as if they had revealed themselves to me first in the flesh and not in the spirit. I think aesthetic teaching is the highest of all teaching because it deals with life in its highest complexity. But if it ceases to be purely aesthetic—if it lapses anywhere from the picture to the diagram—it becomes the most offensive of all teaching. Avowed Utopias are not offensive, because they are understood to have a scientific and expository character: they do not pretend to work on the emotions, or couldn't do it if they did pretend. I am sure, from your own statement, that you see this quite clearly. Well, then, consider the sort of agonizing labour to an English-fed imagination to make art a sufficiently real back-ground, for the desired picture, to get breathing, individual forms, and group them in the needful relations, so that the presentation will lay hold on the emotions as human experience—will, as you say, "flash" conviction on the world by means of aroused sympathy.

I took unspeakable pains in preparing to write Romola—neglecting nothing I could find that would help me to what I may call the "Idiom" of Florence, in the largest sense one could stretch the word to. And there I was only trying to give *some* out of the normal relations. I felt that the necessary idealization could only be attained by adopting the clothing of the past. And again, it is my way, (rather too much so perhaps) to urge the human sanctities through tragedy—through pity and terror as well as admiration and delights. I only say all this to show the tenfold arduousness of such a work as the one your problem demands. On the other hand, my whole soul goes with your desire that it should be done, and I shall at least keep the great possibility (or impossibility) perpetually in my mind, as something towards which I must strive, though it may be that I can do so only in a fragmentary way.

At present I am going to take up again a work which I laid down before writing 'Felix.' It is—*but please let this be a secret between ourselves*—an attempt at a drama, which I put aside at Mr. Lewes's request, after writing four acts, precisely because it was in that stage of Creation or "Werden," in which the idea of the characters predominates over the incarnation. Now I read it again, I find it impossible to abandon it: the conceptions move me deeply, and they have never been wrought out before, There is not a thought or symbol that I do not long to use: but the whole requires recasting, and as I never recast anything before, I think of the issue very doubtfully. When one has to work out the dramatic action for one's self under the inspiration of an idea, instead of having a grand myth or an Italian novel ready to one's hand, one feels anything but omnipotent. Not that I should have done any better if I had had the myth or the novel, for I am not a good user of opportunities. I think I have the right locus and historic conditions, but much else is wanting. . . .

We shall be very glad if you can spare us a sight of you before you go away. I have not, of course, said half what I want to say, but I hope opportunities of exchanging thoughts will not be wanting between us.

Always yours sincerely
M. E. Lewes.

TO ROBERT EVANS III, 10 SEPTEMBER 1866

GE's nephew had invited the Leweses to Nottingham for the meetings of the British Association for the Advancement of Science. His son Alfred became a distinguished physician and was knighted in 1926. William Huggins's report was in the *Proceedings of the Royal Society*. [IV, 306]

The Priory, | 21. North Bank, | Regents Park.
September 10. 66.

My dear Nephew

Thank you for your letter filled with details which are very interesting to me. Memory is keen about those old days which were also our young days, and I am glad of any sign that those I used to care about long ago are well and happy now. It is pleasant to me to think of your Aunt Houghton living with your mother and being in the midst of her nearest friends. Your two younger brothers I have no remembrance of, but all the rest are before me as they used to be more than half my life ago—an image strangely different from what exists now.

I don't know which scientific department you are most interested in among the proceedings of theBritish Association. But we were reading last night a report of Mr. Huggins's lecture on the results of the spectrum analysis, which could hardly be exceeded in impressiveness. It is kind of you to wish we had been there. Instead of that, we have been having a farewell month with our son, who is now on board the mail steamer bound for South Africa.

Always sincerely yours
M. E. Lewes.

TO MRS. CHARLES SANDERS PEIRCE, 14 SEPTEMBER 1866

In correspondence with Americans GE was often more open and confiding than in her letters to English ladies. Melusina Fay Peirce, wife of the philosopher Charles Sanders Peirce, the founder of Pragmatism, who married her in 1862 and divorced her in 1884, wrote copiously in the Boston newspapers and the *Atlantic Monthly* in support of various movements for improving the condition of women. Co-operative housing and farming were her chief interests, and she organized the Cambridge Co-operative Housekeeping Association. Her letter has not been found. [VIII, 383–84]

The Priory, | 21. North Bank, | Regents Park.
September 14. 66.

My dear Madam

I do not usually answer letters unless they demand an answer, finding the days too short for much correspondence; but I am so deeply touched by your words of tenderness and by the details you tell me about yourself, that I cannot keep total silence towards you.

My consciousness is not of the triumphant kind your generous joy on my behalf leads you to imagine. Exultation is a dream before achievement, and rarely comes after. What comes after, is rather the sense that the work has been produced within one, like offspring, developing and growing by some force of which one's own life has only served as a vehicle, and that what is left of oneself is only a poor husk. Besides, the vision of something that life might be and that one's own ignorance and incompleteness have hindered it from being, presses more and more as time advances. The only problem for us, the only hope, is to try and unite the utmost activity with the utmost resignation. Does this seem melancholy? I think it is less melancholy than any sort of self-flattery.

I want to tell you not to fancy yourself old because you are thirty, or to regret that you have not yet written anything. It is a misfortune to many that they begin to write when they are young and give out all that is genuine and peculiar in them when it can be no better than trashy, unripe fruit. There is nothing more dreary than the life of a writer who has early exhausted himself. I enter into those young struggles of yours to get knowledge, into the longing you feel to do something more than domestic duties while yet you are held fast by womanly necessities for neatness and household perfection as well as by the lack of bodily strength. Something of all that I have gone through myself. I have never known perfect health, and I have known what it was to have close ties making me feel the wants of others as my own and to have very little money by which these wants could be met. Before that, I was too proud and ambitious to write: I did not believe that I could do anything fine, and I did not choose to do anything of that mediocre sort which I despised when it was done by others. I began, however, by a sort of writing which had no great glory belonging to it, but which I felt certain I could do faithfully and well. This resolve to work at what did not gratify my ambition, and to care only that I worked faithfully, was equivalent to the old phrase—"using the means of grace." Not long after that, I wrote fiction which has been thought a great deal of—but the satisfaction I have got out of it has not been exactly that of ambition. When we are young we say, "I should be proud if I could do that." Having done it, one finds oneself the reverse of proud.

I will say no more about myself except that you must not imagine my position to be at all like Romola's. I have the best of husbands, the most sympathetic of companions; indeed, I have more than my share of love in a world where so many are pining for it. Mr. Lewes, who cares supremely for science, is interested in what you say of your husband's labours; and he is so delighted when anything good or pretty comes to me that I think he is more grateful to you than I am for your generous, affectionate words. Yet I too am not insensible, but shall remain always

Yours in grateful memory
M. E. Lewes.

TO SARA HENNELL, 29 SEPTEMBER 1866

Gertrude Lewes's first child, born 24 September, was strangled in the cord. [IV, 312]

The Priory, | 21. North Bank, | Regents Park.
September 29. 66.

Dear Sara

Your words of kind feeling for us all were very sweet. The trial is all the greater to poor Gertrude because she had looked forward to her maternity with more than the usual share of serious joy, and she was so well and vigorous to the last moment beforehand, that we were all full of hope. The little one was a fine child, too, and died only from an accident during its birth. We reckon it a great alleviation for Gertrude that she never even heard it cry. She is so precious to us that all regret seems merged in relief at the promise of her speedy recovery. Sometimes it requires an effort to feel affectionately towards those who are bound to us by ties of family, but it is as easy to me to love Gertrude as it is to love the clear air. . . .

Best love to Cara—I wish such a true message were of any use to her. You see, I have disobeyed you about writing—obeyed rather my own impulse which is always that of answering whenever I can.

Yours lovingly
Pollian.

TO JOHN BLACKWOOD, 2 NOVEMBER 1866

This is GE's first mention of the Illustrated or Cheap edition of her novels. Smith & Elder chose as their format under the contract a 2/6 edition of *Romola*, which effectively removed it from Blackwood's series. GHL resigned the editorship of the *Fortnightly* after the number for December 1866. [IV, 313–14]

The Priory, | 21. North Bank, | Regents Park.
November 2. 66.

My dear Sir . . .

I think the project of publishing an illustrated edition of the books—which Mr. William tells me you are entertaining—is a wise one, as likely to assist in their circulation. In the abstract I object to illustrated literature, but abstract theories of publishing can no more be carried out than abstract theories of politics. The form in which books shall appear is a question of expediency to be determined chiefly by public taste and convenience, not by private preference. I am not inclined to be sturdy except about the *matter* of my books, and I shall be glad if a satisfactory plan can be matured for an illustrated edition.

It may be an item for consideration that "Romola" will be at my disposal at the end of 3 years from the beginning of last June, Smith and Elder retaining only the right to publish it always in *one* form—so that from the beginning of June, 1869, it can be included in the series of my books. . . .

Mr. Lewes has broken down again sadly, and I am eagerly looking forward to his renunciation of editorship, which I am sure it is not prudent for him to retain. His brain is quite as much occupied as it ought to be, without those endlessly varying solicitations of editorship, which no one knows better than you.

Always yours sincerely
M. E. Lewes.

J. Blackwood Esq.

TO JOHN BLACKWOOD, 14 DECEMBER 1866

The check for £1,666. 13s. 4d. was the first installment for *Felix Holt*. [IV, 319]

The Priory, | 21. North Bank, | Regents Park.
December 14th 1866.

My dear Sir

I received your precious letter with the cheque enclosed in perfect safety this morning, and am very much obliged to you for remembering me so punctually. I can sincerely say that any satisfaction I have had in the publication of Felix Holt has been heightened by your connexion with it. And I hope you share my wish that health of body and mind may serve me so well as to enable us to look back on some fresh bit of work done or soon to be done, this time next year. Some copies of the 12/ edition came to us last night, and I am much pleased with the taste shown in the getting up. It will be very hard if the public is indifferent to so pretty an edition.

I write in haste, that I may at once acknowledge your letter, so I leave all else that I want to say until I hear from you again. Mr. Lewes is in wretched health, and is longing to get away to the south, but we shall not be able to go till far on in January. He unites with me in kind regards to you and Mr. William Blackwood. Always, my dear Sir,

Yours very truly
M. E. Lewes.

J. Blackwood Esq.

TO MRS. ELIZA LYNN LINTON, 15 DECEMBER 1866

GE had known Eliza Lynn since 1850, when John Chapman refused to publish her novel *Realities* because of the objectionable morality of certain passages. In 1858 Eliza married William J. Linton, the engraver, who had two daughters by his first wife and five by his second, her sister. It was then illegal to marry a deceased wife's sister. In 1866 Linton abandoned Eliza and went with several of his children to America, where he set up a printing press in New Haven, Connecticut. This was doubtless one of the "griefs" Eliza wanted to discuss with the Leweses. She was a frequent caller at the Priory. After GE's death, she wrote vicious untruthful attacks on the Leweses' union, plainly prompted by jealousy. [IV, 319–20]

The Priory, North Bank, Regent's Park,
Saturday, 15th December 1866.

My dear Mrs. Linton,

It was very good of you to write to me. We had thought it particularly unfortunate for us that just the Sunday when you were able to come we should have happened, contrary to rule, to be away. But I hope we shall still see you before we take our longer flight, for Mr. Lewes has some work which he cannot bear to leave unfinished, and his wretched health hinders him so much that we are not likely to get away till far on in January. You know how prompt and quick a worker he is when he is well, but he is often compelled to sit still through the whole morning.

I assure you we both feel a strong interest in everything of moment that befalls you, and we hope you will not keep from us either joys or griefs in which you care for sympathy. Pray come to us the first Sunday you can.

Always, dear Mrs. Linton, yours most sincerely,
M. E. Lewes.

TO JOHN BLACKWOOD, 22 DECEMBER 1866

After much discussion Blackwood decided to try issuing the Cheap edition of GE's novels in 30 sixpenny numbers, ultimately to form four volumes selling at 3/6 each. "The Lifted Veil," which he had published in *Maga,* and "Brother Jacob" he returned as unsuitable. [VIII, 392–93]

> **The Priory, | 21. North Bank, | Regents Park.**
> December 22. 1866.

My dear Sir

I was glad to have your letter this morning, for I was thinking of writing to tell you that we had determined on setting out for the South of France next Thursday. Mr. Lewes's increasing debility, causing him more and more frequent interruptions to the possibility of writing, has made me urge him to leave his work unfinished and let it await his return. This, I feel sure is the only wise course. I am much obliged to you for sending me the estimate of expenses as a basis of judgment. I accept your offer of one thousand pounds (£1000) for my interest in Adam Bede, the Mill on the Floss, Felix Holt, Silas Marner, and the Scenes of Clerical Life, during ten years, with a conditional five hundred pounds (£500), over and above the one thousand, at the end of five years, in case of success according to your estimate. I propose that, if convenient to you, the £1000 should be paid in two instalments together with the two remaining instalments of the sum agreed upon for the five years' interest in Felix Holt.

The estimate for Romola, as you observe, will be best made when the time for its publication has arrived. If a change in our relations with America should open any new prospects, I feel confidence that you would take these into consideration on my behalf as well as your own. As to Brother Jacob and the Lifted Veil, I abide by your opinion.

That two shilling series of Chapman and Hall is among those that make me shudder by the vitiating ugliness of the outside. Even if the profit were considerable, I should feel it a purgatory to see my books published in such a form. A bright colour is certainly desirable, and I should be glad if a cover for the sixpenny series could be chosen with as much taste as the cover of the two-volumed Felix.

Macmillan, talking with Mr. Lewes the other day, said, "If I were to see Blackwood, I would advise him to publish each tale of the Scenes of Clerical Life separately as a shilling volume." Apparently he is one of the special admirers of the "Scenes." . . .

> Always yours sincerely
> M. E. Lewes.

John Blackwood Esq.

TO MRS. RICHARD CONGREVE, 16 JANUARY 1867

As Lewes's health grew steadily worse, they resolved to go to southern France for the winter. They set out 26 December, stayed three days in Paris, and then with brief stops went to Biarritz. Here GE revealed her secret desire to go to Barcelona and Granada, and they bought phrase books to learn a little Spanish. They also read Comte's *Système de politique positive*. Lewes had been one of the earliest Englishmen interested in Comte, but his dissent from its "sacerdotal despotism" had for twenty years made all true Positivists regard him as a heretic. GE tried to persuade him to regard it as a utopia, presenting hypotheses rather than doctrines. [IV, 332–34]

[Biarritz]

Snow on the ground here too—more, we are told, than has been seen here for fifteen years before. But it has been obliging enough to fall in the night, and the sky is glorious this morning, as it was yesterday. Sunday was the one exception since the 6th, when we arrived here to a state of weather which has allowed us to be out of doors the greater part of our daylight. We think it curious that among the many persons who have talked to us about Biarritz, the Brownings alone have ever spoken of its natural beauties; yet these are transcendent. We agree that the sea never seemed so magnificent to us before, though we have seen the Atlantic breaking on the rocks at Ilfracombe, and on the great granite walls of the Scilly Isles. In the southern division of the bay we see the sun set over the Pyrenees; and in the northern we have two splendid stretches of sand, one with huge fragments of dark rock scattered about for the waves to leap over, the other an unbroken level, firm to the feet, where the hindmost line of wave sends up its spray on the horizon like a suddenly rising cloud. . . .

The few families and bachelors who are here (chiefly English) scarcely ever come across our path. The days pass so rapidly, we can hardly believe in their number when we come to count them. After breakfast we both read the 'Politique'—George one volume and I another, interrupting each other continually with questions and remarks. That morning study keeps me in a state of enthusiasm through the day—a moral glow, which is a sort of *milieu subjectif* for the sublime sea and sky. Mr Lewes is converted to the warmest admiration of the chapter on language in the third volume, which about three years ago he thought slightly of. I think the first chapter of the fourth volume is among the finest of all, and the most finely written. My gratitude increases continually for the illumination Comte has contributed to my life. But we both of us study with a sense of having still much to learn and to understand. About ten or half-past ten we go out for our morning walk, and then while we plunge about in the sand or march along the cliff, George draws out a book and tries my paces in Spanish, demanding a quick-as-light translation of nouns and phrases. Presently I retort upon him, and prove that it is easier to ask than to answer. We find this system of *vivâ-voce* mutual instruction so successful, that we are disgusted with ourselves for not having used it before through all our many years of companionship; and we are making projects for giving new interest to Regent's Park, by pursuing all sorts of studies in the same way there. We seldom come indoors till one o'clock, and we turn out again at three, often remaining to see the sunset. . . .

We stayed three days in Paris, and passed our time very agreeably. The first day we dined with Madame Mohl, who had kindly invited Professor Scherer and his wife, Jules Simon, Lomenie, Lavergne, "and others," to meet us. That was on the Saturday, and she tempted us to stay the following Monday by saying she would invite Renan to breakfast with us. Renan's appearance is something between the Catholic priest and the dissenting minister. His manners are very amiable, his talk pleasant, but not distinguished. We are entertaining great projects as to our further journeying. It will be best for you to address *Poste Restante*, Barcelona.

TO MRS. FREDERICK LEHMANN, 3 FEBRUARY 1867

From Biarritz, where they spent three cold, stormy weeks, an excursion of three days took the Leweses to Pau, where Mrs. Lehmann, who had been sent there for a bad cough, formed a friendship with GE that was lifelong. After a few days at San Sebastián they took the new railway to Barcelona, with breaks at Saragossa and Lérida. Miss Volckhausen was Nina Lehmann's governess, to whom GE was kind. [IV, 340–42]

Barcelona, | February 3, 1867.

My dear Mrs. Lehmann . . .

We stayed three days at San Sebastian, and were only troubled with two smells out of the registered twenty-five. We walked for hours on the fine sands of the bay, and each evening the sunset was memorable among our sunsets. I hope you saw Passages [Pasajes], and were rowed out there in the sunshine, listening to the soft splash of the oar. From San Sebastian we went to Saragossa, and I think we never enjoyed landscape so much by railway as on this journey: the reason probably is that the rate of swiftness is much lower, and objects remain before the eyes long enough for delight in them. Until we got into Aragon I thought I had never seen so many pretty women or people with such charming manners as in the few days after we left France. But at Saragossa the people are brusque and the beauty had disappeared. Still they were not rude; the Spaniards seem to me to stare less, to be quicker in understanding what foreigners say to them, and to show more good will without servility in their manners than any other nation I have seen anything of. I longed to be able to sketch one or two of the men with their great striped blankets thrown grandly round them, and a kerchief tied about their heads, who make the chorus to everything that goes on in the open air at Saragossa. They and the far-stretching brown plains with brown sheep-folds, brown towns and villages, and far off walls of brown hills, seemed to me more unlike what we think of as European than anything I had seen before. Looking at the brown windowless villages, with a few flocks of sheep scattered far apart on the barren plain, I could have fancied myself in Arabia.

We stayed a night at Lerida, and here we saw a bit of genuine Spanish life, such a scene on the brown slope of the high hill which is surmounted by the fort— groups of women sitting in the afternoon sunshine, at various kinds of small woman's work, men gambling, men in striped blankets looking on, handsome gypsies making jokes probably at our expense, jokes which we had the advantage of not understanding, and which gave us the advantage of seeing their (the gypsies') white teeth. Then the view from the fort was worth a journey to see, no longer a barren plain, but an olive garden; and the next day, in proportion as we got far into Catalonia, the beauty and variety increased. Catalonia deserves to be called a second Provence, or rather, I should say, it is more beautiful than Provence.

Barcelona is of the class of mongrel towns that one can never care for much, except for the sake of climate, and this we are having in perfection. For the rest we are at a good hotel, the cathedral is fine, the people strikingly handsome, and we have popular theatres, a Spanish opera, and an Italian opera, where we can always get good seats. Yesterday we saw a mystery play, 'The Shepherds of Bethlehem,' at a people's theatre in the little Prado. Except that the notion of decorations was modern, the play itself, in its jokes and its seriousness, differed little from what people delighted in five centuries ago. There was a young actor who played one of the shepherds, with a head of ideal beauty. In the evening we heard a charming Spanish opera, the music really inspiriting, and this evening we are going to hear the Faust at the great Opera House, to say nothing of our being now in a hurry to be ready for a popular drama at 3 o'clock. Pray admire our energy. You can imagine that everything of this sort is interesting to us. We watch the audience as well as the actors, and we try to accustom our ears to the Spanish pronunciation. All this morning we have been bathing in the clear soft air, and looking at the placid sea. If it continues placid till Wednesday, think of us as starting for Alicante in the steamboat, ultimately for Malaga and Granada.

But I am scribbling unconscionably without much excuse—my only excuse is that I like to fancy myself talking to you. George sends his best love, and we both should like the children to be reminded of us. Please ask the rosebud Nina to accept a kiss on each cheek, and think one is from Mr. Lewes and the other from Mrs. Lewes. Our joint good wishes and regards to Miss Volckhausen. Get strong, and like to think of us kindly.

Ever yours, most sincerely,
M. E. Lewes.

We have found no hardships hitherto. Even at unsophisticated Lerida, the odours and insects are hybernating.

TO JOHN BLACKWOOD, 21 FEBRUARY 1867

GHL's Journal gives their itinerary: Córdova ("this dead place"), 23–25 February; Seville, 25 February–1 March; Madrid ("after a 28-hour journey"), 3–6 March; and Biarritz again, 7–14 March. [IV, 347–49]

Granada. February 21. 1867.

My dear Sir

Since I have nothing to say that requires an answer, I write to you without compunction, to tell you something about our wandering selves. Are you astonished to see that we are so far off England? We have been yet farther for we came hither from Malaga. . . .

We are both heartily rejoiced that we came to Spain. It was a great longing of mine, for, three years ago, I began to interest myself in Spanish history and literature, and have had a work lying by me partly written, the subject of which is connected with Spain. Whether I shall ever bring it to maturity so as to satisfy myself sufficiently to print it is a question not settled, but it is a work very near my heart.

We have had perfect weather ever since the 27th of January—magnificent skies and a summer sun. . . . The aspect of Granada as we first approached it was a slight disappointment to me; but the beauty of its position can hardly be surpassed. To stand on one of the towers of the Alhambra and see the sun set behind the dark mountains of Loja and send its after-glow on the white summits of the Sierra Nevada while the lovely Vega spreads below ready to yield all things pleasant to the eye and good for food, is worth a very long, long journey.

We shall start tomorrow evening for Cordova—then we shall go to Seville, back to Cordova, and on to Madrid. It is possible that we may not be at home again until the 20th of March, as we are anxious not to get knocked up by a too rapid journey homeward. Since illness makes us good-for-nothing we find an apology for taking great care of ourselves. . . .

We are allowed to visit the Alhambra (the interior) from 10 till 12 and from 2 to 4, and these two last days of our stay we mean to devote ourselves to this chief object among the historic remains, for we have been tempted to spend the greater part of our time hitherto in seeing the country from various points of view. Mr. Lewes comes to summon me now, and tells me to send you his best regards and wind up my letter. I have written in a hurry while he went to get our places for tomorrow's diligence. I hope you and yours have borne the sad severities of winter without injury.

Always yours sincerely
M. E. Lewes.

TO JOHN BLACKWOOD, 18 MARCH 1867

[IV, 349–50]

The Priory, | 21. North Bank, | Regents Park.
March 18. 67.

My dear Sir

We got home on Saturday evening after as fine a passage from Calais to Dover as we ever had even in summer. Your letter was amongst the pleasant things that smiled at me on my return and helped to reconcile me to the rather rude transition from summer to winter which we have made in our journey from Biarritz. This morning it is snowing hard and the wind is roaring—a sufficiently sharp contrast to the hot sun, the dust and the mosquitoes of Seville. I hope Mr. Lewes will not suffer from the change. At present he is better than he has been for several years before, and he was strong enough to escape a cold from the unwarmed picture galleries at Madrid. I did myself less credit there and carried away a cold which laid me up for a week at Biarritz.

We have had a glorious journey. The skies alone, both night and day, were worth travelling all the way to see. After I wrote to you we went to Cordova and Seville, but we feared the cold of the central lands in the north, and resisted the temptation to see Toledo or anything else than the Madrid pictures, which are transcendant.

Among the letters awaiting me was one from an American travelling in Europe, who gives me the history of a copy of Felix Holt, which he says has been read by no end of people, and is now on its way through Ireland, where he "found many friends anxious but unable to get it." It seems people nowadays economise in nothing but books. . . .

Mr. Lewes joins me in kind remembrances, and I am always

Yours truly

M. E. Lewes.

TO MME EUGÈNE BODICHON, 18 MARCH 1867

Mme Bodichon had come down with Algerian fever and at her husband's suggestion had gone to Paris. There she and Bessie Parkes settled in a chalet at La Celle St. Cloud, rented from Mme Belloc and her only son Louis. Bessie fell in love with Louis, and, overcoming the opposition of her family and friends, married him 19 September 1867. [IV, 351–52]

March 18th 1867.

Dearest Barbara

We got home only the day before yesterday (Saturday the 16th) and there I found Bessie's letter enclosing your own few words in pencil written from Marseilles. That was the first news I had had of your illness, and it was a painful shock to me—all the more because the information I got left me still so ignorant as to the nature of your illness and the reasons why you are moving northward into a horrible climate. Pray let me hear somehow what has been the matter with you, and where you are going.

I know you will like to hear that our journey has been a great success in restoring George's health, but I have no heart to write about anything else while I think of you ill in the horrible cold of Paris. We find hard winter here after having hot summer and mosquitoes at Seville. It is snowing this morning and the wind is howling so as to make one pity every mortal who has to cross the Channel. We were as fortunate as possible, for even in summer we never had a finer passage than on Saturday.

We crowned our delights in Spain with the sight of the pictures at Madrid. They and the Cathedral at Seville are enough to justify western civilization, with all its faults, and transcend any amount of diaper patterns even if they were coloured as the Moors coloured. Not that I mean to be irreverent to the Orientals, but I am thankful that Europe has been filled with ideas over and above what they ever possessed.

But never mind what I think about all that—I care now to know about you. Let me know what you can. Love to Bessie and thanks for her note. If you see Madame

Mohl call me to her remembrance, and say that I wrote to her from Biarritz, before we set out for Spain.

> Ever yours lovingly
> M. E. Lewes.

TO JOHN BLACKWOOD, 21 MARCH 1867

Blackwood's payment included the second installment for *Felix Holt* and £1,000 for the ten-years' copyright of the Cheap or Illustrated edition of the novels. [IV, 354–55]

> **The Priory, | 21. North Bank, | Regents Park.**
> March 21. 1867.

My dear Sir

Your letters, with the valuable enclosure of a cheque for £2166. 13. 4, have come to me this morning, and I am much obliged to you for your punctual attention. I long to see a specimen of the cheap edition of the novels. As to the illustrations, I have adjusted my hopes so as to save myself from any great shock. When I remember my own childish happiness in a frightfully illustrated copy of the Vicar of Wakefield, I can believe that illustrations may be a great good relatively, and that my own present liking has no weight in the question.

The placards have arrived, and seem to me wisely adapted to the times. I fancy that the placarding at Railway stations is an effective measure, for Ruskin was never more mistaken than in asserting that people had no spare time to observe anything in such places. I am a very poor reader of advertisements, but even I am forced to get them unpleasantly by heart at the stations. It is rather distressing to me that the 12s/ edition has not done well. . . . I suppose putting it in a yellow cover with figures on it reminding one of the outside of a show, and charging a shilling for it, is what we are expected to do for the good of mankind. Even then, I fear, it would hardly bear the rivalry of "The Pretty Milliner," or of "The Horrible Secret."

The work connected with Spain is not a Romance. It is—prepare your fortitude—it is—a poem. I conceived the plot, and wrote nearly the whole as a drama in 1864. Mr. Lewes advised me to put it by for a time and take it up again, with a view to recasting it. He thinks hopefully of it. I need not tell you that I am *not* hopeful—but I am quite sure the subject is fine. It is not historic, but has merely historic connections. The plot was wrought out entirely as an incorporation of my own ideas. Of course, if it is ever finished to my satisfaction, it is not a work for us to get money by, but Mr. Lewes urges and insists that it shall be done. I have also my private projects about an English novel, but I am afraid of speaking as if I could depend on myself. At present I am rather dizzy, and not settled down to home habits of regular occupation. . . .

> Always yours truly
> M. E. Lewes.

J. Blackwood Esq.

TO SARA HENNELL, 13 MAY [1867]

After Comte's death in 1857 Congreve became the accepted leader of Positivism in England. On Sunday, 5 May 1867 he founded the Positivist Society with an initial lecture attended by an audience of about 75 people, including Lord Houghton, Lord and Lady Amberley, Mrs. Peter Taylor, Harrison, and the Leweses. The following Sunday saw a much reduced audience, and the third lecture, GE notes in her Journal, was "chilling. New faces in great part." [IV, 363–64]

The Priory, | 21. North Bank, | Regents Park.
May 13.

Dear Sara . . .

Yesterday, we went to the second of a course of lectures which Dr. Congreve is delivering on Positivism, in Bouverie Street. At the first lecture, on the 5th there was a considerable audience—about 75, chiefly men—of various ranks, from lords and M.P.'s downwards, or upwards, for what is called social distinction seems to be in a shifting condition just now. Yesterday the wet weather doubtless helped to reduce the audience, still, it was good. Curiosity brings some, interest in the subject others, and the rest go with the wish to express adhesion more or less thorough. It remains to be seen whether Dr. Congreve's mode of lecturing will secure a continous attendance on the part of experimental comers. But he has now a great opportunity. . . .

With best love to all

Ever yours
Pollian.

TO JOHN MORLEY, 14 MAY 1867

When Morley dined at the Priory 11 May, John Stuart Mill's amendment to secure the franchise for women came under discussion. Feminists, then as now, misunderstanding GE's courageous defiance of the marriage law, tried to enlist her as a champion of reforms. Though she sympathized with many of the movements, the peculiarities of her own position prevented her from speaking openly for them. Morley, who had succeeded GHL as editor of the *Fortnightly*, was publishing articles in support; the one in the *Spectator* attributed free will "to the feminine tenderness of God." [VIII, 402–03]

The Priory, | 21. North Bank, | Regents Park.
May 14. 67.

My dear Mr. Morley

Thanks for your kind practical remembrance. Your attitude in relation to Female Enfranchisement seems to be very nearly mine. If I were called on to act in the matter, I would certainly not oppose any plan which held out any reasonable promise of tending to establish as far as possible an equivalence of advantages for the two sexes, as to education and the possibilities of free development. I fear you may have misunderstood something I said the other evening about nature. I never meant to urge the "intention of Nature" argument, which is to me a pitiable fallacy. I mean that as a fact of mere zoological evolution, woman seems to me to have the worse share in existence. But for that very reason I would the more contend that in the moral evolution we have "an art which does mend nature"—an art which "itself is nature." It is the function of love in the largest sense, to mitigate the harshness of all fatalities. And in the thorough recognition of that worse share, I think there is a basis for a sublimer resignation in woman and a more regenerating tenderness in man.

However, I repeat that I do not trust very confidently to my own impressions on this subject. The peculiarities of my own lot may have caused me to have idiosyncrasies rather than an average judgment. The one conviction on the matter which I hold with some tenacity is, that through all transitions the goal towards which we are proceeding is a more clearly discerned distinctness of function (allowing always for exceptional cases of individual organization) with as near an approach to equivalence of good for woman and for man as can be secured by the effort of growing moral force to lighten the pressure of hard non-moral outward conditions. It is rather superfluous, perhaps injudicious, to plunge into such deeps as these in a hasty note, but it is difficult to resist the desire to botch imperfect talk with a little imperfect writing.

The "Spectator" article is a grandiose specimen of what a journalist can do when *not* "stating his thoughts in a manner below his capacity"—for misrepresentation and wriggling. . . .

Always yours sincerely
M. E. Lewes.

TO JOHN BLACKWOOD, 30 MAY 1867

The illustrated edition of *Adam Bede,* issued in sixpenny numbers, was bound in red cloth at 3/6. [IV, 366]

The Priory, | 21. North Bank, | Regents Park.
May 30. 67.

My dear Sir

I have been explaining to myself that you had not given us the pleasure of seeing you yet, by your being called on to perform some sad duties of friendship. But I hope we shall see you soon. Meantime, I must tell you how pleased I was to receive two copies of the really handsome volume containing Adam Bede. The vignette on the title-page is perfect—almost exactly as I saw the Hall Farm eight years ago in my mind's eye.

I intended to write you a longer letter but the whole morning slipped away at my work, and I don't like to let another post go without carrying to you some sign from me. Hastily—

Always yours
M. E. Lewes.

J. Blackwood, Esq.

TO MRS. PETER ALFRED TAYLOR, 30 MAY 1867

Sir John Karslake had opposed Mill's amendment for the franchise. Mrs. Taylor had attended Congreve's opening lectures with more critical opinions than GE, whose interest in Positivism was influenced by her warm friendship with Mrs. Congreve. [IV, 366–67]

[The Priory]

I do sympathise with you most emphatically in the desire to see women socially elevated—educated equally with men, and secured as far as possible along with every other breathing creature from suffering the exercise of any unrighteous power. That is a broader ground of sympathy than agreement as to the amount, and kind, of result that may be hoped for from a particular measure. But on this special point I am far from thinking myself an oracle, and on the whole I am inclined to hope for much good from the serious presentation of women's claims before Parliament. I thought Mill's speech sober and judicious from his point of view—Karslake's an abomination.

Apropos of what you say about Mr Congreve, I think you have mistaken his, or rather Comte's, position. There is no denial of an unknown cause, but only a denial that such a conception is the proper basis of a practical religion. It seems to me pre-eminently desirable that we should learn not to make our personal comfort a standard of truth.

TO OSCAR BROWNING, 23 JUNE 1867

The Leweses went to Eton 20 June to spend the day with Browning, who gave her *Anthologia Graeca. Passages from the Greek Poets*, edited by F. St. John Thackeray, 1867. In a note (pp. 418–19) Thackeray says that Arnold has translated nearly the whole of Idyll 15 of Theocritus in his essay in the *Cornhill* in April 1864. Browning ordered a chair sent to GE like one she admired at Eton. His mother and sisters lived with him. The MS of this letter is here published complete for the first time through the kindness of Dr. Peter N. Heydon. [IV, 368]

The Priory, | 21. North Bank, | Regents Park.
June 23. 1867

My dear Mr. Browning

Your letter was a welcome after-glow of the pleasure we had in our visit to Eton. I am very much obliged to you for sending me the pretty handy volume of Greek poetry. It came late last night, some hours after your letter; but I have had time to glance through it and to see that the selection is one which I shall be glad to have in that compact form, and that the notes will interest me.

Apropos of the passage which poor Mr. Arnold is accused of mistranslating, I have not his article at hand to refer to, but those parenthetic words are really of disputable and disputed meaning in relation to the context. You see I have a fellow-feeling for writers who may be taxed unfairly.

Thanks many for the trouble you have kindly taken in ordering the chair. It may possibly come while we are away, but we have given orders to our servants to take it in. On Wednesday we start for Niton, and shall probably be absent a fortnight. I wish there were a probability of our being cheered by your smile some Sunday after our return.

I feel it a real good to have been near Mrs. Browning and to have had a glimpse of her bright active life. Pray offer both to her and your sisters my kind and grateful remembrances. Mr. Lewes, alas, is suffering from terrible headache, and I abstain from disturbing him. Otherwise, I know I should have a hearty message to send on his behalf. Believe me,

Yours sincerely

M. E. Lewes

TO EMANUEL DEUTSCH, 13 AUGUST 1867

Deutsch had worked at the British Museum since 1856 as a cataloguer and expert on the Near East. He became acquainted with the Leweses in 1866 through the Lehmanns and was a frequent visitor at the Priory. Born in Silesia, son of a rabbi, he had been taught phrases of ancient Hebrew before he spoke German. The "precious packet" sent to GE was a proof of his famous article "The Talmud," published in the *Quarterly Review* for October 1867, which caused six reprintings of the number and made Deutsch famous. Readers were startled by the parallels revealed between Judaism, Christianity, and other religions. The smooth grace of the style makes one wonder whether some editorial suggestions might have been made by GE. The article on Islam in the *Pall Mall Gazette*, 7 August 1867, showed by quotations from the Koran that Fuad Pasha could not have made a remark about the Crucifixion that the Archbishop of York accused him of. [IV, 384–85]

Ilmenau | August 13, 1867.

Dear Mr. Deutsch

Here we are among our beloved pine forests, renewing past joys—and we like this so well that we do not think of journeying onward till the 20th. Probably on the 22d we shall be at Dresden, so will you please address your (promised) precious packet to me at the Poste Restante there? Ilmenau is somewhat changed in the thirteen years since we first saw it, owing principally to the lengthening ducts of the railway, through which the happy-seeming homely Germans have poured abundantly this year. Houses have multiplied and tables are crowded, but the everlasting hills are large enough to keep us aloof in our walks, and we are chiefly companioned by great silence which has fled to the pine woods far out of the reach of "Slap Bang" and lying after-dinner political speeches.

We get our Pall Mall three days old, and read it duly, so that we have been much obliged to you for the article on Fuad Pasha's Confession. Of course no one else than you could write it, and unless, with that treasure of knowledge you carry within you, you do a great deal more of the same sort, you will deserve the anathemas of men to come, who will lack something you might have given them. Especially, pray return often to that note of reproach for unashamed ignorance, and insist that the conscientious effort to *know* is part of religion. See how I take it on me to tell you your duty! But as a German, you are bound to be reverent to rather silly old women and take them for prophetesses. . . .

Send a Blättchen, as well as the packet, to tell us where you are going for rest. I know now exactly how Heligoland lies, and if you go there I shall know your latitude and longitude. May it be long before you go thither in the mysterious boat and make it heavy with the invisible weight of your soul! Also pray send me any word you can about our friend Mrs. F. Lehmann. Mr. Lewes unites in begging you to accept our kind regards, and I am

Always yours truly
M. E. Lewes.

TO SARA HENNELL, [12 OCTOBER 1867]

[IV, 390]

The Priory, | 21. North Bank, | Regents Park.
Saturday.

Dear Sara . . .

Before I got your letter I was about to write to you and direct your attention to an article in the forthcoming (October) number of the Quarterly Review, on the *Talmud.* You really must go out of your way to read it. It is written by one of the greatest Oriental scholars, the man among living men who probably knows the most about the Talmud, and you will appreciate the pregnancy of the article. There are also beautiful soul-cheering things selected for quotation.

This being said, I proceed to scold you a little for undertaking to canvass on the Women's Suffrage question. Why should you burthen yourself in that way, for an extremely doubtful good? I love and honour my friend Mrs. Taylor, but it is impossible that she can judge beforehand of the proportionate toil and interruption such labours cause to women whose habits and duties differ so much from her own. She would have understood the case if you could have briefly explained it. . . .

Best love,

Thine ever
Pollian.

TO JOHN BLACKWOOD, 18 OCTOBER 1867

In her first draft of The Spanish Gypsy (1864) GE spelled the heroine's name Fedalma, and returned to that name in final proof. The promotion of a junior to under-secretaryship in the Post Office over his head precipitated Trollope's resignation after 32 years of service. GHL had gone off with Herbert Spencer, who introduced him to the Cross family at Weybridge. [IV, 391–92]

The Priory, | 21. North Bank, | Regents Park.
October 18. 67.

My dear Sir . . .

I hope you know from Mr. William Blackwood, whose kind letter lay here so long unanswered, of our being urged to another flight. I am right glad to be at home again. Fidalma is among the gypsies now, and I hope you will be, for some pleasant reason or other, obliged to come to London about Christmas, so that you may renew your acquaintance with her. I have dreadful misgivings lest some mistake not to be amended—like that which Prof. Aytoun recognized in "Bothwell"—should reveal itself further on. But Mr. Lewes says he likes what I have done better on hearing it the fifth time.

I suppose you have seen in the papers that our friend Mr. Trollope has resigned his place in the Post Office. I cannot help being rather sorry, though one is in danger of being rash in such judgments. But it seems to me a thing greatly to be dreaded for a man that he should be in any way led to excessive writing.

Mr. Lewes is gone on a three days' walking excursion in Surrey, and I am rejoicing in the sunshine on his behalf. When we first came home the N. East wind and bitter cold laid hold of his throat and chest, but I hope he will overcome that drawback by help of this milder air.

Pray do not think it needful to write until you are quite at leisure to do so. When you are, I shall be very glad to have a word from you. Mr. Lewes enjoys the New Contributor greatly.

Always yours sincerely
M. E. Lewes.

TO FREDERIC HARRISON, 7 NOVEMBER 1867

In "Culture and Its Enemies" Matthew Arnold had written in the *Cornhill* that Harrison "is very hostile to culture," a charge that the latter answered satirically in the *Fortnightly*. [IV, 395–96]

The Priory, | 21. North Bank, | Regents Park.
November 7. 67.

Dear Mr. Harrison

I suppose it is rather superfluous for me as one of the public, to thank you for your article in the Fortnightly. But "le superflu" in the matter of expression is "chose si nécessaire" to us women. It seems to me that you have said the serious things most needful to be said in a good humoured way, easy for everybody to read. I have not been able to find Matthew Arnold's article again, but I remember enough of it to appreciate the force of your criticism. Only in one point I am unable to see as you do. I don't know how far my impressions have been warped by reading German, but I have regarded the word "culture" as a verbal equivalent for the highest mental result of past and present influences. Dictionary meanings are liable rapidly to fall short of usage. But I am not maintaining an opinion—only stating an impression.

My conscience made me a little unhappy after I had been speaking of Browning on Sunday. I ought to have spoken with more of the veneration I feel for him, and to have said that in his best poems—and by these I mean a large number—I do not find him unintelligible, but only peculiar and original. Take no notice of this letter, else I shall feel that I have made an unwarrantable inroad on your time.

Ever yours sincerely
M. E. Lewes

TO JOHN BLACKWOOD, 9 NOVEMBER 1867

Blackwood wrote: "What would you say to trying some of the drama in type to see how it looked?" In the same letter he suggested that she might write for *Maga* an address to the working men on their new responsibilities in the franchise, signing it "Felix Holt." *The Spanish Gypsy* is about 8,000 lines. Browning's *The Ring and the Book* was published in 4 volumes, 1868–69. The Illustrated edition of GE's novels in sixpenny parts had failed, though they continued to sell bound in one volume at 3/6. [IV, 396–97]

The Priory, | 21. North Bank, | Regents Park.
November 9. 67.

My dear Sir

About putting Fidalma in type. There would be advantages, but also disadvantages, and on these latter I wish to consult you. I have more than 3000 lines ready in the order I wish them to stand in, and it would be good for Mr. Lewes to have them before him in print when he sets to work to read them critically. Defects reveal themselves more fully in type, and emendations might be more conveniently made on proofs, since I have given up the idea of copying the M.S. as a whole.

On the other hand, *could the thing be kept private when it had once been in the printing office?* And I particularly wish not to have it set afloat, for various reasons. Among others—I want to keep myself free from all inducements to premature publication; I mean, publication before I have given my work as much revision as I can hope to give it while my mind is still nursing it. Beyond this, delay would be useless. The theory of laying by poems for nine years may be a fine one, but it would not answer for me to apply it. I could no more live through one of my books a second time than I can live through last year again. But I like to keep checks on myself, and not to create external temptations to do what I should think foolish in another. If you thought it possible to secure us against the oozing out of proofs and gossip, the other objections would be less important. One difficulty is, that in my M.S. I have frequently two readings of the same passage, and being uncertain which of them is preferable, I wish them both to stand for future decision. But perhaps this might be managed in proof.

The length of the poem is at present uncertain, but I feel so strongly what Mr. Lewes insists on, namely, the evil of making it too long, that I shall set it before me as a duty not to make it more than 9000 lines, and shall be glad if it turns out a little shorter. (Imagine—Browning has a poem by him which has reached 20,000 lines. Who will read it all in these busy days?) Will you think over the whole question? I am sure your mind will supply any prudential considerations that I may have omitted.

I am vexed by the non-success of the serial. It is not, heaven knows, that I read my own books or am puffed up about them, but I have been of late quite astonished by the strengthening testimonies that have happened to come to me, of people who care about every one of my books and continue to read them—especially young men, who are just the class I care most to influence. But what sort of data can one safely go upon with regard to the success of editions?

Felix Holt is immensely tempted by your suggestion, but George Eliot is severely admonished by his domestic critic not to scatter his energies. Mr. Lewes has been having some country walks lately, which are equivalents for golf, and he is much better for them.

I think I have not had an opportunity yet of telling you that our boys in Natal go on gloriously—have bought a farm and are thoroughly happy in their partnership. You will be a little glad to think that "Cub" is doing well. Mr. Lewes sends his best regards. He is in high spirits about the poem.

Always yours truly
M. E. Lewes.

TO EMILY DAVIES, 16 NOVEMBER 1867

Describing her first conversation with the Leweses in a letter to Mme Bodichon, Miss Davies wrote: "They thought it desirable that a sentence should be inserted in the Programme about prayers, by way of showing that we do not intend to have a Chapel or a Chaplain," and that only women should serve as resident authorities. They disagreed with Mme Bodichon's suggestion that Elizabeth Blackwell, the first woman physician, should be appointed to the professorship of hygiene; GHL believed that hygiene would come under zoology, and GE that it must depend on the formation of habits in the College, not by direct teaching. [IV, 399]

The Priory, | 21. North Bank, | Regents Park.
November 16. 67.

Dear Madam

In a letter which I received yesterday from Mrs. Bodichon, she assures me that you would like to call on me for the sake of some conversation on the desirable project of founding a College for Women.

I shall be very happy to see you on Tuesday at 4 o'clock if that time will be convenient to you.

I remain, dear Madam

Yours sincerely
M. E. Lewes.

TO JOHN BLACKWOOD, 7 DECEMBER 1867

In sending proof of her "Address to Working Men" Blackwood says the charge that the new franchise makes the working man the master was made as a sarcasm in the House. The printed version reads "sarcastically." The article had no introductory note. [IV, 403–04]

The Priory, | 21. North Bank, | Regents Park.
December 7. 67.

My dear Sir

I return proof by this post. I agree with you about the phrase, "masters of the country." I wrote that part twice, and originally I distinctly said that the epithet was false. Afterwards I left that out, preferring to make a stronger *argumentum ad hominem* in case any workman believed himself a future master.

I think it will be better for you to write a preliminary note washing your hands of any over-trenchant statements on the part of the well-meaning Radical. I much prefer that you should do so. Whatever you agree with will have the advantage of not coming from one who can be suspected of being a special pleader.

What you say about Fidalma is very cheering. But I am chiefly anxious about the road still untravelled—the road I have still "zurück zu legen." . . . Mr. Lewes has to request several proofs of Fidalma—to facilitate revision. But I will leave him to say how many. We shall keep them strictly to ourselves, you may be sure, so that 3 or 4 will be enough—one for him, one for me, and one for the resolution of our differences.

Always yours truly
M. E. Lewes.

TO EMANUEL DEUTSCH, 16 DECEMBER 1867

The article on the Talmud was widely attacked, and during his conversation with the Leweses at the Priory 15 December Deutsch admitted his discouragement. The "frightfully uncertain journey" he refused was a proposal that the British Museum send him with the Army on its Abyssinian campaign in hope of finding manuscripts and antiquities. On 3 December he asked to be released from consideration. [IV, 409–10]

The Priory, | 21. North Bank, | Regents Park.
December 16. 67

Dear Mr. Deutsch

We have been thinking of you much since you parted from us yesterday, and have made ourselves all the more indignant at the buzzing and stinging which is tormenting you. I beseech you not to battle with it. Escape from it—mentally, I mean, by working steadily without reference to any temporary chit-chat, whether silly, ignorant or envious. Of course the noise of admiration is always half of it contemptible in its quality, and as besotting as bad wine if a man lets himself take too much of it. And the spite, the head-shaking, the depreciation that come as a consequence, are the muddier reflux of muddy waters. Get rid of it all by a huge effort of will, and don't run the risk of being maddened by insect stings. Let your articles be what they please—are you accountable to the world for the fuss they have made about it? If wiseacres say it has been over-rated—was it by a conspiracy of yours that the Quarterly went into six editions? Let the quarrel fight itself out, but resolve that no editorial or other influence shall drag you into it. Only when a definite accusation is made, meet it by a definite answer. The ill-nature and nonsense you are suffering from can have no permanent influence against you *except* by your allowing it to determine you to write or act with reference to what I may call a coach-journey as compared to your whole career and purpose. If you keep complete possession of yourself and refuse to lend yourself at small interest, you must be ultimately judged by the knowledge, the ideas, the power of any sort that you give positive evidence of.

It has been a painful thought to me that we should have told you we wavered, and almost wished you gone away from this Babel. It was a sort of figure in Mr. Lewes's speech last night—he only meant to impress on you his sense of the need that you should keep yourself in calm air. You do not believe that we can help, beneath all, rejoicing that you are not gone on that frightfully uncertain journey.

Believe too, if it is worth thinking about, that we at least are not weather cocks—I will not say, "at least"—there are many more who delight to trust in and admire you. I am writing almost in the dark—take everything as the hurried outpouring of sincere regard from

Yours faithfully
M. E. Lewes.

TO MRS. RICHARD CONGREVE, 30 DECEMBER 1867

Mrs. Congreve proposed to stop for GE and accompany her to the Positivist service in Chapel Street. [IV, 413]

[The Priory]
It is very good and sweet of you to propose to come round for me on Sunday, and I shall cherish particularly the remembrance of that kindness. But on reading your letter, Mr Lewes objected, on grounds which I think just, to my going to any public manifestation without him, since the reason for his absence could not be divined by outsiders.

I am companioned by dyspepsia, and feel life a struggle under the leaden sky. Mme. Bodichon writes that in Sussex the air is cold and clear, and the woods and lanes dressed in wintry loveliness of fresh grassy patches, mingled with the soft grays and browns of the trees and hedges. Mr Harrison shed the agreeable light of his kind eyes on me yesterday for a brief space; but I hope I was more endurable to my visitors than to myself, else I think they will not come again. I object strongly to myself as a bundle of unpleasant sensations with a palpitating heart and awkward manners. Impossible to imagine the large charity I have for people who detest me. But don't you be one of them.

TO ARTHUR HELPS, 12 JANUARY 1868

Helps, Clerk of the Privy Council, edited Queen Victoria's *Leaves from the Journal of Our Life in the Highlands* (1868). GE's opinion of the Queen had changed radically since March 1848. [IV, 417]

[The Priory]

I am sincerely obliged by the handsome gift you have sent me. I think I have read the Queen's Journal with more sympathy because I am a woman of about the same age, and also have my personal happiness bound up in a dear husband whose loss would render my life simply a series of social duties and private memories. . . . I like that page in which the Queen prays for the very house which has sheltered her happily. On closing the book I felt that I had been following a thoroughly upright affectionate nature, and I thank you for giving me that healthy pleasure.

Mr. Lewes has just come back from a fortnight's trip to Bonn and Heidelberg to see some of the great scientific luminaries of those universities.

TO EMILY DAVIES, 4 MARCH 1868

The gift to what was later Girton College was entered as from "the author of *Romola.*" [VIII, 414]

The Priory, | 21. North Bank, | Regents Park.
March 4. 68.

My dear Miss Davies

Whenever it will not be a bad example to set down subscriptions of £50 for the Ladies' College, Mr. Lewes begs that you will enter that sum on the list as coming from "the author of Adam Bede," or of "Romola"—whichever title you may prefer. We wish to give our adhesion to the good work: but are afraid of promising more money to an object which many rich people are likely to further, lest we should narrow our means of helping in cases known only to ourselves.

Always yours sincerely
M. E. Lewes.

TO WILLIAM BLACKWOOD, 11 MARCH 1868

Even with 28 lines to the page *The Spanish Gypsy* came to 358 pages. Edward Robert Bulwer Lytton, who published under the pseudonym Owen Meredith, had corresponded with the Leweses since 1862. [IV, 421–22]

The Priory, | 21 North Bank, | Regents Park.
March 11. 68.

My dear Sir

The Revise reached me quite safely yesterday. The specimen pages look very handsome, and the length of 28 lines will prevent undue thickness in the volume.

It is necessary to have patience in the printing of a poem, which is properly subjected to a more frequent and fastidious revision than a prose work. I think I am less troublesome than I hear of other authors being with regard to proofs and alterations, and the printing off of these earlier sheets at present is very much to be deprecated. Mr. Lytton had a whole volume of poems in print by him to meta-morphose as he chose, a long while before he published. But I shall certainly not linger unduly, and the sooner I can have the proof of the second batch of M.S. (which Mr. John Blackwood told me he had forwarded to Edinbro') the better will be my advance, for when I see what I have done as a whole, I am helped to conclusive determinations. Now I have no copy (beyond fragments) of the M.S. in your hands. I do not remember having made any serious accusation against the printers: I only laughed at the drollery of some mistakes, such as "doff all your I sir."

We are going to the coast next week to try and get some health for me and some zoologizing for Mr. Lewes, who desires his kind remembrances to be offered to you. His "hunting" begins, you see, when yours ends.

Always sincerely yours
M. E. Lewes.

TO SARA HENNELL, 22 MARCH 1868

GHL's four important articles on Darwin appeared in the *Fortnightly* in April, June, July, and November. GE was reading Lubbock's *Pre-Historic Times* (1865) as well as the *Iliad*. [IV, 423–24]

Carclew | Torquay | S. Devon March 22. 68.

My dear Sara . . .

Mr. Morley asked Mr. Lewes to write on Darwin for the Fortnightly Review, so, having something that he wanted to say on Darwin and Darwinism, he is finishing two long articles on the subject:—the first will appear in the next Fortnightly.

I am reading about savages and semi-savages, and think that our religious oracles would do well to study savage ideas by a method of comparison with their own. Also I am studying that semi-savage poem, the Iliad. How enviable it is to be a classic. When a verse in the Iliad bears six different meanings and nobody knows which is the right, a commentator finds this equivocalness in itself admirable! Farewell. You see, I had nothing to say, but I wished to make a sign that I had received your note.

Ever yours
Pollian.

TO MME EUGÈNE BODICHON, [?28 MARCH 1868]

[IV, 425]

Carclew | Hesketh Road | Torquay.

My dear Barbara . . .

I think Ruskin has not been encouraged about women by his many and persistent efforts to teach them. He seems to have found them wanting in real scientific interest—bent on sentimentalizing in everything.

What I should like to be sure of as a result of higher education for women—a result that will come to pass over my grave—is, their recognition of the great amount of social unproductive labour which needs to be done by women, and which is now either not done at all or done wretchedly. No good can come to women, more than to any class of male mortals, while each aims at doing the highest kind of work, which ought rather to be held in sanctity as what only the few can do well. I believe—and I want it to be well shown—that a more thorough education will tend to do away with the odious vulgarity of our notions about functions and employment, and to propagate the true gospel that the deepest disgrace is to insist on doing work for which we are unfit—to do work of any sort badly. There are many points of this kind that want being urged, but they do not come well from me, and I never like to be quoted in any way on this subject. But I will talk to you some day, and ask you to prevail on Miss Davies to write a little book which is much wanted.

We are uncertain whether we shall stay here more than a week

Ever thine
Marian.

TO JOHN BLACKWOOD, [?4 APRIL 1868]

In GE's Journal 8 October 1864 (and probably in the original draft of the play) the name appears as *Fedalma*. *Fidalma*, however, is found from 1 June 1867 to 22 April 1868, where *Fedalma* reappears. [IV, 428–29]

Carclew | Hesketh Road | Torquay.

My dear Sir

Mr. Lewes quite agrees with you that it is desirable to announce the poem. His suggestion is, that it should be simply announced as "a poem" first, and then a little later as "The Spanish Gypsy," in order to give a new detail for observation in the second announcement. I chose the title "The Spanish Gypsy" a long time ago, because it is a little in the fashion of the elder dramatists with whom I have perhaps more cousinship than with recent poets. Fedalma might be mistaken for an Italian name, which would create a definite expectation of a mistaken kind, and is on other grounds less to my taste than "The Spanish Gypsy." If you have any preference for the plan of advertising the title at once, let that preference decide. . . .

Mr. Lewes sends his kind regards—and pities all of us who are less interested in ganglionic cells. He is in a state of beatitude about the poem.

Always yours truly
M. E. Lewes.

A sudden consciousness makes me ashamed—namely in a moment of stupidity I somewhere in the proof corrected Fedalma into Fidalma which of course is wrong. It was dreamy muddleheadedness of mine.

TO LADY AMBERLEY, 22 APRIL 1868

Linda, Incidents in the Life of a Slave Girl, Written by Herself was edited and published *"for the Author"* (Boston, 1861) by Lydia Maria Child, who probably gave Lady Amberley the book. It was written by Linda Brent Jacobs. This letter, now in the Beinecke Library at Yale University, is published here for the first time.

The Priory, | 21. North Bank, | Regents Park.
April 22. 68

Dear Lady Amberley

I am very glad to be remembered by you and to receive your kind present of "Linda" which I shall certainly read.

But one thing your letter tells me which I am grieved at. I had heard that you were not quite well, but not that you had had an accident in America, which I fear must cause you much pain, as well as deprive you of that activity which I know you make useful to others.

About the Woman's College, in which I am more sympathetically than practically concerned, I hope we should agree that we must not wait to give our help until we get a plan exactly to suit our own views. It is enough that the balance seems to us to be on the side of a much needed benefit.

I should like to *have been* to America, but should not so well like to go there. The impression from seeing a younger society than our own must, I am sure, be deeply effective in minds with any integrity—anxious to find out and acknowledge the good.

I shall hope to hear—perhaps to see?—that you are released from the sofa before long.

Yours sincerely
M. E. Lewes.

TO JOHN BLACKWOOD, 5 MAY 1868

In reply Blackwood explained that the printing for the poem cost about a third more than for *Silas Marner*, the paper and the binding above a third more, and advertising double. The firm's profit on the 2,000 copies would be a little over £100. [IV, 436]

The Priory, | 21. North Bank, | Regents Park.
May 5. 1868.

My dear Sir

As to the matter of pounds and shillings I had not, before I received your letter, formed any definite idea beyond this: that I was to be paid only for the number of copies *sold*. You appear to offer me £300 unconditionally for 2000 copies printed. This I do not wish. If any of the 2000 remain unsold I do not intend to be paid for the copies left on your hands.

Concerning the proportion of interest in each copy sold, which you propose to me, I am of course ill-instructed as to the present conditions that would determine such a proposal, so I must beg you to understand my demurrer as merely interrogative. The only fact I have to guide me is, that for "Silas Marner," a volume of 265 pp. at 12s/ you offered me £200 per 1000 copies *printed*. I should have thought, therefore, that for a volume of the same size at 12s/6, the proportion of 4s/ on each copy *sold* would not, unless there are some altered conditions of which I am ignorant, be larger than reasonable calculations would allow. But if I am under any illusion, you will set me right. . . .

Mr. Lewes will write tomorrow, when the proofs will be ready. I am a good deal knocked up, and look very much like a persecuted witch.

Always yours sincerely
M. E. Lewes.

John Blackwood Esq.

TO MRS. CHARLES BRAY, 7 MAY 1868

For *The Spanish Gypsy* Blackwood paid a royalty of 3/ a copy sold. From Ticknor & Fields GE received £400 for the American copyright. [IV, 438–39; 498]

The Priory, | 21. North Bank, | Regents Park.
May 7. 1868.

My dear Cara . . .

Yes, I am at rest now—only a few pages of revise to look at more. My chief excitement and pleasure in the work are over; for when I have once written anything and it is gone out of my power, I think of it as little as possible. Next to the doing of the thing, of course, Mr. Lewes's delight in it is the cream of all sympathy, though I care enough about the sympathy of others to be very grateful for any they give me.

Don't you imagine how the people who consider writing simply as a money-getting profession will despise me for choosing a work by which I could only get hundreds where for a novel I get thousands? I cannot help asking you to admire what my husband is, compared with many possible husbands—I mean, in urging me to produce a poem rather than anything in a worldly sense more profitable. I expect a good deal of disgust to be felt towards me in many quarters for doing what was not looked for from me and becoming unreadable to many who have hitherto found me readable and debateable. Religion and novels every ignorant person feels competent to give an opinion upon; but en fait de poésie, a large number of them "only read Shakspeare." But enough of that. . . .

Mr. Spencer returned from Italy sooner than he intended, disappointed in the sanitary effects of travelling. The long railway journeys were eminently unpleasant to him. He is better, however, and talks with much spirit about his experiences, of which you will probably hear when you come to town—so I will not anticipate any of his matter. . . .

Best love all round. You will have the volume at the end of May—but don't write, because I shall probably be gone.

Always thine
Marian . . .

TO EMANUEL DEUTSCH, [17 MAY 1868]

Deutsch lectured on the Talmud at the Royal Institution Friday 15 May, ending with a reference to the legendary vision of the abolition of Hell and Death. [IV, 440]

The Priory, | 21. North Bank, | Regents Park.
Sunday Evening.

Dear Mr. Deutsch

Since I have not seen you today, I must send a line to thank you for remembering me and giving me the possibility of going to the Royal Institution on Friday. You had not a more anxious, sympathetic listener than I was. Indeed, I was too anxious to be able to judge of the effect on outsiders who listened with more indifference.

Pray don't forget Wednesday evening—we are going away so very soon. In haste

Yours ever truly
M. E. Lewes.

TO FREDERIC HARRISON, 25 MAY 1868

In sending Harrison The Spanish Gypsy GE makes plain that it is for his help with Felix Holt, not a prospect of future writing. [IV, 447]

The Priory, | 21. North Bank, | Regents Park.
May 25. 68.

Dear Mr. Harrison

Before we set off to Germany, I want to tell you that a copy of "The Spanish Gypsy" will be sent to you. If there had been time before our going away, I should

have written on the fly-leaf that it was offered by the author "in grateful remembrance." For I especially desire that you should understand my reasons for
asking you to accept the book to be retrospective and not prospective.

And I am going out of reach of all letters, so that you are free from any need to
write to me, and may let the book lie till you like to open it.

I give away my books only by exception, and in venturing to make you an
exceptional person in this matter, I am urged by the strong wish to express my
value for the help and sympathy you gave me two years ago. Always.

Yours most sincerely
M. E. Lewes.

TO FREDERIC HARRISON, [25 MAY 1868]

GE's acceptance of Positivism as a subject anything but Utopian had been declining, and
she recognized the impossibility of using her art to promulgate it. [IV, 448–49]

The Priory, | 21. North Bank, | Regents Park.
Monday.

Dear Mr. Harrison

Yes, indeed, I not only remember your letter, but have always kept it at hand,
and have read it many times. Within these latter months, I have seemed to see in
the distance a possible poem shaped on your idea. But it would be better for you to
encourage the growth towards realization in your own mind rather than trust to
transplantation.

My own faint conception is that of a frankly Utopian construction, freeing the
poet from all local embarrassments. Great epics have always been more or less of
this character—only the construction has been of the past, not of the future.
Write to me Poste Restante Baden-Baden, within the next fortnight. My head
will have got clearer then.

Ever yours sincerely
M. E. Lewes. . . .

TO CHARLES AND GERTRUDE LEWES, 27 JUNE 1868

The Leweses travelled leisurely through Liège, Bonn, and Frankfurt to Baden, where they
stayed nine days, then to Petersthal, where they stayed three weeks. The publisher had sent
GE William Morris's poem. [IV, 454–55]

Petersthal June 27. 68.

Dearest Children . . .

I believe Pater has written to Grandmamma a full account of our proceedings,
ever since our settlement in Petersthal. But I can add that after a fortnight's stay,
we love the valley and the mountains better than ever, and daily rejoice that we
have found such a Cur-ort, suiting both mind and body. It would take us many
more weeks to find out all the walks that wind up the little valleys and round
among the firs and white-barked birches towards the summits of the hills.

Through the main valley the lovely river Rench, rushing clear among grey stones, gives us its music perpetually, and wherever we go we hear and see little rills hurrying to join it. Morris's charming poem, "The Earthly Paradise" has been our companion in our shorter morning rambles, which we have been glad to break by frequent halts and readings. In the evening we walk more vigorously, and, as usual, we have the woods and hills all to ourselves, the Kür-gäste almost without exception lingering the live-long day about the precincts of the "Bad." The ladies are in the majority, and find their paradise in round parties enlivened by fan-cywork and what Pater irreverently calls "cackle." We do a great deal of bowing and occasionally a little friendly small talk with our neighbours at the table d'hôte. Otherwise, as you imagine, our days are spent in our favourite dual solitude. We drink the waters diligently, and bathe at due intervals, and we find these Kür-mittel highly agreeable. The water is nectar-pearly with carbonic acid, and rich in iron and palatable salts. We are both wonderfully stronger, but poor little Pater still pays tribute to his enemy King Liver in the form of headaches that linger on to the second day. Still, he looks well, and rejoices in the ease with which he mounts the hills, feeling none of the uncomfortable palpitation which a walk up to the petty Kranz-berg caused him when we were at Bonn. He is gone now to have his bath, so I have taken his place as scribe meanwhile, but he will have something to add about our future movements, and where we shall hope to find a letter giving us good news of you. And, dear Boy, if there are any letters for me written on thin paper or marked "to be forwarded," please enclose them. I hear his unmistakeable step "upon the stairs," so no more, except love to all and each, including Aunt Susanna, from

Your affectionate
Mutter.

TO JOHN BLACKWOOD, 7 JULY 1868

Blackwood wrote that about 1,500 copies of *The Spanish Gypsy* had been sold, and though there was some difference of opinion among the reviewers, "they all seem to be of opinion that something big is born into the world." Daniel Douglas Home was a spiritualist medium whose frauds of levitation etc. were attacked by Browning in "Mr. Sludge, the Medium." St. Märgen is the scene of GE's poem "Agatha." Robert Patterson, editor of the *Globe*, wrote to Blackwood that *The Spanish Gypsy* seemed to him "to dwarf all other poems that ever were written." [IV, 457–58]

St. Märgen | July 7. 1868.
My dear Sir
We got your letter yesterday here among the peaceful mountain tops. After ascending gradually (in a carriage) for nearly four hours, we found ourselves in a region of grass, corn, and pine-woods, so beautifully varied that we seem to be walking in a great park laid out for our special delight. The monks as usual found out the friendly solitude, and this place of St. Märgen was originally nothing but an Augustinian monastery. About three miles off is another place of like origin,

called St. Peter's, formerly a Benedictine monastery, and still used as a place of preparation for the Catholic priesthood. The monks have all vanished, but the people are devout Catholics. At every half mile by the roadside is a carefully kept crucifix, and last night as we were having our supper in the common room of the inn we suddenly heard sounds that seemed to me like those of an accordion. "Is that a zittern?" said Mr. Lewes to the German lady by his side. "No, it is prayer." The servants, by themselves—the host and hostess were in the same room with us—were saying their evening prayers, men's and women's voices blending in unusually correct harmony. The same loud prayer is heard at morning noon and evening from the shepherds and workers in the fields. We suppose that the believers in Mr. Home and in Madame Rachel would pronounce these people "grossly superstitious." The land is cultivated by rich peasant proprietors, and the people here as in Petersthal look healthy and contented. This really adds to one's pleasure in seeing natural beauties. In North Germany, at Ilmenau, we were always pained by meeting peasants who looked underfed and miserable.

Unhappily the weather is too cold and damp, and our accommodations are too scanty under such circumstances, for us to remain here and enjoy the endless walks and the sunsets that would make up for other negatives in fine warm weather. We return to Freiburg tomorrow, and from thence we shall go on by easy stages through Switzerland by Thun and Vevey to Geneva, where I want to see my old friends once more. We shall be so constantly on the move, that it might be a vain trouble on your part to shoot another letter after such flying birds. We shall probably be at home by the end of the month, and will immediately write to let you know of our arrival, when you may be sure we shall be glad to have a letter from you.

As to the poem I should have been dispirited if you had not sent me Mr. Patterson's letter as well as the news of a steady sale. His letter shows that he at least has received the impression of a whole, with parts wrought in subordination to that preconceived whole.

We dine here at the primitive hour of 12 1/2, and the hour is come. Mr. Lewes unites with me in kindest regards and thanks for your letter.

Always yours sincerely
M. E. Lewes.

TO JOHN BLACKWOOD, 30 JULY 1868

William MacIlwaine, Perpetual Curate of St. George's, Belfast, was the friendly correspondent. His corrections were made in the second printing of *The Spanish Gypsy*. Though it was called the "Second Edition," only 250 copies were printed. [IV, 463–64]

The Priory, | 21. North Bank, | Regents Park.
July 30. 68.

My dear Sir
I enclose a list of corrections for the reprint. I am indebted to my friendly correspondent from Belfast for pointing out several oversights which I am

ashamed of, after all the proof-reading. But among the well-established truths of which I never doubt, the fallibility of my own brain stands first.

I suppose Mudie and the other librarians will not part with their copies of the poem quite so soon as they would part with their more abundant copies of a novel. And this supposition, if warranted, would be an encouragement to reprint another moderate edition at the same price. Perhaps before a cheaper edition is prepared I may add to the corrections, but at present my mind resists strongly the effort to go back on its old work.

I think I never mentioned to you that the occasional use of irregular verses, and especially verses of 12 syllables, has been a principle with me, and is found in all the finest writers of blank verse. I mention it now because, as you have a certain "solidarité" with my poetical doings, I would not have your soul vexed by the detective wisdom of critics. Do you happen to remember that saying of Balzac's— "When I want the world to praise my novels, I write a drama: when I want them to praise my drama, I write a novel." On the whole, however, I should think I have more to be grateful for than to grumble at. Mr. Lewes read me out last night some very generous passages from the St. Paul's Magazine.

Always yours sincerely
M. E. Lewes.

John Blackwood Esq.

TO EMILY DAVIES, 8 AUGUST 1868

GHL was at Oxford for the meeting of the British Medical Association, invited by H. W. Acland, Regius Professor of Medicine, who presided. He had pleasant rooms in Magdalen College and among the doctors found warm welcome for his physiological work. GE was never convinced of the need for equality of the sexes, though she insisted on equal education. In a letter to H. R. Tomkinson Miss Davies wrote: "I will try to be respectful to parents, but how is it possible to describe College life without showing how infinitely pleasanter it will be than home?" [IV, 467–68]

[The Priory]
August 8 1868.

You must have numbered me yesterday among the women of the 'glittering eye' and excited demeanour. Not liking that sort of identification I want to tell you that I had all the morning been mentally agitated and in bodily pain, and that I was additionally restless in the prospect of Mr. Lewes' return. The pleasure of a visit from you made me thrust away all that pre-occupation, but I was not very successful, and I fear I talked on serious subjects in a sadly flurried imperfect way, which makes me feel guilty. Ineffectual rash talk is an offence, only not so bad as ineffectual rash writing. Pray consider the pen drawn through all the words and only retain certain points for your deeper consideration, as a background to all you may judge it expedient to say to your special public.

1. The physical and physiological differences between women and men. On the one hand, these may be said to lie on the surface and be palpable to every impartial person with common sense who looks at a large assembly made up of both sexes. But on the other hand the differences are deep roots of psychological development, and their influences can be fully traced by careful well-instructed thought. Apart from the question of sex, and only for the sake of illuminating it, take the mode in which some comparatively external physical characteristics such as quality of skin, or relative muscular power among boys, will enter into the determination of the ultimate nature, the *proportion* of feeling and all mental action, in the given individual. This is the deepest and subtlest sort of education that life gives.

2. The spiritual wealth acquired for mankind by the difference of function founded on the other, primary difference; and the preparation that lies in woman's peculiar constitution for a special moral influence. In the face of all wrongs, mistakes, and failures, history has demonstrated that gain. And there lies just that kernel of truth in the vulgar alarm of men lest women should be 'unsexed.' We can no more afford to part with that exquisite type of gentleness, tenderness, possible maternity suffusing a woman's being with affectionateness, which makes what we mean by the feminine character, than we can afford to part with the human love, the mutual subjection of soul between a man and a woman—which is also a growth and revelation beginning before all history.

The answer to those alarms of men about education is, to admit fully that the mutual delight of the sexes in each other must enter into the perfection of life, but to point out that complete union and sympathy can only come by women having opened to them the same store of acquired truth or beliefs as men have, so that their grounds of judgment may be as far as possible the same. The domestic misery, the evil education of the children that come from the presupposition that women must be kept ignorant and superstitious, are patent enough. But on that matter your know quite as much as I do.

I have it on my conscience that I did not make a little protest against something that fell from you about 'the family' and also about the hurrying industrial view of life that infects us all in these days—but I should never have done, and I am not well. Come again, when you can, if I did not weary you.

TO THOMAS CLIFFORD ALLBUTT, [AUGUST 1868]

Among the new acquaintances GHL made at Oxford was Dr. Allbutt, who had been turned toward medical studies by reading Comte. After studying at St. George's Hospital and taking his medical degree at Cambridge, Allbutt at the age of 28 was appointed physician to the Leeds General Infirmary. The Leweses accepted his invitation and spent 15–17 September with him at Leeds. GE's acquaintance with him persuaded many people that he must be the "original" of Mr. Lydgate in *Middlemarch.* But there is a much closer parallel in GE's brother-in-law Edward Clarke, who was—like Lydgate—"better born than other country surgeons," studied in Paris but at no university, and went bankrupt. Allbutt had a brilliant professional career, which won him a knighthood and appointment as Regius Professor at Cambridge. [IV, 471–73]

My dear Dr. Allbutt

I had conjectured the fact, that some call of duty had summoned you back to Leeds earlier than you had expected. Since you refer to our conversation, I must tell you that I am always a little uneasy about my share in the talk when it has turned on religion. The weaknesses of one's mind are always taken by surprise in hasty discussion, and the chief result left in the consciousness is that of having misrepresented the dearest beliefs. My books are a form of utterance that dissatisfies me less, because they are deliberately, carefully constructed on a basis which even in my doubting mind is never shaken by a doubt, and they are not determined, as conversation inevitably is, by considerations of momentary expediency. The basis I mean is my conviction as to the relative goodness and nobleness of human dispositions and motives. And the inspiring principle which alone gives me courage to write is, that of so presenting our human life as to help my readers in getting a clearer conception and a more active admiration of those vital elements which bind men together and give a higher worthiness to their existence; and also to help them in gradually dissociating these elements from the more transient forms on which an outworn teaching tends to make them dependent.

But, since you have read my books, you must perceive that the bent of my mind is conservative rather than destructive, and that denial has been wrung from me by hard experience—not adopted as a pleasant rebellion. Still, I see clearly that we ought, each of us, not to sit down and wail, but to be heroic and constructive, if possible, like the strong souls who lived before, as in other eras of religious decay.

I dare not enter on these wide, wide subjects in a letter—for to write a letter at all, except about necessary details, is a difficult overcoming of indolence to me; but in relation to your despairing words that we seem to 'be reaching the limits of our scheme,' I wish you could thoroughly consider (if you have not already done so) whether it is probable that in a stage of society in which the ordinary standard of moral possibility, nay, of moral requirements, is still so low as I think you must recognize it to be, the highest possible religion has been evolved and accepted?

If we were talking again, I should like to express what I fear was far from evident the other night—my yearning affection towards the great religions of the world which have reflected the struggles and needs of mankind, with a very different degree of completeness from the shifting compromise called 'philosophical theism.' But I am sure your favourite Marcus Aurelius would not have approved of my eagerness to say everything. I should try to make use of other interviews rather to get instructed by your rich practical experience—experience grievously wanting to me, whose life is passed chiefly in study and always in domestic ease.

The invitation you give us is very tempting and pretty. If there came some beautiful autumnal weather, and other conditions were favourable in the third week of September, we might perhaps indulge ourselves with a journey into

Yorkshire, get some breezes on the moors, and accept for a couple of days the pleasure your goodness offers us of seeing Leeds in your company. It is just the sort of thing I should like to do—to go over the Hospital with you. . . .

Believe me,

Yours always truly,
M. E. Lewes.

TO CHARLES LEWES, [13 OCTOBER 1868]

[IV, 478–79]

The Priory, | 21. North Bank, | Regents Park.
Tuesday.

Dearest Boy

I forgot to ask you last night to do me a kindness, when you have the necessary time—namely to get me some music from your city man. I think it will be good for me hygienically as well as on other grounds, to be roused into practising. I dare say you know of things by Schumann and Schubert, of the genre, for example, of Schumann's Arabesque. Also I should like to have an arrangement of Verdi's best operas for the Piano. Pater likes hearing those things. These are indications which you can perhaps carry out for me better than I could tell you. If I trust to our getting anything ourselves—except books—I usually end by going without it. So you can—or rather I know you will *if* you can—be of delightful use to

Your loving
Mutter.

TO JOHN BLACKWOOD, 21 OCTOBER 1868

It is regrettable that GE's misaccenting of *Zíncalo* as *Zincálo* was not brought to her attention when she was making corrections in preparation for the electrotyping of what was called the "Third Edition." [IV, 480–81]

The Priory, | 21. North Bank, | Regents Park.
October 21. 68.

My dear Sir

I think the specimen page is very pretty—allowing, as you suggest, for a larger margin. I do not possess Aytoun's Lays, but I have used your permission to ask for a copy of Mr. Langford.—At first Mr. Lewes said, he thought it would be well not to make the next edition dearer than Tennyson's 6s volumes. But on taking down the Idylls we saw that the volume was much thinner than mine could be, and was too shabby-looking to be a good precedent, in these early days of my less assured popularity. Therefore I accept your proposal to bring out an edition at 7/6, and to give me a lordship of 1/6 on each copy sold. If you stereotype, I suppose it will be easy to bring out as cheap an edition as we like, by reducing the cost of paper and binding.—I mentioned to Mr. W. Blackwood, that I should like the cover to be a deep red, like Kinglake or Col. Hamley's Operations of War, unless that colour happens to be appreciably dearer.

Ticknor and Fields have sent me a specimen of their edition. It is small, but handsomely got up, for a dollar and a half. They allow me a shilling on each copy, and have already sold more than 5000. I am happy in having fallen into honourable hands across the Atlantic, where dishonourable hands are abundant. With regard to your obliging proposition about payment, the turn of the year will do quite well for me.

I have gone through the Poem twice for the sake of revision, and have a crop of small corrections—only in one case extending to the insertion of a new line. But I wish to see the proof sheets, so that "revised by the author" may be put in the advertisement and on the title-page. I will send the sheets of corrections to Mr. Simpson with the request for the transmission of proofs. . . .

Always yours sincerely
M. E. Lewes.

TO SARA HENNELL, 20 NOVEMBER 1868

The Leweses had been invited to see the River Don Steel Works of Naylor, Vickers by Ernst Leopold Schlesinger Benzon, whose wife Elizabeth was a sister of Frederick Lehmann. Benzon had been agent for Vickers in the United States, where he got 5 percent on all sales, increasing an already enormous fortune during the railway building after the Civil War. The Benzons gave ostentatious parties at their house, 10 Kensington Palace Gardens, to which the Leweses were often invited. There is delightful irony in GE's remark that Spencer's "feelings are never too much for him." [IV, 488–89]

The Priory, | 21. North Bank, | Regents Park.
November 20. 68.

My dear Sara . . .

Since we saw Cara we have been to Sheffield, at the seducing invitation of a friend who showed us the miraculous iron-works there; and afterwards we turned aside to beautiful Matlock, where I found again the spots, the turns of road, the rows of stone cottages, the rushing river Derwent, and the Arkwright Mills, among which I drove with my Father when I was in my teens. We had glorious weather, and I was quite regenerated by the bracing air: all the molecules in my body seem to have amended their behaviour. Mr. Lewes too is a little better, though not equal to much exertion of brain.

Our friend Mr. Spencer is growing younger with the years. He really looks brighter and more enjoying than he ever did before since he was in the really young, happy time of fresh discussion and inquiry. He always asks with sympathetic interest (*proportion gardée,* for you know his feelings are never too much for him) how you are going on. Unhappily I can never tell him much about you. His is a friendship which wears well, because of his truthfulness: that makes amends for many deficits. He is just come to ask George to walk out with him, and

I wind up my hasty letter, that it may be carried to the post. All blessings to you dear Sara!

Your ever loving
Pollian.

TO JOHN BLACKWOOD, 31 DECEMBER 1868

The check was for £333 18s., royalty on 2,226 copies of *The Spanish Gypsy*. The review of *The Ring and the Book* was not by William Hepworth Dixon, who often attacked GE in the *Athenaeum*, but by Robert Buchanan. [IV, 500–02]

The Priory, | 21. North Bank, | Regents Park.
December 31. 1868.

My dear Sir

Many thanks for the cheque, which I received yesterday afternoon. Mr. Lewes is eminently satisfied with the sales, and indeed it does appear, from authoritative testimony, that the number sold is unusually large even for what is called a successful poem.

The cheap edition of the Novels is so exceptionally attractive in print, paper and binding, for 3/6, that I cannot help fretting a little at its not getting a more rapid sale. The fact rather puzzles me too, in presence of the various proofs that the books really are liked. I suppose there is some mystery of reduced prices accounting for the abundant presentation of certain works and series on the bookstalls at the railways, and the absence of others. Else, surely those pretty volumes would have a good chance of being bought by the travellers whose taste shrinks from the diabolical red-and-yellow-pictured series. We often wonder how that very handsome 7/6 edition of Thackeray sells: perhaps better, in his case, than a cheap one would. I am sure you must often be in a state of wonderment as to how the business of the world gets done so as not to ruin two thirds of the people concerned in it, for judging from the silly propositions and requests sometimes made to me by bald-headed experienced men there must be a very thin allowance of wisdom to the majority of their transactions.

I have been reading "The Ring and the Book" aloud to Mr. Lewes. At present it verifies the fear we have always had when we have heard Browning talk of the poem, namely that the subject is too void of fine elements to bear the elaborate treatment he has given to it. It is not really anything more than a criminal trial, and without any of the pathetic or awful psychological interest which is sometimes (though very rarely) to be found in such stories of crime. I deeply regret that he has spent his powers on a subject which seems to me unworthy of them. But I should not choose to say this in ordinary talk: I should choose to be silent on the whole matter. The review in the Athenaeum especially was a laughable mixture of impertinence and attempted compliment. I thought it bore the stamp of the great Dixonian seal. I recognize the often recurring phrases—"breadth of tone," "warmth of colour" and "certainty of outline." . . .

Mr. Lewes joins me in sincere good wishes to Mr. William Blackwood as well as yourself for the coming year—wishes for general happiness. The chief particular wish would be that we should all in common look back next Christmas on something achieved in which we share each other's satisfaction.

Always yours truly
M. E. Lewes.

John Blackwood Esq.

11

GRIEF AND CRITICAL TRIUMPH
Thornie Dies · Middlemarch

GE first mentioned *Middlemarch* in her Journal 1 January 1869, but aside from planning, did not begin writing it until August. She and GHL were distressingly occupied with poor Thornie. A letter had come from him 6 January telling of severe pains in his back, which the doctor in Natal ascribed to kidney stones. GHL at once sent him money and urged him to come home. On 8 May, weeks before it was thought possible, he arrived, piteously ill with spinal tuberculosis; he died 19 October. For the rest of the year GE worked only fitfully on the novel. She wrote a number of poems, however, which were published in 1874 as *The Legend of Jubal and Other Poems*.

On 2 August 1869 GE's Journal notes: "Began *Middlemarch* (the Featherstone and Vincy part)." Her letters give little information about the writing of the book. "My novel, I suppose," she told Blackwood, "will be finished some day; it creeps on." In November 1870 she began a story called "Miss Brooke," a subject recorded among her possible themes ever since she first wrote fiction, and in December decided to combine it with what she had written of *Middlemarch*. During five quiet summer months at Shottermill in 1871 she finished the third of the eight Books. GHL suggested their publication at two-month intervals to allow readers time to digest them; Book I was published 1 December 1871. The summer of 1872, spent at Redhill, saw GE well into Book VIII, and at Homburg in September she wrote the Finale and sent the last proof. Readers' interest was so keen that it was decided to publish the last two Books in November and December. Most modern critics agree with the reviewer in the *Academy*: "To say that *Middlemarch* is George Eliot's greatest work is to say that it has scarcely a superior and very few equals in the whole wide range of English fiction."

JOURNAL, 1 JANUARY 1869

The Burne-Joneses' friendship with the Leweses began at the Priory in February 1868. The poem on Timoleon, the tyrant of Syracuse, was never written. This is the first mention of *Middlemarch*. [V, 3]

A bright frosty morning! And we are both well. The servants are going to have their little treat, and we are going to see Mr. and Mrs. Burne Jones and carry a Book for their little boy. I have set myself many tasks for the year—I wonder how many will be accomplished?—A Novel called Middlemarch, a long poem on Timoleon, and several minor poems.

TO MME EUGÈNE BODICHON, 5 JANUARY 1869

At the Infirmary in Leeds Dr. Allbutt showed GE how he tried to make the rooms more cheerful with pictures, and she promised to send him a chromolithograph, which Barbara chose for her. Reminding Barbara about the shilling was not meanness, but a matter of principle. [V, 3]

> **The Priory, | 21. North Bank, | Regents Park.**
> January 5. 1869.

Dear Barbara

I enclose a cheque for the Chromo: thanks for the trouble you took.

Do you remember borrowing a shilling from Grace, to pay for your cab, when you brought me the hamper of pretty things in the summer? She told me of it the other day and she is so accurate about money matters that I have no doubt she is right. I forget such things myself, and therefore feel sure that you, like me, will be glad to be reminded. Will you, when you come again, just give Amelia the shilling when she opens the door for you, and say what it is for?

> Yours always
> M. E. L.

TO MRS. CHARLES ELIOT NORTON, 22 JANUARY 1869

Charles Eliot Norton, a Boston Brahmin who spent many years in Europe, lived in Queen's Gate Terrace with his wife and children, his mother, and two sisters. GHL met him at Oxford in August 1868. Norton wrote to an American friend: "As soon as we came to London he came to see us, and asked us to come and see his wife, saying that she never made calls herself, but was always at home on Sunday afternoons. She is an object of great interest and great curiosity to society here. She is not received in general society, and the women who visit her are either so émancipée as not to mind what the world says about them, or have no social position to maintain. Lewes dines out a good deal, and some of the men with whom he dines go without their wives to his house on Sundays. No one whom I have heard speak, speaks in other than terms of respect of Mrs. Lewes, but the common feeling is that it will not do for society to condone so flagrant a breach as hers of a convention and a sentiment (to use no stronger terms) on which morality greatly relies for support. I suspect society is right in this." Yet he and Mrs. Norton came to the Priory to lunch 17 January 1869, and Mrs. Norton and her sisters-in-law were frequent callers on Sunday afternoons. The book Mrs. Norton sent GE was J. R. Lowell's *Under the Willows.* Mrs. Mark Pattison called January 25th. [v, 5–6]

The Priory, | 21. North Bank, | Regents Park.
January 22. 1869.

Dear Mrs. Norton

I thank you for sending me Mr. Lowell's poems. They could not have come to me in a way more pleasantly memorable than as a gift from you and Mr. Norton, and I expect to enjoy the reading of them very highly.

I am wondering whether your charitable judgment of our climate will wear through many more weeks of fog. I lose one half of my minutes in dwelling on my miserable sensations and the other half in shame that I have not heroism enough in me to triumph over such ills. Mrs. Pattison did not come on Sunday, after all, so I am glad to think that you got home without too much fatigue—which you might not have done, if you had waited to see her.

With best regards to all those of your family whom I have had the pleasure of seeing, and whom I hope we shall soon see again, I am

Sincerely yours
M. E. Lewes.

TO MRS. HARRIET BEECHER STOWE, 8 MAY 1869

Mrs. Follen read Mrs. Stowe's letter to GE in March 1853 [II, 92]. The new book, *Oldtown Folks,* laid in Natick, Massachusetts after the American Revolution, concerns a group of eccentric characters and two foundling boys, who are discovered to be members of a wealthy English family. GE's religious view is clearly stated in this letter. [v, 29–31]

The Priory, | 21. North Bank, | Regents Park.
May 8th 1869.

My dear Friend. . . .

I value very highly the warrant to call you friend which your letter has given me. It lay awaiting me on our return the other night from a nine weeks' absence in Italy, and it made me almost wish that you could have a momentary vision of the discouragement, nay, paralyzing despondency in which many days of my writing life have been past, in order that you might fully understand the good I find in such sympathy as yours—in such an assurance as you give me that my work has been worth doing. But I will not dwell on any mental sickness of mine. The best joy your words give me is the sense of that sweet, generous feeling in you which dictated them, and I shall always be the richer because you have in this way made me know you better.

I must tell you that my first glimpse of you as a woman came through a letter of yours, and charmed me very much. The letter was addressed to Mrs. Follen, and one morning when I called on her in London (how many years ago!) she was kind enough to read it to me because it contained a little history of your life and a sketch of your domestic circumstances. I remember thinking that it was very kind of you to write that long letter in reply to the inquiries of one who was personally unknown to you; and looking back with my present experience, I think it was still kinder than it then appeared. For at that time you must have been much oppressed with the immediate results of your fame. I remember too that you wrote of your husband as one who was richer in Hebrew and Greek than in pounds and shillings, and as the ardent Scholar has always been a character of peculiar interest to me I have rarely had your image in my mind without the accompanying image (more or less erroneous) of such a scholar by your side. I shall welcome the fruit of his Goethe-studies, whenever it comes. In the meantime let me assure you that whoever else gave you that description of my husband's History of Philosophy, namely, "that it was to solve and settle all things"—he himself never saw it in that light. The work has been greatly altered as well as enlarged in three successive editions, and his mind is so far from being a captive to his own written words, that he is now engaged in physiological and psychological researches which are leading him to issues at variance in some important respects with the views expressed in some of his published works. He is one of the few human beings I have known who will often, in the heat of an argument, see and straightway confess that he is in the wrong, instead of trying to shift his ground or use any other device of vanity.

I have good hope that your fears are groundless as to the obstacles your new book may find here from its thoroughly American character. Most readers who are likely to be really influenced by writing above the common order will find that special aspect an added reason for interest and study, and I dare say you have long seen, as I am beginning to see with new clearness, that if a book which has any sort of exquisiteness happens also to be a popular widely circulated book, its power over the social mind, for any good, is after all due to its reception by a few appreciative natures, and is the slow result of radiation from that narrow circle. I mean, that you can affect a few souls, and that each of these in turn may affect a few more, but that no exquisite book tells properly and directly on a multitude however largely it may be spread by type and paper. Witness the things the multitude will say about it if one is so unhappy as to be obliged to hear their sayings. I do not write this cynically, but in pure sadness and pity. Both travelling abroad and staying at home among our English sights and reports, one must continually feel how slowly the centuries work toward the moral good of men.

And that thought lies very close to what you say as to your wonder or conjecture concerning my religious point of view. I believe that religion too has to be modified—"developed," according to the dominant phrase—and that a religion more perfect than any yet prevalent, must express less care for personal consola-tion, and a more deeply-awing sense of responsibility to man, springing from sympathy with that which of all things is most certainly known to us, the difficulty of the human lot. I do not find my temple in Pantheism, which, whatever might be its value speculatively, could not yield a practical religion, since it is an attempt to look at the universe from the outside of our relations to it (that universe) as human beings. As healthy, sane human beings we must love and hate—love what is good for mankind, hate what is evil for mankind. For years of my youth I dwelt in dreams of a pantheistic sort, falsely supposing that I was enlarging my sympathy. But I have travelled far away from that time.

Letters are necessarily narrow and fragmentary, and when one writes on wide subjects are liable to create more misunderstanding than illumination. But I have little anxiety of that kind in writing to you, dear friend and fellow-labourer—for you have had longer experience than I as a writer, and fuller experience as a woman, since you have borne children and known the mother's history from the beginning. I trust your quick and long-taught mind as an interpreter little liable to mistake me.

When you say "We live in an orange grove and are planting many more," and when I think that you must have abundant family love to cheer you, it seems to me that you must have a paradise about you. But no list of circumstances will make a paradise. Nevertheless, I must believe that the joyous, tender humour of your books clings about your more immediate life and makes some of that sunshine for yourself which you have given to us. I see the advertisement of "Oldtown Folk," and shall eagerly expect it. That and every other new link between us will be reverentially valued. With grateful affection and high regard

Yours always
M. E. Lewes.

Mrs. H. B. Stowe.

TO ROBERT LYTTON, [8 MAY 1869]

For twenty years Lytton had been in various diplomatic posts, including Madrid and Vienna. In August 1868 he wrote to the editor of the *Edinburgh Review* offering to review *The Spanish Gypsy*. He told John Forster that its faults are obvious, but its genius still more so. "I think it a magnificent failure, better than many small successes." If he had sent word to GHL in 1868, the false accent in Zíncalo might have been corrected before the Cheap edition was electrotyped. The corrections were not made until the Cabinet edition in 1880. [v, 32–33, with corrections from the MS owned by Lady Hermione Cobbold]

Dear Mr. Lytton

I am much obliged to you for mentioning, in your letter to Mr. Lewes, two cases of inaccuracy (I fear there may be more) which you remembered in The Spanish Gypsy. How I came to write Zincálo instead of Zíncalo is an instance which may be added to many sadder examples of that mental infirmity which makes our senses of little use to us in the presence of a strong prepossession. As soon as I had conceived my story with its Gypsy element, I tried to learn all I could about the names by which the Gypsies called themselves, feeling that I should occasionally need a musical name, remote from the vulgar English associations which cling to "Gypsy." I rejected Gitana, because I found that the gypsies themselves held the name to be opprobrious; and Zíncalo—which, with a fine capacity for being wrong, I at once got into my head as Zincálo—seemed to be, both in sound and meaning, just what I wanted. Among the books from which I made notes was

Pott, Die Zigeuner, etc.: and in these notes I find that I have copied the sign of the tonic accent in Romanó, while in the very same sentence I have not copied it in Zíncalo, though a renewed reference to Pott shows it in the one word as well as in the other. But "my eyes were held"—by a demon prepossession—"so that I should not see it." Behold the fallibility of the human brain generally, and especially of George Eliot's. Unhappily the cheap edition of the poem is stereotyped, so I must wait until it be published in a new form before I can correct the error.

As to Don Silva, I was aware that Silva is a family name, as in Juan de Silva, Count of Cifuentes; and I was also aware that it is not right to prefix Don to a surname; but I thought it admissible in Spanish, as in English, to use a name which in one case is a family name, as being in another case a Christian name. I intended Silva for the baptismal name of my Duke, and chose it because the easily pronounced Spanish names have been fatiguingly run upon. I have been questioned about my use of Andalus for Andalusia, but I had sufficient authority for that in the Mohammedan Dynasties, translated by Gayangos.

It may interest you, who are familiar with Spanish literature, to know that after the first sketch of my book was written, I read Cervantes's novel La Gitanilla, where the hero turns gypsy for love. The novel promises well in the earlier part, but falls into sad commonplace towards the end. I have written my explanation, partly to show how much I value your kind help towards correcting my errors and partly to prove that I was not careless, but simply stupid. For in authorship I hold carelessness to be a mortal sin.

We are hoping that your transplantation from Madrid to Vienna is a gain in ways that more than counterbalance any loss from the change. Perhaps there can hardly be a change without some loss. Believe me

Most sincerely yours
M. E. Lewes.

TO JOHN BLACKWOOD, 11 MAY 1869

On 8 May, two days after their return from Italy, the Leweses went together to call on Mrs. Willim. On coming home they were astonished to find that Thornie had arrived, six weeks before it was thought possible. His pain was caused by spinal tuberculosis. Unable to sit up, he lay on the floor, writhing in agony. Grace Norton came on Sunday afternoon to introduce the stammering young Henry James, who after a few minutes kneeling beside Thornie, went off in a cab to take a note to Paget. [V, 34–35]

The Priory, | 21. North Bank, | Regents Park.
May 11th 1869.

My dear Sir

I am much obliged by your letter containing the cheque for £50, received this morning, in consideration of little Lisa's story. The letter, which tells us of your family trouble, finds us also in much sadness. On Saturday evening our poor Thornie surprized us by arriving many weeks before the time at which we thought it possible for him to get to us, and at present we are quite absorbed in cares on his account. His suffering turns out to have arisen from an injury of the spine received four years ago, in a fall while wrestling. The injury was strangely quiescent for a whole year, and he imagined that no harm had befallen him. Then began pains, which he at first supposed to be merely rheumatic. These pains have been gradually becoming more intense and more frequent in the recurrence, but he did not begin to lose flesh and strength until about six months ago. In that short time he has lost 4 stone [56 lbs.] of his weight, and from a fine muscular fellow has become piteously wasted. Paget saw him on Sunday, and evidently judges the case to be a very grave one. It is complicated by a hardening of the glands, which seems dependent on some constitutional weakness. Perfect repose, chiefly lying prone on an inclined couch, is the only measure towards cure that can be adopted. When he is not in pain, he is very cheerful, and likes to be amused with talk and music. You see, I can think and write this morning of nothing but what employed my head and limbs all yesterday. By and by we shall get more used to our trouble. . . .

Yours always truly
M. E. Lewes.

TO MME EUGÈNE BODICHON, [12 MAY 1869]

Charles and Gertrude Lewes, abroad on holiday, were not told about Thornie till their return; Charles fainted when he first saw him. They soon took over much of the burden of sitting with him. Friends of GE who came to call would sometimes slip away from the drawing room to amuse him. On 18 May (and perhaps on other days) when GE was out, Agnes Lewes, his real mother, came and sat two and a half hours with him. [V, 35]

Dearest B.

Thornie is come home in a very precarious state, and we are absorbed by cares about him. Come and see him—in the intervals of pain, he likes to be amused. Thanks for the flowers.

Yours ever
Marian

TO MESSRS FIELDS, OSGOOD, & CO., 20 MAY 1869

James T. Fields offered GE a half share on a uniform edition of her works in America. But Harpers, who had paid £300 for The Mill on the Floss, were sure to reprint. Fields, Osgood published a facsimile of this letter following the title page of the novels in their Household edition. Fields also paid £300 to publish "Agatha" in the Atlantic Monthly for August. [V, 38]

To Messrs. Fields Osgood and Co.

Dear Sirs

Your intimation that my friends in America would welcome a new uniform edition of my novels with the latest corrections, is very gratifying to me. Some of the most intelligent and generous sympathy I have received has come to me from your side of the Atlantic, and has given me a belief in my public there which is a precious source of encouragement. I have also good reasons, not probably peculiar to myself among the English authors whose works you have reproduced, for especially wishing my books to appear under the auspices of your firm; and I therefore gladly authorize you to publish the proposed edition, leaving the form and price to your more experienced judgment. I remain, dear Sirs,

Yours faithfully
George Eliot.

London | May 20th, 1869.

TO EMANUEL DEUTSCH, [24 MAY 1869]

Deutsch had been given leave by the British Museum to go to Cyprus and the Holy Land. He left 7 March and returned 10 May. [v, 39–40]

The Priory, | 21. North Bank, | Regents Park.
Monday Morning.

My dear Mr. Deutsch

Thrice welcome! Keep next Sunday for us, if you can, and come to lunch at 1/2 past 1. We shall not be satisfied with a small allowance of talk. Somebody may have told you that we have a house-trouble—a dear lad lying ill. But that makes our evenings all the more open for conversation, and if you can't come next Sunday and *will* come some evening before then, you will find affection and bring gladness.

Always yours faithfully
M. E. Lewes.

TO MME EUGÈNE BODICHON, [14 JUNE 1869]

Mark Pattison was a valued contributor to many periodicals, writing the theological section for the *Westminster Review* and articles for the *Quarterly,* the *National,* and *North British, Fraser's,* the *Saturday,* the *Fortnightly, Macmillan's,* and *The Times.* He wrote biographies of Isaac Casaubon and Milton, besides briefer accounts for the *Encyclopaedia Britannica* of Bentley, Erasmus, Grotius, Sir Thomas More, Lipsius, and Lord Macaulay. [v, 44–45]

The Priory, | 21. North Bank, | Regents Park.
Monday.

My dear Barbara

I am always rather miserable when I have chanced to seem flippant and irreverent to one who deserves respect, and I felt yesterday that in speaking of Mr. Pattison, my joking way of saying that he was a "general writer" might have seemed a sarcasm on him personally, when in fact it was rather a spurt on the condition of the literary world in answer to Mr. Burton's query "what is he?" The Rector seems to me worthy of high esteem so far as I have seen anything of him, and his tête-à-tête talk is really valuable and unusually genuine.

Pardon me for troubling you with an explanation which is necessary rather for my own ease of mind than for any good of yours. Du reste, I have been so poorly for the last three days, that I was imbecile in conversation yesterday.

Yours ever
M. E. L.

TO MME EUGÈNE BODICHON, [17 JUNE 1869]

John Russell Reynolds was Professor of Medicine at University College, London. In 1855 he published *Diagnosis of Diseases of the Brain, Spinal Cord, and Nerves.* [v, 45]

The Priory, | 21. North Bank, | Regents Park.

Dearest Barbara

The fruit came just in the nick of time—when he was wanting a strawberry and the last supply was all gone.

Dr. Reynolds met Paget last evening. The report given to George is that there is slight curvature of the spine, and inability to move the ribs in breathing—these seeming to Paget to be new symptoms. Reynolds thinks there is tuberculosis in some of the glands. But the case seems to be rather obscure. The only advice is— rest, cod-liver oil, if possible, and morphia in case of pain. He has taken morphia 3 times since last night at 12.

Don't tire yourself to come today, because Gertrude has promised to come early, and he will probably be asleep, from the morphia. I fear you are not at all well. . . .

Thine ever
Marian

TO MRS. MARK PATTISON, 10 AUGUST 1869

Mrs. Pattison was only one of many younger persons for whom GE felt this filial sympathy. She would draw them out in conversation and letters, helping them and at the same time deepening her own knowledge of human nature. [v, 52]

The Priory, | 21. North Bank, | Regents Park.
August 10. 69.

My dear Mrs. Pattison

It has done me good to have a word with you this morning and to know that you are on the eve of a pleasant journey. I am in danger of forgetting that there is enjoyment, as well as suffering, in the world. Our trouble has deepened suddenly. Our poor boy, since Sunday, has shown the most alarming symptoms of paraplegia and the lower part of the body is at present quite helpless. I have had an especial dread of this, not because of the external difficulties, but because of its effect on the poor boy's own spirit. But I will say no more of our affliction. There is this alleviation—that it does not extend beyond our own little group.

I feared after you had left us that I had allowed myself an effusiveness (of that dumb sort which is the more apt to come when one has not full opportunity of speech) beyond what was warranted by the short time we had known each other. But in proportion as I profoundly rejoice that I never brought a child into the world, I am conscious of having an unused stock of motherly tenderness, which sometimes overflows, but not without discrimination. In any case, whatever there may have been of too much or too little, excuse, and believe me always

Your sincerely affectionate
M. E. Lewes.

TO SARA HENNELL, 21 SEPTEMBER 1869

Sara's religious monomania made her writing more and more obscure. Though she lived until 1899, it grew increasingly difficult to communicate with her. The Byron scandal sprang from Mrs. Stowe's article in the September *Atlantic Monthly* and in *Macmillan's* declaring that Lady Byron had confided to her in 1856 that her husband had confessed his incest with his half sister Augusta Leigh. George Browne Macdonald had six daughters: Alice married J. L. Kipling, father of Rudyard; Georgiana m. Edward Burne-Jones; Agnes m. Edward John Poynter; Louisa m. Alfred Baldwin, father of Stanley Baldwin; Caroline died young; and Edith never married. John Sibree was a private schoolmaster at Stroud. [v, 56–57]

The Priory, | 21. North Bank, | Regents Park.
September 21. 69.

Dear Sara

I am so glad you were inspired to write to me and let me have the pleasure of thinking of you under new, health-giving conditions. Do bring yourself to consider these pauses from writing as an absolute duty, and spend all your spare money on them. I have such a horror of a mental break-down, like old Mrs. Trollope's, for example. Her body was strong as iron; but, for years before she died, she had totally lost her memory.

As to the Byron subject, nothing can outweigh to my mind the heavy social injury of familiarizing young minds with the desecration of family ties. The discussion of the subject in newspapers, periodicals and pamphlets, is simply odious to me, and I think it a pestilence likely to leave very ugly marks. One trembles to think how easily that moral wealth may be lost which it has been the work of ages to produce, in the refinement and differencing of the affectionate relations. As to the high-flown stuff which is being reproduced about Byron and his poetry, I am utterly out of sympathy with it. He seems to me the most *vulgar-minded* genius that ever produced a great effect in literature.

The neighborhood of Stroud has acquired an additional interest for me, as the place or district which another friend of mine, Mrs. Burne Jones, the wife of a wonderfully fine painter, has been in the habit of visiting, to see her parents. Her father, who lately died, was a Methodist minister! Another of her sisters married Poynter, also a remarkable painter. But I forget her father's name.

Our poor boy Thornie is still our heavy anxiety. He is recovered from the chief symptoms of paralysis but is unable to walk or even stand long together.

Ever yours lovingly
Pollian. . . .

TO MRS. NASSAU JOHN SENIOR, 4 OCTOBER 1869

Mrs. Senior was the first woman to be appointed Inspector of Workhouses and Pauper Schools. She came often to sit with Thornie and sing to him. Mrs. James Manning was the first Mistress of Girton College, which opened at Hitchin in October 1869. [v, 57–58]

The Priory, | 21. North Bank, | Regents Park.
October 4. 69.

My dear Friend

I am wondering whether you are come home. If you are (and the chance of it makes me fear to address a letter to your Worthing house) your kind heart will make you glad to have this note with its bit of good news about our poor Thornie. He is going on well, we think, in his slow way: passing his days and nights with little suffering, and enjoying his food without frequent symptoms of indigestion. His face has more than ever of the wizened look that has come instead of its old beauty, and that pains me to see; I cannot shake off the impression it creates in me of slow withering. But this is a mere weakness of mine, and I recognize the probability of what Mr. Lewes insists on—that the emaciated look may disappear in a week when once a more rapid assimilation has set in. . . .

I have no personal knowledge of Mrs. Manning and no practical connexion with the proposed college, beyond subscribing to it, and occasionally answering questions which Miss Davies has put to me about the curriculum which would be desirable. I feel too deeply the difficult complications that beset every measure likely to affect the position of women and also I feel too imperfect a sympathy with many women who have put themselves forward in connexion with such measures, to give any practical adhesion to them. There is no subject on which I am more inclined to hold my peace and learn, than on the "Women Question." It seems to me to overhang abysses, of which even prostitution is not the worst. Conclusions seem easy so long as we keep large blinkers on and look in the direction of our own private path.

But on one point I have a strong conviction, and I feel bound to act on it, so far as my retired way of life allows of public action. And that is, that women ought to have the same fund of truth placed within their reach as men have; that their lives (i.e., the lives of men and women) ought to be passed together under the hallowing influence of a common faith as to their duty and its basis. And this unity in their faith can only be produced by their having each the same store of fundamental knowledge. It is not likely that any perfect plan for educating women can soon be found, for we are very far from having found a perfect plan for educating men. But it will not do to wait for perfection.

I write these hasty words to show you that I valued what you said to me. But do not let any one else see this note. I have been made rather miserable lately by revelations about women, and have resolved to remain silent in my sense of helplessness. I know very little about what is specially good for women—only a few things that I feel sure are good for human nature generally, and about such as these last alone, can I ever hope to write or say anything worth saying.

Ever yours affectionately
M. E. Lewes.

JOURNAL, 19 OCTOBER 1869

[v, 60]

October 19. 1869. This evening at half past six our dear Thornie died. He went quite peacefully. For three days he was not more than fitfully and imperfectly conscious of the things around him.

He went to Natal on the 17th of October, 1863, and came back to us ill on the 8th of May, 1869. Through the six months of his illness, his frank impulsive mind disclosed no trace of evil feeling. He was a sweet-natured boy—still a boy though he had lived for 25 years and a half. On the 9th of August he had an attack of paraplegia, and although he partially recovered from it, it made a marked change in him. After that he lost a great deal of his vivacity. But he suffered less pain. This death seems to me the beginning of our own.

TO MME EUGÈNE BODICHON, 22 OCTOBER 1869

The Leweses went to stay at Park Farm in Limpsfield, which Gertrude's mother Mrs. Hill had told them about. The quiet life there for three weeks with the Steer family rested and calmed them after the long ordeal of Thornie's illness. "But I have a deep sense of change within," GE wrote to Barbara, "and of a permanently closer companionship with death." [v, 60–61]

21 North Bank, | October 22. 69.

Dearest Barbara

Thanks for your tender words. It has cut deeper than I expected—that he is gone and I can never make him feel my love any more. Just now all else seems trivial compared with the powers of delighting and soothing a heart that is in need.

We go tomorrow morning to Limpsfield, in Surrey, to nice people in an old-fashioned farm house, that we knew of beforehand. It is an unspeakable comfort to have an immediate retreat. Later on, we shall perhaps go to the Isle of Wight, but, just now we are unequal to journeying and arrangements with new people.

Ever yours affectionately
M. E. Lewes.

TO MRS. HARRIET BEECHER STOWE, 10 DECEMBER 1869

The "Byron question" had filled the papers and magazines, most of them "vindicating" Lady Byron. [v, 71–72]

The Priory | 21 North Bank | December 10. 69.

My dear Friend

The months which have passed since I received your last kind letter, with the signs of remembrance, have been filled for us with deep and often painful experience. Our dear son, of whose illness I wrote to you, died on the 19th of October.

. . . Death had never come near to me through the twenty years since I lost my Father, and this parting has entered very deeply into me. I never before felt so keenly the wealth one possesses in every being to whose mind and body it is possible to minister comfort through love and care. But your experience of this kind has been much greater than mine. I am recovering now from a very shattered state of health, and I cannot feel at ease without writing you a brief letter, first to tell you how my silence has been occupied—I have said enough to give you a conception of that—and next to thank you for all the helpful words that you sent me.

In the midst of our trouble I was often thinking of you, for I feared that you were undergoing considerable trial from harsh and unfair judgments, partly the fruit of hostility glad to find an opportunity of venting itself, and partly of that unthinking cruelty which belongs to hasty anonymous journalism. For my own part I should have preferred that the "Byron question" should not have been brought before the public, because I think the discussion of such subjects is injurious socially. But with regard to yourself, dear friend, I have felt sure that in acting on a different basis of impressions, you were impelled by pure, generous feeling. Do not think that I would have written to you on this point to express a judgment; I am anxious only to convey to you a sense of my sympathy and confidence, such as a kiss and a pressure of the hand would give, if I were near you. . . .

Mr. Lewes unites with me in high regards to your husband and yourself, but in addition to that I have the sister woman's privilege of saying that I am always

Your affectionate friend
M. E. Lewes.

TO EMANUEL DEUTSCH, 18 DECEMBER [1869]

Deutsch published his long article "Islam" in the *Quarterly Review* in October, but his learning was never appreciated properly by the British Museum. In October 1869 the Trustees refused him six weeks leave to accept the invitation of the Viceroy of Egypt to attend the opening of the Suez Canal. His depression, which began at this time, was caused partly by the onset of cancer, from which he died in 1873. The Leweses had him often to dinner and held long conversations about his scholarly work. [v, 73]

December 18th.

My dear Mr. Deutsch

Mr. Lewes rejoices in my having such a privilege as that you offer me. If you can really spare me some time every week, we think the plan that will impose the least gêne on you will be, that you should choose each week the evening which suits you best. When you can come to dine with us, send me a note the evening before, so that I may have enough dinner for three: when you can only come in the evening, there is no need to send word, because I never go out—the other evening being an exception such as occurs perhaps once a year.

If you are thinking of a change of abode, why not take into consideration the advantages of this N. W. region? It is very healthy, there is wider sky, and there are stations of the Underground Railway at short distances from each other. In a word, it is detestable; but less detestable than most parts of London and its suburbs.

Ever yours sincerely
M. E. Lewes.

Many thanks for "The Talmud" in its German clothes.

TO MME EUGÈNE BODICHON, 21 DECEMBER [1869]

The Leweses walked to Rosslyn Unitarian Chapel on Christmas morning and went with Charles to Thornie's grave in Highgate Cemetery. [V, 74]

December 21.

Dearest B.

O what a lovely basket! It is a little oasis in the dreariness of this morning's fog. Bless you for it—and come up to town looking and feeling as well as you deserve—or better if possible.

We are going to dine with our children on Christmas day, and to visit the grave at Highgate in the morning if the weather will let us.

I hope your Christmas will be very happy among the dear kith and kin. I cling strongly to kith and kin, even though they reject *me*.

Ever yours lovingly
Marian.

TO GEORGE FREDERIC WATTS, 11 JANUARY 1870

When they came to lunch, Burne-Jones and Rossetti brought GE a copy sent by Watts of his bust of *Clytie*. For an account of it see "George Eliot and Watts's *Clytie*," *Yale University Library Gazette* 56 (April 1982): 65–69, where this letter was first published.

21 North Bank | Jan. 11. 1870

My dear Mr. Watts

You have sent me the finest present I ever had in all my life, and I wish you knew better than I can tell you how much good it has done me. But Mr. Rossetti was telling me on Sunday that you have long been and still are continually suffering from bad health, and *that* experience is almost sure to include some sadness and discouragement. Therefore, when I tell you that such conditions have made a large part of my history, you will understand how keenly I feel the help brought me by some proof that anything I have done has made a place for me in minds which the world has good reason to value. And this strong proof from you happens to come at a time when I especially needed such cheering.

The Bust looks grander and grander in my eyes now that I can turn to it from time to time. Mr. Burne Jones, who had a generous delight in carrying it, brought me also the message, that we should not be unwelcome if on some fine day we presented ourselves in your studio. Both Mr. Lewes and I desire to have that pleasure, and we shall not forget the permission.

Long ago as one of the public, but now on private grounds also, I can truly call myself

Yours most gratefully
M. E. Lewes

TO FREDERIC HARRISON, 15 JANUARY 1870

In his article in the *Fortnightly* (November 1869) Harrison discussed his differences with Congreve and others who "definitely accept Positivism as a religion, and regard themselves as a community, of whom it should be said the present writer is not one." [v, 75–76]

21 North Bank | January 15. 1870.

My dear Mr. Harrison

I am moved to write to you rather by the inclination to remind you of me, than by the sense of having anything to say. On reading "The Positivist Problem" a second time, I gained a stronger impression of its general value, and I also felt less jarred by the more personal part at the close. Mr. Lewes would tell you that I have an unreasonable aversion to personal statements, and when I come to like them it is usually by a hard process of *conversion*. But—to tell you all just for the sake of telling, and not because the matter can have any weight—my second reading gave me a new and very strong sense that the last two or three pages have the air of an appendix added at some distance of time from the original writing of the article. Some more thoroughly explanatory account of your non-adhesion seems requisite as a nexus—since the statement of your non-adhesion had to be mentioned after an argument for the system against the outer Gentile world. However, it is more important for me to say that I felt the thorough justice of your words, when in conversation with me, you said, "I don't see why there should be any mystification: having come to a resolution after much inward debate, it is better to state the resolution." Something like that you said and I give a hearty "Amen," praying that I may not be too apt myself to prefer the haze to the clearness. But the fact is, I shrink from decided "deliverances" on momentous subjects, from the dread of coming to swear by my own "deliverances" and sinking into an insistent echo of myself. That is a horrible destiny—and one cannot help seeing that many of the most powerful men fall into it. . . .

Always yours most sincerely
M. E. Lewes.

TO DANTE GABRIEL ROSSETTI, [FEBRUARY 1870]

Rossetti wrote to GE 18 February, sending her two sonnets, "Mary Magdalene" and "Pandora," with photographs of his drawings of them and of the "Rosa Triplex" and "Hamlet." [v, 78–79]

[Dear Mr. Rossetti]

I have had time now to dwell on the photographs. I am especially grateful to you for giving me the head marked June 1861: it is exquisite. But I am glad to possess every one of them. The subject of the Magdalene rises in interest for me, the more I look at it. I hope you will keep in the picture an equally passionate type for her. Perhaps you will indulge me with a little talk about the modifications you intend to introduce.

The 'Hamlet' seems to me perfectly intelligible, and altogether admirable in conception, except in the type of the man's head. I feel sure that 'Hamlet' had a square anterior lobe. Mr. Lewes says, this conception of yours makes him long to be an actor who has 'Hamlet' for one of his parts, that he might carry out this scene according to your idea.

One is always liable to mistake prejudices for sufficient inductions, about types of head and face, as well as about all other things. I have some impressions— perhaps only prejudices dependent on the narrowness of my experience—about forms of eyebrow and their relation to passionate expression. It is possible that such a supposed relation has a real anatomical basis. But in many particulars facial expression is like the expression of hand-writing: the relations are too subtle and intricate to be detected, and only shallowness is confident. . . .

[M. E. Lewes]

TO JOHN BLACKWOOD, 7 MARCH 1870

The check was £92 18s. 6d. for 1,259 copies of The Spanish Gypsy. For her poem "The Legend of Jubal," Macmillan's paid £200 and the Atlantic Monthly £50; they published it simultaneously in May. [v, 81–82]

21 North Bank | March 7. 70.

My dear Sir

Many thanks for the cheque announced by your letter which Mr. Lewes has just brought up to me. We were afraid that you might write, or come up to town during our absence, and did not therefore like the thought of going away without sending you word of our movements. You are one of the voices of my conscience asking me, "What have you been doing?" I am obliged to tell my conscience that I have been suffering, in order to apologize for the small doing. But I am now in decidedly better health, and hope to have a tolerably long release from tooth-torments.

My novel, I suppose, will be finished some day: it creeps on. A rather long poem which I finished about Christmas I have been induced to accept an offer for from Mr. Macmillan, who has behaved very handsomely to me. I did not mention it (the poem) to you because I know that you do not care to have exceptional contributions to Maga. And the English worship of Quantity does not allow the separate publication of 800 lines, after the fashion of America (for example, Lowell's "Cathedral"). My poem is not to be published until May, the announcement for April being a mistake. . . .

I am glad that you have got through this severe winter (or latter-winter) without worse evils than a cough. The last time you were with us I thought you looked more robust than I had ever seen you look.

Always yours truly
M. E. Lewes

John Blackwood Esq.

TO MRS. RICHARD CONGREVE, 3 APRIL 1870

In Berlin the Leweses were lionized by the great—scientists, professors, ambassadors, authors, publishers, royalty. Among the callers were Frederick VIII, Prince of Schleswig-Holstein, and George Bancroft, the American Minister, who gave a large dinner for them. After a party given by their old friends the Stahrs GE described the women as waiting like a flock of birds to peck at her. [V, 86–87]

[British Hotel, Berlin]

Our journey has not been unfortunate hitherto. The weather has been cold and cheerless; but we expected this, and on the 1st of April the sun began to shine. As for my *Wenigkeit*, it has never known a day of real bodily comfort since we got to Berlin: headache, sore throat, and *Schnupfen* have been alternately my companions, and have made my enjoyment very languid. But think of this as all past when you get my letter; for this morning I have a clearer head, the sun is shining, and the better time seems to be come for me. Mr. Lewes has had a good deal of satisfaction in his visits to laboratories and to the *Charité*, where he is just now gone for the third time to see more varieties of mad people, and hear more about Psychiatrie from Dr Westphal, a quiet, unpretending little man, who seems to have been delighted with George's sympathetic interest in this (to me) hideous branch of practice. I speak with all reverence: the world can't do without hideous studies.

People have been very kind to us, and have overwhelmed us with attentions, but we have felt a little weary in the midst of our gratitude, and since my cold has become worse, we have been obliged to cut off further invitations. We have seen many and various men and women, but except Mommsen, Bunsen, and Du Bois Reymond, hardly any whose names would be known to you. If I had been in good health, I should probably have continued to be more amused than tired of sitting on a sofa and having one person after another brought up to bow to me, and pay me the same compliment. Even as it was, I felt my heart go out to some good women who seemed really to have an affectionate feeling towards me for the sake of my books. But the sick animal longs for quiet and darkness. . . .

One enters on all subjects by turns in these evening parties, which are something like reading the 'Conversations-Lexicon' in a nightmare. Among lighter entertainments, we have been four times to the opera, being tempted at the very beginning of our stay by Gluck, Mozart, and an opportunity of hearing Tann-häuser for the second time. Also we have enjoyed some fine orchestral concerts, which are to be had for sixpence! Berlin has been growing very fast since our former stay here, and luxury in all forms has increased so much, that one only here and there gets a glimpse of the old-fashioned German housekeeping. But though later hours are becoming fashionable, the members of the Reichstag who have other business than politics complain of having to begin their sitting at eleven, ending, instead of beginning, at four, when the solid day is almost gone. We went to the Reichstag one morning, and were so fortunate as to hear Bismarck speak. But the question was one of currency, and his speech was mere-ly a brief winding up.

Now I shall think that I have earned a letter telling me all about you. May there be nothing but good to tell of! Pray give my best love to Emily, and my earnest wishes to Dr Congreve, that he may have satisfaction in new work.

TO LORD HOUGHTON, 7 MAY [1870]

Lewes had known Lord Houghton for 25 years and was often at his dinner parties. But it was not until June 1869 that Lady Houghton called with him at the Priory, and, in July, invited GE to dinner—a mark of society's acceptance of her anomalous position. [VIII, 473]

The Priory, | 21. North Bank, | Regents Park.
May 7.

My dear Lord Houghton

I read your kind letter only last night, on our return from a long journey which took us as far as Vienna.

We shall be very happy to accept Lady Houghton's kind invitation for the 15th. I am rejoiced to hear that her health has improved.

In our rambles we saw more than one person who spoke to us about you—the Lyttons, for example, who were very good to us at Vienna.

Yours very truly
M. E. Lewes.

TO OSCAR BROWNING, 8 MAY 1870

At Salzburg the Leweses spent a week in fine weather, before going 25 April to Munich to visit old friends. They stopped for a few days at Nuremberg, Würtzburg, Heidelberg, Strasburg, and Paris, so that GHL could call on physiologists, and reached home 6 May. Emerson's *Society and Solitude* (1870) is a collection of essays and lectures, many delivered as early as 1858. [V, 92–93]

The Priory, | 21. North Bank, | Regents Park.
May 8, 1870.

Dear Mr. Browning

Thanks for your kind letter from Rome, which I found on our return home, the other evening. For we too have been vagrants, and have wandered with cold winds for our company as far as Vienna. We set out on the 14th of March and only got back last Friday. . . .

A propos of books, I think very highly of Emerson's new volume. There is enough gospel to serve one for a year in one or two of the Essays—those on Domestic life, Eloquence, Farming etc.

Mr. Lewes unites with me in best remembrances and I am

Always yours sincerely
M. E. Lewes.

TO DANTE GABRIEL ROSSETTI, 8 MAY 1870

Rossetti's *Poems* was inscribed: "To Mrs. Lewes with D. G. Rossetti's kind regards, April, 1870." [v, 93]

The Priory, | 21. North Bank, | Regents Park.
Sunday morning | May 8. 70.

Dear Mr. Rossetti

We returned only the night before last from a two months' journey on the Continent, and among the parcels awaiting me I found your generous gift. I am very grateful to you both as giver and poet.

In cutting the leaves, while my head is still swimming from the journey, I have not resisted the temptation to read many things as they ought not to be read— hurriedly. But even in this way I have received a stronger impression than any fresh poems have for a long while given me, that to read once is a reason for reading again. The Sonnets towards "The House of Life" attract me peculiarly. I feel about them as I do about a new cahier of music which I have been "trying" here and there with the delightful conviction that I have a great deal to become acquainted with and to like better and better.

I hope that you have been having much enjoyment lately in your painting too. Mr. Lewes unites with me in kind regards, and I am

Always yours sincerely
M. E. Lewes.

JOURNAL, 25–28 MAY 1870

Since she first met GE in January 1869 Mrs. Pattison had been urging her to visit them at Lincoln College, where she had formed a sort of salon among her husband's friends. GE, the greatest lion of the day, describes her visit during Eights Week. It was her first visit to Oxford. [v, 99–101]

Wednesday, May 25. We started for Oxford at 1/2 past 9, and arrived at Lincoln College, where we were to stay with the Rector and his wife about 12. After luncheon, G. and I walked alone through the town, which on this first view was rather disappointing to me. Presently we turned through Christ Church into the Meadows and walked along by the river. This was beautiful, to my heart's content. The buttercups and hawthorns were in their glory, the chestnuts still in

sufficiently untarnished bloom; and the grand elms made a border towards the
town. After tea, we went with Mrs. Pattison and the Rector to the croquet ground
near the Museum. On our way we saw Sir Benjamin Brodie; and on the ground
Professor [George] Rawlinson, the "narrow-headed man," Mrs. Thursfield and
her son [James] who is a fellow (I think of Corpus), Miss [Mary] Arnold, daughter
of Mr. Tom Arnold, and Prof. [John] Phillips, the geologist. At supper we had
Mr. [Ingram] Bywater and Miss Arnold, and in chat with them, the evening was
passed.

26. G. and I went to the Museum, and had an interesting morning with Dr.
[George] Rolleston who dissected a brain for me. After lunch we went again to the
Museum, and spent the afternoon with Sir Benjamin Brodie, seeing various
objects in his laboratories, amongst others the method by which weighing has
been superseded in delicate matters by *measuring* in a graduated glass tube. After
Mrs. Pattison took me a drive in her little pony carriage round by their country
refuge—the Firs, Haddington [Headington], and by Littlemore, where I saw J. H.
Newman's little conventual dwellings. Returning we had a fine view of the
Oxford towers. To supper came Sir Benjamin and Lady Brodie.

27. In the morning we walked to see the two Martyrs' Memorial, and then took
a cab to Sir Benjamin Brodie's pretty place near the river and bridge. Close by
their grounds is the original ford whence the place took its name. The Miss
Gaskells [Margaret and Julia] were staying with them, and after chatting some
time, we two walked with Sir Benj. to New College, where we saw the gardens
surrounded by the old city wall; the chapel where William of Wykeham's crozier is
kept, and the cloisters, which are fine but gloomy, and less beautiful than those of
Magdalen which we saw in our walk on Thursday, before going to the Museum.
After lunch we went to the Bodleian, and then to the Sheldonian Theatre, where
there was a meeting apropos of Palestine Exploration. Captain [Charles] Warren,
conductor of the Exploration at Jerusalem read a paper, and then Mr. Deutsch
gave an account of the interpretation, as hitherto arrived at, of the Moabite
Stone. I saw "squeezes" of this stone for the first time, with photographs taken
from the squeezes. After tea we went—Mrs. Thursfield kindly took us—to see a
boat-race. We saw it from the Oriel barge, under the escort of Mr. [Mandell]
Creighton, fellow of Merton, who on our return took us through the lovely
gardens of his college. At supper were Mr. Jowett, Prof. Henry Smith, Miss E.
Smith his sister, Mr. [Thomas] Fowler, author of "Deductive Logic," and Mr.
[Walter] Pater, writer of articles on Leonardo da Vinci, Morris etc.

28. After a walk to St. John's College, we started by the train for London and I
arrived home about 2 o'clock, delighted to be under our own roof again.

TO SARA HENNELL, 13 JUNE 1870

Dickens died 9 June 1870. The railway accident at Staplehurst 9 June 1865 was more terrible to Dickens because his mistress Ellen Ternan was in the carriage with him returning from Paris. [v, 102]

The Priory, | 21. North Bank, | Regents Park.
June 13, 1870.

My dear Sara . . .

Dickens's death came as a great shock to us. He lunched with us just before we went abroad and was telling us a story of President Lincoln having told the Council on the day he was shot, that something remarkable would happen, because he had just dreamt for the third time a dream which twice before had preceded events momentous to the nation. The dream was, that he was in a boat on a great river all alone—and he ended with the words "I drift—I drift—I drift."

Dickens told this very finely. I thought him looking dreadfully shattered then. It is probable that he never recovered from the effect of the terrible railway accident.

With love, always dear Sara

Your faithful
Pollian.

TO MRS. EDWARD BURNE-JONES, 26 JUNE 1870

During the Leweses' fortnight at Whitby they saw Mrs. Burne-Jones every day. Ned was not ill, but working on paintings of Mary Zambaco, commissioned by her wealthy mother Mrs. Ionides. After the Leweses left Whitby, Mrs. Burne-Jones wrote to GE: "I think much of you and of your kindness to me during this past fortnight, and my heart smites me that I have somewhat resembled those friends who talk only of themselves to you. . . . Forgive me if it has been so, and reflect upon what a trap for egotism your unselfishness and tender thought for others is. The only atonement I can make is a resolve that what you have said to me in advice and warning shall not be lost." [VIII, 482–83] GE's good effect on this troubled marriage cannot be overestimated. [v, 105–06]

Albert House | Cromer | June 26. 70.

Dear Friend

I was meditating a letter to you, just when yours came to me, for I wanted to tell you exactly all that could be told about our future movements, so that in as far as your own movements might be determined by ours, you might not be left in an unpleasant state of conjecture. We are to leave this place on the 30th and Mr. Lewes has set his heart on going next to Harrogate, to try the effect of the chalybeate waters there. We should only stay a fortnight there at the utmost, and possibly we may quit it much earlier for Whitby, which is still our goal. I think Mr. Lewes is a little strengthened, but this place is not inspiriting and the weather is just now very cold, so that though I am clad in woollen, I am as cold as if the woollen were my shroud. I must not depreciate Cromer, however. There are fine sands and the inland scenery has much quiet beauty. The sunsets over the sea and the absence of German bands playing out of tune are "local features of no mean order," as the Athenaeum writers would say.

Still I expect Whitby to be far more various and stimulating, and I do hope that nothing will hinder our all meeting there—you, the bairns (and possibly the husband?) with us two grandparents. But I hope with some trembling, because of George's health, the conditions which may suit it defying all prophecy, especially with this changing climate. I shall write at once to you on the slightest change of intention, and of course I shall let you know when we have determined on the day of our departure for Whitby, always supposing that you do not set off in advance of us. You will let me know of that, will you not, dear little Epigram? And, in general, you will be faithful, and keep me well-informed about you?

I am grieved to hear that your great painter is ailing still. Tell him that friends of ours, who know Whitby, give us enthusiastic descriptions of the country around it. And they are old Fellows of Cambridge and Oxford, who are not usually vials of enthusiasm. Let us hope that we shall have a rainy week or so for the good of the country, and that afterwards we shall have sunshine for our good at Whitby. Our united love to all. Keep in mind

Yours ever faithfully
M. E. Lewes.

Write to me at the Priory, because our letters are sent on, and other addresses are uncertain.

TO THE HON. MRS. ROBERT LYTTON, 8 JULY 1870

The death of her uncle, George William Frederick Villiers, 4th Earl of Clarendon, who "had been like a father to her," was the occasion of this letter. [v, 106–07]

[Dear Mrs. Lytton]

I did not like to write to you until Mr Lytton sent word that I might do so, because I had not the intimate knowledge that would have enabled me to measure your trouble; and one dreads of all things to speak or write a wrong or unseasonable word when words are the only signs of interest and sympathy that one has to give. I know now, from what your dear husband has told us, that your loss is very keenly felt by you,—that it has first made you acquainted with acute grief, and this makes me think of you very much. For learning to love any one is like an increase of property,—it increases care, and brings many new fears lest precious things should come to harm. I find myself often thinking of you with that sort of proprietor's anxiety, wanting you to have gentle weather all through your life, so that your face may never look worn and storm-beaten, and wanting your husband to be and do the very best, lest anything short of that should be disappointment to you. At present the thought of you is all the more with me, because your trouble has been brought by death; and for nearly a year death seems to me my most intimate daily companion. I mingle the thought of it with every other, not sadly, but as one mingles the thought of some one who is nearest in love and duty with all one's motives. I try to delight in the sunshine that will be when I shall never see it any more. And I think it is possible for this sort of impersonal life to attain great intensity,—possible for us to gain much more independence, than is usually believed, of the small bundle of facts that make our own personality.

I don't know why I should say this to you, except that my pen is chatting as my tongue would if you were here. We women are always in danger of living too exclusively in the affections; and though our affections are perhaps the best gifts we have, we ought also to have our share of the more independent life—some joy in things for their own sake. It is piteous to see the helplessness of some sweet women when their affections are disappointed—because all their teaching has been, that they can only delight in study of any kind for the sake of a personal love. They have never contemplated an independent delight in ideas as an experience which they could confess without being laughed at. Yet surely women need this sort of defence against passionate affliction even more than men. . . .

[M. E. Lewes]

TO SARA HENNELL, 12 AUGUST 1870

In the opening weeks of the Franco-Prussian War the French had been forced to withdraw to the Moselle, their army divided by the Prussian wedge in Alsace. At first GE's sympathies lay with the Germans, feeling that the French had been misled by Napoleon III. Benjamin Jowett, whom she met at the Pattisons' in May, sent the proofs of his *Plato*, which appeared in 4 volumes in 1871. Froude's *History* had been in course of publication since 1856; Volumes X and XI completed it in 1870. [V, 111–13]

Park Farm | Limpsfield | Surrey | August 12. 70.

Dear Sara . . .

We too, you see, have come back to a well-tried refuge—the same place that soothed us in our troubles last October—and we especially delight in this deep country, after the fuss which belongs even to quiet watering-places such as Cromer, Harrogate and Whitby, which are, after all, "alleys where the gentle folks live." . . . We are excited even among the still woods and fields by the vicissitudes of the War, and chiefly concerned because we cannot succeed in getting the day's "Times." We have entered into the period which will be marked in future historical charts as "The period of German ascendency." But how saddening to think of the iniquities that the great harvest moon is looking down on! I am less grieved for the bloodshed than for the hateful trust in lies which is continually disclosed. Meanwhile Jowett's Translation of Plato is being prepared for publication, and he has kindly sent us the sheets of one volume. So I pass from discussions of French lying and the Nemesis that awaits it, to discussions about rhetorical lying at Athens in the fourth century before Christ. The translations, and Introductions to the Dialogues, seem to be charmingly done.

Also, we are reading Froude's picture of England under the Tudors, which he rather timidly insinuates than maintains to have been a time when Englishmen were far nobler and more unselfish than now. So, you perceive, we get plenty of contrast with that agitated Now, which is the main interest even in this far-away village. I don't quite know when we shall return to Town—probably in September. . . . Always, dear Sara,

Your affectionate
Pollian.

TO MME EUGÈNE BODICHON, 25 AUGUST [1870]

Dr. Bodichon, a radical of Republican sympathies, who had come to Algeria in the 1830s to help the natives, had no sympathy with the Empire as the Germans pushed through MacMahon's army heading towards Paris. [v, 113]

Park Farm | Limpsfield | August 25.

My dear Barbara

We shall return to town on Monday, various small reasons concurring to make us resolve on quitting this earthly paradise.

I am very sorry for the sufferings of the French nation, but I think these sufferings are better for the moral welfare of the people than victory would have been. The war has been drawn down on them by an iniquitous Government, but in a great proportion of the French people there has been nourished a wicked glorification of selfish pride, which like all other conceit is a sort of stupidity, excluding any true conception of what lies outside their own vain wishes. The Germans, it seems, were expected to stand like toy-soldiers, for the French to knock them down. It was quite true that the war is in some respects the conflict of two differing forms of civilization. But whatever charm we may see in the southern Latin races, this ought not to blind us to the great contributions which the German energies have made in all sorts of ways to the common treasure of mankind. And who that has any spirit of justice can help sympathizing with them in their grand repulse of the French project to invade and divide them? If I were a Frenchwoman, much as I might wail over French sufferings, I cannot help believing that I should detest the French talk about the "Prussiens." They wanted to throttle the electric eel for their own purposes.

But I imagine that you and the Doctor would not find us in much disagreement with you on these matters. One thing that is pleasant to think of, is the effort made everywhere to help the wounded. All this scribble is mere fringe to the information I wished to send you as to our whereabouts. With best regards to the Doctor,

Yours always
M. E. L.

TO MRS. ERNST LEOPOLD BENZON, [26 SEPTEMBER 1870]

Besides their house in Palace Gardens, the Benzons had places in Scotland and at Tunbridge Wells. GHL reported in his Diary: "Perfect weather; delightful place. Benzon full of details of his visit to the wounded at Metz." They drove over to Penshurst to call on Naysmyth, inventor of the steam hammer: "Much talk about War and wounded." GHL returned home 28 September to find "Polly in bed, abscess in her gum! Strasburg surrendered." [VIII, 487]

The Priory, | 21. North Bank, | Regents Park.
Monday.

My dear Mrs. Benzon

I am an unfortunate person. Yesterday I was attacked with an aching in the gums, from cold or some other disturbance. It increased during the night, and now I am not well enough to dare the journey which would take me to you. Happily, I know Tunbridge Wells and many of its pretty drives and walks, so that I shall be able to imagine my husband's enjoyment in walking and driving with you. I shall trust to your coming to smile on me when you are once more in town. With best regards

Ever yours affectionately
M. E. Lewes.

TO ROBERT LYTTON, 26 SEPTEMBER 1870

Lytton's uncle Sir Henry Bulwer long served as ambassador at many European capitals and at Washington before retiring from diplomatic service in 1865. [VIII, 487–89]

The Priory, | 21. North Bank, | Regents Park.
September 26. 70.

Dear Mr. Lytton . . .

I am getting more and more gloomy about the War. It seems as if every one were getting the worse for it (I mean morally worse), spectators as well as agents. In my intense dislike for vague blame, it is always a satisfaction to me when any one will speak who (like Sir Henry Bulwer) is practically acquainted with affairs. If you were here I should ask you whether there is any real authority, any evidence beyond Parisian conceptions for the statement that the other neutral Powers hold back from recognition of the French Republic because they wait for England to take the initiative. I find excellent people, in talking of such matters, as free as savages from the need of any evidence for a statement which falls in with their dominant mood. Those who sympathize with the French believe what is discreditable to the Germans, and vice versa. This is to me the most pitiable weakness, and precisely that slavery of the judgment which it is one end of life-discipline to get rid of. To keep the temper also is an accomplishment which people are fast letting slip in this War discussion. Perhaps the aristocratic regions are more serious than the mid-air we are breathing. After all, one is glad that any public question should be a matter of general interest, and hot temper about them is better than the indifference of philistinism.

Mr. Lewes is going to Tunbridge Wells on this beautiful day to visit some friends of ours who have a country paradise there. I was to have gone with him, but have been entered by a demon of tooth-ache and general misery, and am glad to hide myself from the world like a sick crab. This demon, of course, has written a muddled letter, and not allowed me to guide my own pen. . . . The demon allows me to feel lovingly, though not to write clearly, and much of that lovingness goes out towards Mrs. Lytton. To her other self also I am always

His affectionately
M. E. Lewes.

TO SARA HENNELL, 18 NOVEMBER 1870

Charles Haddon Spurgeon was a Baptist preacher whose sermons were so popular that in 1861 the Metropolitan Tabernacle was built to house the 6,000 hearers he attracted. The Leweses heard him at the Park Square Chapel. Ruskin's contribution was 100 guineas. [V, 121–23]

The Priory, | 21. North Bank, | Regents Park.
November 18. 70.

My dear Sara

Think how far we are behind our contemporaries:—yesterday, for the first time, we went to hear Spurgeon! Mr. Lewes, who likes to surprize me with the fulfillment of some half-forgotten wish, had come home a day or two before with tickets for admission to a chapel within five minutes' walk of our house. So the experience was gained by very slight exertion, and certainly it was not worth more. I remembered what you had said about his vulgar, false emphasis, but there remained the fact of his celebrity, and such testimony as that of Ruskin, who after hearing him sent him (I think) £200 for his chapel, saying that he had never heard such preaching before. I was glad of the opportunity. But my impressions fell below the lowest judgment I ever heard passed upon him. He has the gift of a fine voice, very flexible and various; he is admirably fluent and clear in his language, and every now and then his enunciation is effective. But I never heard any pulpit reading and speaking which in its level tone was more utterly common and empty of guiding intelligence or emotion: it was as if the words had been learned by heart and uttered without comprehension by a man who had no instinct of rhythm, or music, in his soul.

And the doctrine! It was a libel on Calvinism, that it should be presented in such a form. I never heard any attempt to exhibit the soul's experience that was more destitute of insight. The sermon was against Fear in the elect Christian, as being a distrust of God, but never once did he touch the true ground of fear—the doubt whether the signs of God's choice are present in the soul. We had plenty of anecdotes, but they were all poor and pointless—Tract Society anecdotes of the feeblest kind. It was the most superficial, Grocer's-back-parlour view of Calvinistic Christianity; and I was shocked to find how low the mental pitch of our society must be, judged by the standard of this man's celebrity. Mr. Lewes was struck with some of his tones, as good actor's tones, and was not so wroth as I was. But just now, with all Europe stirred by events that make every conscience tremble after some great principle as a consolation and guide, it was too exasperating to sit and listen to doctrine that seemed to look no farther than the retail Christian's tea and muffins. He said, "Let us approach the throne of God," very much as he might have invited you to take a chair—and there followed this fine touch: "We feel no love to God because he hears the prayers of others: it is because he hears my prayers that I love him." You see, I am relieving myself by pouring out my disgust to you. . . . Always, dear Sara,

Your faithfully loving
Pollian. . . .

JOURNAL, 2 DECEMBER 1870

GE began working on a story called "Miss Brooke" early in November 1870. [v, 124]

DECEMBER 2. I am experimenting in a story, which I began without any very serious intention of carrying it out lengthily. It is a subject which has been recorded among my possible themes ever since I began to write fiction, but will probably take new shapes in the development. I am today at p. 44. I am reading Wolf's Prolegomena to Homer. In the evening aloud, Wilhelm Meister again!

TO MME LOUIS BELLOC, 20 DECEMBER 1870

Married at 37, Bessie bore two children: Marie, who became the noted author Marie Belloc Lowndes (1868–1947), and Hilary, better known as Hilaire Belloc (1870–1953), an equally prolific author. GHL's mother Mrs. Willim died 10 December, "quite peacefully as she sat in her chair." She was 83. [v, 125–26]

Priory | December 20. 70.

Dearest Bessie

Where do you think we are going in half an hour's time?—To Swanmore Parsonage, Ryde, to stay for a few days with Barbara. We shall be home again next week, and I will write to you immediately on our return to say when I can see you. If you have anything to say meanwhile, write to me at Barbara's.

Alas alas for the sorrows of poor France!—That is the haunting thought, wherever one goes. And I fear you have a large share in these sorrows. I heard of your boy through your own letter to Barbara which she sent on to me in the summer.

Always yours affectionately
M. E. Lewes.

The mourning paper is for Mr. Lewes's Mother.

JOURNAL, 31 December 1870

In a letter to Charles and Gertrude, GHL adds: "Yesterday we had the Mummers; and the ritualistic High Mass in the Church at 12 at night, to which Mad. Bodichon went—we retiring to the less ecclesiastical bed." [v, 127]

December 31. On Wednesday the 21st we went to Ryde to see Madame Bodichon at Swanmore Parsonage, a house which she had taken for two months. We had a pleasant and healthy visit, walking much in the frosty air. On Christmas day I went with her to the Ritualist Church which is attached to the Parsonage and heard some excellent intoning by the delicate-faced tenor-voiced clergyman Mr. Hooker Wicks. On Wednesday last, the 28th, Barbara came up to town with us. We found the cold here more severe than at Ryde, and the papers tell of still harder weather about Paris where our fellow-men are suffering and inflicting horrors. Am I doing anything that will add the weight of a sandgrain against the persistence of such evil?

Here is the last day of 1870. I have written only 100 pages—good printed pages—of a story which I began about the opening of November, and at present mean to call "Miss Brooke." Poetry halts just now.

In my private lot I am unspeakably happy, loving and beloved. But I am doing little for others.

TO ROBERT BROWNING, [?12 JANUARY 1871]

GHL called 12, 15, and 17 January on Gertrude Lewes, who had had a second miscarriage. Browning may have been giving the dinner for Charles Leland, the American author, who lived in London 1869–80 while writing his books on the gypsies. The letter, written on the mourning paper the Leweses used after Mrs. Willim's death, is in the Armstrong Browning Library, Baylor University; I am indebted to the Director, Professor Jack W. Herring, for permission to publish it here for the first time.

Dear Mr. Browning

I asked your messenger to wait for the chance of Mr. Lewes's arrival, because I did not like to take on myself the negative reply to your kind note which I am sorry to say that Mr. Lewes's report of his bodily feelings this morning makes me certain that he would be obliged to give. He went out to see our daughter-in-law, who is an invalid just now, simply because his head would not allow him to read or write. I expect him to return very soon, but I do not like to keep your messenger for an indefinite time, and I hope I am doing the right thing in begging you on Mr. Lewes's behalf not to keep a place for him. Indeed I have no doubt that, much as he would like to see Mr. Leland, he would not venture on the excitement of a dinner away from home. When a fit of dyspepsia lays hold of him, he rarely has the force to throw it off before it has spoiled several days for him.

You will not be hindered from coming to us, spite of the weather I hope. In haste

Yours very truly
M. E. Lewes.

TO MRS. JULIA CAMERON, 17 JANUARY 1871

Julia Cameron, who took up photography in 1865, made famous portraits of Robert Browning, Tennyson, Darwin, and many other Victorians. One may regret that GE was not among them. "Golden Locks" cannot be surely identified. [v, 133]

The Priory | 21 North Bank | January 17. 1871.

My dear Mrs. Cameron

The love which you have so prettily inscribed on the beautiful presents which you have sent me, is the more precious because it is given for the sake of my books. They are certainly the best part of me, save only in the power which my fleshly self has of returning love for love and being grateful for all goodness. It was a surprize to me, but all the more a pleasure, when Mr. Oscar Browning told me that he held some photographs of yours under his arm which were sent by you expressly to me. I have long admired your works of this kind, but I am naturally disposed to think these especially charming—above all the "Golden Locks." I thank you with all my heart. Wise people are teaching us to be sceptical about some sorts of "charity," but this of cheering others by proofs of sympathy will never, I think, be shown to be harmful. At least, you have done me good.

You are happy in being far away from under the London blanket with a sight of the sky above you. I suppose you will some time return to the uglier world here, and in that case I may hope that the kindness which sent the photographs may bring you to me in your own person. Believe me, my dear Mrs. Cameron

Sincerely and gratefully yours
M. E. Lewes.

TO FRANÇOIS D'ALBERT DURADE, 27 JANUARY 1871

William Cross and his brother-in-law W. H. Bullock (later Bullock Hall), a correspondent for the *Daily News*, established a soup kitchen at Sedan. Charles François Daubigny, whom Mme Bodichon had befriended, came with her to lunch at the Priory 22 January 1871. [IX, 8–10]

The Priory, | 21 North Bank, | Regents Park.
January 27. 1871.

My dear Friend

I had a great longing to hear from you, and I confess that I had almost suspected you of having ceased to think of me. . . . This war has been a personal sorrow to every human creature with any sympathy who has been within reach of hearing about it; still more to those who have gone out to see and help the sufferers. Several of our friends have been among these latter. But even we who have stayed at home have seen as well as heard the effects of the great calamity, for the French who are among us are many of them half or wholly ruined. Last Sunday we had the eminent paysagiste D'Aubigny to see us, a grave, amiable simple-mannered man. His house on the Loire, full of his own painting on such objects as his daughter's bedstead and all such family memorials, has been completely destroyed. He is now living with his family in small lodgings at Kensington. This is but a mild sample of the myriad sorrows produced by the regression of Barbarism from that historical tomb where we thought it so picturesquely buried—if indeed one ought not to beg pardon of Barbarism, which had no weapons for making eight wounds at once in one body, and rather call the present warfare that of the Devil and all his legions. Enough! I like better to think how Madame d'Albert would exert herself in all helpfulness as long as she had strength to do so. . . .

Writing does not go on quickly under bodily depression, but Mr. Lewes has lately prepared a new edition of his History of Philosophy, with many changes and additions, and carries on at his leisure his favorite work on physiological psychology. That is his sole occupation now, and he has long given up all other forms of writing. I think my affections grow more intense and my interest in such studies increases rather than diminishes, but physically I feel old, and Death seems to me very near. The idea of dying has no melancholy for me, except in the parting and the leaving behind which Love makes so hard to contemplate.

Goodbye, dear Friend. I trust we shall see each other again. But I hope you will not let so long an interval pass again before you send me news of Madame d'Albert and yourself. . . . God bless both of you, and let me sometimes be assured that you believe in me as

Your affectionate friend
M. E. Lewes.

Our son Charles is well and happy, his wife delicate in health after a second miscarriage. Our last news of Herbert, the son who is in South Africa, was the very good news that he was engaged to be married to a young lady of good education, the daughter of a long-established colonist.

JOURNAL, 19 MARCH 1871

Professor Jerome Beaty in his masterly *Middlemarch from Notebook to Novel* (1960) finds that GE had written the first 18 chapters and what is now Chapter 23 and had already joined the Vincy-Featherstone part with "Miss Brooke." But he shows that the 236 pages were manuscript, not print, for Chapter 23, which was originally 19, ended on p. 236. [v, 137]

Sunday, March 19. 1871. It is grievous to me how little, from one cause or other, chiefly languor and occasionally positive ailments, I manage to get done. I have written about 236 pages (print) of my Novel, which I want to get off my hands by next November. My present fear is that I have too much matter, too many "momenti."

TO MRS. ALEXANDER GILCHRIST, 19 APRIL 1871

Planning to install a new bathroom and make other improvements in the Priory, the Leweses looked at a number of houses in the country before settling on Brookbank, "a queer little cottage" at Shottermill, near Haslemere, belonging to the widow of the biographer of

Blake. They lived there from 2 May to 1 August 1871. A letter from GHL to Blackwood 7 May gives her plan for *Middlemarch:* "Mrs. Lewes finds that she will require 4 volumes for her story, not 3. I winced at the idea at first, but the story must not be spoiled for want of space, and as you have more than once spoken of the desirability of inventing some mode of circumventing the Libraries and making the public *buy* instead of borrowing I have devised the following scheme, suggested by the plan Victor Hugo followed with his long *Miséra-bles*—namely to publish it in *half-volume parts* either at intervals of one, or as I think better, two months. The eight parts at 5/- could yield the 2 £ for the four volumes, and at two month intervals would not be dearer than Maga. Each part would have a certain unity and completeness in itself with separate title. Thus the work is called *Middlemarch.* Part I will be *Miss Brooke.*" [v, 140, 145–46]

The Priory, | 21. North Bank, | Regents Park.
April 19. 1871.

My dear Madam
We are very much obliged to you for your kind, methodical thoughtfulness as to all which is necessary for our accommodation at Brookbank, and also for your hints about the points of beauty to be sought for in our walks. That "sense of standing on a round world" which you speak of, is precisely what I most care for amongst out-of-door delights. The last time I had it fully was at St. Märgen near Freiburg, on green hill-tops whence we could see the Rhine and poor France. . . . The garden has been, and is being, attended to, and I trust that we shall not find the commissariat unendurable. Mr. Ewens wanted to stay till the last day of the month, but that would have been a serious annoyance and retardation for us, as the house cannot be well cleaned without the work of some days. Always, dear Madam,

Sincerely yours
M. E. Lewes.

TO CHARLES LEWES, 4 JUNE [1871]

Charles found Wolff and returned it to the London Library, where this letter is also found now. GHL diagnosed GE's illness as tic douleureux and took her to London to see a doctor 6 June. She says nothing of the visit 31 May of John and Willie Blackwood, who talked over the plan of *Middlemarch* and took away Book I, which John read with intense delight. [v, 149–50]

Shotter Mill | Petersfield. | June 4.

Dearest Boy
I feel myself a culprit, that I have to be troublesome to you and again cause you a détour on your way home. When I came away I unhappily left behind me a volume belonging to the London Library, and it is now required by some other subscriber. The volume is Wolff's Prolegomena to Homer which I have had in my possession ever since November, and had read through a long while ago. But I still kept it, because I wished to read it again, and relied too confidently on the unlikelihood that anyone else would ask for it. Now, however, by way of Nemesis, some student turns up who wants the said volume. You see, all wrong-doing strikes the innocent

more than the guilty, and so in consequence of my mistake you are bothered. I am much afraid lest you should have trouble in finding the volume, but this much is certain: that it is in one or other of the bookcases in my study. It is less certain, but very probable, that it is in the upper shelves, or else in the middle cupboard of the long bookcase which used to be in the drawing-room in Blandford Square. Its appearance is this: an octavo volume with brown calf back split on one side, lettered dully with (I think) *Homerus Wolfii.* When you have found it, will you be so good as to despatch it to the London Library? As Pater says, if I had consulted him, he would have told me to bring it down here, and then we could have returned it immediately on receiving notice that it was wanted. But wisdom has come too late.

I was made happy by your and Gertrude's letters, which gave me an idea that you were enjoying this young time of the year and of life.

Always your loving
Mutter.

I have been ill all week with a cold which I took on Sunday last, and which brought on inflamed gums, headache and general disorder of functions. Pater is jolly.

TO CHARLES LEWES, 20 JUNE 1871

After a painful operation for cancer Emanuel Deutsch lived for many months in the house of the Reverend Hugh Haweis, incumbent at St. James's, Marylebone. He and his wife gave Deutsch a private sitting room near the street door and unless especially invited never saw any of his visitors. H. Buxton Forman became a clerk at the General Post Office at the same time as Charles Lewes in 1860. In 1866 he wrote an article on GE; when he reprinted the essay in *Our Living Poets* (1871), he added four pages of hyperbolic praise of her poem "Agatha." The poem had been privately printed in 1869 to secure the copyright before its publication in the *Atlantic Monthly.* Three forged editions of it are known. Thomas J. Wise, the notorious forger, declared that it "was seen through the press upon behalf of the authoress by Mr. Buxton Forman." It is certain that GHL would never have allowed his son's young colleague to see anything through the press on GE's behalf. If it can be shown that Forman had had the pamphlets printed surreptitiously in 1869, it will exculpate Wise, who was then only ten years old. [v, 154–56]

[Shottermill]
The Priory, | 21. North Bank, | Regents Park.
June 20. 1871.

Dearest Boy

I was delighted to have your pretty letter this morning, and I hope that when you are as old as I am you will be having the same sort of pleasure. Gertrude's letter, too, reassuring me about her health, was very precious, and I have been thinking of you both with much happiness of late, because you seem to be free from anxieties. . . .

We have several times been to see Mr. Deutsch at Mr. Haweis's, but I never met the host. He and his wife must be good people to have taken care as they have done of Mr. Deutsch through an illness which the medical men thought likely enough to be fatal. Helping one's fellow-men in that way is much more difficult than any outdoor charities.

I am sorry that our good friend Forman has republished his criticisms, because I think there is more than enough literature of the criticising sort urged upon people's attention by the periodicals. To read much of it seems to me seriously injurious: it accustoms men and women to formulate opinions instead of receiving deep impressions, and to receive deep impressions is the foundation of all true mental power. Even with so admirable a writer, so accomplished and mature a judge as Lowell, whose Essays we have been reading, I feel how worthless his critical articles are compared with his essays on his "Garden acquaintances" and on "Winter." These are like a pure brook (we have endless brooks about us here!) and the others are like Crystal Palace fountains got up for display and making you feel that there is too much of them. . . .

Is not the weather like April? We have just had a great thunderstorm, and now the sun is sending yellow and blue patches through our painted glass on to my paper. I write always on my knees—that is, with the paper on my knees now, and thus avoid any stooping. I recommend that plan to Gertrude. Good by, dear children.

> Always your loving
> Mutter.

TO EMANUEL DEUTSCH, 7 JULY [1871]

Froude did not resign from *Fraser's* until 1874, when Allingham succeeded him. Mary Wollstonecraft Godwin's wetting her clothes before attempting suicide is imitated by Mirah in *Daniel Deronda*, Chapter 17. [v, 160–61]

> Shottermill | Petersfield | July 7.

My dear Rabbi

I have heard from others that you are "better" and "very well," but I want to have an account of you from yourself. Since I wrote to you last I have been ailing and in the Slough of Despond too, and am only just emerging. Come, be generous, shake off dull sloth and take the trouble to write me a few lines. Is it not the middle of this month that you go back to work? How are you really?

About Fraser, I have had a confirmation of the report that Froude has given up the editorship, but either Longmans will choose some man with a popular name as nominal or show editor, or else, I should think, Mr. Allingham who has been acting as sub-editor will take the entire management.

Pray observe that we want to know how you are physically—whether you get plenty of sleep, and whether the bad symptoms have thoroughly disappeared. If so, encourage Mr. Micawber's philosophy in your soul, and be sure that something will "turn up." Hopelessness has been to me, all through my life, but especially in painful years of my youth, the chief source of wasted energy with all the consequent bitterness of regret. Remember, it has happened to many to be glad they did not commit suicide, though they once ran for the final leap, or as Mary Wolstonecraft did, wetted their garments well in the rain hoping to sink the better when they plunged. She tells how it occurred to her as she was walking in this damp shroud, that she might live to be glad that she had not put an end to herself—and so it turned out. She lived to know some real joys, and death came in time to hinder the joys from being spoiled. Which things are a parable.

We had thought of going to Scotland next month, but we shall not do so, my health not being strong enough for me to incur the fatigues of the journey and the literary mob.

Yours always sincerely
M. E. Lewes.

TO JOHN BLACKWOOD, 15 JULY 1871

GHL sent Book II of *Middlemarch* on 14 July. Blackwood's letter has not been found. GE was apparently to be seated at the head table for the Scott centennial dinner. [v, 164–65]

Shottermill | near Petersfield | July 15. 71.

My dear Mr. Blackwood

I still feel that I owe you my thanks for your kind letter, although Mr. Lewes undertook to deliver them in the first instance. You certainly made a seat at the Commemoration Table look more tempting to me than it had done before, but I think that prudence advises me to abstain from the fatigue and excitement of a long railway journey with a great gathering at the end of it. If there is a chance that "Middlemarch" will be good for anything, I don't want to break down and die without finishing it. And whatever "the tow on my distaff" may be, my strength to unwind it has not been abundant lately. . . .

The continuous absence of sunshine is depressing in every way, and makes one fear for the harvest—so grave a fear that one is ashamed of mentioning one's private dreariness. You cannot play golf in the rain, and I cannot feel hopeful without the sunlight; but I daresay you work all the more, whereas when my spirits flag my work flags too. . . .

Please give my kind regards to Mr. William Blackwood, and believe me

Always yours truly
M. E. Lewes.

TO JOHN BLACKWOOD, 24 JULY 1871

After reading Book II Blackwood suggested that a possible feeling of the lack of continuous interest between the Brooke and Vincy parts did not matter since they were complete in themselves. The cottage at Shottermill had been let to George Smith, a painter, from 1 August; but the Leweses were able to secure a house across the road until 1 September. Mrs. Tennyson's Journal records: *"July 14th.* A[lfred] travelled down from London with

G. H. Lewes, who took him to his home . . . and introduced him to Mrs. Lewes." He called again with Hallam, 22 July: "She is delightful in a *tête-á-tête* and speaks in a soft soprano voice, which almost sounds like a fine falsetto, with her strong masculine face." [v, 168–69]

Shottermill | Petersfield | July 24. 71.

My dear Mr. Blackwood

Thanks for the prompt return of the M.S., which arrived this morning. I have just been making a calculation of the pages and I find, on a liberal estimate, that this second portion is about 190 pp. of the size you usually give to my novels—I think, 25 lines per page, is it not? "Miss Brooke" being about 150 pp. the two parts together would be equal to the larger volumes of Adam Bede and The Mill, which are at least 350 pp. if my memory may be trusted.

Mr. Lewes has been saying that it may perhaps be well to take in a portion of Part II at the end of Part I. But it is too early for such definite arrangements. I don't see how I can leave anything out, because I hope there is nothing that will be seen to be irrelevant to my design, which is to show the gradual action of ordinary causes rather than exceptional, and to show this in some directions which have not been from time immemorial the beaten path—the Cremorne walks and shows of fiction. But the best intentions are good for nothing until execution has justified them. And you know I am always compassed about with fears. I am in danger in all my designs of parodying dear Goldsmith's satire on Burke, and think of refining when novel readers only think of skipping.

We are obliged to turn out of this queer cottage next week, but we have been fortunate enough to get the more comfortable house on the other side of the road, so that we can move without any trouble. Thus our address will continue to be the same until the end of August.

Tennyson, who is one of the "hill-folk" about here, has found us out, so that we have lost the utmost perfection of our solitude—the impossibility of a caller.

Always yours sincerely
M. E. Lewes.

TO THE HON. MRS. ROBERT LYTTON, 25 JULY 1871

Lytton's letter announced the death of their six-year-old son Rowland. [v, 170–71]

Shottermill | near Petersfield | July 25. 71.

Dear Mrs. Lytton

This morning your husband's letter came to us, but if I did not know that it would be nearly a week before any words of mine could reach you, I should abstain from writing just yet, feeling that in the first days of sorrowing it is better to keep silence. For a long while after a great bereavement our only companionship is with the lost one. Yet I hope it will not be without good to you to have signs of love from your friends, and to be reminded that you have a home in their affections,

which is made larger for you by your trouble. For weeks my thought has been
continually going out to you, and the absence of news has made me so fearful that I
have mourned beforehand. I have been feeling that probably you were undergoing
the bitterest grief you had ever known. But under the heart-stroke, is there
anything better than to grieve?—Strength will come back for the duty and the
fellowship which gradually bring new contentments, but at first there is no joy to
be desired that would displace sorrow. What is better than to love and live with
the loved?—But that must sometimes bring us to live with the dead; and this too
turns at last into a very tranquil and sweet tie, safe from change and injury.

You see, I make myself a warrant out of my regard for you, to write as if we had
long been near each other. And I cannot help wishing that we were physically
nearer—that you were not on the other side of Europe. We shall trust in Mr
Lytton's kindness to let us hear of you by-and-by. But you must never write except
to satisfy your own longing. May all true help surround you, dear Mrs Lytton, and
whenever you can think of me, believe in me as

Yours with sincere affection
M. E. Lewes.

TO ALEXANDER MAIN, 3 AUGUST 1871

Main had studied at Glasgow to prepare for the ministry, but changed his mind and
returned to Arbroath to teach, living with his mother. This is GE's reply to the first of more
than twenty letters that he wrote to her in 1871. GHL at first encouraged the correspondence as a help in overcoming GE's morbid diffidence. [v, 174–75]

[Shottermill]
The Priory | 21 North Bank | Regents Park.
August 3. 71.

Dear Sir

You have been rightly inspired in pronouncing Romŏla, and in conceiving
Romŏlo as the Italian equivalent of Romulus. I can assure you that the Italians say
Romŏlo and consequently Romŏla. There is a mountain named Romŏla in sight
from Florence. The music of the name is quite lost in the painful quantity
Romōla. So pray go on defying an evil custom—if custom it be.

I am touched by the sympathy you express with a book which was an intense
occupation of my feelings as well as thought for three years before it was completed
in print. The general ignorance of old Florentine literature, and the false conceptions of Italy bred by idle travelling (with the sort of culture which combines
Shakespeare and the musical glasses), have caused many parts of Romola to be
entirely misunderstood—the scene of the Quack doctor and the monkey, for
example, which is a specimen, not of humour as I relish it, but of the practical
joking which was the amusement of the gravest old Florentines, and without
which no conception of them would be historical. The whole piquancy of the
scene in question was intended to lie in the antithesis between the puerility which

stood for wit and humour in the old Republic, and the majesty of its front in graver matters.

I suppose that our beloved Walter Scott's imagination was under the influence of a like historical need when he represented the chase of the false herald in Quentin Durward as a joke which made Louis XI and Charles of Burgundy laugh even to tears and turned their new political amity into a genuine fellowship of buffoonery.

But I perceive from the remarks in your letter that you have had reason to reflect on the small insight and comparison which go to form the ordinary chit-chat judgments on literature. I remain

Yours sincerely
M. E. Lewes.

Alexander Main Esq.

TO ALEXANDER MAIN, 9 AUGUST 1871

After three or four more letters from him, which GHL volunteered to answer, Main wrote 25 September asking permission to undertake the publication of a selection of "sayings" from her works. GHL, thinking it a good speculation for the publisher, agreed to propose the plan to Blackwood. [v, 175]

[Shottermill]
The Priory | 21 North Bank | Regents Park | August 9. 71.

My dear Sir

I am grateful for—indeed, deeply affected by your assurance that my writings have been long precious to you and others. I like to tell you that my worship for Scott is peculiar. I began to read him when I was seven years old, and afterwards when I was grown up and living alone with my Father, I was able to make the evenings cheerful for him during the last five or six years of his life by reading aloud to him Scott's novels. No other writer would serve as a substitute for Scott, and my life at that time would have been much more difficult without him. It is a personal grief, a heart-wound to me when I hear a depreciating or slighting word about Scott.

I have not much strength and time for correspondence, but I shall always be glad to hear from you when you have anything in your mind which it will be a solace to you to say to me.

Yours very sincerely,
M. E. Lewes.

I was especially gratified to know that the "Life of Goethe" had been a long companion of yours. But my dear husband almost forgets his own books in the sympathy he gives to all that concerns mine.

TO MRS. CHARLES BRAY, 6 OCTOBER 1871

After their return from Shottermill 1 September GE had a severe intestinal attack from which she did not recover for two months. Her servants Grace and Amelia, who had been with her for ten years, gave notice 5 September and left 13 October. GE replaced them with three others. [v, 197–98]

The Priory, | 21. North Bank, | Regents Park.
October 6. 71.

Dear Cara . . .

I think my complaint had nothing to do with brain-work, except so far as this has been diffused over my life at the expense of my bodily capital; for I have not been taxing myself—indeed for many months I have been too ailing to do more than an apology for a morning's work. We are hoping that this crisis may have delivered me from long-accumulating sources of dyspepsia, for I am certainly going on well now in my *eingeweide*. But I am as thin as a mediaeval Christ, and Mr. Lewes is exerting his ingenuity to feed me up. He has been housekeeper, secretary and Nurse all in one—as good a nurse as if he had been trained in a hospital.

Our old servants' going was a shock to me at first. We should never have dismissed them, and we looked forward to taking care of them when they were too old to work. But their oddities were a yoke which we were certain would get heavier with the years, and since they could think of going we are contented now that they should go. To inherit servants from Mrs. Call, who is in all respects an excellent mistress, seems the best fortune that could have happened to us in this matter. But it is difficult for us masters and mistresses to allow enough for the difference between our drawing-room point of view and that of the kitchen. A very good quiet young woman whom we had as nurse for Thornie, soon became an object of dislike and criticism to Grace and Amelia, and they apparently are unable to tolerate any "stranger," though she were hired purely to relieve them from excessive work.

Here is a long spell about myself—the first letter I have written, and probably the last for a good while. With best love to all,

Your faithful
Marian.

TO JOHN BLACKWOOD, 29 OCTOBER 1871

John Walter Cross called at the Priory 22 October with his sisters Emily and Elinor to beg the Leweses to come visit them at Weybridge. They went the following Tuesday and stayed till Saturday. Alexander Main came to lunch with the Blackwoods in Edinburgh. John, who called him "the Worshipper of Genius," described him as "a little fellow, dark with bright clear-looking eyes. He used his knife in a dangerous manner at lunch, but the ladies were all taken with him." GE is "his particular idol," and he "reads her works aloud on the seashore."

Most of the irregularity in the MS of *Middlemarch* came from the weaving of the Brooke-Casaubon into the Vincy-Featherstone parts. Blackwood agreed to try the new form of issuing the novel in 8 Books with paper covers at intervals of two months in an effort to break the monopoly of the circulating libraries, and afterwards in 4 volumes bound in cloth. GE received 2/- for each 5/- book sold, a royalty of 40 percent. An advertising section of 16 pages, added to give bulk, brought GE another £143. [v, 208–09]

> The Priory, | 21. North Bank, | Regents Park.
> October 29. 71.

My dear Mr. Blackwood

Yesterday we returned from Weybridge, where for a few days I have been petted by kind friends (delightful Scotch people) and have had delicious drives in the pure autumn air. That must be my farewell to invalidism and holiday making. I am really better—not robust or fat, but perhaps as well as I am likely to be till death mends me.

Your account of Mr. Main sets my mind at ease about him, for in this case I would rather have your judgment than any opportunity of forming my own. He had told us that he was only 31, but I was without even a conjecture as to his bring-up and occupation. The one thing that gave me confidence was his power of putting his finger on the right passages, and giving emphasis to the right idea (in relation to the author's feeling and purpose). Apart from that, enthusiasm would have been of little value.

Mr. Lewes will see Mr. Langford about the registration at Stationers' Hall. Also, we think of sending the M.S. of Parts II and III to Edinburgh this week, that they may be got into type, to test their proportionate quantities. I am quite ashamed of giving so much trouble by irregularity of writing, but I hope in future to keep my pages tolerably equal, so as not to be in doubt about the size of my two-monthly Parts. . . . I hardly dare hope that the 2d Part will take quite so well as the first—the effects being more subtle and dispersed, but Mr. Lewes seems to like the 3d Part better than anything that has gone before it. But can anything be more uncertain than the reception of a book by the public? . . .

Mr. Simpson says he thinks well of the German plan, and I conclude that your opinion concurs. As for me I get more and more unable to be anything more than a feeble sceptic about all publishing plans, and am thankful to have so many good heads at work for me. Allah illah Allah!

> Always yours sincerely
> M. E. Lewes.

TO MRS. ELIZABETH GARRETT ANDERSON, 31 OCTOBER 1871

Mrs. Anderson, one of the pioneer woman physicians, was raising funds to establish the hospital now known by her name. The Leweses gave £5 in 1872 and 2 guineas each year thereafter. [V, 209–10]

The Priory, | 21. North Bank, | Regents Park.
October 31. 71.

Dear Madam

I am much interested in the prospectus of the Woman's Hospital which you have sent me. From the prospectus itself as well as from the fact that a lady whose name is on the Committee has told me that she is uncertain whether she shall belong to it, I gather that the scheme is at present in a hypothetic state. When it is quite set on foot we shall like very much to be annual subscribers. I assure you, Mr. Lewes and I are glad to be remembered by you in connection with good efforts.

    Always, dear Madam,

Yours sincerely
M. E. Lewes.

TO SARA HENNELL, 15 DECEMBER 1871

The first volume of John Forster's *Life of Charles Dickens* (3 vols., 1872–74), was published 4 December. GHL agreed to write an article on it for the *Fortnightly.* The portrait by Daniel Maclise, painted in 1839, shows Dickens seated in a richly decorated chair, pen in hand, preparing to write. Others who knew him at this time thought it a good likeness. Forster attacked GHL's article violently in Volume III. [V, 226–27]

The Priory, | 21. North Bank, | Regents Park.
December 15. 71.

My dear Sara . . .

If you have not yet fallen in with Dicken's Life, be on the lookout for it, because of the interest there is in his boyish experience and also in his rapid development during his first travels in America. The book is ill-organized, and stuffed with criticism and other matter which would be better in limbo; but the information about the childhood, and the letters from America make it worth reading. We have just got a photo of Dickens taken when he was writing or had just written David Copperfield—satisfactory refutation of that keepsakey, impossible face which Maclise gave him and which has been engraved for the Life in all its odious ⟨namby-pambyness⟩ beautification. This photograph is the young Dickens corresponding to the older Dickens whom I knew—the same face without the unusually severe wear and tear of years which his latest looks exhibited. . . .

    Always, dear Sara

Your loving friend
Pollian.

TO FREDERICK LOCKER, 16 DECEMBER 1871

The widening of GE's social circle as her fame increased appears in the invitation to dine at Lockers with his wife Lady Charlotte (a daughter of the Earl of Elgin), their daughter Elinor, and Dean Arthur Stanley and his wife Lady Augusta. Mrs. Tollemache, whom GE had not met, called at the Priory a few weeks later. [V, 227]

The Priory, | 21. North Bank, | Regents Park.
December 16. 71.

Dear Mr. Locker

Pray thank Mrs. Tollemache on my behalf for her kind gift. I read a long way in "Spanish Towns and Spanish Pictures" immediately on opening the cover, led on by the fascination which the subject always has for me.

Some day, I hope, we shall go to Spain again along the route taken by Mrs. Tollemache, and carry her book with us. We have not yet seen Burgos and the north-western towns. Our course was from San Sebastian to Saragossa and Barcelona, then southward; and we returned from Seville to Madrid. After the pleasant introduction this book gives me to Mrs. Tollemache I shall think agreeably of the possibility that I may make her personal acquaintance.

Your cares about Lady Charlotte are such as I can enter into with much fellow-feeling. We pay a heavy price in anxiety for the blessedness of loving. Our evening which gave me a little vision of her will always be a memory that I shall like to recal. Do not forget us, and believe me

Always sincerely yours
M. E. Lewes.

TO ALEXANDER MAIN, 28 DECEMBER 1871

Wise, Witty, and Tender Sayings, in Prose and Verse, selected from the works of George Eliot by A. Main. [V, 229]

The Priory, | 21. North Bank, | Regents Park.
December 28. 71.

Dear Mr. Main

Your gift—what gift can be more precious than the patient care which helps to save the seed of one's soul from perishing?—has come to brighten a Christmas in which my large share of good has been somewhat dimmed by bad health. One of the memorable events of this closing year to me will always be the acquisition of you as a known friend—a friend of the only sort I now desire much to acquire: one who takes into his own life the spiritual outcome of mine. Let it be a memorable year to you in this light—that you have given me a lasting source of encouragement in those often-recurring hours of despondency which, after cramping my activity ever since I began to write, continue still to beset me with, I fear, a malign influence on my writing. I don't suppose I could assure you of anything better for you to know, than that you have planted something to be a sweet shade and fruit for your elder fellow-traveller.

I have been looking through the 'Sayings' with that sort of delight which comes from seeing that another mind underlines the words one has most cared for in writing them. In one sense the book is marvellously new to me—since I had forgotten the greater part of what I had written. In another sense it is rather startlingly familiar—namely, that I find my old self (meaning my past self) very much like my present self. If there is any progress, I fear it is downhill. I think that I have not yet seen any passage which I am sorry not to have had left out, and I have confidence that I shall not be less completely satisfied with the selecting mind when I have made further acquaintance with the work. Always with gratitude

> Yours most sincerely
> M. E. Lewes.

TO WALTER WILLIAM SKEAT, [?1872]

Skeat was collecting material for his *English Dialect Dictionary* and for the *New English Dictionary*. The MS of this letter is buried among a million others in the cellars of the Oxford University Press. [IX, 39]

[London]

It must be borne in mind that my inclination to be as close as I could to the rendering of dialect, both in words and spelling, was constantly checked by the artistic duty of being generally intelligible. But for that check, I should have given a stronger colour to the dialogue in "Adam Bede," which is modelled on the talk of N. Staffordshire and the neighbouring part of Derbyshire. The spelling, being determined by my own ear alone, was necessarily a matter of anxiety, for it would be as possible to quarrel about it as about the spelling of Oriental names.

The district imagined as the scene of "Silas Marner" is in N. Warwickshire. But here, and in all my other presentations of English life, except "Adam Bede," it has been my intention to give the general physiognomy rather than a close portraiture of the provincial speech as I have heard it in the Midland or Mercian region. It is a just demand that art should keep clear of such specialities as would make it a puzzle for the larger part of its public; still, one is not bound to respect the lazy obtuseness or snobbish ignorance of people who do not care to know more of their native tongue than the vocabulary of the drawing-room and the newspaper.

TO JOHN BLACKWOOD, 18 JANUARY 1872

Blackwood wrote with genuine enthusiasm on reading Book III in proof. For the sake of quantity GE had wanted to add Chapter 34 at the end, but GHL with his sense of the melodramatic saw that it would be better to stop with the death of Featherstone after Mary Garth's refusal to burn his will. Blackwood proposed to give Main £31 10s. for his work on the *Sayings* and give GE half the copyright, but she said that she never expected any interest in the book, and GHL "assented, with less fervour." [V, 236–38]

The Priory, | 21. North Bank, | Regents Park.
January 18. 72.

My dear Mr. Blackwood

It is like your kindness to write me your encouraging impressions on reading the Third Book. I suppose it is my poor health that just now makes me think my writing duller than usual. For certainly the reception of the First Book by my old readers is quite beyond my most daring hopes. One of them, who is a great champion of Adam Bede and Romola, told Mr. Lewes yesterday that he thought Middlemarch surpassed them. All this is very wonderful to me. I am thoroughly comforted as to the half of the work which is already written—but there remains the terror about the *un*written. Mr. Lewes is much satisfied with the Fourth Book, which opens with the continuation of the Featherstone drama. I wanted for the sake of quantity, to add a chapter to the Third Book, instead of opening the Fourth with it. But Mr. Lewes objects on the ground of effectiveness. . . .

I felt something like a shudder when Sir Henry Maine asked me last Sunday whether this would not be a very long book—saying, when I told him it would be four good volumes, that that was what he had calculated. However it will not be longer than Thackeray's books, if so long. And I don't see how the sort of thing I want to do could have been done briefly. . . .

I would not for the world say anything to hurt Mr. Main, who is as keenly sensitive as I am, so that he must have no hint of my criticism, which, indeed, I would not have written to any one but you. Mr. Lewes, who caught a hoarseness yesterday, sends his regards to you dolorously. . . .

Yours always truly
M. E. Lewes.

TO JOHN BLACKWOOD, 21 FEBRUARY 1872

Book IV of *Middlemarch* was finished a few days before Book II was published, 1 February. Main's long letters to Blackwood won him the sobriquet of "The Gusher." [V, 249–50]

The Priory, | 21. North Bank, | Regents Park.
February 21. 72.

My dear Mr. Blackwood . . .

Thanks for the list of sales since February 12th. Things are encouraging and the voices that reach us are enthusiastic. But you can understand how people's interest in the book heightens my anxiety that the remainder should be up to the mark. I want to get the Fourth Book into print and shall send the M.S. when the printers are free from the magazine. It has caused me some uneasiness that the Third Part is two sheets less than the First. But Mr. Lewes insisted that the death of old Featherstone was the right point to pause at, and he cites your approbation of the Part as a proof that effectiveness is secured in spite of diminished quantity. Still it irks me to ask 5/- for a smaller amount than that already given at the same price. Perhaps I must regard the value as made up solely by effectiveness, and certainly the book will be long enough. . . .

Our good Mr. Main sent us a letter four sheets long the other day, and full of really remarkable insight into the bearing of what he reads. He is not simply rhapsodic, but likes to give a reason for his faith. Many little indications tell favourably of his nature—such as his incidental mentionings of his mother.

I am glad to hear of the pleasure Middlemarch gives in your household: that makes quite a little preliminary public for me. Mr. Lewes sends his best regards and I am always

Yours very truly

M. E. Lewes.

TO MRS. HARRIET BEECHER STOWE, 4 MARCH 1872

Mrs. Stowe sent GE her review of *Debateable Land between This World and the Next* by Robert Dale Owen, who came to Indiana in 1825 with the New Harmony commune. He had been deluded by the notorious "medium" Katie King. Mrs. Stowe promised to get his book "read by leading minds in England, particularly by Mrs. Lewes (*Adam Bede*) with whom I correspond." Daniel Douglas Home had recently convinced some notable Englishmen of his ability to be carried by spirits out one window and in another 70 feet above the ground. Early in 1872 Mrs. Samuel Guppy "materialized" live eels and lobsters and spirit "photographs." [v, 252–53]

The Priory, | 21. North Bank, | Regents Park.

March 4. 72.

Dear Friend

I can understand very easily that the two last years have been full for you of other and more imperative work than the writing of letters not absolutely demanded either by charity or business. The proof that you still think of me affectionately is very welcome now it is come, and all the more cheering because it enables me to think of you as enjoying your retreat in your orange orchard—your western Sorrento, . . . I am sure it must be a great blessing to you to bathe in that quietude—as it always is to us when we go out of reach of London influences, and have the large space of country days to study, walk, and talk in. Last year we spent our summer months in Surrey and did not leave England. Unhappily the country was not so favourable to my bodily health as to my spiritual, and on our return to town I had an illness which was the climax of the summer's malaise. That illness robbed me of two months, and I have never quite recovered a condition in which the strict duties of the day are not felt as a weight. But just now we are having some clear spring days, and I am in hope of prospering better, the sunshine being to me the greatest visible good of life—what I call the wealth of life, after love and trust.

When I am more at liberty I will certainly read Mr. Owen's books if he is good enough to send them to me. I desire on all subjects to keep an open mind, but hitherto the various phenomena reported or attested in connexion with ideas of spirit-intercourse, "psychism" and so on, have come before me here in the painful form of the lowest charlatanerie. Take Mr. Hume as an example of what I mean. I would not choose to enter a room where he held a séance. He is an object of moral disgust to me, and nothing of late reported by Mr. Crookes, Lord Lindsay, and the rest carries conviction to my mind that Mr. Hume is not simply an impostor whose professedly abnormal manifestations have varied their fashion in order to create a new market, just as if they were papier mâché wares or pommades for the idle rich. But apart from personal contact with people who get money by public exhibitions as mediums, or with semi-idiots such as those who make a court for a Mrs. Guppy or other feminine personage of that kind, I would not willingly place any barrier between my mind and any possible channel of truth affecting the human lot.

I write to you quite openly, dear friend, but very imperfectly, for my letters are always written in shreds of time, and this must only be taken as a stammering and hurried assurance that I am, and shall always be

Yours with sincere affection and gratitude
M. E. Lewes.

TO ALEXANDER MAIN, 29 MARCH [1872]

Simpson was manager of the Blackwood printing office. GE's curiosity about Main's life is characteristic. She always elicited confidence, no doubt storing it up for future use in novels. [v, 260–62]

The Priory, | 21. North Bank, | Regents Park.
Good Friday Evening.

My dear Mr. Main

The announcement of the fourth Part, Mr. Simpson tells us, was only omitted in the presentation copies, because the slip was not yet ready. My illness would not have prevented the appearance of that part, which is safely in print, and I have not been absolutely disabled. But I have been depressed and retarded by much bodily discomfort, especially during the last fortnight. . . .

Try to keep from forecast of Dorothea's lot, and that sort of construction beforehand which makes everything that actually happens a disappointment. I need not tell you that my book will not present my own feeling about human life if it produces on readers whose minds are really receptive the impression of blank melancholy and despair. I can't help wondering at the high estimate made of Middlemarch in proportion to my other books. I suppose the depressed state of my health makes my writing seem more than usually below the mark of my desires, and I am too anxious about its completion—too fearful lest the impression which it might make (I mean for the good of those who read) should turn to nought—to look at it in mental sunshine. I am very glad you like the passages you quote about Mr. Casaubon's and Caleb Garth's experience. You are right in believing that they gave me much delight while I was writing them. . . .

Some time, perhaps, you will tell us exactly how you spend your days. I like to think of your reading what you enjoy aloud to your mother. But I should like also to know what is the general web of your life—that is, if you are ever inclined to tell. I have established for myself the privilege of being the poorest correspondent in the world, so you see I am fearless in implying that I expect a great deal from you without the least intention of repaying. . . .

Yours with sincere regard
M. E. Lewes.

I was glad to hear from Edinburgh how good the sale of the "Sayings" has been.

TO MME EUGÈNE BODICHON, 4 JUNE 1872

The Leweses took possession of Elversley at Redhill 24 May. The "grand luncheon" given by Lord and Lady Houghton 15 May included Lord Acton, Mr. and Mrs. Henry Reeve, and other notables. [v, 276–77]

[Redhill] June 4. 72.

My dear Barbara . . .

We have been in our hiding place about twelve days now, and I am enjoying it more and more—getting more bodily ease and mental clearness than I have had for the last six months. Unhappily George is rather ailing, having slipped back a few degrees in the hurry and fatigue of book-packing etc. on our migration.

Our house is not in the least beautiful, but it is well-situated and comfortable, perfectly still in the middle of a garden surrounded by fields and meadows, and yet within reach of shops and "civilization." We managed to get to the Academy Exhibition one day before leaving town. . . . Also, we went twice to the opera in order to save ourselves from any yearnings after it when we should have settled in the country.

We have taken our house only till the end of August, and have the option of quitting it at the end of July. . . . We tell no one our address and have our letters sent on from the Priory. I have no other news to tell you. But I must say that it vexed me to miss having you with us to lunch that day when you could have come. We went to rather a grand luncheon which was not a great delight to me—and it is always something pleasanter than that to see you.

Your affectionate
Marian. . . .

TO MRS. HARRIET BEECHER STOWE, [24] JUNE 1872

Mrs. Stowe wrote lengthy descriptions of her planchette "conversations" with Charlotte Brontë's spirit, which lasted more than two hours. [v, 279–82]

[Redhill]

We too are in a country refuge, you see, and this bit of Surrey, as I dare say you know, is full of beauty of the too garden-like sort for which you pity us. How different from your lodge in the wilderness! I have read your description three or four times—it enchants me so thoroughly; and Mr Lewes is just as much enamoured of it. We shall never see it, I imagine, except in the mirror of your loving words; but thanks many and warm, dear friend, for saying that our presence would be welcome. I have always had delight in descriptions of American forests since the early days when I read [Châteaubriand's] 'Atala,' which I believe that you would criticize as half unveracious. I dwelt on the descriptions in 'Dred' with much enjoyment. . . .

Your experience with the planchette is amazing; but that the words which you found it to have written were dictated by the spirit of Charlotte Brontë is to me (whether rightly or not) so enormously improbable, that I could only accept it if every condition were laid bare, and every other explanation demonstrated to be impossible. If it were another spirit aping Charlotte Brontë—if here and there at rare spots and among people of a certain temperament, or even at many spots and among people of all temperaments, tricksy spirits are liable to rise as a sort of earth-bubbles and set furniture in movement, and tell things which we either know already or should be as well without knowing—I must frankly confess that I have but a feeble interest in these doings, feeling my life very short for the supreme and awful revelations of a more orderly and intelligible kind which I shall die with an imperfect knowledge of. If there were miserable spirits whom we could help—then I think we should pause and have patience with their trivial-mindedness; but otherwise I don't feel bound to study them more than I am bound to study the special follies of a particular phase of human society. Others, who feel differently, and are attracted towards this study, are making an experiment for us as to whether anything better than bewilderment can come of it. At present it seems to me that to rest any fundamental part of religion on such a basis is a melancholy misguidance of men's minds from the true sources of high and pure emotion. I am comforted to think that you partly agree with me there. . . .

Dear friend, how much you have lived through both in the flesh and in the spirit! My experience has been narrow compared with yours. I assure you I feel this, so do not misinterpret anything I say to you as being written in a flippant or critical spirit. One always feels the want of the voice and eyes to accompany a letter, and give it the right tone.

TO JOHN BLACKWOOD 4 AUGUST [1872]

GE read the last chapter of Book VII to GHL and sent it to Edinburgh 9 August. Blackwood agreed that it would be well to publish the two last Books in November and December instead of at two-month intervals. After Book I was published the *Spectator* declared that the "spiritual effect of her poems and stories is utterly, blankly melancholy." [V, 296–97]

Park Hill | Red Hill | August 4.

My dear Mr. Blackwood

Your letter found me in the midst of a nasty little bilious attack—a very bad employment of the time which ought to have been given to the last Part of Middlemarch. . . .

I shall send Part VII in a few days, as I wish to see it in print that I may be better able to judge of quantities. It will perhaps be desirable to make a few excisions in order to introduce a little further development and leave larger room in the last Part. Since Mr. Lewes tells me that the Spectator considers me the most melancholy of authors, it will perhaps be a welcome assurance to you that there is no unredeemed tragedy in the solution of the story.

Mr. Lewes examines the newspapers before I see them, and cuts out any criticisms which refer to me, so as to save me from these spiritual chills—though alas, he cannot save me from the physical chills which retard my work more seriously. I had hoped to have the manuscript well out of my hands before we left this place at the end of the month, but the return of my dyspeptic troubles makes me unable to reckon on such a result.

It will be a good plan, I think to quicken the publication towards the end, but we feel convinced that the slow plan of publication has been of immense advantage to the book in deepening the impression it produces. Still, I shudder a little to think what a long book it will be—not so long as Vanity Fair or Pendennis, however, according to my calculation. . . .

Always yours truly
M. E. Lewes.

TO MRS. WILLIAM CROSS, [?19 AUGUST 1872]

William Henry Bullock, husband of Elizabeth Cross, had assumed the surname Hall on succeeding to the estate of his uncle General John Hall and had moved to Six Mile Bottom, about six miles east of Cambridge. Alkie was Alexander Hall, his only son. The shooting had been let to the Prince of Wales for 1872. After several miscarriages Gertrude Lewes had given birth to a daughter Blanche, 18 July 1872. Emily and Florence were Mrs. Cross's younger daughters. "Nephew" Johnnie's paper on "Social New York" was published in *Macmillan's* in June 1872. [V, 301–02]

Park Road | Redhill | Monday Evening.

My dear Mrs. Cross

I am tired of behaving like an ungrateful wretch—making no sign in answer to affectionate words which have come to me with cheering effect. And I want to tell you and Mr. Hall (alas, for the dear old name which had such cherished associations!) that I long too much to see you all, nephew John included, at Six Mile Bottom, to give up utterly the prospect of that good. We imagine that the place is near Ipswich, which is no more than 1h. 50m. from London. If so, the journey would be easily managed and would be worth taking for the sake of one whole day and two half days with you—just as if you were the hour nearer, at Weybridge—before we set our faces towards Germany. I am not hopeless that we might do that in the second week of September, if you are not quite disgusted with the thought of me as a person who is always claiming pity for small ailments, and also if Mr. Hall can secure me against being shot from the other side of the hedge by the Prince of Wales, while we are discussing plantations.

I dare not count much on fulfilling any project, my life for the last year having been a sort of nightmare in which I have been scrambling on the slippery bank of a pool, just keeping my head above water. But I shall be the happier for having told you that I delight in the double invitation for the sake of the love it assures me of, and that I do want to see you all.

Gertrude and Charles are going to bring the Baby for us to kiss its little toes and worship, on Saturday week. I have a little comet's-tail of its hair, and what is more precious, the frequent thought that its tiny life is a great comfort to the dear mother. We could not help being painfully anxious for the last week or two before the Baby came.

You are all gloriously well, I hope—Alkie looking more and more cherubic and Emily and Florence blooming like two tall nymphs of Diana. My best love to all. Particular regards to "Johnnie," and regrets that we were not on his route from Brindisi. I read his paper on New York with much interest and satisfaction.

You are often among my imaged companions both in dreaming and waking hours and always welcome to

Yours affectionately
M. E. Lewes.

TO MRS. WILLIAM CROSS, [25 SEPTEMBER 1872]

After several overnight stops, the Leweses reached Homburg 21 September and took the whole first floor of No. 14 at only 24 florins (£2) per week. GE's impressions of the gamblers at Homburg are recollected in the opening pages of *Daniel Deronda*. Among the "rather grand" acquaintances the Leweses made were Lord and Lady Castletown and their two daughters, Mrs. Wingfield and Lady Murray. [V, 311–13]

No. 14 Obere Promenade | Homburg.

My dear Mrs. Cross

It was a delightful surprize to see your handwriting when we went to inquire at the Poste Restante. . . . We had, on the whole, a fortunate journey, and are especially grateful to Mr. Hall for suggesting the route by Trèves, where we spent two nights and an exquisite day. I was continually reminded of Rome when we were wandering in the outskirts in search of the antiquities, and the river banks are a loveliness into the bargain which Rome has not. We had even an opportunity of seeing some dissipation, for there happened to be an excellent circus where we spent our evening. The pretty country through which we passed had an additional interest for us about Libramont.

We arrived at Homburg on Saturday night and settled in these comfortable lodgings the next morning. The air, the waters, the plantations are all perfect— "only man is vile." I am not fond of denouncing my fellow-sinners, but gambling being a vice I have no mind to, it stirs my disgust even more than my pity. The sight of the dull faces bending round the gaming tables, the raking-up of the money, and the flinging of the coins towards the winners by the hard-faced croupiers, the hateful, hideous women staring at the board like stupid mono-maniacs—all this seems to me the most abject presentation of mortals grasping after something called a good that can be seen on the face of this little earth. Burglary is heroic compared with it. I get some satisfaction in looking on from the sense that the thing is going to be put down. Hell is the only right name for such places.

"Everybody" is going away, or rather gone, except a few stragglers in search of health like ourselves—and the gamblers. Nevertheless we have found acquain-tances, some rather grand, who are going away on Friday, others less grand who are also likely to go in a few days. We don't mind their departure, if the Sun will give us his company. But it was cruel to find the bitter cold just set in as we arrived. For two days we were as cold as in clear winter days at Berlin. Since then, the wind has become milder, and we are hoping that there may still be at least a fortnight, if not three weeks, of healthy dryness in this delicious spot. Damp would drive us away.

We are tolerably prosperous in health, and in sufficiently good spirits to think that we shall be better before we are worse again. There are no amusements for the evening here, and the pleasure of listening to the excellent band in the afternoons is diminished by the chilliness which makes one fear to sit down in the open air. But we like being idle, and the days pass easily.

It is good to have in our memories the two happy days at Six Mile Bottom, and the love that surrounded me and took care of me there is something very precious to believe in among hard-faced strangers. But it has vexed me to think that Mr. Hall lost his morning's shooting owing to my troublesome ailments. My best love to him and all the other young ones. George's love keeps close to mine and flies with it. Chief love to you, dear Friend, and much gratitude for the anticipated letter that will come to tell us more news of you by and by.

Always yours
M. E. Lewes.

TO JOHN BLACKWOOD, 4 OCTOBER 1872

The MS of the Finale of *Middlemarch* was sent off 2 October, and by the 8th the proof had been read and returned. GE underestimates the dramatic "Stoff" she picked up at the Kursaal: the young lady whose gambling fascinated her, Geraldine Amelia Leigh, a daughter of Byron's nephew Henry Leigh, became the germ of Gwendolen Harleth in *Daniel Deronda*. [v, 314–16]

14 Obere Promenade | Bad Homburg | October 4. 72.

My dear Mr. Blackwood . . .

On the whole we are not sorry that we came to this place rather than any other. On dry days the air is perfect, and the waters are really an enticing drink. Then there is a wood close by where we can wander in delicious privacy—which is really better than the company here, save and except a few friends whom we found at first and who have now moved off to Baden. The Kursaal is to me a Hell not only for the gambling, but for the light and heat of the gas, and we have seen enough of its monotonous hideousness. There is very little dramatic "Stoff" to be picked up by watching or listening. The saddest thing to be witnessed is the play of Miss Leigh, Byron's grand niece, who is only 26 years old, and is completely in the grasp of this mean, money-raking demon. It made me cry to see her young fresh face among the hags and brutally stupid men around her. Next year, when the gambling has vanished the place will be delightful—there is to be a subvention from government to keep up the beautiful grounds, and it is likely that there will be increase enough in the number of decent visitors to keep the town tolerably prosperous. One attraction it has above other German baths that I have seen is the abundance of pleasant apartments to be had, where one can be as peaceful as the human lot allows in a world of pianos. . . .

We brought no books with us, but have furnished our table with German books which we bought at Frankfort, from learned writing about Menschliche Sprache and Vernunft to Kotzebue's comedies, so that we have employment for the rainy hours when once our heads are clear of aches. The certainty that the weather is everywhere else bad will help our resolution to stay here till the 12th at least. In the meantime we hope to have the proof of the Finale to Middlemarch. . . .

We mean to return by Paris, and hope that the weather will not drive us away from health and pleasure seeking until the end of the month. I fear, from the accounts of your Scottish weather, that you will have enjoyed Strathtyrum less than usual and will be resigned to Edinburgh before your proper time. How one talks about the weather! It is excusable here where there is no grave occupation and no amusement, for us who don't gamble, except seeking health in walks and water drinking. Mr. Lewes unites with me in kindest regards and I am always

Yours most truly
M. E. Lewes.

TO ALEXANDER MAIN, 4 NOVEMBER 1872

[v, 323–25]

The Priory, | 21. North Bank, | Regents Park.
November 4. 72.

My dear Mr. Main . . .

Yes, we are the better—many thanks for your wish to have that assurance. . . . One healthy condition at least for me is that I have finished my book and am thoroughly at peace about it—not because I am convinced of its perfection, but because I have lived to give out what it was in me to give and have not been hindered by illness or death from making my work a whole, such as it is. When a subject has begun to grow in me I suffer terribly until it has wrought itself out— become a complete organism; and then it seems to take wing and go away from me. That thing is not to be done again—that life has been lived. I could not rest with a number of unfinished works on my mind. When they—or rather, when a conception has begun to shape itself in written words, I feel that it must go on to the end before I can be happy about it. Then I move away and look at it from a distance without any agitations. . . .

I am going now to bathe my mind in deep waters—going to read Mr. Lewes's manuscript which has been storing itself up for me, and to take up various studies which have been to sleep since I have found my strength hardly enough for "Middlemarch." I easily sink into mere absorption of what other minds have done, and should like a whole life for that alone. . . .

Yours always faithfully
M. E. Lewes.

TO SIR JAMES PAGET, 7 DECEMBER 1872

Dr. George D. Brown wrote that it was wrong to describe Lydgate with "bright, dilated eyes" from taking opium, which contracts the pupils. Paget assured her that the eyelids could be wide with excitement even though the pupils were contracted. Nevertheless, she changed the passages in the one-volume edition to read "a strange light in his eyes" and "the peculiar light in the eyes." [IX, 66]

The Priory, | 21. North Bank, | Regents Park.
December 7. 72.

My dear Sir James

Since I saw you a medical man at Ealing has written to me to express his regret that I have "blotted" the correctness of my representation on medical subjects by speaking of Lydgate's "bright dilated eyes" in such a connection as to imply that an opiate would have the effect of dilating the pupil. It is a piece of contemptible forgetfulness in me that when I wrote those passages I had not present in my mind the fact which I had read again and again—that one of the effects of opium is to contract the pupil. What I had in my imagination was the appearance in the eyes which I have often noted in men who have been taking too much alcohol, and who are in the loquacious, boastful, or quarrelsome stage. I am unhappy, as you may imagine, about this said "blot." And what I wish to ask of your goodness now is, to tell me whether you think the matter grave enough to urge my cancelling the two stereotype plates (certainly no great affair) before any more copies are struck off?

I am sure that your sympathy is large enough to take in this small trouble of mine.

Always most truly yours
M. E. Lewes.

TO JOHN WALTER CROSS, 11 DECEMBER 1872

The Leweses had long been seeking a country house where they could work quietly yet be near London. John Cross and his family suggested several. [V, 340]

The Priory, | 21. North Bank, | Regents Park.
December 11. 72.

My dear Nephew

A thousand thanks for your kind interest in our project and for the trouble you have taken in our behalf. I fear the land buying and building is likely to come to nothing and our construction to remain entirely of the aërial sort. It is so much easier to imagine other people doing wise things than to do them oneself! Practically I excel in nothing but paying twice as much as I ought for everything. On the whole, it would be better if my life could be done for me and I could look on.

However, it appears that the question of the land at Shere may remain open until we can discuss it with you at Weybridge. Certainly the possession of an acute Nephew may throw a new light on one's affairs, and there is no telling what we may not venture on with your eyes to see through.

But, oh dear, I don't like anything that is troublesome under the name of pleasure—from eating shrimps upwards. Always

Your affectionate Aunt
M. E. Lewes.

TO MRS. WILLIAM CROSS, 11 DECEMBER 1872

The Leweses spent Christmas at Weybridge with Mrs. Cross. In a copy of Vol. 1 of *Middlemarch* GE wrote: "To Mrs. Cross from her friend George Eliot in remembrance of much precious sympathy, December 1872." [IX, 68–69]

The Priory, | 21. North Bank, | Regents Park.
December 11. 72.

My dear Mrs. Cross

We shall look forward to our Christmas holiday as if London were school and Weybridge home. A London Christmas is always dreary, to me, not being in the least after that country fashion to which I was bred. Please thank Mr. Hall on our behalf for his kind partnership in your hospitality, and feel yourself spiritually kissed by our gratitude. If we have a fine morning on the 24th, George desires me to say, that we will be with you before lunch-time, but in case of rain he will console himself by doing his morning's work at home, and we will start by an afternoon train.

Yours always lovingly
M. E. Lewes.

TO MRS. MARK PATTISON, 16 DECEMBER 1872

Pattison was chairman of the committee considering redistribution of the revenues of Oxford and Cambridge. Deutsch had been growing rapidly worse with cancer. Unknown to him, his friends collected a sum of money to give him a second trip to the East. He reached Alexandria 10 January 1873. [v, 343–44]

The Priory, | 21. North Bank, | Regents Park.
December 16. 72.

My dear Mrs. Pattison

A word in answer to your letter of this morning, before I get ready to start for Hastings, whither we are going for a couple of days, to renew our faith in the sun. When I saw in the Times that the Rector had been presiding at a meeting on University Reform I hastily concluded that you were in town and looked for you at the Concert. . . .

You will be sympathetically glad to hear that I had a note from Mr. Deutsch this morning telling me that he has six months' leave to go again to the East. I have not seen him, femininely speaking, for an age—that is, for seven or eight months. But I have reason to believe that he has been struggling more and more severely under his old wretched symptoms. This journey, which is just what he longed for, gives him the best possible chance of recovery. . . .

Please offer my best regards to the Rector, and believe me, in scribbling haste

Yours always affectionately
M. E. Lewes.

TO SARA HENNELL, 20 DECEMBER 1872

Julia Smith, Mme Bodichon's aunt, used to see GE often at the Chapmans' in the Strand. Her brother Octavius Smith, founder of the Thames Bank Distillery, left his wife an annuity of £8,000, and to each of his daughters £50,000 outright, but made no mention of Julia. Blanche Lewes was christened in the Rosslyn Hill Unitarian Chapel in Hampstead. [v, 346–47]

The Priory, | 21. North Bank, | Regents Park.
December 20. 72.

My dear Sara

The other day we were at Hastings and saw an old friend of yours, Miss Julia Smith. I think you will like to hear a word about her. She is seventy-three, you know, and a very pretty old lady with just the same refined air and expression as that she had twenty years ago. She enjoys life much, says her niece, Madame Bodichon, and we saw lying about with her marks in them various books which I daresay you will recognize as a continuance of her former tastes—Greg's "Enigmas of Life" for example. I spoke to her of you, and told her that I should write to tell you that I had seen her. Between ourselves, I think it was very disgusting of her brother, Mr. Octavius Smith who left a great deal too much money to his wife and children not to make an ample provision for this Sister during her life. . . .

Tomorrow we are going to the christening (in a free Unitarian fashion) of Gertrude and Charlie's baby—Blanche Southwood Lewes. Thus the world travels onward.

Best love to all from

Your always affectionate
Pollian.

JOURNAL, 1 JANUARY 1873

[v, 357]

January 1. 1873. At the beginning of December, the eighth and last book of Middlemarch was published, the three final numbers having been published monthly. No former book of mine has been received with more enthusiasm—not even Adam Bede, and I have received many deeply affecting assurances of its influence for good on individual minds. Hardly anything could have happened to me which I could regard as a greater blessing, than the growth of my spiritual existence when my bodily existence is decaying. The merely egoistic satisfactions of fame are easily nullified by toothache, and *that* has made my chief consciousness for the last week. This morning, when I was in pain, and taking a melancholy breakfast in bed, some sweet natured creature sent a beautiful bouquet to the door for me, bound round with the written wish that "every year may be happier and happier, and that God's blessing may ever abide with the immortal author of Silas Marner." Happily my dear husband is well, and able to enjoy these things for me. That he rejoices in them is my most distinct personal pleasure in such tributes.

TO MRS. NASSAU JOHN SENIOR, 24 JANUARY 1873

The "good news" was the appointment of Mrs. Senior as the Inspector of Workhouses and Pauper Schools—the first woman to hold such a position. A public house called The Duke of Walmer, close to one of Octavia Hill's housing projects, had an obviously bad influence. Finding it impossible to get enough of her friends to buy the premises, Octavia opposed renewal of the lease, rousing great hostility. [v, 372–73]

The Priory, | 21. North Bank, | Regents Park.
January 24. 73.

Dear Friend
We had already been told something, though inaccurately, of the good news, before your letter came; and we had felt it as a New Year's gift to us. Our joy is

without misgiving, we feel sure that your work will be done well. May all blessings attend you in it, over and above the affectionate wishes of your friends, wishes which you will carry with you like a host of encouraging guardian spirits.

The influence of one woman's life on the lot of other women is getting greater and greater with the quickening spread of all influences. One likes to think, though, that two thousand years ago Euripides made Iphigenia count it a reason for facing her sacrifice bravely that thereby she might help to save Greek women (from a wrong like Helen's) in the time to come. There is no knife at your throat, happily. You have only got to be a good faithful woman such as you have always been, and then the very thought of you will help to mend things. Take it as a sign of that, when I tell you that you have entered into my more cheerful beliefs, and made them stronger, because of the glimpses I have had of your character and life. . . .

We are much interested just now in Octavia's new work of buying a public house to have it under good control. I daresay you know all about it. Please offer our best regards to Mr. Senior, and believe me, dear friend,

> Yours with sincere affection
> M. E. Lewes.

TO JOHN BLACKWOOD, 25 FEBRUARY 1873

Middlemarch was reprinted in 4 volumes from the stereotyped plates of the first edition, but only 337 copies were sold at 42/-. The Guinea edition from the same plates with a different binding at 21/- sold 2,386 copies before November, when 500 more were printed. Blackwood explained that *The Times* reserved its "Publisher's Column" for new books. Albert Cohn, manager of Asher's Collection in Berlin, paid £50 for reprinting *The Spanish Gypsy*. GE contrasted Lockhart's *Scott* with Forster's *Dickens*, the last volume of which contained a vulgar personal attack on GHL for his article on Dickens. [v, 378–79]

The Priory, | 21. North Bank, | Regents Park.
February 25. 73.

My dear Mr. Blackwood

I am much pleased with the colour and the lettering of the guinea edition, and the thinner paper makes it delightfully handy. Let us hope that some people still want to read it, since a friend of ours in one short railway bit to and fro saw two persons reading the paper-covered numbers. Now is the moment when a notice in the Times might possibly give a perceptible impulse. By the way, I should like to ask Mr. Simpson—who, I imagine, directs all the advertising—whether the non-use of the "Publishers' Column" in the Times is systematic, i.e., for well-weighed reasons? I understand thoroughly the futility of advertisements (of books) in other columns of the Times, but this front row of reserved places does seem particularly noticeable—even to me, who never make a practice of reading advertisements, and I have observed that most books of any mark make an appearance or two there. But there may be good reasons of which I know nothing.

Cohn, of Berlin, has written to ask us to allow him to reprint the Spanish Gypsy

for £50, and we have consented. Some Dresdener, who has translated poems of
Tennyson's, asked leave to translate the S. G. in 1870, but I have not heard of his
translation appearing. . . .

I have a love for Lockhart because of Scott's Life, which seems to me a perfect
biography. How different from another we know of!

Always truly yours
M. E. Lewes.

TO MRS. C. T. SIMPSON, 2 MARCH 1873

GE apologized for GHL's rudeness when on returning home he found Mrs. Simpson, a
slight acquaintance, who had called without notice, "and gave her 'a bit of my mind' ". [v,
382]

The Priory, | 21. North Bank, | Regents Park.
March 2. 73.

My dear Mrs. Simpson

Many thanks for the lovely photograph. You would have been less surprized at
Mr. Lewes's outburst the other day if you had been able to imagine what a feeble
wretch I have been this winter, and how often he has seen me overdone by weekday appointments—the "boiling over" of receptions beyond the rim of Sunday.
My friends who are kept at home on Sundays usually send me a note or card to ask
if I can see them on a particular afternoon. If at any time you think it worth while
to do so, I will let you know whether there is any obstacle of illness or incompatible engagement; and thus you will be saved a journey in vain. I hope to be less
good-for-nothing by and by. Believe me

Sincerely yours
M. E. Lewes.

TO JOHN BLACKWOOD, 14 MARCH 1873

GE's admirer wrote from San Mateo "to thank you very much for *Middlemarch*, most of all
for the last chapter," signing himself "Your humble admirer, Ralph Q. Quirk." Louisa
Stuart and Blackwood's daughter Mary with lessons in music and French were preparing for
their "coming out." The ministerial crisis was the resignation of Gladstone after his defeat
over the Irish university bill. [v, 387]

The Priory, | 21. North Bank, | Regents Park.
March 14. 73.

My dear Mr. Blackwood

This is good news about the guinea edition, but I emphatically agree with you
that it will be well to be cautious in further printing. I wish you could see a letter I
had from California the other day, apparently from a young fellow, and beginning
"Oh, you dear lady! I who have been a Fred Vincy ever so long . . . have played
vagabond and ninny ever since I knew the meaning of such terms" etc. . . .

That phrase of Miss Stuart's— "fall flat on the world"—is worth remembering. I should think it is not likely to prove prophetic, if she is at all like her cousin, whose fair piquant face remains very vividly before me. The older one gets, the more one delights in these young things, rejoicing in their joys.

The ministerial crisis interests me, though it does not bring me any practical need for thinking of it, as it does to you. I wish there were some solid, philosophical Conservative to take the reins—one who knows the true functions of stability in human affairs, and as the psalm says "would also practise what he knows."

Always yours truly
M. E. Lewes.

TO EDWARD BURNE-JONES, 20 MARCH 1873

The Leweses went on 13 March to see Burne-Jones's *Love among the Ruins* and *The Hesperides* at the Dudley Gallery. [v, 390–92]

The Priory, | 21. North Bank, | Regents Park.
March 20. 73.

Dear Mr. Burne Jones

I suppose my hesitation about writing to you to tell you of a debt I feel towards you is all vanity. If you did not know me you might think a great deal more of my judgment than it is worth and I should feel bold in that possibility. But when judgment is understood to mean simply one's own impression of delight, one ought not to shrink from making one's small offering of burnt clay because others can give gold statues.

It would be narrowness to suppose that an artist can only care for the impressions of those who know the methods of his art as well as feel its effects. Art works for all whom it can touch. And I want in gratitude to tell you that your work makes life larger and more beautiful to us—I mean that historical life of all the world in which our little personal share of her seems a mere standing room from which we can look all round, and chiefly backward. Perhaps the work has a strain of special sadness in it—perhaps a deeper sense of the tremendous outer forces which urge us than of the inner impulse towards heroic struggle and achievement—but the sadness is so inwrought with pure elevating sensibility to all that is sweet and beautiful in the story of man and in the face of the earth, that it can no more be found fault with than the sadness of midday when Pan is touchy like the rest of us. Don't you agree with me that much superfluous stuff is written on all sides about purpose in art? A nasty mind makes nasty art, whether for art or any other sake. And a meagre mind will bring forth what is meagre. And some effect in determining other minds there must be according to the degree of nobleness or meanness in the selection made by the artist's soul.

Your work impresses me with the happy sense of noble selection and of power determined by refined sympathy. That is why I wanted to thank you in writing, since lip-homage has fallen into disrepute. I can't help liking to tell you a sign that my delight must have taken a little bit of the same curve as yours. Looking, àpropos of your picture, into the Iphigenia in Aulis to read the chorus you know of, I found my blue pencil marks made seven years ago (and gone into that forgetfulness which makes my mind seem very large and empty)—blue pencil marks made against the dance-loving Kithara and the footsteps of the Muses and the Nereids dancing on the shining sands. I was pleased to see that my mind had been touched in a dumb way by what has touched yours to fine utterance.

Always yours faithfully
M. E. Lewes. . . .

TO FRANÇOIS D'ALBERT DURADE, 21 MARCH 1873

Though GE continued her resolute reading, she made occasional exceptions to her rule against dining out, now that her fame was recognized and the irregularity of her relation with Lewes ignored. [v, 392–93]

The Priory | 21 North Bank | Regent's Park | March 21. 1873.
My dear Friend . . .
No wonder you have little time for reading, with your life of devotedness to the small needs of others. It always requires some severity of resolution to keep up a course of orderly study, even when the solicitations are no more than those of ordinary society. I can only maintain some repose and intellectual self-possession by making a rule never to pay visits, never to return calls, or go out to dinners. Without that rule all my happiness would be absorbed by futile or rather hurtful occupation with the outsides of social life. As it is, I am compelled to see so many people and with the utmost chariness of correspondence to write so many notes that I always long for that retirement into the country which gives us long days of our sweet semi-solitude. . . .
How long it seems, dear Friend, since we walked together in the old and now vanished walks on the fortifications at Geneva. I had no bright hopes about my life then. But your affectionate heart will delight—has already delighted in the good that has been given to me—and more in that chief gift of having one's life felt to be of some value by others. For the direct personal joy of living can never be intense with me, though it is stronger now than when I was young.
I fall into this egotism because I am recalling old times. How vividly I still see Maman's entering my room and opening her arms to greet me—my pleasant bed-room with the alcove in it, and with her painting of the Bible opened and the flowers hanging on the book. Tell her that Minnie values that memory all the more as the years deepen her impressions of the goodness shown towards her in the past. Life, I find, seems to strengthen, not wither my affections of youth with a comparatively hard unsympathetic period. I dare say Maman remembers that I was always cold and burned an unconscionable amount of wood. I can not pretend that I have reformed in that respect. . . .
Always, dear friend, yours and Maman's,

With grateful affection
M. E. Lewes.

TO CHARLES DARWIN, 31 MARCH 1873

Darwin had called several times at the Priory without his wife. He wrote: "My wife complains that she has been very badly treated and that I ought to have asked permission for her to call on you with me when we next come to London." He asked whether his daughter and son-in-law Richard Litchfield might call too. They came 6 April. [IX, 87–88]

The Priory, | 21. North Bank, | Regents Park.
March 31. 73.

My dear Mr. Darwin

We shall be very happy to see Mr. and Mrs. Litchfield on any Sunday when it is convenient to them to come to us. Our hours of reception are from 1/2 past two till six, and the earlier our friends can come to us, the more fully we are able to enjoy conversation with them.

Please do not disappoint us in the hope that you will come to us again, and bring Mrs. Darwin with you, the next time you are in town.

Yours most sincerely
M. E. Lewes.

TO ALEXANDER MAIN, 22 APRIL 1873

In an effort to help Main GHL unfortunately suggested his making a "life" of Samuel Johnson by selections from Boswell. GE's caution about quotations was evoked by Main's frequent use of extracts from her works to "brighten Boswell's pages"! [V, 404–05]

The Priory, | 21. North Bank, | Regents Park.
April 22. 73.

My dear Mr. Main

Be sure that I shall feel a strong interest in seeing how your powers exhibit themselves in this delightful task of helping to impress on men's minds the life of dear, ever-memorable Johnson. From what Mr. Lewes tells me I am very hopeful that we shall rejoice in the issue of your labours. . . .

As to quotations, please—please be very moderate, whether they come from Shakespeare or any other servant of the Muses. A quotation often makes a fine summit to a climax, especially when it comes from some elder author, or from the Bible, so that there is a certain remoteness in the English as if it came from long departed prophets who lived as citizens of the ages that were future to them and had our thoughts before we were born. But I hate a style speckled with quotations. Nevertheless I enter into what I think is your feeling, that when the consciousness is very full of a particular writer's mode of thought, it is almost a part of rectitude to avow the influence and give a precise quotation rather than melt down the edges and weld the borrowed metal into one's own. I have often, as I daresay you have, experienced a sense of repulsion from a writer who shows an eloquent memory of everything but his own indebtedness. . . .

Good bye. Keep the highest ambition, which doesn't mind worn edges to its coat, and is bent on the quality rather than the rank of its work. . . .

Yours always faithfully
M. E. Lewes.

TO EDWARD BURNE-JONES, 12 MAY 1873

After J. P. Knight resigned in April 1873, it was decided that for the first time in its history the Secretary of the Royal Academy should not be a member. GHL wrote letters to a number of members and called on Millais, Watts, Leighton, and Calderon, who all promised their votes to Pigott. GE wrote several letters in his support. [IX, 91–92]

The Priory, | 21. North Bank, | Regents Park.
May 12. 73.

Dear Friend

I am sure you will be glad to help Mr. Pigott in any way possible to you. The secretaryship of the Royal Academy is vacant, and an acquaintance of Mr. Pigott's has suggested to him to try for the post. It is resolved that *no artist* shall be appointed, and I should think that our old friend has just the requisite accomplishments for such an office. His command of French is rare, and he has a peculiar felicity in letter-writing. Then, his gentlemanly feeling and agreeable manners would make personal relations with him comparatively easy even to artists with grievances.

The prospect of such a post with £600 a year is the prospect of as much affluence, won by useful work, as he would need to give him thorough contentment and he longs very much to get a release from the sort of labour which he has been chained to for the last 13 or 14 years. It seems to me that any effort to get him into this office would be justly bestowed. If you think so too, will you speak on his behalf to artists or other influential persons whom you may judge to lie within your reach, mentally and physically.

I write in great haste in order to post the letter forthwith, as I go out.

Yours always sincerely
M. E. Lewes.

TO BENJAMIN JOWETT, 12 MAY 1873

Jowett invited the Leweses to spend the weekend of 7–9 June with him at Balliol College to meet Charles Roundell and his wife. Before this Oxford visit they went to Cambridge at the invitation of F. W. H. Myers 19–21 May. During the festivities over the boat races they met many of the young Trinity men—Henry Sidgwick, Edmund Gurney, Richard Jebb, Hallam Tennyson, one of the Balfour brothers, Alfred Lyttelton, and many others—all of whom became distinguished. [V, 408–09]

The Priory, | 21. North Bank, | Regents Park.
May 12. 73.

Dear Master

Your kind invitation is too delightful to be resisted. We rejoice to hear of that happy marriage-prospect, and I expect much pleasure in making Mrs. Roundell's acquaintance. Before the 7th we shall probably have retreated into the country, but we shall still be near enough to feel the attraction towards Oxford and be drawn thither. Will you before then kindly instruct us as to times and seasons, in order that we may make our arrangements so as not in any way to disturb yours?

Mr. Lewes, who is just now very busy, pruning his too abundant manuscript, begs me to send you his best regards. Believe me

Very truly yours
M. E. Lewes.

TO LORD HOUGHTON, 13 MAY 1873

Of the 107 applicants eight were listed, including Pigott, but in July F. A. Eaton was elected. [IX, 92–93]

The Priory, | 21. North Bank, | Regents Park.
May 13. 73.

My dear Lord Houghton

I think you know our friend Mr. Edward Pigott, for whom we have a respect founded on an acquaintance of twenty years. It has been suggested that he might possibly obtain the Secretaryship of the Royal Academy which is about to be declared vacant and which is *not* to be given to any artist or art critic.

So far as I can imagine the Duties of the office, Mr. Pigott seems to me to have just the requisite qualifications. He has a perfect command of French both for conversation and correspondence—not an ordinary accomplishment in an Englishman, as you have had reason to complain in a certain essay of yours—and I suppose that this must be a chief demand on a Secretary to the Academy with its present cosmopolitan admissions. Then, he has the sympathetic manners which would make difficult business relations easier, and his letter-writing is peculiarly felicitous. He has a fine literary sense, and in spite of fourteen years hard work at journalism, he retains his finesse of expressions and has not lost the discrimination of epithets.

If anybody asks whom he "boasts himself to be"—he is a younger son of a

Somersetshire gentleman, made a good figure at Eton and Balliol (the present master of Balliol is one of his best friends), spent some time in France, and finally coming to London bought the Leader newspaper in which he sank all the portion that fell to him as a younger son. He took this check of fortune very gracefully, put himself into heavy harness without grumbling, and has ever since been deepening the respect of his friends.

Those who know his value—and among them are some of the best people both French and English—must be heartily rejoiced at his getting a post which would give him both a comfortable maintenance and a suitable change of work. But his success of course depends on his recommendations being straightway made known to those who have the power in their hands. Every day is of importance.

If, from what you know, you believe that his appointment would be a good service to the Academy as well as to himself, will you be so kind as to write a letter to me expressing your favourable wishes on Mr. Pigott's behalf—a letter which might be put in as an informal sort of testimonal? You may possibly have knowledge which would correct my uninstructed suppositions. In that case you will consider my request to be retracted. But I make no apology for trusting in your readiness to give help wherever you can. I remain, my dear Lord Houghton

Yours very sincerely
M. E. Lewes.

TO FREDERIC HARRISON, 20 JUNE 1873

James FitzJames Stephen in his Liberty, Equality, Fraternity (1873) advocated strong central government in the Carlylean vein, grossly parodying the rationalist view. Harrison retorted in "The Religion of Inhumanity" in the Fortnightly. [v, 421–23]

The Priory, | 21. North Bank, | Regents Park.
June 20. 73.

Dear Mr. Harrison

Before receiving your note I had already gone through your article on Fitzjames Stephen's book, but I had not seen the book itself. I have a liking for him personally, and classifying men broadly as 'bad and good,' I should put him far within the borders of the good. Hence I hoped that if I saw the whole context of sentences which had set my teeth on edge when I read them as quotations, their effect might be mitigated. And I was told that he had written a remonstrance against some things said in your article. So I waited until I had read his full statement. I have now both finished his book and re-read your article, and I want to tell you that on this second, more illuminated reading, my sympathy has gone with you almost unswervingly. You are pungent, but he should remember that he has been offensively contemptuous to a large number of thinkers whom any audience in the world would regard as his peers.

I confess that I think the least excusable portions of his book are chiefly due to an inoculation of that shallow undiscriminating scorn, made to seem profound by a 'rimbombo' of rhetoric (like the singing into big jars to make demon-music in an opera) which is the disease of Carlyle's later writing. The new submission of Mr. Stephen's mind to this influence gives strange incongruities to his style. "O bubbles, love each other!" etc., etc. is a sort of question-begging which is evidently a transplantation. Raise the image of a bubble—what can be more ridiculous than fellow-feeling? The objection is, that we are not bubbles, but men and women—and it is for these rhetorical gentlemen to justify their "taste" in finding the eternal duration of their neighbour an indispensable reason for feeling kindly towards him.

There is a great deal in the book which, according to my lights, seems to me wise and wholesome—and you express your own agreement with the parts to which I refer. But (excepting perhaps the paragraph where you do not seem to allow enough for the terrible difficulty of limits which besets us in all moral questions, the ¶ on p. 693—"By insisting" etc.) I think that your criticism is thoroughly justified both in matter and tone.

I do not mean all this in the presumptuous sense of delivering a judgment, but simply in the sense of expressing my fellow-feeling. And the concluding statements from pp. 694 to 699 is what one desires to see put in various forms—a statement which embraces and explains faiths, instead of simply contending against them.

Please offer my kind regards to your wife and believe me

Always yours truly
M. E. Lewes.

We start for the continent immediately and shall be away for two months.

12

THE LAST NOVEL
Daniel Deronda

Though she had said that there was "little dramatic 'Stoff'" to be picked up at Homburg, GE's recollection of Geraldine Leigh, Byron's grandniece, at the gambling table, provided her with the opening chapter of *Daniel Deronda*. Much of her knowledge of the orthodox Jewish element depicted in Mordecai came from her friend Emanuel Deutsch, who had given her lessons in Hebrew and after long suffering from cancer died in May 1873, just as she was beginning to plan the novel. Julius Klesmer, the brusque musician—"German, Slav, and Semite"— whose Jewishness is an important part of GE's argument, was drawn from her acquaintance with young Anton Rubinstein at Weimar in 1854. The Leweses' holiday in Germany during the summer of 1873 was devoted to collecting materials. At Frankfort GHL bought "books on Jewish subjects" for her and made inquiries. They stayed over till Friday so that she might go to the synagogue as Daniel does. At Homburg again, and again at Mainz, where Daniel received his grandfather's papers, the Leweses went to the synagogues to study the congregations and hear the singing. Back in London GE filled notebooks with extracts of Jewish lore. Aware that the theme would be unpopular, she did not mention it in writing to Blackwood that she was "simmering towards another book."

The first sketches were written in January 1874, and during the summer in the quiet of Earlswood Common a "thick slice of manuscript" was finished. The summer of 1875 was spent similarly at Rickmansworth, where the work went more rapidly. In October Books I–IV were printed, the first of the eight Books, published monthly in 1876 from February to September. In June the Leweses read the last pages of proof in the Tuileries garden. After a long rest at Ragatz they returned to the Priory 1 September, the day Book VIII was published. As they expected, the Jewish part of *Daniel Deronda* proved unpopular and brought hostile reviews. But to the pioneers of Zionism the book formed a momentous landmark. Twenty years before Theodor Herzl's *Der Judenstaat* GE had there projected a heroic vision, which, according to the *Encyclopaedia Britannica* (11th ed., 1911) "gave the Jewish national spirit the strongest stimulus it had experienced since the appearance of Sabbatai Zevi" in 1666. Letters of fervent gratitude came to GE from Jews all over the world, including the Chief Rabbi, for her depiction of Jewish life. For others this was "the bad part" of the book; as late as 1948 F. R. Leavis wrote "there *is* nothing to do but cut it away." Sounder critics soon showed the unity of GE's novel. Some rank it higher than *Middlemarch*.

TO MRS. WILLIAM CROSS, 8 SEPTEMBER 1873

The "trouble" was the death of Mrs. Cross's sister of cholera at Salzburg. [v, 433–34]

Blackbrook | Bickley | Kent | September 8. 73.

My dear Mrs. Cross

Just before leaving town we heard from Mr. Pigott an imperfect account of trouble which had befallen you and yours since our parting from you. In my ignorance of details I am afraid to say more than that we bear you all in our hearts and shall think it kind if you will let us hear directly from you.

We got home at the end of August and came down here on Friday. I imagine that you too are among the fields (at Six Mile) and probably more contented than we are with this cold beginning of Autumn. I long to know that you and "the children" are in good health amidst all vicissitudes, for any grievous darkness in your lives would make a shadow in mine.

We wandered quite away from our plan in our travels, and after Fontainebleau went to no one place which we had set down as a goal. Among the happy thoughts I carried with me were the sweet parting words sent to me in a letter from my nephew Johnnie. I will not tell you of any calamities—they were all due to the imperfections of the fleshly tabernacle considered as a vehicle to travel in, and fell rather unfairly on my husband. He unites with me in best love to all.

Faithfully and affectionately yours
M. E. Lewes.

TO MRS. WILLIAM CROSS, 17 SEPTEMBER [1873]

GHL was far from contented with the house. He found it "wretchedly provided with necessaries—not a blanket nor a brush—and most of the things broken or dilapidated." He resolved to change the year's lease. [v, 435–36]

Blackbrook | Bickley, Kent | September 17.

Thanks, dear friend, for the difficult exertion you gave to the telling of what I so much wished to know—the details of the trouble which you have all had to go through either directly or sympathetically. I almost think *your* trial was the worst, when you had no telegram and were uncertain about Eleanor and Emily. But I will not dwell now on what it cost you, I fear, too much pain to recall so as to give me the vivid impressions I felt in reading your letter. The great practical result of such trouble is to make us all more tender to each other—this is a world in which we must pay heavy prices for love, as you know by experience much deeper than mine. . . .

As to our house, spite of beautiful lawn, tall trees, fine kitchen garden, and good invigorating air, we have already made up our minds that it will not do for our home. The house is old and cold and wants rebuilding—in fact is too much like our own bodies. And, as usual, we were too precipitate in our conclusions about practical matters—engaging ourselves without due examination into facts. When we saw the house it was inhabited by a family who had taken it for three months and had brought down some waggon loads of furniture. We imagined that this abundant furniture belonged to the house, and have gone through the disillusion of finding it comparatively bare. Still there is nothing to complain of very bitterly. We have many things to enjoy and the weather is to be grieved over for the sake of the nation and not for our private sakes. We shall not probably remain here longer than to the end of October.

My motherly love to all such young ones as may be around you, from Mr. Hall to Florence, and from Florence to Alkie. I do not disturb George in order to ask for messages from him, being sure that his love goes with mine. Ever, dear Friend

Yours affectionately
M. E. Lewes.

TO MRS. ELMA STUART, 17 SEPTEMBER 1873

Since 1870 Mrs. Stuart had been sending GE presents, mostly of her own making. She had been invited to lunch to meet GE for the first time. [v, 437–38]

Blackbrook | Bickley | Kent | September 17. 73.

My dear Mrs. Stuart

The lovely shawl is come in safety. I suppose that Wordsworth would have rebuked me for calling a shawl 'lovely.' But I think the word is allowable in this case, where the exquisite texture seems to my imagination to hold much love in its meshes. It is really just the sort of garment I delight to wrap myself in—the utmost warmth compatible with the utmost lightness being my ideal of clothing for my feeble body. Thanks, dear Friend. You have made many pretty epochs for me since that epoch of your first letter, when, as Clotilde de Vaux said of her friend, "J'ai eu le bonheur de vous acquérir." . . .

I confess I tremble a little at the prospect of your seeing me in the flesh. At present I have the charms of a 'Yarrow Unvisited.' As to the portrait, I am not one bit like it—besides it was taken eight years ago. Imagine a first cousin of the old Dante's—rather smoke-dried—a face with lines in it that seem a map of sorrows. These portraits seen beforehand are detestable introductions, only less disadvantageous than a description given by an ardent friend to one who is neither a friend nor ardent. But it would be sad if one's books were not the best of one, seeing that they reach farther and last (it is to be hoped) longer than the personality they went out from.

I need say no more now, since we shall soon see you. Only let me thank you once more for all the sweet affection you have manifested towards me, and the valued words you have written me about your own experience so far as it has drawn your heart towards me. Such things are among my reasons for being glad that I have lived. Mr. Lewes and I are keeping a warm welcome for you. We have often observed that Solomon's wise admonition is rarely applied except by those who are the least in danger of being wearisome. The real bore, alas, never dreads boring you. In expectation

Yours maternally
M. E. Lewes.

TO JOHN BLACKWOOD, 19 SEPTEMBER 1873

Blackwood had proposed an edition on paper the same size as that of the 2-volume *Felix Holt*, with a vignette by Birket Foster engraved in steel for an added title page. He offered £50 honorarium for the first 2,000 copies and 1/6 per copy for every copy sold at 7/6 beyond that. The binding was in plum-colored cloth. The title page read: "New Edition—Complete in One Volume." W. L. Collins, who had reviewed *Middlemarch* for *Maga*, wrote that he was moving to a new living actually called Lowick, [near Thrapston, Huntingdon] "where of course I shall carry out all Dorothea's theories, and cherish a tender recollection of Mr. Casaubon, of whom, you remember, I did not think so badly." [v, 441–42]

Blackbrook | Bickley | Kent | September 19. 1873.

My dear Mr. Blackwood

I quite assent to your proposal that there should be a new edition of 'Middlemarch' in one volume at 7/6—to be prepared at once, but not published too precipitately. Mr. Lewes thinks that such an edition as you describe would be likely to answer, if one could make the public well aware of it. I like your project of an illustration. And the financial arrangements you mention are quite acceptable to me. For one reason especially I am delighted that the book is going to be reprinted—namely, *that I can see the proof-sheets and make corrections.* Pray give orders that the sheets be sent to me. I should like the binding to be of a rich sober colour, with very plain Roman lettering. It might be called a 'revised edition.'

Thanks for the extract from Mr. Collins's letter. I did not know that there was really a Lowick, in a midland county too. Mr. Collins has my gratitude for feeling some regard towards Mr. Casaubon, in whose life *I* lived with much sympathy. When I was at Oxford in May, two ladies came up to me after dinner: one said, "How could you let Dorothea marry *that* Casaubon?" The other: "O I understand her doing that; but why did you let her marry the other fellow, whom I cannot bear?" Thus, two "ardent admirers" wished that the book had been quite different from what it is.

I wonder whether you have abandoned—as you seemed to agree that it would be wise to do—the project of bringing out my other books in a cheaper form than the present 3/6—which, if it were not for the blemish of the figure illustrations, would be as pretty an edition as could be, and perhaps as cheap as my public requires. Somehow, the cheap books that crowd the stalls are always those which look as if they were issued from Pandemonium. I cannot understand why W. H. Smith does not use his stalls for better works, when they are known to be popular. He seems not to renew his stock of your publications when the first lot has been sold—at least there is no systematic attention to the supply of the various stalls. . . .

With our united kind regards I remain

Yours very sincerely
M. E. Lewes.

TO MRS. ELMA STUART, 4 OCTOBER 1873

In his Diary 3 October 1873 GHL wrote that he "went to the station to meet Mrs. Stuart—knew her at once. She lunched and stayed with us till 4 and we accompanied her back to the station. Interesting interview." [V, 442]

Blackbrook | Bickley | Kent | October 4. 73.

My dear Elma

Here is the shabby little lock of hair. I want also to say that I love you the better for having seen you in the flesh, and shall always (for the brief time that I shall last) be with motherly interest

Your affectionate Friend
M. E. Lewes.

TO MRS. WILLIAM CROSS, 11 OCTOBER 1873

Mr. Hamilton, the owner of Blackbrook, offered to reconstruct the house, but GHL was not interested in the plan and wrote proposing to replace their year's lease by paying £10 a week, which was agreed. Henry Sidgwick, who advocated the abolition of the Cambridge religious tests for fellows, resigned his fellowship in Trinity College on conscientious grounds in 1869. His colleagues showed their respect for him by permitting him to retain his lectureship. The two tall nephews were John and William Cross. Alexander Hall's father is included among George Eliot's "Nephews." [V, 444–46]

Blackbrook | Bickley | Kent | October 11. 73.

Dear Friend . . .

We like the bits of scenery round us better and better as we get them by heart in our walks and drives. And I regret more and more our disappointment in the house which with all its defects is very pretty, and more delightfully secluded without being remote from the conveniences of the world than any place we have before thought of as a possible residence for us. But we could not make it our sole home without having a great sum of money spent on it, and after all, the result of expensive patchings would be uncertain. But these troubles of ours are of the least pitiable kind, and ought rather to be counted as indulgences if they did not cause one to waste some time and thought. . . .

Mr. Henry Sidgwick is a chief favourite of mine—one of whom his friends at Cambridge say that they always expect him to act according to a higher standard than they think of attributing to any other chief man or of imposing on themselves. "Though we kept our own fellowships without believing more than he did," one of them said to me, "we should have felt that Henry Sidgwick had fallen short if he had not renounced his." . . .

My two tall nephews have promised to come and see us next week, and through them we (you and I) shall interchange a great deal more information about each other than we can write on note-paper. . . .

I dreamed that I saw you the other night and you were looking as well as when we last parted at the railway station—your cheeks the colour of a rose-petal. I

m not hearing the contrary that
And I have some faith that my
... ...ot without an answering memo-
the other side of the wall, so I shall not
i mine, when mine goes towards you, so

Yours always
[Signature cut away.]

TO JOHN WALTER CROSS [19 OCTOBER 1873]

GE was reading intensively on the history of the Jews in preparation for *Daniel Deronda*. [v, 447–48]

Blackbrook Sunday.

My dear Nephew

The chances of conversation were against my being quite clear to you yesterday as to the cases in which it seems to me that conformity is the higher rule. What happened to be said or not said is of no consequence in any other light than that of my anxiety not to appear what I should *hate to be*—which is surely not an ignoble egoistic anxiety, but belongs to the worship of the Best.

All the great religions of the world historically considered, are rightly the objects of deep reverence and sympathy—they are the record of spiritual struggles which are the types of our own. This is to me preeminently true of Hebrewism and Christianity, on which my own youth was nourished. And in this sense I have no antagonism towards any religious belief, but a strong outflow of sympathy. Every community met to worship the highest Good (which is understood to be expressed by God) carries me along in its main current, and if there were not reasons against my following such an inclination, I should go to church or chapel constantly for the sake of the delightful emotions of fellowship which come over me in religious assemblies—the very nature of such assemblies being the recognition of a binding belief or spiritual law which is to lift us into willing obedience and save us from the slavery of unregulated passion or impulse.

And with regard to other people, it seems to me that those who have no definite conviction which constitutes a protesting faith, may often more beneficially cherish the good within them and be better members of society by a conformity based on the recognized good in the public belief, than by a non-conformity which has nothing but negatives to utter. *Not*, of course, if the conformity would be accompanied by a consciousness of hypocrisy. That is a question for the individual conscience to settle. But there is enough to be said on the different points of view from which conformity may be regarded, to hinder a ready judgment against those who continue to conform after ceasing to believe in the ordinary sense.

But with the utmost largeness of allowance for the difficulty of deciding in special cases, it must remain true that the highest lot is to have definite beliefs about which you feel that "necessity is laid upon you" to declare them, as something better which you are bound to try and give to those who have the worse.

Please put this in the fire. It is scribbled in explanation to you only, and not meant for other eyes.

Your affectionate Aunt
M. E. Lewes.

TO THOMAS CLIFFORD ALLBUTT, 1 NOVEMBER 1873

Dr. Allbutt's monograph on the use of the ophthalmoscope was published in 1871 and his pioneer papers on the effect of strain on the heart in 1870 and 1873. Richard Liebreich, an ophthalmic surgeon, called at the Priory with his wife 1 June 1873, and three days later the Leweses went to see his chairs. [v, 450–51]

The Priory, | 21. North Bank, | Regents Park.
November 1. 73.

Dear Dr. Allbutt . . .

Your suggestions about lessening the inconveniences of writing could not come to a more appreciative person. I have for the last three years taken to writing on my knees, throwing myself backward in my chair, and having a high support to my feet. It is a great relief not to bend, and in this way at least I get advantage from the longsightedness which involves the early need of glasses. Mr. Lewes is obliged to stoop close to his desk. But Dr. Liebreich condemns my arrangement as forcing up my knees too much, and he has devised a sort of semi-couch which seems to be perfection so far as the physical conditions of my writing are concerned. But how if I have nothing else worth the writing! It is in vain to get one's back and knees in the right attitude if one's mind is superannuated. Some time or other, if death does not come to silence one, there ought to be deliberate abstinence from writing—self-judgment which decides that one has no more to say. The public conscience about authorship wants quickening sadly—don't you think so? Happily for me, I have a critic at hand whom I can trust to tell me when I write what ought to be put behind the fire.

Mr. Lewes unites with me in best regards to Mrs. Allbutt and yourself. We do not despair of being in your neighbourhood again some day, and taking a glimpse of you in your new home.

Yours always warmly and sincerely,
M. E. Lewes.

TO JOHN BLACKWOOD, 5 NOVEMBER 1873

About 2,300 copies of the Guinea edition of *Middlemarch* were sold, bringing GE £570. The anonymous reviewer of Pater's *Studies in the History of the Renaissance* [Mrs. Oliphant] described the famous Conclusion as "half pitiful, half amusing, in its earnest self-persuasion and attempt to look and feel as if so many fine-sounding words must be true. . . . The book is *rococo* from beginning to end." [V, 453–55]

The Priory, | 21. North Bank, | Regents Park.
November 5. 73.

My dear Mr. Blackwood . . .

Is it not wonderful that the world can absorb so much 'Middlemarch' at a guinea the copy? I shall be glad to hear particulars, which I imagine will lead to the conclusion that the time is coming for the preparation of a 7/6 edition. I am not fond of reading proofs, but I am anxious to correct the sheets of this edition, both in relation to mistakes already standing and to prevent the accumulation of others in the reprinting.

I am slowly simmering towards another big book, but people seem so bent on giving supremacy to Middlemarch that they are sure not to like any future book so well. I had a letter from Mr. Bancroft (the American ambassador at Berlin) the other day—asking me to let him quote something with a slight change from the Sp. Gypsy—in which he says that everybody in Berlin reads Middlemarch; he had to buy 2 copies for his house, and he found the Rector of the University, a stupendous mathematician, occupied with it in the solid part of the day. I am entertaining you in this graceful way about myself, because you will be interested to know what are the chances for our literature abroad. . . .

I agreed very warmly with the remarks made by your contributor this month on Mr. Pater's book, which seems to me quite poisonous in its false principles of criticism and false conceptions of life. . . .

Mr. Lewes sends his kind regards and I am always

Yours most truly
M. E. Lewes.

TO MME EUGÉNE BODICHON, 11 NOVEMBER 1873

George James Howard, an amateur watercolourist, and his wife Rosalind, youngest daughter of Baron Stanley of Alderley, were close friends of the Burne-Joneses; they had been regular visitors at the Priory since 1869. "It is like being in fairy land to inhabit this solitary old castle on the sea-shore," Mrs. Burne-Jones wrote to GE. In 1889, when Howard succeeded his uncle as 9th Earl of Carlisle, they lived in the more wonderful Castle Howard in Yorkshire. Mill's extravagant praise of his wife in the *Autobiography* (1873) is found also on their tombstone in Avignon. Their love affair of more than twenty years was one of the great scandals of the century. [V, 457–58]

The Priory, | 21. North Bank, | Regents Park.
November 11. 73.

My dear Barbara

Glad to hear at last that you have arrived safely in Algiers. I imagined that you must have got there long ago. It is at least something to sing a Jubilate over, that *one* crossing is done. . . .

We have seen few people at present. The George Howards are come from a delicious lonely séjour in a tower of Bamborough Castle!—and he has brought many sketches home. That lodging would suit you—wouldn't it?—The castle is in the hands of trustees, who let one tower to fortunate applicants. A castle on a rock washed by the sea seems to me just a paradise for you.

We have been reading John Mill's Autobiography, like the rest of the world. The account of his early education and the presentation of his Father are admirable, but there are some pages in the latter half that one would have liked to be different.

Goodbye, dear. Send me some word how you are by and by, because I shall be anxious about you. G., I am sure, sends his love with mine—which is that of your faithful

Marian.

TO MRS. MARK PATTISON, 17 NOVEMBER 1873

Swift's metaphor had been given currency by Matthew Arnold's use of it in *Culture and Anarchy* (1869). GE's morning studies were on the history of the Jews. [V, 460–61]

The Priory, | 21. North Bank, | Regents Park.
November 17. 73.

Dear Figliuolina

There was plenty of "sweetness and light" in our country home, but not enough of more prosaic desirabilities. The house is old and needed much repairing and rebuilding. We were sorry to give it up, as we did, at the end of October. Now we are keeping eyes and ears open for any hint of another little country place that will present the antithetic conditions of "the cab-stand before and the desert behind." But we mean to keep this London nook all the same.

Glad to hear a good account of the Rector. Best regards, and congratulations that he is able to carry armour and weapons well.

We are unusually "up" in the literature of our time—have been reading aloud Max Müller's Science of Religions and Mill's Autobiography, and are in the middle of Spencer's Essays on Sociology. But in the mornings my dwelling is among the tombs, farther back than the times of the Medici.

I gather that you are in excellent health, and am glad. We are not without some venerable infirmities.

Yours affectionately
M. E. Lewes.

TO JOHN BLACKWOOD, 21 NOVEMBER 1873

The proofs GE was reading were the beginning of the 1-volume *Middlemarch*. [IX, 112]

The Priory, | 21. North Bank, | Regents Park.
November 21. 73.

My dear Mr. Blackwood . . .

I return today the corrected proofs to p. 64. Of course one cannot like the 7/6 type so well as the original spaciousness, but I see no other fault to be found with it. The page seems rather long, but the size of the proof paper causes some illusion. It is printed with admirable correctness, but I find one or two errors of print which I had allowed to pass in the first Edition, and also an important error of my pen which I am indebted to Mr. Main for pointing out. I had put (p. 50) 'any more than vanity *will help us to be* witty' instead of 'makes us witty.'

I can imagine that you get interesting letters about Parisian affairs—from Lord Lytton for example, and from Mr. Oliphant. Lord L. is one of the most delightful letter-writers I know of in these hurried penny-post days. But we have heard nothing from him for these seven months. He must be quite enough occupied with immediate claims, in a position so much more responsible than that he held at Vienna.

We are having some fine days, which I hope you are sharing. . . .

Yours always truly
M. E. Lewes.

TO MME EUGÉNE BODICHON, [?3 DECEMBER 1873]

For a more extraordinary kindness the Amberleys showed to D. A. Spalding see Ronald W. Clark, *The Life of Bertrand Russell* (New York, 1976, p. 25). The Leweses went to Brighton to see GE's niece Emily Clarke; on 19 November they called on the Peter Taylors. [V, 467]

[The Priory]

[Dear Barbara] . . .

The Amberleys are going to Egypt, and that interesting Mr. Spalding whom you may have seen here and may remember as having made some important experiments on the instinctive actions of birds (published in Macmillan) is going with them as tutor to their son. He is consumptive, and this is the reason for taking him. Pretty—is it not? . . .

We had occasion to go to Brighton a fortnight ago, and called on the Taylors. Mr. T. is apparently quite strong now and they seem very cheerfully settled.

Everyone talks of Mill's autobiography, and I think the effect of the book is good which is what I feared would not be the case when we read it at Blackbrook. I feared then that the exaggerated expressions in which he conveys his feeling about his wife would neutralize all the good that might have come from the beautiful fact of his devotion to her. Not one person to whom I have spoken on the subject has had anything but delight to express about the book. Here and there in the newspapers only I have seen something to verify my fears.

Goodnight, dear. My head is heavy, and I am going to bed. "God bless you" is a favourite word of mine too, and seems to say well what I feel.

Ever your loving
Marian.

TO MRS. LESLIE STEPHEN, 5 DECEMBER 1873

Harriet Thackeray, first wife of Leslie Stephen, came with her elder sister Anne Isabella Thackeray. On their return from Blackbrook the Leweses, with the advice of John Cross and the Druce's coachman, began to look for a carriage of their own. Laura was the Stephens' only child. [v, 468]

The Priory, | 21. North Bank, | Regents Park.
December 5. 73.

My dear Mrs. Stephen
I was much discontented to have missed seeing you and Miss Thackeray when you were kind enough to call the other day.

In case you should be inclined to the pretty action of coming to me again, I write to say that we have taken of late to the aged habit of driving more and walking less, so that we go farther and remain out a little later than we used to do. But after 1/2 past 4 we should not be out on any but a rarely exceptional occasion.

I hope that Switzerland did you all good. With best regards—reverentially including Miss Laura (see Wordsworth),

Yours always sincerely
M. E. Lewes.

TO MRS. WILLIAM CROSS, 6 DECEMBER 1873

[v, 468–69]

The Priory, | 21. North Bank, | Regents Park.
December 6. 73.

My dear Mrs. Cross
Our wish to see you after all the long months since June, added to your affectionate invitation, triumphs over our disinclination to move. So, unless something should occur to make the arrangement inconvenient to you, we will join the dear party on your hearth in the afternoon of the 24th and stay with you till the morning of the 26th.

Notwithstanding my trust in your words I feel a lingering uneasiness lest we should be excluding some one else from enjoying Christmas with you. Our unsociability does not extend to the 'lads'—only to the ladies who spoil conversation. . . .

We have gone through adventures in the purchase of the carriage, and are saving the narrative for Johnnie. His friend Dr. Andrew Clarke has been prescribing for Mr. Lewes—ordering him to renounce the coffee which has been a chief charm of life to him, but being otherwise mild in his prohibitions.

I hear with much comfort that you are better and have recovered your usual activity. Please keep well till Christmas, and then love and pet me a little, for that is always very sweet to

Your affectionate
M. E. Lewes.

TO CHARLES EDWARD APPLETON, 24 DECEMBER 1873

Appleton, who made the acquaintance of GHL through their common interest in Hegel, had been an occasional caller at the Priory since 1869, when he founded the *Academy*, which he edited until his death. GE suggested to him when he called 3 December that he try to get as a contributor Robert Lytton, who succeeded his father as 2nd Baron Lytton in January and was now in Paris as first secretary of the Embassy. [V, 473–74]

The Priory, | 21. North Bank, | Regents Park.
December 24. 73.

Private.

Dear Mr. Appleton

I would willingly help you, but in this case there is an obstacle. It is, that I have never heard from Lord Lytton since the early spring, when he asked us to go down to Knebworth, and we declined. I am not aware that anything can have arisen since then to mar the cordial friendship which had long been expressed towards us by both him and his wife. But it is in my nature and therefore in my habits never to take the initiative in any sort of intercourse with people whose conventional rank is above my own.

Lord L——'s long silence may be due simply to that pressure of occupations which must be incident to his promotion in the diplomatic service. When he was at Vienna, he was not only in a quieter, more humdrum city, but he was also in a less responsible post. This same pressure may account for his not having answered your letter, which in case of his absence would certainly be forwarded with the rest of his correspondence. He may have taken up the rule of allowing a certain number of letters to answer themselves by the fact that they have made silence significant. In this case I think you must take the silence to be significant of his indifference to your proposition. He may hold it to be incompatible with his conspicuous diplomatic position to be writing or rather printing a letter of political news or comment with his signature. I am sincerely sorry if by encouraging the notion that Lord Lytton might consent to be the contributor you need, I have caused you to waste time and trouble. But it seems clearly the wisest course now to seek some other person as a Parisian correspondent.

If you had any favourable means of communication with Lord Arthur Russell, he is likely to know more than any one else of "good" men (or women) in the line of political writing on French affairs. Your letter came just in time to catch me before our departure into the country for our Christmas Day.

Yours very truly
M. E. Lewes.

TO CHARLES EDWARD APPLETON, 5 JANUARY 1874

Lord Arthur Russell was among the dozen callers at the Priory Sunday afternoon. Mme Perronet wrote for the *Pall Mall Gazette.* [VI, 3–4]

The Priory, | 21. North Bank, | Regents Park.
January 5. 74.

Dear Mr. Appleton

I saw Lord Arthur Russell yesterday, and thinking it possible that you might not yet have made a satisfactory and permanent arrangement with a Parisian correspondent I mentioned to him the search that you had been making. He is quite disposed to help you, if he can, and he has allowed me to say to you, that if you still need a correspondent resident in Paris and not only acquainted with affairs but able to write well about them, he will be glad to receive a note from you to that effect, and will take it as a signal for immediately inquiring of the person most likely to know of any available talent such as you want. You are probably aware that Madame Perronet, Lord Arthur's mother-in-law, is one of the very best writers on political and social matters, but it appears that she is not sure of remaining in Paris and that she is no longer inclined to write. However, if you are still seeking, he is ready to do what he can in helping you.

Yours very truly
M. E. Lewes.

TO CHARLES EDWARD APPLETON, 7 JANUARY 1874

Crookes's experiments on the radiation of heat were presented to the Royal Society 11 December 1873. Ellis was publishing his *Early English Pronunciation* in parts. Müller reviewed Isaac Taylor, *The Etruscan Language;* Frances Cobbe, the *Personal Recollections of Mary Somerville;* and George Simcox, Bulwer Lytton's *The Parisians.* [VI, 4–5]

The Priory, | 21. North Bank, | Regents Park.
January 7. 74.

Dear Mr. Appleton

I must tell you that owing to a mistake of our News Agent who sent us the Architect instead of the Academy, we did not get our ordered copy until Monday, so that I wrote my last letter in ignorance of your excellent first number of which both Mr. Lewes and I think very highly. The Parisian letter is nicely done and escapes a certain offensive jauntiness which is in the usual fate of such correspondence. . . . The single paragraph on the pressure of radiation is worth more than the price of the paper to people who care about such subjects, and for tastes of another sort there is work very thoroughly done—the account of Mr. A. J. Ellis's labours, for example, and Max Müller's article. Then, Miss Cobbe and Mr. Simcox have done their criticisms very gracefully.

The particular Sunday on which Lord A. Russell will come again is incalculable, but I need not say that we shall be happy when any chance or purpose brings you among our friends. I gathered from what he said to Madame Peyronnet that her engagement with the P.M.G. was at an end.

Sincerely yours
M. E. Lewes.

TO JOHN WALTER CROSS, 12 JANUARY 1874

John and Emily Cross came to lunch with Myers at the Priory 18 January. The Leweses met him again a few days later at a spiritualist séance at the Erasmus Darwins' with the Charles Darwin family, Mrs. Bowen, and others; but as complete darkness was insisted on, the Leweses left in disgust, followed by the Charles Darwins. Myers was one of the founders of the Society for Psychical Research. Mary Cross had been overshadowed by Mr. and Mrs. Francis Cornish; he was an assistant master at Eton, she (according to the *DNB*) "a brilliant conversationalist." [VI, 6–7]

The Priory, | 21. North Bank, | Regents Park.
January 12. 74.

My dear Nephew

Just after you were gone yesterday, entered Mr. Fred. Myers of whom you may have heard us or others speak with regard and admiration. He is coming to lunch with us next Sunday (at 1/2 past 1). When Mr. Lewes asked him whom he would like to meet, he said, "Do you know the Cross's? I should like to meet some of them." Therefore—will you keep yourself free from other engagements for next Sunday, and will you beg the fair Emily to accompany you *in good time* for lunch?

I was rather miserable yesterday fearing that dear Mary had a very dull visit. My small capacity for looking after my guests is always absorbed by the least interesting persons who happen to be present, and after Mr. and Mrs. Cornish came in, I lost sight of everybody else's fortunes and could only wonder whether they were as little amused as I was. This, in confidence from your venerable aunt. With best love to all

Yours affectionately
M. E. Lewes.

TO ALEXANDER MAIN, 14 JANUARY 1874

Main sent a copy of the second edition of *Wise, Witty, and Tender Sayings in Prose and Verse* inscribed: "To Mr. and Mrs. G. H. Lewes with Alexander Main's loving devotion, Dec. 30th 1873." When he inquired about it a week later, GHL sent a rude letter reminding him that "we have had other things to do than even to look into the book!" The *Athenaeum* had already attacked the *Life and Conversations of Dr. Samuel Johnson* as "a signal example of folly and bad taste," for which GHL did not escape blame. "We cannot understand how a man of his experience came to make such a mistake." GHL's *Problems of Life and Mind* had sold well. [VI, 7–8]

> **The Priory, | 21. North Bank, | Regents Park.**
> January 14. 74.

My dear Mr. Main

On looking at the date of your kind inscription in the new edition of the "Sayings," I see December 30th—fully a fortnight ago. . . . I have just been looking through the extracts from Middlemarch which make the 'differentia' of the new edition, and I find your choice marked as usual by a keen sensibility and penetration. The only objection I see possible to urge is, that there are perhaps too many, and that the work is left too nearly in the condition of the gutted house. The book has now so goodly an embonpoint, that it gives at least this amount of cheerfulness to the probability that I shall never write another book worth extracting from, namely, that the "Sayings" will not bear any addition.

If I had not already allowed so much time to pass before thanking you for what you have done in painstaking judgment applied to Middlemarch, I should have waited to write until I could tell you my impression from your work on Johnson. But I cannot bear to delay my little sign of grateful remembrance longer, especially as I fear that you may have felt a wound from the wantonly expressed *animus* of the notice which the Anthenaeum hurled at you. Yet, you would see that there was no pretence of a judgment determined by examination of your work, and the notice may have been prompted solely by some backstairs influence of a publisher. Happily, Mr. F. Chapman, when Mr. Lewes saw him the other day, laughed at the notice and showed that his publishing withers were unwrung.

> Always yours most faithfully
> M. E. Lewes.

TO SARA HENNELL, 10 FEBRUARY 1874

GE's new pain came from kidney stone. [VI, 15–16]

> **The Priory, | 21. North Bank, | Regents Park.**
> Tuesday Evening | February 10. 74.

Dear Sara . . .

I have been almost constantly an invalid during the last seven weeks or more, and last week I had quite a new form of an ailment which Dr. Andrew Clarke is inclined to dignify with the name of lumbar neuralgia. The pain was very trying while it lasted, but happily it came on in fits and after a few hours would leave me suddenly like a cast out daemon. However, I have now been free for several days and am cheerfully hoping that the enemy will not return. . . .

Best love to all from

Your ever affectionate
Pollian.

TO JOHN BLACKWOOD, 20 FEBRUARY 1874

Sir Alexander Cockburn, Lord Chief Justice, presided at the final trial of the Tichborne claimant, who was found guilty of perjury, 28 February. Gladstone resigned again after the Liberal defeat in the general election. He had published a sample of his translation of the *Iliad* in the *Contemporary Review*, opposing the grand style in favor of the popular. The corrections in *The Spanish Gypsy* were not made until 1878. GE shared the dislike of biography that Tennyson expressed in "You Might Have Won the Poet's Name." Blackwood's nephew William had been injured in a riding accident in November. [VI, 21–23]

The Priory, | 21. North Bank, | Regents Park.
February 20. 74.

My dear Mr. Blackwood

I imagined you absorbed by the political crisis—like the rest of the world, except the Lord Chief-Justice, who must naturally have felt his summing-up deserving of more attention. I who am no believer in Salvation by Ballot, am rather tickled that the first experiment with it has turned against its adherents. And I heartily wish that with the outgoing of this ministry there might go out for ever the fashion of indulging an imbecile literary vanity in high places—as if it were not putting on a fool's cap instead of laurels for a man who has the most responsible business in the country to be turning the Shield of Achilles into doggrel of this sort—"Boötes, hight to boot the Wain."

I have been making what will almost certainly be my last corrections of the Spanish Gypsy, and that causes me to look forward with especial satisfaction to the probable exhaustion of the present edition. The corrections chiefly concern the quantity of the word Zincalo, which ought to be Zíncalo, but there are some other emendations, and altogether they make a difference to more than 70 pages. But it would still be worth while to retain the stereotypes, replacing simply the amended pages, there being about 400 in the whole book. I am sadly vexed that I did not think of having these corrections ready for the German reprint. . . .

I think I have never written to you since I wanted to tell you that I admired very much the just spirit in which the notice of Mill's Autobiography was written in the Magazine. Poor Dicken's latter years wear a melancholy aspect, do they not?—in the feverish pursuit of loud effects and money. But some of the extracts from his letters in this last volume have surprizingly more freshness and naturalness of humour than any of the letters earlier given. Still, something should be done by dispassionate criticism towards the reform of our national habits in the matter of literary biography. Is it not odious that as soon as a man is dead his desk is raked, and every insignificant memorandum which he never meant for the public, is printed for the gossiping amusement of people too idle to re-read his books? "He gave the people of his best. His worst he kept, his best he gave"—but there is a certain set, not a small one, who are titillated by the worst and indifferent to the best. I think this fashion is a disgrace to us all. It is something like the uncovering of the dead Byron's club foot. . . .

I have been ill lately, weeks of malaise having found their climax in lumbar neuralgia or something of that sort which gave fits of pain severe enough to deserve even a finer name. My writing has not been stimulated as Scott's was under circumstances of a like sort, and I have nothing to tell you securely. Please give an expression of my well-founded sympathy to Mr. William Blackwood. My experience feelingly convinces me of the hardship there must be in this. I trust I shall hear of the lameness as a departed evil.

Always yours truly
M. E. Lewes.

TO MRS. ELMA STUART, 8 MARCH 1874

GHL's Diary describes how Elma's friend Mrs. Fitzgerald stopped GE while leaving the concert Saturday, 28 February 1874, "and begged to be allowed to *kiss her hand.* This done, another younger lady did the same, declaring herself 'one of the many thousands.'" [VI, 26–27]

The Priory, | 21. North Bank, | Regents Park.
March 8. 74.

My dear daughter Elma

I must send you a few words, in spite of your considerate prohibition, to say that the pretty little book is arrived with your precious letter, which makes me very grateful—and what feeling is happier than gratitude? since it takes all the good that is given us, as the goodness of others. . . .

I should like to know something else about Mrs. Fitzgerald than that she is rich. But I am uneasy in the sense that at the moment she and her companion appealed to my attention in that pretty way, I was distracted by thoughts of the half-blind lady on my arm, and I fear that I should hardly know Mrs. F. again so as to give the sign of recognition which I owe her. . . .

Farewell, dear. Mr. Lewes is always gladdened by what you write to us, and wafts you many remembrances.

Always yours maternally
M. E. Lewes.

TO EDWARD AUGUSTUS BOND, 19 MARCH 1874

Bond, a librarian in the British Museum, was associated with Octavia Hill in many of her charities. In 1874 a group of friends without her knowledge raised a fund which freed her for the future from earning money as a teacher and left her able to devote her whole time to housing reform. The Leweses contributed £200. [VI, 31]

The Priory, | 21. North Bank, | Regents Park.
March 19. 74.

Dear Mr. Bond

Unless you can let us have the pleasure of seeing you again very soon—which would be quite the most agreeable way for me to learn anything from you—will you kindly let me know whether the plan we talked of has been making progress, and what is the amount already assured?

Sincerely yours
M. E. Lewes.

TO ALICE HELPS, 19 MARCH 1874

GE disliked shopping and welcomed the assistance of her young admirers, among them Alice Helps, the daughter of GHL's old friend Sir Arthur Helps, Clerk of the Privy Council. [VI, 32]

The Priory, | 21. North Bank, | Regents Park.
March 19. 74.

Dear ministering Spirit

I shall be still further grateful if you will order me the cloak lined with squirrel, just like your own. Why it should be dearer now than at the beginning of Winter is one of the mysteries of retail trade, with respect to which I suppose we are to be religiously unenquiring. If the cloak makes a reason for you to come again soon, I shall be doubly a gainer.

Yours always
M. E. Lewes.

TO ALICE HELPS, 31 MARCH 1874

The name not to be mentioned was perhaps that of Barbara Bodichon, whose costumes were loose and original in design. [IX, 121–22]

The Priory, | 21. North Bank, | Regents Park.
March 31. 74.

Dear Ministering Spirit

I want to write to you this morning because I have no other way of trying to let you know that your kindness still keeps me company and makes me the happier. The sweet services and signs of care for me which you call little are to me very great, and create a warm soothing climate for my rather shivering personality—

and it is the result of making other lives than your own easier which I perceive is a chief end of yours. Thinking how I came by them I shall find a spiritual as well as bodily comfort in my warm capote and cloak. But you must not, please, take any tiring trouble for my sake—only let me come into your work as an easy parenthesis.

I trust to your quick kind instinct not to mention the name of my dear friend in connection with the difficulties of my toilette. Her taste is exquisite, but all experimental beginnings are hazardous with my unlovely form, and you saw only a rough tentative representation of her design. Those sleeves which you did not like, are charming on her—or on pretty Mrs. G. Howard. She has a fairy deftness and tact—a bright-glancing wit like your own. . . .

Yours always sincerely
M. E. Lewes.

TO JOHN BLACKWOOD, 2 APRIL 1874

The Legend of Jubal and other Poems was sold at 6/-, of which GE received 1/6 per copy in royalty. In the MS the month and year of writing were later inserted after each poem, but only the year appears in print. The table of contents gives their place of first publication. [VI, 37–39]

The Priory, | 21. North Bank, | Regents Park.
April 2. 74.

My dear Mr. Blackwood

Thanks for your letter and the Revise. I should think that 1500 is a fairly hopeful number for the impression—I don't know whether you mean to prepare for stereotyping. Five shillings as the price, would have been my notion too, but I am no judge in these matters, and Mr. Lewes urges that 6/- is the regular charge for such volumes—vide, the advertisement sheets. Browning's Ring and the Book is even charged 7/- per volume. A royalty seems to us the simpler and preferable plan. If you have any grave doubts as to the propriety or wisdom of the 6/- pray mention them.

When I return the Revise I will write to Mr. Simpson about some points important to be attended to. But perhaps I had better say now that I wish to restore the dates of the poems—*not* the months, but simply the years. And I will put the statement about the reprints in the Table of Contents.

We hope to make our migration into the country at the end of May, but not before, and I am very glad to hear that you will come at a time when you will have no trouble to get to us. That you should have had any pleasure in my poems gives *me* pleasure. I know you always mean what you say about such things.

Yours always truly
M. E. Lewes.

Mr. Lewes has just come up to say that he has gone through the Revise, since I finished reading it, so that he is going to despatch it by post. I wished to beg Mr.

Simpson to attend to certain details, namely, that full stops should not be left where I have marked commas. For some reason or other (probably of a mechanical kind) the printers have constantly made this mistake in printing verse, and in the Spanish Gypsy there are numerous cases. Also, I beg him kindly to compare my corrections himself, as there are various important mistakes in the Revise— chiefly left by my own oversight. The indenting of the final couplets in "Brother and Sister" will make an improvement, and is always done in the Shakespearian sonnet.

TO GEORGE SIMPSON, 25 APRIL 1874

Simpson, Blackwood's printer, had designed the book quite differently from GE's original plan, but she saw that his taste was better than hers. The erratum slip, correcting "songs" to "hugs" in the seventh "Brother and Sister" sonnet, was inserted just after the Table of Contents. [VI, 42]

The Priory, | 21. North Bank, | Regents Park.
April 25. 74.

Dear Mr. Simpson

I am thoroughly satisfied with the red cover which I now return. That sober red, the tone of fine Russia, is a favourite with me, and I should be glad to have all my books put into that colour. I agree with you that it is not desirable to pare off the front edges. You rightly conjecture that my Keats is bound, and I see that a copy in boards pared down to the same size would make a miserable figure when it came to be bound. Is the paper quite as good as that you generally use for poems? That used in the cheaper edition of the Spanish Gypsy seems to me much nicer, and has a creamy tint which I think specially desirable. But I suppose it is too late to make that remark now. The volume looks poorer than I expected, and in my opinion it would be hideously high-priced at 6/-. But I leave that point to be settled by Mr. Lewes and Mr. Blackwood.

The *erratum* is just what it should be. The page is a pretty one, and the printing seems to have been very carefully managed. It is only the dead-white paper that I am rather down-at-heart about. It is the first time I ever thought your choice of paper otherwise than handsome.

Yours sincerely
M. E. Lewes.

TO MRS. WILLIAM GRIFFITHS, 9 MAY 1874

Edith Evans, eldest daughter of Isaac Evans, with some daring defied the family taboo and called with her husband at the Priory 9 April 1874. The Leweses then drove them to the South Kensington Museum. Griffiths was Vicar of St. Nicholas, Birmingham. The College for the Poor was the workhouse in Chilvers Coton built by Sir Roger Newdigate in 1800. [VI, 45–46]

The Priory, | 21. North Bank, | Regents Park.
May 9. 74.

My dear Niece

Many thanks for the photographs which I am delighted to have. Dear old Griff still smiles at me with a face which is more like than unlike its former self, and I seem to feel the air through the window of the attic above the drawing room, from which when a little girl, I often looked towards the distant view of the Coton 'College'—thinking the view rather sublime.

The return of the bitter winds has made me ill and we are longing for our retreat to the country which is not to happen till the end of the month. Town, with its necessity of receiving numerous visitors, soon becomes a weariness to my country-bred nature, and with the first hour of stillness among the fields and lanes and commons I get a delicious sense of repose and refreshment.

I will ask Mr. Lewes about the possibility of sending his carte de visite. I am sure he will send it at your request if he happens to have a copy remaining. With best remembrances to Mr. Griffiths,

Yours always affectionately
M. E. Lewes.

TO MRS. NASSAU JOHN SENIOR, [MAY 1874]

Mrs. Senior's "Education of Girls in Pauper Schools," a long article of more than 80 pages, published in *Parliamentary Reports: Education* in 1874, urged the superiority of foster care over the institutional system. [VI, 46–47]

The Priory, | 21. North Bank, | Regents Park.

Dear Friend

I think your report is admirable for fullness, clearness, and wisdom of suggestion. But I can understand how the pointing out of evils under a system may be regarded by officials as an "attack," and that as the old professor considered Sir Humphrey Davy "a verra troublesome fellow" in chemistry, so a clear-eyed ardent practical woman may be found very troublesome as an inspector.

I confess that the Report deepens my sad conviction that the whole Poor Law System is an evil to be got rid of as soon as possible rather than developed. And on this ground it would seem to me an unspeakable advantage if you could evoke voluntary work quite independently of the Government organization. But though I saw a great deal of the Poor in my early youth, I have been for so many years aloof from all practical experience in relation to them that I am conscious of my incompetence to judge how far it would be wise to use existing arrangements rather than to try and supersede them. I have a dreadfully distinct vision of that typical pauper girl whom you describe—"stubborn, apathetic, capable of violence." And I am not sure that she would be a better mother or sister of the race than one who would be usually ranked as more vicious but who would have a more human sort of passion in her.

I enter so heartily into what you say about the superiority of that home education which calls out the emotions in connection with all the common needs of life, and creates that interest in means and results which is the chief part of cleverness. That is a pregnant little paragraph in which you mention "the germs of all valuable qualities."

Do what one will with a pauper system it remains a huge system of vitiation, introducing the principle of communistic provision instead of provision through individual, personal responsibility and activity. But what evil can be got rid of on a sudden? Only it makes a difference when the evil is recognized as an evil, because then the action is adjusted to gradual disappearance instead of contemplated permanence. And you have very firmly and clearly expressed your recognition of the whole Poor Law System as an unhappy heritage which we have to hinder as far as possible from descending to future generations. Perhaps that is part of your "attack"?

I am chatting with you to please myself—not with the notion of saying anything that you don't already know better than I. My chat is just an outflow of the strong interest your Report has excited in me.

M. E. L.

TO MRS. WILLIAM CROSS, [26 MAY 1874]

On 2 June the Leweses took possession of a house at Earlswood Common, where GE could work undisturbed on *Daniel Deronda*. "I hope there," she wrote in her Journal, "to get deep shafts sunk in my prose book." John Blackwood, who called on them a week before, reported that they were "looking wonderfully well. . . . Her new novel is actually on the stocks, and Lewes thinks she is nearing the point when her doubts, which oppress her so dreadfully at starting, will disappear and she will go full swing at it." Their final week in London included an afternoon musicale at Lady Colville's, a concert by the Grenadier Band, and an evening at the French Play with Mme Bodichon, after which they walked home and "ate supper with appetite." The Crosses came to lunch. [VI, 50–51]

The Priory, | 21. North Bank, | Regents Park.
Tuesday Evening.

My dear Mrs. Cross

Alas, we have no time for anything this week except leaving undone what we want to do. We can see no part of a day on which we could get to you to have a parting kiss. But is that pleasure forbidden to us on another arrangement? Would it be too toilsome for you to come and lunch with us on Sunday—you and my nephew Johnnie? That would be a delight to us, but I know that it is a great exertion to ask from you. I have faith that you will give us this pleasure if you can do so without tasking yourself in any way, which you understand would be a grief to me.

We have an engagement for tomorrow afternoon, on Thursday we expect visitors, on Friday we go to the theatre, and Saturday we must if possible keep open for little preparations towards departure. Thus, you see, we have no choice but necessity to follow in giving up a journey to Weybridge.

Anyhow—whether you can come to us or not—you are with us very effectively in our memory and love. Mr. Lewes is gone to bed, but you believe in his affection without the testimony of a message. Greetings to all my family from

Yours ever affectionately
M. E. Lewes.

TO MRS. CHARLES BRAY, 29 MAY 1874

Mrs. Bray, having failed to interest any publisher in her *Paul Bradley*, was planning to pay for its printing out of the £50 that GE had given her. [VI, 52]

The Priory, | 21. North Bank, | Regents Park.
May 29. 74.

My dear Cara

You must not *please* grieve me by applying any of the £50 which you earned by writing Paul Bradley to what it was never intended for. The plan of printing it is good, but you must let me pay for it as my contribution towards the good ends of your Society for the Prevention of Cruelty to (or the protection of) Animals. I have faith in your affection for me, that you will not set up any difficulty in the way of my doing this small quota towards what you are working for.

We start for our country Hermitage—The Cottage, Earlswood Common—on Tuesday next. We take all our servants else I would have asked you whether you could have made use of our house during any part of your stay in town. But the people in charge are not such as would "do for you." With best love to all,

Your faithfully affectionate
Marian.

TO JAMES THOMSON, 30 MAY 1874

In reply to GE's letter Thomson wrote that he had ventured to send her a copy of *The City of Dreadful Night* "(as I ventured to send another to Mr. Carlyle) because I have always read, whether rightly or wrongly, through all the manifold beauty and delightfulness of your works, a character and an intellectual destiny akin to those of that grand and awful Melancholy of Albrecht Dürer which dominates the City of my poem." It had been published serially in the *National Reformer.* [VI, 53, 60–61]

The Priory, | 21. North Bank, | Regents Park.
May 30. 74.

Dear Poet

I cannot rest satisfied without telling you that my mind responds with admiration to the distinct vision and grand utterance in the poem which you have been so good as to send me.

Also, I trust that an intellect informed by so much passionate energy as yours will soon give us more heroic strains with a wider embrace of human fellowship in them—such as will be to the labourers of the world what the odes of Tyrtaeus were to the Spartans, thrilling them with the sublimity of the social order and the courage of resistance to all that would dissolve it. To accept life and write much fine poetry, is to take a very large share in the quantum of human good, and seems to draw with it necessarily some recognition, affectionate and even joyful, of the manifold willing labours which have made such a lot possible.

Yours sincerely,
M. E. Lewes.

TO MRS. WILLIAM CROSS, 14 JUNE 1874

All her life GE was sensitive to the cold; the delight Charles Kingsley felt in his "Ode to the North-East Wind" was not for her. The search for a permanent country house went on all summer—at Reigate, Dorking, Burstow, Croydon, and Penshurst—guided by John Cross. [VI, 55–56]

The Cottage | Earlswood Common | June 14. 74.
My dear Mrs. Cross

I have so much trust in your love for us that I feel sure you will like to know of our happiness in the secure peace of the country, and the good we already experience in soul and body from the sweet breezes over hill and common, the delicious silence, and the unbroken spaces of the day. Just now the chill east wind has brought a little check to our pleasure in our long afternoon drives, and I could wish that Canon Kingsley and his fellow-worshippers of that harsh divinity could have it reserved entirely for themselves as a tribal god. But we live in hope that the kindlier air which we revelled in for the first week after our arrival will by and by return. Meanwhile I am wearing winter clothing in the middle of June. Perhaps our wide common, which we delight in, gives us an extra share of breeze.

We think this neighbourhood so lovely that I must beg you to tell my nephew

Johnnie we are in danger of settling here unless he makes haste to find us a house in your "country-side." . . .

I confess that my chief motive for writing about ourselves is to earn some news of you, which will not be denied me by one or other of the dear pairs of hands always ready to do a kindness. I hear the dishes rattling for luncheon, which will be the sweeter that we have not to receive Sunday visitors after it. Our Sunday is really a Sabbath now—a day of thorough peace. But I shall get hungry for a sight of some of the Sunday visitors before the end of September. I include all my family in a spiritual embrace and am

Always yours lovingly
M. E. Lewes.

TO JOHN BLACKWOOD, 16 JUNE 1874

Blackwood was staying in London with Mrs. Blackwood and Mary. Comte de MacMahon, a royalist sympathizer, was elected President in 1873; but for the intransigence of Henri, Comte de Chambord, France might have become a monarchy again. The Scotch lady was Elma Stuart who came to lunch 8 June with her son Roland. [VI, 56–58]. He wrote of GE: "Her voice can only be compared with that of Sarah Bernhardt—in her melting moods: its tones were so low and soft, and at the same time so musical, that once heard it could never be forgotten; but above all it was her eyes which impressed you—and she possessed that magnetic power of looking down into your soul and of drawing you out and making you speak of yourself—at the same time giving you the impression that she was deeply interested in your doings and all that concerned you." (*Letters from George Eliot to Elma Stuart* [1909], p. 22.)

The Cottage | Earlswood Common | June 16. 74.

My dear Mr. Blackwood

I had imagined you back at Strathtyrum, but I take your stay in London as a pleasant sign that you are finding much enjoyment there, if not of a direct at least of a fatherly sympathetic sort. We on the other hand are revelling in the peace of the country and have no drawback to our delight except the cold winds which have forced us to put on winter clothing for the last four or five days. . . . We have been hunting about for a permanent country home in the neighbourhood, but no house is so difficult to get as one which has at once seclusion and convenience of position, which is neither of the suburban villa style nor of the grand Hall and Castle dimensions. . . .

Paris—a melancholy word! The restoration of the Empire which is a threatening possibility seems to me a degrading issue. In the restoration of the Monarchy I should have found something to rejoice at, but the traditions of the Empire, both first and second, seem to my sentiment bad. Some form of military despotism must be as you say the only solution where no one political party knows how to behave itself. The American pattern is certainly being accepted as to Senatorial manners. I daresay you have been to Knebworth and talked over French matters with Lord Lytton. We are grieved to hear from him but a poor account of sweet Lady Lytton's health and spirits. She is to me one of the most charming types of womanliness, and I long for her to have all a woman's best blessings. . . .

We have had a Scotch lady (from Brittany) to see us on her way to Scotland, but otherwise our quiet has been uninterrupted, and we mean to give no invitations to London friends desirous of change. We are selfishly bent on dual solitude.

Always yours truly
M. E. Lewes.

TO MRS. MARK PATTISON, 3 JULY 1874

Grasshoppers stand for *burdens* (Ecclesiastes 12:5). Mark Pattison was reading the proofs for his *Isaac Casaubon, 1559–1614.* Earlswood Common was the site of a large Asylum for Idiots. [VI, 66]

The Cottage | Earlswood Common | July 3. 74.

Dear Figliuolina

We retired from the world on the 2d of June and are to remain in strict religious retreat here till the end of September. Our souls and bodies are much the better for it. I waft you a kiss and a blessing. I received your pretty note, but trusted to your comprehension of silence as that of an aged person to whom the necessity of answering letters is the worst of Grasshoppers. Of course I like to receive them, so please let yourself be numbered among the loving creatures who give me in this kind, asking for nothing again. . . . I hope the Rector is dismissing his proof sheets and is as well as can be expected under these circumstances.

I was ill when I came down, but have not for a long while been so well as I am now. Mr. Lewes is gone to town on business this morning, and I am going to have a windy walk by myself. This Common, I suppose, was considered a bracing place for the idiots—which may account for my being so well here.

Faithfully and affectionately yours
M. E. L.

TO GEORGE BANCROFT, 15 JULY 1874

Edward Burlingame, editor of the new edition of the *North American Cyclopaedia,* appealed to Bancroft for facts about GE, even the date of her birth being unknown. In the English *Men of the Time* (1862) she was described as "Mary A. Evans, born about the year 1820, in the north of England." The 6th edition (1865) adds "the daughter, it is said, of a dissenting minister in Derbyshire." The 7th edition (1868) makes him "a clergyman," and in the 9th edition the legend is embroidered: "She is the daughter of a poor clergyman, but in early life was adopted by a wealthy clergyman who gave her a first-class education. When she left school . . . Mr. Herbert Spencer became her tutor and friend, and under his skilful training her mind was developed rapidly and broadly. . . . She became one of the staff of the *Westminster Review.* Here by her intimacy with Mr. John Stuart Mill and others, she became confirmed in their peculiar religious and philosophical views." For GE's denial of these statements see her letter to Elizabeth Stuart Phelps, 13 August 1875. [VI, 67–69]

The Cottage | Earlswood Common | July 15. 74.

My dear Mr. Bancroft . . .

I perceive from the few words—highly considerate words, in which you put Mr. Burlingame's proposal, that I may count on your full understanding and your discreet conveyance of what I say to you on the subject. I am thoroughly opposed in principle (quite apart from any personal reference to myself) to the system of *contemporary* biography. I think it one of the abuses of print and reading that the mass of the public will read any quantity of trivial details about a writer with whose works they are very imperfectly, if at all, acquainted. Even posthumous biography is, I think, increasingly perverted into an indulgence of this time-wasting tendency: for example, a great poet's trash, written when he was a schoolboy, trash which, if he had remembered it, he would have burnt, is brought into quite mortifying publicity at the end of half a century, and poor Dickens's small scraps of memoranda certainly meant for no eyes but his own, are raked from his desk to the amusement of the most contemptible of his readers and (I trust) to the indignation of all who respected him.

I say these things merely to indicate the point of view from which I take my objection to furnishing particulars about myself for any compendium such as our own "Men of the Time." It seems to me that just my works and the order in which they have appeared is what the part of the public which cares about me may most usefully know; and Mr. Lewes declined, on my behalf, to give any information to the editors of that work, who have had the good taste not to insert unauthenticated statements.

In reply to Miss Phelps (the author of 'Gates Ajar') who said that she desired only to know something that would better enable her to illustrate the bearing of my books in some lectures which she expected to give, I stated that I was born in Warwickshire and brought up in the Church of England—the latter point having some importance merely that my sympathetic presentation of dissenters may be understood not as a prejudice of education but as an impartial judgment. Apart from this correspondence with Miss Phelps, I believe that I have in no instance given any other reply to biographical questions than, that I decline to furnish personal information. If I ever did so, I can say without fear of its being interpreted as a hollow phrase, that a request from editors of repute transmitted so delicately through you, would be an instance that could present no obstacles, but rather, every inducement. But I prefer that not only myself, but other authors, should be more read during their lives and have their lives left unwritten till they are dead. Perhaps you may not agree with me, but I am sure you will tolerate my difference, even if you class it as an idiosyncrasy.

With best regards to Mrs. Bancroft and yourself, in which Mr. Lewes heartily joins, I remain, my dear Mr. Bancroft,

Yours most sincerely,
M. E. Lewes.

TO MME EUGÈNE BODICHON, 16 JULY 1874

When chloral was introduced as a sedative in 1869 its habit-forming quality was not known. Matilda Betham Edwards recovered and wrote voluminous trash until her death at the age of 83. The Leweses considered buying the Old Mill House at Holmwood Common but finally decided not to. [VI, 69–70]

The Cottage | Earlswood Common | July 16. 74.

Dearest Barbara . . .

Your picture of poor Miss E is deplorable. I cannot help thinking it a misfortune that she took to writing. But it seems that the only chance of her finding dignity and independence is that she should be left to extricate herself. That chlorale is a very pernicious thing to begin taking: the doctors say that women who begin with it never leave it off. . . .

And now I have two questions to ask of your benevolence. First, was there not some village near Stonehenge where you stayed the night?—nearer to Stonehenge than Amesbury?—Secondly, Do you know anything specific about Holmwood *Common* as a place of residence? It is ravishingly beautiful: is it in its higher part thoroughly unobjectionable as a site for a dwelling? I ask in reference to a house which is built on the higher part of the Common—a thick-walled substantial house, but with no high trees round it. We shall be very grateful if you will answer these questions, so far as you can, by a speedy post.

It seems that they have been having the heat of Tophet in London, whereas we have never had more than agreeable sunniness, this common being almost always breezy. And the country around us must I think, be the loveliest—of its undulating woody kind—in all England.

I remember when we were driving together last, something was said about my disposition to melancholy. I ought to have said then, but did not, that I am no longer one of those whom Dante found in a Hell-border because they had been sad under the blessed daylight. I am uniformly cheerful now—feeling the preciousness of these moments in which I still possess love and thought. . . .

G. sends his love and I am

Always your faithful
M. E. L.

TO JOHN BLACKWOOD, 8 AUGUST 1874

Between December and July 107 copies of *The Spanish Gypsy* were sold, but the many corrections were not made till 1878. The popular novels GE looked into are not named; the only books listed in GHL's Diary at this time are Jane Austen's *Mansfield Park* and *Persuasion*, which GE read aloud to him, and Trollope's *The Way We Live Now*. She met Dean Liddell at Jowett's in June 1873. [VI, 75–77]

The Cottage | Earlswood Common | August 8. 74.

My dear Mr. Blackwood

Thanks for sending me the good news. The sale of Middlemarch is wonderful out of all whooping, and considered as manifesting the impression made by the book, is more valuable than any amount of immediate distribution. I suppose there will be a new edition wanted of the Spanish Gypsy by Christmas, and I have a carefully corrected copy by me containing my final alterations, to which I desire to have the stereotype plates adjusted.

As to confidence in the work to be done I am somewhat in the condition suggested to Armgart, 'How will you bear the poise of eminence, With dread of falling?' And the other day, having a bad headache, I did what I have sometimes done before at intervals of five or six years—looked into three or four novels to see what the world was reading. The effect was paralyzing, and certainly justifies me in that abstinence from novel-reading which, I fear, makes me seem supercilious or churlish to the many persons who send me their books or ask me about their friends' books.

To be delivered from all doubts as to one's justification in writing at this stage of the world, one should have either a plentiful faith in one's own exceptionalness or a plentiful lack of money. Tennyson said to me, "Everybody writes so well now," and if the lace is only machine-made it still pushes out the hand-made, which has differences only for a fine fastidious appreciation. To write indifferently after having written well—that is, from a true, individual store which makes a special contribution—is like an eminent clergyman's spoiling his reputation by lapses and neutralizing all the good he did before. However, this is superfluous stuff to write to you. It is only a sample of the way in which depression works upon me. I am not the less grateful for all the encouragement I get.

I saw handsome Dean Liddell at Oxford. He is really a grand figure. They accuse him of being obstructive to much-needed reforms—but everybody accuses everybody else in that seat of learning. For my own part I am thankful to him for his share in 'Scott and Liddell' and his capital little Roman History. . . .

Yours always truly
M. E. Lewes.

TO MME EUGÈNE BODICHON, 23 SEPTEMBER 1874

The Leweses returned to London 24 September before taking a brief holiday in France. The 2nd volume of GHL's *The Foundations of a Creed* was published in 1875. Among the few visitors at Earlswood Common were Mrs. Congreve and her sister Mrs. Geddes, John Cross, and Lord Lytton, who spent a day and night there. GE gave £50 to Girton College. Most of the charities went to GHL's widowed sister-in-law, his own sons, and to Agnes Lewes and her children by Thornton Lewes. Phoebe Sarah Marks was the nice girl Barbara was helping. [VI, 82–83]

The Cottage | Earlswood Comm. | Sep. 23. 74

My dear Barbara . . .

Glad to hear good news of your establishment. Altogether you give me the impression that you have had a delightful summer. So have we. . . . George has got his 2d volume ready for the press, and we have had daily drives in lovely scenery, looking at the country through the changing months as one looks at a

dear face through the changing years. The children have been to us twice from
Saturday to Monday, and we have had about eight other visitors for a day or half a
day at rare intervals. Otherwise we have had uninterrupted quiet. You know we
are not social creatures, unlike you who have always the real, breathing, talking
world about you. . . .

I dare say you wonder that I have not done more for Girton. The fact is that we
have been devoting a considerable sum of late years to the help of individual needs
which are not published to the world. More and more of such needs disclose
themselves to one—old governesses and other beings having some claims through
the memory of good received in one's youth, and who could only be helped by
such special care. But you will let me know what is to be done for this nice
girl. . . .

Always your affectionate
M. E. Lewes.

TO MRS. HARRIET BEECHER STOWE, 11 NOVEMBER 1874

The "unspeakable troubles" were the accusation of Theodore Tilton that her brother the
Reverend Henry Ward Beecher had committed adultery with Mrs. Tilton. The trial began
in January 1875 and lasted six months. GE got the *Imitation of Christ* by Thomas à Kempis in
1849 and read it frequently throughout her life. [VI, 88–89]

The Priory, | 21. North Bank, | Regents Park.
November 11. 74.

My dear Friend

I feel rather disgraced by the fact that I received your last kind letter nearly two
months ago. But a brief note of mine, written immediately on hearing of you from
Mrs. Fields, must have crossed yours and the Professor's kind letters to me, and I
hope it proved to you that I love you in my heart. We were in the country then,
but soon afterwards we set out on a six weeks' journey, and we are but just settled
in our winter home.

Those unspeakable troubles in which I necessarily felt more for *you* than for any
one else concerned, are I trust, well at an end and you are enjoying a time of
peace. It was like your own sympathetic energy to be able, even while the storm
was yet hanging in your sky, to write to me about my husband's books. Will you
not agree with me that there is one comprehensive Church whose fellowship
consists in the desire to purify and ennoble human life, and where the best
members of all narrower churches may call themselves brother and sister in spite
of differences? I am writing to your dear Husband as well as to you, and in answer
to his question about Goethe, I must say, for my part, that I think he had a strain
of mysticism in his soul,—of so much mysticism as I think inevitably belongs to a
full poetic nature—I mean the delighted bathing of the soul in emotions which
overpass the outlines of definite thought. I should take the "Imitation" as a type
(it is one which your husband also mentions), but perhaps I might differ from him

in my attempt to interpret the unchangeable and universal meanings of that great book. . . .

I am decidedly among the correspondents who may exercise their friends in the virtue of giving and hoping for nothing again. Otherwise I am unprofitable. Yet believe me, dear Friends, I am always with lively memories of you

Yours affectionately
M. E. Lewes.

TO JOHN BLACKWOOD, 11 NOVEMBER 1874

By the end of 1874 GE had written about two-thirds of Volume I of *Daniel Deronda* but had planned most of the novel. [IX, 138–39]

The Priory, | 21. North Bank, | Regents Park.
November 11. 74.

My dear Mr. Blackwood

Don't despair of me. I am settled down now, and the thick slice of manuscript which had passed into the irrevocable before we left Earlswood, had been read aloud to my private critic and was immensely approved by him, I did not think it up to the mark myself, but he vows it is. . . .

Charles is a monumental reminder to us of our venerable years. He is the father of two children, wears spectacles, and has just been appointed head of a department in the P.O. with twenty men under his direction. And it seems to us but the other day when we brought him from Hofwyl looking like a crude German lad of seventeen. . . .

You are rather hard on the Master of Balliol, who is a favourite of mine. But he certainly is not a specimen of muscular Christianity. And he is wonderfully old-seeming for his years. I get on with him delightfully.

If you feel it a grievance to migrate from the country to Edinburgh, think what it is for your wretched fellow Britons who are doomed to London—a much vaster wilderness of brick and mortar without the grand breaks and outlines of Edinburgh. But I suppose that Miss Blackwood thinks the Londoners the more enviable among the doomed, and indeed I am not sure that I should like the Edinburgh life as a whole better than what we get here. As an equivalent for golf, I am going to see some tennis playing which, they tell me, is very fine, and possible as a private institution for ladies.

Always yours truly
M. E. Lewes.

TO MRS. CHARLES BRAY, 23 NOVEMBER 1874

Mrs. Salis Schwabe was interested in preventing cruelty to animals, especially in Italy. GE paid £28 10s. for the printing. [VI, 94]

The Priory, | 21. North Bank, | Regents Park.
November 23. 74.

My dear Cara

I am delighted to have the good news about the books. Especially I enjoy thinking that the little darkies in Hindustan will be the better for the work of your dear fair head.

Yes, I should like to have a proof (if it can be had in pages, for slips are too irritating) of Paul Bradley, just for the chance of getting anything done with it in Mrs. Schwabe's direction. She is not forthcoming just now, and may be in Italy for what I know, but she has a house in Clarges St. Piccadilly to which she comes from time to time, and I dare say she will show herself by and by. She is a dear benevolent widow, up to her chin in wealth, I suppose, and wanting to do good with it.

The plan of getting illustrations is a very happy one. I think, in the case of a book about animals, they will really help the moral effect by giving the children more vivid images of the creatures written about. As to the printing, that is to be paid for irrespective of proceeds or profits, and is my contribution to your Society for the protection of animals. . . .

Your always loving
Marian.

TO THE HON. MRS. HENRY PONSONBY, 10 DECEMBER 1874

A granddaughter of Earl Grey, Mary Elizabeth Bulteel (1832–1916) served as Maid of Honour to Queen Victoria until her marriage in 1861 to Henry Frederick Ponsonby, the Queen's Private Secretary. As a girl she had been an ardent Anglo-Catholic, and once thought of joining a Protestant sisterhood. Reading J. S. Mill *On Liberty* in 1859, she began to have doubts about her religion which remained all her life. George Howard brought her to call on GE 16 March 1873. She was 41 years old and had lived in Court circles all her life, but, she wrote, no Emperor or King had ever made her feel such awe as in approaching GE. "It makes me laugh now to think of the involuntary deep curtsey I greeted her with—rather to George Howard's astonishment." She came to talk privately later, having a feeling from GE's books that she had some secret which made it possible to combine sympathy for modern scientific thought with "approval for moral greatness and beauty and purity in the high ideals you would set before us." In October 1874 she wrote a 24-page letter to GE recounting her religious experience from the age of 16. [VI, 97–100]

The Priory, | 21. North Bank, | Regents Park.
December 10th, 1874.

My dear Mrs. Ponsonby,

For some days after receiving your note with the photographs and accompanying papers, I was head-achy and deferred thanking you in the hope that I might bye-and-bye be able to write something more than—mere acknowledgment.

I am deeply interested in what you have confided to me, and feel the confidence to be a strong link between us. But I fear that any such limited considerations as I could put before you, in the sort of letter which is all that I could manage to write specially to you at present, could hardly have much more efficacy than what you have found in my books, which have for their main bearing a conclusion the opposite of that in which your studies seem to have painfully imprisoned you—a conclusion without which I could not have cared to write any representation of human life—namely, that the fellowship between man and man which has been the principle of development, social and moral, is not dependent on conceptions of what is not man: and that the idea of God, so far as it has been a high spiritual influence, is the ideal of a goodness entirely human (i.e., an exaltation of the human).

Have you quite fairly represented yourself in saying that you have ceased to pity your suffering fellow-men, because you can no longer think of them, as individualities of immortal duration, in some other state of existence than this of which you know the pains and the pleasures?—that you feel less for them now you regard them as more miserable? And, on a closer examination of your feelings, should you find that you had lost all sense of quality in actions—all possibility of admiration that yearns to imitate—all keen sense of what is cruel and injurious— all belief that your conduct (and therefore the conduct of others) can have any difference of effect on the wellbeing of those immediately about you (and therefore on those far off), whether you carelessly follow your selfish moods or encourage that vision of others' needs, which is the source of justice, tenderness, sympathy in the fullest sense? I cannot believe that your strong intellect will continue to see, in the conditions of man's appearance on this planet, a destructive relation to your sympathy: this seems to me equivalent to saying that you care no longer for colour, now you know the laws of the spectrum.

As to the necessary combinations through which life is manifested, and which seem to present themselves to you as a hideous fatalism, which ought logically to petrify your volition—have they, in fact, any such influence on your ordinary course of action in the primary affairs of your existence as a human, social, domestic creature? And if they don't hinder you from taking measures for a bath, without which you know you cannot secure the delicate cleanliness which is your second nature, why should they hinder you from a line of resolve in a higher strain of duty to your ideal, both for yourself and others? But the consideration of molecular physics is not the direct ground of human love and moral action, any more than it is the direct means of composing a noble picture or of enjoying great music. One might as well hope to dissect one's own body and be merry in doing it, as take molecular physics (in which you must banish from your field of view what is specifically human) to be your dominant guide, your determiner of motives, in what is solely human. That every study has its bearing on every other is true; but pain and relief, love and sorrow, have their peculiar history which make an experience and knowledge over and above the swing of atoms.

The teaching you quote as George Sand's would, I think, deserve to be called nonsensical if it did not deserve to be called wicked. What sort of "culture of the intellect" is that which, instead of widening the mind to a fuller and fuller response to all the elements of our existence, isolates it in a moral stupidity?—which flatters egoism with the possibility that a complex and refined human society can continue wherein relations have no sacredness beyond the inclination of changing moods?—or figures to itself an aesthetic human life that one may compare to that of the fabled grasshoppers who were once men, but having heard the song of the Muses could do nothing but sing, and starved themselves so till they died and had a fit resurrection as grasshoppers; and "this," says Socrates, "was the return the Muses made them."

With regard to the pains and limitations of one's personal lot, I suppose that there is not a single man, or woman, who has not more or less need of that stoical resignation which is often a hidden heroism, or who, in considering his or her past history, is not aware that it has been cruelly affected by the ignorant or selfish action of some fellow being in a more or less close relation of life. And to my mind, there can be no stronger motive, than this perception, to an energetic effort that the lives nearest to us shall not suffer in a like manner from *us*.

The progress of the world—which you say can only come at the right time—can certainly never come at all save by the modified action of the individual beings who compose the world; and that we can say to ourselves with effect, "There is an order of considerations which I will keep myself continually in mind of, so that they may continually be the prompters of certain feelings and actions," seems to me as undeniable as that we can resolve to study the Semitic languages and apply to an Oriental scholar to give us daily lessons. What would your keen wit say to a young man who alleged the physical basis of nervous action as a reason why he could not possibly take that course?

When I wrote the first page of this letter I thought I was going to say that I had not courage to enter on the momentous points you had touched on, in the hasty brief form of a letter. But I have been led on sentence after sentence—not, I fear, with any inspiration beyond that of my anxiety. You will, at least, pardon any ill-advised things I may have written on the prompting of the moment.

I hope that we shall see you before very long, and that you will always believe me,

Most sincerely yours,
M. E. Lewes.

P.S. As to duration, and the way in which it affects your views of the human history, what is really the difference to your imagination between Infinitude and billions, when you have to consider the value of human experience? Will you say that since your life has a term of threescore years and ten, it was really a matter of indifference whether you were a cripple with a wretched skin disease or an active creature with a mind at large for the enjoyment of knowledge and with a nature which has attracted others to you? Difficulties of thought and acceptance of what is without full comprehension belong to every system of thinking. The question is to find the least incomplete.

TO FREDERIC HARRISON, 30 DECEMBER 1874

Perhaps GE was considering this course for Sir Hugo Mallinger, who Deronda suspected might be his father. [VI, 100]

The Priory, | 21. North Bank, | Regents Park.
December 30. 74.

Dear Mr. Harrison

Is the legitimization of a son by act of Parliament so rare that it would be out of the probabilities for any Nob, or Snob who could pay for it?

I make no apology for troubling you because I know by experience that you are glad to do a service.

Yours always sincerely
M. E. Lewes.

TO MRS. MARK PATTISON, 3 JANUARY 1875

The final chapter of *Isaac Casaubon* discussing his religious attitudes is the same in both editions, 1875 and 1892. Mrs. Pattison's book was *Renaissance of Art in France*, 1879. [VI, 107–08]

The Priory, | 21. North Bank, | Regents Park.
January 3. 75.

My dear Goddaughter

A happy new year to you in the most prosperous industry! It was very dear of you to remember me and write me an interesting letter. But first about the "Isaac Casaubon." Mr. Lewes and I both cry out against the omission of that final chapter which must be needed as a spire to the edifice. And it is unfair to those who buy the first edition, that such an advantage should be reserved for the second. But I suppose our crying out is in vain now. You should have called in a body of remonstrants before it was too late. What is the use of adapting good books to bad readers? . . .

I enter into the Rector's weariness under his proof and revise reading. All writing seems to me worse in the state of proof than in any other form. In manuscript one's own wisdom is rather remarkable to one, but in proof it has the effect of one's private furniture repeated in the shop windows. And then there is the sense that the worst errors will go to press unnoticed!

I am glad to hear that you are so far on your way in your useful book. Let us all consider ourselves privileged persons to be surviving in comfort while our fellow-men are shattered in railways and burnt at sea. Were there ever such horrors accumulated about one Christmas? . . .

Always your affectionate
M. E. Lewes.

TO FREDERIC HARRISON, 7 JANUARY 1875

In *Daniel Deronda* Sir A. B. Bart. became Sir Francis Mallinger; C, his elder son, Sir Hugo
Mallinger; D, the younger son, who married the heiress Miss Grandcourt and added her
name, became the father of E, Henleigh Mallinger Grandcourt. [VI, 110–11]

The Priory, | 21. North Bank, | Regents Park.
January 7. 75.

Dear Mr. Harrison

Pardon my troubling you to give me one more 'response.' I have been looking
into Williams on Real Property, but cannot get clear as to the frequency and strict
necessity of resettlements of estates in tail. Pray give me a little light on the
following case.

Sir A. B. Bart., having resettled the estate (in tail general) on his marriage, has
issue, two sons C. and D. C. remains unmarried till latish in life, while D. marries
early and has a son E. Afterwards, when his son E. is already of age, C. marries and
has no other issue than three daughters. What resettlements would probably have
taken place? And if E. died without issue while C. was still living, would the
inheritance go to the three daughters equally, spite of the father C.?—the baronetcy becoming extinct—or would the whole power over the estate revert to C.,
so that he could resettle it as he liked? And if the estate went to the daughters
would the baronetcy go off to a distant male branch?

I wish I had all knowledge so as to do without taxing your precious time. And I
might have hunted further, but as that solitary hunting might be unsuccessful
after all, I send this note in time (it is to be hoped) to save you from writing me two
letters instead of one.

Yours always gratefully
M. E. Lewes.

JOURNAL, 13 JANUARY 1875

GE's latest entry was 19 May 1874. Of the 1-volume edition of *Middlemarch* 13,150 had
been sold. Page 234 in the MS of *Daniel Deronda* is the end of Chapter 15. [VI, 116]

January 13. 1875. Here is a great gap since I last made a record! But the time has
been filled full of happiness. Yesterday I received from Blackwood the last year's
account of Middlemarch, Jubal and the Spanish Gypsy, amounting to £860. Of
Jubal a second edition was published in August and the 4th edition of the Spanish
Gypsy is all sold. This morning I received a copy of the 5th edition. The amount of
copies sold of Middlemarch up to December 31 is between 19 and 20,000. . . .

The last year has been crowded with proofs of affection for me and of value for
what work I have been able to do. This makes the best motive or encouragement
to do more; but as usual I am suffering much from doubt as to the worth of what I
am doing and fear lest I may not be able to complete it so as to make it a
contribution to literature and not a mere addition to the heap of books. I am now
just beginning the part about Deronda, at p. 234.

TO THE HON. MRS. HENRY PONSONBY, 11 FEBRUARY 1875

[VI, 124]

Do send me the papers you have written—I mean as a help and instruction to me. I need very much to know how ideas lie in other minds than my own, that I may not miss their difficulties while I am urging only what satisifes myself. I shall be deeply interested in knowing exactly what you wrote at that particular stage. Please remember that I don't consider myself a teacher, but a companion in the struggle of thought. What can consulting physicians do without pathological knowledge?—and the more they have of it, the less absolute—the more tentative—are their procedures.

You will see by the 'Fortnightly,' which you have not read, that Mr. Spencer is very anxious to vindicate himself from neglect of the logical necessity that the evolution of the abstraction "society" is dependent on the modified action of the units; indeed he is very sensitive on the point of being supposed to teach an enervating fatalism.

Consider what the human mind *en masse* would have been if there had been no such combination of elements in it as has produced poets. All the philosophers and *savants* would not have sufficed to supply that deficiency. And how can the life of nations be understood without the inward light of poetry—that is, of emotion blending with thought?

But the beginning and object of my letter must be the end—please send me your papers.

TO OSCAR BROWNING, 2 MARCH 1875

A long feud with the Headmaster of Eton, Dr. J. J. Hornby, ended in Browning's dismissal at the end of 1875. He returned to Cambridge as Fellow of King's College. [VI, 126–27]

The Priory, | 21. North Bank, | Regents Park.
Mar. 2. 75.

Dear Mr. Browning

Your letter shall be sacred. I am glad to know that you have made up your mind to endure and persevere—words easy to write as advice, but hard to follow out in the patient action of days, months, years. Perhaps the most difficult heroism is that which consists in the daily conquests of our private demons, not in the slaying of world-notorious dragons. Certainly it seems to me that the finest course of action you can pursue will be to impose the utmost restraint on impatience, and look at your life simply as the problem of carrying out your ideas of usefulness at Eton as far as may be without dangerous collisions. To further this happiness and beneficence of your life—even apart from that question of your dear mother's feeling—you should have a precise conception of an alternative to your present task, an equivalent social contribution, before you unlink yourself. But I gather that your resolution is thoroughly formed, and I rejoice.

We shall see you at the end of this fiercely menacing March. You are young enough to dare travel at that time of year which we used to find everywhere cruel, south as well as north.

Always truly yours
M. E. Lewes.

TO ALICE HELPS, [8 MARCH 1875]

Her father Sir Arthur Helps died suddenly of pleurisy 7 March 1875. The bottom of the MS has been torn away. A note in Alice Help's hand says: "The double autograph of G. H. Lewes and G. Eliot asked for by the Queen on seeing the letter." [VI, 129]

The Priory, | 21. North Bank, | Regents Park.
Monday.

Dear Alice

A silent pressure of the hand to assure you that the calamity which has fallen on you is felt by us. We know how devoted your love for your father—we know how loveable he was—nothing more to be said!

TO MRS. EDWARD BURNE-JONES, 11 MAY 1875

GE's symptoms of illness were probably subjective, for they usually disappeared as soon as a book was finished. But 3 February 1875 she awoke with excruciating pain in her left side, which Dr. Andrew Clark diagnosed as kidney stone. Another sharp attack two days later was followed by gradual recovery. Sir James Paget concurred with the diagnosis. When GE saw Salvini's Othello twice in April, she was greatly moved, but he was a great disappointment in Altenheim's melodrama *The Gladiator*. Friday afternoons were reserved for Mrs. Burne-Jones for many years. [VI, 142]

The Priory, | 21. North Bank, | Regents Park.
May 11. 75.

Dearest Mignon

The doctors have decided that there is nothing very grave the matter with me, and I am now so much better that we even think it possible I may go to see Salvini in the Gladiator tomorrow evening. This is to let you know that there is no reason against your coming, with or without Margaret, at the usual time on Friday.

Your words of affection in the note you sent me are very dear to my remembrance. I like not only to be loved but also to be told that I am loved. I am not sure that you are of the same mind. But the realm of silence is large enough beyond the grave. This is the world of light and speech, and I shall take leave to tell you that you are very dear to

Your faithfully affectionate
M. E. Lewes.

TO FREDERIC HARRISON, 9 JUNE 1875

Sir Hugo Mallinger and Grandcourt. [vi, 149–50]

The Priory, | 21. North Bank, | Regents Park.
June 9. 75.

Dear Mr. Harrison

I am deeply obliged to you for the full and lucid paper you have written me. By going back and altering a detail or two in what I wrote some time ago, I think I shall be able to make out all I want, by using the possibility of exchange between Sir H. and G.

I suppose that the possible son whose rights cannot be infringed does not disappear from the legal scene until the death of the possible father, who if one wife died could marry any number of wives in succession. He is rather troublesome to me. But I hope that through your kindness I may be able to understand what were the family affairs of my personages—for such understanding is necessary to my comfort, if not to the true relation of that part of their history which I undertake to write. Always

Sincerely and gratefully yours
M. E. Lewes.

TO EMILY CLARKE, 12 JUNE 1875

Emily, the only surviving daughter of GE's sister Chrissey, was a teacher at Lombard House, a school in Brighton. GE had her for occasional visits, gave her gifts, and left her £5,000 in her will. Edward, the black sheep of the Clarke orphans, had been in Australia since 1861; the cause of his disgrace is unknown. James Kittermaster, M.D., a physician at Meriden, corresponded with Edward and Emily. Arnold Ruge fled from Frankfurt to Brighton in 1849 and set up as a teacher there. [vi, 150–51]

The Priory, | 21. North Bank, | Regents Park.
June 12. 75.

Dearest Emily

I am sorry to think of your losing so healthy a change as a visit to Scotland during the Summer Holidays, but the sweet duties of gratitude cannot be neglected without a still greater loss, and you will at least have the relief of rest with your friend Madam Monsigny. . . .

I wish we had been able to manage a little visit to Brighton for a day and a night this spring, for it would have been a great satisfaction to me to have a kiss and a chat with you. But I have been so delicate and so liable to suffer from the slightest draught, that we have been discouraged from railway journeys in which we must have had that undesirable companion the North-East Wind.

I am surprized to hear that your old friend Dr. Kittermaster is still living. The kind old man would be sadly grieved to know of the trouble about Edward in whom he took so friendly an interest. You can hardly expect to hear from that unfortunate Brother, and perhaps silence is the least painful condition in relation to him.

The bit of newspaper you sent me about Dr. Ruge gratified me highly. It is an honour to his fellow-countrymen that they do him honour. I hope that you keep up your connection with Frau Ruge, and are not too much exhausted by other work to have a little appetite for German studies.

All Blessings on you, dear. Your Uncle unites with me in love.

Ever your affectionate
Aunt Polly.

TO MME EUGÈNE BODICHON, 13 AUGUST 1875

Herbert Lewes joined Thornie in Natal on the government's promise of 5,000 acres of land on the Orange River. He married in 1870 the daughter of an old settler and had two children, who were named Marian Evans and George Henry. The glandular disease, probably tubercular like Thornie's, attacked Herbert in 1874, and he died without having seen his son. Alfred Morrison, a millionaire art collector, had called with his wife at the Priory since 1872. Octavia Hill with the Charles Leweses and others had been trying to get money to save Swiss Cottage Fields from the builders and had collected over £8,000, mostly from people of small means. Now as the option was about to collapse GE suggested appealing to Morrison. [VI, 161–62]

The Elms | Rickmansworth | August 13. 75.

My dear Barbara . . .

We have had a trouble, prepared for by a long-standing anxiety. On the 29th of June our poor Bertie died at Durban, where he was staying for the sake of sea-air and medical attendance. The sad news only reached us last Sunday, when we were hoping that we might soon get a letter to tell us of his being able to rejoin his wife. He leaves two little children, the youngest an infant boy, born in May. It is a comfort that we are able to provide for the wife and children, but the consequent claims (in these next months when there will be debts and expenses of uncertain amounts) prevent me from doing what I should like to do, namely, to supply the needed £100 for the new rooms at Girton.

It will be worth while to send the information to Mrs. Alfred Morrison—it can do no harm. But she made no response at all when I sent former circulars to her; she is now ill, and her husband a most unsympathetic mortal. I am determined not to appeal to him again in any way. I lately gave an introduction to Gertrude that she might try to interest him in keeping open the Hampstead fields, and she found the interview a great *crux*. . . .

Poor Bertie had been suffering from the glandular disease of which he showed symptoms when a boy, but which he appeared to have completely outgrown. He had become a splendidly strong man before he went to Natal and continued so till about three years ago, when he began to complain of neuralgia. His death was immediately caused by an attack of bronchitis.

We return to town on September 23. but go off again in two or three days to the Coast—Bournemouth I believe, till about the end of October.

Ever yours lovingly
M. E. L.

TO ELIZABETH STUART PHELPS, 13 AUGUST 1875

Miss Phelps, preparing some lectures on GE at Boston College, planned at one point to lift the letter to show it. But lately she had gone to her travelling bag where the letter was kept and found that a little flask of brandy had leaked out and made it illegible. So she sent the extracts that were in the lecture and asked GE to recopy them. In obliging, GE incidentally corrected the misstatements about Mill and Spencer that were repeated in the latest issue of *Men of the Time*. [VI, 163–64]

The Elms | Rickmansworth | Herts. August 13. 75.

My dear Madam

I am happy to be able to remedy the little accident to your paper by copying the passages you have extracted from my former letter.

"I certainly feel a strong disgust for any readiness to satisfy that idle curiosity which, caring little for the study of an author's works, is pleased with low gossip about his private life and personal appearance. Of every writer worth reading it may be said 'He gave the people of his best; | His worst he kept; his best he gave.' Can we be too severe on the spirit which neglects the 'best,' and eagerly accepts details called biographical, which would be worthless even if they were accurate? Every sentence of your letter assures me that you are at one with me on this point. . . .

It is interesting, I think, to know whether a writer was born in a central or border district—a condition which always has a strongly determining influence. I was born in Warwickshire, but certain family traditions connected with more northerly districts, made those districts a region of poetry to me in my early childhood. I was brought up in the Church of England, and have never joined any other religious society, but I have had close acquaintance with many dissenters of various sects, from Calvinistic Anabaptists to Unitarians.

I never—to answer one of your questions quite directly—I never had any personal acquaintance with J. S. Mill—never saw him, to my knowledge, except in the House of Commons; and though I have studied his books, especially his Logic and Political Economy, with much benefit, I have no consciousness of their having made any marked epoch in my life.

Of Mr. Herbert Spencer's friendship I have had the honour and advantage for twenty years, but I believe that every main bias of my mind had been taken before I knew him. Like the rest of his readers, I am of course indebted to him for much enlargement and clarifying of thought." . . .

I see that I wrote (automatically) 'dear *Madam*' at the beginning of my letter. If that looks chill and formal to you, believe that it does not represent my feeling which is that of sympathetic as well as respectful regard.

Yours, dear Miss Phelps, sincerely
M. E. Lewes.

TO JOHN BLACKWOOD, 10 OCTOBER 1875

On returning to the Priory 23 September, the Leweses found the drawing room still unpapered and the whole house smelling of paint. So they set off for a holiday in Wales, returning 9 October. During this trip GE read aloud Jane Austen's *Emma*, Dickens's *Uncommercial Traveller*, Sterne's *Sentimental Journey*, and Turgenev's *Nouvelles Moscovites* and *Récits d'un Chasseur*. Her plan of publishing Book I in February was accepted. Blackwood assured her that they had a fireproof room at 45 George Street where the MS would be carefully kept. [VI, 171–73]

The Priory, | 21. North Bank, | Regents Park.
Oct. 10. 75.

My dear Mr. Blackwood . . .

You will laugh at our nervous caution in depositing our MSS at the Union Bank before we set out. We could have borne to hear that our house had been burnt down provided no lives were lost, and our unprinted matter, our oeuvres inédites, were safe out of it.

About *my* unprinted matter—Mr. Lewes thinks it will not be well to publish the first part till February. December he says will be too soon for the necessary arrangements with America, and January he maintains is a bad month for publishing anything, whereas February is altogether eligible. The four first monthly parts are ready for travelling now. I am a little uncertain about the way the quantities will turn out, but I have divided these two volumes to the best of my calculation. I found that the first volume—i.e. the first two parts—would turn out enormously thick on my first plan of division, and have therefore revised the arrangement. It will be well to begin the printing in good time so that I may not be hurried with the proofs, and I must beg Mr. Simpson to judge for me in that matter with kind carefulness.

I can't say that I am at all satisfied with the book or that I have a comfortable sense of doing in it what I want to do, but Mr. Lewes *is* satisfied with it and insists that since he is as anxious as possible for it to be fine I ought to accept his impression as trustworthy. So I resign myself. . . .

Yours always sincerely
M. E. Lewes.

TO OSCAR BROWNING, 28 OCTOBER 1875

Browning was dismissed in September 1875 and, after the failure of his appeal in November, left Eton at Christmas 1875 and went abroad. I am indebted to the Librarian of the Eastbourne Public Library for permission to publish this letter for the first time, and to Mr. Ian Anstruther for telling me about it.

The Priory, | 21. North Bank, | Regents Park.
Oct. 28. 75

My dear Mr. Browning

Your letter has brought me very painful news. In my darkness in the whole affair I try to persuade myself that the crisis will turn favourably for you, and that you will be able after November 9th to send me word of your position being confirmed. I imagine with sympathy what the trial would be to Mrs. Browning of having the home broken up, where she has presided so beneficently. We have but lately returned to town and Mr. Lewes saw Mr. Pigott only the day before yesterday, when among their many subjects of chat on a first meeting after many months, your trouble did not happen to be mentioned.

We are now settled for the winter, I hope, and are at home on Sundays for friends who can spare us a little time. But I suppose you are just now under the stress of an opening term as well as of this calamitous duel with the Head Master. Whenever you can give me any intimation about yourself, be sure that Mr. Lewes and I shall be warmly interested.

Always yours sincerely
M. E. Lewes.

TO JOHN BLACKWOOD, 10 NOVEMBER 1875

The original division was after Chapters 11 and 22. As published Book I ends with Chapter 10 (188 pp.), Book II with Chapter 18 (172 pp.), Book III with Chapter 27 (185 pp.), and Book IV with Chapter 34 (173 pp.). On each of the eight Books sold for 5/- GE received a royalty of 2/-. By December 1876 *Daniel Deronda* had brought her £8,195. [VI, 181–82]

The Priory, | 21. North Bank, | Regents Park.
November 10/75.

Dear Mr. Blackwood

I want your opinion about the length of the four first Parts of D. D. Mr. Simpson sends me word this morning that Pts. III and IV make respectively 170 and 175 pp. Pts. I and II being 191 and 180. My original division made the two first parts considerably longer—Pt. I ending at the end of the Archery Ball, and Part II at the end of Mirah's story. But I found that by this arrangement, the first part would be more than 220 pp. and the second at least 190—making the 1st vol. tremendously thick. But I fear that the present division may make the two first parts—the impression from which is of course supremely important—rather poverty-stricken in point of matter.

What do you think? As to the III and IV Parts—there are two Books of Middlemarch which are 175 and 176 respectively, but they don't come together. The question of course is rather of matter in relation to interest than in relation to quantity. If you are for the larger size of Parts I and II and Mr. Lewes concurs, (he is this morning at Cambridge) I could throw the *same* amount into Parts III and IV— not less, I fear, because of the difficulty as to properly dividing the subject matter. Unhappily I cannot drill myself into writing according to set lengths.

Charging 5s per Book makes me dreadfully afraid of giving the Public too little for its money. On the other hand, Too Much is the most thankless form of generosity. Please give me your ideas.

Always yours sincerely
M. E. Lewes.

The 2 first volumes would preponderate in the one case—the 2 last in the other.

TO JOHN BLACKWOOD, 18 NOVEMBER 1875

Blackwood's remarks about the book were cheering. He fixed upon the "psychological notation" in Gwendolen's conversation with Grandcourt that F. R. Leavis praised in *The Great Tradition* (1948). When Blackwood's wife and nephew suggested that Rex's horse was unlikely to break his knees in a field, GE changed it to "a lane lately mended." GHL agreed that the division of parts was the best except for the last five pages of Book II, which were made into Chapter 19 at the opening of Book III. [VI, 187–88]

The Priory, | 21. North Bank, | Regents Park.
November 18. 75.

My dear Mr. Blackwood

Your enjoyment of the proofs cheers me greatly. And pray thank Mr. Blackwood for his valuable hints on equine matters. I have not only the satisfaction of using these hints—I allow myself the inference that where there is no criticism on like points I have made no mistake. As to the division Mr. Lewes has made up his mind decidedly—he will tell you to what effect, among the other points about which he is writing to you.

I should be much obliged to Mr. Simpson—whom I am glad that Gwendolen has captivated—if he would rate the printers a little about their want of spacing. There are really some lines where the words all run into each other as in an ancient Greek inscription. I am anxious that my poor heroes and heroines should have all the advantage that paper and print can give them. Has the colour of the wrapper been at all discussed? The lettering I want to have large, simple Roman.

It will perhaps be a little comfort to you to know that poor Gwen is spiritually saved, but "so as by fire." Don't you see the process already beginning? I have no doubt you do, for you are a wide-awake reader. . . .

I leave all other questions to Mr. Lewes's letter.

Yours always truly
M. E. Lewes.

TO SARA HENNELL, 20 NOVEMBER 1875

Learning Maria Lewis's address somehow, GE wrote to her in September 1874, sending £10, which Maria said, "came opportunely." She added: "My heart has ever yearned after you, and pleasant is it truly in the evening of life to find the old love still existing." Similar payments were made in November each year until GE's death. [VI, 191–92]

The Priory, | 21. North Bank, | Regents Park.
November 20. 75.

My dear Sara . . .

I wonder if you all remember an old governess of mine who used to visit me at Foleshill—a Miss Lewis? I have found her out; she is living at Leamington, very poor as well as old, but cheerful—and so delighted to be remembered with gratitude. How very old we are all getting! But I hope you don't mind it any more than I do. One sees so many contemporaries, that one is well in the fashion. The approach of parting is the bitterness of age.

It would sweeten this birthday very much dear Sara, to be assured that it finds you in serenity—undisturbed by illness or care. Please give my love to Cara and Mr. Bray.

Always your affectionate
Pollian.

TO JOHN BLACKWOOD, 15 DECEMBER 1875

GE was nearly at the end of Book V of *Daniel Deronda*. Simpson had sold the serial rights to the *Australian*. GHL got £1,700 for the North American rights from Harper, who serialized the novel in *Harper's New Monthly Magazine*. GE declined Blackwood's offer to send her some novels of Laurence Lockhart. There were wild rumors in the English papers that *Daniel Deronda* would illustrate American or French life. [VI, 198–200]

The Priory, | 21. North Bank, | Regents Park.
December 15. 75.

My dear Mr. Blackwood . . .

In the sanest, soberest judgment . . . I think the third volume (which I have not yet finished) would be regarded as the difficult bridge. I will not send you any more M.S. until I can send the whole of Vol. III.

We think that Mr. Simpson has conducted our Australian business admirably. Remembering that but for his judgment and consequent activity we might have got no publication at all in that quarter, we may well be content with £200. I am quite satisfied too with the prospect of the wrapper, which I think will be just what I wanted. . . .

When I am writing, or only thinking of writing fiction of my own, I cannot risk the reading of other English fiction. I was obliged to tell Anthony Trollope so when he sent me the first part of his Prime Minister, though this must seem sadly ungracious to those who don't share my susceptibilities.

Apparently there are wild reports about the subject-matter of Deronda—among the rest, that it represents French life! But that is hardly more ridiculous than the supposition that after refusing to go to America I should undertake to describe society there.

It is wonderful how Middlemarch keeps afloat in people's minds. Somebody told me that Mr. Henry Sidgwick said it was a bold thing to write another book after Middlemarch, and we must prepare ourselves for the incalculableness of the public reception in the first instance. I think I have heard you say that the chief result of your ample experience has been to convince you of that incalculableness. . . .

Always yours truly
M. E. Lewes.

TO DR. JOSEPH FRANK PAYNE, 25 JANUARY 1876

GE had known both Dr. Payne and his brother John since 1869. John studied theology, but lost his faith and never took orders. After his sudden death, Dr. Payne discussed religious consolation with GE. On the death of his mother in October 1875, Dr. Payne wrote a long letter, which was not sent till January, again urging GE to offer some hope of a future life in her novels. [VI, 216–17]

The Priory, | 21. North Bank, | Regents Park.
January 25. 76.

My dear Dr. Payne

No word of your unspeakable loss had reached me. . . . You could have done nothing to touch me with more keenness—to move me more deeply, than your writing that letter to me in October. I say so at once on reading it, that you may know I am bearing it in mind even if I keep silence for the present in relation to that supreme subject—how far the religion of the future must be one that enables us to do without consolation, instead of being what religion has been (I think pervertingly) held—chiefly precious as a source of consolation.

Your letter will have associated you with questions which are the most frequently in my thoughts—questions which are my chief prompters to write anything at all. But my writing is simply a set of experiments in life—an endeavour to see what our thought and emotion may be capable of—what stores of motive, actual or hinted as possible, give promise of a better after which we may strive—what gains from past revelations and discipline we must strive to keep hold of as something more sure than shifting theory. I become more and more timid—with less daring to adopt any formula which does not get itself clothed for me in some human figure and individual experience, and perhaps that is a sign that if I help others to see at all it must be through that medium of art.

It is true that I am not very well, and I am just now liable to feel my weakness the more because I am haunted by the fear that everything is done worse in consequence. That is why I write this note at once. I dare not promise myself to answer your letter as I should like to do for the next month or two, and pray trust in me so far as to believe that my silence however protracted will not be one of forgetfulness. . . .

Most sincerely yours
M. E. Lewes.

TO JOHN BLACKWOOD, 25 FEBRUARY 1876

Returning the revises of Book V 23 February, Blackwood refrained from saying that he disliked Mordecai. Henry Mills Alden, editor of *Harper's*, praised *Daniel Deronda*; eagerness to read the story perhaps increased his desire to have copy earlier. Lord Lytton became Governor General of India 1 January. The Leweses dined with the Lyttons 26 February, before they left England 1 March. [VI, 222–23]

The Priory, | 21. North Bank, | Regents Park.
February 25. 76.

My dear Mr. Blackwood . . .

I thought it likely that your impressions about Mordecai would be doubtful. Perhaps when the work is finished you will see its bearings better. The effect that one strives after is an outline as strong as that of Balfour of Burley for a much more complex character and a higher strain of ideas. But such an effect is just the most difficult thing in art—to give new elements—i.e. elements not already used up— in forms as vivid as those of long familiar types. Doubtless the wider public of novel-readers must feel more interest in Sidonia than in Mordecai. But then, I was not born to paint Sidonia.

We are going to dine with Lord and Lady Lytton tomorrow to say a long farewell. It had seemed to us unlikely that we could have a glimpse of them, but I am very glad to have a parting remembrance—which to us old folk has that aspect of being final that begins to predominate in all partings. I am reminded of age by the fact that Mr. Lewes has been laid up with lumbago and is still rickety. . . .

Yours always truly
M. E. Lewes.

TO MRS. MARK PATTISON, 3 MARCH 1876

Discussing the average Oxford prize-man, Pattison wrote that one plainly recognizes that he has suffered from the forcing-house: "mental pallor, moral indifferentism, the cynical sneer at others' effort, the absence in himself of any high ideal." Burne-Jones achieved recognition with the opening of the Grosvenor Gallery in 1877. [VI, 228–29]

The Priory, | 21. North Bank, | Regents Park.
March 3. 76.

Dearest Figliuolina . . .

We are hoping to get away to the continent by the end of May, but I hope also you will have risen above the horizon here before that time. You will find us looking thin and ghastly. The Rector's article in 'Mind' on Philosophy at Oxford pleased us mightily by its vigorous portrait of the Prizeman. He spoke with husband's pride of your having written your last article on the Life of Voltaire without any books at hand.

Burne Jones goes on transcending himself and is rising into the inconvenient celebrity which is made up of echoes as well as voices. I do hope he will be urged into having a collection of his pictures in a separate little gallery for a time, so that his admirers might point to the reason for the faith that is in them.

I have no news worth telling. We go to our one amusement of the Saturday concert, our friends come to see us on a Sunday, and lately we have said goodbye to the Lyttons with many longings for his and her good in their new, distant, trying honours. She is expecting another Baby in August, and one hopes it may be a boy to soothe the poignant memories of the lost ones. . . .

Your affectionate
Madre.

TO JOHN BLACKWOOD, [18] MARCH 1876

Mr. and Mrs. W. H. Hall had lent the Leweses their house at Weybridge for two or three weeks. Blackwood said that complaints about understanding Gwendolen were really the highest compliment. GE, quoting from memory the motto for Chapter 17, wrote: "This is true the poet sings," ascribing it to *In Memoriam.* An erratum slip was inserted before the half title of Book III, quoting the passage correctly as "truth" and from *Locksley Hall.* Henry Reeve's suggestion was followed in later printings. [VI, 232–33]

The Priory, | 21. North Bank, | Regents Park.
March 17. 76.

My dear Mr. Blackwood

We have just come in from Weybridge, but are going to take refuge there again on Monday for a few days more of fresh air and long breezy afternoon walks. Many thanks for your thoughtfulness in sending me the cheering account of sales. I find one—also from Mr. Langford carrying the good news up to the last moment—this morning being marked 25 of B. II.

Mr. Lewes has not heard any complaints of not understanding Gwendolen, but a strong partizanship for and against her. My correspondence about the misquotation of Tennyson has quieted itself since the fifth letter. But Mr. Reeve, the Editor of the Edinburgh, has written me a very pretty note taxing me with having wanted insight into the technicalities of Newmarket, when I made Lush say 'I will *take* odds.' Mr. Reeve judges that I should have written 'I will *lay* odds.' On the other hand, another expert contends that the case is one in which Lush would be more likely to say 'I will take odds.' What do you think?—I told Mr. Reeve that I had a dread of being righteously pelted with mistakes that would make a cairn above me—a monument and a warning to people who write novels without being omniscient and infallible.

Mr. Lewes is agitating himself over a fifth reading of Revise, B. VI, and says he finds it more interesting than on any former reading. It is agreeable to have a home criticism of this kind. But I am deep in the Fourth Vol. and cannot any longer care about what is past and done for—the passion of the moment is as much as I can live in. . . .

> Always yours sincerely
> M. E. Lewes.

TO GEORGE GROVE, 28 MARCH 1876

George Grove, author of *The Dictionary of Music and Musicians*, was instrumental in founding the Palestine Exploration Fund. Of Mirah he wrote GE: "You must have thought of our dear Deutsch when you conceived her character. . . . my memory welled up" [IX, 173]

> **The Priory, | 21. North Bank, | Regents Park.**
> March 28. 76.

Dear Mr. Grove

Many thanks for your kind letter. I am much cheered and comforted by the encouragement it gives me to hope that some of the purpose which has animated me in writing 'Daniel Deronda' may not be without its fulfilment. I shall know at least that in much of what is to follow I shall have you for a sympathetic reader. Mr. Lewes unites with me in best regards.

> Always truly yours
> M. E. Lewes.

TO MME EUGÈNE BODICHON, 30 MARCH 1876

Wolseley served in the Crimean War and the Indian Mutiny and had lately been administrator in Natal. GHL testified before the Royal Commission on vivisection that the amount of pain caused in research was very small. [VI, 235–36]

> **The Priory, | 21. North Bank, | Regents Park.**
> March 30. 76.

My dear Barbara . . .

I am well pleased that Deronda touches you. I *wanted* you to prefer the chapter about Mirah's finding, and I hope you will also like her history in Part III which has just been published. . . .

We have been getting a little refreshment from two flights between Sundays to Weybridge, where Mr. and Mrs. Hall lent us their house and servants. But we have had the good a little drained from us by going out to dinner two days in succession. At Sir James Paget's I was much interested to find that a gentle-looking, clear-eyed, neatly-made man was Sir Garnet Wolseley and I had some talk with him which quite confirmed the impression of him as one of those men who have a power of command by dint of their sweet temper, calm demeanour and unswerving resolution. The next subject that has filled our chat lately has been the Blue Book on Vivisection, which you would like to look into. There is a great deal of matter for reflection in the evidence on the subject, and some good points have been lately put in print and conversation that I should like to tell you of if I had time. Prof. Clifford told us the other Sunday that Huxley complained of his sufferings from "the profligate lying of virtuous women." I am scribbling at the fag end of the day, being short of time not so much because of work as because of my feebleness which makes me incapable of getting through it. . . .

Yours always
Marian.

JOURNAL, 12 APRIL 1876

[VI, 238]

April 12. On February 1 began the publication of Deronda, and the interest of the public, strong from the first, appears to have increased with Book III. The day before yesterday I sent off Book VII. The success of the work at present is greater than that of Middlemarch up to the corresponding point of publication. What will be the feeling of the public as the story advances I am entirely doubtful. The Jewish element seems to me likely to satisfy nobody.—I am in rather better health; having perhaps profited by some eight days' change at Weybridge.

TO JOHN BLACKWOOD, 18 APRIL 1876

Books V and VI came to 196 and 197 pages respectively; Book VII was only 162. GE had reviewed Whitman's *Leaves of Grass* for the *Westminster* in 1856 and doubtless found copies of the book in the house of Mrs. Gilchrist, his most ardent English admirer, at Brookbank in 1871. Regret at having quoted the two lines as a motto for Chapter 29 may have come from recent attacks on Whitman in the *Saturday Review*. GHL contributed £2 for a Whitman fund in 1876. The first performance of Tennyson's play with Kate Bateman as Queen Mary and Henry Irving as Philip II had all the excitement of a First Night, but, according to GHL was "horribly acted throughout." Blackwood confessed that he had sent for a Hebrew dictionary to look up *tephillin*, but didn't know the alphabet. The printers misread *Kalonymos* as *Kalongmos*. [VI, 240–42]

The Priory, | 21. North Bank, | Regents Park.
April 18. 76.

My dear Mr. Blackwood

It was better than I expected to receive the proof of Book VII. so soon in this Easter time. And your sympathetic letter is a welcome support to me in the rather depressed condition which has come upon me with a whole week's internal disorder, from the effect, I imagine of a chill taken in the sudden change from mildness to renewed winter. You can understand how trying it is to have a week of incompetence at the present stage of affairs. I am rather concerned to see that the part is nearly a sheet smaller than any of the other parts. But Books V and VI are proportionately thick, and Mr. Lewes insists that B. VII is thick *enough*. It seemed inadmissible to add anything after the scene with Gwendolen, and to stick anything in, not necessary to development, between the foregoing chapters, is a form of 'matter in the wrong place' particularly repulsive to my authorship's sensibility. . . .

We are rather vexed, now it is too late, that I did not carry out a sort of incipient intention to expunge a motto from Walt Whitman which I inserted in Book IV. Of course the whole is irrevocable by this time, but I should have otherwise thought it worth while to have a new page, not because the motto itself is objectionable to me—it was one of the finer things which had clung to me from among his writings—but because, since I quote so few poets, my selection of a motto from Walt Whitman might be taken as the sign of a special admiration which I am very far from feeling. How imperfectly one's mind acts in proof reading! . . .

People in their eagerness about my characters are quite angry, it appears, when their own expectations are not fulfilled—angry, for example, that Gwendolen accepts Grandcourt etc. etc. One reader is sure that Mirah is going to die very soon and I suppose will be disgusted at her remaining alive. Such are the reproaches to which I make myself liable. However, that you seem to share Mr. Lewes's strong feeling of Book VII being no falling off in intensity, makes me brave. Only, endings are inevitably the least satisfactory part of any work in which there is any merit of development.

We are going tonight to see the first representation of "Queen Mary" which is a literary and dramatic epoch. It is perhaps not likely to be played again, for without transcendant acting of Mary's part the performance will be dreary, and I fear there is no chance of transcendant acting.

Always yours truly
M. E. Lewes.

I forgot to say that the tephillin are the small leather bands or phylacteries inscribed with supremely sacred words, which the Jew binds on his arms and head during prayer. Any periphrasis which would be generally intelligible would be undramatic, and I don't much like explanatory foot-notes in a poem or story. But I must consider what I can do to remedy the unintelligibility.

The printers have sadly spoiled the beautiful Greek name Kalonymos, which was the name of a celebrated family of scholarly Jews transplanted from Italy into Germany in mediaeval times. But my writing was in fault.

JOURNAL, 3 JUNE 1876

On 18 May Book VII and half of Book VIII were sent to press. Despite her fatigue and ill health GE went with GHL to dinner at Lady Portsmouth's, and two days later to Oxford for the weekend with Jowett at Balliol, coming back "none the worse for the lionizing." She worked at the final pages of *Deronda* while GHL took over the rest of the social commitments. At Lord Houghton's the King of the Belgians was much put out by her absence. [VI, 259]

June 3. Book V was published a week ago. Growing interest in the public and growing sale, which has from the beginning exceeded that of Middlemarch. The Jewish part apparently creating strong interest.

JOURNAL, 10 JUNE–1 SEPTEMBER 1876

The last proofs of *Deronda* arrived in Paris 12 June; the Leweses read them sitting in the Tuileries Garden and at home after a drive in the Bois. At the Théâtre Français they saw Coquelin and Sarah Bernhardt in *L'Etrangère*, . At the Russian Cathedral the Grand Duke Michael and his wife were present, and the music exquisite. At Aix-les-Bains they bought Rousseau's *Confessions* and at Chambéry took a three-hours' walk to see his rooms at Les Charmettes. [VI, 263]

June 10.—We set off on our journey, intending to go to San Martino Lantosc in the Maritime Alps. But I was ill at Aix, where the heat had become oppressive, and we turned northwards after making a pilgrimage to Les Charmettes—stayed a few days at Lausanne, then at Vevey, where again I was ill; then by Berne and Zurich to Ragatz, where we were both set up sufficiently to enjoy our life. After Ragatz to Stachelberg, the Klön-Thal, Schaffhausen, St. Blasien in the Black Forest, and then home by Strasburg, Nancy, and Amiens, arriving September 1.

TO JOHN BLACKWOOD, 2 SEPTEMBER 1876

The regime at Ragatz was excellent for GE. GHL wrote to Blackwood that she "is quite another woman, and is recovering her colour and contour." On their walks she began to give Lewes "lessons in Hebrew—reviving our Spanish days." With his letter Rabbi Hermann Adler sent a copy of the *Jewish Messenger* with his review of *Daniel Deronda*. [VI, 274–76]

The Priory, | 21. North Bank, | Regents Park.
September 2. 76.

My dear Mr. Blackwood

We reached home only last night. After we left Ragatz our wanderings became too changeful and uncertain in their direction for me to venture on writing to you with any indication of our coming whereabout, and since the beginning of August our Son has been taking his holiday in the country, so that we arrive as strangers and foreigners to all home affairs, the fortunes of D. D. included.

We had scarcely taken our much-needed dinner before a parcel was brought in which proved to be D. D. in the four bound volumes, and various letters with other "missiles" as an acquaintance of mine once (quite naïvely) called his own favours to his correspondents—which have at present only gone to swell a heap that I mean to make acquaintance with very slowly. Mr. Lewes, however, is more eager than I, and he has just brought up to me a letter which has certainly gratified me more than anything else of the sort I ever received. It is from Dr. Hermann Adler, the Chief Rabbi here, expressing his "warm appreciation of the fidelity with which some of the best traits of the Jewish character have been depicted by" etc. etc. I think this will gratify you too.

We are both the better for our journey, and I consider myself in as good case as I can ever reasonably expect. We can't be made young again and must not be surprized that infirmities recur in spite of mineral waters and air 3000 feet above the sea-level. After Ragatz we stayed at Stachelberg and Klönthal—two lovely places where an English face is seldom seen. Another delicious spot, where the air is fit for the gods of Epicurus, is St. Blasien in the Schwarz Wald, where also we saw no English or American visitors, except such as "übernachten" there and pass on. Amidst all the loveliness of forest and mountain, Mr. Lewes has had frequent attacks of headache and severe cramp; still, he is stronger than he was, and we have done exploits in walking, usually taking four or five hours of it daily.

I hope that you and yours have kept well, and have enjoyed the heat rather than suffered from it. I confess myself glad to think that this planet has not become hopelessly chilly. Draughts and chills are my enemies, and but for them I should hardly ever be ailing. . . .

Always yours truly
M. E. Lewes.

TO EMILY CLARKE, 4 SEPTEMBER 1876

To make up for her neglect GE invited Emily for a four-day London visit 27–30 September, taking her to the Indian Museum, to the Haymarket to see *Dan'l Druce, Blacksmith* (by W. S. Gilbert, partly based on *Silas Marner*), to the Zoo, the National Portrait Gallery, the Opera, and the Kensington Museum. Walter Pearson Evans, son of Isaac Evans, married Constance Mackie in 1877. [VI, 277–78]

The Priory, | 21. North Bank, | Regents Park.
September 4. 76.

Dearest Emily

On returning home from a three months' journey on the Continent I found your letter among the large heap awaiting me. It was written, I see, on the 12th of July, when I had already been a month away and was on the other side of Switzerland, at Ragatz, taking walks and waters in order to get up my strength. I felt very sorry, after I had left home on the 10th of June, that I had not managed to send you a letter, as I had had it in my mind to do. The many details I had to occupy my attention, and my failing strength, caused me to forget what was not at all a matter of indifference to me. I thought of my omission very soon after I had left England, but for a long while I was so poorly that the news I had to tell would not have cheered you, and afterwards I imagined you enjoying your holidays in some place away from Brighton.

Enough of myself and my leaving-undone what I ought to have done. I am very well now, and we are hoping that before the pleasant autumn weather is all gone we shall get down to Brighton for a day to see your dear face, and hear all the little things that you could tell us in conversation so much better than in writing. I long to see you again. I gather from your letter that you have had only a week of change from your Brighton air this summer, and that grieves me. I want to inquire into your finances and plans for other holidays. Pray go on studying your German. It may be of great use to you in many ways. I think Wednesday used to be your half holiday—is it so still?

The last letter you wrote me before I went away contained the news of Walter's engagement, and I imagine that the marriage must have taken place by this time, though it has not occurred to you to mention the fact.

All blessings on you, dear Child. If you saw the many letters I have to open, you would not suppose that my silence to you implies any want of love and care for you. But now I shall be more at liberty, and shall not be in danger of neglecting you any longer. Mr. Lewes sends his best love to you, and unites with me in all tender wishes for you.

Ever your loving and faithful
Aunt Polly.

TO HAIM GUEDALLA, 26 SEPTEMBER 1876

Guedalla, a communal worker, expressed his admiration of *Daniel Deronda* and sent a pamphlet with his vision of Syria again in the hands of the Jews. [VI, 288]

The Priory, | 21. North Bank, | Regents Park.
September 26. 76.

Dear Sir

I thank you heartily for your kind letter, with the copies of your pamphlet and of the Hebrew newspaper. No response to my writing is more desired by me than such a feeling on the part of your great people, as that which you have expressed to me. It is something more than an interesting coincidence—it is a deeply felt encouragement to me, that at the date you mention, last winter, when I happened to be writing precisely that scene at the club, your practical judgment was occupied with projects not in disagreement with my conceptions.

I remain

Sincerely yours
M. E. Lewes.

TO MME EUGÈNE BODICHON, 2 OCTOBER 1876

Modern critics have dismissed the superficial opinion that *Daniel Deronda* could be cut into parts and have demonstrated the unity of GE's plan. [VI, 290]

21 N.B. | October 2. 76.

My dear Barbara

My blessing on you for your sweet letter which I count among the blessings given to me. Yes. Women can do much for the other women (and men) to come. My impression of the good there is in all unselfish efforts is continually strengthened. . . .

I have had some very interesting letters both from Jews and from Christians about Deronda. Part of the scene at the club is translated into Hebrew in a German-Jewish newspaper. On the other hand a Christian (highly accomplished) thanks me for embodying the principles by which Christ wrought and will conquer. This is better than the laudation of readers who cut the book into scraps and talk of nothing in it but Gwendolen. I meant everything in the book to be related to everything else there. . . .

Your affectionate
Marian.

TO HAIM GUEDALLA, 2 OCTOBER 1876

[VI, 288–89]

The Priory, | 21. North Bank, | Regents Park.
October 2. 76.

My dear Sir . . .

Your request that my former letter to you may be published in the Jewish Chronicle I am obliged to refuse, for reasons which I trust you will not misunderstand. I have a repugnance to anything like an introduction of my own personality to the public which only an urgent sense of duty could overcome. But over and above this feeling I have a conviction founded on dispassionate judgment, that any influence I may have as an author would be injured by the presentation of myself in print through any other medium than that of my books. False statements are frequently made both in British and American newspapers about my history and opinions, but I shall never break silence in an effort at contradiction until I perceive that some one else is being injured by those falsities in any way that my protest can hinder.

It is my function as an artist to act (if possible) for good on the emotions and conceptions of my fellow-men. But, as you are aware, when anyone who can be called a public person makes a casual speech or writes a letter that gets into print, his words are copied, served up in a work of commentary, misinterpreted, misquoted, and made matter of gossip for the emptiest minds. By giving occasion for more of this frivolous (if not vitiating) kind of comment than already exists in sickening abundance, I should be stepping out of my proper function and acting for what I think an evil result. . . .

Sincerely yours
M. E. Lewes.

H. Guedalla Esq.

TO MRS. HARRIET BEECHER STOWE, 29 OCTOBER 1876

Mrs. Stowe's son Charles was studying at Bonn. Among the Rugby men GE knew were John Cross and Richard Congreve. In publishing this letter Cross omitted "at Rugby." [VI, 301–02]

October 29. 76.

Dear Friend . . .

As to the Jewish element in 'Deronda,' I expected from first to last in writing it, that it would create much stronger resistance and even repulsion than it has actually met with. But precisely because I felt that the usual attitude of Christians towards Jews is—I hardly know whether to say more impious or more stupid when viewed in the light of their professed principles, I therefore felt urged to treat Jews with such sympathy and understanding as my nature and knowledge could attain to. Moreover, not only towards the Jews, but towards all oriental peoples with whom we English come in contact, a spirit of arrogance and contemptuous dictatorialness is observable which has become a national disgrace to us. There is nothing I should care more to do, if it were possible, than to rouse the imagination of men and women to a vision of human claims in those races of their fellow-men who most differ from them in customs and beliefs. But towards the Hebrews we western people who have been reared in Christianity, have a peculiar debt and, whether we acknowledge it or not, a peculiar thoroughness of fellowship in religious and moral sentiment. Can anything be more disgusting than to hear people called "educated" making small jokes about eating ham, and showing themselves empty of any real knowledge as to the relation of their own social and religious life to the history of the people they think themselves witty in insulting? They hardly know that Christ was a Jew. And I find men educated at Rugby supposing that Christ spoke Greek. To my feeling, this deadness to the history which has prepared half our world for us, this inability to find interest in any form of life that is not clad in the same coat-tails and flounces as our own lies very close to the worst kind of irreligion. The best that can be said of it is, that it is a sign of the intellectual narrowness—in plain English, the stupidity, which is still the average mark of our culture.

Yes, I expected more aversion than I have found. . . . I sum up with the writer of the Book of Maccabees—'if I have done well, and as befits the subject, it is what I desired, but if I have done ill, it is what I could attain unto.' . . .

Always your gratefully affectionate
M. E. Lewes. . . .

TO JOHN BLACKWOOD, 3 NOVEMBER 1876

As his ten-years' lease of the copyright of GE's works would expire in December, Black-wood wrote proposing £4,000, payable over a term of three years, for another ten years. After some consideration the Leweses decided that a royalty would be the best arrangement. [VI, 303–04]

The Priory, | 21. North Bank, | Regents Park.
November 3. 76.

My dear Mr. Blackwood

A cloud of cold having rolled off my brain, it seems clear to me that I owe you a letter. I was much gratified by your handsome proposal about my books, but no one will understand better than you that I incline to keep up a sort of active parental relation to those grown-up children. Also I prefer sharing their vicissitudes and saving everybody from risk as far as anything in this changing world can be saved from that condition. I was uncomfortable about the former arrangement while I feared that it had not answered. We are not greedy, though we are far from being indifferent to money, having relatives to depend on us—a widowed daughter-in-law and two little grandchildren in Natal became entirely our charge last year. We told hardly anyone at the time (because Mr. Lewes dreaded letters of condolence) that his youngest son Herbert died after an illness which ended in severe bronchitis. The sad news came to us when we were at Rickmansworth, quite out of this world, and we did not have it put in the Times. A little boy had been born only a month before the father died. The marriage was a very satisfactory union of two affectionate industrious young creatures who seemed to have a happy life before them till the fatal illness came.

It will be rather interesting to see what is the sale of Deronda compared with Middlemarch. . . . Certainly, if I had not very strong private proofs to the contrary I should conclude that my book was a failure and that nobody was grateful for it, though a certain tenderness was accorded to the production as that of an author who had done more tolerable things. But I am saved from concluding that I have exhibited my faculties in a state of decay by very delightful letters from unknown readers and reported judgments from considerable authorities. A statesman who shall be nameless has said that I first opened to him a vision of Italian life, then of Spanish, and now I have kindled in him a quite new understanding of the Jewish people. This is what I wanted to do—to widen the English vision a little in that direction and let in a little conscience and refinement. I expected to excite more resistance of feeling than I have seen the signs of, but I did what I chose to do—not as well as I should have liked to do it, but as well as I could.

This is an answer, and is not to be answered, so all the chat has at least the agreeableness of being cheap to you and drawing no further on your time than is required for the reading.

Yours always truly
M. E. Lewes.

TO SARA HENNELL, 22 NOVEMBER 1876

Spencer began his *Autobiography* in May 1875. Though it was not published till after his death in 1903, both volumes of it were in print in 1889. Six copies were circulated among his friends after they signed an agreement to keep the volumes under lock and key, not let servants see them, etc. Most of the private letters he used in it were destroyed by Spencer or his biographer David Duncan. Harriet Martineau died 27 June 1876. In GHL's Journal there is an entry on GE's birthday, 22 November 1870: "Bought Polly a lockup book for her Autobiography." It has not been found. [VI, 310–11]

The Priory, | 21. North Bank, | Regents Park.
November 22. 76.

My dear Sara . . .

Perhaps it will amuse you to know that our friend Mr. Spencer, who used to despise biography as the least profitable occupation of brain, is now busily collecting the materials of his own family and personal history! The Spencer family is really interesting. H. S's father was a strong, peculiar character, and there seems to have been a strain of mental force through former generations.

We are waiting with some expectation for Miss Martineau's autobiography, which I fancy will be charming as far as her younger and less renowned life extends. All biography diminishes in interest when the subject has won celebrity—or some reputation that hardly comes up to celebrity. But autobiography at least saves a man or woman that the world is curious about from the publication of a string of mistakes called 'memoirs.' . . .

With best love to Cara. Always, dear Sara,

Your faithfully affectionate
Pollian.

JOURNAL, 1, 11 DECEMBER 1876

The Leweses met John Cross at Waterloo Station and went with him to see a house called the Heights at Witley. "Enchanted with the house and grounds." A week later they bought it for £4,950. [VI, 314]

1 December 1876. Since we came home at the beginning of September I have been made aware of much repugnance or else indifference towards the Jewish part of Deronda, and of some hostile as well as adverse reviewing. On the other hand there have been the strongest expressions of interest—some persons adhering to the opinion, started during the early numbers, that the book is my best—delighted letters have here and there been sent to me, and the sale both in America and in England has been an unmistakeable guarantee that the public has been touched. Words of gratitude have come from Jews and Jewesses, and there are certain signs that I may have contributed my mite to a good result. The sale hitherto has exceeded that of Middlemarch as to the £2/2s four-volumed form, but we do not expect an equal success for the guinea edition which has lately been issued.

11 December 1876. We have just bought a house in Surrey, and think of it as making a serious change in our life, namely, that we shall finally settle there and give up town.

TO MRS. CHARLES BRAY, 21 DECEMBER 1876

The picture was the photograph of GE sent to Cara and Sara. See [29 March 1858]. [VI, 319–21]

> **The Priory, | 21. North Bank, | Regents Park.**
> December 21. 76.

Dear Cara . . .

The 'Sir Charles Grandison' you are reading must be the series of little fat volumes you lent me to carry to the Isle of Wight, where I read it at every interval when my father did not want me, and was sorry that the long novel was not longer. It is a solace to hear of any one's reading and enjoying Richardson. We have fallen on an evil generation who would not read 'Clarissa' even in an abridged form. The French have been its most enthusiastic admirers, but I don't know whether their present admiration is more than traditional, like their set phrases about their own classics. . . .

The other night we went to hear the Bach Choir, a society of Ladies and Gentlemen got together by Jenny Lind, who sings in the middle of them, her husband acting as conductor. It is pretty to see people who might be nothing but empty fashionables taking pains to sing fine music in tune and time with more or less success. One of the baritones we know is a Grosvenor who used to be a swell guardsman, and has happily taken to good courses while still quite young. Another is a handsome young Gurney—not of the unsatisfactory Co. but of the Russell Gurney kin. A soprano is Mrs. Ponsonby—wife of the Queen's Secretary, General P.—the granddaughter of Earl Grey and just like him in the face. And so on. These people of "high" birth are certainly reforming themselves a little.

Mr. Lewes has just come up to me after reading your letter and says, "For God's sake, tell her not to have the photograph reproduced!"—and I had nearly forgotten to say that the fading is what I desired. I should not like the image to be perpetuated. It needs the friendly eyes that regret to see it fade, and must not be recalled into emphatic black and white for indifferent gazers. Pray let it finally vanish. . . .

Do let me know the good news when the Sydenham house is let, and do not forget your promise that you will not suffer any lack which I could hinder—you know, I mean lack of comforts for that difficult breath, such as might come from a sense that expensiveness obliged renunciation. With much affection all round,

> Yours always
> Marian.

TO JAMES SULLY, 19 JANUARY 1877

In his *Pessimism* (1877) Sully writes of the word *meliorism,* "for which I am indebted to our first living woman-writer and thinker 'George Eliot.'" The *OED* cites the earliest use of the word in John Brown, *Horae Subsecivae* (1858). [VI, 333–34]

The Priory, | 21. North Bank, | Regents Park.
Jan. 19. 77.

Dear Mr. Sully

I don't know that I ever heard anybody use the word "meliorist" except myself. But I begin to think that there is no good invention or discovery that has not been made by more than one person. The only good reason for referring to the "source" would be, that you found it useful for the doctrine of meliorism to cite one unfashionable confessor of it in the face of the fashionable extremes.

Always yours sincerely
M. E. Lewes.

TO JOHN BLACKWOOD, 30 JANUARY 1877

Romola was reprinted in the Cabinet edition (1878) and then in one volume (1880) without illustrations. [VI, 335–36]

The Priory, | 21. North Bank, | Regents Park.
January 30. 77.

My dear Mr. Blackwood . . .

What are we to do about 'Romola'? It ought to range with the cheap edition of my books—which, exceptis excipiendis, is a beautiful edition—as well as with any handsomer series which the world's affairs may encourage us to publish. And this edition is sufficiently distinguished from the 2/6 form which Smith and Elder have chosen. Also, I find that 'Romola' will make a volume about 50 pp. thicker than 'The Mill,' which is a sheet or so thicker than 'Adam'—and hence the volume ought to be priced rather higher. The only difficulty lies in the illustrations required for uniformity. The illustrations in the other volumes are, as Mr. Lewes says, not queerer than those which amuse us in Scott and Miss Austen— with one exception, namely, *that* where Adam is making love to Dinah, which really enrages me with its unctuousness. I would gladly pay something to be rid of it. The next worst is that of Adam in the wood with Arthur Donnithorne. The rest are endurable to a mind well accustomed to resignation. And the vignettes on the title-pages are charming. But if an illustrator is wanted, I know one whose work is exquisite—Mrs. Allingham.

This is not a moment for new ventures, but it will take some time to prepare 'Romola.' I should like to see proofs, feeling bound to take care of my text. . . . Mr. Simpson must, I think, have mistaken the intention for the act when he imagined that he had asked me for corrections of 'Daniel Deronda,' which it grieves me sorely to think of as uncorrected even in its melancholy repose.

I have just read through the cheap edition of 'Romola,' and though I have only made a few alterations of an unimportant kind—the printing being unusually correct—it would be well for me to send this copy to be printed from. I think it must be nearly ten years since I read the book before, but there is no book of mine about which I more thoroughly feel that I could swear by every sentence as having been written with my best blood, such as it is, and with the most ardent care for veracity of which my nature is capable. It has made me often sob with a sort of painful joy as I have read the sentences which had faded from my memory. This helps one to bear false representations with patience, for I really don't love any gentleman who undertakes to state my opinions, well enough to desire that I should find myself all wrong in order to justify his statement.

I wish, whenever it is expedient, to add "The Lifted Veil" and "Brother Jacob," and so fatten the volume containing "Silas Marner," which would thus become about 100 pp. thicker.

Will you kindly think and consult over these matters and let me know when you have come to any clear result?

Always yours truly
M. E. Lewes.

TO JOHN WALTER CROSS, [3 FEBRUARY 1877]

GHL noted in his Diary 27 January that "Polly had lumbago and I went to Concert alone." [VI, 337]

Saturday.

Dearest Nephew
When I say that I am delighted with the delicate azalias and deep pansies (pensées) I am showing myself a very greedy person. Ought I to be glad that so much falls to my share? I fear the only excuse for my having these flower-feasts would be that I was lame with lumbago—whereas I am nearly well today and have been enjoying a long drive and walk in the milder air.

Much love to all from

Your affectionate Aunt
M. E. Lewes.

TO WILLIAM ALLINGHAM, 8 MARCH 1877

This is GE's most detailed statement on Midland dialects. [VI, 347–48]

The Priory, | 21. North Bank, | Regents Park.
March 8. 77.

Dear Mr. Allingham
Mr. Lewes feels himself innocent of dialect in general and of Midland dialect in especial. Hence I presume to take your reference on the subject as if it had been addressed to me. I was born and bred in Warwickshire, and heard the Leicester-

shire, North Staffordshire and Derbyshire dialects during visits made in my child-hood and youth. These last are represented (mildly) in 'Adam Bede.' The War-wickshire talk is broader and has characteristics which it shares with other Mercian districts. Moreover, dialect, like other living things, tends to become mongrel, especially in a central fertile and manufacturing region attractive of migration: and hence the Midland talk presents less interesting relics of elder grammar than the more northerly dialects.

Perhaps unless a poet has a dialect ringing in his ears, so as to shape his metre and rhymes according to it at one jet, it is better to be content with a few suggestive touches, and I fear that the stupid public is not half grateful for studies in dialect beyond such suggestions. I have made a few notes, which may perhaps be not unacceptable to you, in the absence of more accomplished aid. . . .

Yours sincerely
M. E. Lewes.

1. The vowel always a double sound—the y sometimes present, sometimes not: either *aäl* or *yaäl*. *Hither* not heard except in *C' moother* addressed to horses.

2. *Thou* never heard. In general the 2d pers. sing. not used in W. except occasionally to young members of a family and then always in the form of *thee* i.e. *'ee. Can't* pron. *Cawn't*. For the *emphatic* nominative *Yo*, like the Lancashire. For the accusative *Yer*, without any sound of the r.

3. Not year but *'ear*. On the other hand with the usual 'compensation' *head* is pronounced yead.

4. "A gallows little chap as e'er yer see."

5. Heres *to* yer, Maäster. Saäme to yo.

6. Never V.

7. The demonstrative *those* never heard among the common people (unless when caught by infection from the parson etc.).

8. *Self* pron. *Sen.*

9. The *f* never heard in *of*, nor the *n* in *in*.

Perhaps, however, these imperfect indications may only determine you to reject all but the faintest signs of dialect in your well-to-do farmers who have been to London.

TO JOHN BLACKWOOD, 20 MARCH 1877

The Advertiser bound with the Books of *Daniel Deronda* brought GE £257. She had gone to Witley with the contractor Mr. Hoole to discuss alterations needed. *Harriet Martineau's Autobiography* was published 1 March 1877. [VI, 350–52]

The Priory, | 21. North Bank, | Regents Park.
March 20. 77.

My dear Mr. Blackwood

We both thank you for your letter of yesterday, enclosing the cheque for the advertisements in Deronda. . . . We are likely still to be in town when you come, for we shall hardly be able to leave till the beginning of June, and for this Summer we shall only make a sort of bivouac in our Surrey house, only putting absolutely necessary things in it, so that we may test its conveniences and inconveniences and have all the needful alterations and the more troublesome cleansings set about after we leave it for the winter. We have made up our minds not to give up our London shell till we have made more complete experiments as to the conditions of life at Witley.

About a more expensive edition of my books, I one day mentioned a plan which Mr. Lewes wants me to tell you of. I was enjoying the fine octavo page of an edition of Fielding which we possess, when it occurred to me that I should like my own books to be published in *eight* volumes of like size with fine type and paper: the six long novels making each a volume, a *seventh* being made by the Scenes of Clerical Life, Silas Marner, the Lifted Veil and Brother Jacob, and the *eighth* by the Spanish Gypsy and the Poems. I don't know how this would do financially. . . . We cannot enter into your objection to coupling the cheerful story with sadder aspects of human experience, the cheerfulness in the one mitigating the impression of sadness from the other which might be too strongly felt in separate publication. . . .

We have been reading Miss Martineau's autobiography, which is pathetic and interesting throughout the childhood and early youth. But afterwards when she has to tell about her writings and what others said and did concerning them, the impression on me was one of shuddering vexation with myself that I had ever said a word to anybody about either compliments or injuries in relation to my own doings. But assuredly I shall not write such things down to be published after my death.

Always yours truly
M. E. Lewes.

TO MRS. CHARLES BRAY, 20 MARCH 1877

GE had been an intimate friend of Harriet Martineau from her *Westminster Review* days, visited her at Ambleside in 1852, and was on the most cordial terms with her until her union with GHL. The quarrels were with her brother James Martineau. [VI, 352–54]

The Priory, | **21. North Bank,** | **Regents Park.**
March 20. 77.

My dear Cara . . .

You must read Harriet Martineau's Autobiography. While I was ill Mr. Lewes took my office of reader and for the most part read the first two volumes to me. The account of her childhood and early youth is most pathetic and interesting, but as in all books of the kind the charm departs as the life advances, and the writer has to tell of her own triumphs. One regrets continually that she felt it necessary not only to tell of her intercourse with many more or less distinguished persons—which would have been quite pleasant to everybody—but also to pronounce upon their entire merits and demerits, especially when, if she had died as soon as she expected, these persons would nearly all have been living to read her gratuitous rudenesses. But I rejoiced profoundly in the conquest of right feeling which determined her to leave the great, sad breach with her once beloved brother in almost total silence, and as I did not read Mrs. Chapman's volume (Mr. Lewes having glanced through it and told me that it was worthless) I was feeling hardly anything about the book but satisfaction in the picture of a life which was on the whole thoroughly virtuous, beneficent and dignified, until I found (what Mr. Lewes had not observed) that this wretched Mrs. Chapman has been so forsaken of all the good as to enter into details and accusations connected with that very quarrelling which Harriet Martineau had willed to bury in silence. Really there is nothing but imbecility to be pleaded as a reason why Mrs. Chapman's conduct should not be called wicked. Then again, she has published H. M's private letters—at the end of the very book which begins with a solemn protest against any such publication!

Browning observed to me that Miss Martineau's procedure in demanding back her own letters, made it the more reprehensible for her to enter into statements about her relations with others, because her own letters being destroyed there remained no evidence to check her statements. And one cannot help being convinced that her representations are often false, not from any untruthfulness in her but from the extremely self-satisfied point of view with which she regarded her transactions with business acquaintances and her intercourse with friends.

Still, in spite of Mrs. Chapman, I hope the book will do more good than harm. Many of the most interesting little stories in it about herself and others she had told me (and Mr. Atkinson) when I was staying with her, almost in the very same words. But they were all the better for being told in her silvery voice. She was a charming talker, and a perfect lady in her manners as a hostess. It is a comfort to think—looking back on the vile treatment she received from the Quarterly and Frasers, making people believe that she was a coarse-minded, repulsive woman— that such blackguardism in print could not be tolerated now, and that it would hardly enter into anybody's mind to conceive such sentences for any form of outward utterance. . . .

Your loving
Marian.

TO JOHN BLACKWOOD, 29 MARCH 1877

On 30 March—Good Friday—Tennyson came to the Priory with his son Hallam and read from 9:30 till 12. There were 21 guests. John Crombie Brown had been proofreader for the Blackwoods over many years. Mrs. Senior died 24 March. [VI, 358–59]

The Priory, | 21. North Bank, | Regents Park.
March 29. 77.

My dear Mr. Blackwood . . .

Before your letter arrived I was going to tell you of a small experience which had shaken my admiration for the 8vo in relation to imaginative works. We went the other day to choose a complete edition of Tennyson—rather in a hurry, because the poet was coming to read to us, and we did not possess quite everything he had written. So we turned into Bumpus's where we could have the various editions displayed to us. We asked first for the Library Edition, meaning to be rather grand, but when a volume of it was put into our hands we were disgusted with its weight and unmanageableness and turned with relief to the next size in five volumes, . . . Since then I have been feeling the advantage of your former idea, that our new edition should have the existing type printed on finer, tinted paper, with more margin and with a nice bit of landscape to each volume.

The loss of Mr. Brown must make a sad breach for you in the long-valued associations of your life. We are grieving for the loss of a newer but also valued friend—Mrs. Nassau Senior, that fair, bright useful woman whom, I remember, Mr. William Blackwood met at our house one day and accompanied or rather conducted helpfully to some destination, finding en route that she was the daughter of an old friend of your family. . . .

I hope you will enjoy your Easter holiday at N. Berwick.

Yours always truly
M. E. Lewes.

TO MRS. EDWARD BURNE-JONES, 28 APRIL 1877

The Burne-Joneses dined at the Priory 18 April. Sir Coutts Lindsay, who had built the Grosvenor Gallery, invited Burne-Jones to exhibit eight of his paintings at the opening, 30 April. [VI, 364–65]

The Priory, | 21. North Bank, | Regents Park.
April 28. 77.

Dearest Mignon

To have a loving note from you is the next best thing to seeing you. . . . If the Lindsays had not happened to send us tickets for the private view, we should have been most grateful for those you offer us, but now we are supplied.

I wonder what I ought to have for a morning dress to wear at breakfasts and walk out in on visits at Oxford and Cambridge. I have just had a black silk, of the robe species, such as I humbly trust you would approve, for my dinner dress. But I want something less heavy and dustshowing for the day-time. I like plain silk better than anything, but it is hard to get the right colour. These remarks are to give you a faint idea of my heavy private anxieties—not to urge you into taking the trouble to write me advice.

Our best love to both.

[Signature cut away.]

TO EDWARD BURNE-JONES, 8 MAY 1877

In 1870, Richard Wagner married Cosima, the daughter of Liszt and the Comtesse d'Agoult. She brought a letter from her father to GHL and the Leweses saw her nearly every day during Wagner's season in London. GE's many engagements included a dinner given by George Goschen, First Lord of the Admiralty, to meet the Princess Louise (at her special request). She told Mrs. Ponsonby "with great glee that she was going to meet us," and showed her pleasure in a very unusual way, for instead of GE's being presented to her, she asked, immediately on arriving, to be presented to GE, and at once sat down beside her and entered into friendly chat. After dinner they had a long talk—"very agreeable." At 11 the Leweses went from the Goschens' to a music party at Mrs. Benzon's, and got home at 1. [VI, 368, 370–72]

The Priory, | 21. North Bank, | Regents Park.
May 8. 77.

Dear Friend

Is the request I am going to make too great? It is, that I may be allowed to bring to you Madame Wagner at a time when you will be personally at liberty. She is, I think, a rare person, worthy to see the best things, having her father's (Liszt's) quickness and breadth of comprehension. Monday is the day we have conditionally proposed to ourselves. Can you confirm our plan by your permission? Madame Wagner will lunch with us, and we could drive to you afterwards so as to be with you about three—or later, if this were more convenient to you.

Yours always truly
M. E. Lewes.

TO MRS. ELMA STUART, 27 MAY 1877

Having spent the weekend of 19–21 May with Jowett at Oxford, the Leweses were at Cambridge visiting the Henry Sidgwicks 31 May–4 June. Lewes's Diary gives a concise account: The Sidgwicks had guests at breakfast, lunch, and dinner. "We visited Girton and Newnham Hall. Lunched with Oscar Browning and went to Trinity Chapel on Sunday afternoon"—probably the occasion of F. W. H. Myers's walk with GE, when by his melodramatic account she pronounced on God, Immortality, and Duty. Among others they met were Arthur Balfour, whose recent reading of *Daniel Deronda* may have spurred his declaration (1917) for a Zionist home in Palestine; Michael Foster the physiologist; Stanford, the Trinity organist; Lord Edmund FitzMaurice; and Reginald Brett, later Viscount Esher. [VI, 377–78]

The Priory, | 21. North Bank, | Regents Park.
May 27. 77.

Dearest Elma . . .

On Thursday the 31st we go to Cambridge while our servants will be busy in removing furniture, and from Cambridge we shall pass straight to our Witley home, where we hope to rest in quiet for four or five months. I think we have told you the address, but I repeat it for security—'The Heights, Witley, Surrey.' We are going to camp there experimentally, merely sending down necessaries. For if we like the house and decide to keep it, there is still a great deal of work to be done to it, so that it must in any case have been emptied again. I wish we never had to think of these outside things. The small remainder of our lives seems all too little for the emotions and ideas which are aloof from our own chairs and tables, dinner-service and paper-hangings. . . .

Always, dearest Elma

Your loving Mother (in the spirit)
M. E. Lewes.

TO DAVID KAUFMANN, 31 MAY 1877

Kaufmann (1852–99) had just become a professor at the Jewish Theological Seminary in Budapest. His article was "George Eliot und das Judenthum." [VI, 378–80]

The Priory, 21, North Bank, May 31, '77.

My dear Sir,

Hardly, since I became an author, have I had a deeper satisfaction, I may say a more heartfelt joy, than you have given me in your estimate of 'Daniel Deronda.' I must tell you that it is my rule, very strictly observed, not to read the criticisms on my writings. For years I have found this abstinence necessary to preserve me from that discouragement as an artist which ill-judged praise, no less than ill-judged blame, tends to produce in me. For far worse than any verdict as to the proportion of good and evil in our work, is the painful impression that we write for a public which has no discernment of good and evil. My husband reads any notices of me that come before him, and reports to me (or else refrains from reporting) the general character of the notice or something in particular which strikes him as showing either an exceptional insight or an obtuseness that is gross enough to be amusing. Very rarely, when he has read a critique of me, he has handed it to me, saying, "*You* must read this." And your estimate of 'Daniel Deronda' made one of these rare instances.

Certainly, if I had been asked to choose *what* should be written about my book and *who* should write it, I should have sketched—well, not anything so good as what you have written, but an article which must be written by a Jew who showed not merely sympathy with the best aspirations of his race, but a remarkable insight into the nature of art and the processes of the artistic mind. Believe me, I should not have cared to devour even ardent praise if it had not come from one who showed the discriminating sensibility, the perfect response to the artist's intention, which must make the fullest, rarest joy to one who works from inward conviction and not in compliance with current fashions. Such a response holds for an author not only what is best in "the life that now is," but the promise of "that which is to come." I mean that the usual approximative, narrow perception of what one has been intending and professedly feeling in one's work, impresses one with the sense that it must be poor perishable stuff without roots to take any lasting hold in the minds of men; while any instance of complete comprehension encourages one to hope that the creative prompting has foreshadowed, and will continue to satisfy, a need in other minds.

Excuse me that I write but imperfectly, and perhaps dimly, what I have felt in reading your article. It has affected me deeply, and though the prejudice and ignorant obtuseness which has met my effort to contribute something to the ennobling of Judaism in the conception of the Christian community and in the consciousness of the Jewish community, has never for a moment made me repent my choice, but rather has been added proof to me that the effort was needed—yet I confess that I had an unsatisfied hunger for certain signs of sympathetic discernment, which you only have given. I may mention as one instance your clear perception of the relation between the presentation of the Jewish element and those of English Social life. . . .

My husband has said more than once that he feels grateful to you. For he is more sensitive on my behalf than on his own. Hence he unites with me in the assurance of the high regard with which I remain

Always yours faithfully,
M. E. Lewes.

TO FREDERIC HARRISON, 14 JUNE 1877

Harrison had been trying since 1866 to get GE to turn her art towards Positivism. Now he wrote that, as his children were growing up, their mother was called upon for some equivalent of family prayer. He hoped that GE, with her sympathy for the inmost emotions of humanity, could help supply something. The poem she refers to was published in *Macmillan's* as "A College Breakfast-Party" in July 1878. [VI, 387–88]

The Heights | Witley | Godalming | June 14. 1877.
Dear Mr. Harrison

I am greatly indebted to you for your letter. It has done something towards rousing me from what I will not call self-despair but resignation to being of no use. . . . I do not quite understand whether you have in your mind any plan of straightway constructing a liturgy to which you wish me to contribute in a direct way. That form of contribution would hardly lie within my powers. But your words of trust in me as possibly an organ of feelings which have not yet found their due expression is as likely as any external call could be to prompt such perfectly unfettered productions as that which you say has been found acceptable.

I wasted some time three years ago in writing (what I do not mean to print) a poetic dialogue embodying or rather shadowing very imperfectly the actual contest of ideas. Perhaps what you have written to me may promote and influence a different kind of presentation. At any rate, all the words of your letter will be borne in mind and will enter into my motives. . . .

Yours sincerely
M. E. Lewes. . . .

TO MME EUGÈNE BODICHON, 2 AUGUST 1877

Barbara was only 50 years old when she had a stroke in June 1877. She lived till 1891. Thackeray's daughter Anne at the age of 40 married her cousin Richmond Ritchie, who was only 23. [VI, 398–99]

The Heights | Witley | Godalming | Aug. 2. 77.

Dearest Barbara

It was a draught of real comfort and pleasure to have a letter written by your own hand, and one so altogether cheerful. I trust that the warmer weather is salutary to you and that you will by and by be able to write me word of continued progress.
. . .

We are enjoying the mixture of wildness and culture extremely, and so far as landscape and air go, we would not choose a different home from this. But we have not yet made up our minds whether we shall keep our house or sell it. Some London friends are also occasional dwellers in these parts. The day before yesterday we had Mr. and Mrs. Frederic Harrison, whose parents have a fine old Tudor house—Sutton Place—about 3 miles beyond Guildford. Mrs. Harrison asked with much interest about you, and was glad to hear of Madame Mario also, of whom Dr. Bridges had spoken very prettily to her. And do you remember Edmund Gurney? He and his graceful bride lunched with us the other day. She was very poor before her marriage and had worked in an exemplary way both to help her mother and educate herself—her father having lost his property and left his family destitute.

And Miss Thackeray's married today to young Ritchie. I saw him at Cambridge and felt that the nearly 20 years' difference between them was bridged hopefully by his solidity and gravity. This is one of several instances that I have known of lately, showing that young men with even brilliant advantages will often choose as their life's companion a woman whose attractions are wholly of the spiritual order. . . .

We are poor creatures—headachy and feeble but not the less affectionate in our memories of our too far-off friend. I often see you enjoying your sunsets and the wayside flowers.

Always your loving
Marian.

TO THE HON. MRS. HENRY PONSONBY, 17 OCTOBER 1877

William H. Mallock was an undergraduate at Balliol 1869–74. Though he won the Newdigate Prize for a poem on the Isthmus of Suez, he obtained a third class degree. Jowett, then Master, regarded him as a mere dilettante. In *The New Republic,* a parody of University life, the principal characters are drawn from well-known people: Jowett is lampooned as Dr. Jenkinson; Arnold is Mr. Luke; Mrs. Pattison, Lady Grace; Pater, Mr. Rose; Huxley, Mr. Storks; etc. [VI, 406–07]

The Heights, Witley, | October 17th, 1877.

Dear Mrs. Ponsonby,

I like to know that you have been thinking of me and that you care to write to me, and though I will not disobey your considerate prohibition so far as to try and answer your letter fully, I must content my soul by telling you that we shall be settled in the old place by the end of the first week in November, and that I shall be delighted to see you there. I long to know how far that purpose for which you made your residence in London months ago has been fulfilled. And there are many other subjects, more common to all of us, that I shall have a special pleasure in talking of with you. . . .

It will perhaps surprise you to know that, having read the *New Republic* I think it one of the most condemnable books of the day; not simply because the Master of Balliol is a friend for whom I have a high regard. If I had known nothing of Mr. Jowett personally, I should equally have felt disapprobation of a work in which a young man who has no solid contribution of his own to make, sets about attempting to turn into ridicule the men who are most prominent in serious effort to make such contribution. With that impression from the *New Republic* I was not inclined to read anything by the same writer until I heard that he had repented and been converted to the emotions of gratitude and reverence. I think that kind of direct personal portraiture (or caricature, for except for Mr. Jowett and one other, the drawing is mere distortion) is a bastard kind of satire that I am not disposed to think the better of because Aristophanes used it in relation to Socrates. Do you know that pretty story about Bishop Thirlwall—that when somebody wanted to bring to him Forchhammer as a distinguished German writer, he replied, "No! I will never receive into my house the man who justified the death of Socrates." . . .

I am so glad you have been enjoying Ireland in quiet. We love our bit of country and are bent on keeping it as a summer refuge always. Dear Mrs. Ponsonby,

Yours affectionately,
M. E. Lewes.

TO JOHN WALTER CROSS, 6 NOVEMBER 1877

The maxim of Cleobulos was "Avoid extremes." Cross had sent a badminton set to the Priory. They set it up on Sunday, 4 November, but the wind was too strong. Among the guests that afternoon were the George Howards, Spencer, Edith Simcox, Norman and Richard Grosvenor, Cobden Sanderson, Leslie Stephen, and Burne-Jones. [VI, 415–16]

The Priory, | 21. North Bank, | Regents Park.
November 6. 77.

My dearest Nephew

If I could find it in my heart I should scold you for not observing a precept of the Seven Sages. Two battledores and a shuttle cock would have been apparatus enough for my skill, or want of skill. And we find that with these we can play a modest game in our little entrance hall. I cannot bear to have that magnificent rainbow of a net and its polished poles exposed to the alternate smoke and rain of this avenue to Tartarus. But with all this grumbling at your too lavish generosity under these morose skies, I am deeply touched by your thoughtful kindness.

Still—which would you choose? An aunt who lost headaches and gained flesh by spending her time on tennis and Badminton, or an aunt who remained sickly and beckoned death by writing more books? Behold yourself in a dilemma! If you choose the plump and idle aunt, she will declare that you don't mind about her writing. If you choose the pallid and productive aunt she will declare that you have no real affection for her. It is impossible to satisfy an author.

Apropos of authorship I was a little uneasy on Sunday because I had seemed in the unmanageable current of talk to echo a too slight way of speaking about a great poet. I did not mean to say Amen when 'The Idyls of the King' seemed to be judged rather 'de haut en bas.' I only meant that I should value for my own mind 'In Memoriam' as the chief of the larger works, and that while I feel exquisite beauty in passages scattered through the Idyls, I must judge some smaller wholes among the lyrics as the works most decisive of Tennyson's high place among the immortals.

Not that my deliverance on this matter is of any moment, but that I cannot bear to fall in with the sickening fashion of people who talk much about writers whom they read little, and pronounce on a great man's powers with only half his work in their mind, while if they remembered the other half they would find their judgments as to his limits flatly contradicted. Then again, I think Tennyson's dramas such as the world should be glad of—and would be if there had been no prejudgement that he could not write a drama.

Perhaps you will reflect that all this scribbling is my Badminton for a wet morning.

Your affectionate Aunt
M. E. Lewes.

TO SARA HENNELL, 16 NOVEMBER 1877

Elinor Southwood Lewes (24 June 1877–3 November 1974), the youngest and last surviving of Charles Lewes's children, was married to Ernest Carrington Ouvry, 25 April 1903 by
Dr. Thomas Sadler, minister of the Rosslyn Hill Unitarian Chapel at Hampstead. [VI, 419–
21]

The Priory, | 21. North Bank, | Regents Park.
November 16. 77.

My dear Sara . . .

We returned from our country home (with which we are much in love) at the
beginning of this month, leaving it earlier than we wished because of the need to
get workmen into it. Our bit of Surrey has the beauties of Scotland wedded to
those of Warwickshire, and in front of our hill we have a valley which would be
equal to what one sees from Richmond Hill—if the river were not wanting. Water
is the one deficiency. During the last two months of our stay there I was conscious
of more health and strength than I have known for several years. Imagine me
playing at lawn tennis by the hour together! . . .

The Saturday before last we went to the christening of a new little Eleanor,
Charles and Gertrude's third baby, born in June last. The christening took place
in Dr. Sadler's chapel where Miss Marshall, eleven years ago, came to look on at
their marriage. Dr. Sadler is a benignant-faced refined man whose voice and
manner make the occasion such as affects one without any moral jar. Our two
little ones at Natal are delicate, and so is their mother, but we are assured that the
climate there gives the best hope of their being reared. The widowed mother
writes with a loving unselfishness which has given us an affection for her all across
the ocean. . . .

Your loving
Pollian.

TO JOHN BLACKWOOD, 22 NOVEMBER 1877

Blackwood wrote that only 400 copies of the 7/6 *Deronda* remained. Main had proposed a
"George Eliot Birthday Book," with extracts from her work for each day of the year.
Blackwood published it in 1878. [VI, 422–23]

The Priory, | 21. North Bank, | Regents Park.
November 22. 77.

My dear Mr. Blackwood

Thanks for your kind letter with its agreeable news. I am much comforted by
the speedy sale of the 7/6 edition. Beforehand, I should have thought 5000 a rash
number to print.

On the specimen title-page for the Cabinet Edition, which Mr. Simpson has
sent, Mr. Lewes has written a suggestion which I think will be found an improvement. The design for the cover we like very much. I had thought of a rich olive
green for the colour—a hue which sets off well both the gold and the black. But

Mr. Simpson promises to let us see specimens. Is it not desirable to omit any numbering of the volumes *according to the series?*—for two reasons: first, because the order of publication is not the chronological, in which they should ultimately be ranged, and secondly, because it would be a disadvantage for the independent sale of the several works. Is it not usual to omit such serial numbering?—for example the volumes of De Quincey's works are not numbered except furtively, by stars, and Thackeray's not at all.

As to Mr. Main's proposition, we have never seen or heard anything of the said 'Birthday Books'—have you? They may be the vulgarest things in the book stalls for what we know. *Entre nous*, I am a little shocked by the tone of Mr. M's letter. How could he be so ignorant as to suppose that any other publishing house than yours could issue such a book? . . . But I must refer the matter to your judgment. Burns and Shakespeare books are no criterion for a living writer. The Tennyson book would be such, and I confess I should like to see its aspect before consenting. I believe that you, as much as I, hate puffing, gaudy, claptrappy forms of publication, superfluous for all *good* ends. But anything graceful which you consider an advantage to the circulation of my works we are not averse to. . . .

[*The rest of this letter is lacking.*]

TO JOHN WALTER CROSS, 13 DECEMBER 1877

On the illness of his mother. [VI, 432–33]

The Priory, | 21. North Bank, | Regents Park.
December 13. 77.

Dearest Nephew

Your note yesterday gave me much comfort, and I thank you for sparing the time to write it. The world cannot seem quite the same to me as long as you are all in anxiety about her who is most precious to you—in immediate urgent anxiety, that is. For love is never without its shadow of anxiety. We have this treasure in earthen vessels. With best love to her and all

Your affectionate Aunt
M. E. Lewes.

DIARY, 31 DECEMBER 1877

The Diary for 1878 has not been found. [VI, 439–40]

Today I say a final farewell to this little book which is the only record I have made of my personal life for sixteen years and more. I have often been helped by looking back in it to compare former with actual states of despondency from bad health or other apparent causes. In this way a past despondency has turned to present hopefulness. But of course as the years advance there is a new rational ground for the expectation that my life may become less fruitful. The difficulty is, to decide how far resolution should set in the direction of activity rather than in the acceptance of a more negative state. Many conceptions of works to be carried out present themselves, but confidence in my own fitness to complete them worthily is all the more wanting because it is reasonable to argue that I must have already done my best. In fact, my mind is embarrassed by the number and wide variety of subjects that attract me, and the enlarging vista that each brings with it.

I shall record no more in this book, because I am going to keep a more business-like diary. Here ends 1877.

13

THE GREAT PARTING
Impressions of Theophrastus Such

It is impossible to overestimate the debt English literature owes to GHL. Nothing but his encouragement could have overcome GE's diffidence about the value of her writing. His shrewd marketing of her work earned her £70,000. In 1863 they bought the Priory. In 1873 they set up their own carriage—that unmistakable token of Victorian success. In 1876 they bought the Heights at Witley as a summer residence. Most of all GHL's vivacity animated and directed the Sunday afternoons at the Priory, when their drawing room was crowded with the most brilliant and famous society of the age. Admiration of GE's genius had borne down disapproval of their irregular union, lived openly, "a virtuous crime." For 24 years they had enjoyed unbroken happiness. The only joy they lacked was good health. In 1874 GE had the first severe attack of kidney stone, which tormented her intermittently for the rest of her days. Though his cheerfulness never faltered, GHL suffered from very serious illnesses that culminated in an intestinal cancer. Returned to London in November, he sent Blackwood his last letter with the MS of the collection of GE's essays called *Impressions of Theophrastus Such*. On 30 November 1878, nine days later, he died.

Overwhelmed with grief, GE did not go out of her room for more than a week; more than a month passed before she even walked in the garden. Though racked with acute pain, she set to work preparing GHL's *The Study of Psychology* for the press, before undertaking the 500 pages of the final volume of his *Problems of Life and Mind*. She had been considering establishing a Studentship in Physiology in GHL's memory and had written to scientific friends about it. For this and the many other business matters that GHL had always attended to for her, she turned to "Nephew Johnnie" Cross, the banker who managed their investments. His mother had died just a week after GHL, and he was trying to find new interests. When he told GE that he was learning Italian by reading Dante, she exclaimed: "Oh, I must read that with you." After she went to the Heights for the summer, they saw each other even more frequently. Though she was 20 years older, Johnnie loved her. In August he said that he wanted to be more than a friend. Twice she refused him. But she discussed the matter with her doctor, Sir James Paget, who said, "Why not?" On 6 May 1880 at St. George's, Hanover Square, she became Mrs. John Walter Cross.

TO JOHN BLACKWOOD, 26 JANUARY 1878

Pascal was in Blackwood's Foreign Classics for English Readers. Blackwood's last dispatch contained a check for £1,006. [VII, 10–11]

The Priory, | 21. North Bank, | Regents Park.
January 26. 78.

My dear Mr. Blackwood . . .

Last night I finished reading Principal Tulloch's small but full volume on Pascal—a present for which I am much obliged. It is admirably fair and dispassionate and I should think will be an acceptable piece of instruction to many readers. . . . My first acquaintance with Pascal came from his *Pensées* being given to me as a school prize when I was fourteen, and I am continually turning to them now to revive my sense of their deep though broken wisdom. It is a pity that *La Bruyère* cannot be done justice to by any merely English presentation. There is a sentence of his which touches with the finest point the diseased spot in the literary culture of our time—"Le plaisir de la critique nous ôte celui d'être vivement touchés de très belles choses." We see that our present fashions are old, but there is this difference, that they are followed by a greater multitude.

You may be sure that I was very much cheered by your last despatch—the solid unmistakable proof that my books are not yet superfluous. . . .

Always yours sincerely
M. E. Lewes.

TO FREDERICK LOCKER, [7 MARCH 1878]

It had not been made clear to the Leweses that they were invited to the reception in the Jerusalem Chamber. Locker sent them a piece of the bridecake later. Lewes noted in his Diary: "At 11 went to the Abbey to attend the marriage of Lionel Tennyson and Eleanor Locker. The Abbey crowded. Many of our friends and acquaintances there. The ceremony very touching and interesting. One of the most interesting points—at least to me—was that as we all came out of the Abbey I saw a lady gazing very devoutly at Polly and then quietly as if unobserved stroke the back of her cloak and person. Du Maurier afterwards told us that Mrs. Kendall was in high spirits at having 'touched George Eliot.' Now the lady I saw was *not* Mrs. Kendall—so that there were two who had the same inspiration." [VII, 14–15]

The Priory, | 21. North Bank, | Regents Park.
Thursday.

My dear Mr. Locker

The bridecake is proudly and gratefully valued as a sign of the sweet Bride's remembrance and yours. I cannot help feeling rather exasperated against unpunishable Chance for leaving us ignorant that we might have gone into the Jerusalem Chamber after the ceremony and had a greeting and parting which would always have been a favourite memory with us. I should have had a real joy in being there. . . .

With cordial thanks from both of us I remain

Yours always truly
M. E. Lewes.

TO JOHN CROSS, 29 APRIL 1878

Cross and his sister Florence had brought the flowers when they came to lunch at the Priory 28 April. [IX, 226]

The Priory, | 21. North Bank, | Regents Park.
April 29. 78.

Dearest Nephew

I had no opportunity yesterday of thanking you for my transcendantly beautiful basket of flowers, which not only cheered me as a sign of your valued affection, but made our table cheerful and supplied some deficit of vivacity in the hostess. It is a precious thought to me that you care for that part of me which will live when the 'Auntship' is gone—'Non omnis moriar' is a keen hope with me. Yet I like to be loved in this faulty, frail (yet venerable) flesh.

My master insists that I shall go out to walk with him. So I have had only three minutes to scribble in.

Always your affectionate
Aunt.

TO MRS. GEORGE GOSCHEN, 24 MAY 1878

The guests of honor were Frederick William, Crown Prince of Prussia, and his wife Victoria, eldest daughter of Queen Victoria, Princess Royal of Great Britain. There were 22 at dinner. The Leweses had read Mme d'Agoult's *Souvenirs de ma Vie* in 1877. [VII, 28]

The Priory, | 21. North Bank, | Regents Park.
May 24, '78.

Dear Mrs. Goschen,

We shall be very happy to dine with you on Friday the 31st at 8 o'clock, according to your kind invitation.

Glad you like *Mes Souvenirs*. The writer's experience is more interesting than her personality.

Yours sincerely,
M. E. Lewes.

TO MRS. CHARLES BRAY, 7 JUNE 1878

Charles and Gertrude Lewes, who had lived since their marriage with Mary and Margaret
Gillies at 25 Church Row, Hampstead, moved into Elm Cottage, Rosslyn Hill. The
Leweses went for their annual visit to Jowett at Oxford 8–10 June, missing the Empress
Eugénie by leaving before lunch. [VII, 29–30]

The Priory, | 21. North Bank, | Regents Park.
June 7. 78.

My dear Cara . . .

The royalties did themselves much credit. The Crown Prince is really a grand
looking man, whose name you would ask for with expectation if you imagined him
no royalty. He is like a grand antique bust—cordial and simple in manners withal,
shaking hands and insisting that I should let him know when we next came to
Berlin, just as if he had been a Professor Gruppe, living *au troisième*. *She* is less
distinguished in physique, but equally good-natured and unpretending, liking
best to talk of nursing soldiers and of what her Father's taste was in literature. She
opened the talk by saying, "You knew my sister Louise"—just as any other slightly
embarrassed mortal might have done. The only complaint one had to make was
that she never sat down till quite late in the evening—a sore trial to plebeian legs
and backs. We had a picked party to dinner—Dean of Westminster, Bishop of
Peterborough, Lord and Lady Ripon, Dr. Lyon Playfair, Kinglake (you remember
Eōthen—the formal old gentleman is a good friend of mine) Froude, Mrs. Ponsonby (Lord Grey's granddaughter), and two or three more 'illustrations'—then a
small detachment coming in after dinner. It was really an interesting occasion.

We have got through our furniture buying to our great relief—and now Charles
and Gertrude are going to leave Miss Gillies and set up a house of their own—
room being deficient for the growing family. But we shall not have to buy for
them, thank heaven, except in the sense of finding the money. We both long for
quiet and a farewell to shops which are my abhorrence. . . .

Your loving
Marian.

We go to Oxford tomorrow, and by the following Saturday we hope that the
flitting will have been made.

TO MRS. THOMAS TROLLOPE, 27 AUGUST 1878

The Trollopes spent two days at the Heights. After lunch on 22 August they went with
GHL to Aldworth, where Tennyson read them two of his new poems. [IX, 237]

The Heights, Witley, | Nr. Godalming.
August 27. 78.

My dear Mrs. Trollope

Mr. Trollope's letter has been a great comfort to us this morning, clearing up
painful doubts. And O thanks for the trouble you took—when you had the
headache too—to get me the impossible Hat! Headache makes me selfish, but in

you apparently it only adds more merit to your good nature. I blame myself for not having reflected that my request might cause you to make an otherwise unnecessary loop in your journey. . . .

I feel sure that Tennyson was highly gratified by the sympathetic audience you made for him. I saw an expression in his face that always reminds me of a large dog laying down its ears and wagging its tail on being stroked and patted. . . .

Good weather and all other possible good attend you in the rest of your journey.

Yours always affectionately
M. E. Lewes.

TO MME EUGÈNE BODICHON, 15 OCTOBER 1878

Cross wrote "At this time I was in the habit of going over occasionally from Weybridge on Sundays. The shadow of trouble was on both our houses. My mother was in her last illness, and Mr Lewes was constantly ailing, though none of us then thought that he would be taken first. But the sharing of a common anxiety contributed to make our friendship much more intimate. In our drives in the neighbourhood of Witley, Mr Lewes used sometimes to be suddenly seized with severe cramping pains. I think he was himself aware that something was seriously wrong, but the moment the pain ceased the extraordinary buoyancy of his spirits returned. Nothing but death could quench that bright flame. Even on his worst days he had always a good story to tell; and I remember on one occasion, in the drawing-room at Witley, between two bouts of pain, he sang through, with great *brio*, though without much voice, the greater portion of the tenor part in the 'Barber of Seville'—George Eliot playing his accompaniment, and both of them thoroughly enjoying the fun." Mrs. Richard Greville, the neighbour, came often and recited poems at the Heights. On 19 October she brought Henry James's *The Europeans*, which Lewes read at once. [VII, 70–71]

The Heights, Witley, | Nr. Godalming.
October 15. 78.

Dearest Barbara . . .

We have been a little better of late but the poor little man has still visitations of cramp and gout. Still he is as joyous as ever, and we are intensely happy in our bit of country—as happy as the cloudy aspect of public affairs will allow any one who cares for them to be, with the daily reading of the Times. . . .

A neighbour of ours was reciting to me yesterday some delicious bits of dialogue with a quaint Surrey woman—e.g. 'O ma'am, what I have gone through with my husband. He is so uneddicated—he never had a tail-coat in his life!" Best love from us both.

Yours ever
Marian.

TO MRS. ELMA STUART, 5 NOVEMBER 1878

GHL's "gouty symptoms" came from a cancer of the bowel, which caused his death 30 November. On 1 November, without warning, Mrs. Greville appeared with Henry James. They found the Leweses sitting beside the fire "in a chill desert of a room." Since there was no preparation for tea, they soon took leave. GHL went with them to the door, but, as James was stepping into the carriage, returned for *The Europeans,* which he wanted to return to Mrs. Greville. In *The Middle Years* James fills several pages (80–84) with his assumption that the Leweses did not connect him with the book and had not read it or realized that he too was doing "her sort of work." [VII, 74–75]

The Heights, Witley, | Nr. Godalming.
November 5. 78.

Dearest Elma . . .

We shall leave this house on the eleventh (11th) and by the 15th we shall be settled in London, at the old Priory again. Mr. Lewes has been much tormented with gouty symptoms, but is bright and enjoying, nevertheless. I am variable, but on the whole better than in the summer. . . .

The larger world is so sad, with its wars and rumours of wars, that one is more than ever in need of the small world of specially beloved ones. I am ashamed to add to the much that I am sure Mrs. Menzies has to do and think of, but her heart is as large as my demands.

Always your loving Mother,
M. E. Lewes.

TO MRS. EDWARD BURNE-JONES, 18 NOVEMBER 1878

The news of the Afghan War was of special interest to GE because Lord Lytton was involved as Viceroy of India. [VII, 78]

The Priory, | 21. North Bank, | Regents Park.
November 18. 78.

Dearest Mignon

At last we are in the old place again, but it vexes my soul a little that if you could come to see us on Friday we might not be at home till 1/2 past 5, having to do parental duty in seeing our children's new house.

I am unhappy about my husband, who is grievously ailing. This anxiety spoils all joy, which would otherwise be abundant with me in spite of the world's calamities. The newspaper makes me sad one part of the day, but I recover myself and find the air sweet nevertheless. I suppose nobody ever committed suicide because the world was full of suffering, unless he felt the fact through some misery of his own.

Love to all from

Yours always
M. E. Lewes.

TO JOHN BLACKWOOD, 23 NOVEMBER 1878

GHL's last letter to Blackwood (21 November) went with the MS of *Impressions of Theophrastus Such*. Sir James Paget, who surely foresaw the outcome, comforted GE by saying that the actual trouble would soon be allayed. [VII, 80–81]

The Priory, | 21. North Bank, | Regents Park.
November 23/78.

My dear Mr. Blackwood

When Mr. Lewes sent you my M.S. the other morning he was in that state of exhilarated activity which often comes with the sense of ease after an attack of illness which had been very painful. In the afternoon he imprudently drove out and undertook with his usual eagerness to get through numerous details of business, over-fatigued himself and took cold. The effect has been a sad amount of suffering from feverishness, headache and sickness, and I have been in deep anxiety—am still very unhappy, and only comforted by Sir James Paget's assurance that the actual trouble will soon be allayed.

I have been telling the patient about your letter and suggestion that he should send a form of slip as advertisement for the Magazine. He says—and the answer seems to have been a matter of premeditation with him—that it will be better not to announce the book in this way at once—"the Americans and Germans will be down on us." I cannot question him further at present, but I have no doubt he has been thinking about the matter, and we must not cross his wish in any way.

Will you kindly send me the calculation as to quantity as soon as you can? I thought that more than 300 pages for a volume in handsome paper might not be desirable. But you know in a work of this unkind—in contrast with the continuous development of a story—"il n'y a pas de raison que cela cesse," except such reason as lies *outside* the author's mind.

I have thought that a good form of advertisement to save people from disappointment in a book of mine not being a story, would be to print the list of Contents which, with the title, would give all but the very stupid a notice to what form of writing the work belongs. But this is a later consideration. I am glad you were pleased with the opening.

Always yours truly
M. E. Lewes.

TO MME EUGÈNE BODICHON, [7 JANUARY 1879]

[VII, 93]

Tuesday.

Dearest Barbara

I bless you for all your goodness to me, but I am a bruised creature, and shrink even from the tenderest touch. As soon as I feel able to see anybody I will see *you*. Please give my love to Bessie and thank her for me—I mean, for her sweet letter.

It was a long while before I read any letters, but tell her I shall read hers again and again.

Your loving but half dead
Marian.

TO JOHN BLACKWOOD, 13 JANUARY 1879

Theophrastus Such had been set up a few days after the MS arrived. Blackwood wrote that he would send her complete proofs 15 January. [VII, 93–94]

The Priory, | 21. North Bank, | Regents Park.
January 13. 1879.

My dear Mr. Blackwood

It was a long while before I read any letters, and as yet I have written none except such as business required of me. You will believe that this has not been for want of gratitude to all my friends for their goodness to me. I can trust to your understanding of a sorrow which has broken my life.

I write now because I ought not to allow any disproportionate expense to be incurred about my printed sheets. To me now the writing seems all trivial stuff, but since he wished it to be printed, and you seem to concur, I will correct the sheets (if you will send me the remainder) gradually as I am able, and they can be struck off and laid by for a future time. I submit this proposition to your judgment, not knowing what may be the most expedient for your printing office.

Only two days before he died he asked me to let him see the specimen page (I had told him of it the morning it came—five days before), looked at it closely and said with a satisfied expression, "O how nice!" Thank you for all your kind words.

Yours always truly
M. E. Lewes.

TO ASHER ISAAC MYERS, 18 JANUARY 1879

Myers, editor of the *Jewish Chronicle*, wrote that he found Mordecai "an unconscious photograph" of the late Dr. Benisch. [VII, 95–96]

The Priory, | 21. North Bank, | Regents Park.
January 18. 1879.

Pray let this letter be strictly private.
Dear Sir

I have but lately begun to read letters and have not answered them unless duty demanded it. But I answer yours because the anxiety you express lest I should feel your writing to me an intrusion should lead you to misinterpret my silence. . . .

I am not in the habit of reading printed observations on my writings, but my husband informed me that various excellent persons had (with the best intention) repeated the mistaken statement that the Jew named Cohn, of whom he gave some recollections in the Fortnightly Review ten or twelve years ago, bore a resemblance to Mordecai, and was thus a guarantee that the character was not an impossible ideal. Mr. Lewes took several opportunities (in conversation) of pointing out that no such resemblance existed, Cohn being a keen dialectician and a highly impressive man, but without any specifically Jewish enthusiasm. His type was rather that of Spinoza whose metaphysical system attracted his subtle intellect, and in relation to Judaism Spinoza was in contrast with my conception of Mordecai.

Such misunderstandings continually arise, and are hardly worth notice. But I mention the subject on this occasion because I believe that my husband would have written this letter for me and would have said nearly what I have said.

> Yours very sincerely
> M. E. Lewes.

TO JOHN CROSS, [22 JANUARY 1879]

GE had written a number of other letters about business which are noted in her Diary but have not been found. [VII, 97]

The Priory, | 21. North Bank, | Regents Park.

Dearest Nephew

Some time, if I live, I shall be able to see you—perhaps sooner than any one else. But not yet. Life seems to get harder instead of easier.

> Yours ever
> M. E. L.

TO JOHN CROSS, [30 JANUARY 1879]

In her Diary GE wrote 19 January: "Ruminating on the founding of some Educational instrumentality as a Memorial to be called by his name." She was working steadily on the MS Lewes left unfinished, called The Study of Psychology. [VII, 99]

The Priory, | 21. North Bank, | Regents Park.
Sunday.

Dearest Nephew

When I said 'some time' I meant still a distant time. I want to live a little while that I may do certain things for his sake. So I take care of my diet, and try to keep up my strength, and I work as much as I can to save my mind from imbecility. But that is all at present. I can go through anything that is mere business. But what used to be joy is joy no longer, and what is pain is easier because he has not to bear it. . . .

You will not mention to anyone that I wrote about seeing you. I know your thoughtful care. But if you feel prompted to say anything, write it to me.

Always yours affectionately and gratefully

> M. E. L.

TO MME EUGÈNE BODICHON, 3 FEBRUARY 1879

The attack began 30 January. Sir James Paget called the next day and prescribed. He also spoke about Sir John Simon's scheme for lectures at the College of Surgeons. Her pain continued until 6 February when Paget came again and "Talked of my darling." [VII, 100]

The Priory, | 21. North Bank, | Regents Park.
February 3. 79.

Dearest Barbara

I had become anxious about your health, not having heard anything of it for so long, and had just told the housekeeper to call and inquire in Blandford Square. Your note relieved my anxiety, and I trust that the thaw will favour your change of air.

I have had an attack of renal pain and have been much disordered by it. My head, however, has become clearer this morning and I am able to occupy myself.

Your always loving
Marian.

TO JOHN CROSS, 7 FEBRUARY 1879

[VII, 101–02]

The Priory, | 21. North Bank, | Regents Park.
February 7. 79

Dearest Nephew

I do need your affection. Every sign of care for me from the beings I respect and love is a help to me. And I did *not* mean that I should prefer you or my dear nieces not to call. Only I fear it takes up valuable time to make this out of the way round. In a week or two I think I shall want to see you. Sometimes even now I have a longing, but it is immediately counteracted by a fear. The perpetual mourner—the grief that can never be healed—is innocently enough felt to be wearisome by the rest of the world. And my sense of desolation increases. Each day seems a new beginning—a new acquaintance with grief.

I have written this just on receiving your kind answer. Love to them all at home.

Your affectionate Aunt
M. E. L.

TO THOMAS CLIFFORD ALLBUTT, 20 FEBRUARY 1879

Allbutt's letter written 19 January said with much other praise of GHL: "More than one of our best young biologists have said to me, 'Other books on Physiology may be more learned or at any rate more comprehensive, but although I knew all school physiology as a lesson, this knowledge never sprang into life within me until I read Lewes. From him I date my real beginnings.'" Pavlov, the great Russian physiologist, said the same thing about Lewes's *Physiology of Common Life.* [VII, 103–04]

> **The Priory, | 21. North Bank, | Regents Park.**
> February 20. 79.

Dear Dr. Allbutt

Your letter is among the most precious signs of sympathy that my kind friends have given me, because of what you say in it about my husband's influence over students. That is what he himself cared for as among the chief aims of life. I am tempted to ask you whether it would be otherwise than repugnant to you—whether you would have any satisfaction in writing, not a eulogistic, but a plain statement of your observation and experience in relation to the effect of my husband's work, to be printed in quotation, but not (unless you wished it) with your name, simply as a testimony of an experienced physician whose judgment is not simply that of a professional man, but of a scientific experimenter. I want, if I can, to write a *'characteristik'* of my loved one—no memoir, but a brief sketch of his mental and moral qualities, and his way of looking at the work he tried to do. Just now I am ill. Sir James Paget and Dr. Andrew Clark say I shall get better, but in the meantime my comparative incapacity for the work I want to do makes me anxious.

Can you help me with any suggestions as to founding (now while I live) some Lectureship or other efficient instrument of teaching Biology (including Psychology) in memory of my husband, and to be called by his name? I am trying to get good advice, knowing how difficult it is to make an endowment a 'good custom' which shall not in the end become corrupt. . . .

> Always yours gratefully,
> M. E. Lewes.

I have not yet seen any one except our son Charles, and am unequal to anything more than feeble thinking and writing in relation to those chief objects. Any word you can send me will be valued.

TO MRS. MARK PATTISON, 20 FEBRUARY 1879

Mark Pattison wrote to GE 18 January 1879 expressing his sympathy. "Nor am I myself without a special share in the common loss of all of us. For the last few years no one's word of approval has been more to me than Mr. Lewes'. I have had the feeling that however others might miss the point of any allusion, there was one friendly house in which every word would be taken as it was meant." [VII, 104]

The Priory, | 21. North Bank, | Regents Park.
February 20. 79.

My dear Daughter
    Your tender words and the other signs of your mindful affection have not been lost upon me. I am not easy without telling you so and blessing you in these inky characters as well as in my heart. But I am ill, dear—have been hindered from using my mind effectively for several weeks, and I am obliged to leave the great goodness of many friends quite unacknowledged. I should like to know how your health is. You say nothing about it.

Always your faithfully affectionate
M. E. L.

I have seen no one yet, except Charles.

TO MRS. ISAAC EVANS, 20 FEBRUARY 1879

No word came from GE's brother Isaac. His son-in-law the Reverend William Griffiths wrote 6 December 1878: "We shall never forget his kindness to us when we took the liberty of calling in 1874." [VII, 105]

The Priory, | 21. North Bank, | Regents Park.
February 20. 1879.

My dear Sarah
    I have been ill in body of late, but that only makes me the more anxious to tell you that your words of sympathy were very deeply felt by me in the first pressure of my sorrow. That sorrow was not the heaviest. I feel the weight more and more in the necessity of living on from day to day and fulfilling the duties of life. Your own health, I know, has long been such as to cause you much suffering. But I know too that you are encompassed with affection and blessed with the sense of having good children.
    Give my love to my Brother and believe me always

Your affectionate Sister
M. E. Lewes.

If you are writing to Mr. Griffiths please thank him on my behalf for his kind letter. I am unable to write the many acknowledgements of my friends' goodness that gratitude would prompt.

TO CI

Since Herbert Lewes's d   etter
announcing that she ha   )6]

                                               ing.

Dearest Boy

The enclosed letters came today. Finding them in the drawer and seeing they came from Natal, I opened them because you were not coming today. The bill drawn on you at the Union Bank will now, I suppose, create no difficulty. But if you had not opened your account there, it might have been awkward. On the back I have made a copy of Eliza's statement of expenses. It is clear, she wants £200 and I must make arrangements to let her have that sum.

Your loving
Mutter.

Food per month £6	78. 0.0
Girl's Wages £1	13. 0.0
Kafir do.	13. 0.0
Kafir's food	6.10.0
(!) Children's Boots	7.16.0
Washing	3.18.0
Seats at Chapel	2. 0.0
	124. 4.0

Doctor's Bill ⎫
             ⎬ Vague
Dress   ⎭

TO JOHN BLACKWOOD, 5 MARCH 1879

Here GE takes up the details which GHL had always attended to. The shortened title was accepted. Before the half title Blackwood had tipped in: "Publisher's Note. The Manuscript of this Work was put into our hands towards the close of last year, but the publication has been delayed owing to the domestic affliction of the Author." [VII, 110–11]

The Priory, | 21. North Bank, | Regents Park.
March 5. 79.

My dear Mr. Blackwood

I send the corrected sheets of 'Theophrastus', and shall be much obliged if you will order a complete Revise to be sent me before they are struck off.

Is it intended that the paper should be of the same size as in these proofs? The margin seems perilously and unbeautifully narrow, especially at the back. I observe that the line is longer than that of the original edition of Silas Marner, and the length of the printed page equally long, while even in Silas Marner the margin is not too wide. My husband was desirous that the book should be nicely got up, and I should plead that the paper should not be an absolute white. I have sent an

alte⟶   plification, or whether
you   and Characteristics or
Imp   : truthfully descriptive,
but they have been much ————,   e called 'Theophrastus
Such.' . . .

The printers seem to have been unusually at a loss with my handwriting in Theophrastus, and the numerous awkward mistakes make it important that I should see a revise. Whenever the book is published (I cannot contemplate its appearing before June, and if that is a bad time, it must stand over till the autumn season) I beg you kindly to write for me a notice, to be printed on the flyleaf, that the M.S. was placed in your hands last November, or simply 'last year.'

Ever since my husband's death, the time in which I have been able to work at all has been occupied with his MSS. and I think you will enter into my feeling when I say that to create a notion on the part of the public of my having been occupied in writing Theophrastus would be repugnant to me, and I shrink from putting myself forward in any way.

I hope you are benefiting by the milder weather. I drive out a little now, but you must be prepared to see me a much changed creature. I think I should hardly know myself.

Always yours truly
M. E. Lewes.

TO MME EUGÈNE BODICHON, 5 MARCH 1879

GE recorded her weight 1 July as 7 stone 5-1/2 [103-1/2] pounds. She saw Cross again 28 February, 2 March, and 11 March, when he brought a register of 90 pages with all her investments neatly written out. On 9 March Henry Sidgwick called to discuss the plan for the Studentship in memory of GHL; on 13 March Michael Foster came, "and we arrived at a satisfactory clearness as to the conditions." He mentioned Huxley, Pye-Smith, Thistleton Dyer, F. Balfour, and H. Sidgwick as suitable trustees. [VII, 113–14]

21 N.B. | March 5. 79.
My dear Barbara

Your letter which tells me that you are benefiting by the "clear sunny air" is very welcome. Yes, here too the weather is more merciful and I drive out most days. I am better bodily, but I never feel thoroughly comfortable in that material sense, and I am incredibly thin. As to my mind, I am full of occupation, but the sorrow deepens down instead of diminishing. I mean to go to Witley in a few months, that I may look again on the spots that he enjoyed, and that we enjoyed together, but I cannot tell beforehand whether I shall care to go again afterwards.

Everybody is very kind to me, and by and by I shall begin to see a few intimate friends. I can do or go through anything that is business or duty, but time and strength seem lacking for everything else. Give my love to Bessie. You and she must excuse my weakness, remembering that for nearly 25 years I have been used to find my happiness in his. I can find it nowhere else. But we can live and be helpful without happiness, and I have had more than myriads who were and are better fitted for it.

I am really very busy and have been sadly delayed by want of health. One project I have entered on is to found a studentship which will be called after my husband's name. I am getting help from experienced men. . . .

Always your loving
Marian.

TO MRS. CHARLES BRAY, 1 APRIL 1879

Eliza Lewes and her two children were already at sea when word reached GE that they planned to come. [VII, 123–24]

The Priory | April 1. 79.

My dear Cara

I have told Charles that I would myself answer your kind letter to him. For a long while I have been saying to myself that I would write to you, but I have shrunk from writing about myself needlessly though I have for the last month and more been answering all business letters.

I happen to have a headache today, but I have been generally better of late. I take the air every day and have no great bodily evil to complain of—only a certain slowness and ineffectiveness of mind which may perhaps be counted as the worst form of bodily languor. The sorrow can't grow less—the sense of the happiness that *was*, and the distaste for life that is and will be. I cannot yet resign myself to the cutting short of that happiness for *him*. He enjoyed it so intensely—And we have had everything we wanted. I can bear my own privation, but I cannot yet bear submissively that he had not a few more years of joy. That was my first feeling and it is still the strongest. But we had 24 years of constantly growing love, and I have this comfort—the belief that he never knew he was dying—never felt that we were parting. But it is better not to write of these things. . . .

I want to tell you—because perhaps it may allay some little anxiety in Mr. Bray, supposing there is any uncertainty about your other sources of income, that you will have by my Will £100 a year for your life. You once laughed at the idea that you should outlive me. That is not so unlikely. But at any rate, while I am here, think of me as a living Will, to provide for any want you may feel. How is the letting of the Sydenham house going on?

I see no visitors yet—only some gentlemen who are helping me in a matter of business which is near my heart. I am going to found a Studentship of Physiology to be called by his name.

Our Bertie's widow, with her two children, is on her way to England, frightened out of Durban by the results of that wicked war. I have plenty to think of, have I not? But my friends are so good and helpful that I am carried through everything. Love to all from your otherwise sadly changed

Marian.

TO MME EUGÈNE BODICHON, 8 APRIL 1879

The Studentship paid £200 a year for three years to enable a student of either sex to devote the whole time to original research. It is still at Cambridge, and many distinguished physiologists, among them Sir Charles Sherrington, have described themselves in their publications as "George Henry Lewes Student." [VII, 128–29]

The Priory | April 8. 79.

Dearest Barbara . . .

The Studentship I mention is to supply an income to a young man who is qualified and eager to carry on physiological research and would not otherwise have the means of doing so. Mr. H. Sidgwick, Michael Foster, and other men of kindred mind are helping me in settling the scheme. I have been determined in my choice of the Studentship by the idea of what would be a sort of prolongation of *His* life. That there should always, in consequence of his having lived, be a young man working in the way he would have liked to work, is a memorial of him that comes nearest to my feeling. It is to be at Cambridge to begin with, and we thought at first of affiliating it to the University, but now the notion is that it will be well to keep it free, so that the Trustees may move it where and when they will. But the Scheme is not yet draughted.

I cannot tell yet when I shall be able to get down to Witley, for our daughter-in-law (Bertie's widow) with her two little children is on her way to England from Natal—terrified into flight by the state of things there—and as she comes in a sailing vessel, the time of her arrival is uncertain. I must stay to see her and the little ones.

I am going to bring out one of His Problems in a separate volume at the beginning of May, and am now correcting the proofs. . . .

Ever your loving grateful
Marian.

TO JOHN CROSS, [22 APRIL 1879]

GE was faced with a number of financial perplexities involving GHL's nephew Vivian Lewes and also Mme Belloc, who wrote asking for a loan of £500. In her Diary GE wrote: "J. came to advise me in the evening. Wrote to Mde. Belloc declining." [VII, 138]

Tuesday | 1/2 past 11.

Dearest N.

I am in dreadful need of your counsel. Pray come to me when you can—morning, afternoon, or evening. I shall dismiss anyone else.

You will probably not get this till the Greek Kalends, for I never know where you are. If I address you at Cornhill, you will be at the club, if I address you at the club, you will be at Weybridge, and if I address you there you will be gone on a distant visit.

Your much worried
Aunt.

TO JOHN BLACKWOOD, 23 APRIL 1879

Harper offered a 10 percent royalty and sent £50 in advance. [VII, 141–42]

The Priory | April 23. 79.

My dear Mr. Blackwood

I think your letter to Mr. Harper quite perfect. A royalty is not the sort of arrangement with him that I expected, but if you think well of it, I rely on your judgment and am satisfied. . . .

I am much stronger than I was, and am again finding interest in this wonderful life of ours. But I am obliged to keep my doors closed against all but the few until I go away. You, however, I shall hope to see.

I am founding a studentship of Physiology to be called 'the George Henry Lewes Studentship.' It will be placed in the first instance at Cambridge where there is the best physiological school in the Kingdom. But the Trustees (with my consent during my life) will have the power of moving it where they judge best. This idea which I early conceived, has been a great stay to me. But I have plenty to think of—plenty of creatures depending on me, to make my time seem of some value. And there are so many in the world who have to live without any great enjoyment.

Always yours truly
M. E. Lewes.

TO CHARLES LEWES, 5 JUNE 1879

GHL had inherited from Mrs. Willim a farm at Eaton Bishop, Herefordshire, which Charles had gone down to examine. GE, who now owned it, writes with the authority of a daughter of Robert Evans. Alkie (Alexander Hall) came to lunch with John and Mary Cross. GE drove to Guildford and ordered the Victoria at 12/6 per week. Mme Bodichon, who came 5 June, reported GE in good spirits, "though she is wretchedly thin, and looks in her long, loose, black dress like the black shadow of herself. She said she had so much to do that she must keep well—'the world was to *intensely interesting.*' She said she would come *next year* to see me. We both agreed in the great love we had for life." The "little baby," Elinor Lewes, had measles. The "Africans" were Eliza Lewes and her children. [VII, 158–60]

The Heights, Witley, | Nr. Godalming.
June 5. 79.

Dearest Boy

I was very glad to have your letter this morning with its satisfactory news. Do not in these times think of any building—only of repairs thorough enough to make the dwellings weather-tight and decent. Under those conditions I prefer old buildings to new. Mr. Oldaker, I suppose, spoke from a sufficient knowledge of actual circumstances and prospects, but I am rather surprised at his recommending to re-let on a yearly tenancy. That mode of holding is in the nature of things not favourable to good farming, and in the present state of agricultural interests I should have thought that one great reason for a lease on the side of the Tenant was transferred to the Landlord's side, namely, that the landlord would be in danger of being left by his Tenant planté là with the law in his own hands. In any case let there be no pulling down to rebuild, no throwing of two cottages into one, but only attention to keep the roofs good and make sufficient windows for light and ventilation.

What weather for the poor people's holiday! On Whitmonday Mary Cross and Johnnie brought down little Alkie whom I had promised to have while his parents are away in France. We had to sit indoors the whole time looking at the rain. It is still very cold here and every morning I come down shivering. But I am getting better in health. . . . I have got the same light carriage that we had last year on the same terms, and the relief to the horse is great. . . .

I am so glad that you are taking to the Latin reading, for it will be a continuous thread of interest for you in the midst of desultory things. Poor little baby—I long to hear that her sweet apple of a face is quite free from specks. Love to all from your faithful

Mutter.

It was delightful news that 'the Africans' had had a visit to the Zoo. Remember to give a message of love from me when you see them.

TO CHARLES LEWES, 18 JUNE 1879

Agnes Lewes and her children by Thornton Hunt lived at 3 Campden Hill Terrace, Kensington. The cheque was for £41 13s. 4d. [VII, 167–68]

The Heights, Witley, | Nr. Godalming.
June 18. 79.

Dearest Boy . . .

Last week I received a letter from Mr. Warren saying that the next court of Manor is to be held on the 26th and sending me Beddoes' account of the Fines and Fees to be paid on the Copyhold. They amount to £364.11.10, and though Mr. W. said there was no necessity for my being entered at this next court, I thought it better to have done with it, and have drawn the £400 from deposit, sending Mr. Warren the cheque. The Succession Duty will not have to be paid till a year from the 30th of November. Mr. Cross has managed the matter for me, as he is constantly at the Bank. His firm has £30,000 in deposit for clients.

I shall enclose with this letter the cheques for your Mamma and Eliza, since I suppose you have ascertained that no extra money is wanted at Kensington. I am ruminating over the possibility of having Eliza and the 2 children along with you and Gertrude etc. in July. If it were decided on I could have Maud in my bed the two nights that you were here. But do not speak of it to Eliza until the thing is resolved on.

The exceptionally fine weather you had on Saturday rejoiced me for your sake, but alas how little of that blessing we have to rejoice in! The hay-harvest is grievously threatened.

I am going to test myself by getting up now, so goodbye. Love to all from

Your loving Mutter.

I was glad to know Mr. Harrison's opinion, for naturally though he has written to me about other things he, no more than other friends, writes about Theophrastus. And now I am alone I need the more assurance that I have not published superfluously. . . .

TO MRS. ELMA STUART, 18 JUNE 1879

[VII, 169–70]

The Heights, Witley, | Nr. Godalming.
June 18. 79.

My poor dear, dear Elma! . . .

The silence and beauty of this spot would be bliss to me but for—what I cannot write about. I have simply to live, and I must live as well as I can, making myself as little as possible a burthen on the earth and trying not to be one of that crowd whom Dante puts in the chill mud, making them confess, "Tristi fummo | nell' aer dolce che'l Sol rallume." There is no virtue in gloom which is the easiest hiding-place for languid idleness.

The African daughter-in-law is going on better, and becoming more reconciled to our non-colonial inferiority. And the little girl now goes every day to the *Kindergarten* with her cousins. Charles writes me word this morning that Eliza is beginning to think better of the Kafirs because she finds our common men so much ruder!

I shall venture to send you a copy of "Impressions of Theophrastus Such"— written by me in the spring and summer of last year and sent in manuscript to the publisher by *His hands* the last morning he sat at his desk. I was not quite certain before hearing from you that you were still at Dinan.

I have published one volume of His, "The Study of Psychology"—a comparatively thin volume, and am now beginning to print the final volume which will be as thick as either of the three first. . . .

Let me hear when you are better, dear, and believe me

Always your loving Mother
M. E. L.

TO HERBERT SPENCER, 27 JUNE 1879

Spencer sent *The Data of Ethics*, the first part of his *Principles of Ethics*. *The Principles of Sociology*, begun in 1876, was completed in 1896. [IX, 270]

The Heights, Witley, | Nr. Godalming.
June 27. 79.

Dear Friend

Thank you for your kind present. I am now at the end of the "Criticisms and Explanations" and am carrying on my reading with an interest which you will infer to be rather strong when I tell you that I have for the last 12 days been going through rather a sharp illness. My reading as well as my correspondence have been chiefly done in bed.

I rejoice not in the cause, but in the fact of your having broken the contemplated order of your series for the sake of securing this portion of your Ethics, and if I did not believe it to be an impertinence to tell an author what one would wish him to do, I should say a little more of the value that many would attach to a continuation of this weft as something more needed than even the completion of the Sociological portion. Of course, as you predict, you will be partly misunderstood and misrepresented. That is destiny unshunnable. All one must care about is that some grains of corrective knowledge or useful stimulus will be here and there swallowed and digested.

I have an evil pleasure in observing that you have as good a crop of little misprints as I should have left myself.

Yours always sincerely
M. E. Lewes.

TO CHARLES LEWES, [7 JULY 1879]

From 20 June GE suffered for nearly a month from recurrent attacks; the strawberry festival, planned for the 12th, had to be cancelled. Many letters were written, like this, in bed. [VII, 178–79]

The Heights, Witley, | Nr. Godalming.
Monday | *Dal letto.*

Dearest Boy

On Saturday I had a rather severe relapse and though I am getting out of the tunnel into daylight, this renewal of weakness taken with the dreary prospects of the weather under which nothing ripens and fruits hardly escape rotting, makes it seem as if we should be wiser to defer the visit till the 19th when the promised Rubicon of the 16th will have been passed. Qu'en dis tu? . . .

Fancy! I am ordered to drink Champagne and am wasting my substance in riotous living at the rate of a pint bottle daily. Meanwhile my bodily substance in the shape of flesh is wasting also. But my doctor is the greatest possible comfort to me, and everything is being done for me that can be done. To counterbalance other pains I have had no headache to speak of all through the illness, and am generally able to get through some work of letter-writing and proof-reading—nay some days I have played an hour on the piano. The relapse, thinks the doctor, may have been due to chills.

Love to all from
Mutter.

TO CHARLES LEWES, 23 JULY 1879

Charles and Gertrude had been planning a holiday in Switzerland, but decided to go to Wales instead. [VII, 184–86]

The Heights, Witley, | Nr. Godalming.
July 23. 79.

Dearest Boy

I will write to dear little Blanche, if not today, tomorrow. No! I do not like your change of plan. I have no belief in the climate of Wales, and your Father and I were altogether disappointed with the places on the W. coast, Barmouth included. I am sure it would not be anything like so good for you as a foreign trip, and by *you* I mean emphatically Gertrude as well. I cannot bear to think of your being fixed for your one good holiday in rainy Wales, where the Methodists sing out of tune and there is a general aspect of moral dreariness.

As to me, you need not, I think, be in the least anxious. Taking the worst view of the case nothing sudden is to be apprehended—I seem to be so thoroughly sound in the chief vital organs. And I am certainly in many respects better than I was. Besides when I am in pain the thought I most sustain myself with, and childishly utter aloud to my own ears alone, is, that the trouble does not interfere with other lives—begins and ends in me. It would really grieve me if your holiday were interfered with on my account. You know, dear, any business at the Bank or with Mr. Warren, Mr. Cross will easily attend to, and he will order anything for me from town. And do not let any fear of a bad telegram haunt you, because as I said, there is no reasonable ground for apprehending anything sudden. It is possible that in a few weeks I may be well. . . .

The news about Eliza is of the dreariest—especially the untruthfulness. I am alarmed still more to find that she has a notion of borrowing money, and since she seems disposed to throw the blame on you, would it not be better after all for me to write to her? The worst of it is, that in my present mood I could hardly help writing to her very severely. Don't take a tone of dissuasion about her going back to Natal or remaining. That effects nothing but harm. . . .

Love to all from
Mutter.

TO BLANCHE LEWES, 24 JULY 1879

Evenings at Home is a series of children's books compiled by John and Laetitia Barbauld, 6 volumes, 1792–96. [VII, 186–87]

The Heights, Witley, | Nr. Godalming.
July 24. 79.

My dear Blanche

I was very much pleased to have a letter from you, and to know all about your Birthday. "Evenings at Home" is a very pretty book. I read it when I was at school, and I think you will like to read many stories in it over and over again till you know them almost by heart. That is very nice to carry pretty things in your mind so that you can say them to yourself in the dark. I am sure you must have liked being on the river in the steamboat for the first time. The wide river, and the bridges, and the great buildings that can be seen a long way by the waterside, are all very beautiful, are they not? It would seem to you like another and grander sort of picture, after seeing the small pictures on the wall at the Exhibition.

Only think! This was your seventh birthday, and when you have lived three times seven years you will be a tall woman aged 21, able to do almost everything for dear Mamma, so that she may rest after doing so much as she does for you and Maud and Eleanor. Please give my love to Maud and tell her that I am very glad to hear of her having been at the head of her class.

Yesterday there was sunshine here; the trees made pretty shadows on the grass, and the flowers lifted up their little faces and looked very happy. But this morning it rains again and the hay that should be nice and dry, ready for the horses to eat, will all be wet through again. This makes people sorry.

I am writing this letter in bed, not being very well, and my paper lies a long way off on a flat board, so it is not easy for me to write well. But I hope the letter is written plainly enough for you to read it without much trouble. Give my love to Papa and Mamma and tell them that I feel a little better. And now good bye, my dear Blanche. Whenever you think of me remember that I am

Your loving
Grandmamma.

TO ALBERT GEORGE DEW-SMITH, 11 SEPTEMBER 1879

Dew-Smith, who was connected with the Cambridge Engraving Co., was seeing the announcement of the George Henry Lewes Studentship in Physiology through the press. The original wording was in the deed transferring £5,000 to the Trustees. The revised form appears in the announcement. [IX, 273]

The Heights, Witley, | Godalming.
September 11. 79.

Dear Sir

Having Dr. Foster's warrant for troubling you on the subject of the paper sent to me yesterday, I venture to ask that you will oblige me by making a correction which I omitted, namely—in the heading instead of *'by Mary Ann Evans Lewes'* simply *'by M. E. Lewes'* known as an author etc.

Yours faithfully
M. E. Lewes.

DIARY, 26 SEPTEMBER–3 OCTOBER 1879

[VII, 202–03]

[The Heights]

26 September 1879

Feeling ill and depressed. Mr. Tennyson and Hallam called.

27 September 1879

Still ailing. Lady Holland called.

28 September 1879

Last proofs came from Dr. Foster and Mr. Sully. Better in the afternoon.

29 September 1879

Sent off last proofs. Madame Bodichon came to stay.

30 September 1879

Wet day—could not drive. Mr. Cross came to dinner with us.

1 October 1879

Letter from a madman in Kansas. Drove Made. Bodichon to Thursley. Mrs. Greville came and recited the Revenge, Delilah from Samson Agonistes, and Jeanne d'Arc.

2 October 1879

Letter from Michael Foster. Madame Bodichon left at 1/2 past 11.

3 October 1879

Tears, tears.

TO JOHN CROSS, [16 OCTOBER 1879]

This letter was addressed to Cross at the City Liberal Club. James Sully's article is a survey of GHL's life and work. Beatrice is the ideal of beauty and goodness celebrated by Dante in his *Vita Nuova* and *Divine Comedy*. [VII, 211–12]

The Heights, Witley, | Nr. Godalming.
Thursday.

Best loved and loving one—the sun it shines so cold, so cold, when there are no eyes to look love on me. I cannot bear to sadden one moment when we are together, but wenn Du bist nicht da I have often a bad time. It *is* a solemn time, dearest. And why should I complain if it is a painful time? What I call my pain is almost a joy seen in the wide array of the world's cruel suffering. Thou seest I am grumbling today—got a chill yesterday and have a headache. All which, as a wise doctor would say, is not of the least consequence, my dear Madam.

Through everything else, dear tender one, there is the blessing of trusting in thy goodness. Thou dost not know anything of verbs in Hiphil and Hophal or the history of metaphysics or the position of Kepler in science, but thou knowest best things of another sort, such as belong to the manly heart—secrets of lovingness and rectitude. O I am flattering. Consider what thou wast a little time ago in pantaloons and back hair.

Triumph over me. After all, I have *not* the second copy of the deed. What I took for it was only Foster's original draft and my copy of it. The article by Sully in the New Quarterly is very well done.

I shall think of thee this afternoon getting health at Lawn Tennis, and I shall reckon on having a letter by tomorrow's post.

Why should I compliment myself at the end of my letter and say that I am faithful, loving, more anxious for thy life than mine? I will run no risks of being 'inexact'—so I will only say 'varium et mutabile semper' but at this particular moment thy tender

Beatrice.

TO MRS. EDWARD BURNE-JONES, 18 OCTOBER 1879

Charles Stuart Roy, the first holder of the Studentship, was from 1884 to 1897 Professor of Pathology at Cambridge. [VII, 212–13]

The Heights, Witley, | Nr. Godalming.
October 18. 79.

Dearest Georgie . . .

You *never did* speak to me of Emily Beattie. But you must do so some Friday afternoon. Remarkable men so often choose a succession of stupid women (if not evil ones) that there should be some tolerance for a remarkable woman who does the corresponding thing. But the core of good news in your letter is that your husband is well again, and again happy in his work. Your collapse is what I feared for you, and you must call the getting change of air and scene—I was going to say 'a duty,' but are you one of those wonderful beings who find everything easier under that name? But at least one prefers doing a hard duty to grimacing with a pretence of pleasure in things that are no pleasure. . . .

I am greatly comforted this morning by the fact that the (apparently) right man is found for the George Henry Lewes Studentship—an ardent worker who could not have carried on his pursuit without this money help. I know you are not unmindful of what touches me deeply.

Go on your visit, dear, and come back well—then show yourself without unnecessary delay to

Your loving Friend
M. E. Lewes.

TO EDMUND EVANS, 22 OCTOBER 1879

Evans, the engraver, a neighbour at Witley, proposed that GE might write a short story of or about children for Kate Greenaway to illustrate. Mrs. Evans, who was a niece of Birket Foster, had brought Miss Greenaway to call on GE and left some of her books 17 September. [VII, 215–16]

The Heights, Witley, | Nr. Godalming.
October 22. 79.

Dear Mr. Evans

It is not my way to write anything except from my own inward prompting. Your proposal does me honour, and I should feel much trust in the charming pencil of Miss Greenaway, but I could never say 'I will write this or that' until I had myself felt the need to do it.

I too was sorry that I did not see Mrs. Evans when I called. The servant kindly invited me to wait, but I was feeling cold after my drive and was afraid of staying out after sundown. I am sure that Mrs. Evans will not think me indifferent to the pleasure of seeing her, and will understand that I avoid being out late in the afternoon in obedience to my doctor's warning against chills.

I return to town next week. Believe me, dear Mr. Evans

Yours most sincerely
M. E. Lewes.

TO CHARLES LEWES, [27 OCTOBER 1879]

John Blackwood died 29 October. [VII, 217–18]

The Heights, Witley, | Nr. Godalming.
Tuesday.

Dearest Boy

I have just had some news that grieves me. Mr. Blackwood is dangerously ill and I fear from Mr. William's letter that there is little hope of recovery. He will be a heavy loss to me. He has been bound up with what I most cared for in my life for more than twenty years and his good qualities have made many things easy to me that without him would often have been difficult.

I wrote to Mr. Trübner to tell him that the printing of the Problems being finished I should be glad if he would arrange with you about the conditions of publication. He is at home now and has answered my letter. So you had better call on him. Bear in mind your Father's wish that the volumes should not be made dearer than necessary.

I am going to Weybridge on Friday, in order to leave the servants free while they finish preparations for departure, and I intend to be at the Priory by Saturday before dusk. But it is *just possible* I may be detained till Monday morning. So if you have any good occupation for Sunday you had better call on your way home on Monday.

Your loving
Mutter.

DIARY, 25–30 NOVEMBER 1879

GE drove to Highgate Cemetery almost every week when she was well. Gertrude, Charles, Eliza, and the five children came to lunch at the Priory 6 December. GE solved the problem of an advance of the quarterly payment to Dr. Roy by sending £50 for him. [VII, 227]

Tuesday 25 November 1879

Dentist at 2. Wrote to Dr. Roy. Another turning point.

Wednesday 26 November 1879

Drove into town in the morning to buy books and toys for the children.

Friday 28 November 1879

Went to the Cemetery.

Saturday 29 November 1879

Reckoning by the days of the week, it was this day last year my loneliness began. I spent the day in the room where I passed through the first three months. I read his letters, and packed them together, to be buried with me. Perhaps that will happen before next November.

Sunday 30 November 1879

Sent £50 to Mr. Balfour for Dr. Roy.

TO MRS. THOMAS TROLLOPE, 19 DECEMBER 1879

Ludwig Haller, a friend of the Trollopes from Berlin, asked them if there was a life of GHL or if GE was going to write one. James Sully wrote the article in the *New London Quarterly*. [VII, 230–31]

> **The Priory, | 21. North Bank, | Regents Park.**
> December 19. 79.

Dear Mrs. Trollope

In sending me Dr. Haller's words you have sent me a great comfort. A just appreciation of my Husband's work from a competent person is what I am most athirst for, and Dr. Haller has put his finger on a true characteristic. I only wish he could print something to the same effect in any pages that would be generally read.

There is no Biography. An article entitled 'George Henry Lewes' appeared in the last 'New London Quarterly.' It was written by a man for whom we had much esteem, but it is not strong. A few facts about the early life and education are given with tolerable accuracy, but the estimate of the philosophic and scientific activity is inadequate. Still, it is the best thing you could mention to Dr. Haller. You know, perhaps, that a volume entitled 'The Study of Psychology,' printed from my Husband's M.S.S. appeared in May last and that another volume (500 pp.) of 'Problems of Life and Mind' has just been published. The best history of a writer is contained in his writings—these are his chief actions. If he happens to have left an autobiography telling (what nobody else can tell) how his mind grew, how it was determined by the joys, sorrows and other influences of childhood and youth—that is a precious contribution to knowledge. But Biographies generally are a disease of English literature.

I have never yet told you how grateful I was to you for writing to me a year ago. For a long while I could read no letter. But now I have read yours more than once and it is carefully preserved. You had been with us in our happiness so near the time when it left me—you and your Husband are peculiarly bound up with the latest memories. . . .

With best love to you both,

Always dear Mrs. Trollope,
Yours faithfully
M. E. Lewes.

TO JOHN CROSS, 24–25 DECEMBER 1879

Elize Lewes and her two children came to lunch. Lady Strangford, after her husband's death in 1869, started a course to train nurses for the poor. Cross had sold £1,200 worth of GE's Gas Light and Coke shares for $2,260. [VII, 234–35]

The Priory, | 21. North Bank, | Regents Park.
December 24. 79.

Bester Mann!

I received the card you kindly posted for me at the Station—your kindness was the chief impression I got from its hieroglyphics. I imagined Mary and you dining cozily after your journey and having a glorious walk in the sunshine today.

My time has been well filled. The grandchildren came with their mamma to lunch and I managed to amuse them till four. Then came Dr. Congreve and Lady Strangford, and yesterday I had Mr. Sully and Burne Jones—the last bringing me beautiful photographs which I may keep as long as I like, so your imagaination may be enlarged with them whenever you feel inclined for self-culture, sweetness and light.

Tomorrow I shall be alone all day smelling the servants' goose and hoping that a fraction of this world's inhabitants are enjoying themselves. . . .

Lady Strangford has settled one young Bulgarian at Oxford, who is to be a teacher in his own country, and she has another of the species in her own house carrying on his studies at King's College and preparing to be a Pastor by learning Chemistry which he will follow up with Agriculture, the Gospel most needed in Bulgaria. I ought to sit in dust and ashes after hearing of her work in these late years—if dust and ashes were regenerative.

Charles is coming to dine with me on Monday, but I suppose that I shall hardly have any company before then, except a stray person glad to escape from "the bosom of his (or her) family." I am quite contented, being out of pain and not (that I know of) annoying anybody. If you return to town in time to dine with me on Tuesday, will you do me that honour? Or perhaps you will prefer Wednesday?

Give my love to any creature who wants that small alms and believe me to remain

Your obliged ex-shareholder of A and C Gaslight and Coke.

Christmasday. It is now mid-day and I am still owing all my light to candles. The fog is dense and one thinks of cab accidents. You are well off to be out of London.

TO WILLIAM BLACKWOOD, 13 JANUARY 1880

Following his uncle John's custom, William Blackwood had the MS of *Theophrastus* bound in the same maroon leather as the other MSS. They are now in the British Library. [VII, 244–45]

The Priory, | 21. North Bank, | Regents Park.
January 13. 80.

My dear Mr. William

I am very much obliged to you for your letter enclosing a cheque for £400, being the remainder of the sum finally awarded to me for the 4 editions of 'Theophrastus Such.' But your punctuality makes me more anxious than I should have been on my own account that the 97 copies still on hand should be completely disposed of. I will be hopeful, however, since the public seems well disposed towards me. Mr. Langford told me that 1000 volumes of the cheap edition had been sold since New Year's Day. This is encouraging for us. . . .

And it was very good of you to send me the little title-page—but I no longer care for the scraps of my writing. It was my other lost self that cared for them. It would have been a pity, though, that the MSS of Theophrastus should have been missing from the row of Russia backs, for Mr. Lewes had set his mind on their going after our death to the British Museum. . . .

Yours always sincerely
M. E. Lewes.

TO MRS. HENRY HUTH, 31 JANUARY 1880

Alfred Henry Huth published *The Life and Writings of Henry Thomas Buckle,* 2 volumes, 1880. I am indebted to Professor John Clubbe, who told me of this letter in the W. Hugh Peal Collection at the University of Kentucky, and to the Librarian for permission to publish it here for the first time.

The Priory | 21 North Bank | Jan. 31. 80

Dear Mrs. Huth

I am very much obliged to you for your kind remembrance of me shown in several ways and now especially in the handsome present to me of your son's book, which I shall look into with much interest.

I hope that you are not at all suffering in health and that your old enemy neuralgia has quite ceased to harrass you.

With best regards to Miss Huth

Yours very truly
M. E. Lewes.

TO GEORGE SMITH, 4 FEBRUARY 1880

The deluxe edition of *Romola* in 2 volumes quarto, was bound in white buckram with the engravings from Leighton's drawings mounted and inserted. [VII, 247]

The Priory | 21 North Bank | February 4. 80.

My dear Sir

I am greatly pleased with your porposal to bring out an 'édition de luxe' of Romola, because I know that Mr. Lewes wished for it.

As to the honorarium, you have already paid me so handsomely for the work and I have so valued a remembrance of the sympathy you gave me in the course of its production, that I would rather not receive more until the complete success of the undertaking has been assured.

I have been often wishing that you would call upon me, and now I hope that I shall soon see you. I am at home to friends every day after 4.30. If Sunday suits you for coming to me better than a weekday, I am at home then throughout the afternoon, but I do not make it a special day of reception, preferring at present to see only one or two friends at a time. Believe me

Yours most truly
M. E. Lewes.

TO WILLIAM BLACKWOOD, 13 FEBRUARY 1880

On the same day that GE wrote, Blackwood sent her a check for £784 and a detailed statement of sales. [VII, 250]

The Priory | 21 North Bank | February 13. 80.

My dear Mr. William

Smith Elder and Co. have now made the proposal of which I spoke to you as probable, namely, to publish an *édition de luxe* of Romola, corresponding with that of Thackeray's works, and I have assented. I mention this to you again, lest in the press of matters on you when you were in town, the fact of our having spoken on this subject may have dropped from your memory. You will now probably recall your having concurred in the idea that such an edition would be rather an advantage to the already existing editions, as bringing the work into relief and aiding in its advertisement.

I see that the new edition of the 'Sayings' is brought out and I should be much obliged if you would order a copy to be sent to me that I may see what Mr. Main has extracted from 'Deronda' and 'Theophrastus.'

I am looking forward to the reception of my account of last year's sales, which you mentioned as being in preparation. Those figures which tell of distribution are the criticism of my books which I most care about. . . .

Always yours truly
M. E. Lewes.

The édition de luxe of Romola is to consist of only 1000 copies.

TO ?, 26 FEBRUARY 1880

I cannot identify the author or the book sent to GE in 1879. I am grateful to Mr. Thomas Lange for sending me a copy of this letter, which is here published for the first time.

The Priory, | 21. North Bank, | Regents Park.
Feb. 26. 80

Dear Madam

I am very gratefully touched by your kind thoughtfulness in having prepared for me the beautiful little gift which came to me yesterday. When I read the volume in the summer I felt as if I had been deprived of something that should have fallen to my share, in never having made the personal acquaintance of your late Husband. And it would have been a great benefit, a great stimulus to me to have known some years earlier that my work was being sanctioned by the sympathy of a mind endowed with so much insight and delicate sensibility.

It is difficult for me to speak of what others may regard as an excessive estimate of my own work, but I will venture to mention the keen perception shown in the note on p. 29 as something that gave me peculiar satisfaction. But why should we shrink from saying that we are glad of any valid testimony to the good of our own doings? We may well be anxious of some assurance that we are not increasing the heap of trash. And after all, our writing is a sort of offspring that may be much better than ourselves and leave us rather poor creatures in our own person.

We are both mourners, dear Madam, and now that I know something of your Husband's mind I can enter into at least a part of your loss. But I trust that your daughter whom you mention (and perhaps other children) may still endear your life to you.

Believe me

Yours sincerely
M. E. Lewes.

DIARY, 28 MARCH–10 APRIL 1880

These brief entries must often be read as if John Cross were with her. GE met Frances Colenso at the Burne-Joneses' in 1870. J. E. Millais the painter lived at 7 Cromwell Place, and Mr. and Mrs. Call at Addison Gardens. Paget had been invited to come, and it was on his advice that GE accepted Cross's proposal. [VII, 258–59]

Sunday 28 March 1880
Went to Weybridge.

Monday 29 March 1880
Brock's wages paid up to this day. Walked on St. George's Hill. Letter from America asking me to read M.S. Revelation.

Tuesday 30 March 1880
Returned from Weybridge early. Maud's birthday. Gertrude, Blanche and Maud to lunch. Miss Colenso came. Much interesting talk. Went to see Mrs. Stuart. Letter from Mrs. Elizabeth Thompson, U.S.A.

Wednesday 31 March 1880
Drove to 7 Cromwell Place and to Addison Gardens. Mrs. Burne Jones from 4.30.

Thursday 1 April 1880
Drove to Hampstead and took cheque to Eliza. Quiet afternoon. Finished Prose Edda etc. Akkadians. Malthus.

Friday 2 April 1880
Alice Helps.

Saturday 3 April 1880
Went to Sydenham.

Friday 9 April 1880
Sir James Paget came to see me. My marriage decided.

Saturday 10 April 1880
To Chelsea to look at No. 4 Cheyne Walk.

TO ELEANOR CROSS, [13 APRIL 1880]

GE had told none of her most intimate friends about her marriage. [VII, 259]

The Priory, | 21. North Bank, | Regents Park.
Tuesday.

Dearest Eleanor
    You can hardly think how sweet the name Sister is to me, that I have not been called by for so many, many years. Without your tenderness I do not believe it would have been possible for me to accept this wonderful renewal of my life. Nothing less than the prospect of being loved and welcomed by you all could have

sustained me. But now I cherish the thought that the family life will be the richer and not the poorer through your Brother's great gift of love to me.

Yet I quail a little in facing what has to be gone through—the hurting of many whom I care for. You are doing everything you can to help me, and I am full of gratitude to you all for his sake as well as my own. The springs of affection are reopened in me, and it will make me better to be among you—more loving and trustful.

I valued Florence's little visit very much. You and she will come again—will you not?—to your

Sister.

TO ELEANOR CROSS, [?14 APRIL 1880]

[VII, 260]

The Priory, | 21. North Bank, | Regents Park.
Wednesday.

Dearest Eleanor

The blessing in your tender note was much needed. Your heart inspired you with just the right words to help me.

The inward struggle, the doubt, the final word—all has been a trial, and I have often wished that my life had ended a year ago. But now what remains of it must have a new consecration in gratitude for the miracle of his love. I am hoping that I shall not take anything from all of you who have been nearest to him, but that I shall bring you an added love that you will not despise in union with his. I am still agitated—terrified, perhaps because I am not well. Your dear letter kept by me is a little lamp in the dimness. I write to Florence as well as to you because she joined you in the blessing.

Yours lovingly
M. E. L.

TO MRS. ELMA STUART, 23 APRIL 1880

GE went to see Mrs. Stuart 20 April. A similar vague warning of the approaching change in her life was given 23 April to Mrs. Burne-Jones; after a long visit GE "seemed loth to go, and as if there was something that she would have said, yet did not." [VII, 262–63]

The Priory, | 21. North Bank, | Regents Park.
April 23. 80.

Dear-good-naughty Elma

What can I say of the 6 beautiful handkerchiefs but that they are ten times too nice for me?—I will not repeat the ungracious (seemingly ungracious) lecture I gave you the other day. I will only beseech you not to imagine me ungrateful for any love or sign of love. The pains of my friends—the pains they take to sweeten my life—are really "registered where every day I turn the leaf to read them." Try to understand what I meant, and do not let me have the grief of thinking that in wishing you to serve me only through serving others, I appeared to you to be repelling your affection.

Why should you compel yourself to cultivate Gertrude's society in order to hear of me, since I am as likely to write to you as to her? And I hope to see you again before I go away. What I would ask of you is, whether your love and trust in me will suffice to satisfy you that, when I act in a way which is thoroughly unexpected there are reasons which justify my action, though the reasons may not be evident to you.

Keep getting better till I see you, and believe in me as always

Your faithfully affectionate
M. E. L.

TO ALBERT DRUCE, 27 APRIL 1880

Cross's brother-in-law, husband of his sister Anna, agreed to give GE away. He wrote to her: "I need not say how glad I shall be to have a small part in completing Johnnie's happiness, and what pleasure I have in knowing that your loving heart has such a tender and reliable companion." [VII, 266]

The Priory, | 21. North Bank, | Regents Park.
April 27. 80.

Dear Albert—

I may call you so may I not?—I am very grateful to you. Your and Anna's sympathy seems to shed a blessing on our union. About the ceremony. Johnnie and I have trusted that you would be willing to come and take me from my house to the church and "give me away." He has told me that you are the man to whom he is most attached and in whom he most confides, and our wish that you should have this part in the act that binds us together seems to follow as a necessary consequence. Johnnie will of course let you know all about times and seasons. Let us hope that the winds will be more friendly next week and that we shall none of us have colds. At present I have a catarrh in the most literal sense—a constant downfall of tears from my right eye.

Our visit to Thornhill has left a very pretty picture in my mind. You will be glad to hear that Mr. Armitage writes with a decorator's rapture about the possibilities of the Chelsea house and promises himself to make it a chef-d'oeuvre.

My best love to Anna. I trust now that I shall always be her and

Your affectionate sister
M. E. L.

TO WILLIAM BLACKWOOD, 5 MAY 1880

[VII, 267]

The Priory, | 21. North Bank, | Regents Park.
May 5. 80.

My dear Mr. William

I know it will be a great surprize to you to learn that I am about to be married to Mr. J. W. Cross, a friend of years, especially loved and trusted by Mr. Lewes. He is of a Scotch family, and is second cousin to Mrs. W. Sellar, of Edinburgh, whom you probably know.

The decision has been made but lately and I have been driven by pressing occupation to write you word only at the eleventh hour. We are going abroad for two or three months and shall return to Witley. But I shall not any more be resident at this house. We shall live, when in town, at No. 4, Cheyne Walk, Chelsea.

I hope you have been well and happy lately. Please let me hear from you in the old way when I return in August, for I shall always be

Yours very sincerely
M. E. Lewes.

TO MME EUGÈNE BODICHON, 5 MAY 1880

By an unfortunate error GE left this and several other letters in a drawer in the dining room. Charles Lewes found and posted it 7 July. [VII, 268–69]

The Priory, | 21. North Bank, | Regents Park.
May 5. 80.

My dear Barbara

I have something to tell you which will doubtless be a great surprize to you, but since I have found that other friends, less acquainted with me and my life than you are, have given me their sympathy, I think that I can count on yours. I am going to do what not very long ago I should myself have pronounced impossible for me, and therefore I should not wonder at anyone else who found my action incomprehensible. By the time you receive this letter I shall (so far as the future can be matter of assertion) have been married to Mr. J. W. Cross, who you know is a friend of years, a friend much loved and trusted by Mr. Lewes, and who now that I am alone sees his happiness in the dedication of his life to me. This change in my position will make no change in my care for Mr. Lewes's family and in the ultimate disposition of my property. Mr. Cross has a sufficient fortune of his own.

We are going abroad for a few months, and I shall not return to live at this house. Mr. Cross has taken the lease of a house in Cheyne Walk (No. 4), Chelsea, where we shall spend the winter and early spring, making Witley our summer home.

You will like to hear that Charles has shown a quite perfect feeling in relation to this unexpected event, and if you would like to write or in any way communicate to him your wish for further knowledge, he will I am sure readily respond to your wish. I indulge the hope that you will some day look at the river from the windows of our Chelsea house which is rather quaint and picturesque.

Please tell Bessie for me, with my love to her. I cannot write to more than two or three persons.

Ever yours lovingly
M. E. Lewes.

TO MRS. EDWARD BURNE-JONES, 5 MAY 1880

Mrs. Burne-Jones received the letter 6 May. At midnight she wrote this reply:

The Grange. | May 6–7 1880. past midnight between | Thursday and Friday.
I have been away with the exception of one clear day until this afternoon, when I returned and found your letter—for which I thank you with all my heart—and I cannot sleep till it is answered. Dear friend, I love you—let that be all—I love you, and you are *you* to me "in all changes"—from the first hour I knew you until now you have never turned but one face upon me, and I do not expect to lose you now. I am the old loving

Georgie.

But she did not post it till six weeks later, when it was enclosed with this letter:

The Grange | June 16: 1880.

Dear Friend,
You will see by the enclosed that I answered your letter at once and that I was grateful for it—but when my answer was written I put it aside, hoping to find more and brighter words to send. Forgive it if they have not come yet, and let me send those first ones—anything rather than you should think my silence a want of respect or feeling—I would rather you were displeased with what I say than that.

Give me time—this was the one "change" I was unprepared for—but that is my own fault—I have no right to impute to my friends what they do not claim. Forgive what would be an unforgivable liberty of speech if you had not said anything on the subject to me or if you had not also looked closely into my life. Edward joins me in love, and I am always

Your loving
Georgie.

[VII, 269–70, 272, 299]

The Priory, | 21. North Bank, | Regents Park.
May 5. 80.

Dearest Georgie
Fate laid me low with influenza last week, a fact only important just now because it has filled the present week with an oppressive crowd of details and made me simply unable to write to you until this eleventh hour. A great momentous change is taking place in my life—a sort of miracle in which I could never have

believed, and under which I still sit amazed. If it alters your conception of me so thoroughly that you must from henceforth regard me as a new person, a stranger to you, I shall not take it hardly, for I myself a little while ago should have said that this thing could not be.

I am going to be married to Mr. Cross whom you may sometimes have seen here. He has been a devoted friend for years, much loved and trusted by Mr. Lewes, and now that I am alone, he sees his only longed-for happiness in dedicating his life to me. This will make no difference in my care for my lost one's family either during or after my life. Mr. Cross has a sufficient fortune of his own. Explanations of these crises, which seem sudden though they are slowly dimly prepared, are impossible. I can only ask you and your husband to imagine and interpret according to your deep experience and loving kindness.

We are going away tomorrow and shall be abroad two or three months. In August we shall be at Witley according to actual intentions. But this house will not again be my home. When in London we shall inhabit 4 Cheyne Walk, Chelsea.

Good bye, dear ones. Always, in all changes either with you or me, I shall be your deeply attached friend,

M. E. L.

Excuse any word that seems the wrong one—any apparent brusqueness or neglect. I have been terribly pressed.

TO MRS. RICHARD CONGREVE, 5 MAY 1880

Mrs. Congreve, one of several friends to whom GE persuaded Charles Lewes to impart the news of her wedding, was a particularly delicate case because of the Positivist doctrine forbidding second marriage. Frederic Harrison, with whom GE had discussed the question, wrote: "I might perhaps have said more than I was able to do under the strong impressions of the moment. . . . I should not presume to think of imposing such opinions on those who stand entirely aloof from our ways and our thoughts. . . . We earnestly desire your happiness." [VII, 270–72]

[London]

A great, momentous change is going to take place in my life. My indisposition last week, and several other subsequent circumstances, have hindered me from communicating it to you, and the time has been but short since the decision was come to. But with your permission Charles will call on you and tell you what he can on Saturday.

Yours and Emily's, ever with unchanging love.

DIARY, 6 MAY 1880

GE had not dared tell Charles Lewes, but made Cross do it. Charles then volunteered to supplant Albert Druce in giving her away. [VII, 270]

Thursday 6 May 1880

Married this day at 10.15 to John Walter Cross, at St. George's, Hanover Square. Present, Charles, who gave me away, Mr. and Mrs. Druce, Mr. Hall, Willie, Mary, Eleanor, and Florence. We went back to the Priory, where we signed our wills. Then we started for Dover, and arrived there a little after 5 o'clock.

14

Mrs. John Walter Cross

After her long open defiance of convention GE's marriage astonished every one. Her more radical friends, who had dared to call on her while she was "living in sin," were the most shocked by this lapse into convention. Afraid to tell them herself, GE enlisted Charles Lewes to explain it to some of the younger women who had confided the secrets of their lives to her and were hurt that she had not told hers. They all underestimated her fundamental conservatism, failed to see her union with GHL as obedience to a morality that would brook no deceit. Few of them knew Johnnie Cross, who, despite the twenty-year difference in their ages, had convinced GE that he could find his happiness only in devoting himself to hers.

On their honeymoon journey through France and Italy she showed him the places she had seen with GHL and carried on the intensive reading they had always followed. Johnnie's schooling had ended after Rugby. He was tall and handsome, an active athletic man of 40, not accustomed to this unremitting course of visits to churches and museums. One day at the Lido when he wanted to have a swim GE deemed it unadvisable, though the weather was warm. On 16 June he suffered a sudden mental derangement and leaped from the hotel window into the Grand Canal. The gondoliers quickly pulled him out. Doctors were called. His brother William came to help GE. They took him by easy stages to Germany to rest. Before the end of July he was back at Witley, playing tennis and chopping down trees to clear the view. He lived till 1924 with no recurrence of the malady.

Cross had taken a house at 4 Cheyne Walk, Chelsea, into which during the summer he oversaw the transfer of books and furniture from the Priory. They moved in 3 December. The next afternoon they appeared together for the first time at the Pop Concert, where the Leweses had long been a cynosure. GE began to invite a few of her old friends to call. Spencer came 19 December, and later in the afternoon Edith Simcox. Though GE's throat was sore, she sat down to write a letter, but before it was finished broke off and went to bed. Two days later she died, and Cross was writing, "I am left alone in this new House we meant to be so happy in."

TO ELEANOR CROSS, 9 MAY [1880]

In her excitement GE forgot her keys and the cameo brooch that she and GHL had bought in Rome in 1860. They arrived at the Russian church too late to hear the music. [VII, 273–75]

Hôtel Vouillemont | Sunday Morning May 9.

Dearest Eleanor,

Your letter was a sweet greeting to us on our arrival here yesterday a little after 5 o'clock. The keys once received, our life was without a cloud (except that little one the size of a brooch, always on the horizon). When we were walking by the sea-side at Dover we agreed either that wedding days had been much maligned or that ours was a marvelously exceptional one, for everything had seemed to us as blessed as it could be. Then the next morning we had a millennial cabin on the deck of the Calais-Douvre and floated over the strait as easily as the saints float upward to heaven (in the pictures). At Amiens we were very comfortably housed at the Hotel du Rhin and paid two enraptured visits, evening and morning, to the Cathedral. I was delighted with Johnnie's delight in it. And we read our dear old Cantos of the Inferno that we were reading a year ago, declining afterwards on 'Eugénie Grandet'. The nice woman who waited on us made herself very memorable to me by her sketch of her own life. She went to England when she was nineteen as a lady's maid—had been much 'ennuyée de sa mère'—detested 'les plaisirs,' liked only her regular everyday work and 'la paix.'

At 1 o'clock we started on our easy journey to Paris, which would have been as pleasant as possible but that half way there came into our carriage a man who combined the facial expression of a crocodile and a Jamaica frog and really made me shudder by fixing his horrible gaze on me. It was some small relief to reflect that he was not an Englishman. At the Station du Nord we got a voiture with two toy horses and mistakenly ordered the coachman to drive to the Hôtel Voltaire, Quai d'Orleans. He took us to the Quai d'Orleans where the Hôtel Voltaire was *not,* and would go no farther without being paid his fare. That time he drove us to the Hôtel Voltaire which is most attractively placed, but had no apartment at liberty. Second colloquy with the coachman who again demanded his fare. Finally he brought us to this Hôtel where we have a very fair apartment and plenty of sunlight, *au premier.* Between after-travel toilet and dinner we walked up to the Arc des Etoiles and back again enjoying the lovely growth and blossoms of the horse-chesnuts which are in their first glory, innocent of dust or of one withered petal. This morning at 12 o'clock we are going to the Russian church, where Johnnie has never been, and where I hope we shall hear the wonderful intoning and singing as I heard it years ago.

This is the chronicle of our happy married life three days long—all its happiness conscious of a dear background in those who are loving us at Weybridge, at Thornhill and at Ranby. You are all inwoven into the pattern of my thoughts, which would have a sad look without you. I like to go over again in imagination all the scene in the church and in the vestry and to feel every loving look from the eyes of those who were rejoicing for us.

534

Write us word about everything, and especially let us know when you think you have found the right house in the right place, so that we as well as Willie, may make our objections. Please commend me to the mercy of the family critic, and consider yourselves all very much loved and spiritually petted by your loving

Sister.

Write next to the Poste Restante, Bourges.

TO CHARLES LEWES, 21 MAY 1880

Barbara Bodichon had written without having received GE's letter. Sir Henry Holland and his wife lived near the Heights at Witley. Robert Benson was Cross's partner. George Otto Trevelyan published the life of his uncle Lord Macaulay in 1876. [VII, 282–84]

Grenoble May 21. 80.

Dearest Boy

Your letter, full of what I wanted to know, was greedily read during those greasy courses of potage and fish on our arrival here. For we have changed our route, and so had written for our letters to be sent hither from Avignon. This place is so magnificently situated, in a smiling valley with the Isère flowing through it, and surrounded by grand and various lines of mountains, and we were so enraptured by our expedition yesterday to the Grande Chartreuse, that we congratulate our-selves greatly on our choice of route. Today we shall take the two hours' journey to Chambéry, and from thence we intend to go through the Mont Cenis and by Turin to Milan, where I should like to hear from you again. Any interesting letters you might send to me. I was very glad to have Barbara's, and such things are quite worth extra postage. I think I told you that I had had a very sweet letter from Miss Simcox. I gathered from your having said that you would send or had sent a card to Mrs. Congreve that you had expected her to write to me at Avignon. But though our first thought this morning was to trot to the Poste there was nothing for me. We shall probably remain two or three days at Milan, and at any rate wherever we go we can order letters to be sent on from thence, so that anything might safely be sent there for me within the next week. . . .

Mr. Benson wrote to J. that Lady Holland wanted to know whether we would let the Witley house to her brother Mr. G. Trevelyan during our absence, but J. is writing that our absence will be too short for that, and also that you and Gertrude will be going down. In any case I would not let it now that our servants are there. . . .

I had but one regret in seeing the sublime beauty of the Grande Chartreuse. It was, that the Pater had not seen it. I would still give up my own life willingly if he could have the happiness instead of me. But marriage has seemed to restore me to my old self. I was getting hard, and if I had decided differently I think I should have become very selfish. To feel daily the loveliness of a nature close to me, and to be grateful to it, is the fountain of tenderness and strength to endure. . . .

Glorious weather always, and I am very well—quite amazingly able to go

through fatigue. . . . There is no knowing what will answer with our strangely
compounded frames. . . .

Always thy loving
Mutter.

J. is deep in letter-writing in his own room, else I would ask him for a message.

TO ISAAC EVANS, 26 MAY 1880

After 23 years of silence after GE told him that she had a husband, Isaac wrote to her:

Griff | Nuneaton | May 17, 1880.

My dear Sister

    I have much pleasure in availing myself of the present opportunity to break the long
silence which has existed between us, by offering our united and sincere congratulations to you and Mr. Cross, upon the happy event of which Mr. Holbeche has
informed me. My wife joins me in sincerely hoping it will afford you much happiness
and comfort. She and the younger branches unite with me in kind love and every
good wish. Believe me

Your affectionate brother
Isaac P. Evans.

Frederick Evans was Rector of Bedworth, and Walter lived at Nuneaton. [VII, 280, 287]

[Milan] May 26. 1880.

My dear Brother

    Your letter was forwarded to me here, and it was a great joy to me to have your
kind words of sympathy, for our long silence has never broken the affection for you
which began when we were little ones. My Husband too was much pleased to read
your letter. I have known his family for nine years, and they have received me
amongst them very lovingly. He is of a most solid, well tried character and has had
a great deal of experience. The only point to be regretted in our marriage is that I
am much older than he, but his affection has made him choose this lot of caring
for me rather than any other of the various lots open to him.

    Emily Clarke has lately sent me rather a sad account of Sarah's health. I trust
that it is now better, for I think it is her lungs that chiefly trouble her, and summer
may act beneficently on them. Please give my love to her, and tell her that I like
the assurance of her share in the good wishes you send me. I have often heard of
Frederick through the admiration of those who have heard him preach, and it has
been a happy thought to me that you and Sarah must feel it a great comfort to have
him as well as Walter settled near you. Edith is the only one of your children
whom I have seen since they have been grown up, and I thought her a noble-
looking woman.

    We are going to remain abroad until some time in July and shall then return to
The Heights, Witley, Surrey. Our home in London will be 4 Cheyne Walk,
Chelsea, looking on a very picturesque bit of the river.

I hope that your own health is quite good now and that you are able to enjoy the active life which I know you are fond of.

> Always your affectionate Sister
> Mary Ann Cross.

TO MME EUGÈNE BODICHON, 29 MAY–1 JUNE 1880

Charles Lewes agreed to explain GE's marriage to Elma Stuart, Mrs. Congreve, and Edith Simcox. Mrs. Richmond Ritchie (Anne Thackeray), who had set the example by marrying a man 17 years younger than she, describes Charles's loyal efforts. She wrote to her husband: "I am still thrrrrrrilling over a conversation I had yesterday with Charles Lewes. Lionel Tennyson was here; he declared that his hair stood on end as he listened. Charles Lewes said he wished to tell me all about the wedding. He gave her away, and looks upon Mr. Cross as an elder brother. I asked him if she had consulted him and he said no, not consulted, but that she had told him a few weeks ago. She confided in Paget who approved and told her that it wouldn't make any difference in her influence. . . . Young Lewes is generous about the marriage. He says he owes everything to her, his Gertrude included, and that his father had no grain of jealousy in him, and only would have wished her happy, and that she was of such a delicate fastidious nature that she couldn't be satisfied with anything but an ideal tête-à-tête. George Eliot said to him if she hadn't been human with feelings and failings like other people, how could she have written her books. He talked about his own mother in confidence, but his eyes all filled up with tears over George Eliot, and altogether it was the strangest page of life I ever skimmed over. She is an honest woman, and goes in with all her might for what she is about. She did not confide in Herbert Spencer. They have taken a beautiful house in Cheyne Walk." [VII, 284, 290–91]

⟨Milan May 29⟩ Verona, June 1. 80.

Dearest Barbara

The change I make in the date of this letter is a sign of the difficulty you well know that one finds in writing all the letters one wants to write while travelling. Ever since Charles forwarded to me your dear letter while I was in Paris I have been meaning to write to you. That letter doubly sweet to me because it was written before you received mine, intended to inform you of my marriage before it appeared in the newspaper. Charles says that my Friends are chiefly hurt because I did not tell them of the approaching change in my life. But I really did not finally, absolutely decide—I was in a state of doubt and struggle until only a fortnight before the event took place and for a week of that time I was ill with influenza, so that at last everything was done in the utmost haste. However, there were four or five friends, of whom you were one, to whom I resolved to write so that they should at least get my letter in the morning of the 6th.

I had more than once said to Mr. Cross that you were that one of my friends who required the least explanation on the subject—who would spontaneously understand our marriage. But Charles sends me word that my friends in general are very sympathetic, and I should like to mention to you that Bessie is one whose very kind words he has sent to me, for you may have an opportunity of giving my love to her and telling her that it is very sweet to me to feel that her affection is constant to me in this as it was in other crises of my life.

I wish, since you can no longer come in and out among us as you used to do, that you already knew my husband better—his character is so solid, his feeling is so eminently delicate and generous. But you will have inferred something of this from his desire to dedicate his life to the remaining fragment of mine. His family welcome me with the utmost tenderness, and they are of the best paste men and women can be made of. All this is wonderful blessing falling to me beyond my share after I had thought that my life was ended and that, so to speak, my coffin was ready for me in the next room. Deep down below there is a hidden river of sadness but this must always be with those who have lived long—and I am able to enjoy my newly re-opened life. I shall be a better, more loving creature than I could have been in solitude. To be constantly lovingly grateful for the gift of a perfect love is the best illumination of one's mind to all the possible good there may be in store for man on this troublous little planet. . . .

> Your always loving
> Marian.

Yesterday we had a drive on the skirting heights of Verona and saw the vast fertile plain around with the Euganean Hills blue in the distance, and the Appennines just dimly visible in the clear margin of the horizon. I am always made happier by seeing well-cultivated land.

TO CHARLES LEWES, 9 JUNE 1880

GE's letter to Mrs. Bray has not been found. On 10 May she sent her best wishes and, "knowing only the bare fact of your marriage," said that it was a comfort to know that there was some one to protect and cherish her. On 17 June Mrs. Bray wrote that she *had* received GE's note the day of the marriage, but that the fact "was so startling and strange that it seemed bare compared to all we wished to know." In Charles's letter to GE at Milan, enclosing one from Mrs. Congreve, he avoided any description of his interview with her, which had been painful. Vittorio Alfieri's autobiography was in 2 volumes, 1804. [VII, 293–95]

Venice, June 9. 1880.

Dearest Boy . . .

To speak of more personal matters I wish you could comfort me a little about the apparent, inexplicable failure of the letters I wrote to some of my friends, letters intended to reach them on the morning of my marriage. I observed that in Mrs. Bray's letter she said "Knowing only the *bare fact* of your marriage"—which I for the moment thought strange but did not follow out to the natural inference that she had not received my letter, telling her various things beyond the 'bare fact.' The other day however I had a letter from Madame Bodichon to whom I had addressed a letter of announcement at the same time with the one to Mrs. Bray. And Mde. Bodichon says that she never received any letter from me before the one I wrote from abroad in answer to hers. She says, by way of explanation, "I think you must have locked the letters you speak of in your drawer." But I feel quite sure that I placed letters to Mrs. Bray, Madame Bodichon, Mrs. Burne Jones and Mr. William Blackwood on the slab, to be taken to the post as usual by Burkin. Will you, when you are next at the Priory, be kind enough to look at Mr. Blackwood's letter to see whether it contains any indication of his having received mine? If they have all missed I can only conclude that Burkin had some misfortune with the letters. The result is very painful to me, and especially that Mrs. Bray and Mrs. Burne Jones should have believed me to be totally silent to them. . . .

Our days here are passed quite deliciously. We see a few beautiful pictures or other objects of interest and dwell on them sufficiently every morning, not hurrying ourselves to do much, and afterwards we have a 'giro' in our gondola enjoying the air and the sight of marvellous Venice from various points of view and under various aspects. Hitherto we have had no *heat*, only warmth with a light breeze. Today for the first time one thinks that violent exercise must be terribly trying for our red-skinned fellow-mortals at work on the gondolas and the barges. But for us it is only pleasant to find the air warm enough for sitting out in the evening. We are at the Hôtel de l'Europe, on the Grand Canal as you remember, just opposite the Dogana. But when you write to me it will be better to send as before to the Posta Restante. We shall not soon run away from Venice unless some plague—e.g. mosquitos—should arise to drive us. We edify ourselves with what Ruskin has written about Venice in an agreeable pamphlet shape, using his knowledge gratefully and shutting our ears to his wrathful innuendoes against the whole modern world. And we are now nearly at the end of Alfieri's Autobiography which serves as an Italian exercise for J. while it is a deeply interesting study of character. . . .

Always your loving
Mutter.

TO MRS. RICHARD CONGREVE, 10 JUNE 1880

Emily Geddes, Mrs. Congreve's sister, lost her husband 9 March 1880. GE's violation of the Positivist dogma of perpetual widowhood intensified the bitterness. Dr. Congreve wrote to a young disciple, outraged at GE's marriage: "Remember that she is not nor ever has been more than by her acceptance of the general idea of Humanity a Positivist." [VII, 295–96]

[Venice]

I wonder whether you have imagined—I believe that you are quick to imagine for the benefit of others—all the reasons why it was left at last to Charles to tell you of the great, once undreamed-of change in my life. The momentous decision, in fact, was not made till scarcely more than a fortnight before my marriage; and even if opportunity had lent itself to my confiding everything to you, I think I could hardly have done it at a time when your presence filled me rather with a sense of your and Emily's trouble than with my own affairs. Perhaps Charles will have told you that the marriage deprives no one of any good I felt bound to render before—it only gives me a more strenuous position, in which I cannot sink into the self-absorption and laziness I was in danger of before. The whole history is something like a miracle-legend. But instead of any former affection being displaced in my mind, I seem to have recovered the loving sympathy that I was in danger of losing. I mean that I had been conscious of a certain drying-up of tenderness in me, and that now the spring seems to have risen again. Who could take your place within me or make me amends for the loss of you? And yet I should not take it bitterly if you felt some alienation from me. Such alienation is very natural where a friend does not fulfil expectations of long standing.

We have already been ten days at Venice, but we hope to remain as long again, not fearing the heat, which has hitherto been only a false alarm in the minds of English travellers. If you could find time to send me word how you all are—yourself, Dr Congreve after his holiday, and Emily, with all her cares about removal—a letter sent to the Poste Restante here would reach me, even if we had left before the next ten days were over. We shall hardly be at Witley before the middle of July: but the sense of neighbourhood to you at Witley is sadly ended now.

TO MARY, ELEANOR, AND FLORENCE CROSS, 13 JUNE 1880

Johnnie, who was very athletic, found the unrelieved study of churches, paintings, and Italian literature rather restrictive. [VII, 296–99]

Venice June 13. 1880.

Beloved Sisters three

I am rather disgusted with myself that I have been so long without finding time to write to you, but please take this omission as a proof that people do not always find time to do what they like, at least when they have many things they like to do and some which they must do. I have been obliged to write to Charlie and some other friends to whom I was in debt. Then our delightful occupations have a *largo* which spreads them over all the large spaces of the day, and in the smaller spaces I have often been ignobly obliged to put stitches into my dress and bonnets.

We have had nothing that we call heat yet—only a delicious sense of sun and a mild breeziness. . . . One gets a new sensation on reaching the other side of the Lido and sitting to watch the line of tidal waves. This is an excellent spot for getting a sea bath and Johnnie rather longs to have a swim there. But though the temperature is agreeable it has not the sort of heat that makes a plunge in cold water as good as a drink to the thirsty. . . . Johnnie has entered with great interest into the art of all the wondrous towns from Milan to Venice, and to me the journey has been a precious revival of memories fifteen or sixteen years old, for it is all that length of time since I was last in North Italy. . . .

Please believe in all sorts of tender thoughts about you in the heart of your loving

Sister.

DIARY, 14–26 JUNE 1880

On 16 June Johnnie fell ill. His note on the episode in *George Eliot's Life* attributes it to the heat, bad air from the canals, and "deprivation of all bodily exercise." One might assume an acute intestinal infection like typhoid. But it is now clear that he suffered a sudden mental derangement. Lord Acton, who later made inquiries, wrote: "At Venice she thought him mad, and she never recovered the dreadful depression that followed. Sent for Ricchetti, told him that Cross had a mad brother. Told her fears. Just then, heard that he had jumped into the Canal" (Cambridge U. Library, MS 5019, item 1571). The gondoliers quickly pulled him out. Dr. Ricchetti called Dr. Cesare Vigna in consultation. They prescribed chloral to calm Cross. These laconic passages from GE's Diary give the only details that have survived. (Haight, *George Eliot. A Biography*, pp. 544–45). From Innsbruck they went to Munich and on to Wildbad, where Willie left them 12 July. Two weeks later they returned to Witley. [VII, 300–01]

Monday 14 June 1880
With Mr. and Mrs. Bunney to the Manfrini Palace and Casa de' quattro Evangelisti.

Tuesday 15 June 1880
To the Accadèmia seeing the Bellinis. Did not go out after lunch.

Wednesday 16 June 1880
Dr. Ricchetti called.

Friday 18 June 1880
Dr. Cesare Vigna called in. Came at 10.30 p.m. Willie arrived in the evening.

Saturday 19 June 1880
Dr. Vigna twice. Better. Wrote to the girls. Sent Telegram. Webley arrived in the evening.

Sunday 20 June 1880
Better on the whole. Wrote telegram. Dr. V. twice.

Monday 21 June 1880
Quiet night, without chloral. Dr. Vigna in the morning, alone.

Wednesday 23 June 1880
Left Venice at 9.5 a.m. and travelled to Verona—"le Due Torri."

Thursday 24 June 1880
To Trent—Hotel Trento.

Friday 25 June 1880
To Botzen—Kaiserkrone.

Saturday 26 June 1880
Arrived at Innsprück at 2 o'clock.

TO CHARLES LEWES, 12 AUGUST 1880

Back at Witley they were soon entertaining friends in the old way. Lady Holland came over to tea and invited Johnnie to come and play tennis with the younger members of her family. He was laying out a court of his own at the Heights. His sisters came from Weybridge; in August they made a round of family visits to Johnnie's married sisters. Charles and Gertrude Lewes came once or twice before going on their holiday in Germany and Switzerland. [VII, 311–13]

The Heights, Witley, | **Nr. Godalming.**
August 12. 80.

Dearest Boy . . .

I am glad that your weather has been temperate, especially for Gertrude's sake who, I know, finds heat very trying. Here we have now had four sunny and really hot days and this morning promises a fifth. That is consolatory as to the harvest and is very agreeable as to our private life. The last two evenings we have walked in the garden after 8 o'clock, the first time by starlight, the second, under a vapoury sky with the red moon setting. The air was perfectly still and warm and I felt no need of extra clothing. I can make you no good return for your pleasant narrative, for our life has had no more important events than calls from neighbours and our calls in return.

The Hollands are very kind and I hope that Johnnie will get some tennis with the young ones, as he much needs to get exercise. He is gone into town again this morning after being there yesterday, and he feels the length of railway rather fatiguing. It is a little unfortunate that we take the railway again tomorrow to pay our visit to the Druces at Sevenoaks, where, you may remember, Mr. Druce has built a beautiful house. But we shall stay till Tuesday and there will be plenty of lawn tennis, so I think of the visit as altogether a sanitary expedition. At the beginning of September we are to visit Mr. and Mrs. Otter at Ranby, and after that I suppose we shall go to Six Mile for a day or two. Then our wanderings will be over.

I suppose you get a glimpse of the papers occasionally and know all about Mr. Gladstone's illness and recovery, the liberal majority *against* the Compensation for Disturbances Bill, and the deplorable railway accident to the Flying Scotchman and worse wreck of the ship with nearly a thousand pilgrims on board—all lost.

I went to the Priory the other day and found a treatise on Blood pressure by Dr. Roy, which he had sent me there and which he has published as the "George Henry Lewes Student." Dr. Roy's mother has lately died. She lived at Arbroath—Mr. Main's town, you remember—all which I only know because a black-edged printed letter was sent to me addressed in Dr. R's handwriting. So I imagine that he has come to pursue his studies in England, as he intended to do. . . .

Johnnie would send his love if he were here, as I wish he were, instead of having to breathe the air of the city.—I hope Gertrude is getting some strength. Much love to her and to you, dearest Boy. You have been a great comfort to your loving

Mutter.

TO WILLIAM BLACKWOOD, 18 AUGUST 1880

William Blackwood's brother, Major George Frederick Blackwood, was killed in July 1880 at Maiwand during the second Afghan War. His two children went to live with the William Blackwoods. Charles Lewes's article in the August *Blackwood's Magazine* was "Hans Preller: A Legend of the Rhine Falls" from the German of Wilibald Alexis. I am obliged to Mr. Alan Bell, who brought to my attention this letter in the National Library of Scotland, and to the Keeper of Manuscripts for permission to publish it for the first time.

The Heights, Witley, | Nr. Godalming.
Aug. 18. 80

My dear Mr. William

I returned home last night after a few days' absence and found your sad letter. I feel for you and with you under this new, bruising sorrow, coming so close on your late trials of various kinds. It is your lot to be heavily laden with responsibilities. Everyone can understand your sense of loneliness in the prospect of being the sole male stay of your family, and there are many friends who will be sharing your anxiety and your faint hope of relief. But in such calamities as this friends can give no help and one is almost ashamed of sending mere words at such a crisis. Forgive me for sending them. It is the stronger impulse that urges me to write them even in the fear that they may be an unwelcome intrusion.

Thank you for exerting yourself to write me a long letter and telling me about more indifferent matters, which you entered into for my sake. The account of sales is good and I am much pleased to see Charles's bit of work in Maga. The jeu d'esprit was worth translating.

Always yours sincerely
Mary Ann Cross.

TO MRS. EDWARD BURNE-JONES, 9 SEPTEMBER 1880

From Westward Ho!, Devon., Mrs. Burne-Jones wrote 31 August: "Today this dreary place is brightened by a visit from Wombwell's Menagerie and its attendant shows and swinging boats, and we watched them put up the tents on the common by the sea." [VII, 320–21]

The Heights, Witley, | Nr. Godalming.
September 9. 1880.

Dearest Georgie

We have just come home after paying family visits in Lincolnshire and Cambridgeshire, else I should have answered your letter earlier. The former one reached me in Venice when I was in great trouble on account of Mr. Cross's illness. I had had reason to believe that my letters ordered to be posted on the 5th of May had not been delivered, so I asked Charlie to inquire about the letter I wrote to you not because it demanded an answer, but because I wished you to know that I *had* written.

I am so glad to know that you have been enjoying our brief English summer healthily. The good harvest makes the country everywhere cheerful, and we have been in great corn districts where the fields full of sheaves or studded with ricks stretch wide as a prairie. Now we hope not to leave this place again till November when we intend to go to Chelsea for the winter and earliest spring.

I almost envy you the opportunity of seeing Wombwell's Menagerie. I suppose I got more delight out of that itinerant institution when I was nine or ten years old than I have ever got out of Zoological gardens. The smells and the sawdust mingled themselves with my rapture—everything was good.

It was very dear of you to write to me before you finished your holiday. My love attends you all, for I am

Your faithfully affectionate
M. A. Cross.

TO MME EUGÈNE BODICHON, 14 SEPTEMBER 1880

Francis Otter, who married Emily Cross in 1875, lived at Ranby Hall and served as J.P. there. In 1885–86 he sat as Liberal M.P. for Lough, Lincolnshire. [VII, 321–22]

The Heights, Witley, | Nr. Godalming.
September 14. 80.

My dear Barbara

Your letter this morning is a welcome assurance about you. We have been away in Lincolnshire and Cambridgeshire, paying visits to Mrs. Otter and the Halls. The weather, which is now broken, was glorious through all our wandering which we made very interesting by pausing to see Ely, Peterborough and Lincoln Cathedrals. The Otters have a very pretty happy household. He is a country gentleman now, called 'Squire' by his tenants, acting as a magistrate and glancing towards parliament. But he keeps up his reading and is delightful to talk to. Emily looks very pretty in her matronly position, with three little children. The Halls too are very pleasant to behold in their home life. He has done wonders in building nice cottages and schools and sinking a well where it was wanted, and founding a cooperative store, and in general doing whatever opportunity allows towards slowly improving this confused world. We saw Mr. and Mrs. H. Sidgwick. Perhaps you know that they have had and have the admirable public spirit to let their house and arrange to live for a year in the new Newnham House, in order to facilitate matters for the double institution.

We are very well. Mr. Cross gets stronger and brighter every day. We often mention you, because you are associated with so many of my memories. He goes to town only once or twice a week, and unhappily is gone today through the rain and cold wind. His unmarried brother and sisters are going to leave Weybridge and live in London. We shall go to our winter nest there at the end of October. Our only bugbear—it is a very little one—is the having to make preliminary arrangements towards settling ourselves in the new house (4, Cheyne Walk). It is a quaint house, and a Mr. Armitage of Manchester, of whom you may have heard has been superintending the decoration and furnishing, but not to the exclusion of old things which we must carry and stow, especially wallings of books. I am become so lazy that I shrink from all such practical work, and pine if I have only to think of furniture.

Charles and Gertrude are very prosperous and happy and are bringing up their three little girls very nicely. They have just come back from a five weeks' holiday in Switzerland.

Here is a gossiping letter!—I wish I had more edifying things to tell you. Please give my kind remembrances to Dr. Bodichon, and my love to Miss Marks whose hand writing is a pleasant sign to me that she is with you.

Always your loving
Marian.

TO CHARLES LEWES, 19 SEPTEMBER 1880

The *Saturday Review* had an article on GHL's *Problems of Life and Mind*. [VII, 325–26]

The Heights, Witley, | Nr. Godalming.
September 19. 80.

Dearest Boy

The Sat. Review arrived and I was very glad to have it. The article, I think, is nicely done. I wonder how the volumes go on selling.

Your 'news-letter' was very welcome, and I was especially glad to know that Gertrude tries to keep up her health by little devices of change, which help to keep the mind from too constant a selfconsciousness. . . . I want to know Eliza's new address, that I may send her the cheque for September, but I suppose that she is sure to send me word when she has decided on her new home. It was a disappointment to me to find that she had quarrelled with her new hosts, for in writing to me she described everything as quite satisfactory.

Johnnie sympathizes with your disgust at the too too solid flesh that will not melt, but at present we are rejoiced that *he* is laying on a little flesh. He improves daily, and we supply the want of regular lawn tennis by in-door battledore and shuttlecock, at which I am becoming an expert with both right and left hand. One advantage of our high drawing-room is its fitness for this exercise, which warms one better, and exercises more muscles, than walking. Our neighbours are very attentive and oblige us to make calls in return, but otherwise we have been enjoying entire quiet since our return from Cambridgeshire. The rain is pouring down steadily again, and Mrs. Congreve writes that there is still wheat out in Warwickshire. It is exasperating that more haste is not made during the fine weather. Did you see in the Times the account of the American farmer who has 75000 acres?

Johnnie unites his love to that of your loving

Mutter.

TO WILLIAM BLACKWOOD, 2 OCTOBER 1880

Details of the death of Major George F. Blackwood and an account of his heroism had just
come from Afghanistan. I am obliged to Mr. Alan Bell for the copy of this letter, which was
recently found at the National Library of Scotland and is here published for the first time.

The Bristol Hotel, Brighton
Oct. 2, 1880

My dear Mr. William

I learn from the 'Times' of today that your sad presentiment of loss is confirmed,
and, however useless it may be, I cannot help writing to say that I am feeling for
you. So many things have conspired to make this trouble fall with peculiar weight
upon you—and you have not only to bear your own share but to help others to
bear theirs. The public testimony to your Brother's value as an officer has at once a
certain bitterness and consolation in it. It makes one feel his death the greater pity
because a fine career has been broken off, and yet it makes the memory of him a
satisfaction.

You are having these things said to you by many, but though I can write nothing
new, I would not ever be absent from the number of those whose regard for you
urges them to make a sign of their sympathy whether in your grief or in your joy.

I have not been well lately, and we have come down here for the sake of getting
a more bracing air than that of Surrey.

Yours always sincerely
Mary Ann Cross

DIARY 1–5 NOVEMBER 1880

[VII, 331]

Monday 1 November 1880

J. to town, to see about moving furniture from the Priory. Played on the piano
for the first time.

Tuesday 2 November 1880

Feeling much stronger. J. cut down trees in the afternoon.

Wednesday 3 November 1880

Bright day again. J. to the city. Wrote to Miss Lewis and sent her cheque. Also
to Mrs. Congreve and Mrs. Greville.

Thursday 4 November 1880

Began Spencer's Sociology.

Friday 5 November 1880

J. to town. Not so well.

TO MRS. ALFRED TENNYSON, 5 NOVEMBER 1880

In the night of 19 September GE's old renal pain returned. When she had slightly recovered, Johnnie took her for ten days to Brighton—without effect. She had another severe attack 17 October; Dr. Andrew Clark came down to see her. [IX, 316–17]

The Heights, Witley, | Nr. Godalming.
November 5. 80.

Dear Mrs. Tennyson

The regret I felt on finding your cards that my drive had happened when I might have had the pleasure of seeing you has been deepened by my inability to get to Aldworth. I have been rather seriously ill, and am not allowed to be out in the open air for more than an hour in the scant sunshine. One seems to be making too much of such facts by writing about them; but I cannot bear to seem unmindful of any friendly sign made to me by you and yours.

Our friend Mrs. Greville has told me—I hope quite correctly—that you are in some respects better in health than you were last year, and that Mr. Tennyson is as energetic and bright as usual. You and he will I trust always believe in the high regard with which I am

Yours most sincerely
M. A. Cross.

Mr. Cross feels himself a loser, that he has missed this year's opportunity of making your and Mr. Tennyson's acquaintance. I am hoping that Mr. Hallam may find his way to us when we are in town at 4 Cheyne Walk, Chelsea.

TO CHARLES LEWES, 23 NOVEMBER 1880

In her Diary 22 November GE ignored her 61st birthday: "Fine frosty day. Having finished Spencer's *Sociology* we began Max Müller's *Lectures on the Science of Language.*" [VII, 338–39]

The Heights, Witley, | Nr. Godalming.
November 23. 80.

Dearest Boy

Thanks for your pretty letter. I do not think I shall have many returns of Novembers, but there is every prospect that such as remain to me will be as happy as they can be made by the devoted tenderness which watches over me. Your years will probably be many, and it is cheering to me to think that you have many springs of happiness in your lot that are likely to grow fuller with advancing time. . . .

When you wrote to me about the Grave, after you had been to see it and pay for tendance on it, you said that the gardener spoke of new ivy being necessary, but you did not say whether you had told him to plant it. I am so disappointed with the ivy-planting and the way in which the grave is now lost among the new ones round it that I am constantly thinking how I could rescue the sight of it by having a new, higher and more distinctive iron railing to replace the present one. It is sad to me to think that the care against exposure to cold which is enforced upon me may prevent me from getting to Highgate for some time, as the cemetery is usually damp or else bleak.

The removal of the books from the Priory has been a very heavy piece of work, and Johnnie has had a hard service in going up and down daily for a week to superintend. At one time when your Father and I thought we should like to leave the Priory the books were always a drag that helped to deter us. However, the book-cases have all been very well fitted into the new spaces, and the books have had the benefit of being well dusted—a work that can never be got done by servants. . . .

A spiritual embrace to your fivefold self from the loving

Mutter.

TO MRS. ALBERT DRUCE, 26 NOVEMBER 1880

They settled at Bailey's Hotel in Gloucester Road until 4 Cheyne Walk was finished. [VII, 339–40]

The Heights, Witley, | Nr. Godalming.
November 26. 80.

My dear Anna

I should have written to you yesterday but that I tired myself out with packing books. For though Johnnie had written in answer to your affectionate wish that we should take refuge with you, I naturally wanted to say my word. It was that I felt a little displeased with circumstances for hindering us from being with you and Albert again after these three months in which I at least have had no glimpse of you and I am afraid you have not seen quite enough of Johnnie to know how well he looks and how stalwart he has become. Did you know that he had been doing exploits in hewing down trees, or was it a pretty chance that the picture which he brought me word of yesterday as your and Albert's very welcome present will be a record to us of his woodmanship as well as your goodness? It seems that a picture was of all things the most needed ornament and illumination for the panelling of our back drawingroom. I am quite a stranger to the house, not having seen it since the painting has been finished. But I am to begin my nearer acquaintance with it next Monday, for Johnnie has finally decided that we shall give up Winchester and simply take up our abode in some Kensington Hotel he knows of, so that we may overlook our servants' preparations, and supply any want that may disclose itself. Your information about Fever at Winchester helps the rain and howling wind to confirm the wisdom of his decision. I shall be so glad for his sake when we are fairly settled, for he has had all the trouble on his shoulders, and I have been unable to help him.

Surely we shall have a chance of seeing you oftener when we are in London. It is rather hard, since people often grumble at seeing too much of their relatives, that we who are with reason very fond of our brothers and sisters should not be able to see enough of them. Much grateful love to you and Albert for all your goodness from

Your affectionate Sister
M. A. Cross.

A man is come to hang up some prints and sconces from the Priory so I have been finishing in a hurry.

TO MRS. CHARLES BRAY, 28 NOVEMBER 1880

Happily Mrs. Bray was very selective in burning letters and papers. Over 600 of GE's letters to her and her family were preserved. [VII, 340–41]

The Heights, Witley, | Nr. Godalming.
November 28. 80.

My dear Cara

I have thought of you all the more because I have not even heard anything of you for several months. You will wonder less why I have not written as a consequence of those thoughts when I tell you that I have been ill and allowed to do nothing but indulge myself and receive indulgence. I am very well now and am every day consciously gathering strength, so that if I could like giving trouble I should look back on my illness as a great opportunity of enjoying the tenderest watching and nursing. I kept my bed only about a week and have always been equal, except at short intervals, to much reading and talking, so that there is no fair cause for any grumbling on my part. It has not been so bad an illness as that of last summer.

You see, we are not yet at Cheyne Walk, but we are to be settled there by the end of next week. It has been a great business to move the books, and the prospect of that always hindered *us* from moving from North Bank as we were often otherwise inclined to do years ago. I have had no trouble, but have remained here on my cushions while Mr. Cross has gone early for several mornings running to superintend the removal. He is exceedingly strong and well now, and cuts down a thickish tree in half an hour, with a special axe which he bought on purpose to make a desirable clearance in our little forest. . . .

I think you are quite right to look over your old letters and papers and decide for yourself what should be burnt. Burning is the most reverential destination one can give to relics which will not interest any one after we are gone. I hate the thought that what we have looked at with eyes full of living memory should be tossed about and made lumber of, or (if it be writing) read with hard curiosity. I am continually considering whether I have saved as much as possible from this desecrating fate.

It is difficult to give you materials for imagining my 'world.' Think of me as surrounded and cherished by family love—by brothers and sisters whose characters are admirable to me, who have for years been my friends, and who adore my husband as a sort of father and brother combined. But there is no excessive

visiting among us, and the life of my own hearth is chiefly that of dual companionship. If it is any good for me that my life has been prolonged till now, I believe
it is owing to this miraculous affection which has chosen to watch over me. Love
to all three from

Your ever affectionate
Marian.

TO MR. CHARLES BRAY, 4 DECEMBER 1880

John Cross, though a handsome man, was shy of being photographed. Charles Bray, born
31 January 1811, was on the brink of 70. Gladstone became Prime Minister for the fourth
time in April 1880. Francis Close, Dean of Carlisle, at the age of 84 had just married his
second wife. [VII, 342–43]

4, Cheyne Walk, | Chelsea, S.W.
November [i.e. December] 4. 1880.

Dear Mr. Bray

Most certainly you shall have the remaining two volumes of 'Problems.' I had
not failed to think of you in connection with them, but I was not at all sure that
you would like to have them, and in such cases questions defeat their proposed
end. But will you excuse a delay of a few days in your getting them from the
Publisher? For I am overwhelmed with details just now. We only got into this
house to dinner yesterday evening, and notwithstanding the much that is done,
chaos still prevails behind the surface. This morning I find myself with the usual
penance on my hands for neglecting letters—the feeling of hurry in making up for
the neglect.

As to your other request, Mr. Cross has no photograph of himself. But I think
you would be satisfied with his coronal arch which finishes a figure six feet high. If
his head does not indicate fine moral qualities, it must be phrenology that is in
fault. He is exceedingly acute, accustomed to deal with men in matters where
their characters are inevitably betrayed, well aware of all our human humbug but
charitable towards it withal as a quality or manifestation in which we have
everyone of us some brother—or—sisterhood. All this is more than you would
learn from a *carte de visite* of the photographic kind, even if he could give it you.

I suppose we may consider 70—not the normal length of human life according
to the mistaken view of the Psalmist but—a comparatively youthful epoch, since
we have our Prime Minister on the one hand doing more work than he is obliged
to do, and Dean Close on the other marrying at 84.

I am writing to Sara this morning.

Yours very sincerely
M. A. Cross.

TO MRS. LIONEL TENNYSON, 8 DECEMBER 1880

Aeschylus's tragedy was performed in Greek by Oxford undergraduates 17 December. [VII, 345]

4, Cheyne Walk, | Chelsea, S.W.
December 8. 80.

Dear Mrs. Lionel

We are both much obliged by your kind thought in sending us the card for Private Theatricals, December 16th. But we have taken a box for the Agamemnon on the 17th and we dare not venture to accept an engagement which would take us into a crowded room on the evening of the 16th, for Mr. Cross, robust as he looks, is obliged to be very careful as to temperature, and is at the moment in bed with a feverish cold which has caused me a very anxious night, though he has all along, I hope, been on the way to recovery.

Always yours sincerely
M. A. Cross.

TO MRS. ELMA STUART, 11 DECEMBER 1880

Mrs. John Stewart Menzies, after the death of her husband in 1867, had lived much with Mrs. Stuart. Her conversion to the Roman Catholic Church was like that of Mme Louis Belloc, which GE had similarly defended against the objections of her friends. [VII, 345–47]

4, Cheyne Walk, | Chelsea, S.W.
December 11. 1880.

Dearest Elma

Your letter received this morning has found me in trouble, Mr. Cross having been ill for the last few days (since Monday evening) with what the doctor declares to be a bilious attack, and he is still in a state of suffering which causes me much affliction. . . .

With regard to the chief subject of your letter, I judge somewhat differently from you. Years ago an intimate friend of mine, then a young woman of little more than thirty took the step on which Mrs. Menzies has resolved. She had very ardent friendships with other women who remained Protestant and plus-quam-Protestant, but no disruption of such friendships occurred in consequence of her becoming a Catholic. After reading Mrs. Menzies' letter I wonder that your acute penetration and habit of reflection are so beclouded by your emotion (with which I sympathize to a certain extent) that you can think this a case for reasoning and remonstrance. How can you by reasoning overturn what is not based on reasoning but on a sense of need which Catholicism seems to supply? I for my part would not venture to thrust my mind on hers as a sort of omniscient dictatress, when in fact I am very ignorant of the inward springs which determine her action. That she has not spoken to you of her intention until now is no proof that it has not been long ripening, and in fact I see in her letter the expression of a long-felt dissatisfaction and yearning—a thirst which has found the longed-for water. To insist on ideas or external reasons in opposition to such deeply-felt inclinations is no more effective than the swallowing of a paper prescription.

Remember, dear, that the reason why societies change slowly is, because individual men and women cannot have their natures changed by doctrine and can only be wrought on by little and little. You are as capable as any one of being patient towards inalterable differences of nature in your friends, and though I understand the painful shock you have felt from this sudden revelation, I feel sure that you will presently have a clear vision of the unfitness manifested by your sweet friend's nature for "voyaging in strange seas of thought" and choosing for herself from among philosophical doctrines. There is so much goodness in her that she will have affinity only for the goodness in Catholicism, and what strikes you as contradiction and folly will have no such perturbing effect on her thought. You speak of 'Protestant sects' as if their ideas were superior to Catholicism, but surely you would have been equally pained if she had united herself with any fanatical Protestant sect which might easily have prompted some line of action inconsistent with *practical* attachment to you. I do not foresee that her actual change will have the effect of dividing her from you, *if* you will only, out of reverence for that sanctuary of inmost feeling which the closest union must leave free from intrusion—if, I say you will only out of such reverence abstain from dictation, remonstrance or worrying argument which can find no corresponding substance to be argumentatively affected. . . . Pardon me, dear if, in my preoccupation of mind, I have used any word that is at all painful to you. That would be the opposite of my wish.

Yours ever affectionately
M. A. Cross.

2 hours later. Mr. Cross is much relieved, and I am more cheerful.

TO MME LOUIS BELLOC, 17 DECEMBER 1880

The Crosses were to spend Christmas with the Druces. Barbara Bodichon had had another stroke. [VII, 347–48]

4, Cheyne Walk, | Chelsea, S.W.
December 17. 80.

Dearest Bessie

Will you or can you come to lunch with us some day—say Monday—at 1/2 past 1 o'clock? That is the only time of day on which I can make an appointment just now. But if that time is inconvenient to you, we shall always be at home between 5 and 6 except on a Saturday. It is so long a journey for you that I have a sort of compunction in writing easily to say 'Come.' For Christmas we go to Sevenoaks to see some of the family, and I suppose you will then be at Slindon.

We have been here a fortnight but are not yet in thorough quietude and freedom from house arrangements. One reason is, that Mr. Cross was ill with a bilious attack one whole week. He is well again now, and I am quite flourishing again in my rickety fashion—a mended piece of antique furniture.

I am deeply grieved to hear of Barbara's partial relapse. We should all feel life the sadder if she were to have another seizure which would narrow her powers still further.

I hope you will have found the children in a satisfactory state of progress, bodily and mentally.

Yours lovingly
M. A. Cross.

TO HERBERT SPENCER, 18 DECEMBER 1880

At the foot of the page Spencer wrote: "I believe this was the last letter she wrote. I called the next afternoon (Sunday) and had a long, pleasant talk with her—thought her looking worn, but she did not seem otherwise unwell. I little thought that I should never see her more!" [VII, 348 and MS at the University of London]

4, Cheyne Walk, | Dec. 18, 1880

Dear Friend

I have been slow to thank you for the kind present of your latest publications, of which I have made ample use, having re-read with Mr. Cross your "Data of Ethics," and the *Study of Sociology*. We saw that you had left your card at the Priory, and therefore we hope that you will find your way to this new home, where you would certainly be welcome.

Yours always sincerely
M. A. Cross.

TO MRS. RICHARD STRACHEY, 19 DECEMBER 1880

Sir James Colvile died 6 December 1880. In *George Eliot's Life* Cross wrote: "Here the letter is broken off. The pen which had carried delight and comfort to so many minds and hearts, here made its last mark. The spring which had broadened out into so wide a river of speech, ceased to flow".

Edith Simcox had a note from GE asking her to come on Sunday the 19th. "She was alone when I arrived. I was too shy to ask for any special greeting—only kissed her again and again as she sat. Mr. Cross came in soon and I noticed his countenance was transfigured, a calm look of pure *beatitude* had succeeded the ordinary good nature. Poor fellow! She was complaining of a slight sore throat; when he came in and touched her hand, said she felt the reverse of better. I only stayed half an hour therefore; she said Do not go, but I gave as a reason that she should not tire her throat and then she asked me to come in again and tell them the news. He came down to the door with me and I only asked after his health. She had spoken before of being quite well and I thought it was only a passing cold—she thought it was caught at the Agamemnon. I meant to call again tomorrow and take her some snowdrops. This morning I hear from Johnnie—she died at 10 last night!" [IX, 320–21]

4, Cheyne Walk, | **Chelsea, S.W.** | December 19. 1880.

Dear Mrs. Strachey

I have been thinking so much of Lady Colvile, and yet I shrank from troubling even your more indirect sympathetic sorrow with a letter. I am wondering how far her health is in a state to endure this loss—a loss which extends even to me, who only occasionally saw, but was always cheered by, the expression of a wise and sweet nature, which clearly shone in Sir James Colvile's manner and conversation. One great comfort I believe she has—that of a sister's affection.

INDEX

The index lists the names of most persons mentioned in George Eliot's letters. Her books are also listed. For her periodical articles see *Essays of George Eliot,* edited by Thomas Pinney (New York and London, 1963). George Henry Lewes is listed only before his union with George Eliot in 1854.

SELECTIONS FROM
GEORGE ELIOT'S LETTERS

George Eliot, 1860. From a drawing in chalks by Samuel Laurence. William Blackwood & Sons Ltd.

Selections from George Eliot's Letters

Edited by Gordon S. Haight

YALE UNIVERSITY PRESS   NEW HAVEN AND LONDON

Published with assistance from the Louis Effingham deForest
Memorial Fund.

Designed by Nancy Ovedovitz and set in Linotron 202 Goudy
Old Style type, by The Composing Room of Michigan, Inc.
Printed in the United States of America by Vail-Ballou Press,
Binghamton, New York.

Library of Congress Cataloging in Publication data
Eliot, George, 1819–1880.
  Selections from George Eliot's letters.
  This is a condensation of the George Eliot letters originally
published in nine volumes, 1954–78.
  Includes index.
  1. Eliot, George, 1819–1880—Correspondence. 2. Novelists,
English—19th century—Correspondence. I. Haight, Gordon
Sherman. II. Title.
PR4681.A4   1985   823'.8   84–13222
ISBN 0-300-03326-5 (alk. paper)

The paper in this book meets the guidelines for permanence and
durability of the Committee on Production Guidelines for Book
Longevity of the Council on Library Resources.

10   9   8   7   6   5   4   3   2   1